Pioneers of Public Sociology:
Thirty Years of *Humanity and Society*

Edited by
Corey Dolgon and Mary Chayko

Pioneers of Public Sociology:
Thirty Years of *Humanity and Society*

Edited by
Corey Dolgon and Mary Chayko

2011
Sloan Publishing
Cornwall-on-Hudson, NY 12520
http://www.sloanpublishing.com

Library of Congress Cataloging-in-Publication Data

Pioneers of public sociology : thirty years of Humanity and society / edited by Corey
Dolgon and Mary Chayko.
p. cm.
ISBN 978-1-59738-026-3
1. Sociology--Periodicals. 2. Association for Humanist Sociology (U.S.) I. Dolgon, Corey. II. Chayko, Mary, 1960- III. Humanity & society.
HM403.P53 2010
301.05--dc22
2010009253

Cover designer: Raul Villarreal

Sloan Publishing, LLC
220 Maple Road
Cornwall-on-Hudson, NY 12520

Printed in the United States of America

10 9 8 7 6 5 4 3 2 1

ISBN 13: 978-1-59738-026-3
ISBN 10: 1-59738-026-1

Dedication

We dedicate this book to the courage and commitment of those whose work shaped the history of humanist sociology—to the Association for Humanist Sociology's founders and members who have given a home to, and tended the flames of, public sociology; to all of the community activists and social movement leaders on the front lines of social justice work whose efforts inspire and inform us; and to the future scholars and activists who will carry on a tradition of public humanist sociology and continue the fight to make this world a better place.

Contents

Section III
Confronting Institutions: Creating Humanistic Practices in Everyday Life   183

Preface

Corey Dolgon and Mary Chayko

The movement toward public sociology is exciting! More and more, scholars and practitioners (especially younger ones) are taking their sociological training directly to—and from—the public in order to change the everyday lives of people and their communities. And it's about time.

For those of us connected to the Association for Humanist Sociology (AHS) and its journal, *Humanity and Society*, both the process and goal of doing sociological work has always been to address social problems and make the world a better place. Every article in this anthology provides a certain insight into this kind of sociology: theories and concepts to help us better understand it, methods used to investigate it, ways to practice it, its future—and how you can be a part of it. And each article is followed by a rejoinder written by a member of the AHS that offers a reflection, critique or update to the original article.

Many of the most important thinkers and researchers in this tradition are represented here: Al McClung Lee, Patricia Hill Collins, Mary Jo Deegan, Ashley "Woody" Doane, Walda Katz-Fishman. They—and the other fine writers and researchers contributing to this volume—have been "pioneering" public sociology for well over a quarter of a century. In this book, they contribute many creative, useful and provocative ideas for bringing sociology to the public and working on behalf of the public.

AHS has been at the forefront of public sociology since its inception in 1976. Our mission statement makes clear this purpose:

> *Humanist sociologists strive as professionals, as scholars and as activists, to uncover and address social issues, working with others to lessen the pain of social problems. We view people not merely as products of social forces, but also as shapers of social life, capable of creating social orders in which everyone's potential can unfold. Difficult times give humanist sociologists opportunities to apply their special skills and perspectives for the purpose of creating a more humane world.*

Now, we see increased publications about public sociology, myriad conferences and workshops dedicated to it, and even entire undergraduate and graduate programs focused on it.

AHS takes great pride in watching the rest of the discipline come around to our way of thinking about (and doing) sociology.

Yet, while we celebrate the increasing "mainstreaming" of public sociology, we also recognize the need to keep what becomes popular grounded in some basic principles. Years ago, Raymond Williams (1989) argued that the institutionalization of radical intellectual practices puts new pressures on those radical intellectuals responsible for such formalization in the first place. Institutions of higher education and professional organizations require a kind of mainstreaming that often depoliticizes work in favor of the demands for funding and grants, institutional assessment and advancement, peer recognition and rewards. The project of radical transformation can be transformed by the bureaucratic and often reactionary forces of conservative institutions and ideologies.

Former ASA President, Michael Burawoy (2004), harkening back to Robert Lynd's question of "sociology for what?" and our own Al McClung Lee's question of "sociology for whom?" asked his own set of framing questions for public sociology and its practitioners:

> Do we take the values and goals of our research for granted, handed down to us by some external (funding or policy) agency? Should we only concentrate on providing solutions to predefined problems, focusing on the means to achieve predetermined ends, on what Weber called technical rationality and what I call instrumental knowledge? In other words, should we repress the question of ends and pretend that knowledge and laws spring spontaneously from the data, if only we can develop the right methods? Or should we be concerned explicitly with the goals for which our research may be mobilized, and with the values that underpin and guide our research? Going further afield, should sociologists be in the business of stimulating public discussions about the possible meanings of the "good society"? (p. 1606)

AHS members and contributors to *Humanity and Society* would respond in much the same way that Bob Dylan's thief "kindly" responds to the joker in *All Along the Watchtower*:

> But you and I, we've been through that,
> And this is not our fate,
> So let us not talk falsely now,
> The hour is getting late.

Or, we would go further back to Albert Camus (1965), whose character Tarrou claimed: "All I know is that there are pestilences and there are victims, and it's up to us, so far as is possible, not to join forces with the pestilences" (p. 301). Camus later says of *The Plague's* hero, Dr. Rieux, that "the tale he had to tell could not be one of a final victory. It could only be the record of what had to be done, and what surely would have to be done again in the never ending fight against terror and its relentless onslaughts, despite their personal afflictions, by all who, unable to be saints but refusing to bow down to pestilences, strive their utmost to be healers" (p. 325). It seems to us that public sociology is *the* principled, moral response to this, as we dedicate our knowledge and abilities to making the world a better, more humane place.

This collection of articles from the first thirty years of *Humanity and Society* reminds us again and again that, in a world filled with pestilence, we must employ all the intellectual and practical tools at our disposal to fight against it, side with the victims of plagues, and comfort the afflicted and afflict the comfortable—especially in cases when the source of comfort is one of the root causes of the pestilence. The scholar activists and activist scholars in this collection (and many others in the Association for Humanist Sociology) are the true "pioneers of public sociology"—practicing public sociology in a wide variety of ways and settings for decades. In other words, AHS was doing public sociology long before it became "cool."

Our job now is to maintain the radical, humanist, politically principled edges of public sociology as it moves from margins to center. We hope that this engaged, motivated, practical approach to sociology fuels your interest in public sociology and in "using" the study of sociology to make the world a better place. And we hope this book gives you specific ideas for how to go about doing so. Using your knowledge of sociology to work directly on behalf of people is a much needed and very rewarding way to make your mark on society. And you should never feel alone. As the rejoinders to these articles show us, we don't follow in these pioneers' footsteps so much as we walk alongside them toward a more humane future.

Acknowledgments

Corey Dolgon would like to thank his many AHS colleagues for making his six-year tenure as editor of *Humanity and Society* and his ten-year tenure on the organization's Executive Board such transcendent and life-changing experiences. He would also like to thank previous editors for all of their years of hard work and excellence that made this collection possible. Finally, Corey would like to thank Deborah, Bailey, and Ruby for allowing him the opportunity to work on this book and sacrificing all the time they could have spent snuggling.

Mary Chayko thanks the AHS for the honor of serving on *Humanity and Society*'s editorial board for the past five years and as the Association's treasurer for four. She thanks the College of Saint Elizabeth, with its warm community of scholars and friends, for its generosity of support, and in particular, Samia Canzonieri, for all-around first-rate assistance. Finally, she thanks her infinitely patient and loving family, especially Morgan, Ryan, Glenn, and Oma.

Both Corey and Mary would especially like to thank Jay Graham, whose work as Managing Editor of *Humanity and Society* has been exemplary and without whose dogged efforts these pages would not have been rescued from the archives.

References

Burawoy, Michael. 2004. "Public Sociologies: Contradictions, Dilemmas, and Possibilities." *Social Forces, 82*, 4 (June); 1603–1618.

Camus, Albert. 1965. *The Plague*. New York: McGraw-Hill.

Williams, Raymond. 1989. *The Politics of Modernism*. London: Verso.

Introduction:
Sociology for Whom?
The "Public" Roots of Humanist Sociology[1]

Chet Ballard
Valdosta State University

The Association for Humanist Sociology (AHS) was launched by Alfred McClung Lee, Elizabeth Briant Lee, Charles Flynn and others in 1976 to promote the practice of sociology in ways that served humanity rather than governments, corporations, or any professional elite. The American Sociological Association (ASA) had experienced an insurgency of sorts within its own ranks as evidenced by Al Lee's election to the ASA Presidency in 1975 as a write-in, protest candidate. Later, AHS would be one of several alternative professional organizations to emerge from this contentious period in the discipline's history—the Clinical Sociological Association (which became the Sociological Practice Association and merged with the Society for Applied Sociology to become the Association for Applied and Clinical Sociology in 2004) began in 1978 and the Society for Applied Sociology in 1983. These groups sought to *revive* the discipline's original mission, not only to produce knowledge *about* the behavior of people in social structures and settings, but more emphatically, to apply that knowledge to *solve* problems and *improve* lives. The AHS in particular pledged to bring "humans back in" and provide an answer to the signature question, "sociology for whom"?

AHS founders and early followers met in New York in the summer of 1976 and discussed what a new association, its newsletter, journal, and annual convention should look like. Al Lee would be its first president while Charles "Chuck" Flynn, a young radicalized romantic and irrepressible humanist, took on the role of Editor of the new AHS journal, *Humanity and Society*. That fall Flynn and Ann Davis, both at Miami University in Ohio, hosted the first annual meeting with sessions held on campus and in Flynn's living room. Al Lee spoke to the small group of assembled humanist sociologists about "A Different Kind of Sociological Society" (Ballard 2003). The inaugural issue of *Humanity and Society* featured, as its lead article, the inspired words of AHS's most luminary figure, Al Lee. Several of those who attended the first annual meeting would write articles that appeared in *Humanity and Society* during its earliest years, including Vicki Rader, Sal Restivo, Chuck Flynn, and Betty Lee.

The Civil Rights Movement, the Vietnam War, the Women's Movement, the Generation Gap, the sexual revolution, Berkeley and Free Speech, riots in Watts, Detroit, and Harlem, Attica State Prison, the Pentagon Papers, Watergate, Manson, assassinations of John F. Kennedy, Martin Luther King, Robert Kennedy, and Malcom X, anti-war protests at Kent

---

[1]This paper originally appeared in *Humanity & Society* Volume 27, Number 3, August 2003.

State and Columbia, police violence, the Black Panthers and songs of war and peace—all were part of the tapestry of American society. Sociology was exploding with new analyses for the myriad of changes around the country and around the world. With America's core institutions under siege, the battles in the streets, campuses, offices, and homes shaped the biographies and stories of the 1960's and 1970's. Professional sociology faced challenges inside and out (from Left and Right) as a radicalized generation of students and teachers wrestled with this question: Are we to be a field of study dominated by a small, insular and self-referential group of academics or can we again become a vibrant intellectual discipline that contributes directly to public dialogue on the fundamental issues and social problems confronting humanity? Those who came together to create the AHS wanted "a different kind of sociological society" whose journal would not be controlled by "entrepreneurs of so-called research institutes in search of grants and contracts" nor by an ASA clique that Lee characterized as a "tightly knit, self-designated, self-perpetuating, and self-verifying ideological elite" (1977: 3).

Al Lee stands as the most charismatic sociologist I've ever known. A visionary and respected crusader, he asked the defining question of humanist sociology, a question that served as the title of one of his most compelling books (1978), *Sociology for Whom?* In "A Different Kind of Sociological Society," Lee articulates an intellectual mandate and historical legacy for AHS's powerful raison d'être. He also forecasts how such commitments will distinguish AHS from the ASA. Tinged with both contempt and unshakeable resolve, Lee insists that *Humanity and Society* will be the place where we "discover all we can about how human beings are made into tools and societies are subjected to costly and even catastrophic scenarios" (1977: 10). Over a quarter century after Lee's address, we pause to reflect on how he and others, some reprinted in this anthology, led by example and published ideas worth reading, teaching, and applying again and again.

AHS founders were committed to publishing a journal that would give voice to marginalized and disenfranchised sociologists whose studies and activism were not generally rewarded inside establishment sociology. As we have watched ASA's mainstream take up the call for "public sociology," and a flurry of books and top tier journal articles have appeared, we are reminded of something that Raymond Williams (1989) said some years ago about the formation of cultural studies as a politically inspired field of interdisciplinary studies combining sociology, communications, literature, and a variety of other disciplines and methodologies. Williams explained that, while cultural studies had developed its own cottage industry and various books and articles had brought a certain status and cache to the field, most of the people who had actually inspired and shaped the origins of cultural studies were forgotten. He expressed sadness that: "the many people who were active in that field at that time who didn't publish, but who did as much as any of us to establish [it]" did not get credit. AHS was fortunate to have established a journal from the outset. *Humanity and Society* and its authors and editors have a strong, substantial record of articulation and achievement in "public sociology." They represent a prototype and prologue to what is happening within the discipline today.

Humanity and Society in its first issue, Summer 1977, and its first complete quarterly volume in 1978, called for the use of sociology to improve humanity. The journal proclaimed an action-oriented, accessible, clearly written and communicated sociology that could be applied at the grassroots level and should be critical of the dehumanizing forces of corporate sociology and elitism in the profession. Themes that emerged from the earliest

H&S articles included human liberation, unity and coalition building, studies of minority and special status groups, analyses of oppression and structures of inequality, essays on the nature of being human, and reports of applied activities from the field. The founders and early members of AHS were indeed the pioneers of public sociology as we know it today.

While Al and Betty Lee were its inspiration, Chuck Flynn, Ann Davis, Vicki Rader, Stu Hills, Lynda Ann Ewen, and Bill Kuvlesky provided the perspiration that resulted in this "different type" of sociological association getting off the ground. Flynn, in particular, served as editor of AHS's first two publications, *Humanity and Society* and *The Humanist Sociology Newsletter* (later to become *The Humanist Sociologist*). In the first AHS newsletter, he published a list of working principles that would guide the new organization (1976):

1. Over-Compartmentalization of the Discipline;
2. Limitations of Empirical Approach;
3. Determinism;
4. Disciplinary Chauvinism;
5. Value-Neutrality Question;
6. Paradigmatic Pluralism and Opposition to Orthodoxy

These guiding ideas would be reflected in the editorial practices of *Humanity and Society* (Ballard 2003). Flynn introduced the journal in the Summer of 1977 saying, "We are pleased to present the first issue of a journal which we hope will provide what many sociologists feel has long been needed: a means for the dissemination of ideas and perspectives focusing upon the value implications and humanistic aspects of the discipline. *Humanity and Society* will publish articles and review books which emphasize the examination of underlying value implications and moral dimensions of sociological theory and research. We will also present explorations of possible connections between sociological perspectives and approaches, and the modes of inquiry of other disciplines such as history and philosophy, so that sociologists might be encouraged to look at familiar sociological issues in new ways. In all this, we seek to be as pluralistic as possible, and thus welcome articles and reviews written from any theoretical or methodological perspective. The unique Reflexive Statement that precedes each article allows the reader to understand where 'the author is coming from' with respect to the value orientations and theoretical or ideological perspectives he/she adopts toward the subject matter of the article."

Some illustrative examples of humanist sociological scholarship are found in the articles and rejoinders in this anthology, many of which were also collected in a 25th anniversary issue of *Humanity and Society*. In "Sociology for People" Lee explores skills students need in order to find fulfilling employment and practice sociology as it should be practiced, that is, a sociology for people. Literacy (the ability to write and communicate well), field experience (a knowledge of the socio-cultural context in which behavior occurs and its meanings), and competency in sociological theory and methods are areas for student instruction by those teaching from a humanist sociology perspective (Lee 1977). Once prepared in the three areas, Lee says students "are likely to have a most fascinating and useful life whether within or without the academic fold" (1979: 91).

The articles and rejoinders presented herein extend Lee's vision of what sociology should be. Vicki Rader in "Teaching Sociology Humanistically" and Patricia Hill Collins in "Perspectivity and the Activist Potential of the Sociology Classroom" provide accounts of how teaching and learning are linked inextricably to the lives of sociology students and their teachers. How should teaching be practiced using the value orientations of humanist sociology? Vicki Rader answers this question in "Teaching Sociology Humanistically." She advises, "No matter how humanistic our course content, we need teaching practices that encourage the student's actual experience of being critically aware, socially creative and cooperatively related to all other living beings" (Rader 1979: 92). The sociology classroom is the place where students and teachers come together to discuss the important social issues of our age. Hill Collins describes the classroom as the place where humanist sociologists train students in the essential political skills needed to engage in and change society (Hill Collins 1986).

How can we integrate analyses of society with humanism to produce a more just society? T. R. Young in "The Sociology of Human Rights" understands that there are no absolutes when it comes to the "right" way to be human (Young 1981). Although disquieting to those who prefer absolutes, essential human rights are embedded in the societal and cultural specifics of time and place. A society that exploits the weak and less advantaged for the profit of the strong and advantaged is unjust and creates conditions of protracted conflict between the haves and the have nots.

David Friedrichs in "Crime, Deviance, and Criminal Justice: In Search of a Radical Humanistic Perspective" explores how the neo-Marxist critique of modern capitalism can be synthesized with humanist values to produce a more productive analysis of crime and punishment. Rejecting the underlying assumptions and values displayed in our contemporary criminal justice system, Friedrichs rejects individual and state-sponsored violence as a systematic response to deviance (Friedrichs 1982). To reshape the justice system, assumptions about what it means to be human as well as which behaviors must be controlled and by what political means, must be openly discussed.

Building competency in critical theory and methods, an objective of "a sociology for people" means challenging the legitimacy of structures of oppression, laying bare the assumptions and value positions underlying social arrangements that deprive people of their basic dignity, and working to change the interaction dynamics that dehumanize and limit individual freedom. Sal Restivo and Michael Zenzen in "A Humanistic Perspective on Science and Society" specify a humanist perspective on the nature of "knowing" and making sense of shared, subjective and multi-faceted social reality (Restivo and Zenzen 1978). Glenn Goodwin in "Toward a Paradigm for Humanistic Sociology" explicates the philosophy of science that guides its use among those who seek to understand and improve society. Humanist sociology values the shared reality of the observer and the observed, in subjective and objective terms, and embraces methods of inquiry that do not reduce humans to mere numbers. It "goes about 'knowing' the social world through placing primary emphasis on the various definitions and constructions of that world as articulated by the subject/actors involved" (Goodwin 1983: 231).

As men and women turn to sociology to answer questions about the nature of social order and change, we see the "sociology for whom?" question raised effectively in, yet also problematized by, the feminist critique of sociology and social order. Mary Jo Deegan explains in "An American Dream: The Historical Connection Between Women, Humanism, and Sociology, 1890-1920" that she wondered who were the women who practiced sociology at its inception and why had she never heard of them in her study of sociology.

Her research identifies women who are "pioneers" and "professionals" in the earliest days of American sociology. She writes, "Their emergence as feminists, leaders in social legislation, and community organizers has been disconnected from their roots in humanist sociology, however, impoverishing our heritage and hiding the power of our vision" (Deegan 1987: 359). Teaching students to look for connections, to ask relevant questions, and to see the relationship between the political structure of society and the life chances of individuals is well demonstrated in Deegan's research.

These articles and the others in this book are a primer on humanist sociology. Lee expected humanist sociologists to train students to be competent practitioners; able to think critically about the nature of society and its social arrangements, communicate effectively with people at all levels of society, and produce a sociology that is for people. It is an abomination when sociology is purchased on demand by plutocrats to further control and subjugate the powerless. Sociology is dehumanizing when it produces sterile analyses communicated in arcane scientific language and reported in narrowly read academic journals. It betrays its founders when sociology permits corporate and governmental technicians to determine what will be studied and by whom. It loses its humanity when it is used to maintain structures of oppression or legitimize arrangements of the unjust.

You can see (and feel) Lee's vision of humanist sociology in these pages. It is cause for celebration and renewal, as we take a collective AHS pause to reflect the value-committed scholarship published in *Humanity and Society*. I must also toast, on this happy occasion, the outstanding service provided to the AHS and its journal by Chuck Flynn, Walda Katz Fishman, Lynda Ann Ewen, David Gil, and Judy Aulette who were editors of the journal during its early years and whose labor and pervasive caring, kept the vision of what sociology should be, alive in the pages of *Humanity and Society*.

References

Ballard, Chet. 2003. "A Select Bibliography of Humanist Sociology Sources" in *Guide to Teaching Humanist Sociology*, 4th ed., Martin Schwartz and Glenn Goodwin, eds., American Sociological Association, Teaching Resources Center Publication.

Friedrichs, David. 1982. "Crime, Deviance, and Criminal Justice: In Search of a Radical Humanistic Perspective." *Humanity and Society*. 6 (3):200–226.

Goodwin, Glenn. 1983. "Toward a Paradigm for Humanistic Sociology." *Humanity and Society* 7(3):219–237.

Hill Collins, Patricia. 1986. "Perspectivity and Activist Potential of the Sociology Classroom." *Humanity and Society* 10(3):341–360.

Lee, Alfred McClung. 1977. "A Different Kind of Sociological Society." *Humanity and Sociology* 1(1):1–11.

Lee, Alfred McClung. 1979. "Sociology for People." *Humanity and Society* 3(2): 81–91.

Rader, Victoria. 1979. "Teaching Sociology Humanistically.' *Humanity and Society* 3(2):92–106.

Restivo, Sal and Michael Zenzen. 1978. "A Humanistic Perspective on Science and Society." *Humanity and Society* 2(4):211–236.

Williams, Raymond. 1989. *The Politics of Modernism*. New York: Verso Press.

Young, T. R. 1981. "The Sociology of Human Rights." *Humanity and Society* 3(4):353–369.

Section 1

What is Humanist Sociology? Theory and Methods from a Humanist Perspective

In the book's first section we build a foundation for the understanding of public sociology as practiced within a humanist sociological framework. While "public sociology" helps people improve their lives in numerous ways, "humanist sociology" provides an ethical and principled guide for such civic engagement. The Association for Humanist Sociology considers humanist sociology to be a commitment to peace, equality, democracy, environmental sustainability and social justice. As you read these articles, however, you will note that many practitioners also believe humanist sociology provides a methodological guide that promotes incorporating people as partners in research and analysis. This means treating individuals "not merely as products of social forces, but also as shapers of social life," including in sociological research and writing itself. The articles in this section help us think about these concepts with more clarity and precision, even as they remind us not to limit possibilities by considering them too narrowly.

1. Sociology for People[1]

Alfred McClung Lee

Brooklyn College and the Graduate Center of the City University of New York

Few new undergraduates know quite what to expect from sociology. Rumors and the mass media associate the discipline with all sorts of ideas and activities. They may identify it with social work or social reform. They may say that it has a strange and useless jargon. They may describe it as involving the sample-surveying of opinions. They may confine sociology to exploring the plight of the poor, the deprived, the deviant, and the criminal. They may limit it to studies of sexual and marital behavior. They may dwell on sociology's allegedly mysterious statistical manipulations that are said somehow to yield figures powerful in guiding politicians and businessmen in policymaking. And some gossips and journalists may even try to confuse sociology—more or less sarcastically—with socialism or communism. This all can give undergraduates rather contradictory images.

Unfortunately high schools rarely provide any comprehensive introduction to or definition of sociology. Thus confusion or an ignoring of the subject persists at least into college years. Then campus scuttlebutt either warns against the difficulties of the discipline or advertises it as a source of easy credits. Fortunately curiosity does entice a fair number of good students to take a chance on at least one sociology course.

In contrast with all this confusion, the interesting thing about the well-trained in sociology—especially those who are literate and experienced in human affairs—is that they are showing up in a wide range of responsible positions. On campuses you can see them not only in sociology departments but also ensconced in the positions of president, college dean, and dean of students. Beyond academic walls, they show up in the offices of newspapers, welfare agencies, and trade unions, of a wide variety of "cause" organizations, of such aspects of business as marketing, advertising, management, planning, and new-product research, and of governmental agencies on all levels from the White House and State Department and of course the H.E.W. Department to the county court house and the city hall. Among other things, sociological training is becoming recognized in a *de facto* way as excellent preparation for administrative positions—in both managerial and policymaking roles.

How can we relate the confused popular image of sociology on the one hand to the increasing social responsibilities of well-trained sociologists on the other? The field is such a complicated and exciting one that its first college course can be one of a number of kinds; it can give one of a number of images of the discipline and of the uses to which the discipline may be placed. Let me give four oversimple examples of what such a first course might be like. Then I'll pursue further the possible practical applications of sociology in a career dedicated to the service of people, of human welfare.

---

[1]This paper originally appeared in *Humanity & Society* Volume 3, Number 2, 1979.

1. The teacher of the first course may be quite philosophically oriented. She or he may spend a lot of time on terms and conceptions said to deal with social life and with the nature of society, but somehow those terms and conceptions may often remain on an abstract level. To illustrate, "social actors" are said to have "roles" in "groups" and to engage in "symbolic interaction," but they do not seem to be quite human and involved in the problems of living. Such terms are supposed to help us understand what happens in actual human groups in bars, in athletic teams, in factories, in corporate board rooms. They may aid the perceptions of the advanced student, and then they might just become verbal substitutes for actually going to look at human behavior and trying to understand it.

2. The teacher may be oriented quite technically toward sociology and try to give that slant to the introductory course being taught. She or he may feel that no one can even start to study sociology without first mastering research methods with which to observe, measure, and record the changing social scene, that only with such methods can one start to understand the nature of human relationships. Such methods yield what are called "hard data." These data are responses to questions or records of human acts that can be fed into computers and manipulated statistically. The results appear to be mathematical and thus "scientific." They must, therefore, be informative about some aspect of the "real" nature of society. Once again, they may aid the perceptions of the advanced student who may know rather precisely the nature of such technical operations. They may also be just pretentious substitutes for actually going to look at human behavior and trying to understand it.

3. In another course possibility, a teacher may in effect take students on a guided reading or even a walking tour of society's and of the local community's chambers of horrors. This can confront protectively raised teenagers chiefly from white suburban ghettos with so-called "social problems," that is, with problems to their own social class, often for the first time in their lives. Thus these students come to realize that there actually are decaying and filthy slums in all their degradation, criminals who have been caught and imprisoned, deprived people, hopelessly handicapped people, and much more. They may also get some glimpse of the fumbling and ineffectual manners in which do-gooders, practical politicians and businessmen, social workers, and bureaucrats try to mitigate or hide or ignore lower-class miseries. Unfortunately such students often come away from such a course with the impression that the problem groups are the "causes" of their own difficulties and not the "victims" of influences they could not be expected to control or counteract. Students may be taught that those groups are to be pitied and helped but that this will not really change them. Students may not be shown what such groups have done for themselves when they have been moved to encouraging social environments. Racists once tried to bar European slum dwellers from our shores on genetic grounds, but their genes must have been all right; the children and grandchildren of those slum dwellers include some of our country's current artistic, political, and business leaders!

4. Then, as another among a great many possible introductory course orientations, a teacher may try to get students to approach the social situation from a quite different angle, that of many a student rap session, that of the basic concerns of perceptive students who are trying to find their way from adolescence into adult participation in society. It is an approach that takes these questions to be central: What has society

done to me and to other people? What purposes and whose purposes are thus served? Should I try to play along with or to counteract these influences in my own life and in that of others? If so, how can I do it? Is so much human misery as exists in my community and in the world necessary? How can I learn how to lead a humane and constructive life?

This fourth approach to sociology I am calling "sociology for people" or "humanist sociology." It is not offered often enough to students in their classrooms. It is too often just a hit-or-miss part of the informal education students work out for themselves in their hangouts. Many teachers of sociology as of other subjects do not wish to face the implication of this approach that they—the teachers—willingly serve as instruments for society's elites rather than as nurturers of autonomous future citizens. They do not want to realize that they are helping to reproduce controllable technicians and bureaucrats for the structures governing our lives.

Many teachers and students find this fourth approach—if they can come to understand it—upsetting, radical, even outrageous and dangerous. Teachers also have inklings that university administrators sometimes worry about teachers who insist upon discussing how competitions and conflicts actually take place in our society. Many deans do not like to think that their sociology teachers might be discussing the principal sources of human problems to the extent to which such problems derive from decisions or neglect and not from uncontrollable natural developments. Those sources are often the decision-makers in the board rooms and offices of society's jerry-built control structures. They are decision-makers similar to those one also finds on university boards of control.

In this fourth or humanist approach, the teacher may dramatize the contribution of sociology somewhat like this: Look, you have been born and assimilated into this society. As you were being absorbed into this society—socialized into it—you learned one and then several other sets of rules in terms of which you were supposed to operate. Presumably the basic set of those rules was the one called the moral or respectable set. They were the rules taught you as a child by your teachers and clergypeople and, depending upon your social class background, also by your parents. Those rules consisted of dogmatic formulas prescribing honesty, fair play, monogamy, respect for the rights and property of others. Then, as you grew up, you joined in the fun, games, competitions, and conflicts of girls' and boys' groups—gangs, clubs, teams, and informal sets of friends. Some groups you valued demanded and got unfailing loyalty to fellow members. You learned that there are necessary ways—etiquettes, as it were—for evading society's moral rules. You discovered that you had to cooperate with friends in covering up delinquencies, lying, sexual experimentations, and perhaps cheating, stealing, and the use of drugs. You also came to observe more clearly the behavior of your parents and of other adults. You saw what they did in contrast with what they advocated that you do. Some of their behavior resembled that of your amoral or immoral peer group members rather than that of idealized moral models.

These conflicts of rules have been called conflicts among the myths by which and with which we live. These conflicts present sensitive people with problems that have far-reaching ramifications not only in our personal lives but also in society. They bother students as they search for paths from adolescence to adulthood. They are problems, as I said, ordinarily discussed with some candor as well as passion only in student rap sessions. They raise questions about how contrived or mythical are the rules by which we are supposed to live. To what extent do those rules serve to hold us still, as it were, so that we can be exploited efficiently by those who do not believe in such rules? How does society face up or evade facing up to these rule contradictions? Must there be what amounts to a slave-morality and a master-morality, as the philosopher Nietzsche contended? What can we do about these contradictions in our own lives? Should we say, "So what?" and try to live in terms of them? or should we demystify such rules and try to help others demystify them? What would all such efforts accomplish for ourselves and for others?

In this approach, the teacher may join with students in developing with them some conception of what it means to strip away some of the comforting myths that enshroud the control and manipulation of themselves and others in society. When they hear talk about a "social justice system," of "equal justice for all," they can ask: Why then are our prisons filled so disproportionately with Blacks, Chicanos, and poor whites? Criminality is rather evenly distributed among the members of all ethnic, "racial," and class groups in our society. Why then does this so-called "social justice system" demonstrate so much greater understanding" for the proportionately numerous white-collar criminals, most of whom continue to walk our streets? And when they hear talk about the promotion of "democracy" and "human welfare" through American international negotiations and military interventions, they can ask: Why do we almost exclusively implement those noble sentiments with arms bases and arms deals around the world which serve chiefly to protect the exploitations of multinational corporations? Why do we spend so little upon trying to develop actual democracy and human welfare in the countries under the shadow of American-centered corporate imperialism?

The teacher may thus, with such illustrations and many more, attempt to reveal to myth-conditioned students something of the hypocrisies and conspiracies of our society. This is not to say that "democracy" and "human welfare" cannot be defined to be highly estimable goals toward which we should struggle. It is to say that such terms can also and have often been used as delusory propaganda to forward quite undemocratic and inhumane goals. Such is often the case today. Similarly, students can start to see how sports and sensational news not only amuse us but also divert our attention and interest from political malfeasances and business exploitations. They can observe how anti-strike propaganda— advocacy of faith in the employer—can make it easy for employers and their cooperating labor leaders to exploit workers. They can learn something about how other manipulations in the name of social welfare, democracy, and Americanism can direct education into narrow industry-serving channels, can counteract efforts to make medical services more available, and can protect the adulterers of food. They can also learn something about the vast manipulations in the name of social welfare, democracy, and Americanism that lead to wars, the overthrow of unfriendly governments, depressions, inflations, stagflations, and the imperialistic exploitation of people in less developed areas, regions, and countries.

In saying all this about sociology for people, I do not mean to insist that there is an integrated and overarching social conspiracy, a carefully constructed worldwide American-centered plutocratic imperialism. On the contrary, what I am saying is that our world is dominated locally, nationally, and internationally by a military-industrial complex of growing proportions, but that it consists of more or less independent and competing conspiratorial units. Those conglomerate corporate units are linked together occasionally by financial ties but more significantly by common class and imperialist interests among their executives and owners. In their competitive manipulating, these conspirators penetrate with their views and values much of society's life, from the school classroom to the pulpit and the mass media, from trade union halls to the civil and criminal courts, from the international-ized markets to the lobbies and political slush funds that control governmental operations.

Sociology can thus help citizens to perceive the mythological or traditionally built up nature of the so-called "social system" upon which we are told to depend. It might aid people to confront their social predicaments shorn of confusing mystifications and then to realize they can organize to cope more directly and effectively with them. Unfortu-nately, if we know much about sociology at all, we are likely to be trapped in one of the first three types of cop-out sociology I mentioned earlier—abstractions, technicalities, or exotic social horrors. Not that abstractions, technicalities, and exotic social horrors might not provide some useful thoughts about society to those who are also motivated to go out and see and hear and even smell what is going on in a variety of social situations. In themselves, however, abstractions, technicalities, and social horrors can merely become diversions from digging into the nature of the human scene. To learn about society, there is no substitute for participant observation. If we do not do such digging, we have to satisfy ourselves with being fed—to state the situation slightly differently than before—(1) ratio-nalizations of or justifications for the "social system," (2) reasons for regarding efforts at more than cosmetic social changes as being either futile or dangerous, and (3) techniques for investigating "deviants" or limited problems that the powerful will appreciate and will subsidize or reward.

How easy it is for many academics and people in business and government to agree on an idealistic statement of the purposes properly to be served by sociologists: Sociolo-gists as scientists discover, verify, and conceptualize what actually exists in society. In the process, they try to understand their findings and to report them so that they will have the benefit of critical appraisals by other sociologists and also be available for social use. Few would disagree that findings so produced and so employed might somehow, in their aggre-gate, serve many purposes including popular human needs and desires.

This is all very well so far as an abstract and idealistic statement might go. Among other things, it neglects a crucial factor in social scientific as well as in other scientific research. It neglects the personality, including the sex, social status, ethnic background, educational and other experiences, and current terms of employment and motivation of the scientist. As a noted physicist, Victor F. Weisskopf, reminds us, "the activity of science is necessarily embedded in a much wider realm of human experience" than is specified traditionally for a discipline itself. He then contends, "Science itself must have a nonscientific base," but he does not seem to realize how the "emotional and social embedding of science" is not only, as he says, "the precondition of the quest for scientific truth," but also it is a powerful influence upon what may be taken to be "scientific truth."[1]

Thus the idealistic statement of purposes for sociology all seems straightforward and uncomplicated enough in an elementary textbook. It very quickly becomes muddled and quite complex when sociologists are observed actually in operation as practitioners in academic or business or governmental circles. The idealistic statement serves to justify a confusing variety of careerist practices that stretch the terms of the statement in many directions. They leave it a shambles.

A very large share of all sociologists contend that they do not knowingly propagan-dize, that is, help create and disseminate anti-social, manipulative myths that serve special interests. They claim that their strivings for academic preferment and for stipends and grants have nothing to do with the form and direction or adhesions to special interests to be found in their teachings or writings. If this claim had enough demonstrable substance, there would be no reason for the existence of the Association for Humanist Sociology. In saying this, I do not mean to try to give the impression that the Association for Humanist Sociology consists of people who have managed somehow to dissociate themselves entirely from any such influences. Quite the contrary. Members of the Association—so far as I have been able to detect—make no such holier-than-others statement or assumption. But the members of the Association for Humanist Sociology appear to realize vividly, I believe, that sociologists need to recognize quite candidly the antisocial pressures under which they operate. The AHS came into existence and thrives because many of us feel the need to reinforce each other in our efforts to serve people. We believe we can serve people by helping to create a sociology stripped of its incrustation of social myths and especially of class, ethnic, and sexist biases. Too many of those biases are integral parts of texts, monographs, and journal articles.

Those of us who belong to that Association are, we trust, dedicated to the doubting or incredulous state of mind, the skepticism, so long typical of creative scientists in all fields and among them the democratic humanists in social science and sociology.

Perhaps it is unnecessary, but I would like to disclaim any similarity between such cleansing and demystifying skepticism in the service of humanity and what is usually called cynicism. The latter is the intellectual stance so typically that of the pillars of the status quo in our society.

Cynicism is the posture common among those who fear to be identified with the creative loneliness of those who do independent work heedless of currently accepted and legitimated views. The followers of the predominant fads in sociology sneer at the presumptuousness, even at what they assert to be the subversiveness, of independent investigation, thinking, and writing. Little wonder that our professional journals often appear so dull and repetitious. Plagiaristic re-embroidery pays off! Little wonder that those journals contain so few surprises, so little that might accurately be called creative. Little wonder that most introductory sociology texts bore students—as evidenced by declining sociology enrollments in a great many colleges and universities.

Cynicism bows to such notions as that little can be done to improve human society and thus give more people opportunities for self-improvement. It goes along with contentions that genetic factors make it impossible to modify human nature. It accepts that elites are powerful because they are the fit while the oppressed and poor are what they are because they are the biologically unfit. Cynicism of a more or less overt sort is a pervasive characteristic of the operating theories not only of business and political entrepreneurs but also of their middleclass lackeys in managerial and professional and technical statuses. Those middleclass lackeys elaborate that posture into palatable myths for mass consumption and thus for mass manipulation. Typically they build cynicism into social myths by focusing attention on society's victims—the women, the nonwhites, the unemployed and underemployed and unemployable, the psychologically disturbed, and the delinquent and criminal. They do not go beyond those societal victims to ask how come they are as they are. They ask what such people have themselves done to be as they are. They avoid the basic question: What has society done to these people to make them as they are?

The spirit of a cleansing and creative skepticism tied to a concern for humane values and for the future of humanity is bringing into existence organizations within the humanist movements of the social scientific fields other than sociology. The Association for Humanistic Psychology, the largest of these, dates from a conference in 1964 held at Old Saybrook, Connecticut. As the psychologist Rollo May recalls, "That conference developed out of a groundswell of protest against the theory of man of behaviorism on the one side and orthodox psychoanalysis on the other."[2] The Society on Anthropology and Humanism (now the Association for Humanistic Anthropology) came into existence in 1974, and then the Association for Humanist Sociology began taking form in 1975.

All three of these organizations are not to be thought of as creating new emphases or movements in their disciplines. On the contrary, they are all efforts to reinforce and update existing humane concerns. As the anthropological society's statement of purpose so well formulates it: "While varied in form and expression and not adhering to any one academic discipline, humanism has historically sought to reaffirm the intrinsic value of the human being by creating other possibilities for human thought and action, and by keeping alive humanity's habit of continually reshaping its own image, hence its own reality."[3]

In closing, I should like to reiterate the *de facto* expansion of opportunities for literate and society-wise sociologists and to answer briefly the question: How can studies in humanist sociology best help to aim a person at an interesting and rewarding type of employment?

Let us assume that the reader knows enough about what a college teacher of any subject undergoes in the way of preparation for a job and what he or she does on that kind of job. In view of restricting academic budgets, I will discuss other types of employment.

The most salable types of training for a sociologist outside of the academy, to judge from the experiences of my students and those of colleagues, are—in the order of their attractiveness to potential *employers*—the following: (1) ability to communicate orally and in writing in the form of uncomplicated English prose, (2) firsthand knowledge of the behavior of a variety of human groups, (3) competence in analyzing current events in terms of social-historical tendencies, (4) methods of sociological research, their potentialities and their limitations, and (5) a good background in sociological theory and in the humanities.

To be able to speak and to write English prose simply and accurately is one of the easiest talents to sell to almost any employer. It is needed in government, business, voluntary agencies of all sorts, and academia. It is a rarity. It is well worth taking the time to learn it. In my estimation, it should be a requirement for any degree in sociology. It is a much more important subject than the usually required statistics. What is the point of learning sociologese as a private language without being able to translate it readily so that students, colleagues, and people of affairs can understand what you are trying to communicate? And in what is called the "real world," you have to communicate.

Concerning the second mentioned salable quality, field experience, I am saying that intimate work in a variety of human groups, a variety of social class, ethnic, and social cause groups, makes society, sociology and the sociologist come to life. Field work gives human affairs new and important dimensions. The cultural anthropologists wisely require one or two years of participant observation in a quite different cultural setting. This then gives a lot of anthropological writing the sense of reality, vividness, and comparability so much of it contains. It was often said of one of our greatest humanist sociologists, Robert E. Park of the University of Chicago and of Fisk University, a former daily newspaper reporter, that he had learned about sociology primarily through walking the streets of the world, talking with a great many sorts of people he found there, and observing their behavior. As some sociological historians put it, "Park represents the unusual combination of literary ability, wide range of experience, insight into personality, keen appreciation of empirical evidence, and a gift for systematic thought."[4] Through his formal training in this country and in Germany and later and less formally in many other countries, Park had a sophisticated grasp of statistical and other sociological methods and of the theoretical literature of the discipline and related fields. But Park never let methods, terms, or theories stand between him and real people. His basic research technique and the one he inspired his students to use was participant observation or what might be more technically called the field-clinical study of human behavior. There is no substitute for what it can teach.

The third quality mentioned, competence in analyzing current developments in terms of social-historical tendencies, is not so academic a matter as it may sound. It depends at least as much upon first-hand observation and accumulated experience as it does upon background reading. Fads and fancies sweep through the commercial and political fields, often orchestrated by the mass media, and they surely penetrate the halls of academe. To be able to place such matters into some sort of sensible social-historical perspective—a reasonably accurate perspective and not at all necessarily a conservative one—can be quite helpful in building the reputation of a rising humanist sociologist to serve as a guide to sound strategies in public affairs and in social action.

I placed the "nuts and bolts" of sociology as it were in my fourth and fifth places in the list of salable qualities. I did not do this because methods and theory are not important. I did so because, from an employment standpoint in the so-called "real world," they are back-ups for the first three items mentioned. You have to know sociological methods and theory to succeed on many a job, but your employer might not even know that you use them or what their names might be. They are not the items most specifically sought by employers. If you have the first two competences mentioned—literacy and field experience—and an academic claim on the rest, the employer is likely to let it go at that—whether you have a B.A., an M.A., or a Ph.D.

Those who learn sociology for quite practical purposes and then gain a lot of experience outside of academic halls might eventually return to a campus to give new life to sociology or to some other academic discipline. From my own standpoint, after having worked at jobs ranging from steel-pouring to printing and journalism, from farming to door-to-door selling, from ghost-writing and press-relations work to managerial consultation, I prefer what is often called "being an old-fashioned professor." In other words, I have preferred to be a full-time university teacher, to encourage my undergraduate and graduate students to do their own work and not to try to get them to do mine for me, and not to bother with trying to set up research enterprises, team-research efforts subsidized by contracts or grants. As one humanist social-historian, Robert Nisbet, puts it, "Grantsmanship, at first a wry joke among academicians, is by now a publicly recognized source of banality, trivialization and pretentiousness."[5] In most universities, one can even yet spend one's summers and one's sabbatical leaves as well as one's spare time on one's intellectual hobbies—which in the case of a sociologist should, in my estimation, be a series of sociological projects about people and for people.

At any rate, those who pursue the five lines of development I have mentioned are likely to have a most fascinating and useful life whether within or without the academic fold.

Endnotes

[1]V. F. Weisskopf, "The Frontiers and Limits of Science," *American Scientist* 65 (1977):405–11, p. 411 quoted. Cf. A. McC. Lee, *Sociology for Whom?* (New York: Oxford University Press, 1978).

[2]Rollo May, "Introduction to the AHP Theory Conference," pp. 40–41 in Carol Guion and Tina Kelly, eds*., Satan Is Left-Handed* (San Francisco: Association for Humanistic Psychology, 1977), p. 40 quoted.

[3]Statement of purpose, Society on Anthropology and Humanism, *Anthropology and Humanism Quarterly,* vol. 2, no. 1 (March 1977), and subsequent issues, inside cover. See A. McC. Lee, *Toward Humanist Sociology* (Englewood Cliffs, N.J.: Prentice-Hall, 1973).

[4]Howard Becker and H. E. Barnes, *Social Thought From Lore to Science,* rev. ed. (Washington: Harren Press, 1952), vol. 2, p. 982.

[5]Robert Nisbet, "Knowledge Dethroned," *New York Times Magazine*, September 28, 1975, pp. 34 ff., p. 46 quoted.

Sociology of Hope[2]

Chris Dale
New England College

I never knew Al Lee personally. I never met him or had a chance to chat with him about his vision of sociology. But I do remember reading some of his work, including this 1979 article, as I neared the end of my graduate education. It helped to affirm my belief that sociology could be more than an abstract academic endeavor, that it could and should be grounded in a commitment to understanding and addressing the real world issues that people struggle with every day. Lee's writings about humanist sociology—a sociology for people—have been important in shaping my own perspective and commitments as a sociologist.

Sociology for people. From where we sit as humanist sociologists today, it might strike us as rather obvious that sociology should be "for people." Of course it should be for people! What, after all, are the options? Although he never gave it a specific name, Lee was concerned about another option that I will call "sociology for the powers that be." In this article, and in two previous books, *Toward Humanist Sociology* (1973) and *Sociology for Whom* (1978) Lee critiques this version of sociology, (which, in effect, was mainstream sociology through the 70s), and offers a vision of an alternative, humanist sociology.

There are a couple renditions of a "sociology for the powers that be." The first corresponds roughly to Lee's first and second examples of how one might teach an introductory sociology course. It is preoccupied with functionalist armchair theorizing and abstract quantitative gymnastics, much as C. Wright Mills described in his 1959 treatise, *The Sociological Imagination*. It is about conducting surveys of research subjects and building data sets as opposed to doing what Lee advises—immersing yourself with diverse groups of people in a broad range of social settings. And perhaps most significantly, it is about sociologists talking to *each other* in esoteric journal articles and other professional venues, far removed from the social issues and concerns that confront real flesh and blood people.

The second rendition is less abstract and detached from human social experience. But the focus of teaching and research efforts is all on society's marginalized, relatively powerless "problem groups"—the deviant and the disadvantaged. In the early 70s, Alex Liazos aptly described and critiqued this approach in deviance studies as "the sociology of nuts, sluts, and perverts." Then, too, Lee makes reference to the scores of studies and courses devoted to the problems of the poor, of those who live in deplorable conditions and struggle every day to make ends meet. All too often, he suggests, virtually nothing is said about the broader structural forces that constrain and impinge on the lives of folks who don't fit in or

---

[2]This paper originally appeared in *Humanity & Society* Volume 27, Number 3, 2003.

make it. So they become spectacles, curiosities, resigned to their lot in life, though worthy perhaps of our pity and charity. (See Lee's third point.)

Sociology for the powers-that-be, then, has nothing to say about societal power arrangements. In the first case, it is abstract and insular and in the second, it focuses on the disenfranchised, thus diverting attention away from society's power brokers. By contrast, Lee advocates a sociology that advances "human welfare" by exposing "society's control structures" and the contradictions between elite interests and those of "the people." A sociology that de-reifies existing social arrangements and demystifies prevailing ideologies.

Underpinning a sociology for people is a commitment to certain values, and more specifically, what Lee considers "humane values." While mainstream sociology posits value-neutrality as a central tenet, Lee advocates a sociology that is quite explicitly values-based. Values help us to clarify our vision of a better, more humane society, and they provide general benchmarks against which to assess current social conditions. In this article, for example, Lee makes reference to the value of democracy. Not an illusory, superficial democracy that is the stuff of elite propaganda, but genuine democracy, where a broad segment of the population—citizens—genuinely have a voice in decisions and policies that affect their lives. And there is a stark contradiction, he suggests, between genuine democracy and a society in which hierarchical institutions prevail and power is increasingly concentrated in the hands of a military-industrial complex, a self-serving elite. For Lee, then, humanist sociology has as one of its responsibilities the work of shedding light on counter-democratic structures and ideologies, thereby laying the foundation for imagining other, more humane, democratic possibilities.

And human possibility lies at the very core of humanism and humanist sociology. In this article, Lee concurs with the Association for Humanist Anthropology's statement that "humanism has historically sought to reaffirm the intrinsic value of the human being by creating other possibilities for human thought and action, and by keeping alive humanity's habit of continually reshaping its own image, hence its own reality" (p. 15 in original). Humanist sociology sensitizes us to the rather fragile and tentative nature of the social world, and posits that nothing about the social order is inevitable. Lee emphasizes the importance of maintaining a healthy skepticism about prevailing/dominant ideologies and institutions, but it is a skepticism that is coupled with an underlying idealism about change. This, as Lee points out, is the obverse of cynicism, the notion that "little [if anything] can be done to improve human society." A sociology for people, then, is a sociology of social critique and of hope.

2. Toward A Paradigm For Humanistic Sociology [1,2]

Glenn A. Goodwin
Pitzer College

"I've known so many of them!" says Sartre's Roquentin of humanists. "The radical humanist is the particular friend of officials. The so-called 'left' humanist's main worry is keeping human values; he belongs to no party because he does not want to betray the human, but his sympathies go towards the humble…. He is generally a widower with a fine eye always clouded with tears: he weeps at anniversaries. He also loves cats, dogs, and all the higher mammals…."

(Jean-Paul Sartre 1964: 116–17)

What is humanistic sociology? How does it differ from other "sociologies"? How does one know when one is *doing* humanistic sociology? Who are the leading "humanistic sociologists" in the profession today? Is there a "non-humanistic" sociology? At the 1980 annual meetings of the American Sociological Association and the Society For the Study of Social Problems in New York city I raised these apparently "simplistic" questions to scores of colleagues from around the country and discovered a great deal of confusion as to the meaning and definition of humanistic sociology. A thorough review of the "humanistic sociology" literature[1] supports such confusion and, indeed, oftentimes sends one away muttering, with Roquentin, "I've known so many of them!" The contribution I wish to make here is to clarify the confusion and achieve some closure on what we refer to so often as "humanistic sociology."

This lack of closure on the nature and meaning of humanistic sociology is particularly troublesome in view of the fact that most sociologists interested in the history and development of sociological theory would argue that humanism in sociology is as old as the discipline itself. Gella et al. (1978: 16, passim), for example, while noting that humanistic sociology is certainly not a " pure vessel," go on to trace the development of humanism in sociology through the works of Dilthey, Weber, Znaniecki, Sorokin, and Mannheim. Arguments similar to those of Gella et al. are, I suspect, partly responsible for the widespread

[1] Many thanks to Rose Ash, Virginia Oleson, Dick Schemerhorn, and Joseph Scimecca for reading earlier drafts of this paper and offering many helpful suggestions for its improvement. As always, any remaining shortcomings are those of the author. Direct all correspondence to the author at Pitzer College, Claremont, CA 91711.
[2] This paper originally appeared in *Humanity & Society* Volume 7, Number 3, 1983.

naive view among sociologists that because we deal with people—human beings—we are all somehow humanistic sociologists. A major purpose of this paper is to take issue with this point of view and to argue that humanistic sociology is a distinct and identifiable perspective, a position that finds agreement with the contention of Seeley (1972: xvi) that to argue that "we are all humanistic social scientists or that none of us is—is patent nonsense." The issue, then, is not that humanistic sociology lacks a history in our profession but rather, that we have been promiscuous with its use and application.

My own inquiries and search of the literature indicate there is certainly no shortage of "self-admitted" humanistic sociology (or sociologists). What *is* missing is a synthesis of main themes—a way of organizing and substantively identifying "humanistic sociology"—in essence, the necessary conditions for the emergence of a paradigm.[2] The lack of such a synthesis has been noted by others. Writing in 1970 (p. 1), Glass noted the absence in sociology of a movement at all analogous to the paradigmatic development of humanist psychology in the late 1950's and early 1960's, and Herman (1980: 1, emphasis in the original) recently wrote that "humanist sociology is *not* value-neutral... *not* elitist, and ... not yet a paradigm."[3] The time to move toward developing a paradigm for humanistic sociology is overdue. In pursuit of this goal, this paper concludes by summarizing the main themes and presenting examplars of humanistic sociology. First, however, it is necessary to comment briefly on the historical roots of humanism, followed by a discussion which attempts to expose the theoretical and methodological approaches of social science work professed to be "humanistic."

A Note on the Historical Roots of Humanism: Emergent Assumptions

While humanism was born in 15th century Renaissance Europe and began to take root as an intellectual current at the turn of the 16th century, it was during the Enlightenment (18th century) that humanism emerged as a widely accepted *weltanschauung* and became institutionalized into Western social thought. As Rotenstreich (1963: 65) points out, it was around the turn of the 16th century that the humanism movement begins to actually codify assumptions, perspectives, and ideas that would later influence the development of social science. Not the least important of these ideas is the "centering" upon humankind, the emphasis toward focusing upon *human* issues and problems. It is then, as Novack (1973: 136) notes, that humanism began to place humanity "in the center of consideration and makes the lot and destiny of our species on earth its prime concern." It is this general "focus" upon human issues and problems that gets increasingly particularized and eventually emerges as a dominant theme of the Enlightenment.

Blackham (1976: 121) has noted that the Enlightenment, by taking reason, tolerance and humanity as its "passwords"—its battle cry—was a golden age of humanism. These values, coupled with what Rotenstreich (1963: 9) calls a "growing consciousness of the sovereignty of man in the world," are the values that begin to "shape the modern mind," to use a phrase of Brinton's (1963), and are fundamental to understanding the contemporary meaning of "humanistic" social science. In addition to the 18th century view of humanism being "associated with the worth, dignity, rights, responsibilities, and fulfillment of man" (Sutich and Vich 1969: 8), it has implicit in it an epistemological perspective equally fundamental to contemporary humanistic social science. This perspective elevates the subject/

actor as the principal unit of analysis and is summarized well by philosopher Howard L. Parsons (1971: v): "Humanism I take to be a theory, an attitude, and a practice which regards man's needs and powers to be central and necessary in the determination of what is real, knowable, and valuable." Thus, Parsons (1971: 164) concludes, humanism refers to "any system of thought that makes the agent and tester of knowledge and value." Contemporary humanistic social science in general, and sociology in particular, have incorporated these and other basic principles into their perspectives.

Underlying Theoretical and Methodological Approaches of Humanistic Sociology

To examine the substance of what gets labeled "humanistic sociology" is, at first blush, to enter a theoretical world seemingly steeped in confusion. The persistent theorist who is willing to dig below the level of "appearance," however, soon discovers a commonality of historical, theoretical, and substantive concerns that lend justification to the view of humanistic sociology as a distinct and identifiable sociological perspective.

Our failure to elevate humanistic sociology to paradigmatic status may be partly related to our overly rigid view of the distinction between the "humanities" ("soft stuff") and "science" ("hard stuff"). To many sociologists, a *humanistic* social *science* is a contradiction in terms. Humanistic sociology begins by eschewing such rigid distinctions and recognizes the significant contributions of the "humanities" to sociology. Peter Berger (1963: 167) puts it well:

> In addition to human values that are inherent in... sociology itself, the discipline has other traits that assign it to the immediate vicinity of the humanities if they do not, indeed indicate that it belongs fully with them... sociology is vitally concerned with what is, after all, the principal subject matter of the humanities—the human condition itself.

In addition to humanistic sociologists acknowledging their familial ties to the "humanities," their work reveals the many themes identified with the historical development of humanism as an intellectual current. Thus, Gella et al. (1978: 16, emphasis in original, brackets mine) write:

> For sociologists *humanism*... is a philosophical perspective which centers on man; it is an attempt to defend the human realm against [that]... which threatens man's dignity freedom and/or self-realization....

and, in a similar vein, Lee (1973: 128) argues that humanist sociology "calls for a man-centered sociology in the service of human needs and goals as they are popularly defined."[4]

There are, in addition to an historical "intellectual current affinity," more substantive concerns that set humanistic sociology apart from other "sociologies." Gella et al. (1978: 169) call our attention to the fact that "all the forbearers of humanistic sociology, in one fashion or another, confronted the issue of values," though I am hard-pressed to identify any substantive sociology that does not confront "the issue of values in one fashion or another." A central hallmark of humanistic sociology is not simply its concern with social values but, rather, as noted by Warshay (1975: 86), its emphasis upon studying the manner in which social values portray various aspects of *human meaning within complex and changing cultural settings*. Further, a major purpose of such emphases is to contribute to the demystification of social phenomena. As Lee (1978: 214) puts it: "Social phenomena that intrigue humanist sociologists include the personal and institutional facades that disguise multidimensional, multifaceted people and groups." Such an undertaking requires, like all sociological theory (cf. Wrong 1961: 193), making certain assumptions about human nature and endorsing a particular image of man/woman. Humanistic sociology is no exception—it makes assumptions about human nature and it has its own unique image of man/woman.

The image of man/woman endorsed and perpetuated by humanistic sociology is one that is true to the heritage of humanism generally. It is a view that focuses upon and emphasizes the human being as a subject/actor who, in the words of Carl Rogers (1963: 47), is an active, choosing responsible architect of self. An "oversocialized view" of man/woman is relinquished here. As Howard L. Parsons (1971) notes, human beings are seen as being more than billiard balls knocked about by circumstances and are conceptualized, rather, as active agents who change circumstances, a view of human nature, Parsons points out, that informs the work of Marx (cf. Marx and Engels 1947: 111). At the same time, while this focus and emphasis represents a departure from other sociological perspectives, humanistic sociology remains true to the sociological tradition by also insisting upon linking the *subject* to socio-cultural context. It is, then, the focus and emphasis upon an *existential, autonomous* being, interacting within complex cultural settings, that is central to humanistic sociology. As Glass and Staude (1972: xi) note: "It is this fundamental consideration for the human person, and the view of man as having a measure of autonomy, choice, and self-determination that is at the root of a humanistic perspective in sociology."

Such an image of the human person as an existential, autonomous and transcending being calls into question many of the assumptions that sociology has commonly made about human nature and hence further establishes the uniqueness of the humanistic sociology perspective. The latter perspective, for example, eschews the traditional sociological image of man/woman as a "consonance/equilibrium seeker" in favor of an image of the human actor as a more complex, even dissonance-creating, and inconsistent being,[5] a view of human life that finds support in the work of Dubin. Dubin (1979: 413) writes:

> the idea of consistency in our total lives is a figment of the imaginations of social analysts and personality theorists…. We are complex selves, manyfaceted, and inconsistent.

The actor as conceptualized by humanistic sociology, then, exists within and is defined by a socio-cultural context, but is also an actor who is capable of transcending that very existence and thus capable of directly influencing and changing it. Rotenstreich (1963: 67, sic) summarizes this point well:

> In establishing man's essential transcendence of given circumstances… humanism shows that man, in his essence, is neither fully dependent upon nor exhaustively defined by the historical process…he alone can determine the

course of external events for he alone has the power to transcend himself and his immediate circumstances so as to criticize and regulate them.

Utilizing this underlying image of man/woman, it then becomes a central task of humanistic sociology, as Glass (1972: 19) notes, to ask which institutions and social arrangements "promote the capacity and ability of groups and individuals to make free and responsible choices in light of their needs to grow, to explore new possibilities, and to do more than simply survive...." The pursuit of such a central task reveals both a substantive theoretical and epistemological direction and an underlying value position, all of which help vindicate the distinctiveness of the humanistic sociology perspective.

The substantive theoretical direction which characterizes humanistic sociology, as I have implied, is one that regards human meaning and consciousness as the critical data upon which interpretations of social life are constructed (Gella et al. 1978: vii). Accordingly, a major emphasis of humanistic sociology is upon the inner-meaning of social action and an inherent preoccupation with the symbolic side of social life, the substance of which is interpreted and analyzed within a socio-cultural context (Gella et al. 1978: 172). It is within this context that humanistic sociology professes to study the human being as a conscious, meaning-creating, intentional agent, thus elevating the epistemological role that intuition and/or empathy plays in informing the research of the humanistic sociologist (cf. Poppen et al. 1975: 5; Glass 1972: 6).

An overriding epistemological concern of humanistic sociology, and one that takes its direction, appropriately, from its substantive theoretical interests, is a focus on the relationship between the subjective and objective modes of "knowing," the underlying orientation to which is grounded in the sociology of knowledge. Thus, a major goal of the humanistic sociologist is to understand the ways in which social reality is "constructed" or "negotiated" by human subjects and to realize that the investigator himself/herself is inherently involved in the process of such "constructions" or "negotiations." Gella et al. in discussing Znaniecki's contributions to the development of humanistic sociology call attention to the importance of this perspective. In commenting upon the significance of Znaniecki's concept of the "humanistic coefficient," the authors (1978: 97) indicate that the essential feature of socio-cultural phenomena, when taken as objects of theoretical reflection, is that they are "data given to somebody in the course of his experience, or activities performed by some conscious subject as viewed by himself or others." Accordingly, the authors (1978: 99) conclude that both the "humanistic coefficient" of Zuaniecki, and humanistic sociology generally, insist that "researchers respect the fundamental idea of the sociology of knowledge that our recognition or perception of reality is socially constructed."

In essence, the distinctiveness of the humanistic *sociology* epistemological perspective lies in a philosophy of science which is not fearful of finding room for the human *person*—both the observer and the observed—in his/her subjective as well as his/her objective made, a frame of reference endorsed by Rogers (1963: 47) nearly two decades ago when he was justifying the development of a humanistic *psychology*. Indeed, perhaps the most easily recognized (and contentious) attributes of humanistic sociology are its underlying value positions regarding "science" and the role of the social science investigator.

It is common in the sociological literature to (wrongly) allege that the humanistic perspective in sociology is somehow "anti-science." Typical of such allegations is Warshay's (1975: 83, parentheses in original) evaluation of my own work in which he first identifies me, appropriately, as representative of the humanistic sociology tradition (what he refers to as the "new humanism!" in sociology) and then goes on to assert that this perspective eschews "scientific rigor (and science altogether)." This type of misconception results, I suspect, from failing to understand the differences between the refusal to accept the canons of a rigid *positivism* while at the same time accepting scientific principles generally on the part of humanistic sociologists. The acceptance of a rigid positivism, referring as it does to the acceptance of classical Scientific Methods as the *only* means of knowing (social) reality—a position that Gouldner (1965) has referred to as a "methodolatry" that results from "an anxiety of reason"—is clearly rejected by humanistic sociologists. What the humanistic sociology perspective does embrace, however, are methods of scientific inquiry that inform the study of the human condition without reducing the essence of man/woman to physicalistic/naturalistic laws or principles. As Glass (1972: 6) notes, "the humanistic social scientist's highest commitment is not a worship of science but a concern for man."

Accordingly, humanistic sociology while clearly anti-positivistic is clearly *not* anti-*scientific*. On the contrary, the major tenets of scientific inquiry, namely, a commitment to rationalism and empiricism and the necessity for replication to verify the accuracy of results are an intricate part of the humanistic sociological perspective. Thomas Ford Hoult (1979: 109, brackets mine), a prominent spokesperson for humanistic sociology, puts it thusly:

> evidence suggests that humanistic and scientific aims can be served simultaneously despite some claims to the contrary... properly controlled science... enhances the possibility of achieving humanistic [sociology] goals... the chief virtue of scientific method is that results of particular investigations can be checked for accuracy. Such checking is made possible by the fact that scientific method calls for full disclosure of procedure in accordance with a well-established series of steps.... Thus, there is a place for empiricism in [humanistic] sociological study... but... 'pure empiricism' [positivism] is often very limited and sometimes dangerous.

Thus, while humanistic sociology does indeed eschew a commitment to a rigid positivism, the general principles of scientific inquiry remain intact.

What the humanistic sociology perspective calls for is a careful, oftentimes *critical*, approach to what especially American sociology has prosaically dubbed "scientific" (i.e., positivistic) research methods. This "call" takes its direction from the insistence that we attempt to synthesize "hard," quantitative, perhaps overly-computerized renditions of social reality, with a more genuine "soft," qualitative version of such reality. Hence, as Matson (1972: 116) warns us, when the human person is the subject "the proper understanding of science leads unmistakably to the science of understanding." The development of such a "science of understanding," a science that is committed to exploring the complex social reality of the *person*, requires an accompanying commitment to empirical and intuitive *and* historical methods. It also requires a redefinition of the role of the sociological investigator.

The humanistic sociology perspective is characterized by an underlying value position which encourages the active involvement and/or engagement of the scientist with the social reality that he/she seeks to investigate. It assumes, in other words, that "humanistic sociology is and must be value-committed, in contrast to the value-free emphasis of the past" (Hoult 1979: 2). Such "value-committed" social science work oftentimes carries with it a personal transformation of the social scientist himself/herself and such work frequently proceeds by acknowledging and endorsing explicit political and/or moral positions.[6] Stein (1972: 165), in summing up what he sees to be major features of humanistic sociology, emphasizes these attributes:

> the humanistic sociologist tries to explore, expand, and transform personal dimensions through his work. [7] Humanistic sociology views society as an historically evolving enterprise that can only be understood through the struggle to liberate human potentialities.

Humanistic sociology, then, in addition to attributes detailed throughout this paper, calls for active engagement and/or participation on the part of the investigating social scientist. There is little room here for the detached, value-neutral sociological positivist.

This paper concludes by summarizing the main themes as well as presenting exemplars of humanistic sociology. Such is the purpose of the next and final section of this essay.

Summary and Conclusions: Main Themes and Exemplars of Humanistic Sociology: Toward A Paradigm

Three general underlying themes emerge from the preceding review of humanistic sociology. These themes are: (1) an emphasis on the unique aspects of human beings, i.e., a view of the human subject as a conscious, relatively autonomous, and existential actor (rather than "reactor"); (2) humanistic sociologists consciously embracing values of freedom, equality, and self-determination for all humankind and encouraging the creation of institutions and social contexts that perpetuate these values; and (3) the rejection of a rigid positivism while accepting scientific principles generally. A brief comment clarifying the consistency between these themes is in order.

That the emphasis on the unique aspects of human beings (theme 1) is compatible with the emphasis on a non-positivistic sociology (theme 3) can be seen by the exemplars of humanistic sociology presented below. Accordingly, those working within a humanistic sociology perspective conceptualize the human actor as a conscious, meaning-seeking *subject* and reject the tendency of positivism to force this conception of social reality into a deterministic and deductive framework. Humanistic sociologists argue, rather, for approaching their subject matter in a manner that allows for adopting whatever methods are judged to be compatible with that subject matter. Method thus becomes a tool to be utilized in research, as opposed to it being determinant of what is "researchable."

The relationships between embracing humanist values of freedom, equality, self-determination, etc. (theme 2) and the themes of human uniqueness (1) and non-positivistic science (3) are also compatible. Humanistic sociology begins by recognizing that there is no social science that is free from value-bias and that ideological axes can be ground in even the most positivistic of research (cf. Rubinoff 1968: 3–21). Given this recognition, humanistic sociology attempts to confront the problem of bias by explicitly identifying the (humanist) value positions that underlie its research. Further, the quality of the values adopted in research (theme 2) is structured by the humanistic sociologist's view of the unique aspects of human beings (theme 1). Thus, the humanistic sociologist who views the human subject as a conscious actor, deserving of dignity, autonomy, and choice, will strive in his/her work to encourage and support the social contexts and institutions that further enhance equality, freedom, and self-determination. What emerges here, given the commitment to scientific principles (theme 3), is a value-*oriented* and, by definition, non-positivistic science.

Having reviewed the essential features of humanistic sociology, it is now possible to summarize the paper by presenting a framework or model that is useful in organizing and substantively identifying humanistic sociology. The foundations of such a framework or model, to be effective heuristically, must identify at least three important characteristics of the subject matter under consideration: underlying presuppositions, theoretical focus and/or emphasis, and methodological/epistemological positions, all of which are to some extent interrelated. It is through the elaboration of these characteristics that the conditions for the emergence of a paradigm of humanistic sociology can be fulfilled.

A. Underlying Presuppositions. To expose the presuppositions that underlie any variety of sociological theory is at the same time to render explicit the underlying ideological positions of that body of theory. As might be expected, the underlying *ideological* commitments of humanistic sociology reflect the history and development of humanism generally.[8] Accordingly, humanistic sociology assumes a commitment to the belief in the dignity and fulfillment of all human beings in their pursuit of equality and liberty and thus also assumes an active pursuit of human values that stress tolerance, self-determination, and free choice for all persons. As Hoult (1979: 1) puts it, humanistic sociology endorses the view that "every person has potential worth and should have the opportunity to develop to the greatest extent possible consistent with the development of others."

Accepting these presuppositions in turn influence the structure and direction of the substantive work undertaken by the humanistic sociologist. Thus, humanistic sociologists begin by accepting the view that sociology must be person-centered (as opposed, for example, to system-centered), critical of existing knowledge, and oftentimes dedicated to social change (cf. Goodwin 1973; Lee 1975). All these presuppositions, of course, structure the theoretical and methodological emphases of humanistic sociology.

B. Theoretical Focus and/or Emphasis. The most prominent dimension of humanistic sociology is its focus on the individual as *perpetually in interaction with a sociocultural context*. It is a focus that elevates the actor/subject to the center of the analytical stage while simultaneously insisting upon analyzing his/her interaction with objective conditions, a theoretical position that has precedence, for example, in much of the work of Weber. Similarly, as Glass and Staude (1972: 184) note, the sociology of C. Wright Mills can be identified as characteristic of such a perspective (see also Mills 1961). The point to be emphasized here is that the chief theoretical characteristic of humanistic sociology is the emphasis it places on examining what Gella et al. (1978: 167) call "the dialectical interplay between objective conditions and subjective existence," an emphasis, it should be noted, that makes inquiry into the nature of human consciousness equally central and distinctive to the perspective. Some exemplars of this approach would be phenomenological sociology, reflexive sociology, critical theory (The Frankfurt School, particularly the work of Reich, Adorno, Marcuse, and Fromm), the sociology of knowledge, and varieties of Marxist sociology.[9]

Moreover, the focus on examining objective conditions and subjective existence and the exploration into the phenomenon of human consciousness also renders symbolic interactionism and varieties of the sociology of the absurd as exemplars of the humanistic sociology perspective. Accordingly, symbolic interactionism, as represented in the work of Strauss (1978), Blumer (1969), Scheff (1968), and Morris (1977), emphasizing as it does the phenomena of reality construction and negotiation, human intentions, acts, feelings, and the symbolic aspects of social life generally, locate it clearly within the perspective. Likewise, the work of Goodwin (1971) and Lyman and Scott (1970) on the sociology of the absurd, particularly as regard its concern with exploring the nature and composition of human meaning, fits into humanistic sociology as outlined in this paper.

C. Methodological/Epistemological Positions. Central to understanding the methodological/epistemological positions of humanistic sociology is its critique of the excesses of positivism and its advocating the utilization of the humanities as a source of information/data in the investigation of social reality. As Gella et al. (1978: 42) point out: "within the discipline of sociology, 'humanism' is a... label that has been attached to almost all those currents of thought which have tried to oppose the excesses of positivism, empiricism, and scientism" and, further, that "humanistic sociologists should impregnate sociological trends with philosophical reflection and defend the role of history as a background for analysis" (p. 192). Moreover, the methodological/epistemological dimensions of humanistic sociology encompasses a commitment to eschewing value-neutrality and encouraging the role of the social science investigator as becoming one of "demystifier" and "critic." Thus, Warshay (1975: 87–9, brackets mine) appropriately notes that humanistic sociology:

> is critical of the emphasis upon formal theory construction and positivistic research methods... a prime duty of [humanistic sociology] is to involve oneself in issues of the day... the humanists continually posit for sociology the task of relevance to such issues... 'involvement' thus comes to have both methodological and activist connotations.

What is clear, then, is that humanistic sociology is value-committed and oftentimes includes a sociology of possibilities i.e., a sociology of what might or can be (cf. Glass, 1970). In essence, humanistic sociologists, as Lee (1978: 36) puts it, should act principally as critics, demystifiers, reporters, and clarifiers.

Various methodological commitments of humanistic sociology take their direction from these guidelines. Thus, phenomenological sociology, emphasizing as it does the subject/actor, observer/observed dichotomies figures prominently in the doing of humanistic sociology, as does an epistemological bias toward the use of *verstehen* and/or intuition as a methodological tool. Accordingly, methods that include the utilization of "the definition of the situation" and that posit the actions of conscious human beings as the ultimate "testers" of knowledge are characteristic of the perspective. Various examplars of such methodological approaches might include participant observation, dramaturgy, what Geertz (1973: 3–30) calls "thick description" in anthropology, and the utilization, when appropriate, of unobtrusive measures.[10] As in its theoretical focus and/or emphasis, humanistic sociology goes about "knowing" the social world through placing primary emphasis on the various definitions and constructions of that world as articulated by the subject/actors involved.

In summary, humanistic sociology presupposes the worth and dignity of every human being and encourages the social scientist to pursue the realization of such values through his/her work; theoretically, it elevates the subject/actor to the center of the analytical stage, emphasizes the examination of subjective existence and objective conditions, and pays close attention to the phenomena of human consciousness and meaning; and, finally, being critical of dogmatic positivism, humanistic sociology argues for the eschewing of value-neutrality and the utilization of research methods that allow for entrance into the symbolic world of reality construction and negotiation.

Like Roquentin's response to humanists generally, we in sociology risk being overwhelmed by "knowing so many of them!" Unlike Roquentin, however, we have the emergence of a framework which may be useful in distinguishing between those who are "particular friends of officials" and those who "weep at anniversaries" and those who....

Endnotes

[1]Subsequent to the original drafts of this paper in early 1981, Joseph Scimecca's fine text, *Society and Freedom: An Introduction to Humanist Sociology* (1981) appeared, a text which I immediately adopted for my Introductory Sociology class. However, though both Scimecca and I share fundamental frames of reference on the nature and meaning of humanistic sociology (see especially pp. 166–81 of his text), the article before you addresses specific paradigmatic or "pre-paradigmatic" issues and themes.

[2]As one would expect, the term "paradigm" continues to be contentious among both the adherents to a humanistic sociology and others among us who wish to eschew the "soft" label of "humanistic," and both for precisely antithetical reasons. Our "humanistic" sisters and brothers eschew the term because it "connotes natural science" and others among us argue that "humanistic sociology" cannot possibly be "paradigmatic" because humanistic sociology fails to meet what they see to be the "rigors" of Science. Consequently, various reviewers have suggested I substitute the terms "model," "frame of reference," "orientation," and even "outline" in place of paradigm. As the title of this article suggests, I believe we are moving toward a paradigm of humanistic sociology, perhaps currently residing in what Kuhn (1970) or Friedrichs (1972) would call a "pre-paradigmatic" stage, and for that reason have retained the contentious term "paradigm" throughout.

[3]Both Class and Herman, it might be noted in passing, are "self-admitted" humanistic sociologists.

[4]In this same work Lee (1973: xii) identifies himself as an "existential-humanist," meaning that his "intellectual focus is upon what exists and upon what is most relevant to man." Further, he maintains (1973: 128) that the "existential-humanist" perspective is a "rough paradigm" in sociology.

[5]The development and elaboration of such an existentialist conception of the human actor was the subject matter of two of my earlier articles (1971; 1973) in which, among other things, I attempted to reformulate our traditional sociological conceptions of human nature.

[6]The acknowledging of political and/or moral positions in the work of some humanistic sociologists has led, I suspect, to commonly confusing the humanistic sociology perspective with radical sociology. As I have argued throughout, the distinctiveness of the humanistic sociology perspective lies in its unique conceptualization of the human actor

and its specific commitments to theoretical and methodological modes of inquiry, qualities that separate it clearly from varieties of "radical sociology." Compare, for example, the "radical sociologies" of Colfax and Roach (1971) and Deutsch and Howard (1970) to the perspective outlined in this paper. For an example of confusing humanistic sociology with radical sociology see Warshay (1975: 75, emphasis mine) where he refers to my own work as humanistic "*and/or radical sociology.*"

[7]This point of view has an affinity to Gouldner's (1970: 481–512) conception of "reflexive sociology."

[8]In addition to the general ideological perspective that underlies humanistic sociology, it is important to be aware of the manner in which that perspective is *utilized*. Thus, as Hoult (1979: 4–5) warns us, sociologists must "remain constantly alert to the possibility that even the most humanistically intended studies can be used for demagogic purposes." Similarly, Michael Goldstein (1980: 581), in his recent review of the work of Thomas Szasz, writes that "an empirical assessment of this point of view may reveal that ideologies that claim to be humanistic…can provide justifications for dehumanizing policies and practices."

[9]The issue of whether or not Marxist sociology (or "Marxist humanism") fits into the perspective developed in this paper is a complicated one and deserving of systematic analysis in its own right. There is abundant evidence in the original writings of Marx and Engels that qualify their work for inclusion within humanistic sociology. At the same time, there is much sociological work done by self-professed "Marxists" that ignores or distorts Marx and Engels' original commitments to a humanistic perspective. For a scholarly and insightful analysis of the original writings of Marx and Engels and the ways in which their work "fits" into humanistic sociology see Howard L. Parsons (1971). An example of the ways in which the original writings of Marx and Engels can be distorted is found in Petrosyan (1972). The point I wish to make here is that the argument one frequently hears from some "Marxist" colleagues that their sociology is ipso facto humanistic because of its professed allegiance to classical Marxism is simply ridiculous.

[10]It should be noted that these methodological exemplars do not always meet *all* the criteria of the humanistic sociology perspective. Participant observation, "dramaturgy," and the use of unobtrusive measures, depending on how they are used by various investigators, for example, do not always criticize existing knowledge or advocate social change. What they do have in *common* with the humanistic sociology perspective, however, is their *collective commitment* to a "person-centered" inquiry, to demystification, reporting, clarifying, and to "knowing" the social world by appeal to the definitions and constructions of that world as articulated by the subjects/actors involved.

References

Berger, Peter L. 1963. *Invitation to Sociology: A Humanistic Perspective*. Garden City, New York: Anchor Books.

Blackham, H. J. 1976. *Humanism*. New York: International Publications Service.

Blumer, Herbert. 1969. *Symbolic Interactionism: Perspective and Method*. Englewood Cliffs: Prentice-Hall.

Brinton Crane. 1963. *The Shaping of Modern Thought*. Englewood Cliffs: Prentice Hall.

Colfax, J. David and Jack Roach (eds.). 1971. *Radical Sociology*. New York: Basic Books.

Deutsch, Steven E. and John Howard (eds.). 1970. *On Where It's At: Radical Perspectives in Sociology*. New York: Harper and Row, Publishers.

Dubin, Robert. 1979. *"Central Life Interests: Self-Integrity in a Complex World."* Pacific Sociological Review, 22, 4 (October), 405–26.

Friedrichs, Robert W. 1972. *A Sociology of Sociology.* New York: The Free Press.

Geertz, Clifford. 1973. *The Interpretation of Cultures.* New York: Basic Books.

Gella, Aleksander, Sue Curry Jansen, and Donald F. Sabo, Jr. 1978. *Humanism in Sociology: Its Historical Roots and Contemporary Problems.* Washington, D.C.: University Press of America.

Glass, John. 1970. "Toward a Humanist Sociology." Newsletter of the Association for Humanistic Psychology VI, 4 (April)

—— and John Staude (eds.). 1972. *Humanistic Society: Today's Challenge to Sociology.* Pacific Palisades, CA.: Goodyear Publishing Co., Inc.

——. 1972. "The Humanistic Challenge to Sociology." In Glass and Staude, Ibid.

Goldstein, Michael S. 1980. "The Politics of Thomas Szasz: A Sociological View." *Social Problems*, 27, 5 (June).

Goodwin, Glenn A. 1971. "On Transcending the Absurd: An Inquiry in the Sociology of Meaning." *American Journal of Sociology*, 76, 5 (March), 831–846.

——. 1973. "The Emergence of Various Theoretical Trends and Their Prospects in Sociology." *Sociological Focus*, 6, 2 (Spring), 1–9.

Gouldner, Alvin W. 1965. *Enter Plato.* New York: Basic Books.

——. 1970. *The Coming Crisis of Western Sociology.* New York: Basic Books, Inc.

Herman, Robert D. 1980. "Toward Humanist Social Theory: A Personal Agenda." Paper presented at the annual meetings of the Association for Humanist Sociology, October 9–12, Louisville, Kentucky.

Hoult, Thomas Ford. 1979. *Sociology For A New Day.* New York: Random House 2nd ed.

Kuhn, Thomas S. 1970. *The Structure of Scientific Revolutions.* Second Edition, enlarged. Chicago: The University of Chicago Press.

Lee, Alfred McClung. 1973. *Toward Humanist Sociology.* Englewood Cliffs: Prentice Hall.

——. 1978. *Sociology For Whom?* New York: Oxford University Press.

——. 1975. "Humanist Challenges to Positivists." *The Insurgent Sociologist,* 6, 1 (Fall) 41–50.

Lyman, Stanford and Marvin B. Scott. 1970. *A Sociology of the Absurd.* New York: Appleton-Century Crofts.

Marx, Karl and F. Engels. 1947. *The German Ideology, Parts I & III.* New York: International Publishers.

Matson, Floyd. 1972. "The Human Image: Science and the Understanding of Man." In Glass and Staude (eds.), op. cit

Mills, C. Wright. 1961. *The Sociological Imagination.* New York: Oxford University Press, First Evergreen edition.

Morris, Monica. 1977. *An Excursion into Creative Sociology*, New York: Columbia University Press.

Novack, George. 1973. *Humanism and Socialism.* New York: Pathfinder Press.

Parsons, Howard L. 1971. *Humanism and Marx's Thought.* Springfield Ohio: Charles C. Thomas, Publisher.

Petrosyan, M. 1972. *Humanism: Its Philosophical, Ethical, and Sociological Aspec*ts. Moscow: Progress Publishers, First printing, trans. from the Russian by Bryan Bean and Robert Daglish.

Poppen, Paul J., Abraham Wandersman, & Lois Pall Wandersman. 1975. "What Are Humanism and Behaviorism and What Can They Say to Each Other?" In Wandersman et al. (eds.), *Humanism and Behaviorism: Dialogue and Growth.* New York: Pergamon Press.

Rogers, Carl R. 1963. "Toward A Science of the Person." In Anthony Sutich and Miles A. Vich (eds.), *Readings in Humanistic Psychology.* New York: Free Press.

Rotenstreich, Nathan. 1963. *Humanism in the Contemporary Era.* The Hague, The Netherlands: Mouton and Company.

Rubinoff, Lionel. 1968. *The Pornography of Power.* Chicago: Quadrangle Books.

Sartre, Jean-Paul. 1964. *Nausea.* New York: New Directions Library. Trans. by Lloyd Alexander.

Scheff, Thomas J. 1968. "Negotiating Reality: Notes on Power in the Assessment of Responsibility." *Social Problems,* 16 (Summer), 3–17.

Scimecca, Joseph A. 1981. *Society and Freedom: An Introduction to Humanist Sociology.* New York: St. Martin's Press.

Seeley, John R. 1972. "Humanizing the Superconscious: A Foreword to Humanistic Society and a Prelude to a Humane Society." In Glass and Staude (eds.), op. cit.

Stein, Maurcie R. 1972. "On the Limits of Professional Thought." In Glass and Staude (eds.), op. cit.

Strauus, Anselm. 1978. *Negotiations: Varieties, Contexts, Processes and Social Order.* San Francisco: Jossey-Bass.

Sutich, Anthony J. and Miles A. Vich (eds.). 1969. *Readings in Humanistic Psychology.* New York: Free Press.

Warshay, Leon H. 1975. *The Current State of Sociological Theory.* New York: David McKay Co., Inc.

Wrong, Dennis H. 1961. "The Oversocialized Conception of Man in Modern Sociology." *American Sociological Review,* April, 183–93.

My Twenty Cents Worth on Paradigms[3]

Corey Dolgon
Stonehill College

I recently received a query from a learned colleague who asked if I could help him define what humanist sociology is. I suggested that it was an approach to sociology that recognized the inherently human, and therefore subjective, conditions of our work. Thus, humanist sociologists openly engage the subjectivity of research from the outset and commit to engage in work that will improve the human condition as our goal. I also pointed him towards the Association for Humanist Sociology website that spells out the framework of our mission: "we view people not merely as products of social forces, but also as shapers of social life, capable of creating social orders in which everyone's potential can unfold. Difficult times give humanist sociologists opportunities to apply their special skills and perspectives for the purpose of creating a more humane world."

Had my colleague wanted more than a few words, I would have pointed him towards Glenn Goodwin's excellent article published by *Humanity and Society* in 1983. Goodwin's "Toward a Paradigm for Humanistic Sociology" not only offers humanists and others insight into what humanist sociology is, but effectively presents the historical, theoretical and methodological foundations for such an approach. In the way that good scholars always do, Goodwin not only tells us where we are, but he explains how we got here. Twenty years later, we may be in a different place, but the examination itself is now an integral historical document necessary for analyzing where we are now and how we got here.

The first thing Goodwin makes clear is that there is no single humanist sociology. In fact, by moving "towards a paradigm," the author simply wants to present a "synthesis of main themes—a way of organizing and substantively identifying 'humanistic sociology'—in essence the necessary conditions for the emergence of a paradigm." He recognizes that there may be "many" humanist sociologies, but crucial elements fundamental to both humanism and sociology should and do distinguish the field. In a powerful summary, Goodwin proposes that our endeavor "presupposes" universal human dignity and worth and "encourages" social scientists to "pursue the realization of such values" in our work.

This kind of declaration of identity and purpose is always important. As I read through the past twenty-five years of *Humanity and Society* in order to produce two special anniversary issues, I found that editors periodically looked to reaffirm or even reshape the project of humanistic social science by presenting articles intended to define humanist sociology. What distinguishes Goodwin's exploration though is how much he offers us about the content and form of such inquiries themselves. His work continues to be a guide in our search for both intellectual and practical identities as humanist sociologists.

---

[3]This paper originally appeared in *Humanity & Society* Volume 27, Number 3, 2003.

I am particularly struck by what Goodwin gives us in the way of grappling with the science/humanism dichotomy. First, the author reminds us of the Enlightenment's commitment not only to science and reason, but also to human rights, dignity and responsibility. Reason itself was not solely the purview of scientific exploration, but was integrally linked to the inalienable rights and worth of all people. Goodwin implies that, in fact, science and humanism as somehow contradictory may simply be a more modern (and mistaken) conceptualization than an inherently epistemological incompatibility. I would pose the possibility that, as the Protestant Ethic facilitated Capitalism's triumph, capitalism itself may have ushered in the promotion of a scientific rationality obsessed with profit maximization and power, as opposed to an intellectual and cultural paradigm in the service of humanity.

Thus I would argue that Goodwin's greatest contribution to humanist sociology is not just a reaffirmation of the importance of inspiring our sociological work with the spirit of humanism, but is a clarion call for the reintegration of science and humanism. Such a theoretical proposition then sheds light into one of the murkier corners of humanist sociology—that of methodology. Because humanists embrace subjectivity and value-laden research, both mainstream sociologists and some of our own members create a dichotomized universe where research must either zealously adhere to the scientific method or passionately reject such methods outright. Goodwin, instead, suggests we navigate the waters between a disciplinary Scylla and Charybdis by reminding us of John Glass's caution, "the humanist social scientist's highest commitment is not the worship of science but a concern for man." Thus, Goodwin contends that humanist sociologists reject rigid positivism and classical scientific methodology as the "only means of knowing social reality," but we should embrace the "methods of scientific inquiry that inform the study of the human condition without reducing the essence of man/woman to physicalist/naturalistic laws of principles."

Inspired by Goodwin, I might go one step further to argue that humanist sociology ought to be able to re-inscribe science into humanity. In other words, we ought to be able to practice a science that recognizes its theory and application as inherently ensconced in the human condition of subjectivity and struggle, just as we might engage a humanism that embraces science as a profound intellectual and practical tool for the improvement of the human condition. This was, of course, at the heart of Marx's historical materialism; a recognition that scientists and their research were always shaped by the material conditions that framed their work, and instead of posing as value-free, his call was to embrace the inherent dialectic of material conditions and social life—of structure and agency—as well as commit ourselves to not just understanding the world, but to changing it.

3. A Humanistic Perspective on Science and Society[1,2]

Sal Restivo and Michael Zenzen
Rensselaer Polytechnic Institute

Reflexive Statement

Prior to turning our attention to the sociology (Restivo) and philosophy (Zenzen) of science in graduate school, we were on the threshold of careers in engineering and science. Our turn toward sociological and philosophical studies has progressively revealed the naiveté of the views we had internalized about science as "free" and "pure" inquiry. We have come to view science as a social activity and process which has radical political implications relative to ordinary political economy. We view "humanistic science" science unified with other modes of inquiry and other social processes in a human community founded on caring, cooperation, self-actualization, ecological consciousness, and evolutionary vision. Our view of the future of science can be described in Marx's terms (1956: 110–111; 1973: 699ff) as the negation of science-as-it-is, and its transformation into wholistic, unitary (not Unified), global, and delineated science. The adjective "humanistic" is a reminder that as humanists fostering scientific inquiry, we are engaged in the general struggle to revolutionize a society that is producing crippled and crippling "monstrosities" (to recall Marx's tough vocabulary) instead of nurturing loving, lovable, liberated, and wise human being.

Introduction

The sociology of science is dominated by the Mertonian paradigm and a research emphasis on science as an autonomous social system (Merton 1973). Mertonian sociology of science (e.g., Storer 1966; Cole and Cole 1973: 235ff; Gaston 1973: 3–7, 174) self-exemplifies its subject matter by affirming modern science as the paradigmatic system of inquiry,

[1] This paper is a revised and expanded version of "Foundations for a Humanistic Sociology of Science," presented by Restivo at the 7th Annual Alpha Kappa Delta Sociological Research Symposium, held at the Jefferson Hotel in Richmond, Virginia, February 17–19, 1977. We want to thank John Schumacher of Rensselaer Polytechnic Institute's philosophy department for helping us think through the ideas on wholistic science we discuss in this paper; Joseph Needham of the East Asian History of Science Library in Cambridge, England, for reading and commenting on the earlier version of this paper; physicist David Bohm of Birbeck College in London for sharing his insights on wholism with us; and David Gil of the Heller Graduate School at Brandeis for his help and encouragement in preparing this paper for publication.
[2] This paper originally appeared in *Humanity & Society* Volume 2, Number 4, 1978.

discovery, prediction and explanation (cf. Bourdieu 1975 and Johnston 1976). It affirms the same science that humanist, counter-culture, and radical critics have identified with modern industrial-technological society and attacked as alienating and dehumanizing. We are sympathetic to this criticism of science, but consider it relevant to science in modern society and not to science as the evolutionary unfolding of the human potential for open inquiry. We consider science part of the humanistic orientation to enhancing the conditions of human living.

The humanistic perspective on science and society we outline in this paper is associated with an emerging global world view. The articulation of this world view is affecting and reflecting transformations in the scientific world view occurring at the frontiers of physical theory, and at the interfaces between science and philosophy, religion, and social criticism. These changes are bringing into question assumptions about the nature of science so deeply rooted that they are taken for granted among humanistic critics of science as well as by orthodox scientists and students of science.

In the first part of this paper, we criticize several orthodox ideas about science which we need to liberate ourselves from in order to foster humanistic inquiry. The second part of the paper deals with the "new physics." Parts one and two are the background against which we sketch a paradigm for humanistic research, theory, and social action in the sociology of science.

New Perspectives on Science

Freedom, Responsibility, and Scientific Laws

Orthodox scientists generally assume that there is a discoverable harmony in nature which can be formulated as "laws of nature." This assumption is usually restricted to physical reality. Persons with a humanistic orientation often embrace this assumption in their struggle against mechanistic and reductionist views of human behavior. This apparently reasonable position, however, has unreasonable political implications. Consider, for example, physicist Brian Easlea's (1973) proposal for a "liberatory, socialist science." Easlea assumes that physical reality is governed by laws but that social reality is not. This implies, he argues, that (1) physical scientists can search for and discover "harmony," or "lawfulness" in physical reality, and (2) social scientists can only "find" harmony by creating it in the real social world. Since physical scientists cannot change nature, Easlea notes, physical reality can never be problematic on moral, ethical, or political grounds; it is only problematic when theory and experience must be reconciled. Social scientists, Easlea claims, can alter social reality. Therefore, social scientists, unlike physical scientists, must always deal with the value implications of their work. Easlea finally concludes that social scientists are more responsible than physical scientists for the present and future of our world. This conclusion is untenable. It rests on two related misconceptions: (1) that "laws of nature" are incompatible with human freedom and individual responsibility; and (2) that the harmony of nature is manifested in abstract laws and in the real world.

Much, if not all, of the confusion about the significance of "natural laws" for human behavior is rhetorical. Behavioral terms such as "obey" should be avoided when referring to what physical things like planets "do" with respect to laws of nature. This rhetoric of obedience will inevitably offend our sense of logic, self, or autonomy when it is transferred to the realm of human behavior. The rhetoric of "feeling" and "free will" is another source of confusion. We do not "feel" the earth move; yet, as Tolstoi (1957: 1443–1444) noted, absurd consequences would follow if we held, based on that feeling, that the earth does not move. The feeling of behavioral freedom does not entail freedom from external conditions, time, and some form of causality.

The mechanistic and deterministic rhetoric of classical science is an important source of confusion about the concept of "lawfulness." The conventional conception of a scientific law is based on viewing nature as a set of closed systems. It is understandable that lawfulness is widely considered irrelevant to the complex and often unpredictable world of human behavior, and a threat to the ideas of freedom and responsibility in human affairs. There is, however, an alternative way to think about scientific laws.

In the first place, a causal law does not have to uniquely determine a given effect. It may establish a range of possibilities within which a given effect must remain. Causal laws are always limited and conditioned by external contingencies and necessary causal connections are present in all phenomena. Statistical laws can be viewed as regularities which arise from the cancellation of change fluctuations in a large aggregate of things. If we conceive a statistical aggregate as a single entity, statistical laws can be conceived as approximate causal laws (Bohm 1971a: 28–32).

Lawfulness is associated with constant conjunctions among variables, and is discoverable only when some approximation to closure in a given system can be observed in nature or manufactured in the laboratory (Bhaskar 1975). Laws operate in open as well as closed systems; but we can only discover them under conditions of closure. Experimental science is possible because regional closures can be created in a world that is an open system. The complex determination of physical and social phenomena allows for different degrees of freedom and constraint in mechanical operations and in human behavior. It is the separation of laws from the phenomenal flux of reality that makes lawfulness consistent with the effectively infinite potential for evolving forms of action and consciousness, and the necessity for acting to effect social change. The search for "harmony" in science is an exercise in abstracting from the complex harmonies and disharmonies of a world of flux. There is no reason to suppose that this search can be fruitful in physics and not in sociology. The open system nature of the world, and the fact that all phenomena—including human behavior—are simultaneously controlled by a set of laws allows for self-determinations with constraints. The more complex the system, the more difficult it is to clearly identify (and the less meaning we attach to the notion of) constraints. This would explain the source of the feeling that human behavior is not constrained by natural laws.

The problem of individual responsibility and laws of human behavior is more difficult to resolve than the problem of freedom. Individual responsibility is problematic whether we adopt a strictly deterministic or an open systems view of lawfulness. In social terms, individual responsibility may only make sense in a society characterized by coercive laws, widespread oppression, structured inequalities, and a false sense of individual liberty. In a liberated society, the notion of individual responsibility might be meaningless. Some method of accounting for an individual's actions would be necessary; but rather than the simplistic calculus of responsibility that operates in contemporary society based on the labels "criminal," "deviant," and "mentally ill," a calculus based on knowledge about the sources of human behavior might be developed. Such a calculus might be manifested in communal responses to problematic behavior.

Harmony in Theory and Reality

Physical scientists do not pass judgment on whether a scientific law should be what it is. But they can judge whether certain manifestations of that law should be what they are. Simplicity and beauty in laws do not alter the destructive potential of physical or social phenomena. Neither does the chaos of a windstorm, or of a riot, preclude the operation of simple and beautiful laws. Imagining and working to create alternative futures does not entail the normative criticism of scientific laws, and is therefore as much a possibility and a responsibility in physics as it is in sociology. Creating the future is a process of actualizing physical as well as social potentials. It is possible to think about, propose, and create alternative natures inside and outside the laboratory, all of them consistent with a set of simple and beautiful laws. Physical scientists can and do make judgments implicitly and explicitly, about the nature of nature; they therefore do confront a morally, ethically, and politically problematic reality. This has not been widely appreciated because just as the sociological imagination has not been ascendant in social science, the physical imagination has not been ascendant in physical science (cf. Mills 1959: 20).

Physical scientists are no more likely than social scientists to speculate—or theorize—about alternative futures. Physical and social scientists internalize the norms, values, and beliefs of the sociocultural systems in which they live; and they internalize the norms, values, and beliefs of their respective professional communities. The relative impermanence of societal and scientific revolutions suggests that these processes of internalization lead to a certain degree of "over-socialization" beyond what is necessary for social cohesion. Kuhn's (1970) view of "normal science," interpreted as a description of science-as-it-is, supports this idea of science. Furthermore, the domination of the Mertonian paradigm has obscured the extent to which science is guided by norms, values, and beliefs derived from—if not exactly like—those of the wider society. Easlea (1973: 177), for example, is not persuasive when he writes that physical scientists are free to be as "revolutionary" as they wish, or that the more revolutionary they are the more likely they are to win Nobel Prizes (cf. Clark 1971: 363–364). The Kuhnian paradigm precludes easy, or permanent, revolutionary activity in science. We will consider this problem and its implications for humanistic science in more detail shortly.

It is not unusual to find humanistic proponents of science joining orthodox colleagues in arguing that "capitalist" society distorts the products of physicists who generally practice physics in pursuit of aesthetic pleasure and not power (e.g. Easlea 1973; Ravetz 1971). This attempt to separate physics from other societal activities (including social science) which are believed to be guided by the prevailing values of capitalist or industrial society is sociologically naive. It is not easy to deny Marx's observations that an alienated reality cannot give rise to a non-alienated science. Certainly, "capitalism" is a sufficiently heterogeneous system in a sufficiently heterogeneous world so that some individuals and groups can and do internalize and develop values and lifestyles that deviate, sometimes radically, from those associated with ideal capitalism. It is not reasonable, however, to assume that physicists are completely independent of the norms, values, and beliefs that prevail in their society, and that their products flow simply out of their aesthetic motives, only then to be sullied by managers, manufacturers, and consumers.

The Myth of Pure Science

Adherence to the pure science myth encourages the aloofness of scientists from the struggle for human liberation. This is curious when it occurs among humanistic science advocates such as Easlea (1973) and Ravetz (1971). Scientists closer to the political mainstream have been arguing recently that scientists are (1) responsible for regularly informing themselves, each other, and the public of the nature, potential, successes, and failures of their work, (2) responsible for instilling a "fondness for nature" among their students, as well as for communicating technical information, (3) accountable for human life in the present and in the future, and (4) responsible for criticizing and evaluating the values that direct their work and their lives (Brown 1971).

Science, conceived as a never-ending process of open, unfettered inquiry, is not compatible with the values of private property, profit, productivity, and power politics that guide contemporary industrialized and industrializing societies. Merton (1973: 275) recognized this to some extent when he noted in 1942 that the norm of communism in science is not compatible with the definition of technology as "private property" in a capitalistic economy. He failed to develop the radical implications of this observation for the education of scientists, the organization of scientific work, and the relationship between science and society. Some of his students, exaggerating the errors of their teacher, are now defending the intellectual viability of a science increasingly characterized by capitalist or industrialist values (e.g., Cole and Cole 1973). The inhibiting effects of industrialization, bureaucracy, and professionalism are invisible to individuals who interpret *technological* growth, *material* benefits, and *internalist* and *elitist* evaluations of science as indications of scientific vitality and progress. This problem reflects the inability of many scientists and students of science to recognize or deal with the conflict between alienated and non-alienated science, and the political impotence of science. The power of science and scientists in capitalistic, industrialist and high-technology societies is increasingly co-opted by and integrated with state power. The powerlessness of scientists as social critics and agents of social change is reinforced by the Kuhnian paradigm.

The Myth of the Kuhnian Revolution

Kuhn's discussion of "sociological" factors in scientific change represents a significant departure from positivistic and idealistic histories and philosophies of science. These factors, however, are not problematic for Kuhn. He notes, for example, that normal science is educationally narrow, rigid, and ill-designed to stimulate creativity (Kuhn 1970: 166). These problems, Kuhn argues, accrue to individuals, and individual rigidity is compatible with scientific progress. Kuhn fails to acknowledge that rigidity is a social as well as a psychological fact. His view of scientific progress is sociologically untenable because it rests on the assumption that the supply of scientific innovators—young scientists and scientists new to their fields, according to Kuhn—is independent of social conditions within and outside of organized scientific activity. Social controls imposed by political authorities, bureaucratization, and professionalization are some of the factors that can cause rigidity to accrue to the collectivity (Restivo 1975: 158–162).

Kuhn is a functionalist in the ideological sense of that term. He focuses on what science "is," supports an elitist distribution of power in science, roots his optimism about science in individuals who can act independently of social forces, and relies on a model—the modern political revolution—that is resistant to *fundamental* change. His conception of a scientific revolution is better characterized in "circulation of elite" terms than egalitarian or liberatory terms.

Kuhn (1970: 92–110) argues that there are parallels between scientific and political revolutions. Both are inaugurated by a "sense of malfunction" in existing institutions among a "narrow subdivision" of the relevant community. This is a precondition for the "crisis" associated with the revolutionary period. The aim of the revolution is to change institutions in ways prohibited by those institutions. This viewpoint stresses "sensing" malfunction; it thus obscures, if it does not entirely ignore, the "unintended consequences" of earlier social actions, and the dialectical sources of change inherent in social structural contradictions. In Kuhn's model, the period of crisis is characterized by a polarization of competing parties (in political revolutions) or paradigm advocates (in scientific revolutions), with defenders of the old order on one side and innovators on the other. At this point, political recourse (or, in the case of science, normal methods and logic) fails to resolve differences. Institutional governance disappears. The competing groups (1) disagree about the institutional context for achieving and evaluating change, (2) reject a supra-institutional framework for resolving differences, and (3) must, given the first two conditions, finally resort to "mass persuasion," and often "force." Kuhn stresses the "extra-institutional" nature of political and scientific revolutions because it is this that gives revolution a vital role in the *evolution* of institutions. In the end, the revolution is successful in science when the process of paradigm choice is accomplished based on the "highest standard," the "assent of the relevant community."

The Kuhnian paradigm is problematic for the humanistic sociology of science because the political imagery Kuhn adopts draws on the history of revolutions over the last several hundred years, revolutions which have failed to fully institutionalize worthy ideals introduced in revolutionary rhetoric. Political revolutions have cumulatively introduced ideas about a new world order without overturning the "Grand Paradigm" of inequality, dehumanization, and alienation that has dominated modern history. Kuhn binds science to a Grand Paradigm of methods, logic, and rationality that goes unchallenged in Kuhnian revolutions. Furthermore, Kuhn (1970: 174–210) seems to have responded to his critics by removing more and more of even this sort of political content from his conception of conflict in science. There is no room in Kuhn's model for a revolutionary Revolution, one that is structurally incompatible with "restorations" and the circulation of elites. This is an increasingly recognized political economic imperative, as well as a scientific imperative. A new, open-ended Grand Paradigm is needed in science and society.

The concept of science in permanent revolution is more appropriate than the concept of paradigm revolutions to the idea of a humanistic science and sociology of science. This conception links an ever-changing, critical science to an ever-changing, critical society. Hooker (1975), for example, extends Popper's (e.g. 1972) ideas on the open society just far enough to hint at permanent revolution in science and society:

> there is no guarantee for any culture that it will not suffer from the following twin defects: (i) a systematically wrongheaded scientific tradition, (ii) a cul-

tural environment which precludes either thought or recognition of this fact. Therefore no one is justified in reposing any positive degree of rational belief in any scientific tradition, no matter how long and glorious... development of our cultures, just as much as our science, are risks which we take in the hope that they will lead toward increasing understanding, freedom, etc. (i.e., that they will fulfill humankind's potential) and risks taken in the knowledge that we are in uncharted seas and could be led subtly but disastrously astray at any time.

David Bohm is more explicit. Bohm (1973: 140) notes that the emphasis in physics, captured in the Kuhnian paradigm is mainly on accommodating to "already existing frameworks of order." In this context, Bohm's concept of "order" may be understood to be equivalent to Kuhn's notion of "paradigm." Bohm opposes the state of physics-as-it-is and the normative force of the Kuhnian idea of normal and revolutionary periods in science. He argues that sensitivity to and perceptions of new orders (paradigms) should be integrated with accommodating activities so that things do not become so confused and chaotic that they can only be cleaned up through the revolutionary destruction of the old order. Bohm's argument is, in fact, the only one possible if we assume—as he does—that the universe is an open, evolving system (Bohm 1971a: 164 ff). If we want to comprehend such a universe, our systems of knowledge, our cultures, and our lifestyles and personalities must be, ideally, open-ended.

The Myth of Universal Science

Perhaps the most privileged and at the same time pernicious myth about modern science is that it is universal, world, de-ethicized science, generating perfected, genuine, pure, neutral, and objective knowledge. When combined with some form of humanistic consciousness, this can lead to questionable conclusions about the relationship between science and society. Ravetz (1971), for example, expresses a concern for the social implications of science side by side with a defense of pure science. On the one hand, he applauds the disappearance of the illusion of pure science. On the other, he defends the delicacy and power of pure science. He is upset by the fact that the only alternative being proposed to "illusory" pure science is "industrialized science." But he shows a surprising readiness to accept the continuing industrialization of science and its transformation into an institution designed to meet the technical needs of society as defined by industry and the state. Ultimately, it is the dangers to science, not the perils of humankind, that Ravetz believes demand our immediate attention.

By narrowly defining morality and responsibility in terms of the technical applicability of scientific research, Ravetz is able to exempt many scientists from moral, ethical, and political accountability. This is logically consistent with his tendency to separate science from society, and the scientist from the total person. He acknowledges Francis Bacon's admonition that the angels fell from "lust of power," humans from "lust of knowledge." But Bacon's notion of using science for the benefit of humankind was a form of noblesse oblige; Baconian "charitable inquiry" is paralleled by Ravetz's "philanthropic science."

Ravetz conceives "society" as an environment within which science either flourishes or degenerates. Science itself always retains a capacity for purity which can and must be defended and upheld against the incursions of society and "immature" disciplines such as sociology. Ravetz's commitment to an internalist view of science is reflected in his description of Hagstrom's *The Scientific Community* (1965), a study of pure science based on a small sample, as the best example of a new understanding of science as work.

The humanistic dimension of Ravetz's argument enters in his call for an "effective ethic" in science that is more refined than professionalism. He sees the source of such an ethic in a sophisticated humanitarian commitment. Following Barry Commoner (1966), he conceives a new kind of science, "critical science," which integrates scientific research and humanitarian functions. Critical science involves (1) collaborative research on the damaging impact of "run-away technology" on people and environments, (2) public exposure of the research, and (3) political action to abolish the offending tools, techniques, and processes (Ravetz 1971: 422–436). There is no vision of a new future here. It is easy to see why Ravetz (1971: 355) finds Weinberg's (1966) sociologically naive concept of the technological fix "cogent." There are no images of social structural changes in this version of critical science. This is reinforced by a life-cycle image of the sciences. Ravetz sees particular sciences, and even whole sections of scientific and scholarly inquiry, going through stages of immaturity, maturity, and senescence. He does not entertain the possibility of "science as a whole" going through these stages and "dying out," being "negated," or being otherwise radically transformed.

Ravetz claims that he failed to find clear and specific guidelines for studying problems of science and society in Marxism. But he identifies Scheler's *Die Wissensformen* und *Die Gesellschaft* as the earliest attempt to analyze the metaphysics of science as a cultural product (Ravetz 1971: 387). He does not mention Marx, whose observations on science and society—though somewhat fragmented—would have made profitable reading.

Joseph Needham conceives modern science as the latest and (in a certain sense) the last stage in the evolution of science. It does not, in contrast to primitive and medieval science, have an "ethnic stamp." The Scientific Revolution of the sixteenth century introduced the "basic technique of discovery," the "full method of scientific investigation," the "absolute universality of mathematics," the "universal language of mathematized hypotheses," and the power of generating incontestable and universally acceptable scientific truths (e.g. Needham 1959: 448; cf. Restivo 1979). Modern science is "science in the fullest sense," the "perfected world-view of natural science," and "universally valid world science." It is not clear, however, whatever the triumphs of modern science, how universal world science could make its appearance in anything less than a universal world culture. We might want to argue that modern science is, perhaps, "less ethnicized" than primitive or medieval science simply because modern society is the product of a higher level of civilizational transactions. The universality of modern science, however, lies in the material realm, the realm of things and their manipulation. Modern science is better described as "bourgeois," "capitalist," or "industrial-technological" than "world science." To the extent that the world is, or is becoming "modern" in this sense it is moving toward an evolutionary dead-end. An evolving world society cannot be "modern" or settle into any form of ultimate unity. De-ethnicized science can be conceived as the system of inquiry that emerges from the development of closer and closer links among the world's cultures, and ultimately of a world culture, or Ecumene. A viable world system will, however, be a system in permanent revolution. The "death" of our sun places a physical limit on the process of evolution, assuming it does not meet its end earlier. Escaping this limit may mean expanding into space, and perhaps contacting extraterrestrial cultures which will confront us with the problem of terrestrial ethnocentrism.

Needham (1970: 417–418) conceives universalistic science, potentially open and comprehensible to all human beings, as the foundation of a new universalism which is preparing the way for the unification of all working people in a catholic, cooperative community. But this science is neutral (Needham 1956: xxvi). Human nature is the root of the good and evil that attend the development of science. Needham assumes that in order to insure benevolent results in pursuing knowledge, some scientists must occasionally engage in non-benevolent acts. This is, he argues, a *sine qua non* of scientific method (Needham, 1956: 49). He also defends the idea that we cannot do science if we divide the world into sacred and profane domains. Everything must be profane if we are going to avoid setting up arbitrary barriers to inquiry (Needham 1975: xxv). Neutrality, non-benevolence, and profanity are inconsistent with humanistic values. Needham is on a schizoid path when he tries to defend these characteristics of modern science and at the same time advocate a socialist world founded on modern science.

Experimentation—the manipulation of things under controlled conditions—may be rooted in part in an aggressive orientation that has had survival value for human beings. As we look toward new stages in evolution, we may have to re-evaluate our views on healthy manifestations of aggressive or assertive motives, and the function of experimentation in stimulating a sense of conviction about the truth-value of hypotheses. Lying to or otherwise misleading subjects in medical experiments, and the general reliance on "naive" subjects in the social sciences are inconsistent with socialistic or humanistic commitments. The problem is not restricted to the human and social sciences as the ecological sciences dramatically illustrate. Manipulating the physical environment in the interest of "pure" science is morally problematic; testing nuclear devices above or below ground in the interest of advancing knowledge is not inherently "right" or "moral" for people who are mindful of their unity with nature.

Human beings are experimental by nature; they must be to survive and to grow. We would not therefore argue that experimentation should be suspended. It is not unreasonable, however, to suggest that perhaps in the future a less domineering and manipulative approach to nature and to ourselves and others should be cultivated. This might be realized by carrying Popper's (1972: 84) notion of letting hypotheses die in our stead to its extreme conclusion. We might invest new and highly sophisticated statistical and logical substitutes for manipulating material and living things. The possibility of relying on states of consciousness as criteria of confidence in testing hypotheses and creating the regional closures that lead to the discovery of scientific laws should also be explored (cf. Tart 1973; Ravindra 1975). Such explorations are indispensable in developing cognitive strategies to deal with emerging problems of survival and growth that are new in type and scale. The new wholism in physics encompasses novel ideas about physical reality, experience, and consciousness and may herald a new cognitive strategy being elicited by transactions between evolutionary forces and human imagination.

The Transformation of the Scientific World View

The object of inquiry in classical physics is *nature-in-itself*. Modern physics deals with a more complex level of inquiry, the *relationship* between humans and nature. Recent efforts by physicists to develop cognitive strategies adequate to this complexity have converged on a wholistic approach. We have discussed this in some detail elsewhere (Restivo 1978c;

Restivo and Zenzen 1978). Our objective here is to give a brief non-technical account of wholism in contemporary physical theory. This necessarily requires conceptual compromises and condensations in the interest of conveying an *image* of developments in physics relevant to sociology and the sociology of science. We discuss wholism in micro- and macro-physics, and David Bohm's proposal for a new order in physics.

Wholism in Micro-Physics

In both macro- and micro-physics, the notion of a consistent, self-determining structure plays a central role. Chew's (1968, 1970) "boot-strap hypothesis" represents a wholistic approach to micro-physics. The logic of his approach to elementary particle theory is as follows: if the sub-microscopic world goes no deeper than the class of aub-atomic particles called the hadrons (protons, neutrons, etc.); if there are an infinite number of individual hadrons and types of hadrons; and if no particular individual or class is more fundamental than any other; then, the laws of nature (descriptions of hadron behavior) may be infinite. This is where the bootstrap notion enters. The single requirement that the universe must form a self-consistent whole might uniquely determine *one* set of equally self-consistent laws of nature. In practice, this proposal requires that we check micro-physical theory against the classical observable world in order to reveal the constraints of logical uniqueness. This means that the "bootstrap" operation will, in practice, always be partial and characterized by successive approximations. Chew, however, is acutely aware of the implications of a complete and extended bootstrap. Observation and perhaps consciousness may have to be confronted, thus leading to a new form of human intellectual activity that will transcent physics and even the descriptive label "scientific."

Wholism in Macro-Physics

General relativity is essentially a field theory of gravitation and as such it provides the theoretical context for exploring the phenomena of macro-physics. Cosmological theories describe the origin and development of the universe. The meanings of space-time and matter-energy depend on a program which seeks to unify various field theories (gravitational, electromagnetic, etc.).

Geometrodynamics is a theoretical program which seeks a unified field theory guided by the intuition that the "geometry" of space-time is sufficient for physics and that "matter" is not ontologically distinct from space-time. Wholism emerges as a methodological necessity in these theoretical efforts. It appears that general relativity (and geometrodynamics as a possible extension of it) cannot have any arbitrarily specifiable boundary conditions. This requires that "we must always deal with the universe as a whole, as the only truly legitimate physical system" (Graves 1971: 154). Thus, unlike other physical theories which contain differential equations whose solutions require initial and boundary conditions which may be arbitrary, general relativity as a cosmological theory requires initial and boundary conditions which cannot be specified from "outside" the universe and may not be arbitrary. Again, we see that the notion of a self-consistent whole has emerged as a crucial determinant in a physical theory.

Physicists continue to be frustrated in their attempts to unify micro- and macro-physical theories. Indeed, it may not be possible to unify the theories in their present forms. It seems likely, however, that the wholism which is common to each will be preserved in any "grand synthesis."

David Bohm and Holonomy Physics

The cognitive imperative in "bootstrap physics" and "general relativity" is clearly wholistic. Bootstrappers and relativity theorists, however, have worked within well-defined disciplinary boundaries and the constraints implied by the adjective in "modern physics." They have generally carried their inquiries to but not beyond the threshold of self-reflection. Chew is aware of the threshold but seems hesitant to cross it. Quantum physicist David Bohm is less timid about integrating self-reflection and physical theory.

The idea of "individual wholeness in flowing movement," or "the holomovement, "is the cornerstone of the Bohmian world-view (Bohm 1971b: 1973). This "universal flux" can be known only implicitly in terms of the explicitly defined forms and shapes (each of which is only relatively stable) which can be abstracted in our experiences from the flux. In Bohm's view, observer and observed are merging and interpenetrating aspects of a reality which is indivisible and unanalyzable. This is a radical extension of the notions which have drifted from modern physics into other intellectual domains (often in seriously distorted form) regarding the role of the observer in quantum physics.

Bohm argues that thought is a *formative activity* in the universal flux; thought sustains or dissolves forms and shapes. He contends that the prevailing trend in modern physics is to ignore those aspects of relativity and quantum mechanics which suggest the need to give primacy to formative activity. Instead, these aspects are treated as "problems" which arise in the mathematical formalism and have nothing to do with the real nature of things. But if reality is a whole, then this fragmented treatment cannot be adequate. The formalism of physics is, ultimately, inseparable from informal (real) descriptions. This, according to Bohm, is what Niels Bohr was trying to express when he formulated his notion of complementarity. The reflective function of the theorist cannot be ignored in an experimental situation since the design and structure of the experiment (including instruments) determine the limits of the structural features of the universe which it can reflect.

For Bohm, the situation in microphysics so eloquently discussed by Bohr is a special case of the *general property* of mutual reflection in all levels of reality. In harmony with this, a theory is not merely an algorithm but rather an organizing activity. This idea suggests a new order in physics. To illustrate what is meant by a new order, Bohm contrasts a lens with a hologram. The lens brings an object into sharp relief and shows detail at the expense of the whole. However, any region of the holographic plate when illuminated yields a three-dimensional image of the object originally photographed. The holographic plate "unpacks" the implicit order contained in each region of space-time. Thus, there is a new sense here of a total order which transcends the notion of order as a regular arrangement of objects or events.

Theorizing is essentially a creative, perceptive activity in which some aspect of the implicit order of the holomovement is made explicit by forms of thought in harmony with their content. There is no fundamental theory on which all of physics can find a permanent basis. Each theory abstracts a certain aspect which is relevant only in some limited context. Physics has, for the most part, treated the universe as a collection of relatively autonomous things related only externally and more or less mechanically. In the Bohmian world-view, there is no externality but rather implicate structure; "things" are enfolded and unfolded in the holomovement. Process and content of thought are not distinct; thought and "reality" are integrated. Holonomy, the law of the whole, or of the holomovement, replaces heternomy, or classical deterministic, externalist, and mechanistic lawfulness. It entails, as does wholism in general, the ideas of hierarchy and relation to which we now turn our attention briefly.

Hierarchism and Relationalism

The new wholism is associated with hierarchical and relational thought. These two ideas overlap with, and are mutually implicated in, the Bohmian idea of holonomy. They are associated with a view of the universe as an infinity of things in becoming (Bohm 1971: 164), an unfolding of morphic processes, and the never-ending emergence of new diversities and higher levels of organization (Whyte 1974). Hierarchy is itself the core of a new conceptual synthesis being developed as a cognitive strategy among general systems theorists (e.g. Koestler and Smythies 1971; Whyte and Wilson 1969). The essence of hierarchization is in this sense not a set of ranks but a process of morphic evolution. Iberall (1972: 388) conceives it as a process in which related series of things are connected in levels by a coupling that introduces a qualitative change without destroying the relatedness and connectedness of the system. It implies increasing structural diversity at higher levels of organization, with specific transformations reflecting basic invariances common to all levels. Koestler (1971: 193) symbolizes hierarchy as a living tree, multi-leveled, stratified, and organized into systems of systems; there are structures within sub-structures, and processes activating sub-processes. He assumes that hierarchies in complex physical, biological and social systems are isomorphic. These ideas are consistent with the notion of a heterarchy, which contains a link that cuts across conventional and otherwise hierarchical (in the ordinary sense) orders (Ogilvy 1977: 112–113).

Whyte argued that twentieth century scientific and philosophical thought has moved toward relationalism, but that a truly relational theory has not yet appeared in any of the sciences. In such a theory, Whyte (1974: 141) noted, "...experienced qualities and measured quantities could both be derived from a single basis, particular qualities being experienced and quantities measured in certain contrasted circumstances..." Whyte suggested that subjective experiences and objective measurement can both be comprehended in terms of changing patterns of spatial relations.

Holonomic Transformations

Having sketched the notion of wholism, its specification in the Bohmian concept of holonomy, and the mutual entailment of wholism, hierarchy, and relationalism, we now consider some social implications. If reality, including social reality, is holonomous, then we should be watchful for holonomous transformations in areas outside of physics. In fact, hints of holonomy can be found in Maslow's (1969) humanistic psychology of science, Bateson's (1972) cybernetic anthropology, and the Ten-Houten and Kaplan (1973) theory of inquiry as the dialectical interaction of analytic and synthetic rationalities. More specific and detailed holonomic perspectives have been outlined in Hooker's (1975) evolutionary naturalistic realism philosophy of science, Radnitzky's (1970) hermeneutic-dialectic metascience, Robinson's (1975) relational metaphysics, Koestler's (1971) holon theory,

Dunn's (1971) social learning metaphor, Land's (1973) philosophy of transformations, and Jantsch's (1975) design approach to evolutionary theory. Pribram (1969) has specifically speculated on a holographic theory of the brain, and T. and D. McKenna (1975) have developed a holographic theory of mind. On a more phenomenological level, we are beginning to recognize the need for local, regional, and global ecological strategies in politics, economics, and religion that can be described as components of an emerging "social holonomy" (cf. Effendi 1955). The development of open systems theory has raised the possibility of a generalized schema capable of symbolically unifying the various holonomous models (Restivo 1978b). And at a more abstract level, nonlinear and nonsummative mathematics, topology, and Bohm's (1973) algebraization of the new order in physics promise a quantitative and qualitative systematization of holonomy theory.

Comparable developments have occurred at the interface of physics and mysticism. Capra (1975) considers the essence of the Eastern world view to be an orientation to the oneness and mutual interrelation of all things in the universe. The parallel he draws with physics is based on the view that quantum theory has (1) abolished the idea of separated entities, (2) introduced first the observer, then the participant, and more recently consciousness into the heart of physical description and explanation, and (3) stimulated the articulation of a wholistic conception of the universe (cf. Siv 1964). There are numerous semantic, ideological, and other pitfalls in this approach (Restivo 1978c). Nonetheless, Capra's strategy is another example of a growing tendency across disciplines to break down traditional barriers between and among cognitive strategies.

Finally, we suggest that a holonomous cognitive strategy may constitute a key to global survival and the further evolution of life and consciousness. It may be a basis for the emergence of the first culturally-derived species, homo ecumenicus (world person), and of a diversified, cooperative global culture (Ecumene). In this new pluralistic society, humanistic science may transcend both itself (to become "inquiry") and the dilemma expressed by William Blake (Erdman 1970: 270) when he christened art "the tree of life" and science "the tree of death."

Conclusion: Paradigm for a Humanistic Sociology of Science

The new perspectives on and transformations in science we have discussed suggest a new perspective on and transformation of the sociology of science. Bohm, perhaps more than any other contemporary physicist, has revealed that scientific theories are world views. Hooker (1975) has explicitly shown that philosophies of science under labels such as empiricism, realism, and Popperianism can be construed as world views. Similarly, sociologies of science under labels such as Mertonian, or neo-Marxist (Sklair 1973) can be construed as world views. Revealing underlying world views in science, or philosophies and sociologies of science, involves a meta-inquiry into, for example, theories of reality, consciousness, and knowledge. In concluding, we want to sketch a humanistic sociology of science construed as a world view. A complete and systematic meta-inquiry is beyond our present capabilities. We can, however, briefly outline the paradigm which is both guiding and emerging from our research. Our notion of paradigm follows Merton (1973: 11 ff: "Paradigm for the Sociology of Knowledge") insofar as it introduces a basis for comparing sociologies of science. We follow Kuhn to the extent that he uses paradigm and world view synonymously.

Our objectives in presenting the following paradigm are to (1) introduce and elaborate the categories for a meta-inquiry proposed by Hooker (1975) in his analysis of world views and philosophies of science, and (2) suggest content for those categories that links humanistic concerns and wholistic perspectives. The unifying cognitive theme in our paradigm is wholism. We sketch the possibilities for approaching the various "regions" of the paradigm wholistically. Ideally, the paradigm itself should be a self-consistent whole and constitute a world view.

The paradigm regions we identify and discuss are (a) subject of inquiry, (b) frameworks of knowledge and comprehension, (c) theory of action, (d) nature of reality, (e) theory of inquiry and comprehension, (f) consciousness and communication, (g) basic queries, (h) the meta-meta principle, and (i) the negation principle.

The subject of inquiry. The humanistic sociology of science focuses on the social organization of science and its guiding norms, values, and beliefs in relation to society and culture. Science is conceived to be a social activity and process. It is also a cognitive strategy, a mode of thought responsive to problems of survival and evolution. Science, scientists, and sociologists of science are assumed to be interrelated, interdependent, and in flux. We need a schema that identifies the social frameworks within which human beings develop systems of comprehension. Gurvitch's (1971) schema is exemplary, and his list of "knowledge frameworks" is reproduced here for illustrative purposes: (a) microsociology: (1) masses, (2) communities, and (3) communions; (b) groups: (1) families, (2) small-scale local groups, (3) factories, (4) states, (5) churches; (c) classes: (1) peasant, (2) bourgeois, (3) proletarian, (4) techno-bureaucratic; (d) global societies: (1) archaic, (2) theocratic-charismatic, (3) patriarchal, (4) city states, (5) feudal, (6) nascent capitalism, (7) democratic-liberal, (8) organized capitalism, (9) fascist techno-bureaucratic, (10) centralized state collectivism, (11) decentralized pluralistic collectivism. Ultimately, the subject of inquiry in the humanistic sociology of science is inquiry itself. The humanistic sociology of science is a process of self-reflexion in human beings acting as epistemic agents. This leads directly to a theory of action.

Theory of action. Human beings are epistemic agents, or inquiring organisms capable of self-reflection. Inquiry is the paradigmatic action of humans as epistemic agents. It is a process of exploration in which humans actively engage in order to survive, grow, evolve, and expand consciousness. This is a humanizing process, that is, a process in which human potentials are identified, clarified, evaluated, actualized, and experimented with. The humanistic sociologist of science is concerned with identifying alienating, dehumanizing, and destructive aspects of science and inquiry, and helping to eradicate them, or otherwise transform them according to humanistic values. We posit the existence of an evolutionary imperative (syntropic or morphic principle) moving human beings to actualize their potential for identifying, processing, and utilizing information effectively; and to actualize their capacity for comprehension. The level and quality of this process of actualizing human information and comprehension potentials is dependent on the form of, social organization and the associated norms, values, and beliefs. Human beings are epistemic agents who realize and create their identity by actualizing their potential for learning about and comprehending themselves, others, and the universe. They maximize this potential, as Restivo (1975, 1978b) has argued elsewhere, when psychological, sociocultural, and broader environmental systems approach openness in the sense formulated in open systems theory. The need for an open systems orientation is rooted in the picture of reality as an infinity of things in becoming.

We include under the theory of action a theory of love as an evolutionary mechanism. This theory is built on the notion that love expresses and facilitates intimacy, promotes communication and cooperation between and among human beings, and therefore enhances learning and comprehension. From this perspective, the humanistic ethos takes on a new significance; it emerges as the value system associated with surviving the current ecological and evolutionary challenges and reaching a new stage in sociocultural evolution. This idea appears later in this paradigm as a meta-meta principle, and is discussed in more detail elsewhere by Restivo (1978a).

The nature of reality. In our view, reality is best conceived as a never-ending process of unfolding in which new "things" (hierarchies, relations, wholes) are continually emerging (e.g. Bohm 1971a; Hooker 1975). In accordance with the preceding discussion, this reality is complexly determined. It is lawful but indeterminate. Discoverable laws are "mechanisms" which "produce" the phenomena of nature and the phenomenal flux of ordinary experience. It is a multi-level, hierarchical, open system. Laws operate throughout reality and on every level, but can only be discovered by creating or recognizing approximations to closure in regions of the universe. Closures can be approximated experimentally, experientially, or through states of consciousness. Reality is thus conditionally comprehensible. Any given "thing" is "knowable" in principle, but the universe as a whole is, at any given time, incomprehensible. And any given thing, though knowable in principle, will itself always have an "incomprehensible fringe," that is, something about it will (because the universe as a whole is in flux and because everything in the universe is connected to everything else) be incomprehensible in principle.

A theory of inquiry and comprehension. Our conception of comprehension encompasses information, explanation, understanding, knowledge, and appreciation. This should be understood as a warning against mistaking calculability, formalisms, and algorithms for the "compelling reasonableness" that tells us we "know" something (Rietdijk 1971: 11). This sense of "knowing" emerges out of the collective efforts of human beings. It is always incomplete, tentative, and in flux. The process of achieving comprehension can be described, following Toulmin (1973), in terms of variable minds discovering variable principles about variable nature. We posit, tentatively, four basic levels of comprehension: (a) rational, (b) intuitive, (c) no-knowledge, and (d) realms beyond the realm of no-knowledge. Comprehension of any given thing at any given time is a dialectically changing configuration of rationality, intuition, no-knowledge, and realms beyond knowledge. In the process of inquiry, the non-rational levels are continually being systematized, modified, and rationalized. This is continually generating new configurations of comprehension. As we rationalize the non-rational, new non-rationalities emerge reflecting the continuing unfolding of the universe. The domain of rationality is also continually changing and expanding, and is not restricted forever to what we now refer to as "modern science," or to realms accessible to conventional symbols or language. Language, ordinary or formal, is not preferred *a priori* as the medium of comprehension and communication. This follows from the holographic theory adumbrated above, and the recognition of the significance of non-symbolic consciousness in human experience. Furthermore, there are no philosophical or meta-philosophical statements or systems which are logically or epistemologically prior to or independent of the theory and practice of inquiry, that is, the actions of humans as epistemic agents (cf. Hooker 1975). No-knowledge and realms beyond knowledge are, finally, considered links with the implicit order (potential, including potential for change) of the brain and the universe.

Consciousness and communication. The levels of comprehension must eventually be correlated with a wholistic theory of consciousness and communication. Such a theory is yet to be developed, but there is some promising work in progress on a holographic theory of consciousness which posits telepathy as the ultimate mode of human communication (cf. Bentov 1977). The idea behind this approach is to develop a theory of consciousness that is consistent with a wholistic theory of reality (cf. Chang 1971). We can consider this from a less abstract point of view. In the first place, the imperative for a wholistic theory of consciousness is rooted in an awareness of the fragmentation of our individual and social lives. Fragmentation creates problems because the world is not really made up of autonomous and independent parts. At the same time, the fragmentation in our lives is reflected in fragmented thinking; and fragmented thinking cannot lead to the insights or theories necessary to solve problems in a wholistic universe. Historically, fragmentation did follow from and lead to some insights about the nature of reality. The notion of local cause and effect, and the experimental analysis of dependent and independent variables, led to notable advances in our understanding of the world. Under the earlier historical conditions of "frontiers," ecological consciousness was slow in emerging. As frontiers have disappeared, the degrees of freedom available to us have been reduced and we have come face to face with ecological and wholistic reality as a global—and even universal—phenomenon.

Secondly, we are beginning to realize that we have not been utilizing the brain's full potential for grasping wholistic reality. Whether we think in terms of left and right brain, or dichotomized modes of thought variously described in such terms as lineal-nonlineal, subordinative-coordinative, and rational-nonrational, it appears that a more "whole brain" approach to identifying, formulating, and solving problems is called for by emerging ecological and evolutionary challenges.

Basic queries. Two sets of basic queries are proposed as the motive force behind humanistic sociology of science:

1. The Mills (1956: 6–7) Sub-Paradigm of Global Queries

    (a) What is the structure of this particular society as a whole? What are its essential components, and how are they related to one another? How does it differ from other varieties of social order? Within it, what is the meaning of any particular feature for its continuance and for its change?

    (b) Where does this society stand in human history? What are the mechanics by which it is changing? What is its place within and its meaning for the development of humanity as a whole? How does any particular feature we are examining affect, and how is it affected by, the historical period in which it moves? And this period—what are its essential features? How does it differ from other periods? What are its characteristic ways of history-making?

(c) What varieties of men and women now prevail in this society and this period? And what varieties are coming to prevail? In what ways are they selected and formed, liberated and represented, made sensitive and blunted? What kinds of "human nature" are revealed in the conduct and character we observe in this society in this period? And what is the meaning for "human nature" of each and every feature of the society we are examining?"

2. Directed Queries

(a) What are the sociocultural bases of processes and products of inquiry?

(b) What are the objectives of a given system of inquiry?

(c) What is the scope of a given system of inquiry?

(d) How are information, explanation, understanding, knowledge, and appreciation achieved?

(e) What is the relative epistemic status of inquiring systems within, between, and among microsocieties, groups, classes, and global societies?

(f) What is the relative epistemic status of the components of inquiring systems?

(g) What are the existential, social structural, and axiological sources and consequences of different modes of inquiry: how do modes of inquiry effect and reflect lifestyles and styles of consciousness; whose interests do they serve; how do they effect and reflect the distribution of power?

(h) What are the sociocultural conditions for an evolving comprehension of reality?

(i) What strategies can be developed to enhance the conditions of living—and concomitantly of inquiry—and what actions must be taken to carry out these strategies?

Finally, we cap our paradigm with (a) a *meta-meta principle* taken from the Sufi wisdom (Shah 1970), which equates love, action, knowledge, and thought; love = thought = knowledge = action = love...; and (b) a principle of negation which instills our paradigm with the power of permanent revolution; there is no justification for investing this paradigm, which is a conjecture, with positive or absolute belief; everything in it is in flux, and subject to criticism and change (cf. Hooker, 1975).

Some concluding words of caution are necessary concerning the idea of "wholism" and the role of science in transforming our world view. Wholism has sometimes been associated with the subordination of the individual to the "group," the "state," on some form of over-arching consciousness. Paul Forman (1971), for example, has superbly narrated the history of physics and society in Germany from 1918 to 1927, and revealed the link between wholism and totalitarian politics. The wholistic viewpoint we advocate, however, is a reaction to both the fragmentation of human lives and the absorption of individuality in "greater wholes." We are in accord with G. W. Morgan's (1968: 320) view that individuals oriented to wholism participate in the complexities and difficulties of human living; they are neither rare parts of social systems nor isolated individualists. They do not suppress their multidimensionality to the authority of one or a few parts of their selves; nor do they surrender themselves to external authorities. As in the case of Bohm's hypothesis of "wholes emerging from wholes," the wholeness of the individual is conceived to be dynamic (cf. Ogilvy 1977). It is not something he or she achieves and then maintains in a static, final, and perfected form. Morgan (1968: 330) captures the Bohmian notion in his statement that

> Every moment of life, each new experience, each new encounter has to be taken into the self, and each may call for a wholeness more encompassing and more profound than has yet been attained.

There should also be no misunderstanding about our view of the role of science in the transformation of our view of reality. Physics is not the autonomous source of the wholism we discuss. In fact, wholistic physics is as much a product as a source of transdisciplinary wholistic intellectual currents. Bohm's views, for example, have not emerged out of considerations restricted to physics; his relationship with the mystic Krishnamurti has strongly influenced the direction of his recent physical theory. In reviewing developments in physical theory, we have tried to indicate why we believe that science should not be rejected as incompatible with humanistic values.

Finally, we want to stress that we have sought to explore the potential of a particular way of viewing the world. Our views are not a dogma. They are offered as a contribution to the continuing struggle to discover reasoned and humane ways of living in and thinking about our world. The people we have cited give evidence that we are neither original nor alone in our quest.

References

Bateson, G. 1972. *Steps to an Ecology of Mind.* New York: Ballantine Books.

Bentov, I. 1977. *Stalking the Wild Pendulum: On the Mechanics of Consciousness.* New York: E. P. Dutton.

Bhaskar, R. 1975. *A Realist Theory of Science.* Leeds: Leeds Books Ltd.

Bohm, D. 1971. *Causality and Chance in Modern Physics.* Philadelphia: University of Pennsylvania Press.

———. 1971. "Quantum Theory as an Indication of a New Order in Physics. Part A. The Development of New Orders as Shown Through the History of Physics." *Foundations of Physics* 1,4: 359–381.

———. 1973. "Quantum Theory as an Indication of a New Order in Physics. Part B. Implicate and Explicate Order in Physical Law." *Foundations of Physics* 3,2 (June): 139–168.

Bourdieu, P. 1975. "The Specificity of the Scientific Field and the Social Conditions of the Progress of Reason." *Social Science Information* 14, 6: 19–47.

Brown, M. (ed.) 1971. *The Social Responsibility of the Scientist.* New York: The Free Press.

Capra, F. 1975. *The Tao of Physics.* Berkeley: Shambhala Press.

Chang, C. 1971. *The Buddhist Teaching of Totality.* University Park: The Pennsylvania State University.

Chew, G. 1968. "'Bootstrap': a Scientific Idea?" *Science,* 161 (May) 762–765.

———. 1970. "Hadron Bootstrap: Triumph or Frustration?" *Physics Today,* 23 (October): 23–28.

Clark, R. 1972. *Einstein: The Life and Times.* New York: Avon Books.

Cole, J. and S. Cole. 1973. *Social Stratification in Science.* Chicago: University of Chicago Press.

Commoner, B. 1966. *Science and Survival.* London: Gollancz.

Dunn, E. 1971. *Economic and Social Development.* Baltimore: The Johns Hopkins Press.

Effendi, S. 1955. *The World Order of Baha'u'llah.* Wilmette, Ill.: Baha' Publishing Trust.

Erdman, D. 1970. *The Poetry and Prose of William Blake.* Garden City, N.Y.:Doubleday Anchor.

Easlea, B. 1973. *Liberation and the Aims of Science.* Totowa, N.J.: Rowman and Littlefield.

Forman, Paul. 1971. "Weimar Culture, Causality and Quantum Theory, 1918–1927: Adaptation by German Physicists and Mathematicians to a Hostile Intellectual Environment." *Historical Studies in the Physical Sciences,* 3: 1–114.

Gaston, J. 1973. *Originality and Competition in Science.* Chicago: University of Chicago Press.

Graves, J. 1971. *The Conceptual Foundations of Contemporary Relativity Theory.* Cambridge, Mass.: M.I.T. Press.

Gurvitch, G. 1971. *The Social Frameworks of Knowledge.* New York: Harper Torchbooks.

Hagstrom, W. 1965. *The Scientific Community.* New York: Basic Books.

Hooker, C. 1975. "Philosophy and Meta-Philosophy of Science: Empiricism, Popperianism, and Realism." *Synthese,* 32: 177–231.

Iberall, A. 1972. Toward *a General Theory of Viable Systems.* New York: McGraw Hill.

Jantsch, E. 1975. *Design for Evolution.* New York: George Fraziller.

Johnston, R. 1976. "Contextual Knowledge: a Model for the Overthrow of the Internal/External Dichotomy in Science." *Australian and New Zealand Journal of Sociology,* 12,3 (October): 193–203.

Koestler, A. and J. Smythies. (eds.) 1971. *Beyond Reductionism.* Boston: Beacon Press.

Koestler, A. 1971. "Beyond Atomism and Holism—The Concept of the Holon." In A. Koestler and J. Smythies (eds.), *Beyond Reductionism.* Boston: Beacon Press, 192–232.

Kuhn, T. S. 1970. *The Structure of Scientific Revolutions.* 2nd ed.; Chicago: University of Chicago Press.

Land, G. Lock. 1973. *Grow or Die.* New York: Random House.

Marx, K. 1956. *Economic and Philosophic Manuscripts of 1844.* Moscow: Foreign Languages Publishing House.

——. 1973. *Grundrisse.* New York: Vintage Press.

Maslow, A. 1969. *The Psychology of Science.* Chicago: H. Regnery.

McKenna, T. and D. McKenna. 1975. *The Invisible Landscape.* New York: Continuum Books.

Merton, R. K. 1973. *The Sociology of Science.* Chicago: University of Chicago Press.

Mills, C. W. 1959. *The Sociological Imagination.* New York: Oxford University Press.

Morgan, G. W. 1968. *The Human Predicament: Dissolution and Wholeness.* Providence: Brown University Press.

Needham, J. 1956. *Science and Civilization in China.* Vol. II; Cambridge: Cambridge University Press.

——. 1959. *Science and Civilization in China.* Vol. III; Cambridge: Cambridge University Press.

——. 1970. *Clerks and Craftsmen in China and the West.* Cambridge: Cambridge University Press.

——. 1975. *Science and Civilization in China.* Vol. V, Part 2; Cambridge: Cambridge University Press.

Ogilvy, J. 1977. *Many Dimensional Man.* New York: Oxford University Press.

Popper, K. 1972. *Objective Knowledge.* Oxford: The Clarendon Press.

Pribram, K. 1969. "The Neurophysiology of Remembering." *Scientific American* 220,1 (January): 73–86.

Radnitzky, G. 1970. *Contemporary Schools of Metascience.* 2nd ed.; New York: Humanities Press.

Ravetz, J. 1971. *Scientific Knowledge and its Social Problems.* Oxford: The Clarendon Press.

Ravindra, R. 1975. Experiments and Experience: A Critique of Modern Scientific Knowing." *Dalhousie Review* 55: 655–674.

Restivo, S. 1975. "Towards a Sociology of Objectivity." *Sociological Analysis and Theory,* 5,2 (June): 155–183.

——. 1978. "An Evolutionary Sociology of Love." *International Journal of Sociology of the Family,* forthcoming.

——. 1978. "Elements of a General Theory in Macrosociology." *International Journal of Contemporary Sociology,* forthcoming.

——. 1978. "Parallels and Paradoxes in Modern Physics and Eastern Mysticism: I—A Critical Reconnaissance." *Social Studies of Science,* forthcoming.

———. 1979. "Joseph Needham and the Comparative Study of Chinese and Modern Science: A Critical Perspective."In R. A. Jones (ed.), *Research in the Sociology of Knowledge, Science, and Art*. Vol. II; Greenwich, Conn.: JAI Press, forthcoming.

Restivo, S. and M. Zenzen. 1978. "Holonomy in Physics and Society." *Consciousness and Culture*, forthcoming.

Rietdijk, C. W. 1971. *On Waves, Particles, and Hidden Variables*. Assen, Holland: Van Gorcum and Company.

Robinson, H. 1975. *Renascent Rationalism*. Toronto: Macmillan.

Shah, I. 1970. *The Way of the Sufi*. New York: E.P. Dutton.

Siu, R. G. H. 1964. *The Tao of Science*. Cambridge, Mass.: M.I.T. Press.

Sklair, L. 1973. *Organized Knowledge*. St. Albans Herts, G.B.: Paladin.

Storer, N. 1966. *The Social System of Science*. New York: Holt, Rinehart and Winston.

Sutherland, J. 1973. *A General Systems Philosophy for the Social and Behavioral Sciences*. New York: George Braziller.

Tart, C. 1973. "States of Consciousness and State-specific Sciences." In R. Ornstein (ed.), *The Nature of Human Consciousness*. San Francisco: W. H. Freeman.

Ten Houten, W. and C. Kaplan. 1973. *Science and its Mirror Image*. New York: Harper and Row.

Tolstoi, L. 1957. *War and Peace*. 2 vols.; Baltimore: Penguin Books.

Toulmin S. 1973. *Human Understanding*. Vol. 1; Oxford: Clarendon Press.

Weinberg, A. 1966. "Can Technology Replace Social Engineering?" *Bulletin of the Atomic Scientists* 22 (December): 4–8.

Whyte, L. and D. Wilson. 1969. *Hierarchical Structures*. New York: American Elsevier.

Whyte, L. L. 1974. *The Universe of Experience*. New York: Harper Torchbooks.

When Culture Met Science: Revisiting "A Humanistic Perspective of Science and Society"[3]

Mary Chayko
College of Saint Elizabeth

When Sal Restivo and Michael Zenzen developed their "Humanistic Perspective of Science and Society," the sociology of science was dominated by Robert Merton's view of science as an autonomous, self-affirming social system. Directly challenging this view, Restivo and Zenzen proposed an alternative and more humanistic way to think about science, calling for the study of the social and cultural conditions in which scientific knowledge is produced and for its humane and ethical applications. They put forth an argument not only wide in scope and ambition but prescient as well, for it provided and continues to provide an excellent foundation for understanding a number of still-unresolved debates between science and sociology.

Several of these debates—flat-out battles, really—between scientists and sociologists of scientific knowledge (SSK) had just begun to percolate around the time of the publication of this article. Sociologists of science, in an effort to examine more fully the social conditions that influence the production of scientific knowledge, were putting forth the notion that a set of scientific ideas do not necessarily reflect objective "fact" or "truth" but, rather, are simply the products of a particular belief system—a culturally influenced system of ideas which might not hold or be considered scientifically valid in another belief system. Scientific laws, they pointed out, and the scientific method itself, were cultural creations, subject to change or to widely differing interpretation in a different time or place (Collins 1998, 1982; Barnes, Bloor and Henry 1996). Many scientists, of course, took issue with some (or all) of this (Gross and Levitt 1994). They stated firmly that scientific laws can and do hold across cultures and domains if they have been properly and reliably proven. This dispute was popularly referred to as the "science wars" (a rather unfortunate term, given the meaning and specter of actual human war), inspiring strong reactions and harsh words from many in the sociology and scientific communities (it even inspired a "hoax" article by physicist Alan Sokol which inflamed tempers further; see Sokol 1996a and b).

In the wake of all of this debate, however, a middle ground began to emerge. The role of cultural factors in influencing scientific production and the sociological underpinnings of such processes as the formulation of theories and the interpretation of data became increasingly visible and appreciated (see Labinger and Collins 2001, Mermin 1997 and Schweber 1997). Today, sociology has become a critical contributor to the understanding of such issues as the appropriate uses of biotechnology, ecological and environmental

[3]This paper originally appeared in *Humanity & Society* Volume 27, Number 3, 2003.

challenges, the trajectories and treatment of diseases, the phenomena of synchrony, the conceptualization of consciousness, mind and "reality," and the global impact of a variety of technologies. And it is in this interdisciplinary spirit that "A Humanistic Perspective of Science and Society" has so much to say and so much to offer.

Restivo and Zenzen's article helps us to understand just how culture and society belong in and must be brought into scientific investigations. Impressively broad in its scope and logical in its construction, it argues for the development of an interdependent academic and human community that operate in harmony with the laws of the physical/natural world and with social/cultural laws, with both sets of findings unified in a kind of meta-analysis dedicated expressly toward "enhancing the conditions of human living" (1978: 212). Implicitly rejecting extreme positions that the authors believe result in the hierarchical and subversive separation of people from one another, they describe exactly how this harmony can be achieved: by identifying the set of physical laws that constrain us, imagining the full complement of options available to us and then creating the conditions in which both scientific and cultural laws are most humanely realized. "It is possible," Restivo and Zenzen explain, "to think about, propose, and create alternative natures inside and outside the laboratory, all of them consistent with a set of simple and beautiful laws" (1978: 214). These "simple, beautiful" laws must be identified and tested, yet always respected: they should be used to create a harmonious and ethical (as opposed to a politicized or commercialized) future which enhances individual and societal potentials. The agenda outlined in the article leaves plenty of work to go around, plenty for scholars in all disciplines to do, scorning interdisciplinary conflict in favor of cooperation and collaboration.

Restivo and Zenzen give a wealth of examples and suggestions for how a more humane future might be collaboratively imagined and realized. They discuss the roles played by cognition, love, consciousness, communication, and human relatedness, among other components of life, fluidly and thoughtfully. They tackle, for example, the tricky concept of "reality" and the way in which it is "lawful, but indeterminate"—subject to a series of physical laws which are never entirely discoverable by scientists but are legitimately and satisfactorily approximated nonetheless. Reality, in their capable hands, is described as only "conditionally comprehensible": a province of both the physical and social worlds, too wide-ranging for any one discipline to colonize, yet too complex and important to conceptually (lazily?) dismiss. It is an appropriate way of considering a concept that has always begged for adequate definition while veering dangerously toward the indefinable. Fluently addressing this and other critical issues in which sociology and science both have a stake, Restivo and Zenzen demonstrate that there are many aspects of life which cut across the sociological, philosophical, and physical/natural realms, and that understandings gained in one area need not supplant or threaten that in another. Thus, the mounting of an overly rigorous defense (and defensiveness) regarding the boundaries of a given discipline is counterproductive to amassing and using knowledge intelligently and humanely. We are in this together.

The authors recommend we move from embracing a strictly scientific worldview to a more explicitly humanistic worldview encompassing wholism, a term used in both micro- and macro-physics to indicate the centrality of a consistent, self-determining structure within a boundless larger system (or universe) of which it is a part. They connect this idea to the Bohmian notion of holonomy which holds that the universe is an ever-unfolding infinity of interrelated things and processes (Restivo and Zenzen 1978: 223–224; Bohm 1971, 1973; see also Capra 2002). With the adoption and application of a worldview which embraces wholism and holomony, knowledge generated in any field can be seen as part of a connected whole which can (indeed, must) be coordinated with that in other fields and used for the benefit of all in the human community. To achieve this, they believe, is to achieve true wisdom in any field and to find liberation from polemical or oppressive thinking and behavior. To fail to do this, to settle for "science-as-it-is," is to further our alienation from one another and the world around us (Restivo and Zenzen 1978: 211; Marx 1956, 1973); to further the "fragmentation of human lives" (Restivo and Zenzen 1978: 231).

Since academic disciplines will probably always be, to some extent, in competition over turfs, definitions, and funding dollars, the lessons of Restivo and Zenzen remain fresh and compelling and well worth revisiting. They point the way toward a sociologically sensitive, humanistic science and a scientifically sensitive, humanistic sociology—and they make the convincing case that the sum of these is much greater than what either part could accomplish alone. The implications of their argument venture far beyond the bounded "worlds" of physical science and sociology and into the realms of philosophy and psychology; all the sciences, social sciences, arts and humanities; and, indeed, all arenas for study and thought. In short, this article serves as a valuable resource for how to approach any endeavor humanistically—to remain engaged in "the continuing struggle to discover reasoned and humane ways of living in and thinking about our world" (1978: 232). For these far-reaching reasons, "A Humanistic Perspective on Science and Society" remains endlessly vital and timely, and richly deserving of this opportunity for a re-reading.

References

Barnes, B., D. Bloor and J. Henry (eds). 1992. *Scientific Knowledge: A Sociological Analysis.* London: Athlone Press.

Bohm, D. 1971. "Quantum Theory as an Indication of a New Order in Physics. Part A. The Development of New Orders as Shown Through the History of Physics." *Foundations of Physics.* 1:4:359–381.

_____. 1973. "Quantum Theory as an Indication of a New Order in Physics. Part B. Implicate and Explicate Order in Physical Law." *Foundations of Physics.* 3:2:139–168.

Capra, F. 2002. *The Hidden Connections: Integrating the Biological, Cognitive, and Social Dimensions of Life Into a Science of Sustainability.* New York: Doubleday.

Collins, H.M. 1982. *The Sociology of Scientific Knowledge: A Sourcebook.* Bath: Bath University Press.

_____. 1998. "The Meaning of Data: Open and Closed Evidential Cultures in the Search for Gravitational Waves." *American Journal of Sociology.* 104:2:293–491.

Gross, P.R. and N. Levitt. 1994. *Higher Superstition: The Academic Left and Its Quarrels With Science.* Baltimore, MD: Johns Hopkins University Press.

Labinger, J. and Collins, H. 2001. *The One Culture: A Conversation About Science.* Chicago: University of Chicago Press.

Marx, K. 1956. *Economic and Philosophic Manuscripts of 1844.* Moscow: Foreign Languages Publishing House.

_____. 1973. *Grundrisse.* New York: Vintage Press.

Mermin, N. D. 1997. "Reference Frame." *Physics Today.* October. 50:11.

Merton, R.K. 1973. *The Sociology of Science.* Chicago: University of Chicago Press.

Restivo, S. and Zenzen, M. 1978. "A Humanistic Perspective on Science and Society.*"* *Humanity and Society.* 2:4:211–136.

Schweber, S.S. 1997. "Reference Frame." *Physics Today.* March. 50: 73.

Sokol, A. 1996a. "A Physicist Experiments With Cultural Studies." *Lingua Franca.* May/June. 62–64.

_____. 1996b. "Transgressing the Boundaries: Hermeneutics of Quantum Gravity." *Social Text.* 46/47. 217–256.

4. Feminist Sociology: Methodology and Politics in Disciplinary Change[1,2]

Marietta Morrissey
University of Toledo

Reflexive Statement

In recent years my research and writing have focused on gender in comparative, historical perspective. I have been especially interested in gender relations in Caribbean slavery and the relationship between women's work and family organization in Latin America and the Caribbean. The following paper is part of an on-going search for ways to conceptualize gender and women's position in research that is heavily influenced by Third World nationalist and feminist politics. These latter views have an increasing if still indirect impact on American sociology. They will, in time, I believe, contribute to the transformation of the discipline and thus to a more meaningful feminist sociology.

Introduction

In 1985, Judith Stacey and Barrie Thorne published a major critical article in which they argue the provocative point that sociology has not been transformed by feminist thought to the same degree as many other disciplines. Stacey and Thorne contend that three characteristics of sociology are responsible for its "missing feminist revolution": its dominant functionalist theoretical tradition; the inclusion of gender in many sociological studies, but as a variable and not a "central theoretical concept"; and the separation of feminist work from mainstream studies.

In this paper I review their argument and consider two other, impediments to the feminist transformation of sociology: our dualistic methodological tradition and related commitment to political reformism. These points are explored first through a discussion of feminist methodologies current in sociology. I then examine political and epistemological differences between sociology and disciplines more readily able to incorporate feminist ideas. Finally, I suggest that only the development of a praxis-based interpretive feminist methodology will generate more meaningful sociological theories of gender relations. This

---

[1]The author thanks Judith Lorber, Barrie Thorne, Randy Stocker and the reviewers of *Humanity and Society* for helpful criticisms of earlier drafts of this paper.
[2]This paper originally appeared in *Humanity & Society* Volume 16, Number 3, 1992.

development may depend ultimately, however, on the radicalization of politics and accompanying discourse in the United States.

Whither the Missing Revolution?

Stacey and Thorne contend that in contrast to history, literature, and anthropology, feminist sociology has failed to challenge fundamental disciplinary assumptions. In history and literature, heavily male-focused traditions and broadly accepted canons have been central targets of feminism, and alternative epistemologies and methodologies compatible with feminist critiques have been developed (Gordon 1986; Kelly 1984). In literature, women have been in the forefront of struggles to incorporate psychoanalytic, deconstructionist and other novel approaches to literary analysis (Kolodny 1988; Robinson 1985; Snitow 1989; Stacey and Thorne 1985: 302; Stimpson 1988). Anthropological studies have been influenced by feminist reinterpretations of women's status and position in production and reproduction, revolutionizing our understanding of changing social formations in non-Western societies (Collier and Yanagisako 1987; Lamphere 1987; Morgen 1989; Moore 1988).

Sociology, in contrast, has not produced a transformative feminist theory, one that acknowledges and explains the essential place of gender in social interaction and in the construction of social institutions. Interpretive and process-focused strands in American sociology have been significant for decades and have affected much feminist thinking in sociology (Acker, Barry and Esseveld 1983; Stacey 1988). But resulting insights about gender relations have not yet formed theories sufficiently influential to stimulate a paradigmatic shift in mainstream sociology. In a similar way, while Marxist studies may increasingly seek ways to consider gendered social relations in production and reproduction, their influence on American sociology is only beginning to become clear (Acker 1989; Morrissey and Stoecker, forthcoming).

If established sociological paradigms have not generated more feminist or women-focused research, it is not then, argue Stacey and Thorne, because fundamental categories or methods of analysis are missing. Rather, male-dominated conventions and characteristics of the discipline itself have blocked the full conceptualization of gender as a fundamental social relation. When included in research and publication, women and gender issues appear in the form of a variable in a larger study, or traditional research questions are recast or modified to reflect women's experience into their analysis but without essential change (Ward and Grant 1985; Grant and Ward 1991).

Stacey and Thorne's analysis raises a number of significant questions about the feminist impact on sociology and on the academy in general. I argue in this paper that the identification of women's position and interests by sociologists will necessarily take longer than the parallel process in other disciplines for two reasons. First, American sociology has a broad and pervasive commitment to a particular form of empiricism—positivism, a methodology not always incompatible with feminist theory but intrinsically less sensitive to the subjectivity of observer and research subject than some other ways of knowing. Second, positivist methodology is closely linked to the reform tradition in American sociology, never a universal imperative, but always vital in sectors of the field (Bernard 1987). The wish of many sociologists to effect social change has reinforced the disciplinary dominance of positivist methods.[1] Within this context the study of women inevitably focuses on gender (usually termed "sex") as a variable rather than an intrinsic component of social organization (Acker 1989). Interpretive methodologies have played a continuing if often minor role in the discipline. They have given a voice to once invisible subjects and social processes.[2] Too often the study of "new" social relations and constituencies is mainstreamed, however, leaving interpretation to seem no more than the preliminary step in a larger, positivist research design.

Feminist Sociology: Methodological Paths and Crossings

Feminists in sociology have opposed the discipline's conventional politics and methodology in several ways. Their alternative visions are elucidated in the burgeoning literature on feminist epistemology and its place in the social sciences (Brewer 1989; Flax 1987; Harding 1987a, 1986; Hekman 1987; Snitow 1989).

Many feminist social scientists have embraced a "feminist empiricism" (Harding 1987a, 1986). Its practitioners accept conventional social science methods and techniques but select topics of study pertinent to women and feminist struggles. Feminist empiricists reject the claims to objectivity of standard sociology, arguing in effect that "facts are theory laden; theories are value laden" (Haraway 1981: 477). The limitation of this approach for feminist theory creation is that feminist ideology eventually conflicts with positivist assumptions about how to know (Bernard 1987; Harding 1986). Feminist empiricism in sociology depends largely on survey research and other techniques geared to large populations, and hence limits the degree to which women as both observer and research subject can mould investigation. For feminist sociologists empiricism has often taken a policy turn and led to intense debate about the impact of ideas, e.g., comparable worth, on feminist politics (see, for example, England and Norris 1985; Steinberg 1987), and how to stretch the boundaries of positivist methodology to accommodate feminist interests.

A second approach to feminist theory follows from adherence to a "standpoint." A feminist standpoint assumes that gender relations are an essential organizing principle of society (Harding 1986; Hartsock 1987). Advocates of this epistemological view also consider the development of gender consciousness and the struggle to bring about the liberation of women from oppressive social relations inseparable from the analysis of women's social position. This posture resembles other "critical" theories, in particular the way in which class relations and the elevation of class consciousness orient Marxist analysis and praxis (Farganis 1986; Smith 1987). Both researcher and subject consciousness are explored by feminist standpoint theorists, often through interpretive research methods, e.g., ethnographic, interviewing, documentary analysis. But penetrating the layers of subjects' consciousness is hindered by the assumption that a valid and true consciousness of gender exists. Proponents of a feminist standpoint have responded by stretching "gender" to include other categories of analysis and consciousness such as race, class, and age divisions (Brewer 1989; Hartsock 1987; see, for example, Cannon, Higgenbotham and Leung 1988; Collins 1986). And advocates of other standpoints (e.g., Marxism) have tried to identify the articulation of capitalism, patriarchy and other forms of gender inequality (see review of Marxist-feminist literature by Morrissey and Stoecker, forthcoming). Some scholars, notably Smith (1987), argue that women themselves can define their situations and that the accumulation of such "situated knowledge" is finally the basis for collective action.

Post-modern feminism offers a more fully relativistic approach to knowledge than feminist empiricism or standpoint theories (Harding 1986). Post-modernism embodies many methodological strategies, joined by doubt about the transcendence and universality of truth, reason and other Western cultural and philosophical values (Flax 1987: 624; Harding 1986; Hekman 1987; Yeatman 1990). Particularly as manifested in deconstructionist and related semiotic approaches now current in literature and the humanities, post-modernism "converges with hermeneutics, an interpretive analysis" with a long if marginal tradition in the social sciences (Collins 1988). As represented by some figures in the Frankfurt School, some structural Marxists, and phenomenologists such as Alfred Shutz, hermeneutic analysis follows three broad tenets.

First, hermeneutics as practiced by sociologists attends to issues of social process and social dynamism.[3] Second, its practitioners acknowledge the complexity and interconnectedness of social phenomena within groups. And third, even while employing highly interpretive research methods, advocates of hermeneutic modes of analysis doubt that either subjects' or observers' consciousness can be fully penetrated or understood (Collins 1988; Farganis 1986). Critiques of post-modern feminism reflect the same concerns that mark critical evaluation of the hermeneutic tradition in sociology, that without a standpoint or fundamental category of analysis consciousness appears to be unpatterned, researcher subjectivity unchecked and social analysis untenable (Fergusen 1991; Flax 1987; Harding 1987a; Jansen 1990; Mascia-Lees, Sharpe and Cohen 1989). Nevertheless, postmodern approaches express an strong conviction among feminist sociologists that theories of women's position need to be inductively built and deep structures of social understanding carefully and reflexively deconstructed (see, for example, Stacey 1990; see also discussion in Stacey 1988; Acker, et al. 1983).

Within feminist sociology, feminist empiricism most directly expresses American sociology's reformist and policy-oriented tradition. As noted above, the frequent focus of feminist empiricism on large-scale institutional trends provides information adaptable to policy formation and implementation (see, for example, the important body of research on occupational segmentation and discrimination by Reskin 1984, Roos 1981, England 1984 and others). Social policy influenced by feminist empiricism has been critically scrutinized by other feminists, reflecting doubt about its ultimate benefits to women. But the origin of both criticisms and policy in advanced industrial countries confounds still further the quest to bring together what may be a more purely interpretive approach to scholarship and politically meaningful action. That is, many critical questions about apparently progressive policies touching women's lives come from feminists using or referring to the same methodological apparatus as the originators of concepts and constructs leading to new policies (Sprague and Zimmerman 1989). Interpretive research often reveals elements of social organization that contradict policy formulations (e.g., ethnographic study of AFDC recipients reveals little resistance to paid work while social policy is constructed on the assumption that women must be compelled to work [Ambramovitz 1988]). But much feminist political dialogue takes place on a stage with large and expensive data sets, analyzed by means of inferential statistics, and leading to policies through slow, cumbersome and ultimately compromising political bargains and exchanges. Whatever the doubts of many feminist sociologists about these means to knowledge and change, to abandon them, particularly as feminists become actors in the piece, is daunting and draws a hesitant response (Jansen 1990).

Feminist Paradigms and Disciplinary Methods: Finding a Match

The challenge of developing interpretive methodologies in sociology is more complex, however, than is suggested by discussion of political imperatives and methodological preferences alone. Sociology is an empirical discipline, focusing on group relations and dynamics. In fact it is generally advocacy for and against particular groups that provides the basis of our political and policy-related positions. Our empirical focus on social phenomena, combined with the discipline's historical accommodation of political concerns, distinguishes sociology from other academic disciplines and shapes the way that feminists contribute to the field.

If we design a continuum from pure interpretation and the related possibility of characterizing behavior as unique to the positivist drive to generalize and objectify, feminist methodologies necessarily span it, for they represent many conceptions of what can and should be known. At one end is literature and other areas of the humanities, where feminist methods have accompanied other strategies to allow the observer's politics to supersede the author's intentions. The deconstruction of a text is not an empirical exercise, for no external object is acknowledged. The subject of scholarly work is the reader, his or her reactions to what may lie at many levels within the text. Here, feminist politics have invaded theoretical territory because feminist thought has eclipsed the text itself and allowed pure interpretation to emerge as a methodology (Robinson 1985; Snitow 1989; Stimpson 1988).

At the other end of the spectrum is positivism, perhaps most suitable to the natural sciences. The claim is that all observers will reliably report on the same objective phenomenon that itself can be found in the same form in other settings. The unique nature of events and the means of knowing them both differ dramatically from the other extreme where humanities discourse is found. The social sciences, including sociology, have not traveled far from this positivist extreme. In political science, for example, research focuses on political attitudes and behavior, measured in the aggregate. The major alternative focus of work in the discipline has traditionally been theoretical (Hawkesworth 1987). Like many feminist sociologists, feminist political scientists have called for more qualitative research to identify invisible groups and slighted group interests, with the intention of refining the quantitative study of politics (Ackelsberg and Diamond 1987; Hawkesworth 1987; Kelly, Ronan and Cawley 1987).

In between literature and the social sciences we find among other disciplines, anthropology and history. These fields accept empirical methods of research and analysis. Even in their more reflexive and interpretive forms, history and anthropology respect the integrity of subjects' definitions of reality and put limits on the role of observer and interpreter in research (Gordon 1986; Strathern 1987). Yet, at the same time, anthropologists and historians acknowledge that the cases and situations they study may be unique. There is thus agreement in both fields that generalization has its limits and must never overwhelm the particularity of the case.

Stacey and Thorne suggest that the depth of historical and anthropological knowledge, achieved through ethnographic, labor-intensive, case-focused methods, may be what feminist sociologists need to achieve a more valid and profound understanding of gender. Anthropology seems to have incorporated feminist insights into the discipline and in the process experienced significant modifications of key areas of research and analysis

(DuBois et al. 1985; Morgen 1989; Moore 1988). Thus there is a coherence to the feminist anthropological enterprise that seems lacking in sociology.

Since the beginnings of feminist anthropology, its proponents have agreed about the issues that need further thought in light of feminist ideas and that these themes are key to the discipline (see, for example, Rosaldo and Lamphere 1974). Among these questions are the degree and consistency of gender autonomy and gender equality cross-culturally, the relationship between the two, the ways in which various kinship systems increase or make diffuse women's status, and a culture's value on production and reproduction (DuBois et al. 1985; Lamphere 1987; Mukhopadhyay and Higgins 1988). While feminist anthropologists scarcely agree about the details of their elaboration historically, there is agreement that fundamental axioms of anthropology are altered by feminist judgments (Morgen 1989).

Moreover a central analytical principle has emerged in feminist anthropology, superseding the study of particular dimensions of gender in relation to production, reproduction and the symbolic order. That is, feminist anthropologists increasingly see the sex-gender system as integral to the social formation as a whole. Gender is structured into the mode or system of production: It is not an epiphenomenoa or in any other way separable from material and cultural life (Collier and Yanagisako 1987; Morgen 1989; Mukhopadhyay and Higgins 1988).

Why has anthropology been successful in bringing gender squarely into disciplinary concerns where other disciplines, including sociology, have failed to do so? First, women's lives and experiences are built in a fundamental way into anthropology, given the discipline's long and strong interest in lineage and kinship. Not all anthropologists come easily if at all to feminist concerns (DuBois et al. 1985; Strathem 1987), but women have been visible in scholarly work, particularly in studies of cultural groups, e.g., foraging societies, where women's production-related activities are critical to the group's survival (Mukhopadhyay and Higgins 1988; Rosaldo and Lamphere 1974; Sacks 1982). Second, feminist anthropology borrows heavily from materialism, which has a respected place and coherent corpus of resulting research in anthropology (Ortner 1984). Finally, anthropology's case-study approach, accompanied by the ethnographic method, is well suited to the intellectually radical enterprise of interpretive, process-focused and systemic analysis many feminist sociologists seek (Mascia-Lees, Sharpe and Cohen 1989; Stacey 1988; Strathem 1987). So compatible is anthropology with feminist and other schools of post-modernism that some anthropologists have recently questioned colleagues' embrace of this highly reflexive approach, claiming that it threatens to move anthropology away from radical and feminist politics and from the construction of analytical categories for understanding gender (Mascia-Lees, Sharpe and Cohen 1989; see also Strathern 1987).

The suitability of anthropological methods to a certain kind of feminist analysis, and the apparent hostility of mainstream sociology to the same, reminds us that the quest for methodological consistency among feminists in the academy is problematic (Harding 1987a, b). We are all bound by the epistemological goals and methodological customs of our disciplines, although the range of disciplinary approaches to knowledge is generally wider than acknowledged and often marked by internal debate. And we are sometimes challenged by methodological movements in sister disciplines that seem to open doors that have remained stubbornly closed to us, yet may finally violate embedded epistemological and/or political visions.

Sociology: The Special Case

Since its start in the nineteenth century, sociology's epistemological as well as policy-driven goals have incited—and contained—enduring conflict between advocates of process-focused, interpretive methods and proponents of now-dominant positivism (Ritzer 1988). The symbiotic relationship between the two methodologies can be said to define sociology more certainly than any single research strategy. As noted above, interpretive sociology has acted as a catalyst for the study of new themes by survey researchers in particular, and as a critical force modifying and questioning positivist research. Less obvious, perhaps, is the way that positivism has pushed interpretation to account for the social structural bases and implications of particular group characteristics and processes.

Contention between proponents of interpretive and positivist modes of sociological analysis has led to conceptual compromises, and to occasional conceptual estrangements and separations. The historical split of anthropology and sociology into distinct fields and academic departments in some respects recalls the current rift between feminists seeking an interpretive methodology and those who accept the dominance of positivism (Turner 1978). The deep divide between the structurally oriented symbolic interactionists influenced by Manfred Kuhn and those inspired by the process-oriented approach of Herbert Blumer and survey researchers is a second precedent feminist sociologists may find familiar (Turner 1978).

At this time feminist sociologists share a particular if broadly defined ideology over and above any affinity with sociology's reform tradition. While this ideology may not constitute an epistemological "standpoint" it is, as Ferree and Hess (1987: 13) note, a common "conscious partiality" (see also Cook and Fonow 1986). Our shared feminist values reflect and reinforce a commitment to the study of gender, a social category. We may quarrel about how much generalization is good but we agree that some is assumed, particularly if we want to make political statements. In the same way our disputes about researcher subjectivity ultimately yield agreement that as practitioners of an empirical system of analysis, some objectivity is required to study social relations (Sprague and Zimmerman 1989).

The range of acceptable methods among feminist sociologists is currently wide. Such methodological flexibility may reflect the unsophisticated state of our disciplinary knowledge about gender: the less we know, the less likely we are to debate about how to know more. Yet the epistemological differences between interpretive and positivist methodologies and all they imply about subjectivity and generalization are substantial and may become more acute as our certainties about gender and its place in politics become more precise and highly differentiated.

The problem for feminist sociology is not finally, however, that two research traditions, interpretive and positivist, dominate sociology's empiricism, or that for feminists, advocacy of the former implies some kinship with the latter. It is rather that interpretive sociology, necessary to a more profound understanding of social processes generally, is too seldom undertaken. How can feminist sociologists be encouraged to embrace interpretive methods? Urging feminist sociologists to do so is finally gratuitous. The academy rewards positivist research and often defeats those who seek academic career success through the pursuit of alternative research strategies (Grant and Ward 1991).

The history of sociology suggests that political mobilization and change facilitates methodological risk-taking. The Civil Rights Movement of the 1960's, the New Left and emergent counterculture inspired ethnographic studies of social movements, minority and alternative communities. American Marxist sociology was also constituted in this era. Recent calls for more diversity in curriculum and research funding demand new knowledge, more readily acquired through interpretive than positivist means. If enduring, this movement could, perhaps, revitalize interpretative sociology. A transformation in the sociological study of gender cannot take place, however, until interpretive methodologies are as influential in the field as positivism. Interpretive research and analysis must not only provide the basis for aggregated group study, but more vitally, must offer a competitive mode of analysis, with clear-cut theoretical and political implications and goals.

To the extent that interpretation focuses on what appear to be singular phenomena, the sociological quest for generalizable knowledge, often with political implications, is frustrated. On the other hand, an interpretive methodology that provides a praxis-based alternative to reformist policy analysis is consistent with the political goals of much conventional sociology. The assumption of group relations directing praxis is consistent with sociological epistemology. Feminist political economy offers a promising epistemological and political counterpoint to mainstream sociology (Acker 1989). As the post-modern project influences feminist political economy to broaden its grounds of interpretation and deepen subjectivity and reflexivity in analysis, it is more satisfying to many feminist critics of positivism (see, for example, Smith 1987; Stacey 1990). In any case, feminist political economy and more highly subjective approaches to interpretation share a methodological orientation that is more likely to yield conceptual advances in our understanding of gender relations than debate between positivism and interpretation has thus far produced.

Feminist political economy has been strongly influenced by the work of European and Canadian feminist sociologists (Morrissey and Stoecker, forthcoming; Acker 1989). The need to go outside the United States for paradigmatic principles suggests political roadblocks to developing meaningful theories of gender relations in the U.S. The respect for materialist, in particular Marxist categories of analysis elsewhere, makes possible the strong and influential status of an interpretive feminism grounded in political economy. Although international exchange is fruitful in radical studies, the endurance of feminist political economy without a basis in national politics is problematic. It may finally be that the feminist transformation of sociology requires a transformation in U.S. politics. While in other academic disciplines theoretical and epistemological debate alone may advance feminist theory, sociology's conceptual progress may await the radicalization and mobilization of external political forces.

Endnotes

[1]This is in contrast to European and Latin American sociology, where disciplinary political interests form from class action and analysis. The bias in this approach is materialist and historical, macro-sociological and more inclusive of the economic treatment of gender than "policy" considerations of American sociology. But it may also be less sensitive than other perspectives to the study of individual emotions and interaction.

[2]Fergusen (1991: 324) notes that hermeneutic epistemology, associated with interpretive methodologies in sociology, is "at odds with authority, inclined to the side of the powerless and marginal."

[3]The hermeneutic "project" is not monolithic. Fergusen (1991) suggests a crucial distinction between interpretation, assuming an ordered universe to be uncovered through research, and genealogy, allowing for "flux and discord" and focus on difference, the particular, the anomalies. Among sociologists, interest in "post-modem" ways of knowing is applied to groups, assuming some uniformity of experience and thus pushing sociologists closer to the interpretation than to genealogy.

References

Abramovitz, Mimi. 1988. *Regulating the Lives of Women*. Boston: South End Press.

Ackelsberg, Martha and Irene Diamond. 1987. "Gender and Political Life: New Directions in Political Science" Pp. 504–525 in *Analyzing Gender: A Social Science Handbook,* edited by M.M. Ferree and B.B. Hess. Newbury Park: Sage.

Acker, Joan. 1989. "Making Gender Visible." Pp. 65–81 in *Feminism and Sociological Theory*, edited by Ruth Wallace. Newbury Park: Sage.

Acker, Joan, Kate Barry and Johe Esseveld. 1983. "Objectivity and Truth: Problems in Doing Feminist Research." *Women's Studies International Forum* 6 (4): 423–435.

Bernard, Jessie. 1987. "Re-viewing the Impact of Women's Studies on Sociology." Pp. 193–216 in *The Impact of Feminist Research in the Academy*, edited by Christine Farnham. Bloomington: Indiana University Press.

Brewer, Rose M. 1989. "Black Women and Feminist Sociology: The Emerging Perspective." *The American Sociologist* 20 (1): 57–70.

Cannon, Lynn Weber, Elizabeth Higgenbotham and Marianne L. A. Leung. 1988. "Race and Class Bias in Qualitative Research on Women." *Gender & Society* 2 (4): 449–462.

Collier, Jane Fishburne and Sylvia Junko Yanagisako. 1987. "Introduction; Toward a Unified Analysis of Gender and Kinship." Pp. 3–13; 14–50 in *Gender and Kinship: Essays Toward a Unified Analysis*, edited by J.F. Collier and S.J. Yanagisako. Palo Alto: Stanford University Press.

Collins, Patricia Hill. 1986. "Learning from the Outside Within: The Sociological Significance of Black Feminist Thought." *Social Problems* 33 (6): 14–32.

Collins, Randall. 1988. *Theoretical Sociology*. New York: Harcourt Brace Jovanovich.

Cook, Judith and Margaret Fonow. 1986. "Knowledge and Women's Interests: Issues of Epistemology and Methodology in Feminist Sociological Research." *Sociological Inquiry* 56 (1): 2–29.

DuBois, Ellen C., Gail P. Kelly, Elizabeth L. Kennedy, Carolyn W. Korsmeyer, and Lillian Robinson. 1985. *Feminist Scholarship: Kindling in the Groves of Academe*. Urbana: University of Illinois Press.

England, Paula. 1984. "Wage Appreciation and Depreciation: A Test of Neoclassical Economic Explanations of Occupational Sex Segregation." *Social Forces* 62 (3): 726–749.

England, Paula and Bahar Norris. 1985. "Comparable Worth: A New Doctrine of Sex Discrimination," *Social Science Quarterly* 66 (3): 627–643.

Farganis, Sondra. 1986. "Social Theory and Feminist Theory: The Need for Dialogue." *Sociological Inquiry* 56 (1): 50–68.

Ferguson, Kathy. 1991. "Interpretation and Genealogy in Feminism." *Signs* 16 (2): 322–339.

Ferree, Myra Marx and Beth B. Hess. 1987. "Introduction." Pp. 9–30 in *Analyzing Gender. A Handbook of Social Science Research*, edited by M.M. Ferree and B.B. Hess. Newbury Park: Sage.

Flax, Jane. 1987. "Postmodernism and Gender Relations in Feminist Theory." *Signs* 12 (4): 621–643.

Gordon, Linda, 1986. "What's New in Women's History." Pp. 20–30 in Feminist Studies/Critical Studies, edited by Teresa de Lauretis. Bloomington: Indiana University Press.

Grant, Linda and Kathryn B. Ward. 1991. "Gender and Publishing in Sociology." Gender & Society 5 (2): 207–223.

Haraway, Donna. 1988. "Situated Knowledges: The Science Question in Feminism and the Privilege of Partial Perspective." *Feminist Studies* 14 (3): 575–599.

____. 1981. "In the Beginning Was the Word: The Genesis of Biological Theory." *Signs* 6 (3): 469–481.

Harding, Sandra. 1987a. "Introduction; Conclusion." Pp. 1–14; 181–190 in *Feminism and Methodology*, edited by S. Harding. Bloomington: Indiana University Press.

____. 1987b. "The Instability of the Analytical Categories of Feminist Theory." Pp. 283–302 in *Sex and Scientific Inquiry*, edited by S. Harding and J. F. O'Barr. Chicago: University of Chicago Press.

____. 1986. *The Science Question in Feminism*. Ithaca: Cornell University Press.

Hartsock, Nancy C. M. 1987. "The Feminist Standpoint: Developing the Ground for a Specifically Feminist Historical Materialism." Pp. 157–180 in *Feminism and Methodology*, edited by S. Harding. Bloomington: Indiana University Press.

Hawkesworth, Mary E. 1987. "Feminist Epistemology: A Survey of the Field." *Women and Politics* 7 (3): 115–127.

Hekman, Susan. 1987. "The Feminization of Epistemology: Gender and the Social Sciences." *Women and Politics* 7 (3): 65–83.

Jansen, Sue Curry. 1990. "Is Science a Man? New Feminist Epistemologies and Reconstruction of Knowledge: A Review Essay." *Theory and Society* 19 (2): 235–246.

Kelly, Joan. 1984. *Women, History and Theory: Feminism and Methodology*. Chicago: University of Chicago Press.

Kelly, Rita Mae, Bernard Ronan and Margaret E. Cawley. 1987. "Liberal Positivistic Epistemology and Research on Women and Politics." *Women and Politics* 7 (3): 11–27.

Kolodny, Annette. 1988. "Dancing between Left and Right: Feminism and the Academic Minefield in the 1980's." *Feminist Studies* 14 (3): 453466.

Lamphere, Louise. 1987. "Feminism and Anthropology: The Struggle to Reshape our Thinking about Gender." Pp. 11–33 in *The Impact of Feminist Research in the Academy*, edited by Christine Farnham. Bloomington: Indiana University Press.

Mascia-Lees, Frances E., Patricia Sharpe, and Colleen Ballerino Cohen. 1989. "The Postmodernist Turn in Anthropology: Cautions from a Feminist Perspective." *Signs* 15 (1): 7–33.

Morgen, Sandra. 1989. "Gender and Anthropology: Introductory Essay." Pp. 1–20 in *Gender and Anthropology*, edited by S. Morgen. Washington, D.C.: American Anthropological Association.

Moore, Henrietta L. 1988. *Feminism and Anthropology*. Minneapolis: University of Minnesota Press.

Morrissey, Marietta and Randy Stoecker. Forthcoming. "Marxist Sociology and Gender." In *Marxist Sociology: Surveys of Contemporary Research*, edited by Patrick McGuire and Donald McQuarie. New York: General Hall.

Mukhopadhyay, Carol C. and Patricia J. Higgins. 1988. "Anthropological Studies of Women's Status Revisited: 1977–1987." *Annual Review of Anthropology* 17: 461–495.

Ortner, Sherry B. 1984. "Theory in Anthropology Since the Sixties." *Comparative Studies in Society and History* 26 (1): 126–166.

Reskin, Barbara (ed.) 1984. *Sex Segregation in the Workplace*. Washington, D.C.: National Academy Press.

Ritzer, George. 1988. *Contemporary Sociological Theory*. New York: Knopf.

Robinson, Lillian S. 1985. "Treason Our Text: Feminist Challenges to the Literary Canon." Pp. 105–121 in *The New Feminist Criticism*, edited by Elaine Showalter. New York: Pantheon.

Roos, Patricia. 1981. "Sex Segregation in the Workplace: Male-female Differences in Returns to Occupations." *Social Science Research* 10 (3): 195–224.

Rosaldo, Michelle and Louise Lamphere (eds.) 1974. *Women, Culture and Society*. Stanford: Stanford University Press.

Sacks, Karen. 1982. *Sisters and Wives*. Urbana: University of Illinois Press.

Scott, Jean Wallach. 1987. "Women's History and the Rewriting of History." Pp. 34–52 in *The Impact of Feminist Research in the Academy*, edited by Christine Farnham. Bloomington: Indiana University Press.

Smith, Dorothy E. 1987. *The Everyday World as Problematic: A Feminist Sociology.* Boston: Northeastern University Press.

Snitow, Ann. 1989. "Basic Divisions in Feminism." *Dissent* 36 (2): 205–224.

Sprague, Joey and Mary K. Zimmerman. 1989. "Quality and Quantity: Revolutionizing Feminist Methodology." *The American Sociologist* 20 (1): 71–86.

Stacey, Judith. 1990. *Brave New Families* New York: Basic Books.

_____. 1988. "Can There be a Feminist Ethnography?" *Women's Studies International Forum* 11 (1): 21–27.

Stacey, Judith and Barrie Thorne. 1985. "The Missing Feminist Revolution in Sociology." *Social Problems* 32 (4): 301–316.

Strathern, Marilyn. 1987. "An Awkward Relationship: The Case of Feminism and Anthropology." *Signs* 12 (2): 276–292.

Steinberg, Ronnie. 1987. "Radical Challenges in a Liberal World: The Mixed Success of Comparable Worth." *Gender & Society* 1 (4): 466–476.

Stimpson, Catherine R. 1988. *Where the Meanings Are.* New York: Metheun.

Turner, Jonathan H. 1978. *The Structure of Sociological Theory.* Homewood, Illinois: The Dorsey Press.

Ward, Kathryn B. and Linda Grant. 1985. "The Feminist Critique and a Decade of Published Research in Sociology Journals." *Sociological Quarterly* 26 (2): 139–157.

Yeatman, Anna. 1990. "A Feminist Theory of Social Differentiation." Pp. 281–299 in *Feminism/Postmodernism*, edited by Linda J. Nicholson. New York: Routledge.

A Rejoinder to Morrissey's "Feminist Sociology: Methodology and Politics in Disciplinary Change"[3]

Mary Patrice Erdmans
Central Connecticut State University

To do feminist sociology is to do humanist sociology, and mainstream sociology does neither very often or very well. While the discipline has incorporated gender as a variable and more women as practitioners and objects of the research gaze, Marietta Morrissey explains that unlike the fields of anthropology and history where feminism has produced paradigmatic shifts, sociology has incorporated feminism without being transformed by it. In this article she examines two "impediments to the feminist transformation of sociology: our dualistic methodological tradition and related commitment to political reformism," and argues in favor of "a praxis-based interpretive methodology."

The scientific assumptions of the discipline that limit feminism's impact also minimize the importance of humanism. In short, the discipline is premised on methodological and policy models that hierarchically separate the object and the subject while humanism and feminism are predicated on their egalitarian integration. As Morrissey notes, interpretive feminist methodology rejects a positivist model, which posits a duality between object and knower and instead promotes practices that bring the researched into the research process in order to both minimize objectification and make evident the subjectivity of the researcher. This resonates with practices of humanist sociology, and the significance of subjectivity is embodied in the reflexive statement that precedes articles published in *Humanity and Society*. Unfortunately, when this reflexive statement is simply tacked onto the article for the purposes of publication, then humanist sociology resembles the state of feminist sociology in that it is additive rather than transformative. Reflexivity should be integrated into our research practices from the emergence of the research question (in collaboration with the researched), to the interpretation and presentation of the findings (both inside and outside the academy), to the praxis-based implementation of the findings in policy proposals.

Interpretive methods allow more voice to the participants and are more mindful of subjectivity. As such, these methods can potentially challenge the hierarchical relations within the academy as well as between the researcher and the researched. Unfortunately, these methods are not used as often as positivist methods, and when they are, they "seem no more than the preliminary step in the larger, positivist research design." It is particularly important that sociologists employ interpretive methods because of the discipline's policy-oriented tradition. Empirical research "even feminist empiricism" is often misguided

---

[3]This paper originally appeared in *Humanity & Society* Volume 27, Number 4, 2003.

because it is based on "expensive data sets, analyzed by means of inferential statistics, and leading to policies through slow, cumbersome, and ultimately compromising political gains and exchanges." Instead, theories and policies about women "need to be inductively built and deep structures of social understanding carefully and reflexively deconstructed."

The data interpretive methods yield are, like human life itself, often messy, complicated, and loaded with contradictions. Social actors have emotions as well as behaviors, consciousness as well as resources, and perceptions as well as opportunities. Interpretive methods are more suitable for studying emotions, consciousness, and perceptions than survey methods, but survey findings are more easily reported in the limited spatial and temporal dimensions of sociology journals and conference presentations. Moreover, these journals and conferences are designed almost exclusively for sociologists. Material and cultural capital, as well as professional elitism (manifest in jargon) create effective barriers between the researcher and the researched. Despite well-meaning attempts to employ humanist and feminist practices, when we write articles and papers solely for academic venues we are maintaining the hierarchical relations of traditional science. We may have added humanist and feminist practices but we have not transformed the discipline.

Morrissey recognizes the power of mainstream sociology to limit the revolution that feminist and humanist sociology threaten. The academy preferences positivist quantitative work in a variety of ways: quantitative studies are more often awarded large research grants; the tenure and promotion clocks discourage lengthy ethnographic studies; journal articles are boiler-plated for quantitative research designs. Given these structural limitations, she understands that rah-rahing sociologists to employ interpretative methods can be "gratuitous." We are left with the option of either adding bits and pieces of humanist and feminist practices to the discipline (a reflexive statement here, a gender variable there) or engaging in "a transformation in U.S. politics" because the hierarchical relations of the discipline are situated within patriarchal, racist and imperialist structures of U.S. society. The contemporary challenge to Feminist-Humanist Sociology remains the goal of praxis— carrying on engaged, critical scholarship in the larger context of radical politics.

5. Embracing Social Activism: Sociology in the Service of Social Justice and Peace[1]

Chris Dale
Dennis Kalob
New England College

Reflexive Statement

For many years, we have personally and professionally, individually and together, struggled with what it means to be a sociologist today. We wondered what the mission of sociology should be given the hardship and suffering in the world and the urgent need for significant social change. We have found the answer in two places. First, we started with our shared vision of a better world—a world that is substantially more just and peaceful. Second, we thought about what it will take to get us closer to that new world and realized that part of the answer lies in certain key historical moments in, and particular contributions of, the sociology of the past. The promise of sociology has not been fulfilled, but we can change that by learning from these lessons of our past and envisioning the exciting possibilities for the future—a future in which sociology plays an active role in healing and transforming our world.

Introduction

Many of the pioneers of American sociology were inspired by an impulse to social reform and a vision of a better society (Coser 1978; Deegan 1988). Ideas about specific reform priorities varied. There were calls for women's suffrage and gender equality, an end to racism, the banning of child labor, the right of workers to organize unions, resistance to militarism and war, immigrant rights, educational reform, and a host of other issues. These early sociologists were based in universities and community organizations, notably urban settlement houses (Lengermann and Niebrugge-Brantley 2002), and for many, sociology's basic mission included a commitment to help improve the quality of life that people experienced.

There were different perspectives, however, on just what sociology's role should be in serving the public interest and fostering reform. Some, like Lester Frank Ward, wanted to establish a social science that would bring to light general laws about social life and use this knowledge to help shape enlightened social policy. Sociologists would, in their "applied" capacity, serve as arms-length social engineers, providing public leaders with general suggestions for ameliorative change. Any involvement in the actual politics of

[1]This paper originally appeared in *Humanity & Society* Volume 3, Number 2, 2006.

social reform, however, was considered strictly off-limits as it would presumably contaminate and compromise sound scientific work. In the words of Ward:

> Applied sociology... is a science, not an art. The most that it claims to do is to lay down certain general principles as guides to social and political action. But in this it must be exceedingly cautious. The principles can consist only of the highest generalizations. They can have only the most general bearing on current events and the popular or burning questions of the hour. The sociologist who undertakes to discuss these, especially to take sides on them, abandons his science and becomes a politician (Ward 1906: 9–10).

Other sociologists adhered to the progressive-era notion that efforts to unveil ugly truths about injustices in U.S. society would arouse public sentiment and ultimately incite ameliorative action. There was a strong faith in the belief that if sociologists (and other reform-minded folks) could document and disseminate information about conditions that violated what they presumed were basic standards of human decency and justice, then the public would rally to change those conditions. W.E.B. DuBois held this position in the early part of his career as a sociologist (Wortham 2005: 78), and he worked assiduously to research and describe the abysmal social and economic conditions that African Americans experienced in the U.S. However, within a few years of taking a position at Atlanta University, where he taught history, economics and sociology, DuBois became increasingly involved in political activism (Broschart 2005). He served as a leader of the Pan African Congress starting in 1900, and five years later, as he grew more impatient with the power of his pen alone, played a key role in the inauguration of the militant Black civil rights initiative known as the Niagara Movement. In 1909, he helped launch the NAACP, and a year later left his academic position at Atlanta to direct research and publication activities for the organization, which would include the founding and editing of *The Crisis*. He would also become more directly involved in the political struggle against lynching and colonial exploitation, as well as the fight for "women's rights, Jewish rights, and worker's rights" (Zuckerman 2004: 3). DuBois returned to Atlanta University for a decade in 1934, but his sociological teaching and scholarship were inextricably coupled with political activism on many fronts (Lewis 1993; Lewis 2000).

Still other sociologists always viewed and practiced their craft as a dialectic process of social analysis and social action. Jane Addams is perhaps the most prominent case in point. For her, these were complimentary ways to pursue social justice. While she had affiliations with Albion Small, Charles Henderson, George H. Mead, and other members of the faculty at the University of Chicago, Addams never accepted an academic position there, and instead worked out of the Halstead Street settlement house that she and Ellen Gates Starr had established in 1889. In her work at the Hull House and in national campaigns (for women's suffrage, for racial justice, for international peace), Addams was deeply engaged in investigative research, scholarly and popular writing, public lecturing, social service work, community organizing, and political activism. For Addams and other "settlement sociologists" (Lengermann and Niebrugge-Brantley 2002), there was no divorcing social science and social activism. Unfortunately, as Deegan (1988) has so forcefully suggested, Addams' action-oriented brand of sociology was largely written out of sociological history and sociology texts.

While concern about social problems and visions of a better society continued to inform sociology well into the early decades of the 20th century, an influential cadre of university-based men became increasingly preoccupied with the field's status and credibility as a *real* science. They promoted sociology as the exclusive domain of university-based, value-neutral scientists. The extent to which the knowledge they produced might actually be relevant in addressing public issues like poverty, racism or war seemed to matter less and less. This narrower version of sociology left no room for value commitments or social reform work. *Real* sociology was an objective scientific enterprise that had nothing to do with politics, reform initiatives, or social activism (Deegan 1988).

Academic Sociology

By the 1920s, the work of social amelioration was essentially relegated to a whole new profession—social work.[1] While sociology had become the domain of university-based, (mostly) male thinkers, social work had become the work of female doers, or, to use the pejorative term thrown around by some academics at the time, do-gooders. The sociology/social work distinction became standard fare in the curricula of the respective disciplines. Sociology was defined as an intellectual enterprise charged with conducting research and producing knowledge while social work was about "helping people" and making the world a better place.[2]

In its academic version, sociology was conceptualized as an intellectual pursuit which had as its central, if not sole, task the creation of social science knowledge. It was defined as a field of study that would, above all, yield generic insights about human social experience. The fruits of this intellectual labor would be presented in scholarly books, journal articles and other publications.

William F. Ogburn, a prominent, widely respected member of the profession in the late 20s, exemplified the academic orientation. In his 1929 presidential address to the American Sociological Society (later, the American Sociological Association), he exclaimed that:

> Sociology as a science is not interested in making the world a better place in which to live, in encouraging beliefs, in spreading information, in dispensing news, in setting forth impressions of life, in leading the multitudes, or in guiding the ship of state. Science is interested directly in one thing only, to wit, discovering new knowledge. (www.asanet.org/governance/OgburnPresidentialAddress.pdf)

Ogburn went on to acknowledge that, "As a human being, I...may want to seek for knowledge that will be of benefit to mankind...[and] to spread this new knowledge far and wide..." (ibid). But in doing so, he insisted, he would no longer be "functioning" as a scientist/sociologist. Clearly, then, Ogburn saw a radical distinction between doing the work of social science and social amelioration. You could not have it both ways, or more precisely, you could not do both things under the rubric of sociology.

This version of sociology continued to prevail into the mid-century with the ascendance of sociologists who dedicated themselves to what Mills (1959) called grand theory and abstracted empiricism. For critics like Mills, sociology had become an elaborate exercise in conceptual and quantitative gymnastics, far removed from very real and pressing social problems like poverty and the threat of nuclear war. For the most part, it was abstract, often quite esoteric and, to put it bluntly, all but irrelevant.

Even in the 60s, when various forms of critical and Marxist sociology began to challenge the hegemony of academic sociology, this orientation held its own. Consider, for example, what Peter Berger had to say in his very popular, and now classic, *Invitation to Sociology*. Early in this book, which interestingly enough is subtitled *A Humanistic Perspective*, Berger tries to clarify what sociology is by delineating it from social work. In his words: "Social work…is a certain *practice* in society. Sociology is not a practice but an *attempt to understand*…" (1963: 4). He continues:

> The interest of the sociologist is primarily theoretical. That is, he is interested in understanding for its own sake. He may be aware of or even concerned with the practical applicability and consequences of his finding, but at that point he leaves the sociological frame of reference as such and moves into realms of values, beliefs and ideas that he shares with other men who are not sociologists (1963: 17).

Here, Berger articulates the dominant understanding of sociology of his time. The sociologist is a detached social *scientist* whose responsibilities are merely to observe, record and make generalizations about human social interaction. Questions about the relevance of this knowledge (i.e. how and by whom it might be applied) fall outside of the sociologist's purview.

The sociologist produces knowledge in a power- and value-neutral vacuum and then dispenses/releases this knowledge (via academic publications) into the public domain, making it accessible to anyone who might find it useful, for whatever purpose they might see fit. To quote Berger once again:

> Sociological understanding can be recommended to social workers, but also to salesmen, nurses, evangelists and politicians—in fact, to anyone whose goals involve the manipulation of men, for whatever purpose and with whatever moral justification (1963: 5).

Today, the purely academic version of sociology remains a powerful force within the profession. While there is more talk now than in Talcott Parsons' day about connecting sociology to real-world issues and problems (as we will discuss later), it is still defined as a field of *study* by the ASA and virtually every major Introduction to Sociology textbook. Sociology is still depicted in essence as an intellectual endeavor. Moreover, as we will discuss later, there is a solid core of folks who remain committed to the idea that sociology should concern itself solely with scientific inquiry, not with the social and political affairs of the world.

Critical Sociology

The reformist impulse in sociology was marginalized with the ascent of the academic orientation, but it did not atrophy and die.[3] It found expression in various alternative perspectives. One of these was critical sociology.

As the term implies, critical sociology takes as its central task the critique of society, particularly the prevailing structure of power and privilege. Current social structural arrangements are analyzed and critiqued in relation to specific values, and by extension, to a vision of a more humane society, one that is more likely to foster human dignity and social justice. In his book *Sociology and Critical Inquiry*, John Walton offers this description:

> Critical sociology provides a revealing description of social reality and interpretively explains the forces that brought it about, evaluates the (intended and unintended) consequences of that reality against the explicit value star⸱dards of freedom and equality, and proposes alternative policies or social arrangements that, based on arguments from research, would more fully realize the values. The second and third tasks require that the sociologist has clearly in mind an alternative, preferable state of affairs... (1990: 67).

The critical sociologist serves as a public intellectual who interprets and clarifies social problems or injustices, and perhaps offers suggestions or proposals to reform, if not to transform, society. In essence, s/he lays the conceptual groundwork for social change.

C. Wright Mills exemplifies the critical perspective in sociology. He wrote extensively about the increasing concentration of power in the economic, political and military sectors of U.S. society. And he did this not simply by way of an observation, but out of a concern about the rapid erosion of anything resembling a genuine democracy. For Mills, democracy—the idea that "those vitally affected by any decision [people] make have an effective voice in that decision"(1959: 188)—was a core value that informed his vision of the good society.

Mills' trenchant sociological critique was widely read, and had a powerful influence in some public circles. Most notably perhaps, his work resonated with Al Haber, Tom Hayden, Bob Ross, and others in the new left who were looking for a way to frame their disillusionment and aspirations for change in the 1960s. Mills served as an intellectual guru of sorts for members of the nascent Students for a Democratic Society (SDS), and his thinking had a strong impact on the organization's crafting of its manifesto, the Port Huron Statement (Miller 1987: 78–91; Trevino and Ross 1998).

There is a key point to be made here: Mills provided the SDS with a coherent and compelling framework for interpreting their concerns and guiding their work as social activists. However, he did not work in collaboration with SDS members, or with the members of any other radical organizations of the time. He did not engage in any movement activities. Mills saw himself, and sociologists generally, as public intellectuals, and quite emphatically, not social activists. In *The Sociological Imagination*, for example, he writes:

> The role of reason I have been outlining neither means nor requires that one hit the pavement, take the next plane to the scene of the current crisis, run for Congress, buy a newspaper plant, go among the poor, set up a soap box. Such actions are often admirable, and I can readily imagine occasions when I should personally find it impossible not to want to do them myself... [He never did so.]... But for the social scientist to take them to be his normal activities is merely to abdicate his role, and to display by his action a disbelief in the promise of social science and in the role of reason in human affairs. This role

requires only that the social scientist get on with the work of social science and that he avoid furthering the bureaucratization of reason and discourse (Mills 1959: 192).

Again, then, critical sociology lays the groundwork for social activism. But ultimately, it leaves the on-the-ground struggles for change to others.

Humanist sociology, at least as it was initially conceived by Al Lee, also falls under the umbrella of critical sociology. A pioneer in the humanist sociology tradition, Lee called for a sociology that serves humanity, and in so doing extolled specific values like individual and national *self-determination*, *democracy* (vs. plutocracy), and *non-violence* (Lee 1978: 16). But how precisely was sociology to serve humanity? According to Lee, humanist sociologists would "develop knowledge of direct service to all classes of people as citizens, as consumers, and as neighbors." Further, he wrote in *Sociology For Whom?*:

> This means knowledge of social behavior that can and will be communicated by its developers through all appropriate media to those who can best use it. It includes studies of ways in which people can protect themselves from undesirable manipulation by those in positions of power, of how to achieve more livable homes and communities, of constructive alternatives to family, civil, and international violence, and of much more. In serving humanity, sociologists act principally as critics, demystifiers, reporters, and clarifiers. They review critically the folk wisdom and other theories by which people try to live. In doing so, they strip away some of the outworn clutter of fictions about life and living that make the human lot even more difficult than it might be. Then they try to report more accurate information about the changing social scene and with it to help clarify ways of understanding human relations and of coping with personal and social problems (1978: 36).

Here, humanist sociology is essentially depicted as an intellectual craft. Yes, it is far more relevant and connected to real world social problems than mainstream academic sociology. But it is still mainly about intellectual work. As Stoecker (1996) has noted, Lee posits a sociology that remains distressingly disconnected from social change groups and initiatives. At its most relevant, sociology is the province of a civic-minded intelligentsia whose members expose important social problems or help to inform public policy. There is certainly no indication that sociology is about engaging in advocacy work, community organizing or political activism, as it so clearly was for Addams and others in the earlier activist tradition.

Having said this about Lee's work, it is important to note that there are many folks today who consider activism to be an important, if not essential, aspect of humanist sociology—including the present authors. A good share of the Association for Humanist Sociology's members today are in fact engaged in social activism, and the organization's website (www.humanistsoc.org) does include this statement: "Humanist sociologists strive as professionals, as scholars and *as activists* to uncover and address social issues, working with others to lessen the pain of social problems" (emphasis ours).[4] Just how much attention humanist sociologists give, or should give, to activism is a subject that we focus on later in the article.

Applied and Clinical Sociology

The post-1920s hegemony of academic sociology meant, among other things, the devaluation of sociological work that had immediate public relevance; that might meet the needs or serve the interests of specific groups or organizations. Nevertheless, some sociologists continued to embrace a more applied orientation, putting sociological concepts, insights and skills to use in a variety of settings. They engaged in efforts that today would fall under the rubrics of applied sociology and clinical sociology, and more broadly, "sociological practice."

The idea of distinguishing between sociology as an intellectual vs. applied endeavor first surfaced in the early years of the discipline. Lester Frank Ward, for example, contrasted what he called "pure sociology," which dealt with "facts, causes and principles," and "applied sociology," which concerned the purposes and uses of sociology. Applied sociology, he argued, had to do with "social ideals," "what ought to be," and the "improvement" of society. It is important to remember, however, that Ward (1906), unlike Addams and others in the early activist tradition, imposed strict limits on the way that the sociologist could legitimately practice his craft in the public domain.

Over the years, the term "applied" has been used broadly to refer to a wide range of sociological work that is oriented to an audience outside of academia, in private and public sector settings. While this generic usage continues, "applied" has recently been given a more specific meaning, namely research done "for practical purposes" (Fritz 2005: 41), to serve the needs of some interested party or "client." The American Sociological Association (2003: 1) describes it this way:

> Applied sociology refers to methodology and includes the research model of problem solving, the research model of formulating and testing options, and the research model of evaluation…. The applied sociologist is a research specialist who produces information that is useful in resolving problems in government, industry and other practice settings.

On its website, the Association for Applied and Clinical Sociology (2006) includes as examples of applied sociology: "evaluating the effectiveness of various educational [or criminal justice] policies/ programs," "investigating the social norms promoting or inhibiting the spread of AIDS," "analyzing employment records for evidence of discrimination," and "planning medical services and facilities for a target population."[5] One gets the distinct impression from these descriptions that the applied sociologist essentially works as a technical advisor to any client-employer who might have a use for, and be able to pay for, their research skills. In sharp contrast to critical sociology, which stands on a values-based critique of existing power arrangements, applied sociology brackets these concerns and focuses on the instrumental tasks of trouble-shooting or problem-solving for whoever pays the bills. And while this may be a "client" that is committed to social justice, to values like freedom, equality and democracy, it may not be. The applied sociologist, it would seem, is equally comfortable working with a corporate marketing firm as with a low income advocacy group. Applied sociology can claim public relevance, something that its academic counterpart can hardly do. Yet, as Stoecker (1996) has noted, it offers "practice devoid of critique." As such, it differs markedly from the brand of "applied sociology"—that is, activist sociology—that Addams and her colleagues embraced.

The idea of clinical sociology first emerged just as academic sociology was solidifying its preeminence within the discipline. Courses with this term in their title were being taught in the late 1920s, and in 1931, Louis Wirth published the first article explicitly describing this new, and as he saw it, up-and-coming area of specialization within sociology. As he described it, "clinical sociology…is a convenient label for those insights, methods of approach, and techniques which the science of sociology can contribute to the understanding and treatment of persons whose behavior or personality problems bring their case under the care of clinics for study and treatment" (1931: 50). Wirth saw clinical sociologists as part of a professional team (consisting also of psychologists, psychiatrists and social workers) that would help maladjusted clients in "child guidance clinics." What he describes is an applied sociology that essentially entails providing therapy or treatment regimens for youngsters who suffer some form of psycho-social pathology. In Wirth's early interpretation, then, clinical sociology is about changing "deviant" individuals, and certainly not social structures.

By the 1950s, some sociologists were talking about a clinical sociology that focused on the problems of groups and organizations. For example, Al Lee wrote in a 1955 article entitled "The Clinical Study of Society" that this endeavor involves painstaking observation and analysis of a group's problem(s), and of any "therapeutic" attempts to address the problem(s). It essentially entailed research aimed first, at the diagnosis of a group's problem, and second, at the evaluation of efforts to rectify the problem. The task of the clinical sociologist, then, includes the monitoring and assessment of group change initiatives, but *not* the instigation of, or direct participation in, these initiatives. He or she will *study* the "therapeutic" measures that others attempt (Lee 1955: 651). Some other sociologists seemed to embrace a more "hands-on" approach to clinical sociology in the mid-50s. At Antioch College of Ohio, Alvin Gouldner offered a course in "Foundations of Clinical Sociology," the description of which included the following: "A sociological counterpart to clinical psychology with the group as the unit of diagnosis and therapy. Emphasis on developing skills useful in the diagnosis *and therapy* of group tensions" (quoted in Fritz 2005: 46; emphasis ours). It would seem here that the role of the clinical sociologist extended beyond research.[6]

The present-day incarnation of clinical sociology surfaced in the 1970s, and its advocates at the time clearly called for an enterprise that encompassed more than research, useful as that research might be. John Glass, who, along with Al Lee, Jan Fritz and others, was at the forefront of the resurgence, reflected in a recent article that he had "envisioned clinical sociology as the direct application of sociological thinking and knowledge to problem solving and change at the individual, group, organization and community level. The clinical sociologist is essentially a change agent *rather than* a researcher or evaluator" (Glass, 2001: 76). This description parallels the American Sociological Association's current definition of clinical sociology, and the distinction made between clinical and applied sociology. To quote from one recent ASA document: "…Clinical sociology is the application of the sociological perspective to facilitate change. The clinical sociologist is primarily a change agent who is immersed in the client's world" (ASA 2003: 1). The applied sociologist, by contrast, is basically a "research specialist."[7]

The most recent version of clinical sociology differs from earlier, pre-70s conceptualizations in a couple ways. First, intervention efforts extend beyond the individual and group to broader contexts, including (but not limited to) communities. In the current vernacular, clinical sociologists may work at the micro-, meso- or macro-levels of intervention. Second, clinical sociologists are actively engaged as agents of change, whichever level(s) of intervention they work at (ASA 2003; Bruhn and Rebach 1995; Glass 2001; Rebach and Bruhn 2001).

What are the parameters for these change efforts? A look through the literature suggests that they are very broad indeed—from efforts aimed at helping individuals navigate and cope with unjust conditions, to helping organizational managers and state elites address problems as they see them, to working collaboratively with grassroots groups who seek change at the community or national level. Social activism directed at challenging entrenched power structures and promoting fundamental change is generally given scant and superficial attention (see e.g. Gaventa 1992). For example, in its 2003 publication *Careers in Clinical Sociology*, the ASA mentions that the clinical sociologist may engage in advocacy work but cautions that this may put the practitioner in an awkward position: "Advocacy requires that clinical sociologists "take a position" and make their values and beliefs known to others. Advocacy may be an uncomfortable role initially and be seen as antithetical to a sociologist's training… Advocacy can be a positive role, but it involves risk taking and taking a position of leadership" (ASA 2003: 12). It would seem from this description that advocacy looms at the margins of professional legitimacy. Still, clinical sociology does at least allow some latitude for sociologists to engage in this kind of work.

One can also glean from the literature in clinical sociology that social justice figures prominently as a value-orientation for at least some practitioners. In the words of Fritz:

> As clinical sociology focuses on the improvement of people's lives, social justice, with its emphasis on fairness and equity, is an important consideration. A number of clinical sociologists have made justice and equality central to their choice of work (e.g., full employment or affordable housing advocate) and their approach to that work (e.g., participatory) while others think justice is important but is not the main focus (2005: 42).

There are, then, some facets of clinical sociology that approximate the early activist sociology of Addams and others. We would also argue that there are some serious limitations, not the least of which include a tendency to elitism as evidenced by the pervasive characterization of clinical sociologists as experts vis-à-vis their clients, and the preoccupation with special credentialing. Nevertheless, clinical sociology offers at least a partial glimpse at what activist sociology might look like today.

Liberation Sociology and Participatory Action Research

In recent years there have been some promising signs within the discipline's largest and most prominent organization, the American Sociological Association, that there is substantial support for a sociology that is more relevant to various publics beyond the academy and for sociological work that is rooted in a commitment to social justice (and related values). The question of relevance dates back many decades, but the post-'70s ASA rendition was largely related to growing student concerns about how their increasingly expensive college degrees would translate into specific career/income opportunities. (This also accounts, in part, for the expanding interest in applied and clinical sociology.) But the simultaneous emergence of an explicit and broadly supported emphasis on relevance and social justice is quite new for the ASA.

One clear indication of this shift came when Joe Feagin, who has a long record of radical scholarship, was elected to serve as the ASA's president for 2000. In his presidential address, published the following year in the American Sociological Review, Feagin talked in no uncertain terms about the need for a sociology that is fully committed to social justice:

> Unquestionably, social justice appears as a recurring concern around the globe...We sociologists must vigorously engage issues of social justice or become largely irrelevant to the present and future course of human history (Feagin 2001a: 6).

Importantly, Feagin points out that we are not exactly breaking new ground in embracing such a commitment. Many of the early U.S. sociologists left us with this legacy, a legacy that we would do well to acknowledge and resurrect in our work today. In his words:

> Contemporary sociologists should...recognize the importance of, and draw more from, the ideas of early U.S. sociologists like Jane Addams and W.E.B. DuBois...These pioneering U.S. sociologists offer solid role models in their dual commitments to social scientific knowledge and social justice, equality and democracy (Feagin, 2001a: 11).

Feagin elaborates his critique and vision of sociology with co-author Hernan Vera in *Liberation Sociology* (2001). To engage in liberation sociology, the authors argue, is to gear social science research and analysis to problems of the oppressed, exploited and dominated (2001b: 23). A key task is to expose oppressive conditions to public scrutiny so that they can be changed. As Feagin and Vera put it:

> The point of liberation sociology is not just to research the social world but to change it in the direction of democracy and social justice... [Its] practitioners... study reality so they and others can better transform it (2001: 1, 23).

This, of course, raises the pivotal question of exactly how the liberation sociologist contributes to the process of social change/transformation. Feagin and Vera describe a variety of examples of liberation sociology in action, so to speak. One is Project Censored, which is directed by sociologist Peter Phillips at Sonoma State University. It essentially has as its agenda researching and making public cases of media bias, censorship and concentration. The website for Project Censored posts news stories that one is not likely to find in the mainstream media, and provides links to many progressive sources like AFL-CIO Now, the Action Coalition for Media Education (ACME), and The New Standard. Apart from providing much needed diversity to media coverage of important issues of the day, Project Censored serves as an important resource and perhaps inspiration for teachers, activists and others who are engaged in the struggle to democratize the media.

Feagin and Vera cite Project South as another example of liberation sociologists in action. Sociologists Walda Katz-Fishman and Jerome Scott created and now help to run this organization. Quite like the Highlander Research and Education Center in rural Tennessee,[8] Project South uses a popular education model for supporting, through research, workshops and printed material, the work of grassroots community activists. As noted on the organization's website:

> Project South creates popular education tools, conducts action research, and publishes accessible curriculum to provide grassroots organizations with the resources to develop stronger analytic skills, leadership capacity, and sustainable strategic plans. We develop leadership from within low income communities of color to build a strong bottom-up movement for social and economic justice (www.projectsouth.org).

Project South routinely networks and collaborates with myriad social justice organizations in its work, which currently includes the planning and facilitation of the 2007 U.S. Social Forum.[9] Project South's work also involves coordination of, and participation in, legislative campaigns, community organizing initiatives, and various kinds of protest, including direct action. That is to say, Project South acts as a resource to activists, but unlike Project Censored, it also engages directly in social justice activism.

Another aspect of "doing" liberation sociology that Feagin and Vera discuss is participatory action research (PAR). Partly in response to the limitations of positivist approaches to research, PAR surfaced as an explicit social science research practice in various countries of the global South and in North America by the early 1970s (Hall 1992; Park 1992). Interest in, and uses of, PAR has expanded significantly since that time (Park et. al. 1993; Stoecker 2005). In its most robust form, PAR involves collaborative research and action between sociology (or other social science) researchers and marginalized people/communities. That is to say, community members take part in all phases of the research on the problem(s) they identify, from question formulation to analysis and articulation of the results. Conversely, the sociologist/researcher engages with community members in activism—the social change process—that grows out of the research.

In practice, and for a variety of reasons, things quite often don't work out exactly this way. Community members may end up playing little or no role in the research process (Cancion 1993; Stoecker 2005: 37), and/or the researcher is not really involved, or only peripherally involved, in on-the-ground struggles for change. In fact, most of the examples of PAR that Feagin and Vera describe (and all of the U.S. examples they use) have sociologists providing their research findings to marginalized/progressive groups as a way of helping them to pursue their agenda. Community members do not (except as "subjects") participate in the research process, nor does the sociologist join community members in the implementation of action plans. Many of the cases that Feagin and Vera describe seemed to more closely resemble "applied research," albeit for marginalized or progressive "clients," than an authentic PAR.[10]

For sociologists engaged in PAR, social activism is embedded in the research experience itself. The first is embedded in the research experience itself. In discussing "research as action," Stoecker has observed that "…the research process is a community organizing process… A main goal of the process is to produce a larger, tighter-knit group or organization…" (2005: 150). In his/her capacity as researcher/organizer, the sociologist helps to raise consciousness, connect people and organizations to one another (as Stoecker did in his work in the Cedar-Riverside neighborhood of Milwaukee), and build local skills, partly in research, but also in leadership and other areas as well. Thus, the sociologist helps to empower oppressed community groups, and "enhance [their] public presence...[They] will [then] be seen as more competent, stable and influential, which will attract allies and at least give pause to potential adversaries" (Stoecker 2005: 150).

One last point about Feagin and Vera's take on the practice of liberation sociology and PAR: Almost every example they cite involves *college- or university- based researchers* working with or for disenfranchised people. The one exception is their chapter-long discussion of Saul Alinsky (Chapter 5, *Sociology in Action*), whom they variously refer to as an "intellectual activist," a "sociologically informed activist," and a "practicing sociologist." The same can be said of much of the literature relating to PAR; the focus is the community-oriented work of researchers who are tied in one way or another to colleges or universities. Unfortunately, this would seem to imply that, with rare exception, one needs to have an academic position to practice liberation sociology or PAR. We will return to this point later in the article.

Public Sociology

A few years after the publication of *Liberation Sociology*, ASA members, again signaling the changing face of the organization, elected prominent leftist sociologist Michael Burawoy to the presidency.[11] In his 2004 presidential address (Burawoy 2005a), and in a number of other articles published that year and the next (e.g., Burawoy 2004a; 2004b; 2005b; 2005c) Burawoy forcefully advocated for the legitimation of a sociology that engages various publics beyond the discipline and academy, an enterprise he referred to as "public sociology."

Burawoy draws a distinction between "traditional" and "organic" public sociology. In the first case, the sociologist serves as a public intellectual who, by means of offering up widely accessible books, op ed pieces, magazine articles, and radio or television commentary, stimulates or contributes to public discussion and debate about social issues.[12] By contrast, organic (or grassroots) public sociologists work "in close connection with... active, local, and often counter- (vs. mainstream) publics [like] a labor movement, neighborhood associations, communities of faith, immigrant rights groups, [and] human rights organizations" (Burawoy 2005a: 7–8). We would include in the many examples of organic public sociology the work of sociologists like Al Gedicks (1996; 2001), Randy Stoecker (1991; 1996; 2005), and Clare Weber (2002; 2006). While most public sociology is of this type, Burawoy notes, it gets much less visibility and carries less professional prestige than traditional public sociology. This, he argues, must change: "The recognition of public sociology must extend to the organic kind which...is often considered to be apart from our professional lives... [We must] validate the organic connections as part of our sociological life" (2005a: 8). We wholeheartedly agree!

Public sociology is delineated from what Burawoy calls "policy sociology." This, he contends, "is sociology in the service of a goal defined by a client" (2005a: 9). "The relationship between sociologist and client is often of a contractual character in which expertise is sold for a fee" (Burawoy 2004a: 1608). Examples would include acting as an expert witness in a trial case, or perhaps conducting research on the causes of unemployment for a public agency. This, it seems to us, bears a striking resemblance to applied and (at least mainstream) clinical sociology, with its emphasis on the sociologist as expert who gets paid to address the need(s) or problem(s) of a client. This is also what seems to differentiate policy sociology from organic public sociology. While the later may also involve remuneration for the sociologist, it is predicated on a dialogic, reciprocal, and egalitarian relationship between the sociologist and a marginalized group or community.

Burawoy's campaign for public sociology has resonated with a good share of the ASA membership. The 2004 annual meeting in San Francisco, which had "public sociology" as its theme, drew a record number of participants. In many ways, Burawoy's general message is not terribly new, echoing as it does a call for sociological relevance that dates back to Lee and other founders of the SSSP, Mills, Gans, and many others. Nor is it terribly radical insofar as it posits public sociology as only one aspect of a discipline which Burawoy says is ultimately anchored in, and dependent upon, professional (or what we earlier called academic) sociology.[13] Moreover, Burawoy at least implies that public sociologists are situated in the academy, that colleges and universities serve as the home base for the sociology they practice.

Even so, there are sociologists in the ASA and the discipline generally who have serious reservations about Burawoy's vision of public sociology. The criticisms range from polite disinterest or skepticism (Brady 2004; Tittle 2004; Nielsen 2004) to vitriolic condemnation. Wagner (2005), for example, contends that: "public sociology is little more than pseudo-Marxist leftist advocacy." In one 2004 commentary published in an ASA section newsletter, Deflem (2004) refers to public sociology as a grave danger to, and "perversion of, our discipline." Under Burawoy's leadership, he argues, "the Association has, instead of seeking to develop and practice sociology, resorted to a populist perspective of subsuming sociology under a quest for justice and popular activism." For Deflem, public sociology is "a benign-sounding label that conceals the particularistic politics and sociological Marxism advocated by the ASA president." At the ASA meeting in San Francisco, Deflem fumed, "The advocates of public sociology… encouraged sociologists…not merely to investigate, but to 'challenge' the world. Sociologists, in other words, were asked to not be sociologists" (Deflem 2004). And finally this:

> With the currently popular wave of activist sociologists, a substantial part of sociology has rendered itself more irrelevant today than ever before in the now more than hundred-year history of the discipline. Whereas the roots of scientific sociology are deeply embedded in our society's commitment to advance humanity, many sociologists have betrayed the very mission of the science they promised to nourish and practice. However much we may regret it, today it is often true that sociologists are mere activists in disguise. That is an insult to sociology… (Deflem 2004).

As it turns out, Deflem is so distressed by the "invasion" of public sociology (and related "perversions" of the field) that he established a website to disseminate his views. Called "Save Sociology" (www.savesociology.org), it is, in his words, "an attempt to safeguard the academic status and integrity of sociology."

Deflem is not exactly a nationally renowned, highly visible sociologist. But his strident views on public sociology do reflect a perspective that more than a few sociologists—including some very prominent sociologists—embrace. Specifically: There is one legitimate sociology and it is an objective, value-neutral, apolitical science which has as it core, if not sole, mandate, the search for and discovery of sociological truths. It emerged as the discipline's dominant paradigm in the 1920s, peaked in the 1950s, and, despite the post-'50s blossoming of alternative perspectives, continues to be a potent force in the field to this day.

Peter Berger, for example, is as firmly committed to this perspective as he was when he penned his classic *Invitation to Sociology* over four decades ago. Berger, who considers the 1950s to be the "golden age of sociology," is mortified by what he sees as the transformation of the discipline from a rigorous science to an empty ideological brew of Marxism, multiculturalism and feminism. In his words:

> The ideologization of sociology has been...devastating....The ideologues who have been in the ascendancy for the last thirty years have deformed science into an instrument of agitation and propaganda, (the Communists used to call this "agitprop"), invariably for causes on the left of the ideological spectrum. The core scientific principle of objectivity has been ignored in practice and denied validity in theory (Berger 2002).

James Davis, another prominent sociologist who is rigidly wed to the scientific perspective, describes sociology today as an unhealthy organization with a "weak immune system" that has "a hard time rejecting foreign objects" (1994: 188). Sociology, he suggests, has been entirely too tolerant of bogus intellectual developments in the discipline. As he puts it:

> We have put up with an appalling amount of bunk, ("...feminist methodology," "humanistic sociology," "critical theory," "ethnomethodology," "grounded theory," and the like), simply because we cannot draw a firm line between what is legitimate sociology and what is not (Davis 1994: 188).

Berger, Davis and others (e.g., Cole, 2001; Horowitz 1993) are convinced that sociology has veered badly off course and betrayed its once noble mission. In this view, there is no room for many of the developments in sociology that we have discussed so far in this article. There is no place for critical or humanist sociology, for liberation sociology or participatory action research, for social justice advocacy, for organic public sociology.

We cannot accept such a monolithic view of sociology. We believe instead that the various sociological perspectives that have emerged since the 1950s (including those that Davis condemns) have greatly enriched the discipline (see e.g. Fitzgerald 1995). And if we were to imagine some "golden age of sociology," it would certainly not be the 1950s, when sociology was all but smothered by the hegemony of structural functionalism and "abstract empiricism" (Mills 1959). In our view, sociology can and should accommodate multiple perspectives and approaches. Having said this, the kind of sociology that we find most compelling is an action-oriented humanist sociology. We next sketch out what we mean by this.

Humanist Sociology Revisited

We shall begin with this premise: Humanist sociology is a value-committed enterprise (Glass 1970; Hoult 1979; Ballard 2002; DuBois and Wright 2002; Goodwin 2003). The specific values that inform the work of humanist sociologists vary somewhat, but a general list would most likely include freedom/self-determination, democracy, non-violence, equality, peace, and social justice, among others. In essence, humanist sociology is grounded in what are generally agreed to be core *humanist* values. This is not the place for a lengthy discussion about what all of these values are or should be. We offer the following as a rough (and emphatically *not* definitive) list of core humanist values or premises:

- All people share a common humanity and have inherent dignity and worth.

- Human beings are interdependent and should act toward one another with respect (vs. mere tolerance), mutual care and compassion.

- Within this context, all people should have the freedom and opportunity to pursue their aspirations and to develop their full potential as individual human beings.

- All people should enjoy equal rights, most of these rights being articulated in the Universal Declaration of Human Rights.

- Genuine democracy should prevail in human affairs. (The Universal Declaration only addresses formal political democracy.)

- All people have the right to a safe, healthy environment, and an obligation to practice environmental stewardship and ecological sustainability. (Not mentioned in the Universal Declaration.)

- People should address or resolve conflict without resorting to violence.[14]

Implied in this list, we believe, is the value of social justice, a value that is central to humanist sociology, liberation sociology, and (organic) public sociology, as well as to the work of many who practice clinical sociology.

There is broad consensus that humanist sociology is "about making a better world" (DuBois and Wright 2002)." As Corey Dolgon puts it, "Making the world a better place for the practice of humanism and social justice is…our unabashed goal" (2001: 109). The humanist values we have just identified provide a general vision of what that world might look like, and how people would relate to one another in a "good society." But a crucial question is: What is the role, or better yet, the responsibility, of humanist sociologists in contributing to a society that is more in line with humanist aspirations?

Surely one responsibility is social inquiry aimed at making sense of the social order, and more precisely, analyzing social and cultural arrangements to assess the extent to which they do (or don't) nurture and support human dignity and well-being (Glass 1972). In what ways do they foster or undermine peace vs. violence? Equality vs. dominant group privilege? Social justice vs. oppression? These, along with many other related questions, humanist sociologists investigate by means of systematic research and analysis. And they do so not by adhering to the "canons of a rigid positivism" (Goodwin 2003: 346), but by drawing from a palate of diverse qualitative and quantitative methodologies. Humanist sociology is a creative endeavor which respects, but does not limit itself to, traditional forms of scientific inquiry. It is predicated upon rational and rigorous analysis, but within this framework, insists that there are multiple paths to, and ways of, knowing.

It is a fundamental premise of humanist sociology that the purpose of critical social inquiry is to produce knowledge that serves humanity. Humanist sociology, as Lee (2003) put it, is a "sociology for people." It is not a sociology that merely speaks to, or for, society's most powerful interests. Nor is it a conversation that remains within the domain of a privileged and insulated intellectual elite. Humanist sociology is a *public* sociology insofar as it engages, and is relevant to, people who are struggling to make sense of the world and to make their way in a world that is fraught with injustices and assaults on their dignity and well-being.

Recall, however, that Burawoy (2005a) distinguishes between two types of public sociology—traditional and organic. In our estimation, the humanist sociology that emerged in the 1970s, most notably in the work of Lee, can be described as a form of traditional public sociology. As we noted earlier, Lee depicts humanist sociologists as public intellectuals who "act principally as critics, demystifiers, reporters, and clarifiers" (1978: 36). That is, they perform the important task of exposing and shedding light on inhumane social structures and conditions, but leave it to others to dismantle or change them.

This brings us to the matter of social action or activism. Social critique and analysis are vitally important. However, it is our belief that humanist sociology has a responsibility that extends beyond critical inquiry, no matter how compelling and relevant the fruits of that inquiry may be. It has a responsibility to translate words into actions, to fully embrace social and political activism aimed at fighting injustice and creating a more humane social order. This means that its practitioners make common cause and work collaboratively with others—activist academics, neighborhood residents, progressive policy makers, labor leaders, members of social justice groups, and so on—to address social problems. They engage in participatory action research, community organizing, popular education, social justice advocacy, electoral politics work, and social protest, including civil disobedience. This, we believe, is largely what Burawoy (2005a) has in mind when he refers to organic public sociology.

But Burawoy suggests that the organic public sociologist is based in academia. Feagin implies the same thing with regard to liberation sociologists. We argue that the humanist sociologist may be situated in a college or university, in any number of applied/community settings, or in some combination of the two. Here we share the premise of clinical sociology (discussed earlier) that one need not have a university post, or even affiliation, to practice sociology, and in our case, humanist sociology. Thus, one example of a humanist sociologist would be a full-time community organizer who is committed to humanist values and whose social justice work is informed by a solid background or education in sociology. What we are saying, in essence, is that humanist sociology encompasses both social inquiry *and* social activism; these are its twin responsibilities. This is not to say that every humanist sociologist will be deeply involved in activism, or in inquiry. The work of specific individuals will fall somewhere along the continuum between inquiry and activism, and quite often involve some combination of both.

There is in fact a clear precedent for an action-oriented humanist sociology, and one that goes back well before the 1970s, to the roots of U.S. sociology. It was embodied in the work of various reform-minded pioneers like Jane Addams. Addams, whom Scimecca and Goodwin (2003) refer to as "the first humanist sociologist,"[15] was deeply committed to humanist values. She engaged in wide-ranging scholarship, and conducted cutting-edge research, often in collaboration with Hull House associates, on social conditions in Chicago and elsewhere. In terms of activism, Addams led or took part in many struggles for social justice, including local and national campaigns for the rights of workers (unions), women (suffrage), youth (child labor, juvenile courts), immigrants, and African Americans. She was also a relentless advocate of nonviolence and peace, taking a firm (and ultimately, very unpopular) stand against U.S. involvement in the first World War (Addams

1961; Deegan 1988; Elshtain 2002a; Elshtain 2002b; Wheeler 1990). And we must not forget that Jane Addams was only one of the most prominent and prolific figures that was practicing what we are calling an action-oriented humanist sociology. Clearly there were others, folks like Emily Balch, Ida Wells-Barnett, W.E.B. DuBois, and Florence Kelley, who were similarly inclined and engaged. No doubt, there were still others whose names we barely know or have yet to "discover" (see e.g. Blasi 2005; Deegan 2003; Deegan 2005; Deegan, this volume).

All of this is certainly not to suggest that humanist sociology today is devoid of activists, or that most folks focus exclusively on social inquiry, far removed from the activist struggles of the day. We know that a good many of our colleagues in the Association for Humanist Sociology, including various authors in this volume, are fierce advocates for social justice. And again, despite what Lee and others may have written in the 1970s, the AHS website proclaims that, "Humanist sociologists strive as professionals, as scholars and as activists to uncover and address social issues, working with others to lessen the pain of social problems" (www.humanistsoc.org).

Nevertheless, we would submit that there are today substantial and growing pressures in academia that can discourage folks from engaging in activism *as part of* their professional responsibilities. For some, there is the "publish or perish" grind, and the knowledge that activism, whether related to scholarship or not, is rarely rewarded by promotion or tenure review committees. For others, there are subtle and not-so-subtle messages about keeping our politics and our scholarship separate, about being "unbiased" professionals. For still others, there may be admonitions from colleagues that politics and activism have no place in sociology. Given these and other constraints, there is a very real possibility that activism might, at least for humanist sociologists who are tied to the academy, increasingly fade to the periphery of their commitments. We must do all that we can to challenge this tendency. In our view, social activism, along with critical inquiry, form the core of humanist sociology's mission. Activism and inquiry are equally important means by which humanist sociology serves humanity.

Teaching and Curricular Activism

We have noted that it can be a real challenge for college- or university-based sociologists to practice, to truly commit to the inquiry and activism responsibilities of, humanist sociology. Institutional pressures, largely associated with the corporatization of the academy (White and Hauck 2000), are part of the problem. But so too are deeply entrenched ideas and assumptions in the broader discipline about the nature and purpose of sociology. Despite some of the heartening changes in the ASA and its leadership that we have mentioned, there is little to suggest that the discipline generally supports a commitment to activism, particularly as a central part of its mission, as it is for humanist sociology. When it comes to teaching sociology, something that we (Dale and Kalob) are passionate about and have in fact done for a combined forty plus years, we frequently feel like we are swimming upstream against a powerful current of traditional academic sociology. In our view, the standard undergraduate curriculum in sociology does not even come close to reflecting, to say nothing about embracing, the commitments of humanist sociology, at least as we have described them. There is a yawning gap between the sociology curriculum to which most undergraduates are exposed and basic humanist aspirations.

Consider, for example, Wagenaar's study (2004) in which he surveyed several hundred sociologists to assess their views regarding the sociology curriculum. Respondents were asked to rate the importance of various concepts, topics and skills for the sociology curriculum, and specifically for the introductory course as well. Not surprisingly, the items that got the lowest ratings included: "promote social change," "social responsibility," and "how to bring about social change." Among the highest rated items were "sociological critical thinking" and "how to use and assess research." Writing and speaking skills were also considered to be very important. We would certainly agree that it is crucial for students to learn critical thinking, writing and communication skills. But we would also argue that sociology is equally about "social responsibility" (related specifically to humanist values) and "promoting social change." Indeed, the curriculum should include skills (like social justice organizing and advocacy) that are needed to foster change.

But the most compelling support for our thesis is perhaps the texts that are typically used to introduce students to sociology. Over the years, we have reviewed scores of these texts, and have found first, that they are remarkably homogenous, and second, that they generally undermine rather than facilitate the teaching of humanist sociology.

Virtually all introductory texts define sociology (generally in the first chapter) as the study of something…social interaction, human societies, and so on. This has become the orthodox understanding of sociology. It is clearly reflected in the ASA's definition of the field: "Sociology is the study of social life, social change, and the social causes and consequences of human behavior" (www.asanet.org). As such, sociology is depicted as a perspective, a set of ideas, an intellectual endeavor aimed at producing knowledge and understanding about human social experience. There is no reference to the idea that sociology also encompasses a commitment to social action or activism. So, right away, we're off to a bad start!

The notion that sociology is essentially an intellectual enterprise is reinforced when, generally in the first chapter, there is some discussion of sociology's founders and /or most influential figures. They are typically referred to as "theorists," "scholars," or "thinkers"—people (and until quite recently men) of ideas. The brief descriptions of these folks focus on their intellectual contributions. Marx, for example, is noted for his views on, and critique of, capitalism, but rarely for his participation in on-the-ground struggles for the communist society that he envisioned. In the U.S. context, Mead is credited with founding the symbolic interaction perspective and developing the concepts of the "I," the "me," and the "generalized other." But nowhere will the reader find any discussion of Mead's social justice activism on behalf of women's suffrage, workers' strikes, and other issues (see e.g. Deegan 1988: 105–134; Feagin and Vera 2001: 53–55).

We have said that humanist sociology is grounded in a commitment to humanist values. Yet in many, if not most, texts, readers learn that the preeminent value in sociology is "objectivity" or "value-neutrality." This point is made early in the text, often in the context of the chapter on research. The other place that the issue of values is raised is generally in the chapter on culture, and here the discussion is about dominant American values, and perhaps cross-cultural differences in values. But it is certainly not about values that might, or should, inform the work of sociologists. One does find occasional reference to sociological concern about social problems, or about helping to make the world a better place. But there is no discussion about the value standards that we might use to identify social problems, or the values that might/should frame and guide the quest for a better world.

Introductory sociology texts typically suggest that the key skill you need to practice sociology is the ability to conduct (and interpret) research. There is inevitably an early chapter on research, and in fact, this chapter is sometimes titled "Doing Sociology." The message, of course, is that doing sociology is basically doing research. Moreover, the text usually covers a very traditional, positivist model of research, where the sociologist *qua* scientist identifies variables, forms a hypothesis, collects data, and so on. While one finds occasional reference to research that sheds light on a social problem or informs public policy, there is certainly no indication that it might be the sociologist's role to couple the research process or findings with social activism, as would be the case, for example, in participatory action research.

There are, of course, other skills that students/sociologists need. One that we mentioned earlier is critical thinking. We would suggest, however, that introductory sociology texts are normally so crammed with terms and definitions that they invite rote memorization more than they inspire a critical thinking process. In the case of humanist sociology, there is a need to teach advocacy and other skills that are essential to becoming an effective agent of social change. And of course these are not mentioned in introductory texts because this would imply that sociology is not just about doing research; it is about actively participating in change initiatives and movements that are swirling all around us.

It is our view that the text that introduces our students to sociology should provide a reasonable glimpse of what they might do with their lives with a sociology degree, or as a sociologist. The ASA has become much more attuned to career prospects for sociology graduates, and this is reflected in recent literature on clinical and applied sociology, or what is now broadly referred to as sociological practice (ASA 2003). Introductory texts have increasingly picked up on this trend, and now commonly incorporate some material, in boxed vignettes, appendices, etc., on what people might do with sociology degrees. Still, this subject is barely broached, and given the content of the standard text, it is very difficult for most sociology students to imagine what in the world they would actually do for a living if they got an undergraduate sociology degree. Many get the impression that their options are either teaching (college) or conducting research, and that both of these options require an advanced degree. Certainly for students who come from low or modest income families, it is more than a little demoralizing to think that a four-year degree costing $100,000 or more won't really prepare you for a job that is related to your interests in sociology. There is, we would argue, a radical disconnect between the way introductory texts present sociology, as an academic or intellectual enterprise, and student needs to earn a living and (often very idealistic) aspirations to help make the world a better place.

We have described just a small sample of the concerns we have about the use of a mainstream sociology curriculum to teach humanist sociology. Hopefully, we have said enough to make this clear: Those of us who are committed to humanist sociology must work to create an alternative curriculum that is compatible with, and inspires interest in, our vision of sociology. What should this curriculum look like? How is it to be implemented? These and related questions are part of the conversations about teaching that we should be having with our colleagues.

It might be useful to start by thinking about how we should introduce students to (humanist) sociology. Briefly, we would strongly suggest beginning this process by jettisoning the standard introductory sociology text. (If there are folks who know of a text that reflects the concerns of humanist sociology, and doesn't follow the format that we have described, please let us know!) Our sense, again, is that these texts frame sociology in a way that is incompatible with a humanist perspective. We can, and should, make note of different approaches to, and definitions of, sociology. But we must make it clear that humanist sociology is grounded in a humanist value orientation, and is equally committed to social inquiry and social activism change. In contrast to what normally happens in an introductory course, we suggest that there should be a robust discussion of the values that lie at the heart of humanist sociology. There should also be coverage of the various ways that people can "do" sociology, here including various kinds of research (academic, applied, participatory, etc.), but *also* social justice advocacy, community organizing, conflict negotiation, and so on. In this regard, we feel that it is very important to bring in guest speakers who are involved in this work, perhaps in local non-profit organizations, and/or connect students with these people/organizations as part of a class assignment or project. We strongly recommend that students be offered opportunities for community-based learning experiences (Dale 2005). Early on and throughout their education, students need to see what sociological work (apart from academic teaching and research) might look like.

We should engage students, too, in meaningful discussions of various career/work options. And it is important that these discussions be tied to a consideration of humanist sociology's core values. Indeed, this is where humanist sociology generally diverges from applied or clinical sociology. One gets the sense from reading the ASA's material on sociological practice that students can use their sociological concepts and skills in virtually any field. The sociology student may elect to work in marketing for a drug or junk food company just as well as he/she might work as a homeless advocate. From the perspective of humanist sociology, however, students explore their job options within the context of humanist values. And given this context, ethical considerations would rule some job possibilities out. Clearly, there are some jobs (in some organizations) where one's responsibilities would inevitably require their compromising basic humanist value commitments. This is a conversation that we should have with our students.

As we move forward with curricular changes where we teach, we will do well to share our experiences.[16] What has worked and what hasn't? Those of us who have been involved in the process of curricular change before know that this is no easy task, particularly when the changes run contrary to well-established standards and expectations. Resistance will surely come from some of our colleagues in sociology, and curriculum committees and deans will likely provide healthy doses of skepticism. Nevertheless, we need to assertively make the case for humanist sociology and a curriculum that does it justice. This is an important part of what we must do as activists *within* the academy and our discipline.

Concluding Remarks

One can find threads of a commitment to social justice activism in U.S. sociology from its beginning in the late 19th century to the present. They appear, for example, in the activist sociology of the progressive era, in humanist sociology, in liberation and (organic) public sociology, and to at least some extent, in clinical sociology. We believe that it is time to weave these threads together into a sociological tapestry that showcases social activism. In recent years there has been evidence of growing support for a sociology that will truly promote human dignity and liberation. It has been spreading and has sparked the imagination of sociologists around the country (e.g. Burawoy 2005a; Feagin 2000; Reese 2001).

We must build on this movement and, as Stoecker (1996) has so eloquently put it, work to "restore the dignity of social action in sociology."

As sociologists, we need to *be* activists, not just admire and advocate for activism. As teachers, we should engage in activism as mentors to our students (Reese, 2001). We must stimulate the activist impulse in the often idealistic and energetic women and men we teach. Indeed, as Feagin has noted, "As teachers of sociology, we should make clear to the coming generations of sociologists not only that there is plenty of room for idealism and activism in the field, but that these qualities might be required for humanity to survive the next century or so" (2001: 14). In the words of Jipson, "We must carry [the] legacy of [social amelioration and activism] proudly and fight to alter the world not just with our ideas but also with our actions inside and outside the classroom" (2002: 76). This must include offering our students a range of action options that illustrate the work that is necessary to bring about meaningful social change. And we must be clear with our students that one does not have to work in academia to "do" sociology.

We call upon the Association for Humanist Sociology to take the lead in this work, in the creation (or, perhaps more accurately, the resurrection) of sociology as not only a critical and politically progressive discipline, but also as a grassroots, activist field. In our view, there is no better organization prepared to lead the way in this endeavor than the AHS.

As we have suggested, this struggle will not be easy for a good many reasons. One significant barrier is the fact that many of us work in institutions that do not value and share this vision. So, we need to take this fight to not only our departments, our students, and our professional associations. We need to take it, too, to the college and university committees and administrators and the other powerful gatekeepers we face. Scholarly publications and artistic creations have value in the pursuit of university missions and individual tenure decisions. That is widely understood. What we must make clear is that social activism has value, including value to university missions, and therefore should have value in decisions regarding tenure and promotion. In demonstrating that activism is a defining characteristic of our discipline, we can more easily make that case.

Finally, we want to reiterate that the sociology we envision is not based solely in the academy. Much as it was for Addams, DuBois and others, sociology should be a collaborative effort on the part of folks in academia and various "applied" or community settings. It is together that we will create a more humane and just society.

Endnotes

[1]The University of Chicago launched its Graduate School of Social Service Administration in 1920; this marked the beginning of social work as a profession requiring a distinctive regimen of academic preparation and training.

[2]Social work lost its radical/progressive edge, as it became increasingly aligned with psychotherapy/clinical work, and less with the community and political advocacy work that Addams was so well known for (see e.g Specht and Courtney 1995).

[3]An interesting irony is that there were sociologists who championed a positivist vision of the field, and even railed against reformist inclinations, but were themselves involved in reform work. As Deegan (1988) notes, Robert Park is a perfect example.

[4]This statement would certainly seem to suggest that activism is at least part of what humanist sociologists do with their lives. But it also may imply that "professional,"

"scholar," and "activist" are distinct—and perhaps even mutually exclusive—identities. Moreover, we have no way of knowing precisely what the author of the statement meant by "activist" and thus, what activism might actually entail.

[5]Other examples found via links on the AACS website reveal a broader interpretation of the term, "applied," and suggest substantial overlap (or blurring) between the allegedly distinct areas of applied and clinical sociology.

[6]The mid-century advocates of clinical sociology, Lee and Gouldner included, suggested that it could be fruitfully (and legitimately) applied to the problems confronting a diverse range of groups and organizations, including businesses, labor unions, prisons, schools, and so on. In contrast to critical sociology, and like applied sociology, there is not a commitment to, or prioritization of, the problems (social injustices) that less powerful (social and economic minority) groups face. In this regard, it is interesting to note that just before he joined the faculty at Antioch, Alvin Gouldner was employed as a consultant to Standard Oil of New Jersey for a year (Fritz 2005: 450).

[7]The ASA and other sources suggest that the distinction between applied and clinical sociology is not a clear-cut dichotomy, but more a matter of emphasis, this being research in the case of applied sociology and change-oriented intervention in the case of clinical sociology. As Fritz notes, for example: "For some clinical sociologists…research is an important part of their own work. Other clinical sociologists may concentrate on the intervention and leave the research activities to others. Clinical sociologists use and combine a variety of research approaches…, but there is considerable interest in participatory, evaluative, and case study research" (2005: 41). Still, the clinical/applied distinction doesn't seem to allow for sociological work where research and intervention (for change) are inextricably linked, as in the case of participatory action research.

[8]The Highlander Research and Education Center was established in 1932 by Myles Horton, who had among his teachers and friends, Jane Addams. Sociologist John Gaventa, well-known for his pioneering participatory research in the Appalachian coalfields, served as director of the center from 1993–1996. For more information on the Highlander Center, check its website at: www.highlandercenter.org.

[9]For more information on this event, go to the U.S. Social Forum website at: www.ussf2007.org.

[10]We are not suggesting that this approach is somehow inappropriate or misguided, only that it is perhaps better characterized as progressive applied research than as PAR per se.

[11]A year earlier, in 2003, another sign of change became evident when a solid majority of the ASA's membership voted in favor of a resolution to condemn the U.S. war in Iraq. As Burawoy (2005a: 6) has observed, a similar resolution in 1968 against the Vietnam War had been soundly defeated.

[12]This, it might be noted, was what former ASA president Herbert Gans had in mind by his use of the term "public sociology" (Gans 1989, 2002).

[13]Burawoy writes about public sociology as one of four different strains of sociology, which also include professional, critical and policy sociology. See any of Burawoy's work cited in the bibliography for more detail.

[14]Obviously, our list draws heavily on the Preamble and articles of the Universal Declaration of Human Rights. We realize that this is an imperfect document and quite controversial in a number of respects. Just the same, it does capture important core elements of what we see as a humanist value orientation/perspective. We should also note

that our list reflects key points laid out in the American Humanist Association's Humanist Manifesto III (www.americanhumanist.org/3/HumandItsAspirations.htm).

[15]We have reservations about referring to Addams as the first humanist sociologist. Other less prominent pioneers at the time (e.g. Emily Balch, Florence Kelley) shared essentially the same perspective as Addams and engaged in myriad intellectual and political activities just as she did (Deegan 2003). We should note, too, that even Addams remained a relatively obscure sociological figure until the 1980s when Deegan's path-breaking work brought to light her brilliant and inspired contributions to sociology.

[16]We (the authors) have been engaged for roughly a decade now in conversations about building a curriculum where we teach that aptly reflects the spirit and mission of humanist sociology. Gradually, we are making some changes but there is still much work to do. For more information on the curricular changes that we have implemented, contact us at either cdale@nec.edu or dkalob@nec.edu.

References

Addams, Jane. 1961. *Twenty Years at Hull House*. New York: Penguin Putnam, Inc. /Signet. (Originally published, 1910.)

American Humanist Association. 2003. *Humanism and Its Aspirations—Humanist Manifesto III*. At: www.americanhumanist.org/3/HumanismandItsAspirations.pdf.

American Sociological Association. 2003. *Careers in Clinical Sociology*. Washington, D.C.: ASA.

Ballard, Chet. 2002. "An Epistle on the Origin and Early History of the Association For Humanist Sociology," *American Sociologist* 33, 4: 37–61.

Bell, Lee Ann. 1997. "Theoretical Foundations for Social Justice Education." Chapter 1 in *Teaching for Diversity and Social Justice Education: A Sourcebook*. Maurianne Adams, Lee Anne Bell and Pat Griffin, eds. New York: Routledge.

Berger, Peter L. 2002. "Whatever Happened to Sociology?" *First Things* 126 (October): 27–29.

Brady, David. 2004. "Why Public Sociology May Fail," *Social Forces* 82, 4: 1629–1638.

Broschart, Kay Richards. 2005. "An Intellectual Wasteland or Garden of Eden? Sociology in the American South Before 1950." Pp. 228–249 in *Diverse Histories of American Sociology*, edited by Anthony Blasi, Boston: Brill.

Burawoy, Michael. 2004a. "Public Sociologies: Contradictions, Dilemmas, and Possibilities," *Social Forces* 82, 4: 1603–1618.

Burawoy, Michael. 2004b. "Public Sociology: South African Dilemmas in a Global Context," *Society in Transition* 35, 1: 11–26.

Burawoy, Michael. 2005a. "For Public Sociology," 2004 ASA Presidential Address, *American Sociological Review* 70 (February): 4–28.

Burawoy, Michael. 2005b. "The Critical Turn to Public Sociology," *Critical Sociology* 31, 3: 313–326.

Burawoy, Michael. 2005c. "Rejoinder: Toward a Critical Public Sociology," *Critical Sociology* 31, 3: 379–390.

Bruhn, John G. and Howard M. Rebach. 1996. *Clinical Sociology: An Agenda for Action*. New York: Plenum Press.

Cancian, Francesca M. 1993. "Conflicts Between Activist Research and Academic Success: Participatory Research and Alternative Strategies," *American Sociologist* 24, 1: 92–106.

Cole, Stephen (ed.). 2001. *What's Wrong with Sociology?* New Brunswick, NJ: Transaction Publishers.

Coser, Lewis. "American Trends." Pp. 283–321 in *A History of Sociological Analysis*, Edited by Tom Bottomore and Robert Nisbet, New York: Basic Books.

Dale, Christopher. 2005. "Community Based Learning," *Humanity and Society* 29, 3/4: 192–208.

Davis, James A. 1994. "What's Wrong with Sociology?" *Sociological Forum* 9, 2: 179–197.

Deegan, Mary Jo. 1988. *Jane Addams and the Men of the Chicago School, 1892–1918.* Transaction Books. New Brunswick, NJ.

Deegan, Mary Jo. 2003. "An American Dream: The Historical Connections Between Women, Humanism, and Sociology, 1890–1920," *Humanity and Society* 27, 3: 378–389. (Originally published in *Humanity and Society* 11, 3, 1987.)

Deegan, Mary Jo. 2005. "Women, African Americans, and the ASA, 1905–2005." Pp. 178–206 in *Diverse Histories of American Sociology*, edited by Anthony Blasi, Boston: Brill.

Deflem, Mathieu. 2004. "The War in Iraq and the Peace in San Francisco: Breaking the Code of Public Sociology," Peace, War and Social Conflict, Newsletter of the ASA section. November.

Dolgon, Corey. 2001. "Revisiting the Three R's—Reading, Writing and Revolution: The Role of Humanist Scholars and the Future of *Humanity and Society*," *Humanity and Society* 25, 2: 100–113.

DuBois, William and Dean R. Wright. 2002. "What is Humanistic Sociology?" *American Sociologist* 33, 4: 5–36.

Elshtain, Jean Bethke. 2002a. *Jane Addams and the Dream of American Democracy.* New York: Basic Books.

Elshtain, Jean Bethke. 2002b. *The Jane Addams Reader.* New York: Penguin Books.

Feagin, Joe R. 2001. "Social Justice and Sociology: Agendas for the 21st Century," 2000 ASA Presidential Address, *American Sociological Review* 66 (February): 1 20.

Feagin, Joe R. and Hernan Vera. 2001. *Liberation Sociology.* Boulder, CO: Westview Press.

Fitzgerald, Tina; Alice Fothergill, Kristin Gilmore, Katherine Irwin, Charlotte A. Kunkel, Suzanne Leahy, Joyce M. Nielsen, Eve Passerini, Mary E.Virnoche, and Glenda Walden. 1995. "What's Wrong Is Right: A Response to the State of the Discipline," *Sociological Forum* 10, 3: 493–498.

Fritz, Jan Marie. 2005. "The Scholar-Practitioners: The Development of Clinical Sociology in the United States." Pp. 40–56 in *Diverse Histories of American Sociology*, edited by Anthony Blasi, Boston: Brill.

Gans, Herbert J. 1989. "Sociology in America: The Discipline and the Public," 1988 ASA Presidential Address, *American Sociological Review* 54 (February): 1–16.

Gans, Herbert J. 2002. "More of Us Should Become Public Sociologists," *Footnotes* July August. American Sociological Association.

Gaventa, John. 1992. Review of Handbook of Clinical Sociology, Rebach and Bruhn, (eds.). *Social Forces* 70, 4: 1127–1128.

Gedicks, Al. 1996. "Activist Sociology: Personal Reflections," *The Sociological Imagination* 33, 1.

Gedicks, Al. 2001. *Resource Rebels: Native Challenges to Mining and Oil Corporations.* Cambridge, MA: Beacon Press.

Glass, John. 1972. "The Humanist Challenge to Sociology." In *Humanistic Sociology, Today's Challenge to Sociology*, edited by John Glass and John Staude, Pacific Palidases, CA: Goodyear Publishing Company.

Glass, John F. 2001. "The Founding of the Clinical Sociology Association: A Personal Narrative," *Sociological Practice* 3, 1: 75–85.

Goodwin, Glenn A. 2003. "Toward a Paradigm for Humanist Sociology," *Humanity and Society* 27, 3: 340–354.

Hall, Budd L. 1992. "From Margins to Center? The Development and Purpose of Participatory Research," *American Sociologist* 23, 4: 15–28.

Horowitz, Irving Louis. 1993. *The Decomposition of Sociology.* New York: Oxford University Press.

Hoult, Thomas Ford. 1979. *Sociology for a New Day* (2nd ed.). New York: Random House.

Jipson, Art. 2002. "Using Humanist Sociology in the Classroom," *Humanity and Society* 33, 4: 74–85.

Lee, Alfred McClung. 1955. "The Clinical Study of Society," *American Sociological Review* 20, 6: 648–653.

Lee, Alfred McClung. 1978. *Sociology For Whom?* New York: Oxford University Press.

Lee, Alfred McClung. 2003. "Sociology for People," *Humanity and Society* 27, 3: 282–292. (Originally published in Humanity and Society in 1979, Vo. 3, No. 2.)

Lengermann, Patricia Madoo and Jill Niebrugge-Brantley. 2002. "Back to the Future: Settlement Sociology, 1885–1930," *American Sociologist* 33, 3, Fall.

Lewis, David Levering. 1993. *W.E.B. DuBois: Biography of a Race, 1868–1919.* New York: Henry Holt.

Lewis, David Levering. 2000. *W.E.B. DuBois: The Fight for Equality and the American Century, 1919–1963.* New York: Henry Holt.

Miller, James. 1987. *Democracy is in the Streets: From Port Huron to the Siege of Chicago.* New York: Simon and Schuster.

Mills, C. Wright. 1959. *The Sociological Imagination.* New York: Oxford University Press.

Nielsen, Francois. 2004. "The Vacant "We:" Remarks on Public Sociology," *Social Forces* 82, 4: 1619–1627.

Park, Peter. 1992. "The Discovery of Participatory Research as a New Scientific Paradigm: Personal and Intellectual Accounts," *American Sociologist* 23, 4: 29–42.

Park, Peter, Mary Brydon-Miller, Budd Hall and Edward T. Jackson (eds.). 1993. *Voices for Change: Participatory Research in North America.* Westport, CN: Greenwood Press.

Perrucci, Robert. 2001. "Inventing Social Justice: SSSP and the Twenty-First Century," *Social Problems* 48, 2: 159–167.

Rebach, Howard M. and John G. Bruhn, (eds.). 2001. *Handbook of Clinical Sociology.* New York: Plenum Press.

Reese, Ellen. 2001. "Deepening Our Commitment, Hitting the Streets: A Call to Action," *Social Problems* 48, 1: 152–157.

Scimecca, Joseph and Glenn Goodwin. 2003. "Jane Addams: The First Humanist Sociologist," *Humanity and Society* 27, 2, May: 143–157.

Specht, Harry and Mark E. Courtney. 1995. *Unfaithful Angels: How Social Work Has Abandoned Its Mission.* Free Press. New York.

Stoecker, Randy. 1994. *Defending Community: The Struggle for Alternative Redevelopment in Cedar-Riverside.* Philadelphia: Temple University Press.

Stoecker, Randy. 1996. "Sociology and Social Action: Guest Editor's Introduction," *The Sociological Imagination* 33, 1.

Stoecker, Randy. 2005. *Research Methods for Community Change: A Project-Based Approach.* Thousand Oaks, CA: Sage Publications.

Tittle, Charles R. 2004. "The Arrogance of Public Sociology," *Social Forces* 82, 4: 1639–1643.

Trevino, A. Javier and Robert J.S. Ross. 1998. "The Influence of C. Wright Mills on Students for a Democratic Society: An Interview with Bob Ross," *Humanity and Society* 22, 3: 260–277.

Wagenaar, Theodore C. 2004. "Is There a Core in Sociology? Results from a Survey," *Teaching Sociology* 32, 1: 1–18.

Wagner, Kenneth. 2005. "Is Sociology Stuck in the 60s?" History News Network, George Mason University. Retrieved from: http://hnn.us/articles/14564.html.

Ward, Lester Frank. 1906. *Applied Sociology: A Treatise on the Conscious Improvement of Society by Society.* Boston: Ginn and Company. (Available on the web at: http://de.share.geocities.com/ralf_schreyer/ward/download/applied_sociology.pdf)

Weber, Clare. 2002. "Latino Street Vendors in Los Angeles: Heterogeneous Alliances, Community Based Activism and the State." In Marta Lopez and David R. Diaz (eds.) *Asian and Latino Immigrants in a Restructuring Economy: The Metamorphosis of Los Angeles.* Stanford, CA: Stanford University Press.

Weber, Clare. 2006. "An Activist and a Scholar: Reflections of a Feminist Sociologist Negotiating Academia," *Humanity and Society* 30, 2: 153–166.

Wheeler, Leslie A. 1990. *Jane Addams.* Englewood Cliffs, NJ: Silver Burdett Press.

White, Jeffrey D. and Flannery C. Hauck (eds.). *Campus, Inc.: Corporate Power in the Ivory Tower.* Amherst, New York: Prometheus Books.

Wirth, Louis. 1931. "Clinical Sociology," *American Journal of Sociology* 37, 1: 49–66.

Wortham, Robert A. 2005. "The Early Sociological Legacy of W.E.B. DuBois." Pp. 74–93 *in Diverse Histories of American Sociology,* edited by Anthony Blasi, Boston: Brill.

Zuckerman, Phil (ed.). 2004. *The Social Theory of W.E.B DuBois.* Thousand Oaks, CA: Pine Forge Press.

New Tools for a Humanist Public Sociology Curriculum: A Response to Dale and Kalob's "Embracing Social Activism: Sociology in the Service of Justice and Peace"

Kathleen Odell Korgen
William Paterson University

Jonathan M. White
Bridgewater State College

Chris Dale and Dennis Kalob provide a powerful argument for bringing sociology back to its social justice roots with "Embracing Social Activism: Sociology in the Service of Social Justice and Peace." We thoroughly agree with their assessment of the foundations of the discipline and the renewed focus on social justice that has come with the public sociology movement. We second their call for the Association for Humanist Sociology "to take the lead in this work, in the creation (or, perhaps more accurately, the resurrection) of sociology as not only a critical and politically progressive discipline, but also as a grassroots, activist field." Public and humanist sociology are intrinsically bound to one another. If we care about the interests and welfare of humans, we must work toward making sociology useful to society. In this response, we spell out why we believe that teaching sociology students a *humanist* public sociology that is useful, accessible, and aimed at improving society is vital to this endeavor and acknowledge the recent creation of tools that can help us accomplish this goal.

Sociology, an increasingly popular major among undergraduates (Spalter-Roth 2008), has the potential to empower millions of citizens if a humanist public sociology curriculum, like the one Dale and Kalob envision, can reach more students. It is up to us, humanist sociologists keen on making a difference in the world, to make our curriculum reflect our vision of what our discipline should be. If we do so, we can influence not just the field of sociology but the millions of Americans who take or are connected to those who take sociology courses. Imagine a world in which the majority of people have experienced a sociology course that provided tools to understand society *and* make it more just! However, to make this impact, we must both convince our colleagues of the merits of moving away from a stale, positivistic, academically-focused curriculum *and* provide the resources needed to carry out a humanist public sociology curriculum.

One of the major road-blocks to changing curriculum has been a lack of textbooks on the market that reflect a humanist public sociology perspective. While other disciplines, such as communications and social epidemiology have connected their respective disciplines to social change efforts with such books as Lawrence Frey's *Communication Activism: Communication for Social Change* (Hampton Press 2007) and Julie Cwikel's *Social Epidemiology: Strategies for Public Health Activism* (Columbia University Press 2006), sociology, has, up until very recently, not produced such texts. Ironically, the vast majority of sociology texts tend to give students the impression that sociology is to be used to study society from a distance, so as to be sure sociologists do not impact it in any way. This message is far from the one Dale and Kalob and other humanist sociologists would like to present to their students. In fact, Dale and Kalob lament that introductory textbooks "are remarkably homogenous, and… generally undermine rather than facilitate the teaching of humanist sociology." They request that "folks who know of a text that reflects the concerns of humanist sociology… should, "please let [them] know!"

We are pleased to let Dale and Kalob (and all other sociologists) know that humanist public sociology resources now exist. Fortunately, in the few years since they wrote their article, some sociologists have created books that offer students a vision of sociology as a useful discipline that provides tools for those interested in creating a more just world. For example Anna Leon-Guerro's *Social Problems* text contains "What Does It Mean to Me" pieces in each chapter that enable students to think about how the social problem covered impacts them and, in some cases, take steps to address it. Corey Dolgon and Chris Baker's new Social Problems book, *Living Sociology: Social Problems, Service Learning and Civic Engagement* (Pine Forge 2010) provides a clearly humanist public sociological perspective. Their explicit goal for the book is to "present information and analytical frameworks for both understanding social problems and taking action to address them."

Our book, *The Engaged Sociologist: Connecting the Classroom to the Community* (Pine Forge 2010, 3rd edition), is another new book that provides a humanist public sociology vision of our discipline. The overriding message in *The Engaged Sociologist* is that sociology can help people become effective citizens who can strengthen our democracy. The book begins: "Have you ever wanted to change society? Do you want to have a voice in how things work throughout your life? If so, you have come to the right discipline. Sociology helps you to understand how society operates and, in turn, how to make society better."

Throughout *The Engaged Sociologist*, we focus on carrying out what Randall Collins (1998) describes as the core commitments of sociology (combining the sociological eye with social activism). These commitments are humanistic to the core. Once we understand how society operates, we are obligated to participate actively in efforts to improve it. Dale and Kalob yearned for a text that spoke of the activism of sociology's founders and not just their thoughts. *The Engaged Sociologist's* theory chapter teaches students that sociology was founded by social scientists eager to (a) understand the major social changes of the late 19th and early 20th centuries and (b) make society better. The book brings forward how the founders of sociology—such as Karl Marx, Max Weber, Émile Durkheim, George Herbert Mead, W.E.B. DuBois, and Jane Addams—carried out the two core commitments of sociology. Each of the theorists, in his or her own way, was a humanist public sociologist. They looked underneath the surface of society to understand how it operates and used this knowledge to improve society.

Kalob and Dale also pointed out the importance of modeling professional sociologists who use sociological tools to effect social change. In every chapter of *The Engaged Sociologist*, we feature professional or student "sociologists in action" to provide students with concrete examples of their peers, or professional public sociologists using sociological tools to improve our society. In our forthcoming book, *Sociologists in Action* (Pine Forge), we provide longer first-person narratives of sociologists who have used sociological tools in social justice efforts that cover a wide range of sociological subjects. In synch with Kalob and Dale's emphasis on giving students opportunities to use sociological tools in the course, every chapter in *The Engaged Sociologist* also contains numerous easy-to-follow exercises and resources geared toward pushing students to *use* the sociology they are learning to work for a more just world. Every chapter in *Sociologists in Action* will also provide resources though which students can learn more about and participate in social change efforts

So, while we totally concur with Kalob and Dale's history and critique of the discipline, we want readers to know that progress has been made since their article was published. Humanist public sociologists have begun to carry out their call to bring sociology back to its social justice roots both inside and outside the classroom. We hope that the texts mentioned in this article are just the beginning of the creation of innumerable texts with a humanist public sociology perspective. If we teach our students a humanist public sociology, they will *practice* sociology in the service of social justice and peace and join the growing movement to bring sociology back to its activist roots.

References

Spalter-Roth, Roberta. 2008. "What is Happening in Your Department?" ASA Research an20surveyd Development Department, November. Retrieved on September 24, 2009 (http://www.asanet.org/galleries/default-file/dept%20survey%20brief%20FINAL.pdf).

Section 2

Confronting Inequalities: Class, Race, Gender, Sexuality and the Fight for Social Justice

The United States has a long history of discrimination against non-whites, women, gay men and lesbians, and the poor and working class of this country. But with the election of Barack Obama, many pundits espoused a new, post-civil rights era where we would be free of the oppressive prejudices that plagued our nation's past. While many might disagree with this claim, even progressive sociologists sometime fall victim to conflating specific victories against prejudice with actually achieving a world in which various race, class, ethnic, gender, transgendered and sexual identities do not result in inequality, discrimination, violence and oppression. Obama's victory may have symbolized a change in certain cultural values and political norms, but we have a long way to go. The articles in this section not only document some of the history of various forms of discrimination, they demonstrate how racism, sexism, and other forms of oppression get reconfigured in ways that imply such inequalities have been resolved when in fact they have simply been recast. But even more importantly, these articles give insight into how understanding the complexities of discriminatory discourse and practices can inform new ways of challenging oppression and inequality. By calling on us to take our new knowledge and understanding into the streets and the workplace, the authors help create a new discourse and practice of human rights. Such must be the goal of any humanist scholarship and especially a public sociology.

1. An American Dream:
The Historical Connections Between Women, Humanism, and Sociology, 1890–1920[1]

Mary Jo Deegan
University of Nebraska-Lincoln

Reflexive Statement

In 1975 I had a very modest wish. I wanted to write a short popular paper on an early woman sociologist. At that time, women social scientists, theorists, novelists, and natural scientists were being "discovered" by women professionals, but I had never read anything about a female sociologist. Surely, I thought, there must have been at least one woman who did something during the founding days of the discipline. To my great surprise, I discovered several dozen women. I now had several questions to answer: Who were these women? Why did they publish in sociology journals? Why had I never heard of them? I have spent the intervening years trying to answer these questions.

Introduction

The humanistic study of women, their lives and experiences, is deeply rooted in the founding of American sociology. During the 1890s, when sociology was emerging as a discipline, social change was occurring with great rapidity and stress.

> For the 1890s was a decade of perceived national crisis, of economic upheaval, of surging political debate. Working-class needs stirred middle-class consciences; grassroots politics merged with intellectuals' concerns; and a women's movement soared side by side with broadly based campaigns for reform (Hill 1980: 4).

Thus, both males and females turned to sociology to help explain the tumultuous social world and point to new ways of planning and conceiving a more just and liberating social order (Addams 1910). They wanted to enact an American dream of justice for all, and sociology was integral to its enactment. This humanist vision of sociology (Becker 1971) was gender linked, however (Deegan 1978, 1987), and it represented only one type of soci-

---

[1]This paper originally appeared in *Humanity & Society* Volume 11, Number 3, 1987.

ology. Humanist sociologists were in conflict with another faction who wanted an "objective" study of society based on the natural science model. This latter faction was more patriarchal and aligned with elite interests vested in the academy (Schwendingers 1971).

In this paper, I focus on the flowering of thought and action generated by women sociologists between 1890 and 1920 during a period I call "a golden era of women sociologists" (Deegan 1985). Twenty-six women of two generations are introduced, and their epistemology and institutional setting examined. I then briefly present their connections to their male, humanist colleagues and the mainstream of sociological thought and practice after 1920. For the golden era of women sociologists is a particular age that began with enthusiasm and ended with ostracism. This sociological erasure of our founder's knowledge and practice has robbed contemporary humanist sociologists of their heritage as major intellectuals and activists who have altered the nature of American life and dreams. I start by introducing the first generation of women sociologists, whom I call the "pioneers," and their successors, the "professionals."

Introducing the Women Pioneers and Professionals

The first women to enter sociology in the United States were born around the time of the Civil War (i.e., 1855–1865). I am calling them "the pioneers."[1] I have singled out ten women as the most eminent pioneers, whom I briefly introduce as individuals and then discuss them as a group. (Their names, along with their successors, are found in Table 1).

Jane Addams is the most outstanding leader; intellectually, institutionally, and politically. Her analysis of American values, thought, and programs for action provides us with a rich corpus of humanist sociology (Deegan 1987). As the co-founder of the social settlement Hull-House (to be discussed in depth below), and as a pacifist in war-time, Addams provided the institutional home for humanist sociology in the community and an international model for sociological pacifism. She and her colleague Emily Greene Balch (Deegan 1983) developed a cooperative view of society that was so controversial, it led to their ostracism from sociology as well as their ultimate vindication as the only American women to be awarded the Nobel Peace Prize. Charlotte Perkins Gilman, another eminent pioneer, generated a major body of thought on the role of family in maintaining the economic subservience and repression of women as a class (Gilman 1898, 1935; Degler 1956).

The achievements of other pioneers are also remarkable. Thus, Marion Talbot co-founded the American Association of University Women and helped institutionalize the position of Dean of Women in universities (Talbot 1936; Talbot and Rosenberry 1931). Florence Kelley translated portions of Frederick Engels' work into English (Blumberg 1964, 1966); Kelley and Addams, in turn, were major figures behind the first urban mapping in Chicago, *The Hull House Maps and Paper* (Residents of Hull-House 1895). In addition, they were part of the famous Pittsburgh Survey documenting the exploitation and suffering of the steel workers and poor of that city.[2] Mary McDowell and Jane Addams helped start the mammoth 19-volume *Investigation into the Wages of Women and Children* (U.S. Congress 1910–1911). Finally, the pioneer sisters include Anna Garlin Spencer who was a noted Unitarian minister, pacifist, and theorist; Mary E. B. Roberts Smith Coolidge who was a leading theorist on Chinese, Mexican, and Indian lives in the United States[3]; and Lucy Salmon who studied domestic work. (See biographies noted in Table 1 for information on specific individuals.)

Table 1   Easily Accessible Biographical Information on Early Women Sociologists

Name	Notable American. Women (Vol: PP)	National Cyclopedia of Biography (Vol: PP)
Pioneers		
Addams, Jane	I: 6–22	C: 83; 27: 248
Balch, Emily G.	IV: 41–45	G: 504
Gilman, Charlotte	II: 39–42	13: 112
Kelley, Florence	II: 316–19	23: 111
Lathrop, Julia	II: 370–72	C: 92; 24: 298
McDowell, Mary	II: 462–64	B:355; 29:86
Salmon, Lucy	III: 223–24	NO
Smith, Mary E. B.	NO	NO
Spencer, Anna G.	III: 331–33	B: 41; 9: 548
Talbot, Marion	III: 423–25	36: 425
The Professionals		
Abbott, Edith	IV: 1–3	C:517
Adams, Elizabeth	NO	NO
Breckinridge, Sophonisba	I: 223–36	37: 65
Davis, Katherine	I: 439–41	A: 263
Donovan, Frances	NO	NO
Eastman, Crystal	I: 543–45	NO
Eaves, Lucille	NO	A: 506; 41: 67
Hewes, Amy	NO	NO
Hollingworth, Leta	II: 206–08	NO
Kellor, Frances (Name spelled "Kellar")	IV: 393–5	15: 248
Kingsbury, Susan	II: 335–6	NO
MacLean, Annie M.	NO	NO
Parsons, Elsie C.	III: 20–22	NO
Paul, Alice	NO	NO
Taft, Jessie	IV: 673–75	NO
Van Kleek, Mary	IV: 707–09	NO

* The literature on these women is so vast that it literally takes volumes to enumerate it. Entries in Notable American Women and The National Cyclopedia of Biography, moreover, are significant indicators of national importance and influence. For convenience, I label the most recent volume of Notable American Women Volume "IV."

** There are two types of listings in this reference series. One series is alphabetical (cumulative) and the other series is numerical (annual).

All the pioneers were members of the American Sociological Society, and eight of the ten presented work at the annual meetings, and two held offices in the organization (Deegan 1981). Each pioneer worked with male colleagues in sociology, especially with the faculty at the University of Chicago (Deegan 1987). (This is not surprising since this faculty was the most powerful group of male sociologists. See Kurtz [1984] for a review of the literature on this school.) All the pioneers called themselves sociologists.

In general, the pioneers were unmarried, white[4], Protestant, and middle class. Their educated parents were often political activists who supported women's education and suffrage; they opposed slavery and were active in the Abolition Movement.

The pioneers were soon followed by a new generation, generally born in the next decade between 1866 and 1876. This new cohort adopted the academic model of earning advanced graduate degrees in order to become "professionals." (See Table 1 for their names and biographical resources.) Thus, thirteen of the professionals earned doctoral degrees in sociology and the remaining three earned master's degrees. They were strongly motivated by the pioneers and strove to emulate them in ideas and legitimacy. The most notable professional, however, is the only woman to completely reject a professional career: Alice Paul. As a militant feminist and author of the Equal Rights Amendment, Paul was openly hostile to the academy (see Willis 1983). Other professionals also achieved eminence, but they did not parallel Paul's renown or that of the pioneers.

Rather than leading the nation, the professionals developed numerous qualitative and quantitative studies documenting inequality and buttressing the more persuasive and dramatic work of the pioneers (e.g. Breckinridge 1933). Thus, Edith Abbott documented the role of women in industry (1910); her work was supported and amplified by that of Annie Marion MacLean, Amy Hewes, Lucille Eaves, Mary Van Kleek, Frances Kellor, Elizabeth Adams, and Frances Donovan. Their colleague Sophonisba Breckinridge similarly revealed that women's inequality was rooted in our legal system.

Yet another thrust within this group was the study of women's specific gender problems. Leta Hollingworth and Elsie Clews Parsons (discussed in Rosenberg 1983) showed that marriage, and myths about child-bearing and menstruation, were forms of discrimination directed solely at women. Katherine Davis documented the varieties of women's sexual behaviors, and Jessie Taft developed a symbolic interactionist therapy for helping women and children (Deegan 1986). (References to the professionals' work, lives, and writings can be found in their biographies noted in Table 1.)

The pioneers and professionals worked together to generate a powerful focus for changing women's social status based on a particular humanist vision and workplace. Not only were they attracted to the emerging discipline of sociology, but they were oriented towards practical change emerging from an alliance between sociologists and the community. Their epistemology explained and supported these activities, and this worldview is examined next.

The Women's Epistemology: Critical Pragmatism and Cultural Feminism

The early women sociologists articulated their views in two major streams of thought: cultural feminism and critical theory that defines traditional feminine values as superior to traditional male values. The second branch, "critical pragmatism," is a social theory that emphasizes the need to apply liberal values, especially democracy and education. Their concept of "democracy" meant that equality must extend beyond citizenship rights and pervade all aspects of life. Thus "democracy" referred to the political right to vote, the economic right to fair and full employment, and the social right to have the mores and customs of one's social group respected by others. Their concept of "education" referred to continuous learning that expanded and augmented each of these rights. As critical pragmatists they sought not only answers to problems, but those answers that were in the best interests of all, including the poor and disenfranchised (Deegan 1987).

Between 1890 and 1915, it appeared to the women and their male colleagues that these two branches were fundamentally compatible. Critical pragmatism was an epistemology widely shared by both male and female humanist sociologists (e.g. Becker 1971; Diner 1980; Small 1896; Ward 1883, 1906): Cultural feminism, however, was largely adopted by women, not men.[5]

The radical import of cultural feminism was not understood, because it coexisted with a very different, sexist vision of the world: the Doctrine of the Separate Spheres (Deegan 1987). In this latter theory, men and women specialized in different ideas, values, and actions. Supposedly these divisions were "separate but equal," but actually it meant that men controlled the public sphere including the economy, government, formal education, the church, and the state, while women were allowed some control in the private sphere of home and family. It was only when the female sociologists openly fought America's entry into World War I that cultural feminism appeared to the public in general and male sociologists in particular as truly different from the Doctrine of the Separate Spheres. The ostracism of the women sociologists that resulted built major barriers between male and female sociologists that the men would not remove. Before examining this end of the Golden Era, however, I want to present the setting in which both streams of thought flourished for a time: in the social settlement.

The Institutional Home of Early Women Sociologists

A new institutional form, the social settlement, employed and housed these women and became the agency for their ideas and activities. It was designed as a neighborhood center to mediate the differences between social factions. Women sociologists with the demographic characteristics previously given represented the established Americans and they articulated an effort to heal the divisions between ethnic groups, classes, races, and ways of life.

In 1889 Jane Addams co-founded the most powerful American social settlement, Hull-House, in Chicago (Addams 1910, 1930). It epitomized the ideal work of women sociologists because of the vibrant leadership of Jane Addams and the women who lived with her. As a Hull-House group, including nine of the ten pioneers and nine of the sixteen professionals, these women established major social institutions such as the Juvenile Court and the Psychopathic Institute; governmental bureaus such as the Women's and the Children's Bureaus; national legislation for minimum wages, the eight-hour day, and child labor laws; and international organizations such as Women's International League for Peace and Freedom. They wrote hundreds of books and articles; they offered college courses; public lectures; controversial debate, defended the civil rights of the oppressed, and fought against the censorship; and ostracism of radicals and immigrants (Davis 1973; Costin 1983; Fish, forthcoming; Sklar 1985).

These women lived in the settlements, they spent their lives together writing, traveling, speaking before governmental committees, organizing, lobbying, protesting, laughing, crying, and arguing. Smith-Rosenberg (1975) has already noted the world of love and ritual that existed among women before their era. The women sociologists extended this world into one embracing a public life centered on women, social action, and professional commitment. They created a new form of professional and personal life based on unity between the self and the other; the workplace and the home; social thought and action; ideas and their implementation; the privileged and the underprivileged, the American Dream and the continuing struggle to enact it.

These humanist sociologists were national leaders advocating social settlement for the poor, children, women, immigrants, laborers, juvenile delinquents, and blacks. Their eminence as feminists, leaders in social legislation, and community organizers has been disconnected from their roots in humanist sociology, however, impoverishing our heritage and hiding the power of our vision. The reasons for their academic erasure are briefly examined next.

Women Sociologists and New Barriers to Their Advancement

The professionals intended to expand the powerful base established by the pioneers. The professionals wanted to be better trained and equipped to claim the titles and rights of sociologists as well. In many ways they accomplished their goals. Their writings are more structurally rigorous and documented by data. They produced an impressive array of studies about women's life and labor. But in more fundamental ways, they failed. They received only token statuses in sociology, low pay, and little recognition. They came to maturity in the period that was a backlash to the power of the first generation of women sociologists, immediately prior to and following World War I.

The Red Scare of 1919 and the ensuing Red hunt of the next decade haunted the work of both cohorts (Davis 1973, 1967). Their belief that women voters would change the political climate was in error. The age of Freudian distain of unmarried women was also in ascendancy (Addams 1930). Simultaneously, American sociology was aligning itself with the German and French models of the University and the profession. The British view of sociology, most compatible with the women's, was defined as less and less desirable (Deegan 1987). Sociology was also disentangling itself from controversies and becoming a somewhat respected, male-dominated, academic field of study (Becker 1971).

Indeed, the profession itself was undergoing increasing resistance to female colleagues. As it became a more legitimate profession for men, the need to draw on the prestige of the pioneer women sociologists decreased. The women were becoming increasingly problematic also, because of their unpopular resistance to World War I. Social work was becoming a more structured occupation and advancing professional claims, and it welcomed women social scientists instead of creating barriers to their acceptance (Lubove 1965). The women wanted more social action, more professional control, and were increasingly estranged from their male colleagues. A systematic reordering of professional alignments occurred. The majority of women sociologists became identified with social work, and a golden era for women sociologists had come to an end.

The Quick Decline and Disappearance of the Golden Era

The mainstream male sociologists working after 1920 were particularly hostile to cultural feminism. For example, Chicago Sociology became know in the 1920s for its theory of human ecology based on competition, conflict, accommodation, and assimilation. The social values of nurturance and co-operation were absent in this new male model (see Park and Burgess 1921; Park, Burgess, and McKenzie 1925; Faris 1967). Critical pragmatism was absorbed and transformed under the language of "urban sociology," "human ecology," and "social policy." The women's authorship, intellectual contributions, and heritage were denigrated, distorted, or claimed as innovations by men (Deegan 1978). This intellectual violence and appropriation continued for decades, and it is only the recent work of feminist scholars that challenges their claims.

A New American Dream: Reconnecting the History of Women, Humanism, and Sociology

Although the golden era of women sociologists has languished for years, the potential for a renewal of their dream is possible. Fortunately, the written work of the women remains, their profound effect on society and legislation continues, and archival records can help us piece together much of the story. The women were temporarily shoved out of sociology, but they will not remain outside the annals of sociological history.

There are a number of reasons for my deep optimism about the fate of early women sociologists, for their ideas and contributions have stood the test of time. Their innovations strike a chord in contemporary lives as society undergoes rapid social change, new definitions of professional activities emerge, and the role of sociology is once more questioned. Women scholars also have a new voice to articulate the dreams and inspirations of their predecessors. In addition, the high cost of competitive and violent models for social life is increasingly apparent in a nuclear age. It is in our own self-interest to understand the work of early women sociologists. And last, but not least, the growing articulation of humanist sociology creates a bridge between the gold era of the past and the possibility of a humanists' renaissance in the sociology of the future.

Acknowledgments

This paper emerged from another, "The Golden Era of Women Sociologists," presented at Brandeis University to Shula Reinharz's class on "The Intellectual Work of Women in Sociology." Their enthusiasm and interest spurred me to write this longer paper which I have wanted to do for a decade. My thanks to Wilbur Watson, Michael Hill, Virginia Kemp Fish, and Steven Beuchler for comments and support of other drafts. This portion of that paper was presented at a plenary session of the Association for Humanist Sociology Eleventh Annual Conference, November 8, 1986, Philadelphia, PA. My particular thanks to Jerry Starr for his support for this work.

Endnotes

[1]Jill Conway wrote an excellent article on some of the women included here. See Women Reformers and American Culture: 1870–1930," *Journal of Social History* 5 (Winter 1971), 164–82. In this piece she defines these women as either "Victorian sages" or "professional experts." "The first is a borrowing from European culture, the type of the sage or prophetess who claimed access to hidden wisdom by virtue of feminine insights. The second is the type of the professional expert or the scientist, a social identity highly esteemed in American culture but sexually neutral (p. 167)."

Contrary to Conway, I see both groups as professional women and, in addition, a particular type of professional, a sociologist. She collapses generational differences whereas I see these groups as more profoundly affected by their age of birth and cohort. I also interpret the classifications differently. She defines Florence Kelley, for example, as a "scientist"; one who did not capture the popular imagination or become a model for other women (pp. 167–68). I think this underestimates the end popularity of Kelley and her impact on women. A discussion of the influence of the group she headed, the National Consumers' League, is found in Sophonisba Breckinridge, *Women in the Twentieth Century* (New York: McGraw-Hill, 1933). For an excellent biography of Kelley that documents her fiery personality and power, see Dorothy Rose Blumberg, *Florence Kelley* (New York: Augustus M. Kelley 1966). In addition, Conway describes Addams as the ideal "sage," tending in my opinion to uncritically accept Addams' popular image more than her intellectual role. It is the latter aspect I empathize here.

[2]The Pittsburgh Survey was a massive undertaking resulting in six books and numerous amides. It is the forerunner of large-scale, survey research using a team to collect the data. It resulted in legislative changes, a raised public consciousness, and academic innovations. The process of generating the survey, its impact on American life, and results is discussed in Chambers (1971: N.B. 33–45).

[3]Mary Elizabeth Burroughs Roberts Smith Coolidge is a major sociologist who has been overlooked in both women's history and professional annals. Her name, and its different forms over the course of her career, partially accounts for her invisibility. She was structurally discriminated against within academia, however, and her life is a triumph over its limitations. I am in the process of writing her intellectual history, and I would appreciate hearing from anyone who knew her.

[4]June Sochen has discussed many of this groups' characteristics in *Movers and Shakers* (New York: Quadrangle, 1973). These women worked within an Anglo world although some of them made efforts to work with women of color, especially Jane Addams, Mary McDowell, and Frances Kellor. I have tried to find early sociologists who were women of color, and Wilbur Watson first suggested to me the name of Ellen Irene Diggs. In my attempts to find women of color, I discovered another generational difference. The first black professional women sociologists I have documented are Dr. Marion Cuthbert (1896–), Dr. Zelma Watson George 1903–), and Dr. Ellen Irene Diggs (1906–). They all came of age in the generation following the one I am studying here. Although their academic careers tended to be within a racially segregated academic network, their applied careers were shared with and similar to those of their contemporary, white, female colleagues. See *In Black and White*, Volume I, 3rd Edition, edited by Mary Mace (Detroit: Gale Research Co. 1980) for Cuthbert, p. 229 and Diggs, p. 262. See *In Black and White*, edited by Mary Mace Spradling (Kalamazoo, MI: Kalamazoo Public Library, 1976); for George, see p. 149.

[5]Only a few men worked closely with the theory of cultural feminism. Lester Ward, who was a colleague and inspiration to Charlotte Perkins Gilman, was one of these men. Another was W. I. Thomas. The latter frequently had intellectual ties with the women of Hull-House, as an intellectual peer to Jane Addams and as a professor to Edith Abbott, Sophonisba Breckinridge, and Jessie Taft. See Klein (1946) for one of the few positive analyses of Thomas' work on women, also Deegan (1987).

References

Abbott, Edith. 1910. *Women in Industry*. New York: D Appleton.

Addams, Jane. 1930. *The Second Twenty Years at Hull-House*. New York: Macmillan.

——. 1910. *Twenty Years at Hull-House*. New York: Macmillan.

Becker, Ernest. 1971. *The Lost Science of Man*. New York: George Braziller.

Blumberg, Dorothy Rose. 1966. *Florence Kelley*. New York Augustus M. Kelley.

——. 1964. "'Dear Mr. Engels,' Unpublished Letters, 1884–1894 of Florence Kelley (-Wischen-wetzky) to Friedrich Engels.'" *Labor History* 5 (Spring): 103–33.

Breckinridge, Sophonisba. 1933. *Women in the Twentieth Century*. New York: McGraw-Hill.

Chambers, Clarke. 1971. *Paul U. Kellogg and the SURVEY*. Minneapolis: University of Minnesota Press.

Conway, Jill. 1971. "Women Reformers and American Culture: 1870–1930." *Journal of Social History* 5 (Winter 1971): 164–82.

Davis, Allen F. 1973. *American Heroine*. New York: Oxford University Press.

——.1967. *Spearheads for Reform*. New York: Oxford University Press.

Deegan, Mary Jo. 1987. *Jane Addams and the Men of the Chicago School. 1892–1918*. New Brunswick, NJ: Transaction Press.

——. 1986. "The Clinical Sociology of Jessie Taft." *Clinical Sociology Review* 4: 30–45.

——.1985. "The Golden Era of Women Sociologists, 1892–1920." Unpublished Paper presented at Brandeis University, November.

——.1983. "Sociology at Wellesley College, 1900–1919." *The Journal of the History of Sociology* 6 (December): 91–115.

——.1981. "Early Women Sociologists and the American Sociological Society." *American Sociologist* 16 (February 1981): 14–24.

——.1978. "Women in Sociology: 1890–1930." *The Journal of the History of Sociology* 1 (Fall 1978): 11–34.

Degler, Carl. 1956. "Charlotte Perkins Gilman on the Theory and Practice of Feminism" *American Quarterly* 8 (Spring): 21–39.

Diner, Steven. 1980. *A City and Its Universities*. Chapel Hill, NC: University of North Carolina Press.

Faris, Robert E. L. 1967. *Chicago Sociology*. Chicago: University of Chicago Press.

Fish, Virginia Kemp. In Press "The Hull-House Circle." In Janet Sharistanian, ed., *Women's Public Lines*. New Haven, CN: Greenwood Press.

Gilman, Charlotte Perkins. 1935. *The Living of Charlotte Perkins Gilman*. New York: D. Appleton-Century.

——.1966, c. 1898. *Women and Economics*. New York: Harper Torchbooks.

Hill, Mary. 1980. *Charlotte Perkins Gilman: The Making of a Radical Feminist, 1860–1896*. Philadelphia: Temple University Press.

Klein, Viola. 1948, c. 1946. *The Feminine Character*. New York: International Universities Press.

Kurtz, Lester. 1984. *Evaluating Chicago Sociology: A Guide to the Literature, with an Annotated Bibliography*. Chicago: University of Chicago Press.

Lubove, Roy. 1965. *The Professional Altruist*. Cambridge, MA: Harvard University Press.

Mace, Mary, ed. 1980. *In Black and White*, Volume, I, 3rd Edition, Gale Research Co.

Park, Robert E. and Ernest W. Burgess. 1921. Chicago: University of Chicago Press.

Park, Robert E. and Roderick D. McKenzie. 1925. *The City*. Chicago: University of Chicago Press.

Residents of Hull-House. 1895. *Hull-House Maps and Papers*. New York: Crowell.

Rosenberg, Rosalind. 1982. *Beyond Separate Spheres*. New Have: Yale University Press.

Schwendinger, Herman and Julia Schwendinger. 1971. *The Sociologists of the Chair*. New York; Basic Books.

Sicherman, Barbara. 1984. *Alice Hamilton*. Cambridge, MA: Harvard Press.

Sklar, Kathryn Kish. 1985. "Hull House in the 1890s." *Signs* 10 (Summer): 658–677.

Smith-Rosenberg, Carol. 1975. "The Female World of Love and Ritual." *Signs* 1 (Fall): 1–29.

Small, Albion W. 1896. "Scholarship and Social Agitation." *American Journal of Sociology* 1 (March): 564–582.

Sochen, June. 1973. *Movers and Shakers.* New York: Quadrangle.

Spradling, Mary Mace. 1976. *In Black and White*, 2nd Edition. Kalamazoo, MI: Kalamazoo Public Library.

Talbot, Marion. 1936. *More Than Lore.* Chicago: University of Chicago Press.

Talbot, Marion and Lois K. M. Rosenberry. 1931. *The History of the American Association of University Women, 1881–1931.* Cambridge, Mass: Houghton Mifflin co.

U.S. Congress, Senate. 1910–1911. *Report on Conditions of Woman and Child Wage Earners in the United States.* volumes 1–18, S. Doc. 645, 61st Congress, 2nd Session.

Ward, Lester. 1906. *Applied Sociology.* New York: Ginn and Co.

——. 1910, c. 1883. *Dynamic Sociology.* New York: Appleton and Co.

Willis, Jean L. 1983. "Alice Paul: The Quintessential Feminist." In *Feminist Theorists,* ed. by Dale Spencer. New York: Pantheon Books. pp 285–295.

Reflections on Deegan's "An American Dream: The Historical Connections Between Women, Humanism, and Sociology, 1890–1920"[1]

Jill M. Bystydzienski
Iowa State University

I first heard Mary Jo Deegan present a version of this paper at a session of the 11th annual Association for Humanist Sociology (AHS) conference in 1986 in Philadelphia. This was pioneering work in sociology, including humanist sociology, as very few sociologists at the time had acknowledged the contributions of women and feminism to the field's foundations, and no one, to my knowledge, had made the connection between women, humanism, and early sociology.

A few years ago, I heard Mary Jo Deegan present another pathbreaking piece of research in a keynote speech at an annual meeting of the Iowa Sociological Association. She spoke about the contributions of African American women to sociological foundations. In her H&S article, Deegan acknowledged that all the early women sociologists she had researched up to that point were white and upper middle class. In an endnote, she mentioned that she found several women of color sociologists (Ellen Irene Diggs, Marion Cuthbert, and Zelma Watson George) but did not include them in her analysis because they were of a later generation. She was able to remedy this omission, however, in her more recent work (see, e.g., Deegan 2002) which focuses on the role of race and contributions of women of color to early sociology.

Since the publication of Deegan's paper in *Humanity and Society* in 1987 (and several related pieces in other journals during the 1980s and early 1990s), a number of sociologists started doing research on women founders. During the late 1980s, throughout the1990s and beyond, sociological texts increasingly began to include the intellectual work of Jane Addams, Caroline Bartlett Crane, Charlotte Gilman, Elsie Parsons, Sophonisba Breckinridge and others (see, Wallace and Wolf 1989; Lengermann and Niebrugge-Brantley 1998; Myers, Anderson and Risman 1998; Rynbrandt 1999; Romano 2002).

Humanist sociologists, however, have not readily embraced these women as intellectual founders of humanist sociology. While numerous articles published in *Humanity and Society* and papers presented at the annual AHS conferences in the late 1980s and throughout the 1990s focused on those thinkers who laid the foundations of humanist sociology, only a few mentioned any of the women discussed by Deegan. A recent content analysis of H&S publications and AHS conference programs revealed that humanist sociologists still consider the founders of the field to be largely white males such as Karl Marx, W.I. Thomas, C. Wright Mills, and Al Lee (Bystydzienski 2002).

[1]This paper originally appeared in *Humanity & Society* Volume 27, Number 3, 2003.

Elsewhere (Bystydzienski 2001), I have discussed the limitations of humanism and the need to incorporate work by women and feminist knowledge. While both feminism and humanism challenge hegemonic sociology, they have also been integral to the discipline. By offering each other corrective perspectives, and carrying on a much needed dialogue, humanism and feminism could achieve a synthesis and further strengthen humanist sociology. The integration of humanist and feminist intellectual legacy of the women founders into humanist sociological theory and practice is one example of how such a synthesis could be achieved.

The significance of Deegan's work for humanist sociology should not be underestimated. As she shows in her 1987 article, the women founders embraced a critical pragmatism and cultural feminism that emphasized participatory democratic values in politics and citizenship, "the economic right to fair and full employment, and the social right to have the mores and customs of one's social group respected by others" (p. 357). Their commitment to an openly value-based sociology and to seeking solutions to social problems that were in the interest of all (including the poor and disenfranchised) clearly place them in the best tradition of humanist sociology. The recognition of these women, as well as the women of color she cites in her later work, as being among the founders of humanist sociology is essential. Their contributions remain to be integrated more fully into the research and teaching of humanist sociologists.

References

Bystydzienski, Jill M. 2002. "Women and Feminism in the Association for Humanist Sociology." *American Sociologist* 33(4):66–73.

————. 2001. "Connecting Humanist Sociology and Feminism: Recognizing our Global Humanity in its Local Diversity." Presidential Address. *Humanity & Society* 21(3&4):209–218.

Deegan, Mary Jo. 2002. *Race, Hull-House and the University of Chicago: A New Conscience against Current Evils.* Westport, Conn.: Praeger.

Lengermann, Patricia and Jill Niebrugge-Brantley. 1998. *The Women Founders: Sociology and Social Theory, 1830–1930.* Boston: MacGraw-Hill.

Myers, Kristen A, Cynthia D. Anderson and Barbara Risman (eds.). 1998. *Feminist Foundations: Toward Transforming Sociology.* Thousand Oaks, Calif.: Sage.

Romano, Mary Ann (ed.). 2002. *Lost Sociologists Rediscovered.* New York: Edwin Mellen.

Rymbrandt, Linda. J. 1999. *Caroline Bartlett Crane and Progressive Reform: Social Housekeeping as Sociology.* New York: Garland.

Wallace, Ruth A. and Alison Wolf. 1989. *Contemporary Sociological Theory: Continuing the Classical Tradition.* Englewood Cliffs, N.J.: Prentice Hall.

2. Workplace Democracy and Occupational Health[1,2]

Bennett M. Judkins
Meredith College

Reflexive Statement

I spent the first sixteen years of my life split between a small cotton textile town and a coal mining community in southern Virginia. My mother was a company nurse for the textile industry and later traveled throughout Appalachia for the United Mine Workers Welfare and Retirement Fund taking care of sick miners. As a graduate student I became interested in the black lung movement where disabled miners were struggling not only for compensation but to challenge the whole health care system for coal miners and their families.

After completing my dissertation on the Black Lung Association, I took teaching positions in the heart of the southern textile industry to begin research on the emerging brown lung movement. Comparative analysis to these two movements resulted in the publication of *We Offer Ourselves as Evidence: Toward Workers' Control of Occupational Health* (1986). Research for this book and subsequent inquiry have led me to explore the possible impact of increasing worker participation in decisions about occupational health.

Introduction

The issue or worker participation in industrial decision making has been a subject of growing interest in the United States, as well as many other industrialized nations. Although not a new phenomenon, such ideas as "the team concept" (Parker and Slaughter 1988), "workplace democracy" (Lindenfeld and Rothschild-Whitt 1982), "economic democracy" (Carnoy and Shearer 1980) and "industrial democracy" (Woodworth, Meek and Whyte 1985) have found their way into the literature on the modern workplace over the last couple of decades. This worker participation "movement" has encouraged an increase in quality circles and quality of working life (QWL) programs, "labor-management" committees, Employ Stock Option Plans (ESOPS), worker cooperatives, and worker ownership. Each reflects a different variation on the movement, which in turn reflects a different ideological position and anticipated outcome.

[1]An earlier version of this paper was presented to the Society for the Study of Social Problems, Atlanta, Georgia, August 21–23, 1988. The author would like to thank economist Bill Van Lear and sociologists Frank Lindenfeld and John Leggett for their comments in the preparation of this paper.
[2]This paper originally appeared in *Humanity & Society* Volume 14, Number 1, 1990.

The last two decades have also witnessed a separate movement to address the issue of occupational health in the workplace. Although several writers have suggested a relation between the two movements (Deutsch 1981b; Dorman 1985; Gevers 1985; Navarro 1983; Mergler 1987), little research has been devoted to exploring this linkage. The underlying question is deceptively simple: Would increasing workers' control over the means of production improve the quality of health and safety in the workplace? Although common sense, several recent government programs, and some initial research would suggest a positive response, the issue may be more complex than would initially appear.

This paper begins to explore this question by looking first at the general idea of increasing workers' control over occupational health. This will be followed by a section on the possible contribution of workplace democracy to improving worker health and safety. A third section will look at some of the empirical research, including analyses of worker controlled occupational health programs in other countries, which might inform possible efforts in the United States. A final section will explore the future prospects of workplace democracy and occupational health.

Toward Workers' Control of Occupational Health

Like most issues, it is difficult to consider occupational health as an isolated phenomenon. Broader factors, many times ideological as well as structural, impinge on our ability to seek resolutions. As one business professor has lamented, it is difficult to talk about health and safety in the United States when we haven't resolved whether an American worker even has a right to a job (McLaughlin 1982).

Since the value of labor, at least to industry, changes with economic fluctuations, will and should there be a change in the value of human health and life? The bottom line of this dilemma is cost, and who bears it. The regulation of health and safety is essentially the process of making costs which are external to the market into internal costs. Someone has to bear the monetary 'burden of these costs: government, industry, workers, or the consumer. The experiences of many industrial laborers—especially those who work in coal, chemicals, cotton textiles and asbestos—suggest that these costs can be very high, if not in regulation, then in the costs of compensation and medical care.

But there are other costs that must also be considered. There is the cost to workers who develop occupational diseases and lose many years of their productive lives. There is the cost to their families, economic and otherwise, and their communities, which must bear some of the responsibility for their care. Although these costs are difficult to quantify, we find ourselves forced in this direction as we attempt to evaluate the costs and benefits of any policy directed towards the solution of occupational health issues. Even more controversial is the possible requirement of putting a value on human life, and differentiating the value of different people's lives. Some would argue that putting the value of human life on the same economic scale as the dollar costs of implementing protective standards is necessary because human life is a risky affair and there is no way of eliminating all risks. In addition, the material resources required for the prevention of risks are limited.

Philosopher Anselm Min suggests that this process raises many of the complex moral issues and dilemmas of modern industrial capitalism. Is it technically possible to put a price on human life? Is it morally justifiable to do so? Under what conditions is it ethically defensible to risk health and life? And what is the moral right and responsibility of the community and its official expression, the government, in case of a conflict between the human and the economic costs of doing business (Min 1982)? Journalist Coleman McCarthy suggests that the political debate over government's role has put aside even more crucial questions of ethics: What is the moral obligation of an employer whose worker comes down with a work related disease, and what is a socially acceptable risk when what is gambled is the health of the worker next to the coke oven and not the owner in the boardroom (1978)? Underlying these questions are fundamental controversies about control over the workplace in general and decision making in the area of occupational health in particular.

Workers' control, a significant ideological component of the European labor movement, has not had the same status, or success, in the American labor movement. Although evident in the early struggles, American workers, through their unions, have often conceded to management the right to direct the workplace and then devoted their energies to wrestling various concessions from management in return. Workers' power evolved from the ultimate threat of shutting down production by going on strike. By the 1930's, this system, known as collective bargaining, had become the philosophy of most major unions in the United States.

For the first half of this century, unions have endured often violent battles with management to develop what many consider to be the most elaborate, extensive and complex system of collective bargaining in the world. Labor union membership as a share of the total labor force has declined since 1950, however, and today the American labor movement enrolls one of the smallest percentages of the labor force among industrialized countries (Carnoy and Shearer 1980). Although the movement has been successful in numerous collective bargaining agreements and has been an important force for legislation on welfare, social insurance, and civil rights, it has never moved out of its production base to develop an overall political program. As historian David Montgomery notes, the effects of the New Deal in the 1930's essentially completed a long historic process of reducing the American labor movement to a trade union movement, "an immobile and isolated aggregation of legally certified bargaining agents" (Montgomery 1980: 171).

Montgomery's assessment is not shared by all labor historians. In addition, even though the dominant work of union leaders may have been in collective bargaining, the role of rank-and-file workers reflects a more diverse association with American industry, one where worker's control is not a completely absent ideological perspective. This has certainly been the case with the recent occupational health movement. The passage of the Occupational Safety and Health Act of 1970 is generally credited to rank-and-file discontent over health and safety hazards in the late 1960s. Although many union officials remained indifferent to these demands, several labor activities, working with public health professionals, were able to build a movement around the workers dissatisfaction (Noble 1986: 70; Epstein 1987: 404–412).

Part of this struggle has encompassed a battle over the actual definition of occupational health and the conceptualization of the problem of illness. As Dan Berman points out, this has been greatly influenced since the turn of the century by an overemphasis on compensation at the expense of prevention (1978: 117). Vicente Navarro argues that this resulted primarily from a broader need within the capitalistic system that all struggles at the point of production be shifted to the area of consumption, where attention is drawn to the cost of labor-personal and social wages-rather than control over the process of production. Not only did labor unions accept this shift, but, consequently, the unalterability of the process of work and damage created at the workplace as unavoidable. Compensation became the accepted alternative, and occupational medicine developed to define for management the size and damage which needed to be compensated (Navarro 1983: 17).

It is this traditional system by which occupational diseases have been identified, measured and defined that is now being challenged. Two grass roots components to the broader occupational health movement that demonstrated this were the Black Lung Association in the coal industry and the Brown Lung Association in the southern textile industry. Coal worker's pneumoconiosis, or "black lung," and byssinosis, or "brown lung," are pulmonary diseases caused by the inhalation of workplace dust into the respiratory system. These coalitions, composed primarily of retired and disabled workers, along with activists labor supporters, sought to gain recognition for their respective occupational diseases, compensation for those affected, and changes in the workplace to prevent future generations from contracting the same illnesses. Their battle required the formulation of "political definitions" of occupational diseases that challenged the traditional "scientific definitions." According to medical anthropologist Janet Bronstein (1983), these scientific definitions were used primarily in medical diagnosis and treatment, while the political definitions were used to create and monitor health and safety regulations and make compensation eligibility determinations. She suggests that while we must accept separate scientific and political definitions of occupational diseases, in reality these definitions are generally formulated in the context of constant interaction between scientists and politicians. Not only are political actions both stimulated and threatened by scientific findings, but the direction and credibility of scientific research are influenced by political interests.

With regard to both black and brown lung, the guiding questions for research were the by-products of political concern. Even though scientific facilities were available in the United States when Britain did much of its research in the 1930's, political interest did not exist here until the 1960's. Scientific findings also affected the political process, as research observations provided support for labor groups' claims that dust in both the coal mines and textile mills made them unhealthy places to work. Scientific findings were in turn affected by the political process because information gathered from workers was influenced by economic considerations. Coal miners were said to exaggerate their symptoms in order to win black lung benefits while cotton textile workers were said to minimize their symptoms in order to avoid losing their jobs (Bronstein 1983).

Others have suggested that the politicalization of defining occupational diseases must go much farther. Vicente Navarro suggests that understanding the evolution and causality of black lung in the United States must come not from just the natural history of the disease, but from an understanding of the class power relations and how that class struggle shaped "both the scientific definition, recognition and knowledge of black lung in the United State and the actual production and distribution of that disease" (p. 30). While Navarro recognizes the achievements of occupational health legislation based upon political definitions, the limitations of legislation result from manipulation by the components and strata of the capitalist class who are affected by the legislation. He argues that there needs to be not only continuous pressure from the working class on the legislative process but also a working class science to complement traditional science. This is necessary because "the power relations in society appear also within scientific knowledge, and the bourgeoisie ideological dominance appears and is being reproduced in the production of knowledge itself" (p. 31).

"Scientific" documents about both black lung and brown lung had concluded that either neither existed in the United States or that they were not causally linked to the workplace. These findings were considered trustworthy because they were scientific, but the knowledge accumulated by generations of coal miners and textile workers, knowledge which appeared in their culture as folk sons and popular writings—that work in the mines or the mills was destroying their lungs—was considered "cultural, folksy, ideological, and, in summary, untrustworthy" (Navarro 1983: 25). Consequently, not only was this knowledge not recognized as legitimate, but for decades little attention was given to the serious loss of health which resulted.

Navarro argues for a mass democratization in the process of the creation of knowledge and a deprofessionalization of science. This would result in a change in the method and creation of knowledge, i.e., "knowledge created not by the few—the scientists—but the many—the working classes and popular masses." This would require not only a change in the power relations in the creation of knowledge, with the working class being the agents and not the objects of that knowledge, but also a professional and political commitment by scientists to the working class. More importantly, it would require a struggle for democracy in the workplace and in our society, to include participation by the working class in all economic, political and social institutions, including medical/scientific institutions (p. 25).

A similar idea is gaining some acceptance in the social sciences under the topic of "participatory research." The basic idea of what political scientist John Gaventa has called "research by the people" is to "break down the distinction between the researchers and the researched, the subjects and objects of knowledge production by the participation of the people-for-themselves in the process of gaining and creating knowledge." Research, then, is not only a process for creating knowledge, but for "education and development of consciousness, and of mobilization for action" (Gaventa, forthcoming).

In the area of occupational health, this idea is best reflected in the many "right-to-know" movements which have challenged the corporate and medical communities' control over information about toxic chemicals and hazardous waste. Both coal miners and textile workers not only had difficulty gaining access to knowledge controlled by these institutions but also found their own experience was not highly valued by those who maintained this control. Interestingly, much of their "folk knowledge" turned out to be true, and ultimately verified by both the medical community and government policy. The question, then, is how do we integrate both scientific knowledge and the knowledge of workers themselves about occupational health issues? More specifically, what kind of structure in the workplace would facilitate this process? The concept of workplace democracy is one possible alternative.

Workplace Democracy: An Alternative Approach?

Some support for these ideas, even if for different reasons, has emerged within more traditional, and even conservative, elements within society. Although its initial proponents came from the academic community, many corporations have investigated at least some of the ideas behind the concept of "workplace democracy." Sociologist Severyn Bruyn (1983) maintains that the trend has generally developed at three levels of corporate activity: in the formation of quality circles and autonomous work groups at lower levels of management; in the establishment of labor management committees which are concerned with productivity and improving working conditions at middle levels of administration; and in the provision of opportunities for employee ownership and employee representation on boards of directors at top levels of management.

As of 1984, the International Association of Quality Circles reported a membership of over 2000 companies. Harvard Business Review estimated that over 90% of the Fortune 500 companies had quality circles in 1985. As of 1987, it is estimated that there were 8,000 companies with Employ Stock Option Plans, with approximately 8 million worker participants (Noble 1988: 4). However, only 1,000 to 1,500 of these are majority employee owned firms. Only about 3 in 10 have full voting rights and only about 4 percent include non-managerial employee representatives on their boards of directors (Noble 1988: 202).

The more radical fringe of this movement has suggested that the transformation necessary is not simply "workplace" but national "economic" democracy, which would transfer capital from the corporations to the public, so that people who work and consume can collectively and democratically decide what to do with it (Carnoy and Shearer 1980). Workplace democracy and economic democracy do not necessarily coincide, however. Public ownership of industry and reforms that shift power over investment decisions to workers and consumers do not necessarily produce firms which are democratic and nonhierarchical in structure. Democratic decision-making, therefore, requires worker control at the plant level (Carnoy and Shearer 1980: 27).

Although still an emerging perspective, the trend toward workplace and economic democracy adds an alternative to the traditional approaches to occupational health through collective bargaining and government regulation. The significance of government intervention has been well established, particularly since the passage of the 1970 Occupational Safety and Health Act. Even if we accept the argument that it may have been passed as only a symbolic gesture by the Nixon administration to win support from labor (Calavita 1983), its impact on the development of the occupational health movement has been substantial. As Lloyd McBride, President of the Steelworkers of American put it, OSHA "uncorked a bottle of knowledge on workplace hazards and unleashed an educational process which has awakened workers to the dangers they confront on the job" (quoted in Calavita 1983: 444).

The general approach to OSHA has been through rule based strategies of state regulation which generally specify what conditions are to be allowed and disallowed. However, as Carmen Sirianni points out,

> the limitations of rule-based strategies have become more and more apparent, and the rights of workers themselves to participate in the process of making workplaces more healthful and safe, as well as their competence in establishing appropriate norms for the work environment, have been increasingly recognized (1987: 18).

These limitations are evident in a 1985 report by the Congressional Office of Technology Assessment (OTA) which shows that, in its then thirteen years of existence, OSHA had issued only twelve new or revised standards for chemical substances, and inspections were extremely rare, even in the most dangerous types of workplaces. The agency was able to inspect only about 4 percent of the 4.6 million workplaces each year and only about 20 percent of manufacturing establishments, which are more hazardous (OTA Report 1985: 1, 5). Even though 7,000 people die each year from work related accidents, OSHA has referred only 42 cases for criminal prosecution since 1970. Of these, only 14 cases have been prosecuted, and convictions have been handed down in only 10 (Committee Critizies OSHA 1989: 18). Part of this failure can be attributed to insufficient resources and funds, which are cut substantially during the Reagan administration. However, OSHA's situation points to the problem of a primary dependence on the government for protection, because, in a relatively short period of time, changing administrations can undo much of what has been accomplished (see Szasz 1984).

The major means by which unions have attempted to improve safety and health conditions since 1970 have been to amend and improve the law, expand standards, and improve administrative practices. Many OSHA proposals have infringed upon collective bargaining agreements, which made OSHA more responsive to trade unions programs for input into their process of rules, regulations, and enforcement programs. Also, the complexity of occupational health and safety issues has resulted in more sophisticated language during contract time, as workers have continued to use established forms of labor relations to address occupational hazards (Goldsmith and Kerr 1982). However, research by Lawrence Bacow (1980) suggests that bargaining is generally confined to rather narrow safety issues and that little bargaining activity is directed at specific occupational hazards.

A survey done prior to OSHA's formation revealed that union leadership thought that money rather than working conditions deserved the most attention, although unionized rank and file workers felt that good health and safety practices and worker's compensation were top priorities. Similar studies have documented that employed persons in general stress the importance of health and safety conditions (Berman 1978; Noble 1986).

Even if union leaders do continue to stress health and safety, the dwindling number of unionized employees not only limits the potential power to affect change, but also means that over four fifths of our nation's employed would not be able to avail themselves of this power. Furthermore, are the economic conditions always going to encourage bargaining for health, particularly in a recession economy with jobs in demand?

Although it is anticipated that government regulations and union activity will continue to play important roles in advancing the cause of occupational health, those who have been able to organize effectively around safety and health issues have increasingly found that the fundamental requirement for social change is democracy in the workplace (Calavita 1983). They argue that workers have a right to know about dangers in the work environment but they also need to be able to participate in the detection, evaluation, and reduction of workplace hazards (Deutsch 1981; Sirianni 1987). The main goal of the Occupational Safety and Health Act of 1970, "to assure as far as possible every working man and woman in the nation safe and healthful working conditions and to preserve our human resources," (*All About OSHA* 1976: 1) may be possible to achieve only if workers are active participants.

A Cross-Cultural Perspective

Although a few firms have adopted policies increasing worker participation in decision making, true workers' control is very rare in the United States. Much of what we do know comes from West Germany, France, Italy, Sweden, Norway, and Canada. According to Yassi, "worker participation, worker rights, and worker control in occupational health and safety matters" has become increasingly entrenched in many of these countries (1988: 689).

One of the more interesting worker experiments is occurring in Italy, which in the late 1960s began to develop a worker-based model of occupational health. Homogeneous groups of workers who experience similar exposures to hazards and work related health problems work collectively to gain knowledge about occupational health problems and exercise power to correct hazardous conditions (Reich and Goldman 1984). The model legitimized worker's subjective reactions to workplace exposures and identification of symptoms and workplace hazards as important as statistical and experimental verification of health conditions. Similar efforts to seek worker's knowledge as informational input have been utilized in France and Canada (Mergler 1987).

In Italy, this movement eventually resulted in the formation of regional occupational health programs, built upon the worker based model, which provided an important link between traditional health services and workers. This decentralization was viewed as compatible with the principles of participatory democracy and worker input. However, research by Calavita (1987) found that those regions which had implemented these new programs had health and safety records which differed little from those regions which did not have decentralized programs. She attributes the failure of decentralization to a fundamental contradiction within a capitalist economy between the drive to maximize profits and the health of workers who produce those profits. In addition, uneven economic development forced regional agencies to frequently choose between jobs and safety.

Occupational health worker-controlled centers have emerged in three Canadian provinces in the last decade. One of the main differences between these and traditional programs is that there is less of a concern with absenteeism or the reduction of compensation claims (usually concerns for management) and more with exposure to long term hazards. In addition, instead of focusing on programs which physicians are capable of implementing, the centers are designed to allow for "time, energy, and multidisciplinary expertise needed to educate workers about hazards, control measures, and their rights under the law" (Yassi 1988: 692).

Although little data are available yet to measure changes in occupational health and safety statistics, there is some evidence that worker-controlled occupational health centers may have a substantial impact on the occupational health community. Mergler (1987), an occupational physiologist working with a worker participatory occupational health research group in Canada, points to several projects in fish processing plants and poultry slaughterhouses where worker input, both in information and project design, has been critical to conclusions reached about occupational health issues. Yassi (1988) found a significant increase in the number of government advisory committee reports, discussion papers, and conferences which have addressed issues in occupational health services in Canada. He also points out that, in contrast to the Italian worker-based model, Canadian centers have not created tensions between workers and experts and the diversity of workers involved has generally enhanced, rather than inhibited, the collective ability to identify and address common occupational health problems.

In the United States, no comparable movement for workers' control of occupational health, through centers or otherwise, has evolved. The plywood industry, which has had worker cooperative firms for several years, does provide some evidence, although not necessarily promising. Research by Leon Grunberg (1987) found that worker cooperative firms tend to have both worse productivity and accident records than conventional firms. Grunberg points out that the values and orientations of the external environment, in this case industrial capitalism, have tended to swamp and submerge the values of the democratic workplace. It is only when there is generalized workers' control (on a national and perhaps international level) that workers' safety and health will not be subjected to these systemic limits (Grunberg 1983: 633). Similar results were found by Edward Greenberg (1986) in a study of the Pacific Northwest plywood cooperatives.

One other form of worker participation that is expected to have an impact on occupational health and safety in the United States is the labor-management health and safety committee. In 1982, OSHA promulgated regulations fostering experimental work in this area. Sweden is a good role model for such committees, where more than 110,000 union health and safety representatives have been trained for 40 hours or more in worker health and safety. Union-management committees have the power to hire and fire health and safety personnel, to stop the production process when they see a hazard, and to plan aspects of production using chemicals. Statistics which indicate that Sweden appears to have a lower death rate and a lower occupational injury and illness rate are provided as evidence of the program's success (Lichty 1983).

In the United States in 1970, 31% of industrial contracts covering 1000 or more workers had provisions establishing joint union management committees. By 1983, this percentage had increased to 45%. Research by Kochan, Dyer, and Lipsky (1977) concluded that such committees were most successful when OSHA pressure and the local union were perceived to be strong and the rank-and-file involvement in health and safety issues was substantial. However, research by Cooke and Gautschi (1981) in Maine and Boden et al. (1984) in Massachusetts suggest that the existence of joint labor-management health and safety committees had virtually no effect on the number of OSHA complaints or workplace hazardousness, as measured by OSHA serious citations (Boden et al. 1984).

Perhaps somewhat more promising is the recent growth of grassroots coalitions for occupational safety and health (COSH). Funding and support from OHSA's New Directions Program, which supported worker education programs, in the late 1970s, spurred the growth of COSH groups all over the country, most of which emerged outside of the framework of organized labor. Like many of the European examples mentioned above, they stress the legitimacy of worker knowledge and develop structures which encourage cooperation between health and safety professionals and workers (Levenstein et al. 1984).

Access to information about occupational health, a key first step to worker participation programs, has been facilitated by several recent state "right-to-know" laws and the 1983 Federal Hazard Communication Act. However, to this date, no evaluation of the 1983 program has been conducted (Niemeier 1988). Also, enforcement of this program has not been stringent and resistance by industry has encouraged a "right-to-act" campaign to give workers greater legal protection against employer retaliation and creating broader rights to monitor and demand action about hazards (Pratt 1989).

Perhaps the best evidence to support the need for greater, worker participation in research and decision making about occupational health matters comes from those companies where workplace democracy is absent. Samuel Epstein chronicles this problem in his classic account of health research in the asbestos industry. In the 1970s, the industry supported major scientific studies at several research centers and universities, all of which minimized the danger of working with asbestos. One of the most controversial of these studies, involving more than 11,000 employees and ex-employees of Quebec asbestos mines, was carried out by J. Corbett McDonald, then in the Department of Epidemiology and Public Health at McGill University. As Epstein points out:

> Major objections were directed not only at the design of the study, but at the statistical analysis of the data as well. McDonald had selected a method of

computing death rates which seemed to ignore the long latency period of lung cancer. (Epstein 1978: 90)

McDonald eventually resigned from McGill amidst the controversy and challenge from independent scientists. Similar misinformation was promulgated by a 1975 British Petroleum Corporation study which concluded that the longer one worked in a Vinyl Chloride plant, the less was the risk of getting cancer. Closer examination by NIOSH, however, questioned the interpretation of the data. Expected death rates were artificially reduced, and rates in workers with lesser exposures were artificially inflated. Re-analysis of the data by NIOSH, using standard methods, showed a clear excess of mortality from all causes and all cancers (Epstein 1978).

The control of occupational health knowledge by industry has only recently been challenged by government, universities and the medical profession. How much workers themselves know and how much this might contribute to a better understanding of worker health and safety, is still unknown. Although communication of risk to workers is currently "fashionable in the Washington regulatory community as well as among scholars" (Kasperson et al. 1988), researchers Nelkin and Brown (1984) point out that worker understanding of risk is often very deficient.

A Look Toward the Future

Although the available empirical evidence suggest mixed results for increasing workers' control as a means to improve workplace health and safety, the strength of the idea has much to recommend its continued pursuit. Still, the United States is very far behind many European countries in even laying a foundation for workers' control. Elling argues that U.S. workers are still struggling for the right to know and have not yet raised the right to refuse or the right to stop hazardous production seriously (1988). But the European situation may not be that far advanced. Gevers points out that worker representatives in the European Economic Community, whose members are obligated to implement worker participation programs, have generally been "agents of communication and information" rather than "agents of control" (1985).

Why, then, should this concept be pursued in the United States? First, the experience of coal miners, textile workers, asbestos workers, and many others suggest that rank-and-file workers, with the opportunity to participate in the decision-making process, could bring the problems of occupational disease to the attention of the medical, research, and governmental communities much earlier than they are. More specifically, they could bring to that process of deliberation a type of knowledge not available through traditional scientific avenues. This is important not just for the moral justification outlined earlier in the paper, but for very pragmatic reasons as well. The identification, detection, and treatment of most occupationally caused diseases are dependent upon the subjective knowledge which workers themselves have about the workplace and their own bodies. This does not preclude, however, as pointed out by Mergler, the use of traditional scientific information such as environmental measurements, health status, or job analysis. However,

> from a scientific point of view this information [worker's knowledge] cannot be neglected or overlooked. Furthermore, this information provides an inte-

grated perception of the work situation or of health, while measurements provide an analysis of the components (1987: 159).

A second reason is that it is consistent with the ideas of workplace and economic democracy, and these ideas are merely an extension of the basic foundations upon which our political system is built. Although the specific nature of programs that will best serve the health and safety needs of workers is yet to be determined, current experimentation with everything from joint labor-management committees to worker cooperatives seems promising. At the same time, we must keep in mind that some of the strongest resistance to workplace democracy has come from American labor unions. Many union representatives have argued that the underlying theme of cooperation rather than conflict is nothing more than management's attempt to reduce or eliminate the power of established worker organizations. It also blurs the distinction between employees and employers—the distinction which gives unions and union officials their identity (see Parker and Slaughter 1988).

Writing in a recent issue of *Labor Notes*, Kim Moody (1989) argues that the quality of working life programs and the "team concept" have actually resulted from the failure to fulfill the democratic promise of unionism on the job. The new cooperation will not make a more democratic workplace, just a less democratic union. However, as Gevers points out, worker representatives will have to collaborate with employers or occupational health care may be left to "institutions over which they will have only indirect and limited control" (1985: 228).

The significance of the active rank and file worker must also be underscored. Although the Black Lung and Brown Lung Associations were important to advancing the occupational health movement, it must be remembered that almost all of the members of both movements were retired and disabled workers. Their participation was facilitated by the fact that they had very little to lose (such as their jobs) and much to gain (worker's compensation). Also, neither the black lung nor brown lung movements had prevention as their primary goal. Although much attention was given to the cotton dust standard, retired and disabled mill workers were more easily mobilized in the struggle for compensation. The Black Lung Association was almost totally dedicated to the issues of worker's compensation and the Black Lung Benefits Program. Sociologist Barbara Smith suggests that, for miners, "this was partly due to the initial, erroneous view that the cost of state compensation (financed by industry) would force the companies to improve health conditions in the mines." Smith recognized that industrial democracy might have been a better preventive strategy:

> A lasting and effective preventive campaign would have required a tighter alliance between working miners, disabled miners and widows; a much firmer conviction that black lung [was] not inevitable, and, at least eventually, a political vision of how miners might improve their occupational health by asserting greater control over the workplace (Smith 1983: 51).

A third reason is that increasing workers' control, at least at a certain level, may help to shift our priorities from profits and productivity to a greater concern for health and welfare. Philosopher Mary Gibson (1983) asserts that the real issue behind workplace health and safety in general and specifically the right of workers to know about the hazards with which they are working is control of the workplace.

Employers correctly foresee that recognition and implementation of the right to know threatens to undermine what has long been recognized as the employers' prerogative to make all decisions about what to do and how to do it. It threatens also to reverse the trend of ever-increasing division and routinization of tasks with its attendant de-skilling and relative interchangeability and replaceability of workers, which in turn keeps the workforce disciplined and makes the employers' decision-making prerogative seem natural and inevitable (Gibson 1983: 53).

But an ideological shift must also be accompanied by creation of structures which encourage active worker participation, particularly in the identification of yet undiscovered hazards in industry. One of the most recent strategies for addressing this problem is the use by large companies in the United States of computer based systems to store and integrate information on worker exposures and medical illnesses. As one observer has pointed out, these sophisticated systems were designed with input from a number of professionals: "industrial hygienists, epidemiologists, physicians, information scientists, programmers, systems analysts, toxicologists and nurses" (Joiner 1982: 863–866). Michael Reich and Rose Goldman observe that "noticeably absent... [is] any mention of workers—the most intimately involved persons in the work process, whose experience could contribute significantly to the development of systems for gathering and using the data" (1984: 1038).

Finally, we must keep in mind that creating worker participation, even worker control, within one firm, or perhaps even a number of firms within an industry, will not automatically alter the structure sufficiently to allow workers to make decisions that will dramatically improve their health and safety. As labor historian Alan Derickson has concluded, "No worthwhile purpose is served by romanticizing the prospects for workplace democracy" (1988: 221). The experience of the plywood firms studied by Greenberg and Grunberg are instructive here. Perhaps the only large enterprises in the United States where workers have been in control—of everything from the work process itself to what is produced—the plywood firms do not seem to produce either better records of health and safety or even better attitudes on health and safety among the workers. In effect, the experience of "democracy, equality and self management" in the plywood firms did not produce attitudes and behaviors which are consistent with democratic self government but which were consistent with the prevailing climate in the United States. Workers became more committed to basic values associated with market capitalism and grew less willing to support democratic control of the economic institutions in America (Greenberg 1986). However, Greenberg argues that, in a more hospitable economic and political environment, workplace democracy could flourish. Consequently, it can be achieved in the United States only if it is part of a "larger struggle for popular democracy and equality" (p. 171). The struggle for worker control of occupational health, then, must not be viewed as an isolated effort, but must be incorporated into a broader venture for economic as well as workplace democracy, to include a transformation of medical, educational, and research institutions as well as industrial policy.

References

All About OSHA. 1976. Programs and Policy Series, U.S. Department of Labor.
Bacow, Lawrence S. 1980. *Bargaining for Job Safety and Health*. Cambridge: MIT Press.
Berman, Dan. 1978. *Death on the Job*. New York: Monthly Review Press.

Bernstein, Paul. 1982. "Necessary Elements for Effective Worker Participation in Decision-Making," in *Workplace Democracy and Social Change*, edited by Frank Lindenfeld and Joyce Rothschild-Whitt. Boston, MA: Porter Sargent Publishers.

Boden, Leslie I., et al. 1984. "The Impact of Health and Safety Committees," *Journal of Occupational Medicine*, Vol. 26, No 11, November.

Bronstein, Janet. "Science and Policy: Controversies in the Definition of Black Lung and Brown Lung," paper presented at the AAAS Meetings in Detroit, May, 1983.

Bruyn, Severyn T. 1983. "On Becoming a Democratically Managed Firm," *The Social Report,* June.

Calavita, Kitty. 1983. "The Demise of the Occupational Safety and Health Administration," *Social Problems*, April.

Calavita, Kitty. "Political Decentralization and Worker Safety in Italy," in *International Journal of Sociology and Social Policy*, edited by Bennett M. Judkins, February, 1987, Vol. 6, No. 4.

Carnoy, Martin and Derek Shearer. 1980. *Economic Democracy*. White Plains, New York: M.E. Sharpe.

Derickson, Alan. 1988. *Workers' Health, Workers' Democracy. The Western Miners' Struggle, 1891–1925.* Ithaca, NY: Cornell University Press.

Deutsch, Steven. 1981. "Introduction: Theme Issue on Occupational Safety and Health." *Labor Studies Journal*, Spring, p. 128.

Deutsch, Steven. 1981. "Extending Workplace Democracy: Struggles to Come in job Safety and Health." *Labor Studies Journal,* Spring.

Dorman, Peter. 1985 A Negotiable 'Workers-Rights' Model of Occupational Safety Policy," November, (Unpublished).

Elling, Ray. 1988. "Workers' Health and Safety (WHS) in Cross National Perspective," *American Journal of Public Health*, July, pp. 769–771.

Epstein, Samuel S. 1978. *The Politics of Cancer*. Sierra Club Books, San Francisco.

Gevers; J.K.M: 1985. "Worker Control Over Occupational Health Services: The Development of Legal Rights in the EEC," *International Journal of Health Services*, Volume 15, Number 2, pp. 217–229.

Gersuny, Carl. 1981. *Work Hazards and Industrial Conflict*. Hanover, NH: University Press of New England.

Gibson, Mary. 1983. *Workers' Rights*. Totowa, NJ: Rowman and Allanheld.

Goldsmith, Frank and Lorin E. Kerr. 1982. *Occupational Safety and Health*. New York: Human Sciences Press, Inc.

Greenberg, Edward S. 1986. *Workplace Democracy: The Political Effects of Participation*. Ithaca, NY: Cornell University Press.

Gries, M. Walton. 1984. "Safety Professional's Role as Health Educator," *Occupational Health and Safety*, February, pp. 42–43.

Grunberg, Leon. 1987. "Safety, Productivity and the Social Relations in Production: An Empirical Study of Worker Cooperatives," *International Journal of Sociology and Social Policy*, edited by Bennett M. Judkins, February, Volume 6, Number 4.

_____. 1983. 'The Effects of the Social Relations of Production on Productivity and Workers' Safety: An Ignored Set of Relationships," *International Journal of Health Services*, Volume 13, Number 4, Baywood Publishing.

Grunberg, Leon, et al. 1984. "Productivity and Safety in Worker Cooperatives and Conventional Firms," *International Journal of Health Services*, Volume 14, Number 3.

"If Not Now, When?" *Social Policy*, January/February, 1981, p. 3.

Joiner, R.L. 1982. "Occupational Health and Environmental Information Systems: Basic Considerations," *Journal of Occupational Medicine*, Volume 24, pp. 863–866.

Judkins, Bennett M. 1979. "Social Movements and Social Structure," in research on *Social Movements, Conflicts, and Change*, vol. II, edited by Louis Kriesberg, JAI Press, pp. 105–129.

_____. 1982A. "Mobilization of Membership in Social Movements," in *Social Movements of the Sixties and Seventies*, edited by Jo Freeman, Longman, pp. 35–51.

____. 1982. "Occupational Health and the Developing Consciousness of Southern Textile Workers," *The Maryland Historian*, Volume XIII, Number 1, Spring/Summer, pp. 55–71.

____. 1986. *We Offer Ourselves as Evidence: Toward Workers' Control of Occupational Health*. New York: Greenwood Press.

Judkins, Bennett M. and Bart Dredge. (Forthcoming.) "The Brown Lung Association: Grass Roots Organizing in the Textile Industry, "Chapter 9 of *Hanging by a Thread: Social Change in Southern Textiles*, edited by Jeffrey Leiter, Michael Schulman, and Rhonda Zingraff.

Krause, Elliot. 1977. *Power and Illness: The Political Sociology of Health and Medical Care*. New York: Elsevier.

Levenstein, Charles, et al. 1984. "COSH: A Grass Roots Public Health Movement," *American Journal of Public Health,* September.

Levi, Lennart. 1981. *Preventing Work Stress*. Reading, Mass: Addison-Wesley.

Lichty, Mark E. 1983. "Avoid Litigation through Cooperation," *Occupational Health and Safety,* September, pp. 42–47.

McCarthy, Coleman. 1978. "Industry's Assault of Workplace Safety." *The Washington Post,* September 19.

McLaughlin, Curtis P. 1982. "Perspectives on the Cotton Dust Standard," paper presented at conference sponsored by the North Carolina Humanities Committee, September 25, Durham, North Carolina.

Mergler, Donna. 1987. "Worker Participation in Occupational Health Research," *International Journal of Health Services,* Volume 17, Number 1.

Min, Anselm. 1982. "Human Life: Its Value and Price," paper presented at conference sponsored by the North Carolina Humanities Committee on the cotton dust standard in Charlotte, North Carolina, September, 19.

Montgomery, David. 1980. *Workers' Control in America.* Cambridge, MA: Cambridge University Press.

Navarro, Vicente. 1983. "Work Ideology and Science: The Case of Medicine" in V. Navarro and Dan Berman, editors, *Health and Work Under Capitalism*. Farmingdale, New York: Baywood.

Niemeier, Richard. 1988. Acting Director, Divisions of Standards Development and Technology Transfer, NIOSH, letter to author dated December 9.

Noble, Charles. 1986. *Liberalism at Work? The Rise and Fall of OSHA*. Philadelphia, PA: Temple.

"OTA Report is Critical of Workplace Protection," *The Nation's Health*, May/June, 1985.

Parker, Mike and Jane Slaughter. 1988. *Choosing Sides: Unions and the Team Concept*. Boston: South End Press.

Pratt, David. 1989. "'Right to Act': Next Goal of Health and Safety Organizers," *Labor Notes,* January.

Reich, Michael E. and Rose H. Goldman. 1984. "Italian Occupational Health: Concepts, Conflicts, Implications." *American Journal of Public Health*. September, Vol. 74, No. 9.

Sirianni, Carmen. 1987. "Worker Participation in the Late Twentieth Century: Some Critical Issues." In *Worker Participation and the Politics of Reform*, ed. by Carmen Sirianni. Philadelphia: Temple University Press, pp 3–33.

Smith Barbara. 1983. "Black Lung: The Social Production of Disease," in Navarro and Berman, *Health and Work Under Capitalism.*

Szasz, Andrew. 1984. "Industrial Resistance to Occupational Safety and Health Legislation: 1971–1981," *Social Problems*, Vol. 32, No. 2, December.

Whitt, Richard. 1985. "Black Lung Program is Costly for States, Lucrative for Miners," *Louisville-Courier Journal*, January 27.

Wildavsky, Aaron. 1988. *Searching for Safety*. New Brunswick: Transaction Books.

Yassi, Annalee. 1988. "The Development of Worker-Controlled Occupational Health Centers in Canada," *American Journal of Public Health*, June.

Zwerdling, Daniel. 1980. *Workplace Democracy.* New York: Harper and Row.

Reflections on Judkins' "Workplace Democracy and Occupational Health"[1]

Charles Koeber
Wichita State University

Occupational health and safety is a sadly neglected issue. As Jeffrey Reiman points out in his classic critical criminology text *The Rich Get Richer and the Poor Get Prison*, occupational disease and hazard are most often (mis)construed and (mis)understood as accidents and tragedies—the result of carelessness and error, and not as preventable dangers, often imposed by employers who knowingly expose workers to unnecessary risks.

According to Reiman, in 1997 more than 31,000 United States workers died and 3,600,000 were injured or became ill as a result of occupational disease and accidents. Those numbers are staggeringly larger than the 18,000 deaths and 1,000,000 injuries that occurred from conventional street crime during the same year (Reiman 2001: 82). These statistics suggest that contrary to popular belief, the gravest threat to life and limb may not be posed by street criminals lurking in dark alleys with guns and knives, but by employers and unsafe workplaces.

Judkins is not only keenly aware of this significant threat and danger, but is driven by a progressive vision of and desire for a safer and more democratically controlled workplace. His interest is not only academic, but grounded in life experience, growing up in southern Virginia where he witnessed the detrimental health effects of work in the mining and textile industries.

By tracing the historical development of two social movements—one for increased worker participation and the other for occupational health and safety—Judkins poses and addresses an important and original question: "Would increasing workers' control over the means of production improve the quality of health and safety in the workplace?"

According to Judkins, the results are mixed, but perhaps more importantly, point to several pressing issues and questions. These include:

- How do we know what serious dangers are in the workplace when "scientific" research has been politically biased?
- Given their institutional limitations, to what extent can government rules and agencies (such as OSHA) ensure safer workplaces?
- Can a dwindling number of unionized workers effectively participate to make workplaces safer and more democratic?
- Without broader economic democracy in society, can democracy confined to the workplace bring about significant improvements in occupational health?

[1]This paper originally appeared in *Humanity & Society* Volume 27, Number 4, 2003.

- Is occupational health limited by the differing labor histories and levels of worker power across cultures?

- Within a capitalist economy, where profit is a requirement of doing business, might workers who control their own workplace choose to sacrifice their health and safety for the financial interest of the enterprise?

Occupational health and safety is a not only a generally neglected topic, but is also absent from most worker participation studies. For example, *Manufacturing Advantage* (Applebaum et al. 2000), a comprehensive study of high performance work systems, does not attempt to measure health and safety, accident rates, etc., in more participatory "high performance" work environments. Like many studies of worker participation, it does address workers' levels of job satisfaction and job stress. However, these concerns tend to be subsumed by and linked to larger concerns about efficiency and productivity.

Therefore, Judkins offers fresh and sorely needed perspective: rather than looking at occupational health and safety in conventional terms of business cost versus benefit, or by examining performance measures of workplace participation, he views the problem humanistic terms—that is, he explores how workers might better control the conditions of their work and in so doing improve their health and safety?

More than ten years after publication, I am skeptical that the current kind of worker participation, most often practiced in large business organizations, can make adequate improvements in workplace health and safety in the United States. In fact, much research has shown that participation in the workplace is mainly limited to that which will improve efficiency and productivity. For example, Kaizen or Continuous Improvement can be understood as a form of participation in which workers offer suggestions to management about ways in which to "hyper-Taylorize" their work. When accompanied by new Just-In-Time inventory systems, teams of workers may participate under a form of "management by stress" that may *increase* the risk for "accidents" and repetitive motion injuries.

Under current economic conditions characterized by both cyclical and structural unemployment, many workers fear that voicing concerns about safety may jeopardize their jobs. These fears are warranted. In addition to a shortage of jobs, employers have become freer to increase their control over the workplace and reduce their business costs (including those incurred by health and safety requirements) by simply moving facilities elsewhere in the world.

Finally, the conservative political climate is a hostile one in which to forge safer and more democratic workplaces. The Bush administration has opposed policy that would make workplaces safer. For instance, it worked diligently to strike down ergonomic standards carefully crafted by the Department of Labor over a period of many years. The administration rejected them primarily because of the monetary cost on employers.

Given recent political and economic developments, it is all too tempting to become cynical and apathetic. However, Judkins reminds us that, historically, social movements can and have increased control by workers and improved workplace health and safety. Unions, especially those attempting to organize low-wage and immigrant workers, continue to place occupational health and safety high on their agenda of concerns. Len Krimerman and Frank Lindenfield (1992) document many successful workplace democracies in the increasing number and diversity of employee-owned and controlled cooperatives.

These examples offer not just rhetorical participation but actual workers' power. The situation is far from hopeless.

Therefore, conclusions reached by Judkins remain not only valid, but all the more pressing in the 21st century. Workers must push on to increase their control of workplaces as a means by which to improve workplace health and safety. They must build not only the structures that give them more control, but also the ideological frameworks that prioritize health and welfare over profits and productivity.

References

Appelbaum, Eileen, et al. 2000. *Manufacturing Advantage: Why High Performance Work Systems Pay Off.* Economic Policy Institute. Ithaca: ILR Press

Krimerman, Len and Lindenfeld, Frank. 1992. *Workplace Democracy Takes Root in North America.* Philadephia: New Society Publishers.

Reiman, Jeffrey 2001. *The Rich Get Richer and the Poor Get Prison*, Ideology, Class and Criminal Justice. Boston: Allyn and Bacon.

3. Healing Brokenness:
Gay Volunteerism and AIDS[1,2]

Philip M. Kayal
Seton Hall University

Reflexive Statement

AIDS is social and medical disaster played out, for the most part, in the bodies of gay men. Often overlooked, is the good news in AIDS—the voluntary response and commitment of the gay community to People with AIDS (PWAs), without regard to race, sex, or sexual orientation. This story of what volunteers have done against great odds to contain AIDS and to bear witness to those suffering horrendous mental and physical pain (as well as discrimination) needs to be told while the memories and people who bear them remain alive. The only way to capture the experience of "uncertainty" in AIDS was to volunteer myself and listen to the stories of the dying, the worried-well, and their volunteer care-partners. If life is precarious, AIDS is infinitely more so. People with AIDS die many deaths, going from health to illness, fear to hope, daily. Living with the fear of AIDS is equally crippling. Having virtually lost my entire social network to this disease, I have committed myself to recognizing and celebrating the help and assistance PWAs received at New York City's Gay Men's Health Crisis, Inc. This paper attempts to identify the significance of gay/AIDS volunteerism in the transformation of gay relationships, the healing of homophobia, and the empowerment of the gay community.

Introduction

AIDS is as much a social problem as it is a crisis in individual health and medical care. Because it primarily affects whole classes of people (gay men and minority drug-users), it is, of necessity, an illness rooted in social structure and interpersonal relationships. Solving the "problem of AIDS" requires healing the brokenness and maladaptive behavior that living on the margins causes, and which being diagnosed or associated with AIDS, increases (Cohen and Weisman 1986).

Being surrounded with moral meanings, AIDS, as an illness, is distinctively American (Osborn, 1989). Because both gays and drug-users live daily with stigma and social approbation, it is not surprising that these populations would be the most susceptible to a disease

---

[1] This paper is part of a larger study of gay/AIDS volunteerism begun in 1986 at New York's Gay Men's Health Crisis, Inc. Titled *Bearing Witness: Volunteerism in AIDS*, the manuscript is being prepared for publication.
[2] This paper originally appeared in *Humanity & Society* Volume 14, Number 3, 1990.

causing pathogen like HIV while at the same time being blamed for its occurrence. It is, therefore, the social context and character of AIDS which allows the disease to fulminate unchecked. Virtually everyone with AIDS is a member of a disenfranchised minority, the "heterosexualization of AIDS" notwithstanding (Fumento 1989).

Equally unique is the distinctive reaction to AIDS by American gays. AIDS united the gay community in a common struggle for survival, producing the phenomenon of gay/AIDS volunteerism. Not only is AIDS volunteerism a response to "deafening silence" (Denneny 1990), but being willing to do "dirty work" in an epidemic is, more importantly, a proclamation of communal and self-pride. Hence, it is a political activity. This is especially significant because of the mixing of "morals" with medicine in the social construction of AIDS (Kayal 1985). This fact, more than any other, has legitimated the social distancing from both gays and People with AIDS (PWAs), with the former, as a group, being held most responsible for its occurrence and spread. In this paradigm, of course, gays are now being punished for their deviance.

If AIDS, as an illness, primarily affects the "disinherited," often turned into "others" by the stigma surrounding both sexual activity outside marriage and/or drug-use, then, AIDS must be acknowledged and challenged publicly by gays to be contained. This cannot be done until homophobia, the inordinate fear and loathing of homosexuals, is healed.

Homophobia is the central issue in AIDS and gays have had to fight both its internalized and institutionalized form to survive. Unintentionally, the overlap of homosexuality and AIDS has joined the interests of the individual with that of the community and its needs. Both became politicized in reaction to the prevailing homophobic social environment. AIDS is, therefore, responsible for the contemporary phenomenon of AIDSHOMO-PHOBIA, which, itself, has transformed AIDS into a social event. In AIDS, "both the individual and the community are threatened with irreparable loss (Denneny 1990: 16)." This is why and how AIDS is social in character.

Gays are the most vulnerable, most desperate, and, hence, the most likely and able to respond to AIDS. They are also the most capable and motivated because the political truly becomes personal in AIDS, which threatens gay life, culture, and civil rights in their entirety. For many mainstream "insiders," one disease (homosexuality) merely produces another (AIDS). If left alone, each would simultaneously resolve the other problem. In any case, gays would lose.

Given its social positioning, any identification with AIDS means being perceived as either a gay activist/supporter, or a person with AIDS. This is stigmatizing because gays suffer with moral oppression and are subsequently perceived as deficient social misfits, threatening the ideologies and interests of the "moral majority." AIDSWORK, directly or by association, thus, becomes suspect work, done by deviants for "outsiders."

Yet, AIDS associated problems cannot be successfully managed or addressed by individuals for private benefit alone. If the solution to all social problems is in the political domain, then, AIDS must become a public issue, on the terms of the affected as a community, for the crisis to be resolved. Because AIDS is an illness of specific populations, problems and needs are met only when an effective community of interest and concern is both established and sustained. With community, challenges to prevailing social arrangements can be mounted.

Until the recent democratization of AIDS, popularized by Dr. Matilda Krim, co-founder with actress Elizabeth Taylor, of AmFar, the American Foundation for AIDS Research

(Johnson 1988), virtually no heterosexuals were publicly involved with or concerned about AIDS on any level of competence or scholarship (Ships 1987). The "now, no one is safe" scare of *Newsweek* and *Time* magazine, however, increased interest, if only in esoteric academic and scientific areas. While gay people and life became acceptable subjects of research and concern, they did so only through the lens of disease and illness.

Social science interest in AIDS rose dramatically as funding projects became less identified with gays and more with AIDS as a generalized problem. The loyalties and sympathies of researchers would remain unquestioned, identity and commitments unspoiled, perhaps even enhanced, for being concerned about a "public health crisis," rather than a "gay plague."

The stigma of AIDSWORK is evidenced by the fact that virtually everyone and anyone associated with AIDS is a gay male. Over 80% of all volunteers in the United States dealing with AIDS are gay men with a vast remainder of volunteers being heterosexual women (Appleby and Sosnowitz 1987; Kreiger and Appleman 1986; Kayal 1987). Even on the medical, nursing, and scientific levels, insider gay doctors, researchers, and health care providers have pushed more than anyone for cures and improved social service delivery.

Often buttressed by the AIDS Coalition to Unleash Power (ACT-UP), the newest and now most powerful AIDS advocacy agency in the country (Gamson 1989), researchers, social scientists, policy makers, as well as medical institutions, have been forced by the growing AIDS lobby to confront their biases and prejudices.

Discrimination in AIDS is grounded in its "sin" association with homosexual behavior, a situation which Hunt (1987) attributes to "theological pornography," or the forced union of sexuality with reproduction and its separation in patriarchal religion from feelings and desires. Because it is non-reproductive, same-sexing is perceived of as inherently narcissistic and, thus, peculiarly suspect (Kayal 1985).

What the definition of AIDS as justified retribution for sin has done is to increase, sustain, and institutionalize homophobia. Fear of AIDS becomes the most contemporary excuse for the political majority to again, and further, depoliticize gays while legitimating their own power. Writing in 1984, Ann Guidici Fettner, co-author of *The Truth About AIDS*, identifies the relationship between AIDS, minority status, and public concern:

> I never realized the depth of prejudice against gays, Haitians and junkies... The lack of conscience on the part of this government has bothered me worse than anything, but it's just a crystallization of the lack of concern for the health of the population outside the politically or financially advantaged.

If the fear of AIDS is anything it is the fear of homosexuality, the guilt that comes with association with stigmatized outsiders. This is why the gay response to AIDS is so important; it confronts both internalized (on the part of gays) and institutionalized homophobia by forcing a commitment and confrontation, willingly and unwillingly, between the whole community and those filled with contempt, hate, and fear of homosexuals.

Bearing Witness

By bearing witness to PWAs, gays make AIDS a political issue defined on community terms. Bearing witness refers to what volunteers actually do and accomplish. It means "taking on the cross," or the suffering of others. "To "witness," notes Petit (1989: 43), "is not simply to make note, not simply to record, although there is a power in that. It is to go out and see what is going on."

Through volunteerism, the gay community becomes the biblical "anawin," the poor of God or the prophetic community which calls people out of isolation and into commitment to one another in a way that challenges the structural sources of AIDS indifference and discrimination.

Nothing is more surprising or threatening to "gay-bashers" and homophobes than gay pride and gay politicization. In his 1989 review of the art show Excommunication: Some Notions of Marginality, at New York University (11/7–12/22), depicting how alienation results from being hidden and pushed into a caste of undesirables, David Hirsh (1989: 36) summarizes the view of gays by the fundamentalist right wing.

> 'Abberrants' should not be recognized and should die in silence. Clearly, the censoring of marginalized populations has become a major issue, as it must when any small but highly organized minority assumes the identity of primal mover.

Why should gays, or any minority, not be primary actors in the spiral of their own lives, especially during AIDS? Identifying the response to AIDS, Kubler-Ross (1987: 155) notes that gays, who have born the stigma of the disease the longest, have, in fact, assumed the responsibility for AIDS care, having to bury hundreds of friends, often without the support of organized religion or family. "At the same time," she writes, "they have educated themselves and have organized extraordinary support systems that now serve as examples to other cities and other countries."

Of the thousands of patients she has seen all over the world, Kubler-Ross (1987: 11) notes that no one has shown such mutual support and solidarity as the AIDS patients themselves and their partners.

> Young men risked their lives in the early days of the epidemic when we were quite ignorant about the transmission of the disease. They were willing to hold those young dying men in their arms so they would not feel unloved and deserted at the end of their lives. In those days they were unaware that one could not catch the disease by sheer proximity, yet they are still willing to risk their young lives to ease their friends' suffering.

Nothing distinguishes AIDS from other diseases more than its social character as a minority illness and problem. Because people suffering with AIDS, and those bearing witness to them, are "outsiders," they are perceived of as interchangeable and are put upon in the same accusatory, suspicious, and demanding way.

It is the social contours and meaning of AIDS (Conrad 1986) and its exigencies, then, as primarily a homosexually transmitted disease, which necessitated an immediate community response on the part of gays. No one else would, no one else could, and given American ideology about community problem-solving on the local level, it is believed that no one else should.

In New York, this mobilization was begun by the Gay Men's Health Crisis, Inc. (GMHC), the largest and most successful AIDS social service and advocacy organization in the world (Lopex and Getzel, 1987). The agency had its informal beginnings in the fall of 1981 after *The New York Times* announced that an unexplainable illness was attacking homosexual men. Since that time, GMHC has grown into a corporation with its own head-quarters in the Chelsea section of Manhattan, a paid staff of 125 administering a budget of $13 million, and a reserve volunteer corps in the thousands. It now serves the psychic, financial, legal, and social welfare needs of over 35% of all cases of AIDS in New York without regard to sexual orientation, age, gender, race or nationality. Yet, nearly 80 percent of its funding comes solely from the gay community (See 1987).

By calling itself The Gay Men's Health Crisis, GMHC succinctly defines and locates the political component in AIDS. Its naming occurred concomitantly with the early identi-fication of AIDS as Gay Related Immune Dysfunction (GRID). GMHC co-founder, play-wright, Larry Kramer immediately recognized that AIDS represents a crisis in emotions, in relations, in community mental health and well being. It went well beyond science and problems in social service delivery. AIDS threatened an identity, a way of life, a com-munity, and a culture. All gay rights, not just medical entitlements, were at risk in AIDS, whether one had the disease or not.

Researching GMHC and Gay Volunteerism

In the summer of 1986, on sabbatical leave and with a grant from Seton Hall University, I begin researching what gay/AIDS volunteerism meant for the community. By becoming a volunteer myself, and, for all practical purposes, living the life of both a care-partner and PWA, I became an "insider." Even though I had not known at the time that I was HIV negative, I was able to secure the trust of the volunteers and the agency staff, unwittingly becoming myself an object of study.

Adler and Adler (1987) note that an ethnographer must be an insider when sub-cultural or "deviant" groups are involved. For me, the problem was determining the best way of understanding the volunteer experience. My instincts favored the *verstehen* (experientially intuitive) approach, but my desire for "objectivity" and accuracy pushed me into a more traditional methodology. I soon realized, however, that this could only be useful in combi-nation with my intuitive sense of what was going on.

It soon became apparent that writing about AIDS and volunteerism would not be easy. The presence of stigma, denial, stereotypes, the criminal law, etc., made it virtually impos-sible to conduct or trust traditional research or writings on gays; social, medical, philo-sophical, or otherwise. But I did learn that my *verstehen* approach to AIDS was not only central to AIDS research, but was one of the main methodological and political questions surrounding AIDS in general. Both Lessor (1987) and Murray (1987) support this thesis that the contingencies of AIDS renders typical survey research less informative or accurate than one would expect.

The question, then, of who can know, understand, and even resolve the problems of AIDS better, the outsider or the insider, remains a primary research issue. The gay commu-nity, people with AIDS themselves, so called "impartial" scientists, policy makers, moral-ists, ethicists, and bureaucrats all lay claim to "the truth about AIDS."

I similarly had to wonder whether my own experiences at GMHC and my interpreta-tions of them were generally representative of all volunteers. All I can say is that I have lived within the shadow of AIDS, GMHC's development, the volunteer experience serving

PWAs, my friends, my community, who are at risk and who responded the most desperately and devotedly. AIDS brought the reality of homophobia (whether institutionalized, internalized, communal, or personal) home to roost in a dramatic way. Fear of the disease led to an increase in violence against gays and lesbians, already settled civil rights issues were again raised, and access to employment and medical insurance became more difficult, etc. Homophobia easily become the context within which I would study and interpret AIDS volunteerism.

Studying volunteers, the afflicted with AIDS and GMHC also required subtle, yet accurate, measurements of realities not necessarily or even consciously known to either the volunteers or to GMHC staff. Indeed, it was the researcher, not the subjects, who was interpreting their behavior and its effects on gay life in atypical political terns. To be sure, there is evidence supporting my claim that by linking the self to the community as its extension, volunteerism destroyed homophobia. My problem, however, was how to conceptualize and accurately operationalize and measure concepts such as community, homophobia, nurturing, transformation, healing, and political behavior.

My choice of roles, then, from "detached observer" to "complete member" or participant observer has, in fact, affected my perspective on volunteerism. It also influenced the type of information collected, the way it was gathered, and how the volunteer experience in AIDS would be interpreted. Being a sociologist simply informed my own volunteer experience which, obviously, I believed to be typical of GMHC volunteers.

It is my impression, supported by the data (Kayal 1987), that all volunteers receive benefits and "healings" the more they lay claim to AIDS by serving and bearing witness to PWAs. By accepting all PWAs, being non-judgmental (open to all gays and lesbians, and PWAs), and defending the goodness of gay sexuality, GMHC is the setting within which an on-going process of personal and social transformation occurs for the benefit of both.

GMHC as Voluntary Association

GMHC was born in the context of a deep emotional commitment to protect "gayness" as an alternate and reasonable way of life. It is, therefore, the primary setting within which the gay civil rights movement and AIDS come together to produce a positive response against an unmitigated evil. The agency was founded by people trying to decipher the implications of a then unnamed disease striking friends and neighbors (Shilts 1987). GMHC fills the need to respond to AIDS and gives the gay community a chance to vent both anger and frustration while taking control of the situation through delivering needed and missing social services to PWAs.

On one hand, GMHC is an informal, empathetic, and activist group of volunteers, and on the other, it is a complex social agency performing all of the organizational roles that voluntary associations normally do. The difference is that GMHC does them all, rather than specializing in one, as other voluntary agencies often do.

In its vanguard role, GMHC innovates, pioneers, experiments and demonstrates alternate community based programming. As an advocator, GMHC serves as a critic and watchdog as it pressures government agencies to improve or supply services. In reflecting and sustaining American ideological beliefs about volunteerism and community, GMHC also performs a value-guardian role. GMHC's other, if not primary, institutional role is as service provider, delivering services not tended to by government (Kramer 1981: 9).

The agency exemplifies within itself most of the diversified criteria and characteristics of a successful and relevant voluntary organization. But as a community organization, it also performs many apparently paradoxical functions: it is social yet political, purposive yet pragmatic, effective yet instrumental.

GMHC has all the qualities of a "mutual-benefit" association combined with a "service organization" ethic. The public at large benefits, but so also do the clients, staff, and board of directors.' This is so because everyone involved owns the corporation. Since it bargains with prevailing social and governmental institutions, it is an interstitial social mechanism cooling out and channeling gay protest.

As a social service agency it is engaged in the production and delivery of needed social services. Yet, it also reflects and implants gay consciousness and values. The services that it performs, the direct relationship it has to clients, and the rewards it offers are the real measurement of its success.

In many ways, GMHC is like any other voluntary organization whose membership has a "specific cause" to help a specific constituency. What is so extraordinary about gay volunteerism at GMHC, however, is the organization's ability to continually harness the energy of "tarnished outsiders" to help severely "tarnished others." For all practical purposes, GMHC is a minority group effort on behalf of minority groups. This fact is the most critical for understanding the political nature and meaning of volunteerism in the age of AIDS.

Because gay/AIDS volunteerism is a social movement for justice and self-preservation, GMHC is able to sustain and be sustained by the gay community. It primarily remains, despite its growing organizational structure, a community based voluntary association. Because GMHC is its volunteers, and its volunteers are gay men, the agency is, for the longest time, the gay community interest encapsulated. By emphasizing the collective political rights of gays and medical needs of PWAs, GMHC both articulates and represents community concerns and interests.

To be sure, GMHC volunteers do perform a multitude of institutional roles ranging from the internal administration of programs and services to political advocacy and public education in the general community. As they work, volunteers protest the mistreatment of PWAs, actively and loudly demanding an end to AIDS. Volunteers also take personal care of the sick and dying, giving hope to those even more disheartened.

Moreover, in acknowledging AIDS unashamedly, GMHC volunteers destroy stereotypes and give credibility to the community. In developing supportive and innovative service programs, GMHC volunteers lighten the burden of PWAs and reaffirm the reasonableness of their need to be treated like persons and citizens.

As a social movement, GMHC began with affectivity. It has been able to maintain its expressive character because AIDS affects everyone similarly, democratizing relationships between volunteers, supporters, members, staff, and PWAs. Hierarchical barriers to communication are contained because AIDS is a shared social event, a communal crisis.

It is not that GMHC lacks bureaucracy, for it doesn't. Rather, it is the phenomenon that the care-partners and PWAs are each other that both distinguishes and characterizes gay/ AIDS volunteerism. Living daily with the human face of AIDS sets the tone and quality of the volunteer experience. GMHC's genius and usefulness, therefore, does not lie in its administrative adaptability or in its ability to successfully tap the financial resources of the gay community, but in its effect on creating self-acceptance by transforming interpersonal relationships.

These "transformations" in consciousness and linkages to "the other" means the larger gay collectivity is politically invigorated through volunteerism and the healing of homophobia. Focusing, therefore, on GMHC as solely a formal agency, will neither capture the significance of this achievement nor identify accurately the political nature of the voluntary care-partner-PWA interaction.

Volunteerism, Transformation, and Homophobia

Looking at GMHC volunteers instrumentally, as organizational members, makes gay volunteerism in AIDS seem utilitarian. This would be the conclusion in traditional research which seeks to be scientific by its reliance on quantitative methods. Such functional analyses of behavior and society makes the personal, the transformative, appear less significant. For this researcher, volunteering in AIDS is a unique phenomenon in the affective and relational domain. A social order analysis of the gay community's AIDS mobilization cannot capture the transformation in gay consciousness coming from new connections to the community as the extension of the personal self.

It is this need to establish linkages that makes gay/AIDS volunteerism in AIDS a uniquely "sacred," that is, a fundamentally political activity. Gay/AIDS volunteerism restores gays to themselves and to the community as mutual sacred sources. It politicizes by replacing broken connections to the self, and instrumental relations with the community, with more life-giving ones.

Characteristically, gay/AIDS volunteerism is political because it allows the self to confront the self in "the other." With acceptance, community (the well-spring of political action) is established and homophobia healed. Overt and traditional political activity is born in the collective experiences of people or the personal experiences of individuals as validated by a community.

AIDS brings the volunteer back to his or her sacred sources because acknowledging AIDS forces basic questions to be asked. "Perhaps unwittingly," writes Toby Johnson (1988: 77), "a major consequence of the AIDS tragedy in gay culture has been the awakening of what might be called spiritual concerns." He continues:

> For many gay people, AIDS has brought a premature acquaintance with death and a consciousness of serving the sick and needy. Such awareness of the fragility and transitoriness of life has long been considered a foundation for spiritual development. Spiritual here does not mean religious. It means seeing oneself and one's life in a larger context in which it makes sense to ask personally transcending and otherwise meaningless questions such as "What is life for?" "What's the meaning of all this?" and "Why do we die?"

When AIDS is accepted as a threat to the collective well-being of the gay community, when it is identified with and embraced as a challenge, the individual is made free of guilt and fear. By creating connections to the heart, the psyche, to the body and soul, and by making linkages to the "other" and the community which sustains them both, volunteering becomes the vehicle through which the personal and individual self is liberated and actualized. Volunteering is a statement about connections to the larger gay collectivity.

For gays, and those who live in and with community, volunteering turns "giving witness" to others into acceptance and integration of the total self. In the paradigm of transformation, this is a basic, hence, radical political act because the inner sources of sacredness are discovered through relationships to now accepted, and included, others. Through transformation, legitimacy in being a gay person is established. Justice can now be demanded. Self-acceptance requires respect, not permission.

By connecting the community and PWA in a common journey of hopeful self-discovery, volunteering reclaims sacred sources and allows the community to determine justice and truth. The existential crisis caused by AIDS is thus tempered by the willingness and ability to be empowered. So doing restores purpose because it allows the volunteer and PWA to participate as equals in the mystery of mutual self-discovery.

AIDS forces all those concerned with justice and truth back to fundamental questions: "who am I, who are "my people," why am I here, why is this happening, why is it or is it not happening to me, what should I do?" etc. In addressing these questions, the value of the personal self is rediscovered and its sacredness internalized. Volunteerism in AIDS is transformative because the sacred is recognized in commitment to others.

Since AIDS is an existential nightmare touching on feelings, sexuality, behavior, values, and relations, confronting its implications requires a redefinition of both personal and gay identities. Because of its virulence, AIDS challenges all assumptions about the overall purpose of life and the goodness of God (Gordon 1988) and society. The volunteer confronts these issues head-on and, as a result, is forced daily to replace despair with hope and faith in resurrection.

AIDS requires a journey inward, to the depths of the soul. For the gay person, it goes to the core precisely because it touches on sexuality, the desire for intimacy. This is why the religious or cultural stigma is such an important issue. As long as it is present and internalized, it restricts the development of psychic and social wellness or hope and faith in resurrection. Stigma destroys community and hinders political activity (Fortunato 1987). This is why reclaiming the sacred, or the self, through volunteerism is so necessary in AIDS: it restores the relationship between being and doing, the self and community, identity and activity, and sexuality and intimacy (Hunt 1987).

Women and gay men identifying with AIDS, therefore, challenge the cosmology of the whole western cultural tradition of white, heterosexual, male privilege. Gay people creating and living in community fundamentally threaten the social status quo. Gay/AIDS volunteerism at GMHC is about social change by making the political personal. It is about community pride and self-actualization, the best, if not the only, solution to discrimination, homophobia, and abandonment.

Because gays are considered either sinful, abnormal, or socially destructive, and therefore, totally expendable, AIDS is the perfect physical and internalized metaphor for institutionalized homophobia. For gays to disassociate from AIDS, as a collective "identity" crisis, would bring both personal and communal annihilation.

Discussion

AIDS supplied the opportunity for the gay community to actualize itself, to be and become what it must, in a life-threatening situation. This is to say, to heal itself of its own brokenness, or depoliticization and homophobia. In the need to respond to AIDS, GMHC forced a confrontation in the hearts and minds of gay men. A decision had to be made about how to live in the world, if to live at all. Volunteering in this context, thus, becomes a life-giving activity, reaffirming the goodness and authenticity of gayness itself. GMHC simply becomes the place, and volunteering the experience, within which new relationships develop, attitudes change, and the experience of AIDS and being gay become integrated, redefined, and understood.

GMHC has been able to create and maintain an "autonomous jurisdiction" in the service of personal and social change by simply being non-judgmental and accepting, and by offering an opportunity to give witness. The activities of its "wounded healers" (Nouen 1979), its volunteers, are based on compassion, commitment to the cause, and identification with the Person with AIDS.

It is the daily trauma of death and displacement, fear and loneliness, desperation and hope that keep the volunteers committed and which make transformation ever necessary. In AIDS, everyone becomes everyone else, with the care-partner and PWA being the mirrors of one another. The volunteer role in AIDS politicizes by bringing people to the truth about themselves at critical autobiographical moments. It does this by forcing people out of themselves, out of their own closets and silence, and leading them to their creativity.

This process of transformation (Abalos 1986) takes place at breaking points like the confrontation with unwarranted death for a whole network of friends. Change and growth are, thus, a central part of the process of becoming fully human. It is implicit in our humanity that we die to ourselves, grow and change, have hope, and seek resurrection. By doing "dirty work," gays in AIDSWORK have risen to the occasion.

Transformation is, therefore, a conscious choice made again and again at each moment of involvement in the process of continuous creation. The process of change is nurtured both informally and unintentionally and is the reason and way that individual and collective gay politics today differ from their historical precedents. GMHC, to date, has been able to sustain its charisma, its affective qualities, because it allows volunteers to turn inward and heal their own brokenness through the realization of the link between their own lives and social arrangements.

This emphasis on linkages (the relationship of the individual to their own sacred source or inner self and to others they recognize as community) makes gay volunteerism a fundamental, hence radical, political experience. Because its starting point is the position and condition of those who have traditionally been most powerless in society, claiming sacredness is an act of "liberation."

For all practical purposes, stressing interior personal transformation through connectedness and bearing witness reflects and creates a new "sacred humanism." Volunteerism, thus, becomes the justifying ideology allowing gay people to lay claim to community authenticity. As an activity, gay/AIDS volunteerism allows the community to come together to confront both social and internalized homophobia.

If AIDS supplies the reason to be political, gay volunteerism becomes the method and way of demonstrating the radical politics of healing or transformation. Gay pride, then, forces the redefinition of AIDS as a medical and public health emergency rather than a "curse from God." AIDS also succeeded in integrating already existing gay social networks, binding further and dramatically individual and communal concerns.

GMHC stemmed the spread of AIDS by making health an individual and communal commitment. By addressing the problem of transmission and prevention rather than causation, GMHC not only forced the issue of sexual behavior out into public, but it fostered responsibility by emphasizing the reward and value of changing behavior for the sake of the community, not just for the individual's well-being.

Since volunteers generally supply direct services to clients whose fortunes were tied up with their own (Knoke 1987), gays and GMHC were immediately bonded together by a desperate situation. Volunteers, thus, laid to rest the prevailing "wisdom" that gays were sinful or shameful, and gay life hedonistic and selfish. Volunteerism put an immediate end to these beliefs because confronting AIDS required a decision about the personal self and the community as a sacred source. GMHC, by joining hope and justice to dignity, thus, publicly united gayness with sickness, but in a positive way.

In order to function effectively, AIDS volunteers need to be free of guilt/shame, a fear of death, and personal selfishness. The most dramatic and powerful medium for achieving these needs is the creation and experience of community because community provides the context for transformation. Self-pride, defined as identification with the values and aesthetic of the community, and communal pride, manifested in the joy of being both oneself and part of a people, are both made possible in and through gay/AIDS volunteerism.

References

Appleby, George A. and Barbara G. Sosnowitz. 1987. "From Social Movement to Social Organization: Voluntary Aids projects in Connecticut." Paper presented at the annual meetings of the Society for the Study of Social Problems. Chicago.

Cohen, Mary Ann and Henry W. Weisman. 1986. "A Biopsychosocial Approach to AIDS," *Psychosomatics*. 27(4): 245–249.

Conrad, Peter and Rochelle Kern. 1989. *The Sociology of Health and Illness*. New York: St. Martins Press.

Conrad, Peter. 1986. "The Social Meaning of AIDS," *Social Policy*. (Summer), pp. 51–56.

Denneny, Michael. 1991. "A Quilt of Many Colors: AIDS Writing and the Creation of Culture," *Christopher Street*. Issue # 141, 12(9): 1521.

Dunne, Richard. 1984. "Vetoing Vito," (Letter to the editor). *The New York Native*. #215 (June 1), p. 6.

Fortunato, John E. 1987. *AIDS. The Spiritual Dilemma*. San Francisco: Harper and Row.

_____. 1983. *Embracing the Exile*. New York: Seabury Press.

Fumento, Michael. 1989. *The Myth of Heterosexual AIDS*. New York: Basic Books.

Gordon, Kevin. 1988. "Can There Be Faith and Theology After AIDS,"? (Unpublished Paper), Presented in James Memorial Chapel, Union Theological Seminary, April 16th.

Hirsh, David. 1989. "On Marginality," *The New York Native*. Issue # 347, December 11th, p. 36.

Holleran, Andrew. 1987. "Reading and Writing: AIDS is Not the Only Thing Spread by a Virus," *Christopher Street*. Issue #115, 10(7): 5–7.

_____. 1987b. "Trust." *Christopher Street*. Issue #117, 10(9): 4–8.

Hunt, Mary E. 1987. "Theological Pornography: From Corporate to Communal Ethics," Paper presented at a seminar to The Consultation, Union Theological Seminary, New York.

Johnson, Toby. 1988. "Celibacy - The Case for: Monks, Mystics and Men's Communities," *Outlook*. (Summer), pp. 15–19.

Kayal, Philip M. 1987. "Doing Good, Doing "Dirty Work:" The AIDS Volunteer." Paper presented at the annual meetings of the Easter Sociological Society, Boston.

_____. 1986a. "Healing Maladaptive Sexual Behavior." Paper presented at the annual meeting of the Society for the Study of Social Problems. New York.

_____ . 1986b. "The Sociology of Religion and AIDS." Paper presented at the Society for the Scientific Study of Religion." Washington, D.C.

_____ . 1985. "Morals, Medicine and the AIDS Epidemic," *Journal of Religion and Health.* 24(3): 218–238.

Kramer, Larry. 1987. "Dear Richard," *The New York Native.* Issue #197, (January 26th), pp. 12–15.

Kramer, Ralph. 1981. *Voluntary Agencies in the Welfare State.* Berkeley: University of California Press.

Knoke, David. 1987. "Incentives in Collective Action Organization." Paper presented at the annual meeting of the Society for the Study of Social Problems, Chicago.

_____ and David Prensky. 1984. "What Relevance Do Organization Theories Have for Voluntary Associations?" *Social Science Quarterly.* 65: 3–320.

Krieger, Nancy and Rose Appleman. 1986. *The Politics of AIDS.* Oakland: Frontline Press.

Lessor, Roberta. 1987. "AIDS and Social Science: The Case for *Verstehen* Research Methodology." Paper presented at the annual Meetings of the Society for the Study of Social Problems, Chicago.

Lopez, Diego and George S. Getzel. 1987. Strategies for Volunteers caring for Persons With AIDS," *Social Casework: The Journal of Contemporary Social Work.* (January), pp. 47–53.

Murray, Stephen O. 1987. "A Note on Haitian Tolerance of Homosexuality." In *Male Homosexuality in Central and South America.* O. Murray (ed) New York: Gai Saber Monographs #5.

Nichols, Tom. 1988. "Taking the Initiative," *The New York Native.* Sept. 19th, #283, p. 14.

Nouen, Henri. 1979. *The Wounded Healer.* New York: Doubleday.

Ortleb, Charles. 1984. "An 'Elegant' Disease: An Interview with Ann Guidici Fettner," *The New York Native.* Issue #95, pp. 27–28.

Osborn, June E. 1989. "Public Health and the Politics of AIDS Prevention." *Daedalus.* 118(3): 123–144.

Petit, Sarah. 1989. "Bearing Witness," *Outweek.* No. 25, Dec. 10th, p. 43.

See, Bernard. 1987. "Treasurer's Report," GMHC Newsletter. Vol. 4:4, (July/ August), p.2, 19.

Shilts, Randy. 1987. *And the Band Played On.* New York: St. Martin's Press.

Reflections on Philip M. Kayal's "Healing Brokenness: Gay Volunteerism and AIDS"[1]

Victoria Rader
George Mason University

On a research trip in Juarez, Mexico, I made the acquaintance of Violeta, a transgendered sex worker with AIDS. It was 1995 and Violeta had come down with an easily treatable opportunistic infection, but every hospital in the city refused treatment. No doctors would help. And there were no grass roots organizations serving people with AIDS. So Violeta lay dying in a small rented room, with no doctor, no antibiotics, not even morphine to soften the pain. At one point during the family's deathwatch, Violata's mother sat down next to me, leaned over, and whispered in my ear: "He is dying for his sins."

Thankfully, Philip Kayal tells a very different story. While the AIDS crisis exacerbated prejudice in the U.S., it also pulled the gay community into volunteer service and political activism, resulting in a widespread support network for people with AIDS. In the process, gay relationships were transformed and the community was empowered with a new sense of pride and unity. This is the story of a brutally oppressed people fighting for their lives and for their liberation, central themes in humanist sociology.

Humanist sociologists assume that individuals are not merely hapless products of big social forces, but subjects of their lives and shapers of history. Thus, Kayal examines the social process by which "tarnished outsiders" came to help severely "tarnished others," rejecting the punitive moral baggage attributed to AIDS. Remember Susan Sontag's examination of the symbolism around cancer, the sexist notion of women "romantically fading away" from tuberculosis in the nineteenth century, and the more recent interpretation of AIDS as a sign of retribution for sin? "Illness is not a metaphor," writes Sontag," and the most truthful way of regarding illness-and the healthiest way of being ill— is the one most purified of, most resistant to metaphoric thinking." Therein lays the gift within the AIDS disaster: The gay community was forced to confront both internalized and institutionalized homophobia. Kayal found that gay men identifying with AIDS came to challenge the cosmology of the whole western cultural tradition of white, heterosexual, male privilege. (Perhaps volunteers were not only healing their internalized homophobia, but the early masculine conditioning that leaves men so ill-prepared for all the tender, humdrum "dirty work" that nursing care entails.)

But how do you study the complex process of a collective change of consciousness? Not from a stance of value neutrality, certainly. On the contrary, values of justice, equality, freedom and the preciousness of life are deeply imbedded in the research designs and clearly articulated in the writing of humanist sociologists. Kayal's values are fiercely

[1]This paper originally appeared in *Humanity & Society* Volume 27, Number 4, 2003.

transparent: he refuses impartiality about an entire population placed in peril, and he celebrates the spiritual, emotional and political empowerment resulting from "bearing witness." Reducing his academic distance, he submerges himself in the anguish, confusion, and outrage of an AIDS volunteer, working within the prophetic flagship organization, New York's Gay Health Crisis, Inc. It may be necessary, Kayal suggests, for the researcher to be an insider when sub cultural or deviant groups are involved, largely because intuitive and experiential ways of knowing are more valuable in such situations than mainstream methods such as survey research. He also challenges the reactionary role academics too often play in the emergent dialogue around urgent social issues: In the early years, only gay men were willing to take on the moral stigma and apparent medical risk of getting close to the AIDS crisis. Later, the issue was "democratized" and gay life became an acceptable subject of research and concern for academics and scientists, although always through the "outsider" lens of disease and illness. In my own experience in the homeless movement, academics were oblivious as advocates struggled for years to name the problem and raise public awareness. Once "discovered," sociologists decided to document "the extent of the problem," employing sophisticated statistical research designs that massively undercounted homeless people and justified further political inaction. A second generation of homeless scholars focused on personal dysfunction, reinforcing the ideology of blaming the victim while ignoring the wholesale decimation of affordable housing and decent work for a living wage. Kayal's research makes us think: If we wait for government grants and then come in as outsiders—What will we learn? What will be the political impact of our research?

Kayal's findings left me inspired and grateful for the powerful mobilization of the U.S. gay community in serving anyone with AIDS. I was also filled with sorrow for my friends in Mexico who are sex workers and gays, still unable to openly organize support. Stigma destroys community and hinders political activity, as Kayal suggests. I hope the U.S. gay community extends its solidarity to oppressed groups in other countries, because life is sacred everywhere, and so is the community-building that enables us to look out for one another.

4. Contested Terrain: Negotiating Racial Understandings in Public Discourse[1,2]

Ashley W. Doane, Jr.
University of Hartford

Reflexive Statement

As a teacher and scholar in the area of race and ethnic relations, I have become increasingly interested in how Americans talk about race in public, in the classroom, and in private conversations. This research stems from my involvement in the school desegregation process in the town in which I reside. As I attended meetings and hearings, I was repeatedly struck by such phenomena as the presentation of non-racist credentials, the deliberate avoidance of issues of race, and the rhetorical strategies which were employed when race was discussed. I firmly believe that we will make little progress in resolving the racial problems of the United States until we undertake a more introspective examination of our racial understandings and come prepared to engage in a more open discussion of issues of race. I hope that this examination of our current public discourse on race will contribute to such a process.

Introduction

In their influential theory of racial formation, Omi and Winant (1986: 68–69) assert that race is an "unstable and decentered complex of social meanings constantly transformed by political struggle." The racial understandings of a society are continually being rearticulated as intellectuals and social movements challenge and defend current ideologies. This has been particularly true in the case of the United States. Over the past few decades, social understandings regarding the role of race in American society have undergone a series of transformations. From the 1950s through the early 1970s, the Civil Rights Movement and related social movements succeeded in recasting racial politics to achieve the elimination of state-supported segregation, a decline in the acceptability of overt expressions of racism, and the increased legitimacy of group-based claims upon the state for redress of inequality. These changes were accompanied by the increased acceptance of minority participation in American society by the white European-American dominant group—as has been repeat-

---

[1] An earlier version of this paper was presented at the Annual Meeting of the Eastern Sociological Society, Boston, Massachusetts, March 28-31, 1996. Special thanks to Lelia Lomba De Andrade for her many insightful comments on an earlier draft.
[2] This paper originally appeared in *Humanity & Society* Volume 20, Number 4, 1996.

edly documented by survey data (Schuman, Steeh and Bobo 1985; Firebaugh and Davis 1988). In the 1970s, 1980s and 1990s, conservative counter movements, fueled by increasing economic and social insecurity and perceived threats to dominant group hegemony, have launched an attack on affirmative action, the welfare state, and the role of the state as guarantor of minority rights (Omi and Winant 1986; Steinberg 1995). Throughout this period, the re-articulation of racial meanings has been grounded in a persistent material reality: U.S. society continues to be marked by pervasive economic and political inequality along racial lines. Each of these dynamics has an important effect upon racial discourse—how Americans talk about race.

Discourse can be conceptualized as occurring across a range of levels of interaction. The most general level, social discourse, can be viewed as the collective whole of the text and talk of a society. Discourse can also be analyzed in relation to a specific context or genre (van Dijk 1993: 28), from media discourse, legislative discourse, and elite discourse to the everyday discourse of face-to-face interaction. With respect to the analysis of social discourse pertaining to social problems or public issues, the bulk of the research (e.g., Gamson and Modigliani 1989; van Dijk 1993) has focused upon media and/or elite discourse. In contrast, the focus of this study is upon *public* discourse, which I define as the oral and written statements of average citizens (the "general public") in public arenas. My purpose is to draw upon insights from discourse analysis and social constructionism to analyze how Americans talk about race in public.

I believe that there are significant advantages to the analysis of public discourse on racial issues. As Omi and Winant (1986: 66–67) assert, racial meanings are manifest on both the micro and macro levels, as a matter of how individuals view the world and interact with others, and as a matter of group and institutional processes. Moreover, these levels have a "reciprocal" influence upon each other: macro level racial meanings—the racial understandings of society—provide the context for individual interpretation, while the collective impact of individual racial understandings shapes institutional and political action. This is a dynamic process. Individual and collective racial understandings are continuously being contested, disrupted and redefined through everyday experience, cultural images and political struggle. This is particularly evident in debates over public issues with significant racial implications, issues such as affirmative action, political representation, immigration policy, police and judicial conduct, and school desegregation.

While elite and media discourse may have a broader influence, the analysis of public discourse provides an opportunity to view the racial understandings of society as articulated by average citizens. Public discourse is a visible connection between the macro-level elite and media discourses and the everyday discourse of the masses. In addition, discourse analysis transcends the study of public opinion via attitude statements in surveys and opinion polls. It encompasses the nature and use of symbols and rhetorical strategies as well as their incorporation into more complex explanatory models. Thus, we can study not only individual attitudes but also how they are linked to interpretative frames and how these "common sense" understandings are employed in debates over social issues. Consequently, the analysis of public discourse is essential to understanding the contestation and re-articulation of the social meaning of race in the United States.

Finally, I would like to emphasize that discourse is more than "talk and text." Negotiated meanings provide a context for thought and action. Code words, labels, claims and mental models are—absent an armed uprising—the "weapons" of political struggle. They can be used to challenge the existing order, or to legitimate and defend privilege. Rhetorical strategies can be used to cloak positions in politically palatable language (cf. Horton 1995: 82 on overt vs. covert sentiments) or to defuse or negate the claims of opponents. Given the racial politics of the 1990s—the debates over affirmative action, immigration restriction, welfare "reform" and school desegregation—racial discourse will become increasingly important in shaping political outcomes.

Analytical Strategy/Methods

In this paper, I use a case study—the debate over school desegregation in West Hartford, Connecticut —to examine the nature of *public* discourse on racial issues in the mid 1990s. Data for this analysis are drawn from public statements—letters to the Board of Education, letters to local newspapers, and statements at public hearings—made during the process of development, adoption, and implementation of a school desegregation plan for West Hartford, a time period which ranged from July 1994 until October 1995. Given the public nature of this process, data gathering was unobtrusive inasmuch as letters and statements were a matter of public record. In addition, I had a public role in the proceedings as a member of the Racial Balance Advisory Committee to the West Hartford Board of Education. This provided both access to documents and an explanation for my presence and note-taking at meetings and hearings.

To provide a context for assessing the research findings, several characteristics of the participants in this discourse should be taken into consideration. First, subjects were self-selected in that they consisted of persons who chose to write letters or speak at a hearing. Moreover, persons participating in public discourse are conscious of writing/speaking for public consumption, which may influence the nature of their statements, especially on matters of race. On the other hand, given the unobtrusive nature of data collection, subjects would be unaware of being studied and, given the scope of the issues under consideration, less self-consciously centered upon issues of race. Finally, based upon observation at public hearings, it is important to note that participants in this discourse were almost exclusively white, which means that findings should be viewed as essentially a white-dominated discourse.

Inasmuch as the focus of this study is essentially descriptive—mapping modes of talking about race in public discourse—the analytical strategy involved reflexively deriving concepts from the data (cf. Altheide 1987 on ethnographic content analysis) as opposed to a more formal discourse or content analysis. The general approach to the data was informed by discourse and social constructionist approaches (van Dijk 1993; Gamson and Lasch 1983; Gamson and Modigliani 1989; Wilmoth and Ball 1995) in that I examined both individual elements of discourse and their aggregation into larger interpretative packages or frames. More specifically, I begin by analyzing the use of symbols—code words, depictions and visual elements (cf. Gamson and Lasch 1983: 399–400)—and the rhetorical strategies through which these elements of discourse are employed in public debate. A second focus of analysis involves the explanatory models or "reasoning devices" (Gamson and Lasch 1983: 399–400) employed by participants in the public discourse; that is, the "theories" and value frameworks through which individuals explain the origins of the issue, predict the consequences of various solutions, and evaluate competing claims. The final step of the analysis is to move from the individual elements of discourse to an assessment of the general interpretative frames through which members of the general public view racial issues.

Context: School Desegregation in West Hartford

Clearly, public discourse does not occur in a vacuum. The larger context for the West Hartford debate begins with the national media/elite discourse on racial issues, which itself is influenced by the transformations of racial meanings initiated by the Civil Rights Movement and reshaped by the "backlash" of the past two decades. Particularly significant for the case of West Hartford is the ongoing discourse on school desegregation, from the *Brown v. Board of Education* decision in 1954 through desegregation struggles in various U.S. cities, including debates and court decisions involving busing. On the local/regional level, the West Hartford debate was situated in a larger controversy involving segregation and educational disparities between Hartford (whose school population is 95% minority) and its suburbs. This culminated in a civil suit—*Sheff vs. O'Neill*—which periodically emerged in the local media throughout the 1990s and which held the potential for court-ordered metropolitan desegregation plans.[1]

The emergence of school desegregation as an issue in a suburban community such as West Hartford was the result of interaction between a larger social dynamic, the nation-wide trend of increasing minority populations in suburbs, with local patterns of residential segregation. In April of 1994, West Hartford was notified by the State Board of Education that its elementary schools were in a state of noncompliance with a state racial balance law governing the distribution of minority students within a school district and that it would be required to submit a racial balance plan.[2] During the summer of 1994, the West Hartford Board of Education developed a desegregation plan, known locally as K-2/3–5, which attempted to address imbalance by pairing elementary schools from different areas of town. Under the K-2/3–5 plan, all students from the two paired districts would attend one school from kindergarten through second grade and the other for grades three through five. Racial balance would be achieved by pairing schools having relatively large minority enrollment with those having relatively low minority enrollment.

The K-2/3–5 plan met with intense public opposition, in response to which the local board tabled the plan and initiated a review process which included two citizen committees (one of which was required by the state racial balance law) and a series of public meetings and hearings). The end result was the development of a racial balance plan which involved redistricting and the creation of magnet schools; this plan was adopted by the Board of Education in February 1995 and submitted to the state in April.[3] This entire process (July 1994–April 1995) was accompanied by intense public involvement and media coverage—manifest in turnouts at public hearings, letters to local and regional newspapers, and media coverage which went beyond the town and even the region.

Concurrent with this process was an attempt—spearheaded by legislators from West Hartford and other suburban communities which had come under the purview of the state racial balance law—to suspend or rescind the Connecticut racial balance law. Proponents were ultimately successful in suspending the law from July 1995 until July 1997. In antici-pation of this action the State Board of Education acknowledged but did not formally accept the West Hartford plan, thus placing the town under no legal obligation to implement the plan. Nevertheless, the West Hartford Board of Education proceeded with implementation of the plan. Redistricting went into effect in September of 1995 and two magnet schools were opened in September 1996, with the opening of the third magnet school currently scheduled for September of 1998. One result of these developments was that the issue of racial balance remained in the public eye, as reflected both in attempts by plan opponents to delay or modify plan implementation and in campaigns for the November 1995 elections for the West Hartford Board of Education.[4]

Symbolic Struggle: Code Words and Contested Meanings

Debates over social issues can be viewed as a competition between opposing interpretative packages or frames, the objectives of which are to mobilize supporters and build social movement organizations, attract nonaligned persons, and neutralize or discredit opponents. One of the core elements in this "public relations" struggle to enhance the power of an interpretative package is the use of "code words" or catchphrases—powerful symbols which effectively summarize the position of the speaker and, what is more important, evoke support by connecting to core social and cultural values (Gamson and Lasch 1983: 399; Gamson and Modigliani 1989: 5). For example, the most frequently used catchphrase by opponents of the racial balance plans—the familiar "neighborhood schools"—conjures up images of a traditional way of life, of children walking to a school which serves as an anchor for a community which may be presumed to be homogeneous. Another popular set of code words, "state mandates" or "social engineering," tap into the strong antigovernment discourse of the 1980s and 1990s by conveying images of "Big Brother-like" bureaucratic forces which threaten the existence of community. The power of these and other code words employed by both sides in the West Hartford debate—forced busing, bureaucracy, government intervention, quotas, diversity, multicultural, equal opportunity—lies in their familiarity. They can readily be traced back to earlier civil rights and desegregation conflicts or current general political discourse.

In the course of the racial balance debate, symbolic struggle involved not only the use of code words or catchphrases, but also the contestation of the meaning of the symbols invoked by the opposing side. Thus, a code word such as "neighborhood school" can become a "contestable moral notion" (Madsen 1991: 50–52); that is, a word whose positive (or negative) value is generally recognized, but which is sufficiently vague so that its specific meaning may be redefined in accordance with the interests of the speaker. For example, given the residential segregation which exists in many metropolitan areas, the notion of "neighborhood schools" has historically served as a vehicle for opposing integration without making reference to race. In contrast, one plan proponent attempted to counteract the symbolic power of the notion of "neighborhood school" by articulating a broader conception of neighborhood:

> It is well and good to call for the preservation of the neighborhood school. However, shouldn't the neighborhood be the town of West Hartford and not just a few blocks of houses?

Similarly, another supporter of desegregation sought to defuse the affective strength of the term busing:

> The kids may be taking the bus, but they are not being bused. This is one town, we're not busing across town lines.

In both instances, the purpose of this tactic was to strengthen the position of the speaker by redefining one of the core symbols of the opposition in more favorable terms.

'Racist': The Ultimate Symbolic Struggle

One of the most significant effects of the Civil Rights Movement upon racial discourse was a dramatic decline in the acceptability of displays of overt racism. Consequently, one of the core elements of current racial discourse is the extreme negative valuation attached to the label of "racist." Indeed, the "racist" label serves as the ultimate rhetorical weapon with which to discredit those opposed to changing the existing racial order. Plan proponents in West Hartford made effective use of this label:

> No, the sad part is that anyone would still argue that educational policy must coddle to racist, classist, elitist motives. It's 1994. How can you argue 'don't adopt this plan or some white people may pull their kids out of our schools?'

One of the most interesting elements in the West Hartford school desegregation debate was the struggle over the use of "racist" in public discourse. The label "racist" has developed such extremely negative connotations in contemporary American society that its application effectively places the recipient beyond the pale of civilized society. Given the potential impact of being labeled a "racist," recipients are unlikely to let this label go unchallenged. Thus, the use of the "racist" label will predictably evoke a strong defensive reaction from the recipient—"how dare you call me a racist!" To quote one letter-writer:

> I also strongly resent the implication that people opposed to the K-2/3–5 reorganization are 'racist' or 'rich.' We are neither racist or rich.

The effect of this response is to make the use of the "racist" label problematic in public discourse. In essence, the label "racist" has become so negative and so powerful that its interjection into a debate changes the focus; that is, the issue is no longer the behavior of the subject, but rather the "hostile" act committed by the use of the label.

Inasmuch as the "racist" label is unassailable in itself—that is, few will argue that it is desirable to be racist—participants in the West Hartford public discourse employed defensive tactics to preempt the use of the racist label or to neutralize its effects. One defensive strategy was to attempt to inoculate oneself against being called a racist by making claims to the contrary. For example, one writer concluded his criticism of the plan by asserting that "racism has nothing to do with it." Another strategy is to seek to devalue the "racist" label by dismissing it as "name calling":

> My anger is increasing with each ridiculous letter I read about 'Haves' and 'Have nots' and people calling each other racists. What are we coming to with this kind of finger pointing and name calling?

Also significant in the school desegregation debate was the emergence of "racist" as a contested concept. There seemingly was a consensus that racist was a negative label; however, there was disagreement as to what exactly constitutes a "racist." As Jaret (1995: 128–29) has observed, formal definitions of racism in American society range from individual adherence to doctrines of superiority and inferiority to individual and institutional practices which maintain white privilege; informal conceptions may exhibit even greater variation. One striking component of the West Hartford debate was the attempt by opponents of desegregation to redefine the "racist" label and to apply it to supporters of integration:

> Proponents of the plan fail to see that their position is firmly rooted in racial stereotypes. They claim that this plan will improve the quality of all schools. If certain schools are performing below our quality expectations, why not redirect funding towards those schools to fix the problem? Are they saying that the racial and ethnic mix of students determines the quality of a school? While they certainly won't say that, it is the logical implication of their position. And that my friends is a racist position.

Another letter writer turned his sights directly upon the state racial balance law:

> State-mandated racial balance, which in my opinion is a form of racism....

A third participant articulated a case for a "color blind" society, implying that racism persists because of attempts at integration:

> Their (the Board of Education) agenda categorizes us, the people of the town of West Hartford, by the pigment of our skins, by the amount of money we make, by the language our parents speak, and then gerrymanders our school districts to create their misguided version of what is meant by equal access—homogenized ratios. To some of us who believe that people should be judged on their strength of character, and who believe that racism will not be eliminated until our nation, states, and towns become color blind, this agenda is repugnant.

In essence, this new conceptualization of racism reduces a racist to someone who is aware of race. Within the confines of the West Hartford school desegregation debate, this rhetorical strategy both dilutes the power of the "racist" label and even makes it available for use by opponents of integration. On a broader level, the equating of racism with race consciousness places racial balance in the public schools on a par with actions by the Ku Klux Klan or white supremacist groups. This rearticulation of the notion of racism has important political consequences, for if racism is the same as race consciousness, then all forms of racism are considered equal (i.e., "black" racism="white" racism) and racism is reduced to a neutral political claim instead of a historically grounded social problem. The potential power of this attempted change in racial discourse parallels that of the notion of "reverse discrimination"—a countermovement whose claims are now viewed in many quarters as equal to or even greater than discrimination against members of minority groups (Gamson and Modigliani 1987; Burstein 1991).

The Strategic Avoidance of Race

Another element of the public discourse on school desegregation was the often complete avoidance of any mention of race. During the process of plan consideration, it was at times possible to sit through a three-hour public hearing without hearing any reference to the word "race." Given the contested nature of race described above, both proponents and opponents of school desegregation had an interest in minimizing race as an issue, the former because of the emphasis on race-neutral policies by plan opponents, the latter because of fear of being labeled "racist." For example, the process was generally referred to by both sides as "elementary school reorganization" (or diversity or imbalance/balance) as opposed to the more politically charged "desegregation." Several writers spoke of changing "demographics" rather than racial imbalance. Also significant was the focus on the issue of redistributing "impacted" students (defined as students eligible for free or reduced price lunches or in need of English for Speakers of Other Languages services) as opposed to racial balance. For example, one writer was clearly thinking of race but preferred the term "impacted":

> Many in West Hartford will question the value of diversity. Some may even prefer to keep those wonderful, talented 'impacted students' away from their own children, preferring to maintain the status quo, even if it is separate and unequal and ultimately, racist.

This strategy seemingly began with the Board of Education; however, it served the objectives of both sides in the debate to downplay race. In essence, racial discourse has become so politically charged that avoidance of any mention of race has become a popular strategy.

Claims Making: Redefining the Problem

On a broader level, each issue package is centered around a core frame or central organizing idea and an agenda which is implied or advocated by the frame (Gamson and Lasch 1983). Claims making is the process through which advocates attempt to promote a particular definition or "construction" of the problem. The ability to define a problem is a crucial component of public discourse in that certain definitions favor various solutions or policy options. Consequently, problem definition is a central arena for symbolic struggle.

In the West Hartford school desegregation debate, plan proponents had the luxury of linking their position to a well-established desegregation frame. The core position of this frame asserts that unequal opportunity grounded in racial segregation is inherently undesirable and unconstitutional. This frame has been elevated to icon status in American culture by the *Brown* decision and by decades of civil rights struggle. Consequently, simple references to "inequality" or "racial imbalance" evoked this entire package:

> There is no question that in the names of fairness and equity (values which I am sure that we all want our children to adopt through our example), and the educational welfare of all our children, changes have to be made.

Another writer explicitly emphasized the connection between segregation and denial of opportunity:

> The spirit of the law is to give minority children an equal opportunity for an education, and that opportunity does not occur in schools that reflect segregation in our culture.

A second claim made by advocates of desegregation moved beyond condemning the negative effects of segregation to emphasizing the advantages of integration. In fact, the argument is advanced that racial balance is necessary in order to prepare students to live in a more diverse society:

> But, as shown by the richness of the Whiting Lane community, diversity offers West Hartford strength, empowering all of our children to face the twenty-first century society they'll know as adults.

Or, as expressed by another writer:

> We can only hide in our little neighborhood enclaves for so long. In doing so we are not helping our children prepare for their adult lives in a diverse society. We are teaching them nothing about fair play and what it means to be part of a community.

The existence of these frames presented a problem for plan opponents inasmuch as such notions as desegregation, diversity and equal opportunity are essentially immune from any meaningful attack. Thus, plan opponents were forced to begin by accepting the core values of the opposing package. This meant that plan opposition could only be advanced by advancing a definition of the problem where some other value was more desirable than diversity or equal opportunity. Strategically, this led to the creation of *dichotomies*—either/ or propositions where values were arranged in a clear order of preference and with the implication that the choice of one value precluded attainment of the other. One example of this comes from a letter which placed racial balance in opposition to educational excellence:

> Racial balance should not be the issue. Instead quality of education for all students should be. The K–2/3–5 system is a racial balancing system which is unlikely to improve the educational quality for students, and is likely to retard it.

A second writer arrayed education against diversity and integration:

> It is undeniably true that children as well as adults need to appreciate and understand the diversity of race, religion and culture which exists not only in this community but also throughout the world. However, the primary focus of the schools should be education, not integration.

In the same vein, a third letter placed equality and diversity at odds with the well-being of children:

> First, may I applaud your efforts to address issues of educational equality and diversity. But your plan is a bad one. You should not use children to solve these problems.

In each case, a socially-valued ideal such as diversity or equity is accepted; however, it is simultaneously devalued by setting it against a presumably more valued ideal—educational quality—in what is asserted to be a mutually exclusive relationship. This enables the writer/speaker to contest ideals which would otherwise appear to be unassailable by setting them aside while recognizing or at least paying lip-service to their value. Thus, diversity and equality are to be valued, but not at the "expense" of education or the well-being of children. Indeed, one hallmark of these statements was the use of the words "*but*" or "*however*" to introduce a clause which asserted that the cost of integration and equality is too high.

A second strategy employed by plan opponents was the redefinition of the problem as "unfairness" to those who were not members of minority groups. This strategy avoids any direct confrontation with the unassailable ideals of integration and equality; however, it advances the counterclaim that the means for achieving these ends (i.e., the school desegregation plan) inflict harm upon the majority:

> We are a hard-working double-income family…We bought our house in a nice neighborhood based on the school. Twenty-five years ago my father did the same thing. For as long as I can remember the tradition and appeal of West Hartford has been based on its neighborhood schools and top-ranked public school education. Why are we being punished for choosing where we want to live and can afford to live?

A speaker at a hearing raised the issue of unfairness to whites by referring to the makeup of the Board appointed Racial Balance Advisory Committee:

> How is this representative of a town which is 98% white? We are not hyphenated, just small letter whites.

At the core of each of these statements is an assertion of harm (punishment, decline in education, underrepresentation) which will befall innocent (children) or even praiseworthy (hardworking, "not hyphenated") victims. The logic of these claims is very similar to the "reverse discrimination" argument; that is, that wrongs should be redressed, but not at the expense of someone else.

Mental Models: Causes and Consequences

In addition to core claims, the other major elements of frames or issue packages are the mental models or reasoning devices which justify a position or proposed plan of action (Gamson and Lasch 1983; van Dijk 1993). Such models are the logical linchpins of an issue package inasmuch as they constitute the main rationale for the central position. During the course of the West Hartford desegregation debate, there were two central issues for which models were constructed: (1) explanations for the *causes* of racial imbalance and (2) assumptions regarding the *consequences* of proposed policies.

Throughout the course of school desegregation in the United States, the issue of the cause of segregation has had significant implications for legal and social remedies. Consequently, one opponent of racial balance sought to portray residential segregation as the outcome of a natural process:

> Families of similar racial, social, and or economic backgrounds by nature settle together in various neighborhoods throughout our town.

Another letter-writer emphasized the unintentional nature of this process:

> What this all boils down to is that at the heart of every citizen, every human is the desire to live in communities where they feel most comfortable. This may result in a racially imbalanced neighborhood, but this is not always a bad or wrong thing. It is bad when residents try to keep others out.

The constant theme here is the assertion that racial imbalance/segregation is unintentional; that is, that it just "happened" or that it reflects individual preferences for living with people who are similar, an occurrence which is viewed as "natural" and acceptable. The crucial corollary is that unintentional discrimination need not be remedied, a point which was explicitly stated by one writer who draws a connection to the ongoing legal debate regarding the distinction between *de jure* and *de facto* segregation:

> The Supreme Court has consistently found that racial balance remedies are only required where there has been previous racial discrimination in establishing attendance zones. I have been assured by the Board of Education that West Hartford has never intentionally discriminated in establishing its attendance zones.

In response, proponents of desegregation sought to link racial imbalance and inequality in the schools to past inaction on the part of the town, with the implication that some remedy was necessary:

> For too long now, several of the elementary schools, and the children who attend them, have been allowed to bear the weight of changing demographics because of the area in which they were located and because the calls for help were easy to ignore. But over the last five years, the special educational needs of some schools have increased so rapidly in comparison to others that the numbers, limited space and physical condition of these schools is severely limiting their ability to meet the needs of the average and exceptional students attending these schools.

Another plan proponent made an explicit connection to residential segregation:

> The long range solution could possibly include redistricting and a pro-active program to encourage a pattern of housing diversity, which is a basic problem of which the present school situation is only a symptom.

Perhaps the ultimate rejoinder to the "unintentional segregation" model was the assertion that segregation needed to be remedied regardless of the cause:

> The State's own studies have shown that school children suffer from segregated school systems. If segregation is harmful to our children, does it really matter if it results from accident or intent?

The other major area where frames came into conflict involved the consequences of possible desegregation plans. For opponents of the desegregation plans, the consequences were clear —educational decline, white flight, declining property values, and the ultimate destruction of the community:

> My understanding is that prospective home buyers have shown little interest in West Hartford lately. I would not be surprised to see real estate values drop by as much as 20 percent.

In some instances, specific references were made to "white flight":

> If we adopt a plan which, whether in reality or merely in perception, lessens the quality of education in West Hartford, I fear, based upon experiences across the United States where this has occurred, that there will be a significant removal of white students from the West Hartford public school system, whether to private education or to other towns.

As van Dijk (1993) observes, mental models are often as revealing in terms of their implicit assumptions. In addition to the explicit arguments about property values and white flight are the assumptions that desegregation will lead to a real or perceived decline in educational quality and that white parents do not want their children to attend schools with significant percentages of minority students. This connection was made more explicitly by a large advertisement which appeared in the major metropolitan daily as the town council prepared to vote on whether or not to support a voluntary regional desegregation planning effort: "Wake Up West Hartford! Do You Want Guns, Gangs, and Graffiti in Your Schools?"[5] The clear image that was presented here was that school desegregation would lead to this outcome—a frame made more dramatic by the demagogic portrayal of a demonized racial other, a portrayal which invoked images perpetuated by the media. Interestingly, while the advertisement evoked condemnation as "racist," it also reflected the avoidance of race in public discourse in that there was no explicit reference to race. However unsubtle the presentation, the reader was still left to make the final inference.

The thesis of educational decline and white flight was challenged in several ways by supporters of racial balance, who in some cases argued that not to adopt a desegregation plan would be more harmful to the community because educational inequality and neighborhood instability would affect the entire town. On the other hand, the arguments of plan proponents in some cases revealed their own contradictory images of race:

> You want reality? Here's a real thought. If we continue to keep the impacted students bottled up in a few schools in one end of town for the first six years of their schooling, then mix them in with the rest of the student population in the sixth grade, know what we'll get? Guns and gangs in the schools.

This quotation is interesting in that we find a supporter of integration employing an image of the racial other which is similar to the stereotypes used by plan opponents. The difference is the causal reasoning: in this case the implication is that integration is necessary to "save" impacted/minority students from "guns and gangs." This indicates that racial attitudes in the 1990s are more complex than a racist-non racist dichotomy, and that individual frameworks or understandings of racial issues may draw upon a range of sources and contain elements which are seemingly contradictory. As is evident in the above quotation, racist constructions are sufficiently pervasive in the racial understandings of American society that they can emerge in what is ostensibly "anti-racist" discourse. This is a point which bears further examination.

Conclusion

What does the West Hartford school desegregation debate tell us about the role of race in American public life in the 1990s? At the most general level of abstraction, there appear to be two competing discourses or interpretative packages. The *integrationist* package incorporates a call for government intervention to facilitate increased racial integration and, presumably, enhanced equality of opportunity. This package contains a set of well-established claims about the inherent inequality and undesirability of segregation buttressed by catchphrases and moral claims grounded in values of equality, antiracism, and diversity. Set in opposition is a *status-quo* package which maintains that state action to increase integration is both unnecessary and illegitimate. Central to this package are explanatory models which assert that segregation is the result of natural or "accidental" processes and that extensive state intervention would produce such outcomes as educational decline and white flight. The status quo package is also supported by strong images of neighborhood schools and unjust government intervention.

Simply outlining the opposing packages, however, would contribute little to our knowledge of the racial understandings of American society. Some form of the integrationist and status quo packages have dominated American public discourse about racial issues for at least four decades. Nevertheless, the complexity of American racial understandings transcends a simple integrationist-status quo dichotomy, for as was evident in the West Hartford case, both packages contain contradictory elements. The vehemence with which racial matters have been contested in American society has left racial understandings as complex and contested terrain. In addition, the interpretative packages themselves are constantly evolving as a result of ideological conflict and social change. These changes are manifest in the various elements of discourse contained in the West Hartford school desegregation debate.

One interesting development is the continuing evolution of the status quo frame. Given the increased prevalence of attitudes of racial egalitarianism in public opinion polls and the rising social intolerance for overt racism, opponents of change have developed an explanatory framework where contemporary racial segregation is "accidental," that it is the outcome of social processes other than racism. This supports the contention—which was explicitly made by one participant in the West Hartford debate—that in the absence of *intentional* discrimination, no change is required. Yet the argument does not stop here. An additional element is added in that integration and equality are asserted to have a "cost" to whites in terms of declining educational quality and real estate values, thus implying that whites are being asked to bear a burden in the absence of any wrongdoing. The outcome of this line of reasoning is the position that one can reasonably oppose integration without being "racist." As Feagin and Vera (1995: 135) have observed, these "sincere fictions" enable whites to act in racist ways while maintaining a non-racist presentation of self.

This "non-racist" racism is compatible with poll results which show whites supporting integration in the abstract, but opposing specific government action to promote integration (McAneny and Saad 1994; Schuman and Steeh 1996).

This form of opposition to school desegregation in many ways reflects what has been termed "modern" or "symbolic" racism (Kinder and Sears 1981; Jaret 1995: 180–81). The notion of symbolic racism describes a more general racial discourse in American society which begins with the assertion that racial discrimination is essentially a historical phenomenon and that there are no meaningful barriers to the full economic and political participation of minorities (Klugel 1990). The "common sense" understanding is that race no longer "matters." In this discourse, demands such as school desegregation and affirmative action are "unwarranted" given the "open" opportunity structure. This position effectively replaces structural constraints with individualism; it is often accompanied by assumptions that the explanations for inequality lie in the values and motivational orientations of individual members of minority groups or in the impersonal working of market forces. While the overt content is "color blind," the covert message is grounded in racial stereotypes. In the West Hartford debate, assumptions about desegregation leading to a decline in the quality of education were seemingly tied to racial stereotypes; however, this issue requires more direct examination in that speakers/writers never clarified the causal link. Nevertheless, this more subtle form of racism is an important component of the discourse on desegregation.

In addition to the assertion that segregation is unintentional, the status quo package contains an increasingly aggressive attempt to undermine both the use of racism as a label and the validity of race-based claims. As described above, the dismissal of charges of racism as "name-calling" is a strategic attempt to devalue what has historically been a powerful rhetorical weapon for forces challenging racial privilege. Even more significant is the attempt to "reverse" the use of the charge of racism to apply it to those who are using race-based claims to promote integration (cf. Blauner 1992: 57). This has significant social implications, for if racism is reduced to a political claim torn from its historical roots, then it will become increasingly possible to equate dominant group racism with "minority racism," which in turn will essentially negate the power of the charge of racism as a political force. Under this redefinition, racism will no longer be a structural or historical force, but merely a label for individual behavior. This represents a significant—and understudied—change in the racial understandings of American society.

Closely connected to the contested meaning of the notion of racism is the presentation of desegregation as unfair to whites. This claim is tied to an emerging larger discourse which portrays whiteness as a liability and whites as victims (cf. Gallagher 1994: 176). In this discourse, whites are "victimized" by affirmative action, false accusations of racism and attempts to hold them accountable for the deeds of their ancestors. If this discourse is successful in placing white victimization on a par with the oppression of peoples of color, then much of the historical basis for group claims on the part of subordinate groups will be effectively undermined.

The major new element in the integrationist package is the increasing assertion of the positive value of diversity. This is significant in that it expands the integrationist package to go beyond the emphasis upon racial justice to assert the benefits of desegregation for whites as well as blacks. As presented by pro-integration forces in the West Hartford debate, without desegregation white students will be handicapped in terms of their ability to deal with a United States which is becoming increasingly diverse. A second, and closely related pro-integrationist argument asserts that racism and racial inequality are harmful to all of society (cf. Feagin and Vera 1995: 7–9 on racism as "societal waste") and thus must be addressed in the interests of everyone. Given that desegregation has historically been viewed as more beneficial to people of color than to whites (cf. McAneny and Saad 1994), this is a significant change in the integrationist package. At the same time, to the extent that diversity is used as an argument to advance integration, we can expect that it will come under attack (see, for example, Krauthammer 1995).

For both packages, the West Hartford experience suggests that race remains a sensitive issue in American society. Both sides displayed a desire to tread lightly when dealing with issues of race. For the forces opposed to integration, this involved attempts to establish non-racist credentials or to assert that race was "not the issue." Both sides exhibited a willingness to shift away from issues of racial balance to discussion of "impacted" students or "demographics" or even to avoid the issue of race altogether. This is a significant trend, for to the extent that we remain unwilling to engage issues of race, it will become increasingly difficult to solve America's race problem.

The above analysis has important implications for those striving to build a more racially just society. Perhaps the core issue highlighted in the West Hartford experience is the continuing emergence of racism as a "contested concept." The question of who is a "racist" has increasingly become a focus of racial discourse. I recognize that this is a sensitive area—"racist" and "racism" have become such emotionally charged labels that their use virtually precludes further dialogue—however it is one which must be confronted. As noted earlier, the equation of racism with race consciousness or simple prejudice and the notion that subordinate group "racism" is equivalent to the racism of the dominant group have profound implications for the racial understandings of American society, implications which mask the importance of power differences in shaping racial oppression in the United States. In a useful definition, Wellman (1993: emphasis added) defines racism as *"culturally acceptable* beliefs that defend social advantages based on race." I interpret this to mean that in the U.S. experience, while anyone may be prejudiced or bigoted, racism is a *white phenomenon*—it is a defense of white privilege. This being said, the point is not to encourage the use of "racist" as a rhetorical weapon or to demonize persons as "racists." As Seldon (1995: C14) reminds us, we need to use racism as a descriptive term, one which characterizes behavior and not the innate characteristics of the actor. The effect of the racist label should not be to demonize "racists," but instead to illuminate ways in which actions—"culturally acceptable" beliefs and the normal functioning of institutions—are serving to perpetuate race-based advantages.

Sociologists—particularly humanist sociologists—need to play a role in highlighting the ubiquity of racism as a fundamental feature of American society. If the status quo discourse continually emphasizes the "unintentional" causes of segregation, then it is incumbent upon progressive forces to illuminate the persistence of institutional racism in American society. For example, given the importance of residential segregation for the school desegregation debate, it is particularly important to ensure that the racial understandings of American society include an awareness of the forces contributing to residential segregation—as Massey and Denton (1993) have documented—to show that segregation did not just "happen." Likewise, to the extent that racial discourse begins to incorporate the depiction of whites as "victims," it is essential that we strive to challenge these new myths and to place the debate over racial equality in its proper social and historical context. As has been made clear by the West Hartford experience, the racial understandings of American society are in a state of constant flux. If current trends continue to gain momentum, the struggle for racial justice in the twenty-first century will be all the more difficult.

Endnotes

[1]The original suit was filed in 1989, trial proceedings occurred in the fall of 1992 and the winter of 1993, and final arguments were made in late 1994. In the initial *Sheff* decision on April 12, 1995, Superior Court Judge Hammer ruled that in the absence of proof that the state created racial isolation, no court-ordered integration or other remedial action would be imposed. The plaintiffs appealed to the Connecticut Supreme Court and on July 9, 1996, the Court, by a 4–3 verdict, overturned the lower court decision and found for the plaintiffs. The question of remedy, however, was placed in the hands of state government and currently remains unresolved. For a discussion of the legal rationale for the plaintiffs' case, see Brittain (1993).

[2]Under the Connecticut State Board of Education regulations to implement the Racial Imbalance Law (Connecticut General Statutes 10–226e) a district is determined to be in a state of racial imbalance when the proportion of minority students in any school is outside of a range of twenty-five percentage points from the proportion of minorities for the entire school district. In the 1993–94 school year, one elementary school in the West Hartford school district had a minority enrollment of 48.5%, which was more than 25% above the district (town) average of 19.3%.

[3]Following the decision to table the K-2/3–5 proposal, the plan development process involved the establishment of a committee to review alternative plans (Committee to Review Alternatives). Plans were then submitted to the Racial Balance Advisory Committee (mandated by state law), which was charged with reviewing proposals for compliance with state law and making necessary revisions. Proposals were then submitted to the Board of Education, which made further modifications and conducted a series of public hearings before adopting a plan in February 1995. The actual end product of the citizen review process was a recommendation for a "controlled choice" plan (cf. Alves and Willie 1987) where parents would have the option of enrolling their children in any of the town's elementary schools (each of which would be organized as a theme or magnet school to maximize alternatives) subject to caps designed to ensure and maintain racial balance. I was a member of the Racial Balance Advisory Committee which made this recommendation to the Board of Education. For a more detailed discussion of the plan and the process through which the plan was developed, see West Hartford Board of Education (1995).

[4]Several subsequent events merit mention. In response to vocal opposition, the West Hartford School Administration decided in August 1995 to drop the use of racial balance criteria for magnet school enrollment for 1995–96. The November 1995 municipal elections led to the replacement of three retiring Board of Education members (out of a seven member board) with three new members, two of whom were active in leading opposition to the desegregation plans, while the other was affiliated with an organization which supported the desegregation plans. The reconstituted Board of Education is currently engaged in further modification of the magnet school selection criteria.

[5]This advertisement appeared on page B3 of the November 28, 1994 edition of *The Hartford Courant*.

References

Altheide, David L. 1987. "Ethnographic Content Analysis." *Qualitative Sociology* 10(1):65–77.

Alves, Michael J. and Charles V. Willie. 1987. "Controlled Choice Assignments: A New and More Effective Approach to School Desegregation." *The Urban Review* 19:67–88.

Blauner, Bob. 1992. "Talking Past Each Other: Black and White Languages of Race." *The American Prospect* 10:55–64.

Brittain, John C. 1993. "Educational and Racial Equity Toward the Twenty-First Century—A Case Experiment in Connecticut." Pp. 167–83 in *Race in America: The Struggle for Equality* edited by Herbert Hill and James E. Jones. Madison, WI: University of Wisconsin Press.

Burstein, Paul. 1991. "Reverse Discrimination' Cases in the Federal Courts: Legal Mobilization by a Countermovement." *The Sociological Quarterly* 32:511–28.

Feagin, Joe R. and Hernan Vera. 1995. *White Racism.* New York, NY: Routledge.

Firebaugh, Glen and Kenneth E. Davis. 1988. "Trends in Anti-Black Prejudice, 1972–1984: Region and Cohort Effects." *American Journal of Sociology* 94:251–72.

Gallagher, Charles A. 1994. "White Reconstruction in the University." *Socialist Review* 24: 165–187.

Gamson, William A. and Kathryn Lasch. 1983. "The Political Culture of Social Welfare Policy." Pp. 397–415 in *Evaluating the Welfare State*, edited by Shimon E. Spero and Ephriam Yuchtman-Yaar. New York, NY: Academic Press.

Gamson, William A. and Andre Modigliani. 1987. "The Changing Culture of Affirmative Action." *Research in Political Sociology* 3:137–77.

_____. 1989. "Media Discourse and Public Opinion on Nuclear Power: A Constructionist Approach." *American Journal of Sociology* 95:1–37.

Horton, John. 1995. *The Politics of Diversity.* Philadelphia, PA: Temple University Press.

Jaret, Charles. 1995. Contemporary Racial and Ethnic Relations. New York, NY: HarperCollins.

Kinder, Donald R. and David O. Sears. 1981. "Prejudice and Politics: Symbolic Racism Versus Racial Threats to the Good Life." *Journal of Personality and Social Psychology* 40:414–31.

Klugel, James R. 1990. "Trends in Whites' Explanations of the Black-White Gap in Socio-economic Status." *American Sociological Review* 47:518–32.

Krauthammer, Charles. 1995. "Diversity is Hot, But It's Also Morally Bankrupt." *The Hartford Courant* September 5:A13.

Massey, Douglas S. and Nancy A. Denton. 1993. *American Apartheid: Segregation and the Making of the Underclass.* Cambridge, MA: Harvard University Press.

McAneny, Leslie and Lydia Saad. 1994. "America's Public Schools: Still Separate? Still Unequal?" *The Gallup Poll Monthly* (May):23–29.

Omi, Michael and Howard Winant. 1986. *Racial Formation in the United States.* New York, NY: Routledge & Kegan Paul.

Schuman, Howard, Charlotte Steeh, and Lawrence Bobo. 1985. *Racial Attitudes in America: Trends and Interpretations.* Cambridge, MA: Harvard University Press.

Schuman, Howard and Charlotte Steeh. 1996. "The Complexity of Racial Attitudes in America." Pp. 455–69 in *Origins and Destinies*, edited by Silvia Pedraza and Ruben G. Rumbaut. Belmont, CA: Wadsworth.

Seldon, Horace. 1995. *Convictions About Racism in the United States of America.* Boston, MA: Community Change.

Steinberg, Stephen. 1995. *Turning Back: The Retreat from Racial Justice in American Thought and Policy.* Boston, MA: Beacon Press.

van Dijk, Teun A. 1993. *Elite Discourse and Racism.* Newbury Park, CA: Sage.

Wellman, David T. *Portraits of White Racism.* 2nd ed. Cambridge: Cambridge University Press.

West Hartford Board of Education. 1995. *A Three-Year Plan to Achieve Racial Balance in the West Hartford, Connecticut Public Schools.* West Hartford, CT: West Hartford Public Schools.

Wilmoth, John R. and Patrick Ball. 1995. "Arguments and Action in the Life of a Social Problem: A Case Study of `Overpopulation,' 1946–1990." *Social Problems* 42:318–340.

Rejoinder to Doane's "Contested Terrain: Negotiating Racial Understandings in Public Discourse"[3]

Gina Petonito
Miami University

Former President of the Association for Humanist Sociology Ashley W. Doane, known as Woody, made his mark on the race and ethnic constructionist literature with numerous articles. "Contested Terrain: Negotiating Racial Understandings in Public Discourse," is but one of them. Placing the discourse of average person at his analysis' center makes this article of particular interest to humanists.

Omi and Winant's (1986) seminal concept, racial formation tells how elites or social movement activists transform racial definitions. When these definitions, forged by political contest, filter down to the masses, they are subject to further re-definition at what Woody defines as the "public" level of race. He notes that "public discourse is a visible connection between the macro-elite and media discourses and everyday discourses of the masses" (p. 33). This concept, "public discourse," introduces reflexivity to the racial constructionist process: constructs created at the elite level are contested at the public level, which in turn can transform elite level constructs. This reflexivity is evident throughout Woody's case study of the school desegregation controversy in West Hartford. Operating within ongoing political discourses dealing with desegregation, the participants in this local debate constructed their own meaningful arguments within this frame.

The participants' arguments about racism are of particular interest, since they are reflective of a more general discourse about race. For some participants, the moniker of racist is a detestable one that "effectively places the recipient beyond the pale of civilized society" (p. 38). Other participants construct racism as mere awareness of racial difference. When these constructs are so employed, "racism" is stripped of its linkages to structures of discrimination and power, and becomes an odious individual characteristic. Since racism is such a contested concept, participants employ new constructs to symbolize race, such as "impacted students." When race is eliminated from everyday talk, racism is similarly obscured. Hence, Woody shows not only how people construct racial meanings, but also how they use these constructs to deny the very existence of power. Humanists interested in dismantling racism will find this insight useful. Rather than directing their efforts solely on elite actions, humanist activists must simultaneously sensitize the average person to the existence of racism. Woody's analysis demonstrates how difficult this task can be, as one must make people transcend the concrete ("racist" as insult) to the abstract, first in seeing

---

[3] An earlier draft of this paper originally appeared in *Humanity & Society* Volume 27, Number 4, 2003.

"racism" as an institutionalized system of power and second in recognizing their role in allowing this system to retain its invisibility.

Woody's analysis, grounded in the ideational social movements literature, could have been deepened by insights drawn from the simultaneously emerging literature outlining the constructionist approach to social problems. This approach describes and analyzes how people construct claims about putative problems (in this case, school desegregation), using rhetorical strategies available in any given discourse. While one can hardly fault him for not drawing from a concurrent literature, insights from a constructionist approach could allow him to more fully describe the particular rhetorical strategies claimants' used to advance their argument within any given frame, or to show how claimants' arguments can bridge frames and draw from different discourses.

Regardless of his theoretical stance, Woody's conception of "public discourse" is a significant contribution to the race and ethnic constructionist literature. The concept's applications go beyond a discussion of claims about a perceived problem, such as desegregation, but can also provide an analytic bridge between racial identities and elite discourse. Identities, often negotiated in the public arena, can affect political discourse and vice versa. While people place themselves into racial categories based, in part, on what constructs exist in the larger discourse, racial identities are also affected by the experiences of dealing with others in everyday life. For example, Nagel's (1996) exploration into "ethnic renewal," or the process by which new ethnic identities, communities or cultures emerge, discusses the connection between individual and collective ethnic renewal, and one arena for this interplay to occur is the public one. So, Woody provides constructionists with a site for locating public discourse between political discourse and individual identity. Further, he gives humanists an analytic tool to place the everyday actor into the race and ethnic constructionist project, allowing for a more complete understanding of how racism persists in everyday life. As he notes, the emphasis in the literature on racist discourse produced by elites, ignores the ways average people understand, use and transform racist rhetorics to advance their particular interests. Woody's introduction of "public discourse" allows the analyst to locate the activities of everyday racism, the first step in realizing its transformation.

References

Nagel, Joane, 1996. *American Indian Ethnic Renewal: Red Power and the Resurgence of Identity and Culture.* New York: Oxford University Press.

Omi, Michael and Howard Winant, 1986. *Racial Formation in the United States.* New York: Routledge & Kegan Paul.

5. The Sociology of Human Rights[1]

T. R. Young
Colorado State University

The concept of human rights is much abused. In the U.S. and the Western Bloc, human rights as a concept refers to the inability of dissidents in the Soviet Union, Bulgaria, Poland and elsewhere to criticize the stupidities and failures of party bureaucrats. In the Soviet Union, Hungary and the Eastern Bloc, human rights is conceived of in terms of access to enough food, shelter, health care and the occupational structure which produce these. Human rights are not seen to include the right to travel freely, to publish freely, to criticize the party outside of party ranks, nor is the concept wide enough to buy and sell the labor of others for a profit. Each social formation, in order to be that social formation, must tailor the concept of human rights in such a fashion as to limit challenges and to maintain legitimacy. A fair analysis of human rights starts with that generalization.

The U.S. government does not care to couch the concept of human rights in terms of the ordinary consequences of capitalism which debases the family, makes crime seem sensible, distorts human sexuality and pollutes every niche of physical space. The U.S.S.R. seems unable to include public criticism, public discourse, local initiative or a generous spirit in its conceptualization of human rights. A second generalization one can make with respect to the present usage is that each social formation conceives of human rights in such terms as to make itself look good in contrast to its chief rival.

The concept of human rights belongs to the entire human collective and not to those nation-states which occupy one small part of the planet in one small fragment of time. There are, perhaps, good reasons for the U.S.S.R. to restrict human rights in this historical epoch but there are no good reasons for the U.S.S.R. to so constitute the concept of human rights as to preempt all subsequent progressive revolution in the Soviet Union or in other socialist countries. And the U.S.A. does have good reason to be proud of its record on human rights—but again not at the expense of the historical record. The many freedoms of some, more advantaged persons developed in context of the political needs of an emerging capitalist class to use freedom of speech to delegitimate feudal relationships. Still less may one overlook the unfreedoms imposed by the capitalist systems on workers, consumers, third-world nations, and upon the surplus population in order to ensure the private freedoms of a privileged minority. A third preliminary generalization we can set as part of the current sociology of human rights encompasses this point: The partisan use of the concept of human rights requires a highly selective, and thus distorted, use of the historical record.

---

[1] This paper originally appeared in *Humanity & Society* Volume 5, Number 4, 1981.

The Concept Itself

A bit of critical reflection is necessary to move the question of human rights outside of its present partisan usage and elevate it as a transocietal measure of performance such that the human project is improved. The process by which the concept of human rights is constituted and enters into the political praxis of a people may be justified only upon the grounds of the human project as a historical whole. Anything short of the interests of the human collective is better served by a different, less ambitious concept. In so doing, the first problem one encounters is whether the concept of human rights contains stable and indisputable content. The nature of language itself warns against an attempt to freeze the meaning of a term for all times and places. No two situations involving people are ever identical and, so, the usage of a given term to convey the notion of both situations is impossible. Many theorists circumvent this problem (falsely, I think) by differentiating between essence and actuality, between ideal and real, abstract and concrete. I think the better position is to understand that meaning must be contextual and variable. This is not very satisfying for those of us who prefer absolutes but the structure of language is designed to create shared meaning; not comfort the insecure.

I should like to set forth some views on a concept of human rights which might be a useful place to start:

1. Human rights might refer to those activities which all humans could do by virtue of their status as humans. Among these are usually found: to live in peace, to make choices of a meaningful sort, to hold property, to gain personal satisfaction, to free association, to equal opportunity, to effective dissent, and to movement which does not harm others.

2. Another way to think about human rights is in terms of those things a person must do in order to properly claim the status of an actual human being. Such a list would include an obligation to help and respect others, to live a productive life, to exhibit a capacity to love as well as to affirm the humanity of another. One must retain also enough personal courage to offer firm and constructive critique even in the face of considerable personal risk. The second appears to be, even in its obligatory nature, more important than the first. The quest for brains, a heart, courage and community in the Wizard of Oz resonates with this set of human rights.

3. A third way to conceive of human rights is in more narrow political terms. They can be seen as: The right to hold office, nominate, make laws, or form parties; the right to speak out; the right to vote approval of candidates and policies once a year or so; and the right to be critical of those candidates and policies.

4. A fourth way to conceive of rights is in terms of economic rights—the right to a decent lifestyle and some choice among consumer goods. Also consumer and financial rights such as: the right to buy and sell labor, goods, and services as well as the right to move capital around the world. For some the concept of human rights is reduced to very few limitations on market behavior. For some, in the Western world, in international terms, human rights center around the right of the multinational corporation to enter and leave an economy as it pleases.

5. Perhaps the least human set of rights which gains considerable emphasis include those rights to sexual novelty, drug use as well as unusual amounts, styles, and

character of wardrobe or body adornment. Some place considerable importance upon psychological experience in various combinations.

These five sets of human rights, as far as I am able to determine, complete the everyday approaches found in the substantive discussions of human rights. There are at least two major issues which one finds in these listings and from which I should like to generate a couple of tentative theses.

In the first instance, one wonders why these rights tend to occur in relatively exclusive sets. A second question concerns the preferred set to which people give allegiance. The sociology of knowledge affords us some insight into these concerns. We can readily surmise that one's position in society (as well as the position of one's society in the international scheme of things) determines one's conceptualization of which "human" rights are of paramount importance. If one can take material welfare for granted, then one (individual or group) can assert other rights as important. If one is in a highly privatized society such as that of the U.S., one can assert the primary of the fifth set. If one is in a highly communal society, the second set above will appear to be fundamental. If one is in a society which is highly stratified and organized in terms of ancient exploitative relations, then political and economic freedoms will appear as singularly salient. Generally, the set chosen will be closely related to the social position a group (or a society) occupies. A competent sociology of human rights will have to sort out the various relationships of a given set to socio-cultural conditions as and when such a sociology develops. One guess is that the themes themselves are related to the political requirements of given social formations. Each social formation has different problematics with which to deal. This variation might well pattern the survival or emphasis of one theme over another theme. For example, the emphasis on political rights to the exclusion of economic rights makes sense for persons with economic security but excluded from the structure of power—just the conditions in which an emerging capitalist class found itself. All elements of "human" rights centering upon the creation of new social relations using the lawmaking instrumentalities have special cogency in such situations. The right to nominate, hold office, vote, initiate legislation, organize political parties, and expunge old legal codes all have special saliency for an emerging capitalist class which naturally prefers the instrument of law to that of violence for the radical transformation of feudal constraints. Violence and coercion have a double liability—they interfere with business and they may not be successful against more powerful social groupings: i.e., feudal lords or organized workers.

The point here is an explication of the selective emphasis on certain human rights in certain social conditions in certain historical periods. To do this, one could equally select the Soviet Union, the Union of South Africa or on northern India during the Moghul period. In capitalist societies, the process of concentration of wealth and the growing desperation of those who are unable to sell their labor power—at rates commensurate with prevailing living standards—lead to emphasis upon another set of human rights: economic rights. The right to work, the right to organize unions, the right to access to various distributive systems: health care, food, shelter, transport all bespeak a new historical formation in which a special set of rights out of a larger universe take on extra importance.

On Necessary Repression

A balanced and transocietal sociology of human rights then must reflect upon the kinds of questions raised in this first section. Such a sociology must also generate conceptual schemes in which given forms of repression come to be seen as sensible in society. In considering repression, one may take the Freudian position that some repression of the individual is necessary in order that the "forces of life" be diverted to the production of various forms of social and cultural life. Or one might take the Marxian position that some social repression is necessary in order to make the transition from exploitative societies to communal societies in which the potential of people to become fully human is realized. And we must consider Marcuse's point that exploitative societies must use surplus repression in order to maintain cooperation in unequal social relations. The other face of a sociology of human rights is a sociology of repression. We must examine the arguments for repression as we attempt to constitute an adequate sociology of human rights: In a later section, I will offer a sociological basis for defining human rights which is more satisfactory than the five sets listed earlier but right now, one must understand that repression and human rights dwell in the same theoretical domain. A theory of one requires a corollary theory of the other.

One must be very careful and very empirical in any discussion on the necessity of repression—which entails constraints of human rights. Any slip, any unguarded statement will be picked up and used as a gloss to legitimate surplus repression—that repression necessary to preserve exploitative structures but not necessary to the human condition. With that caveat ever in mind, one can agree that the process by which human nature is generated is necessarily a process requiring constraints on individual and social behavior. Just as a voiced language requires constraints on pronunciation; tone, pitch, volume, rhythm and speed in order for meaning to be generated, a human society requires constraints on behavior in order for a human to emerge. The rules which constrain the written form have their counterpart in the rules which generate clearly recognizable social forms. If we were to permit the concept "form" to be spelled "farm," "fomr," "from," or "Rofm," as whim dictated, meaning would be less readily established—and other possibilities forclosed. English teachers properly stress correct spelling. Parents properly constrain behavior. Societies properly establish social control mechanisms to create the human project. The question of social repression is not debatable if one accepts the desirability of human society. What is debatable is how much repression is necessary, the forms of repression to be used, and, certainly, the objective results obtained by repression. These questions are well known and frequently researched. The psychology discipline has done a lot of useful work on the question of social control under the general rubric of "motivation" studies—they really mean repression and control. In the sections which follow, I want to explore some less obvious questions and give some ideas which might be useful in orienting research in this area.

Insufficient Repression

Before I leave this topic, I want to emphasize that an adequate sociology of human rights—as theory and praxis united requires a discussion of areas of social organization in which there is a deficiency of repression. The human condition requires enough repression to guarantee that praxis, community and the integrity of the ecological system be guaranteed. With bands of semi-socialized young people roaming the streets of Detroit, Philadelphia, Dallas and Los Angeles, it is easy to argue for such repression as is necessary to socialize these youngsters. The incidence of corporate crime in the U.S. (Clinard 1979) warrants additional repression. The harm done to the environment as billions of pounds of toxic waste each year are put into the good earth, the clear air or the clean waters of the land warrant still more repression. The continued transfer of wealth from poor capitalist countries to rich (Cereseto 1980) warrants repression.

One could make such repression more palatable by using terms such as socialist discipline, the realm of necessity, negation of these negations or more simply liberation movements but we should not deceive ourselves. Repairing the harm done to the social process by several generations of privatized greed, distorted growth, neglected lines of production and excluded ranks of surplus persons requires more repression than we like to think about in liberal circles.

The task of rebuilding Los Angeles, socializing the criminal and the privatized elements, suppressing narcotics, eliminating the elements of organized crime, replacing the autos with low energy, low polluting mass transit as well as improving health, education and housing all are tasks which require, for some generations, at least as much repression as is found in the modern corporations. On a national level, the need for repressing right-wing armies, the various police agencies, all forms of industry and commerce accustomed to friendly regulation, unrestrained pollution and state support in exploiting the economy warrants repression. At the international level, the task is still greater. The multinational corporation (Barnet and Muller 1974), the various military and civil dictatorships, the handful of countries which live off the wealth of the world all need to be the subject of socialist discipline. The next few centuries will see many struggles to change the structure of repression from one which exploits the human process to one which facilitates it. The next several generations will see many theories and theses which are adduced to scholar and politician alike to legitimate that structure of repression oriented to their special vision of necessary repression. The role that a value-full sociology of human rights can play is to critique, evaluate, test, and transform repressive structures to more human and humane purpose. It will not be easy to transcend the ethnic, class, national, and professional interests which cloud and obscure that purpose. Some start is possible with genuinely cross-cultural collaboration in the field.

The Structure of Repression in the Capitalist Bloc

If one gauges the character of human rights in capitalist formations, one must be careful to set the boundaries of the formation properly or one will generate a distorted understanding of this historical formation. Most analysts take the nation-state as the relevant unit of analysis—as indeed one should for certain purposes. But the whole picture requires one to consider all parts of the system in order to determine its full character. The major thesis in this section is that the rich capitalist nations obtain their liberties and guarantees at the expense of the poor capitalist countries which bear the social costs of freedom elsewhere found.

If we think about the freedoms and human rights as are found in the United States, we must consider the possibility that these freedoms rest on the unfreedom of third-world nations. It is an empirical fact, readily established, that the U.S. supports—indeed institutes—repressive regimes in the third world in the name of stability and national interest (Chomsky and Herman 1979; Stockwell 1978). Stability translates to suppression of nationalistic liberation movements especially those with socialist ambitions. Jamaica, Cuba, Nicaragua currently are the objects of great concern in the U.S. State Department, the C.I.A. as well as the U.S. Military. National interest translates to market freedom for the 200 multinational corporations based in the U.S. as well as guaranteed access to energy supplies and strategic minerals for the U.S. economy. A very curious notion of national security—a better phrase is capitalist security.

The magnitude of U.S. support for repressive regimes and the concrete connections between the welfare of U.S. based corporations, interest and dividend income, the jobs of U.S. workers as well as the tax base of the federal government which to maintain welfare programs are all very clear. That these relations are not incorporated in the discussions of human rights by the U.S. press, the various candidates and officials and by U.S. scholars is a most grievous fault on their part. In the U.S., it is easy to apprehend the possibility that the genteel liberalism of 19th century Great Britain depended upon the most savage repression of native peoples in Uganda, Kenya, South Africa, India, and Ireland. It is less easy to consider that present freedoms in the U.S. were purchased by a savage suppression of other capitalist foes (Germany and Japan) and by the most impersonal savagery against Vietnam, Chile and Indonesia. Most historical recollections of World War I and World War II are oriented to a theory of democracy versus fascism. A better view is that, as capitalism became a global system in the 19th century, the less competitive nations—Germany, Italy, Spain, and Austria-Hungary—resorted to fascism to control workers in their desperation and resorted to military expansion to satisfy the national bourgeoisie in their desperation. Had England, France, Poland and the U.S.S.R. not been the target of that aggression, fascism would have come earlier as it is surely coming around a gain in these countries and in the U.S. Fascism is the natural ally of capitalism. Democracy is only a convenient, expedient device and always a luxury for capitalism. The grounding of democracy is in the dynamics of class struggle in the present century as workers slowly consolidated social, economic and political power (Gintis 1980: 225). Just as the emerging capitalist class saw a limited democracy as a political means to delegitimate crown, church and aristocracy, an emerging working class in coalition with other elements saw democracy as a political means to assert its rights against the property rights of the owner. And when it was convenient to labor, labor supported more fascist forms of governance.

The point of all this is that commitment to democratic forms, human rights and non-exploitative relations is most often a variable which correlates to changes in political and economic conditions for both nation-states and class strata within them. Any sociology of human rights must examine the variation in an interest to democracy as it appears in everyday strategies. Generally, a concern for human rights and democratic forms has so far been a highly variable phenomenon. In capitalist relations between states, it has been used as a gloss for less noble interests.

I reiterate two of the points made earlier before going to the major point in this section. First, democratic forms are advocated by excluded sectors whether bourgeoisie in one period or workers in another. Second, human rights and repressions are both necessary to the social process—the operative question is one of necessary and surplus repression. The major point I wish to develop next is that, in a bourgeois democracy, the division between the state sector and the civil sector provides for an extensive and unrecognized system of repression. Just as the freedoms found in one part of the international system of capitalism are, in large part, a result of the unfreedom in other parts of that system, the same is true within a capitalist country. It is quite possible to find political freedoms in the state sector but rare to find these same rights in the civil sector. And, since the vast majority of decisions are made in the civil sector, the human rights found in the state sector, important as they are, are small indeed in proportion to the unfreedom at work, school, market, and family. I would like to sketch out the structure of repression in contemporary civil domains in the U.S. in order to give the sociology of human rights in this country some perspective hitherto not well integrated into such discussions.

Among the social organizations found in the civil sector are labor unions. Very few, if any of them, are authentically democratic. One of the most persistent violators in this sector is the Teamsters' Union. Its history of coercion, exclusion, corruption and violence is a matter of public record. Not so well known is the Laborer's International Union. Its history is even worse than the Teamsters. According to Barnes and Windrem in Mother Jones (August, 1980: 34), the Laborer's Union is controlled by the Mafia, dissent is brutally repressed, pension funds siphoned off, workers are sold out to the bosses, murder is used against challengers and widows are cheated.

The record of human rights suppressed by employers matches that of the more corrupt unions and constitutes a hidden history of capitalism. A recent documentary on television charged employers with spying on employees via informers, wiretaps and private detectives. A news report on Denver KLIR today (20 July 1980) says that two employees at Denver Stapleton airport have been fired for criticizing security procedures there. Montgomery Ward's has a policy forbidding employees to talk to each other except on company business. Ward's in Fort Collins, Colorado, invented reasons to fire the eight employees who tried to organize a union—a right instituted in the state sector but not observed in the civil sector. Ward's also has complaints pending alleging violation of the rights of women employees. A full history of repression in U.S. industry, commerce, and finance is not widely available. However, some sense of the extent can be found in selected studies (Mattes and Higgins 1974; Smith 1969; Hampden-Turner 1973).

In the American university—even those in the state sector—violations of civil, academic and human rights are endemic (*Business Week* 1980). Fred Block, a Marxist, has been denied tenure at the University of Pennsylvania; Bertell Ollman, another Marxist, was appointed Chair of the Political Science department at the University of Maryland by a search committee only to be vetoed by the President of that university. Freiberg and others at Boston University, Schwendinger at Berkeley, and many others whose work reflect a conflict perspective are routinely denied tenure at U.S. universities. However one need not be a Marxist to find oneself *non grata* in the eyes of the administration of the academic corporation. Persons who object to sexist practices commonplace in academia, those who critique the structure of racism in the college town, those who adopt other lifestyles as well as those who object to distortions in the curriculum all have subjected, to the petty vengeance of one's colleagues who take their cues from the lower levels of bureaucratic control. Poor teaching hours, large classes, unpopular courses, salary, tenure, summer teaching or exclusion from the life of the department are all used selectively on those who express dissent in the university. It is only that the Marxists are especially penalized for class and conflict analysis of crime, inflation, unemployment and other forms of social distress.

The church and the sect are also in the civil sector. Each represses their membership far beyond that which is necessary to the social process. The most celebrated case in recent times is the expulsion by the Mormon Church of a woman active in the women's movement. The most bizarre case in recent times of religious repression was, to be sure, the order by the Rev. Jim Jones for mass suicide—and the murder of those who resisted divine command. The history of repression in religion and within religious organization is well known and would be of little new interest except that remembrance of this area of repressive activity helps clarify the thesis that where private parties repress, the state need not.

In the home, one out of seven families experience violence as a way of life. About five million children are beaten seriously enough to require medical attention. About one million are beaten cruelly while some three thousand die from their injury each year. About one million women flee from the repression found in the home each year. All in all, the family is a citadel of surplus repression. An adequate sociology of human rights would conceive this experience to be germane to its analysis.

The most extensive repression occurs in the various total institutions. It is arguable whether this repression is surplus or necessary. It is certainly necessary to a total institution. The prior question is whether military, asylums, convents, prisons, concentration camps, and schools need be so organized. Whether the corrective, process, the therapeutic process, the religious or educational process requires as a social form the total institution contains the answer to the question of whether such repression is surplus or not. If not; then not. It well might be that the repression serves staff purposes rather than therapeutic, justice or educational purpose. In any event, in a total institution, one is restricted to one and only one presenting identity, all routines of life are organized in minute detail, people are processed objectively en masse, and the source of behavior is located externally to the self system in the agency of a cadre itself subject to the dictates of a governing elite. A total institution is hostile to the human process and the notion of human rights therein is a nonsense notion. If there is any such thing as animal rights, the concept might apply to inmate life in a total institution.

In church, at work, in the school and university, in the home and in various forms of play and sports, there is an extensive and endemic surplus repression far beyond that required to create and maintain human forms of social organization. Disregard for this set of private repressive practices permits a society to claim it is a "free" society. Such freedom is confined to one small niche in society while the arena in which the vast majority of people live out the greatest part of their lives is excluded from an appraisal of that society. An adequate sociology of human rights must consider both private and public spheres of life to be relevant.

It is at this point that the sociology of law and of human rights converge and overlap. There are over five million laws in the U.S. and various law-making bodies produce about 150,000 new laws each year. Each law has significance for human rights. Many of these laws are oriented to the human process. Some protect workers, consumers, and the environment. As such, they improve the social and physical conditions in which each must function. Some laws attack ancient wrongs of racist and sexist oppression. Some laws are designed to regulate the conditions of trade, travel and communication; activities historically positively organized. And some laws attempt to regulate the activities of political parties—also in the private sector. The number and kind of laws proliferated bespeak a thoroughgoing conflict within the private sector which the state attempts to mediate. These laws also comprise the battleground upon which the balance between surplus and necessary repression is determined.

The intrusion of the state into the civil sector is widely understood on the right to the unnecessary repression of business and industry. On the left it is viewed as a necessary repression of repressive activity in the private sector. Whatever the case, each law, each rule, each policy, each program is a form of repression. Someone will lose his/her freedom for every law created. If every person complied with a given law out of nature, instinct or wisdom, that law would be superfluous. The very notion of law implies repression. With each law, the state further intrudes into the civil sector but the main thesis remains valid at this time: The remission of necessary repression by the state sector is more than made up by unnecessary repression in the private sector. Indeed, the very life of private capitalism requires the state to abrogate repression in the civil sector and cede repression, as a part of social life, to the private sector—thus are the privileged structures of class, race, and sex reproduced in "free" societies. In unfree societies, the state joins forces with private elites in order to produce still more surplus repression—itself absolutely essential to the survival of exploitation in unstable societies.

The level of surplus repression in the civil sector varies across institutions and varies, as with, among different establishments within the same institution. Generally, the surplus repression of workers is the greatest in society although there are some few corporations in the U.S. which try to minimize surplus repression through participatory governance as well as profit-sharing (Hunnius, Garson and Case 1973). The educational institution, the health and medical care system, the military, the family, religion, and welfare all exceed the minimal repressive requirements of a society in order to maintain class, ethnic and sexist stratification.

The bureaucracy is the archetypical instrument of surplus repression and as Perrow (1980) suggests, the bureau is becoming the central unit of social organization replacing the family, the team, the neighborhood, the community and other primary groups. The bureaucracy is designed as an instrument of surplus repression. The rules of decision-making, of authority, of echelon, of communication and of material resources all generate surplus repression. Communication rules repress consciousness in many ways. To whom one might talk, the appropriate topic of thought and talk, the weight of one's words, the kind of words one may use are all carefully constrained in the interest of those who run the bureau. To the extent Perrow and others are correct, to that extent is the capacity for surplus repression in both civil and state sectors augmented. The bureau thrives simply because it is the best device for surplus repression developed so far. The internal structure of U.S. society finds far more repression than one sees. Since the repression is done quietly by private parties, it is thereby easier to speak of political freedom in the U.S.—freedoms greatly exaggerated in the interest of mystification, alienation, and reproduction of privilege.

The Human Project

The central project which distinguishes humans from animals and which undergirds any sensible notion of human rights is the production of ideological, political and material culture. Exclusion from any one of these realms of production is a violation of the human project and warrants naming as such. The production of ideological culture is central to the human project. By ideological culture is meant all forms of language, art, science, religion, play and sports. Ideological culture includes both the idea and the embodiment of social relatedness. All social forms are ideological culture. Marriage forms, work forms, forms of games and forms of kinship as well as forms of governance are part of the human project. To be human is to be involved in the construction of social reality—in the process by which the idea of a social form is transposed into the reality of that form...at least to such an extent that one can reasonably call that activity an instance of a marriage, a friendship, or a team. The primary set of human rights concerns the right to constitute ideological culture. But as these social forms all require cooperation, certain forms of behavior are not permissible. One must follow rules of grammar if one is to produce language since others are involved in the constitution of meaning. Language is not a private matter subject to personal freedom. It is a social process which opens up a realm of collective freedom.

Access to the process by which social reality is constituted together with the material base required for such construction is, at once, a human right and a human requisite. In the sense that one is not human unless one produces such forms of culture and in that all forms of culture are collective, human rights is not so much a matter of freedom but a matter of necessity. Freedom bears a very special connection to the human project. Freedom—for human beings—is always a collective right. Once again, the nature of language, of social reality, of social relationship is collective. One cannot speak alone, create gods alone, be a parent or a spouse alone or be a teacher or a president alone. Social life is collective life and freedom is a collective right.

Freedom, for human beings, is further constituted in the process of criticizing and changing social forms. When a given social form or any part of the current inventory of ideological culture of a group becomes inappropriate, a given social collective must have the option to adopt other social forms. Human rights imply freedom to transform to some new ways of relating but it is a nonsense statement to hold that freedom includes the option to become a slave or to impose unfreedom on others. Genuine freedom, in its social—i.e. human—mode has a directional bias as well as a collective bias. It must always proceed in the direction of participation. Efforts to transform the structure of racism, sexism, elitism or any division of ideological production which excludes people is progressive. Any effort to produce social forms which increase the stratification of power, privilege or which withholds the material base for social activity is hostile to the human project.

More particularly, any action which fragments social life, which strips language of its human dimension, which excludes people from productive labor, from access to health and medical services, from housing or food delivery systems is a violation of distinctly human rights. The concept of human rights, set forth in this section bears more affinity to the concept found in socialist countries than in capitalist countries. Having said that, I want to emphasize the need for political praxis distributed extensively across a population. Many of the bourgeois freedoms used for privatized and elitist purposes in a capitalist context have a different character when located in a socialist context constrained as they are by the "moment of sociality" (Markovic 1974).

The Dialectics of Human Rights

In this section, I should like to suggest necessary and variable dialectics which must be considered in any nonpartisan, nonpolitical treatment of the Human Rights topic. First is the dialectic between, as Marx put it, the realm of necessity and the realm of freedom. That dialectic is a very general one which subsumes a lot of other dialectics but generally it means that one must first feed, shelter, and cloth the human body before one can go on into the realm of freedom. The preoccupation of undeveloped socialist countries with agriculture, heavy industry as well as technology and management bespeaks a preemptive concern with the realm of necessity. The abiding concern of the developed capitalist countries as England, the U.S. and, perhaps, France with the realm of freedom probably stems more from the different positions in which these two sets of societies are found than in any moral superiority of one people as contrasted to another. Historical conditions always constrain the size and shape of the realm of freedom. Historical conditions always constrain the challenge of the realm of necessity. Geography, geology, climate and the shifting forces of nature collide to press upon a society the realm of necessity. Floods, earthquakes, drought, as well as astronomical events the size and momentum of which we only dimly grasp all render the realm of necessity more intractable and serve to reduce, in human terms, the importance of personal preferences as well as collective plans and programs.

It was, perhaps, concern for this dialectic which led Marx to focus upon the means of production as a central concept in his analytic schema. It was certainly a concern for one's relationship to the means of production (of food, shelter, of health care, of clothing and transport) which led Marx to spend so many years examining the anatomy of capitalist and so many more years excoriating the class system. The whole point of Marxian methodology—as historically limited as it is—the whole point of Marxian social philosophy—as primitive as it was—is simply to change the relationship between the realm of necessity and, through class struggle, expand the realm of freedom. This struggle—always a class struggle—is itself in the middle ground between necessity and freedom. Sometimes people are free to struggle and they fail to live up to the human promise. Sometimes people struggle when the odds are against them so that they become martyrs to their own folly. That this folly often invokes a sense of the heroic and stands as a beacon to hope is true enough but one should, at some level of understanding, realize that even in the appeal of such heroism there are limits to struggle. Today only a fool would suggest that the forces of class struggle openly challenge the forces of repression in the Southern Cone of the Americas. At the same time, only a hopeless coward would bespeak the effort to organize an underground opposition in Bolivia, Chile, Argentina, Paraguay, Brazil and Uruguay.

In those societies, the class relations place the means of production in the hands of fewer and push the realm of human freedom even farther from the masses. A woman who works from five in the morning until nine at night to feed the workers whose labor frees the children of the middle classes to study philosophy, dance the disco, jog or meditate simply has not the time or energy to read, dance and jog. A man whose labor in the mines or fields puts food and energy in front of the doctors, lawyers, and lawmakers simply cannot study medicine, law or politics in his spare time. The children who slowly die on corn or potatoes cannot find the energy to compete with children in the rich capitalist countries who eat the beef, milk, chocolate, coffee, tea, fruit and vegetables exported from the poor nations to those rich countries. Concern with the realm of private capital to invest, divest, or waste is a freedom which lies outside the dialectics of emancipation. Such a freedom must be severely narrowed in progress toward human rights.

A second dialectic important to any discussion of human rights is the necessary and proper dialectic between individual and collective rights. Again, the status of this dialectic is historically conditioned. In any discussion of this dialectic, one must understand that it is empirically the case that neither the human individual nor the human society is possible without that dialectic. There is a large body of evidence, natural and contrived which affirms that the individual Homo Sapiens does not automatically become a human being. Studies of sensory deprivation, of children in orphanages, nurseries, hospitals, asylums and studies, as well, of feral children attest to the need of loving interaction with others for human development. Harlow's monkeys, the studies of bird calls, of isolated horses, ducks, and geese all asseverate the importance of others for "normal," i.e., competent growth.

At the same time, the fully human being can be dehumanized when the dialectic is dominated by the collective. In its most brutal form, the case reports from concentration camps assert the fact that individual freedom is necessary to the human condition—both prisoners and wardens alike become inhuman when a set of social relationship permit no individual variation. This point is readily visible in concentration camps where brutality brutalizes both. However, people become inhuman in the nice comfortable offices of the liberal bureaucracy as well. The lower echelon personnel give up and find expression for their humanity outside the officially given structures—in the interstices and understructures of the bureau. And, at the top, the "superiors" find their power a corrupting and insidious influence.

The conditions under which it is appropriate to demand and to concede the individual abrogate personal choice, personal belief or conviction, personal reservation or personal benefits do, in principle, exist. It is possible to accept that there are times in all societies when the individual must humble himself or herself before the hard exigencies which threaten the survival of the society hence the possibility of humanity itself for those concerned. This stipulation is often abused. False sacrifice is demanded all too often by incompetent governments and self-indulgent privileged persons. To say no to these false demands is at once an act of rare courage and simple wisdom. Apart from the false appeals to personal sacrifice, there are authentic appeals to sacrifice the individual interest of perhaps every single person in that society. This form of the dialectic must be carefully studied and the conditions clearly set out for collective discourse and private reflection.

I am not able to treat this case here other than to accept in principal such a one-sided dialectic. In times of natural calamity, in times of relentless exploitation—an exploitation not directed to the collective good but rather to the benefit of a class or ethnic elite—in these first two cases, one might accept the sacrifice of one's own private freedoms... it is important to note that I have not conceded the right for collective *discourse* or private *reflection* even in the most dire circumstance.

There is, of course, the opposite form of this dialectic. One must wonder whether there is ever a time when the individual may be entirely free from the constraints placed on one by others: constraints of obligation, of reciprocity, of unsolicited generosity or even of common courtesy. The question is whether such a form of the dialectic can ever be justified in terms of the human warrant. It is trivial to point out that this form of the dialectic is commonplace in the privatized world of commodity capitalism, in slavery, and in ethnic and gender stratification. The question I raise here is whether ever one is justified to extricate oneself from the bonds of collective endeavor and go one's own way. Mind, self, language and society are always collective products. Is there ever a time when a private mind, a private language or a private self is possible? A fully developed sociology of human rights would treat such a situation and, perhaps, produce some insights or would admit such a possibility. The movie, A Majority of One, suggests the affirmative but, again, such an easy uncritical answer feeds into the fascist impulse and it is well to remember the fascist solution subverts the human project just as surely as neglect and abandonment of children distorts it.

A third dialectic is that between the present and the future. The urge toward freedom in this generation must always be constrained by the need for freedom in the next generation. Modes of production which use natural resources in profligate manner, despoil the earth, pollute the air or trigger natural calamity provides an unnecessary limitation on choice for those alive 200 or 2000 years hence. It does not suffice to assert that necessity is the mother of invention—that is clearly not the case; there is too much need to support that absurdity. At one extreme one can contemplate the case in which there is no consideration for the present generation. Socialist societies have made much of the need for workers and peasants to defer their personal needs and wants in the interest of a socialist future. After four or five generations of such justifications, it loses its warrant. Still in countries ravaged by colonial or economic imperialism, there is a warrant for real sacrifice as the imperialist forces are expelled. A return of some of the surplus value with a wide deployment of that capital is all too often not in the realm of the possible so the present must sacrifice. At the other extreme of this dialectic is the case in which the present gives no thought to the future generation. Apart from the privatized world of the consumer society, one could support such a case in a rich and renewable environment. There may be a place where such conditions still hold but one wonders. More clearly is the case where conditions are so bleak that every ounce of food and every stick of fuel must be used at once else life itself subsides. In Eskimo life, such times occur. In the barrios of Mexico City, it is an idle luxury to think of the morrow. In times of famine or in the aftermath of war, such a foreshortening of history makes sense. It is too often the case that those who have tomorrow fail to provide for it and the welfare of the future is sacrificed to the petty wants of the day. History will judge harshly the role of advertising and advertisers in creating such a solipsistic society.

A particularly virulent form of such an abortive approach is that embodied in the work of Paul Ehrlich and other population polemicists. They would sacrifice the generations to come of the poor and those in the third-world to maintain the undisciplined consumption of the privileged today. In the name of birth control are the politics of consumption secreted. As many have noted, if it is truly the future one wishes to protect, birth control for one American affords more benefits than the abortion of 20, 60, or 200 persons in the third world depending upon the energy system in use. One American child wastes more than 60 children in Afghanistan, yet the Rockefeller Institute pushed dangerous contraceptives there as in Africa and South America. There is something to be said for population planning but, as with human rights, such decisions should transcend elitist interests.

There are many other such dialectical oppositions which require situated analysis and variable affirmation. No one formula suffices for all time and place. Such is the challenge to and field for human genius. I have mentioned three dialectics in which valued objectives clash and produce struggle—and in which struggle a fair amount of humanity may emerge. There are other dialectics equally of moment to the human project. The dialectics of social organization must be considered—which institutions get which support under what conditions. It seems that in all social formations, the institutions of war and state conflict with other essential structures. The dialectics of social control; self-control against and in conjunction with external controls have a separate, related history. The dialectic between technology and culture—sometimes conceived as the dialectic between instrumental and substantive rationality—requires exposition as a consideration in the sociology of human rights. Quinney and others assert a renewal of the dialectic between things of the spirit (understood as part of nature) and things of the flesh. I support such renewed interest as fully compatible to the human project. I expect the reader can provide a further list of dialectical oppositions which are essential to a considered human rights prospectus. And certainly the discussions above reflect the limitations of knowledge and wisdom of the present writer but, for all that, there is a framework of a sociology of human rights found here which I have no doubt surpasses that used in the rhetoric of a Jimmy Carter, a Ronald Reagan or a Chamber of Commerce.

Conclusion

Human rights, when embodied, create human beings. A society must be organized in such a way as to distribute human rights throughout its population if it is to justify a claim to be a good and decent society. The name we assign to this distribution of human rights in these days is social justice. A just society is known by the health and good spirits of its population. A zest for life and enthusiasm for work is widespread in the population. A society which is poorly organized for social justice is measured by crime rates, desertion rates, child abuse rates, morbidity and mortality rates and by the concentration of wealth. There are objective measures by which a society may be adjudged adequate the human project.

These same measures are appropriate to compare the socialist bloc as an entity with the capitalist bloc as an entity. Measures of inequality, of infant mortality rates, of income concentration and of health and medical indices all suggest that socialist countries, as a group, do better than capitalist countries as a group (Cereseto 1980). In the capitalist bloc, the indicators of social justice continue to deteriorate. Crime, poverty, starvation, infant mortality, as well as military fascism are concentrated in the capitalist bloc and daily grow worse. While this doesn't redeem the surplus repression in socialist countries, it does bespeak a time for discarding capitalism as an economic, political, and social formation. From a major force for human rights in the 17th century, capitalism has become its chief obstacle in the 21st century.

References

Amin, Samir. 1977. *Imperialism and Unequal Development*. New York: Monthly Review.
Barnes, Ed and Bib Windrem. 1980. "Six ways to take over a union." *Mother Jones* (August):34 et passim.
Barnet, Richard and Ronald Muller. 1974. *Global Reach*. New York: Simon and Schuster.
Business Week. 1980. "Marxists on the Campus—in the Faculty." 28 April:126–128.
Cereseto, Shirley. 1980. *Critical Dimensions in Development Theory*. Red Feather: The Red Feather Institute.
Chomsley, Noah and Edward Herman.1979. *The Political Economy of Human Rights*. Vols. I and II. Boston: South End Press.
Clinard, Marshall, et al. 1979. *Illegal Corporate Behavior*. Washington, D.C.: The Justice Department.
Gintis, Herb. 1980. "Communication and politics." *Socialist Review* 10 (2/3) March-June:189–232.
Girvan, Norman. 1976. *Corporate Imperialism: Conflict and Expropriation*. New York: Monthly Review Press.
Hampden-Turner, Charles. 1973. "The factory as an oppressive and non-emancipatory environment." In Hunnius, Garson and Case (eds.), *Worker's Control*. New York: Vintage Books.
Hunnius, Garson and Case (eds.). 1973. *Worker's Control*. New York: Vintage Books.
Marchetti, Victor and John Marks. 1975. *The C.I.A.* New York: Dell Books.
Markovic, Ludwig. 1974. *From Affluence to Praxis*. Ann Arbor: University of Michigan Press.
Mattes, James and James Higgins. 1974. *Them and Us, Struggles of the Rank and File*. Englewood Cliffs: Prentice-Hall.
Perrow, Charles. 1980. *Organization Theory in a Society of Organizations*. Red Feather: The Red Feather Institute.
Smith, Gibbs. 1969. *Joe Hill*. New York: Grosset and Dunlap.
Stockwell, John. 1978. *In Search of Enemies*. New York: W. W. Norton and Sons.
Syzmanski, Albert. 1980. *A General Theory of Civil Liberties*. Red Feather: The Red Feather Institute.
Wise, David and Thomas Ross. 1964. *The Invisible Government*. New York: Vintage Books.

A Sociology of Human Rights[2]

Stephen Adair
Central Connecticut State University

"Human rights" are articulated and pursued by widespread social movements and revolutions. All social movements and collective political actions involve advocates who claim some value or ethic, but only occasionally have people sought to universalize access to a "resource" or a privileged status by making claims to a human right. Therefore, a sociology of human rights ought to address the social conditions under which people willingly express an interest in sharing a resource or a status with all human beings.

By situating the emergence of human rights within a particular set of political conditions, I do not mean to diminish the good work that many have engaged in to specify inalienable rights or to discover transocietal rights. Indeed, T.R. Young maintained that a core objective of humanist sociology was to "elevate" human rights to "a transocietal measure of performance such that the human project is improved." This is a large task for sociology. If an identified human right is to have social and political legitimacy, then it must have a legal, public and official standing that greatly exceeds the authority that can be bestowed by sociology. The Universal Declaration of Human Rights, adopted and proclaimed in 1948 by the General Assembly of the United Nations, is certainly the most important and most comprehensive example. One might try to assess the adequacy of the Declaration in terms of the dialectical tensions Young raises. Though valuable in its own right, this exercise could only inform how human rights are realized in the social world if the Declaration itself was universally recognized.

Young opens his paper by noting that the U.S. and the former Soviet state emphasized different categories of human rights, and that, in general, nations have selectively identified particular rights to bolster its own interests. This is true enough, yet it implies that it is the state or other forms of organized power that define, protect and insure human rights. Human rights, however, are not generated by the state; and the fact that agents of the state must occasionally resort to the language of human rights to justify or to obscure its practice is itself a victory of sorts for humanism. The state can justify its practices in many ways-appeals to the glory of a warrior elite, God's will, manifest destiny, national interests - that will incur much lower social costs than the granting of rights. Human rights constrain organized power (cf. Sjoberg, Gill and Williams 2001), and reasserting them may well inspire pesky patriots who insist that the state live up to its stated ideals.

Overlapping Young's five categories of human rights, T.H. Marshall (1964) had previously suggested three major types: civil rights, political rights, and social (or economic) rights. Like Parsons (1967), Marshall suggested that human rights evolve alongside the development of citizenship as processes of inclusion became less dependent on ethnic-

[2]This paper originally appeared in *Humanity & Society* Volume 27, Number 3, 2003.

ity. Marshall (also like Parsons) associated this inclusiveness with the strengthening of the modern nation state. However, consider briefly the advancement of civil, political and social rights in the context of American history: Major advances in civil rights (equality before the law; freedom from undue forms of organized power) developed through the American Revolution, the Civil War (and the abolitionist movement) and the Civil Rights Movement. Political rights (the right to vote, petition, and to run for office) were articulated and realized because of the American Revolution, the Civil War, the Women's Suffrage Movement, and the Civil Rights Movement. The meager efforts to address *social* rights in the U.S.—the right to basic human needs and a minimum quality of life—followed the union and labor movement in the 1930s, and the Civil Rights and associated political actions of the 1960s. In all cases, the spread of human rights occurs when social movements forced the state (or overturned it) to accept the ethical value of its central claim. In a much broader sense, the language of human rights may have become embedded in the history of the West as Judaism and later Christianity formed and grew by articulating a more humane ethic in opposition to Egypt and to Rome respectively.

Social movements are often generous. To be successful, they must build solidarity against organized power interests by addressing issues of injustice that are widely perceived. For non-participants, the emergent ethic may appear as an expedient expression of self-interest, but for adherents, this struggle feels like a battle of the ethical against organized power. Social movements may thereby inspire a genuine idealism and a universalism—the language of human rights. Whether the articulated human rights really are universal, or whether they are merely the exuberant idealism of a particular historical and cultural juncture may largely depend on who gets to write the history. Stuck, as we all are, in a particular historical condition, I do not know how this question can be reconciled.

The development of civil, political and social rights over the last two centuries has not necessarily led to a more humane world. The twentieth century was almost certainly been the most deadly in the history of humanity, even though many of the most egregious forms of abuse and human cruelty have waned. Slavery and direct forms of colonial exploitation are less prevalent, but domination has become more global, insular, capillary and multi-dimensional. In the past, domination was typically explicit. Slavery required whips, chains, and a crude ideological apparatus. In early industrialism, owner and worker confronted each other, so that the worker could see his own poverty in the owner's wealth. Today, many of the most privileged are unable to recognize their own condition in the condition of the other. They no longer have to justify an explicit cruelty. Their privilege likely depends on indirect forms of exploitation or "merely" the reproduction of impoverishment, but they might reasonably imagine that they are doing good because they are unable to perceive fully the relations that they create and perpetuate. Likewise, poverty today seems more like the result of negligence and personal irresponsibility, rather than the result of an appropriation of labor and value by a few.

As I see it, identifying and describing the indirect relations that constitute the global, insular, capillary and multi-dimensional forms of domination is at the core of humanist sociology today. By doing so, we serve those who seek to come to terms with the current relations of production and reproduction. Perhaps a more universal understanding of human right awaits our ability to articulate current relations, so that a large number of people can gather in generosity and solidarity to challenge the system that does well for only a few.

References

Marshall, T. H. 1964. Class, *Citizenship and Social Development; Essays*. Garden City, NY: Doubleday.

Parsons, Talcott. 1967. *Sociological Theory and Modern Society*. New York: Free Press.

Sjoberg, Gideon; Elizabeth A. Gill and Norman Williams. 2001. "A Sociology of Human Rights." *Social Problems* 48(1): 11–47.

Section 3

Confronting Institutions:
Creating Humanistic Practices
in Everyday Life

How do we act humanistically, in fair and just ways, day in and day out? How do the major institutions responsible for framing reality, socializing our values and norms, and empowering us with information and knowledge tend to fall short in their charge? The group of articles and rejoinders in this section describe how we can make humanistic choices at the everyday, microinteractional level even in the midst of large, complex, mostly uncaring and unfeeling, social structures and institutions. Examining at the educational system, the criminal justice system and the media, these authors provide new ways of looking at old practices and attitudes. In their critiques of traditional forms of socialization and knowledge production, each author provides a critique of conservative approaches to education, criminal justice and the media. But these writers also suggest intriguing, inventive ways that we can create humanistic practices in perhaps unlikely settings, and remind us that we can create them anywhere, anytime. From classrooms to prison cells to internet web sites, humanist sociologists carry on the struggle to inform public institutions and public spaces with analytical tools in the service of social justice. We critique conservative and hierarchical pedagogy, we challenge punitive and oppressive systems of criminal punishment and inhumane incarceration, and we dismantle reactionary mythologies about military prowess and machismo. But more importantly, articles such as these inspire us all to take our best sociological imaginations and change the world.

1. Teaching Sociology Humanistically[1]

Victoria Rader
George Mason University

Statement of Values

I believe that we human beings have the capacity to build social lives that truly delight us. We are more likely to create such a world when we see ourselves as essentially the creators rather than the victims of society; when we develop our imaginations to envision a more satisfying social life; and when we experience an underlying alignment with all human beings. I am especially interested in the ways that my classes, the discipline of sociology, and schooling in general influence these aspects of consciousness and reality. I argue in this paper that to teach students humanist sociology we need to practice humanist values in our classroom procedures. No matter how humanistic our course content, we need teaching practices that encourage the student's actual experience of being critically aware, socially creative and cooperatively related to all other living beings.

It is the thesis of this paper that classroom processes, like theoretical models, are never value neutral. In fact, they vary significantly to the extent that they embody values of responsibility, divergent thinking and human cooperation. We have the opportunity in our sociology courses to encourage practices in which students experience themselves as becoming more critically aware, less limited in the recognition of options and more skilled in personal and cooperative action. At the same time we can select course content that gives a conceptual base for understanding the social influences on these values.

Yet, most sociologists begin their teaching career with little or no training in the problems of learning or teaching and have conventionally made their educational goals those of their predecessors, the conveyance of a body of material called "Sociology." This material often involves hidden or explicit assumptions of scientific objectivity (The Truth), material and linear causation (social determinism) and a bias toward social order rather than change. The material is conventionally taught through standard lectures and competitive exams. When most students do not seem particularly interested in "doing sociology" this way, professors develop a special interest in the few students, who, for various reasons, connect up with the subject matter and teaching practices. Those few, labeled the "bright students," presumably justify the present system and give personal satisfaction to many sociology professors in American colleges today. The most we can say about such a debilitating set of conventions is that they are consistent. The mystification, determinism, and ultimately, the pessimism that is found in much of conventional sociology are reinforced in the meta-messages of typical classroom procedures.

---

[1] This paper originally appeared in *Humanity & Society* Volume 3, Number 2, 1979.

As humanist sociologists become reflexive teachers, we tend to modify course content. We argue that human behavior is not completely determined but may be the partial result of choice and voluntary value orientations. On the other hand, we suggest that the sociologist is a human being who necessarily has internalized world views which condition his or her orientations, so that total "objectivity" is not attainable. We believe that moral and ethical implications are legitimate concerns for sociology. In short, humanist sociologists are concerned with asking questions and exploring answers about social conditions which encourage or limit human choice, responsibility and cooperation, and our course syllabi probably reflect this focus. But how are we going to teach sociology so that values of freedom, responsibility and alignment are experienced in the learning process itself?

Most college teachers participate in a mass standardized system of socialization where students acquiesce to sit in our required courses and give up deciding for themselves what is worth learning (Becker, Geer and Hughes 1968; Clark 1962; Kozol 1970). Students have learned to compete with one another, to fear "failure" and to distrust their own experience in the face of experts (Holt 1974; Hentoff 1977). They have learned to adapt to a system that requires students to obey rules and learn information for which they see no reason (Bowles and Gintis 1976). Given this context, what do humanist sociologists teach students by our required reading lists, competitive testing and grading, one way communication patterns, and standard array of abstract answers to unasked questions? In sum, do our teaching practices contradict our humanist goals? Paulo Freire put the issue quite cogently: "To affirm that persons should be free, and yet to do nothing tangible to make that affirmation a reality is a farce" (1969: 7).

I have developed four experimental learning methods in the last four years to explore further some of the possibilities and problems of trying to incorporate humanistic values in the teaching process itself. Teaching practices that encourage responsibility, social imagination, and cooperation involve certain basic assumptions about human nature, the nature of learning and the nature of knowledge. First I would like to review the underlying premises and assumptions and then describe the four methods. Then I will raise relevant issues from current critics who argue that such concern over teaching methods is misguided.

With these methods I assume that the human being is a whole person with the possibility for rational choice and motivated to make his or her life more satisfying. I also assume that the teacher needs to attend to the set—the beliefs and interests of students coming into the course, and the setting—the social environment created in the course, to maximize learning. In fact, all of these premises and assumptions are about learners; that is, people changing their awareness, whether they are in the role of student, teacher, department chairperson or college president. There have to be reasons for the instructor to want to expand his or her teaching style, and for the administrator to alter his or her rules to support new learning approaches. I assume that we are working with active "meaning makers" in our classrooms, not "empty jugs" or "fertile gardens," and that what students perceive is largely a function of their previous experiences, assumptions, and perceived purposes. The student's life experiences and purposes operate as the environment in which any learning will take place.

Since our perceptions come from our past experience and currently perceived needs, each individual will perceive in a somewhat unique way. This premise, if accepted, would greatly affect the kinds of expectations we have for students, our course structure and our forms of student evaluation.

On the other hand I assume that while students come from varied backgrounds, hold widely different interests and make different connections with course material, they share some general concerns. Human beings share the desire to increase their und?rstanding and control over their own identities, their relationships with other people and their location in the world. They want to learn skills that encourse survival and growth (Freire 1969; Maslow 1976; Jung 1959). We also know that such learning is more likely to occur if the student believes he or she can learn it and if the learning situation is not perceived as threatening. Peer norms, role expectations and classroom atmosphere will influence these perceptions (Thomas 1928; Mead 1934; Rosenthal and Jacobson 1970).

If we take these assumptions and apply them to teaching practices, we would develop an array of approaches that work for different teachers, students, institutional contexts, and program purposes. I have developed four experimental learning methods in a public commuter university, and would like to describe the methods and the initial opportunities and limitations that I have observed in relation to values of responsibility, critical thinking and cooperative action. The first method is the process journal; the second is a series of critical analysis papers; the third is a series of improvisational theater workshops; the fourth is the contract learning system. I have kept careful records of all course planning and modifications as well as detailed observations of each class section taught as a control or experimental class for each method and their combinations. I have extensive student evaluations of each of the four methods over three and sometimes four semesters. Further, with the permission of students, I have retained copies of critical analyses, student observations as well as photographic slides and videotapes of improvisational workshops and entries from the process journals. This exploratory data suggest areas that must be explored further.

The Process Journal

The process journal is a means by which students are encouraged to think and act sociologically. Through the journal, the learner continually initiates contact with the course material. Students write entries in a notebook considering sociologically, issues that interest them. The instructor suggests exercises which increase the student's awareness of his/her own way of experiencing social life as well as the perspective of others. For example, there are such exercises as "A Dialogue Between Selves" (e.g., the wife-mother self talks with the college student self) or "Shifting Perspectives" (e.g., the student takes up something important to him/her in her imagination and creates a dialogue with a guest speaker or someone we have read, like Malcolm X). Other exercises are designed to engage students in looking at their own language, assumptions, and values, and relate them to the institutional contexts which have influenced them.[1]

Other exercises are designed to make connections between sociological issues raised in class and the student's life experience. For example, an examination of the stratification system of one's own high school frequently clarifies such concepts as mobility, ascribed and achieved status, reward systems, and life consequences, as well as frequently inducing skepticism about the ways in which society assigns, as Berger comments, some human beings to darkness and others to light. Some of these exercises are derived from Ira Progoff's work on the process journal (1975). Students and I have developed other exercises to fit our particular course purposes.

I have observed considerable motivation and seriousness invested in the journals. The learner knows that he/she is not simply "covering the material." Whatever the student produces is going to represent a unique statement about him or herself. For example, here is an excerpt from a journal in which the student relates her reading of Asylums to her own experiences.

More Goffman –

Goffman speaks of a drastic form of contaminative exposure when an individual is forced to witness a "physical assault upon someone to whom he has ties and suffers the permanent mortification of having taken no action."

This certainly occurs frequently in the institution of education. In the past, it was physical. You watched the teacher cruelly bash the knuckles of a "misbehaving" boy (usually) that you liked and yet you said nothing and somehow this experience of no action is even more degrading than the person suffering the blows. Today it is more subtle. The teacher verbally and skillfully thrashes while students, afraid for themselves, look on. In the class that I recently dropped, the professor skillfully put down a girl who voiced a disagreement. We all sat there seething but did nothing. I did not respect myself for doing nothing.

> Peggy Keefe, 1977
> George Mason University

As students see their own understanding of social issues evolve on paper, they frequently report a clarification of their values and a new realization that they have many resources to draw upon and much to say and do about their world.

Dear Scriptwriter(s):

You have been composing a generally pleasant but sometimes flawed script. All the scenes you have written into the play have molded me into who I am. You have introduced characters in the roles of family, friends, and adversaries. You have made me fall in and out of love, taken away the use of an eye, made we "win" and "fail." *But did you think I wouldn't learn?* You left the scissors just a little too near and now I've cut the string.

> Sincerely,
> Edward D. Bull
> Citizen, Earth 1976
> George Mason University

Frequently, journal entries are photocopied or read in class. Students begin to teach and learn from one another. Sociological consciousness expands when students and teachers communicate aspects of reality in which they have a personal interest.

Moreover, periodic readings of student journals allow the instructor frequent feedback on what is actually being "learned," decreasing the amount of one way communication. The journal also gives excellent indications as to what could follow in group or individual work. In other words, the journal can allow for frequent, detailed, and non-threatening feedback for the student and teacher concerning the learning experience. The major problem with the journal approach has been in finding a productive way of grading. Since most of the work is a much more personalized expression of student views, the usual quandaries of grading become even more difficult. I have found that no matter which standards are used, the teacher must be clear from the beginning of his/her approach for journal evaluation. A second disadvantage to the journal is the time consumed in reading student work, making frequent feedback less possible in large classes.

The Critical Skills Papers

There are two important reasons why the sociological perspective cannot be considered merely in terms of students knowing a particular "subject matter." The sheer amount of information is progressing and changing at phenomenal rates, and learning the information alone does not help students learn to critically analyze, synthesize, evaluate and make use of the information as they so choose. As Nat Hentoff suggests, one way of defining growing up absurd is growing up ignorant (1977). Students who have focused on recall of information in sociology classes even five years ago may now be largely "ignorant" of the body of information generally conveyed in sociology classes today. With this rationale I have experimented with a series of critical thinking papers in which students practice the cognitive skills of inquiry (Bloom, 1956). They learn to analyze, synthesize and evaluate any model of social life, whether it comes from a popular movie with The Godfather, a public policy like the War on Poverty, the remarks of a guest speaker or teacher, or a "factual" news account. For example, last semester, some students in a social problems class studied and analyzed the War on Poverty as a social program. They argued that the major premise of the program was that a "paradox" of poverty existed which could be remedied by social reforms built around increasing the individual's competitive chances in the market place. Some of the assumptions of such a program uncovered by students included the following: the belief that poverty was not necessary to the economic system; the belief that poverty was the result of a vicious cycle of poor family life; pathological neighborhoods and deprived schooling which led to underemployment which led back to poor family life; the belief that this cycle could be broken by reform efforts at any one point; the belief that individuals would be motivated to use the reform services. Students then examined the research reports of such programs as Head Start, Job Incentive Training and Community legal services. In their conclusions, they became aware of the political aspect of defining the "success" or "failure" of programs.

Students report increasing awareness of the process of breaking down an argument into it's logical parts, uncovering the implicit assumptions, analyzing the limits of evidence, pulling together their own conclusions, and then enlarging the perspective to examine any significant implications for understanding and improving social life. Recognizing this process and learning these skills has resulted in many students beginning to take themselves seriously as critical thinkers. As they see progress from one analysis to the next, students report increased confidence that they can, indeed, learn to understand themselves and their social environment. Social analysis becomes less of a mystery left to the "experts." Students also report feeling that they are taking more responsibility for and control over what they learn and what they come to believe. It has been surprising to find how many students in each of my classes have never been asked to think analytically, or who hold beliefs that they cannot think systematically, "they are not the type." Some students choose to have individual conferences to review their papers and to develop self-confidence.

Improvisational Theater Exercises and the Sociological Imagination

In a series of improvisational theater workshops students are encouraged to see themselves as researchers who are seriously exploring the ways human beings create meaning for themselves and others. The work encourages the commitment, discipline and cooperation found in serious acting. In the basic exercise, the instructor suggests a problematic situation to small groups of actors. The actors created the social context and develop individual characters with specific personal and social characteristics. The interaction then takes place without a planned ending. The scene develops spontaneously as each character responds to the situation, and creates meaning in the scene. All performance is considered work in progress, for the major purpose of the three-hour workshop is personal and group discovery.

For example, in an introductory sociology class, we may be discussing relationship patterns of exchange, conflict, cooperation and competition. In the workshop, one group of actors is asked to create any simple, concrete situation where there is a problem of perceived scarcity. Students, after eight minutes of planning, put themselves into the situation as specific characters of their own making and act out of an intuitive understanding of what is frequently an entirely different personal and social situation than that to which they are accustomed. After the improvisation, students explore the conditions under which cooperative, exchange, conflict or competitive relationships or combinations develop in the scene as solutions to the problem of perceived scarcity. They explore the meaning of the value systems their actions implied.

In the course of discussion, they sometimes decide to replay the scene, changing one or more variables. Throughout the work and discussion, it is emphasized that there is no "right" way to experience a problematic situation, and that individuals will sometimes experience the same situation quite differently. The process of sharing quite different perceptions of an improvisation, like good class discussions, increases student awareness of the wide range of selection and interpretation of "reality." They experience directly that there is more than one way (*their* way) of seeing or understanding a situation.

The exercises raise basic questions about social life which are experienced in a number of different situational contexts. In the discussion, students also relate the exercises to their own life experience. We then take the initial awakening experiences and begin to trace, in group discussion, the social-historical forces that led to such conventions and, sometimes, to notice alternatives. For example, this student writes of the connection he made with a hand touching exercise and a past experience.

> Knowing that one of the hands I held was male, and then overcoming my aversive reactions was important to me. Several years ago my very closest and life-long friend died after a two year battle. In the years since, I have often regretted that I was never able to express in other than the most neutral terms the way I felt about him and our friendship. Had I been able to hold his hand, maybe our level of communication would have been enhanced. Maybe I could

have told him how much I would miss him. An experience like this one can help cross over artificial barriers.

Robert Burklow, 1977

Improvisational exercises have several advantages for developing the sociological perspective. To begin with, the exercises involve the student fully in intellectual, experiential and intuitive modes of knowing. Some students who have developed learning blocks with rational methods in the classroom, often readily grasp important sociological principles intuitively and experientially.

Secondly, improvisational theater is valuable as a pure form of play. While the exercises are real and produce real ideas, feelings and sensations, their limits provide a way of trying out behavior without taking the full consequences which might result in everyday life. For example, another student writes about his experience in the hand exercise mentioned earlier.

> Being male, especially in America, requires a great deal from a person, if he is to gain acceptance and approval. The framework of his role is built with rituals, rules and taboos; on Monday I was asked to violate one of these prohibitions; thou shalt not touch another man. My first gut reaction to blindly holding hands, was an overwhelming desire that a woman be seated on each side of me. This feeling became so significant that I began to analyze its meaning and its implications. Experiencing hands as separate entities, I found that I was not able to imagine them sexually neutral, at least in the beginning of the exercise. After my hands "met" their companions... they explored and found some evidence of gender.... My conclusions are irrelevant; the most damning fact is that I needed a conclusion at all. The obvious implication is that I require a label before I can begin communication. Please tell me your sex, so that I know how to deal with you, so that I can pull out the appropriate script. Of course, beyond the world of hands, we demand a multitude of labels which describe an individual; his education, his job, his family, his politics.... Social interaction seems to rest on sets of expectation; we put the cart before the horse in wanting to know who a person is before we allow ourselves to know him... I am now more aware of the amazing complexity of the roles we play in order to maintain social identities.

Peter Dozier, 1977
George Mason University

In doing various exercises, a person recreates him or herself, re-experiencing the problems which beset him/her, tests our social boundaries and tries alternatives.

A further important advantage to this method is the spontaneous development of community. As students share their initial nervousness and serious work they develop common bonds. The group provides a support system for students in their efforts to know more about themselves and their social world. There is a sense of peer acknowledgement that is seldom as forcefully experienced in other classroom activities. The experience of playfulness, personal growth and group bonds are accepted as natural benefits of our work.

> Alone in the workshop, one unlearns old roles and tries new ones on. One unlearns mistrust, sometimes the other person has to help you, and you have to believe that. One unlearns that it's every person for themselves, whole groups become dependent on each other. One unlearns conventional language, communication is possible through mime and jibberish.

> Ann Knowles, 1975
> George Mason University

Students also report more self-confidence to explore social patterns and alternatives outside of the workshop. Social patterns become transparent as agreements rather than taken-for-granted reality. One indication of this is that students who participate in the improvisations frequently become more active in other class activities; they seem to transfer the involvement and initiative that develops within the workshops to demand more for themselves in other classroom activities.

One disadvantage to this approach is that it appeals to some students and not to others, so is always made optional in my classes. This means that several three-hour time blocks must be arranged outside of regular class scheduling.

The Contract System

The contract system is a way of structuring the grading and range of activities in a sociology course. The learner and teacher recognize a variety of legitimate purposes that students may bring with them into the course. The instructor suggests a number of alternative options for fulfilling learning goals, with a point system designed to allocate credit for different options. Students consider their purposes in the course, the possible options to achieve their goals and the desired grade. Student and instructor then negotiate until a contract satisfactory to both is developed. This approach places the responsibility for what is worth knowing and the commitment or choice for learning much more visibly in the hands of the student.

Several advantages to the contract system are worth noting. Many students begin to develop independent and highly responsible strategies for determining and fulfilling their own goals for the course. Students have frequently created options that meet their unique scheduling, career or life stage interests. Students report more individual self-confidence, more group cooperation and more instructor-student trust. They sense that they have more control over what they learn, how to learn and the grade that they will earn. The point system is helpful in that it indicates the instructor's value system before work is initiated. Evaluations are continuous and progressive throughout the semester. And the system is non-competitive. Grading is based on a student's work in relation to somewhat more personalized goals. The disadvantages of such a system include a tendency of students to emphasize quantity over quality. Also, some students have difficulty moving from a traditional teacher-oriented process to one based on his or her own self-discipline, commitment and purposes. In this case the approach itself becomes a vital part of the learning process.

The contract system can be modified to many forms of teacher-styles, student interests, and varied institutional frameworks.

Summary and Discussion

Teaching methods, like theoretical models, are never value free. Moreover, they have consequences in the way students come to understand their everyday world. Each teaching practice embodies values that encourage or discourage the experience of becoming more capable and responsive to building a viable social world, less limited in the recognition of options, and more skilled in cooperative action. These are the reasons why our methods as well as content should be continually reviewed and revised.

Considering these values, some advantages in the four experimental methods are clear. I have found that when people are encouraged to assume responsibility for their own reality, the results in their education are surprising. The process journal encourages a serious and independent examination of world views, including the sources of one's own belief system. Developing critical thinking skills makes people less dependent on the experts. Improvisational workshops operate out of a respect for one's self and others, and encourage a free community exploration of alternative definitions of reality. The contract system encourages self determination and initiative.

Limitations to these methods are also apparent in relation to humanistic teaching. The critical analysis papers, the journal and the contract system encourage essentially individualistic rather than cooperative approaches to learning. Other methods, such as Professor Sal Restivo's "Mao Midterm Festival" at Renssaeler Technological Institute, encourage students to jointly prepare for exams, and thus embody cooperative learning values. Another limitation to the four experimental methods is the minimal opportunity students have to test their understanding and build skills in cooperative action in the community. Courses structured around action/research projects, such as those Professor Fred Millar is developing at George Mason University, embody such a value.

Thus, an argument has been presented logically from sociological premises and assumptions and experientially, from the development and close observation of four experimental learning methods, that there exist significant advantages in some teaching practices over others. Some sociologists and educators would disagree. There have been several arguments recently presented that a concern for improved teaching methods is misguided. The most popular positions are that 1) empirically, different teaching methods have fairly equal results; 2) teacher qualities are more important than teaching methods; 3) students actually teach themselves using their own methods; and 4) educational problems will not be solved by focusing on classroom procedures but on institutional reform. Each of these positions is considered seriously enough in the literature and the personal belief systems of teachers to merit review.

Several researchers using conventional survey designs have reported that they find no important differences in the learning results of various teaching methods. Dubin and Taveggia, for example, in their re-analysis of survey data from 91 comparative colleges found no significant differences in effectiveness of various conventional methods to convey subject content to students (1968). Such survey results may tell us something about comparative ability of different methods in relation to student recall of information. It tells us nothing about the values and attitudes reinforced or modified by the class experience.

To test the social beliefs and values of students we could do better using an attitude survey approach such as in Rotter's work, to study changes in perceptions of personal or external control, social expectations and the sense of relationship with others (1966). However, if methods are fairly equally effective in conveying subject matter, that is all the more reason to choose and develop methods on the basis of the values inherent in the learning process itself, as Dewey (1936), Jencks and Bane (1972) and others have argued.

A second position is that choice of teaching methods is not as significant as the qualities of the teacher. Reece McGee articulates this position when he suggests that teachers teach, not teaching methods. McGee speculates that good teachers are probably those who, whatever their teaching methods, liked students, were excited about their subject matter and enjoyed communicating it to others. I would argue that, although no particular methods are going to single-handedly change a teacher's personality, the qualities of liking students and the enjoyment of communicating one's subject matter is deeply affected by the approach taken in the classroom.

Methods are also the conditions which encourage or inhibit the teacher in making meaningful connections with students—their natural wisdom, their interest in understanding their world, and their life experience. Learning methods can be evaluated as to whether they give students an opportunity to contribute aliveness to the instructor as well as the reverse, for learning is a subtle and profoundly interactive process where excitement is exchanged among participants to support expansion and change. I have found the process journal and the improvisational workshops extremely important to me in this respect. (Many faculty gain some sense of this connection with their students through informal talks before and after class.) In other words, the isolation of teachers and students from one another is not just detrimental to student performance but teacher performance. I would argue that in general regularly facing a room full of blank faces deadens interest and the desire to communicate, often serves to decrease teacher expectations, and lowers respect and liking of students. It is true, on the other hand, that teaching methods, to be effective, must fit the personal style of the teacher, the institutional context and program purposes as well as student characteristics. This is to suggest that much more attention and experimentation, rather than less, be given teaching methods.

A third hypothesis is that neither teachers nor teaching methods teach: They merely create the conditions in which students teach themselves (1974). McGee argues that teachers structure the possibilities and constraints on learning. Within these conditions each student will have his own intentions and very personal array of learning methods. Again, McGee makes a good point and draws the wrong conclusion. Since students, to a large degree teach themselves that is all the more reason to examine methods. If each student has his/her own ways to generate interest, connect with materials, and learn skills, then we would greatly favor approaches that allow a variety of choices, learning contexts and time options. The contract grading system, the process journal and the improvisational workshops rate highly in the ways they provide latitude and choice, and encourage learning material in experiential and intuitive as well as rational ways. Of course, these experimental approaches only broaden the usual range of alternatives within the very constraining context of a letter grading system. What is clearly inadequate about these three criticisms is the total concern for content and total lack of concern for what is learned by the course experience itself.

A final criticism worth mentioning is the argument that conforming and alienating learning exists, not as a result of mindlessness (we can do better if we tried) but because schooling is bound to be alienating in the kind of society in which we live (Wasserman

1971; Michaels 1970). The values of competition, individualistic achievement, and consumerism will mold students regardless of what a minority of teachers attempt within the shelter of their individual classrooms (Weinberg 1976). Of course, this analysis is correct on one level. But surely, this doesn't mean that we would not develop the most humane and powerful learning processes in our classrooms as possible? It seems nihilistic not to act positively at every level of our experience. As humanist sociologists we can attempt to ask questions and explore answers that clarify what living in these times and in this culture involves. As humanist teachers we can devise non-cooptable processes which offer students the experience of increased degrees of self-determination, and whet the desire for more. And as humanist members of educational institutions and communities, we can work for humane institutional change. Again, this radical criticism ignores an important aspect of the care and feeding of teachers as well as students. One definition of integrity is undividedness. I gain strength from the consistency of treating myself and students as free, responsible, and cooperative human beings, as well as reading and discussing theoretically these possibilities. It feels increasingly absurd to discuss the human capacity for critical awareness, social vision and the common human impulse to support life, while unconsciously or helplessly conforming to teaching practices that do not work; that isolate and render more passive the very human beings that participate in them.

Sheldon Kopp, in his narrative history of great teachers, suggests that the best teachers of any historical period are not the individuals who have the answers, but those who most embody in their own lives the crucial issues of their day (1971). I find it a relief to allow students to see that I am continually learning in the same ways as they are; by building skills and practicing them, by continually exploring alternatives, and by risking mistakes while facing the consequences of my actions. As Gouldner describes so well, one's self is transformed in this reflexive process. I would not attempt to tell students how to re-build our world. As Mariampolski remarked, sociologists' solutions are often as fuzzy and as frightening as anyone else's (1978). But I can encourage students in the classroom experience to expand their own awareness and skills for living in this historical time and in this society as they so choose.

Endnotes

[1]Harry Wagachal and C. A. Bowers both use a journal method more directly phenomenological, in which students are asked to keep a journal of their intellectual and daily life experiences, out of which taken-for-granted assumptions can be identified and analyzed in terms of historical-social roots.

References

Becker, Howard, Blanche Geer and Everett C. Hughes. 1968. *Making the Grade.* New York: Wiley.

Bowles, Samuel, and Herbert Gintis. 1976. *Schools in Capitalist America.* New York: Basic Books.

Clark, Burton. 1962. *Educating the Expert Society.* San Francisco: Chandler Press.

Dewey, John. 1936. *Experience and Education.* New York: Collier Books.

Dubin, R., and T. C. Taveggia. 1968. "The Teaching-Learning Paradox: A Comparative Analysis of College Teaching Methods." Eugene: University of Oregon Center for the Advanced Study of Educational Administration.

Freire, Paulo. 1969. *Pedagogy of the Oppressed.* New York: Seabury Press.

Hentoff, Nat. 1967. *Our Children Are Dying*. New York: Viking.

Holt, John. 1974. *How Children Fail*. New York: Dell.

Jencks, Christopher, Mary Jane Bane, et al. 1972. *Inequality: A Reassessment of the Effect of Family and Schooling in America*. New York: Basic Books.

Jung, C. G. 1959. *Aion: Researches into the Phenomenology of the Self. Collected Works*, Vol. 9, part 2, translated by R. F. C. Hull. New York: Pantheon Books.

Kopp, Sheldon. 1971. *Guru*. Palo Alto: Science and Behavior Books.

Kozol, Jonathan. 1970. *Death at an Early Age*. New York: Bantam.

Mariampolski, Hyman. "Teaching Introductory Sociology," *Teaching Sociology* (forthcoming).

Maslow, Abraham. 1976. *The Farther Reaches of Human Nature*. New York: Penguin.

McGee, Reece. 1974. "Does Teaching Make Any Difference?" *Teaching Sociology* 1 (April).

Mead, George Herbert. 1934. *Mind, Self and Society*. Chicago: University of Chicago Press.

Michaels, Patricia. 1970. "Toward a Movement." *No More Teachers' Dirty Looks*, BARTOC.

Mills, C. W. 1961. *The Sociological Imagination*. New York: Grove Press.

Progoff, Ira. 1975. *At a Journal Workshop*. New York: Dialogue House Library.

Rosenthal, Robert, and Lenore Jacobson. 1968. "Teacher Expectations for the Disadvantaged." *Scientific American* 218 (April).

Rotter, Julian. 1966. "Generalized Expectancies for Internal Versus External Control of Reinforcement." *Psychological Monographs: General and Applied* 80:1–28.

Wasserman, Miriam. 1971. "School Mythology and the Education of oppression." *This Magazine is About Schools* 5 (Summer):24–36.

Weinberg, Carl. 1976. *Education as a Shuck*. New York: Morrow.

Wheelis, Allen. 1969. "How People Change." *Commentary* 47 (May):56–66.

Creativity and Pedagogy:
A Humanistic Sociological Legacy[1]

Steve McGuire
Muskingum College

What about this piece makes it humanist sociology? Let's cut to the chase, with an excerpt:

> I have found that when people are encouraged to assume responsibility for their own reality, the results in their education are surprising (Rader, p. 102 in original).

Pretty direct if you ask me. Think about it. And notice the emphasis on the process of humanist teaching, rather than the content. I suspect that many of us sociologists are good at selecting the right content replete with punchy details regarding emancipation, but not so good at embodying an emancipatory process itself. Thus, we invite the worst sort of cynical defeatism on the part of students. "Uh, let me see, he wants us to be non-racist, so the answer to question 23 must be..."

In fact, this excerpt is exemplary of the "Big Distinction" that continues to distinguish the Association for Humanist Sociology (AHS) from mainstream sociology and animates this volume.

What I wonder is how often mainstream sociology thinks about whether the discipline should be involved in encouraging people to assume responsibility for their own reality. In other words, the matter of empowerment is nothing other than another topic for most sociologists, one that many mainstream practitioners might want to advocate for in their private lives, but not as their model of, say, science, or sociology.

Mainstream sociology has a bad case of role conflict; it advocates nothing except science as harnessed by the values of its practitioners. Mainstream sociologists might, in their private lives, favor people taking responsibility for their own reality, but as sociologists the issue is tangential to their discipline.

Here I point in contradistinction to AHS's defining philosophical statement: "Humanists view people not merely as products of social forces but also of shapers of social life, capable of creating social orders in which everyone's potential can unfold." It's the kind of self identification and declaration that addresses how to live wholely, as examiners of social reality and as practitioners working to create the kind of social reality we envision. As Rader puts it, "I believe that we human beings have the capacity to build social lives that truly delight us." How many sociology articles begin this way?

---

[1]This paper originally appeared in *Humanity & Society* Volume 27, Number 3, 2003.

Humanist sociology advocates for "assuming responsibility" at the very core of its being. Having done so, it immediately points toward outcomes that celebrate the magic we sometimes engender. For mainstream work, responsibility is either a technical point or an arbitrary personal topic; the values toward which science is harnessed are likewise technically arbitrary, personal.

Current mainstream work on the teaching of sociology does advocate, albeit implicitly, for certain outcomes such as critical thinking. But the rationale for such goals rarely transcends cultural platitudes about education as a social value and, therefore, critical thinking as a good thing. Rader advocates more widely than that, instead promoting a pedagogy that educates for the freedom and responsibility that human beings need as whole persons to make their lives more satisfying. In this connection, it does not take a humanist sociologist to point to education's current functioning, in which it subordinates students to the needs of a rationalized, McDonaldized, toxic economy. But it is almost a hallmark of humanist sociology to try to move education intrinsically toward generating more satisfying, holistically healthy lives.

Similarly, most advocates for active learning and critical thinking do so within a fetishized scientific model of thinking. Rader wisely points out the hidden assumptions of scientific objectivity, and material and linear causation. Fortunately, truly independent examinations of world views lead to wider conceptions of evidence than those extolled by mainstream work, and more activist notions of the roles of social scientist, citizen, and their relationship. Two diverging positions on the relationship between commitment and social science largely underwrite the distinctiveness of humanist sociology and teaching. Here the whole rhetoric of "value-free" and "non-value-free" probably leads to some mutual demonization between mainstream and humanist sociology, but that's a whole other article. With the exception of a very few practitioners, the traditional position actually admits that the questions sociological work addresses are governed by practitioners' values. Also acknowledged is that the impact of the work non-neutrally affects the subject matter. But again, both are thought to be arbitrary, not amenable to the purported certainty of objectivist science itself.

In various ways, humanist sociologists have worked to embody a less arbitrary tie between commitment and sociology. Whole lives so embodied transcend the role conflict of the mainstream scientist/citizen. Humanist practitioners either seek to heal that rupture or transcend it entirely. They refuse to treat their sociology and teaching as determined by science, and refuse to treat those studied as mere victims with lives completely determined by abstract social forces. Humanist sociologists operate with wider models of evidence and critical thinking, and such models elicit the deeper foundational problems built into higher education today.

Rader notes the claims that schooling is alienating and bound to be so in the toxic society in which we live. Here, again, it would be possible to infer that individually we are miniscule victims buffeted about by advanced corporate capitalism. On such a model, educational reform is misguided. We might better wait for the revolution. The sociologist acutely describes the toxic economy and concludes that action is hopeless until that economy is taken down—by someone else. I'm put in mind of the Al-Anon term for such a faltering of the will, "analysis paralysis."

As creators rather than victims, we imagine and act otherwise. Rader concurs with the problem, but not the quietist conclusion.

> But surely, doesn't this mean that we would not develop the most humane and powerful learning processes in our classrooms as possible? It seems nihilistic not to act positively at every level of our experience. (p. 104 in original)

We imagine and create social lives that delight us, especially when faced with toxic higher education. One can just describe the beast, analyze it to death (the death of student interest and professor hubris), or one can "practice humanist values in our classroom procedures." What one says, however emancipatory its inspiration, is light years less important than what one does.

> It feels increasingly absurd to discuss the human capacity for critical awareness, social vision and the common human impulse to support life, while unconsciously or helplessly conforming to teaching practices that do not work; that isolate and render more passive the very human beings that participate in them. (p. 104 in original)

Energy that might go into analyzing the problems of mass cattle car lectures and McCarthyist containment of radical teaching too readily dissipates into rationales, when it should be redirected to emancipatory teaching methods themselves.

The concerns raised by the article have not withered away during the decades since it was published, even though sociology overall has become more radical and self-critical. When it comes to teaching, passing on its substance, mainstream sociology has certainly moved in the direction of active student involvement and even empowerment. However, such initiatives are extensively countered by the move toward standardized assessment, as well as the increasing corporatization of higher education.

Today we need as much clarity regarding teaching humanistically as we can muster. No one article can begin to scratch the surface of a pedagogy that will enable us all to live more whole, satisfying lives. The beauty of Victoria Rader's article lies not just with its invocation of four helpful strategies or tools, but more fully with its absolute and very explicit, articulate embodiment of the distinctive vision of teaching sociology humanistically. Think of sociology as a dance, alternately one of analysis, paralysis and despair, or a terribly risky and painful, yet challenging dance of delight.

2. Perspectivity and the Activist Potential of the Sociology Classroom[1]

Patricia Hill Collins
University of Cincinnati

Reflexive Statement

To me, teaching is much more than the passive transfer of technical skills from teacher to learner. Rather, teaching has political implications that reach far beyond the classroom.

I sensed this when, in 1970, I first taught Black women's studies to eighth grade girls in an embattled public school in the Roxbury section of Boston. The following six years that I spent as teacher/curriculum developer at three Black community schools solidified my conviction that by teaching, one becomes an activist, whether by intention or default. My years as an administrator at Tufts University and my current faculty responsibilities at the University of Cincinnati have convinced me that the process of teaching and learning has universal elements that extend beyond the content offered or the combination of individuals who encounter that content. Thus, I think that it is important that humanist sociology examine the philosophical and political implications of the pedagogies that are used in teaching sociology. This essay takes a first step at doing just this.

Introduction

"Some days," sighed a colleague of mine, "teaching is just like any other job. You punch the time clock, put in your hours, and try to make it through." My colleague's industrial metaphor of the assembly line of interchangeable students, flowing by year after year, to be filled up with information and then routed to the next operator, is a revealing one. Far too many educators feel trapped in their own classroom, hiding behind the deference accorded their titles, credentials, and established disciplines, mechanically teaching the same material over and over. Somehow, for both teacher and students, the classroom is not the "real world" in the sense that you can be yourself. Rather, the classroom is a place where you become what others expect you to be.

Sociology classrooms have not been immune to this pedagogy of alienation. Ironically, while many of sociology's goals and much of sociological course content may be labeled "humanist," the very structure of the sociology classroom frequently undermines humanistic goals.[1] For example, Lee contends that one of the aims of sociology should be to help people feel that action and change are desirable and possible, and certainly preferable to an anxious attachment to an illusory stability (1973: 36). Yet when students are lectured

---

[1]This paper originally appeared in *Humanity & Society* Volume 10, Number 3, 1986.

that change is possible but allowed minimal opportunity to act as change agents in their classrooms, when professors of sociology spend time with students yet appear unwilling to change course structures, when material, no matter how radical, revolutionary, or humanist, is taught as if it were a static, timeless reality, sociological pedagogy contradicts the goal that action and change are what is really wanted. In short, humanist rhetoric is no substitute for humanist action.

This pedagogy of alienation is especially problematic for humanist sociology. The sociology classroom is a major link in the knowledge validation process, and as such is a primary means of teaching people either to fit into the existing system or to act to improve it. The teaching process is much more than the benign transfer of knowledge from its producers (researchers) to its consumers (students). Rather, the validity of knowledge cannot be separated from the social contexts in which it is produced and reproduced (Mannheim 1936). Ideas do not stand alone—it matters who created them, and it matters how they are shared. The two interlocking components of content and process—what is taught and the pedagogy used to teach—must work in tandem for a humanist sociology to avoid inadvertently validating some of the ideas it allegedly rejects.[2]

This article tackles the rather slippery topic of defining a humanist pedagogy in sociology by focusing on the role of perspectivity in the teaching/learning process. It is argued that perspectivity, defined as the holistic angle of vision produced by the merger of an individual's (1) unique biography, (2) cultural and group experiences, and (3) formal, disciplinary training,[3] is systematically denigrated in the educational institutions that are the primary reproducers of Eurocentric, patriarchal thought. Moreover, this suppression of perspectivity is far from benign, for denying the perspectivity of less powerful peoples is crucial in maintaining systems of domination. If humanist sociology aims to help people feel that action and change are possible, it must sanction perspectivity as a valid way of knowing, especially for less powerful peoples, by developing pedagogies that validate and incorporate teacher and student perspectivity in the sociology classroom.

This article approaches this task in the following manner. First, perspectivity is defined, with attention to its relationship to thought and social action. Second, the article discusses the treatment of perspectivity in Eurocentric social science and argues that an attenuated versus a holistic notion of perspectivity is needed to maintain systems of domination. Third, the current state of perspectivity in the sociology classroom is reviewed. The essay concludes by discussing two considerations when using perspectivity in the teaching/learning process.

Perspectivity and Social Action

Defining Perspectivity: The Personal, the Cultural, and the Disciplinary Contexts

Perspectivity, one's angle of vision or stance, is shaped by three interlocking categories. First, each individual has a unique personal biography that includes a specific set of concrete experiences, values, motivations and emotions. No two individuals occupy the exact same social space, thus no two biographies are identical.

A second component of perspectivity is the cultural context formed by those experiences, thoughts, statuses, roles and ideas that are shared with other members of a group and that give meaning to individual biographies. Each individual biography is rooted in several overlapping cultural contexts, eg., groups defined using race, social class, age, gender, religion or other types of boundaries. The cultural component of perspectivity contributes, among other things, the concepts used in thinking and acting, group validation of an individual's interpretation of concepts, the "thought-models" used in the acquisition of knowledge, and standards used to evaluate individual thought and behavior (Mannheim 1936).

A third component of perspectivity consists of the training offered by socializing institutions external to the experienced group cultural context, namely, schools churches, the media, and other formal organizations. Such disciplinary training exposes individuals to ideas, knowledge, and angles of vision that go beyond an individual's experienced personal reality.

An effective social actor is one who understands and uses his or her individual, group, and disciplinary ways of knowing, while seeing the strengths and limitations of each. Mills (1959) identifies this holistic way of knowing as the "sociological imagination" and identifies its possibilities. He notes, "the sociological imagination enables us to grasp history and biography and the relations between the two within society. That is its task and its promise" (1959: 60). Moreover, using one's perspectivity, engaging one's sociological imagination, can empower the individual. For example, Audre Lorde, a Black feminist scholar, points out, "my fullest concentration of energy is available to me only when I integrate all the parts of who I am, openly, allowing power from particular sources of my living to flow back and forth freely through all my different selves, without the restriction of externally imposed definition" (1984: 120–1). A holistic perspective is the source of Lorde's energy.

Ideally, effective social action both informs and is informed by thought, which in turn is a reflection of the synthesis of the three components of perspectivity.

The Role of Sociology in the Thought/Social Action Nexus

Sociology is, in a sense, a microcosm of the type of, disciplinary training that an individual encounters in a variety of institutions. But sociology has a special mission. For while its structure is similar to that of other disciplines—physics, mathematics and chemistry all expose people to knowledge that goes beyond an individual's experienced reality—sociology's subject matter is the familiar terrain of human social interaction. The sociological stance used in studying human social interaction can have a direct effect on human social interaction itself. Sociology, like other social disciplines, can be a double-edged sword.

On the one hand, sociology has the potential of revealing to the individual how personal history is actually shaped by cultural and group contexts, how the unique is part of the universal, and how the everyday and ordinary are part of large, generalizable human concerns. This type of sociology can be a powerful catalyst in forging a dialectic of thought and action. Sociology can simultaneously affirm the personal and cultural components of individual perspectivity yet reveal the limitations of individual experience as the sole route to understanding and as the sole foundation for action. In his classic work *The Pedagogy of the Oppressed*, Paulo Friere clearly alludes to the power of perspectivity in the teaching/ learning process. He points out that the line dividing the subjective and objective worlds (the distinction between the personal and cultural contexts being the "subjective," and the disciplinary context being the "objective,") is arbitrary, and that positioning oneself via perspectivity in the objective disciplinary world deconstructs it, and opens up possibilities of negotiation and action. Friere notes, "in problem-posing education, men [and women] develop their power to perceive critically the way they exist in the world with which and in which they find themselves; they come to see the world not as a static reality, but as a reality in process, in transformation" (1979: 71). Like Lorde, Friere suggests that validating a holistic perspectivity by rejecting externally imposed realities, especially those that present a static, "finished" world, simultaneously fosters the power of human intentionality and action. For a reality in process is one in which a human can act.

On the other hand, sociology can be equally powerful in breaking the consciousness that individuals have of their own power as actors. Sociological stances that alienate learners from their personal and cultural experiences, that label these ways of knowing as less valid, effectively erode the primary base that we all stand on as social actors, namely, what we know to be true through our own experiences. Severing the connections between the personal, cultural, and disciplinary components of perspectivity, and replacing a holistic perspectivity with, in Lorde's words, "externally imposed definition[s]" or, in Friere's terms, "the world... as a static reality," weakens the alliance between thought and action. In this sense, sociology becomes an ideology used for domination, an agent of social control.

The discipline of sociology thus is highly political, for it can serve as a key link in the synthesis of a holistic perspectivity (thought) with informed action—action directed by a holistic perspectivity. Or it can serve as a major barrier in this synthesis, by suppressing the personal and cultural components of perspectivity and presenting a narrow framework for action that fits the angle of vision of those who define what is and is not important in sociology. Whether sociology alienates or empowers its learners depends on researcher and teacher decisions about what and how to teach, and this, in turn, is shaped by the treatment of perspectivity in sociology itself.

The Treatment of Perspectivity in Sociology

Perpsectivity and Sociology: An Assessment

Morgan and Smircich (1980) point out that sociology accommodates a wide range of basic assumptions about ontology and human nature, of epistemological stances, and of research methods grounded in these frequently implicit assumptions and epistemologies. In spite of this diversity, positivist approaches to social science predominate, with attendant efforts to render an objective description of reality as a concrete structure by constructing an objective social science.

The predominance of positivist approaches in sociology sends a clear message to prospective and current sociologists that the personal and cultural components of perspectivity are inappropriate for sociology's mission of building a science of society. Moreover, sociologists are taught that, not only is one's own personal and cultural history inappropriate for sociological discourse, it may actually have a negative effect on one's effectiveness as a scholar. For example, quantitative research methods are viewed as more appropriate for constructing a positivist sociology because such methods better control for "bias," generally defined as researcher intrusion into the research process. From the positivist view, those studies that can be replicated by anyone possessing acceptable technical training are those deemed most accurate, reliable, and valid. The race, gender, age, etc. of the researcher should have no effect on the research process or findings. In short, in order to render an "objective," "true" version of reality, positivist approaches favor methodological approaches that explicitly exclude the personal and cultural components of researcher perspectivity.

Much has been written about the value-laden nature of allegedly value-neutral, positivist sociology (Gouldner 1970; Bash 1979; Papcke and Oppenheimer 1984). In essence, positivist sociology presents itself as being different than it actually is. While positivist approaches claim to be "universal" and "unbiased," they actually reflect the personal and cultural values of one group's angle of vision. Positivist sociology reflects the stance of its Eurocentric, patriarchal, financially comfortable practitioners and their converts, and it is this group's perspectivity that pervades the discipline. Rather than being objective, it is thus highly subjective.

In essence, the predominant mode of discourse in sociology is to deny that personal and cultural components of perspectivity profoundly affect the questions asked, the issues identified as being worthy of sociological attention, the way research is conducted, and the way findings are presented to the scholarly community and to students. This is not only dishonest, this denial of personal and cultural perspectivity weakens the protest of those who would challenge the "truth" by using their personal and cultural perspectives as the foundation for dialogue. Those who do not share the perspectivity of those in power simply cannot participate, and are effectively silenced. The irony is that, while the different are silenced because their personal and cultural perspectives are labeled subjective, and there-fore inferior in a system based on value-neutral objectivity, they are being silenced by an "objective" social science that itself is highly subjective.

Explaining the Denial of Perspectivity

Describing the suppression of the personal and cultural components of perspectivity in sociology is one thing. Explaining why this condition is so tenacious is another. It appears that the denigration of perspectivity in sociology finds it origins in some of the key tenets of Eurocentric, patriarchal, capitalist thought, and that this thought, in turn, reflects the socio-historic origins and cultural contexts of its creators.

Several ideas/constructs apparently pervade this body of thought. First, dichotomous categories are prominent in Eurocentric social science. For example, Richards (1980) and Irele (1982) both discuss the dichotomous definition of the ideology of race in Western societies where Blacks (Africans) are defined as being fundamentally different than Whites (Europeans). Using this dichotomous construct, one must be either Black or White. Similarly, feminist scholars point to the dichotomous definitions of male and female that pervade gender-based social science (Eisenstein 1983). Knowing is another dichotomous construct. Distinctions between mind/body, thought/feeling, culture/nature, fact/value, and knowledge/judgment, are all variations of an objective/subjective dichot-omy in knowing.[4]

A second tenet of Eurocentric social thought of direct relevance to the suppression of perspectivity is the concept of objectification and its role in oppositional difference. The key issue here is not dichotomous difference per se, rather, the issue is how difference is valued. The thread that draws the above dichotomies together is that difference is defined in oppositional terms, i.e., one part is not simply different than its counterpart, it is inher-ently opposed to its other. In this system, Blacks and Whites, males and females, thought and feeling are not complementary counterparts—they are fundamentally different entities related only through their definition as opposites. Thus, feeling cannot be incorporated into thought or even function in conjunction with it, because in this system, feeling retards thought, values obscure facts, and judgment clouds knowledge.

Objectification is central to this process of oppositional difference. In dichotomous thought, one element is objectified, or viewed as an object to be manipulated, worked upon, or controlled. For example, a Marxist assessment of the culture/nature dichotomy argues that history can be seen as the history of production in which human beings constantly objectify the natural world in order to control and exploit it (Britain and Maynard 1984: 198). Culture is defined as being the opposite of an objectified nature, a nature that, if left alone, would destroy culture. Similarly, feminist scholars have pointed to the identification of women with nature, and their subsequent objectification by men as sex objects and wives (Eisenstein 1983). Black scholars have described the denial of subjectivity cf African and Asian peoples, their definition as being less human or objects, as being a central component of systems exploiting people of color (Asante 1980).

A third tenet of Eurocentric social thought tied to the suppression of perspectivity concerns the unstable nature of these relationships of oppositional difference. The inherently unstable relationship can only be resolved if one side of the dichotomous pair is subordinated to the other. Thus, women are subordinated to men, Blacks to Whites, nature to culture, body to mind, feeling to thought, and value to fact. The foundations of a complex social hierarchy thus are tied to the concepts of dichotomy, oppositional difference, objectification, and domination, with domination based on difference forming one essential pillar of this entire system of thought. As Brittan and Maynard contend, "it is domination (oppression) which objectifies the world. Domination always involves the objectification of the dominated; all forms of oppression imply the devaluation of the subjectivity of the oppressed" (1984: 199).

This leads us back to the significance of the denial of the personal and cultural components of perspectivity as valid ways of sociological knowing. Specifically, attenuated versus holistic notions of perspectivity appear central in maintaining systems of domination. The effects of the denial of a holistic perspectivity are especially significant for those who want to challenge the prevailing wisdom. First, personal and cultural experiences are used as alternative ways of knowing than the "objective" stance of positivist sociology. For those denied access to prolonged, technical training, personal and cultural experiences provide the primary way of knowing. If these are invalidated and seen as "inappropriate" regardless of content, then there is no effective challenge to the perspectivity of the powerful. Second, gaining access to the technical training and perspectivity of the powerful is no solution either. For an oppressed person, taking on the perspectivity of a dominant group involves accepting a perspectivity that denies self, because the perspectivity of the dominant group is based on opposition to and objectification of the subordinate group. There is simply no space in such a world view for the "other" unless the "other's" objectionable characteristics are somehow explained away or conveniently overlooked. Audre Lorde expresses this constraining notion by noting, "the master's tools will never dismantle the master's house. They may allow us temporarily to beat him at his own game, but they will never enable us to bring about genuine change" (1984: 112).

It appears that the treatment of perspectivity in positivist sociology has implications far beyond the simple power-elite model of a self-conscious, interest group of sociologists who deliberately try to exclude others from the field via their control of funding, publication sources, and hiring. The issue is much deeper than one that can be fixed by diversifying the race-gender composition of those in power, or by adding in the experiences of a previously omitted group to a curriculum reflecting a pre-existing, "objective" view of reality. It appears that the very constructs of sociology, e.g., race, man, nature, knowledge, have been shaped by the not so benign tenets of Eurocentric social science. Until these basic assumptions are challenged and alternatives presented, sociological discourse will continue to be constrained by its very language, methods, and way of validating truth. In short, perspectivity will continue to be judged a less valid way of knowing.

The Current State of Perspectivity in the Sociology Classroom

The devaluation of a holistic perspectivity as a valid way of knowing in sociology classrooms should come as no surprise in that classroom strategies are but visible parts of the "hidden curriculum" of Eurocentric thought.[5] Classrooms are designed to teach people to think and act in accordance with the wishes of those in power. Quite simply, Eurocentric social science devalues perspectivity, and its classrooms merely reflect its ideological core. Students are justifiably leery of sociology professors who explicitly embrace a holistic perspective for themselves or for students, for such behavior flies in the face of years of accumulated instruction. Overall, both the formal curriculum and the "hidden curriculum" contain clear rules governing perspectivity's role in the teaching/learning process.

First, the terms "perspective" and "opinion" are frequently used interchangeably, with the accompanying devaluation of both concepts. As Westkott (1983) points out, Eurocentric social science compartmentalizes "knowledge" and "judgment" as being two separate functions in the process of knowing. Opinion (and the related concepts of judgment, values, and feelings) is subordinated to the better way of knowing—the rational, value-free approach. According to Westkott, this process is far from benign.

> Separating seeing from judging dilutes the power of "seeing" so that it becomes an enfeebled process of blind observation and bland description. Thus released from the full range of human perception and understanding, judgment itself becomes trivialized as mere "opinion." We reject this enfeebling approach... (1983: 211).

For students, who generally accept this dichotomous notion, opinion is an inferior way of knowing. Any class where the teacher appears to be expressing his or her "opinion" is deemed less valid than one where an abundance of "knowledge" is on the syllabus. Generally, classrooms reinforce the belief that opinions and perspectives are best left to students. The popular notion is one where educated people, such as professors, express "knowledge" while less educated people, such as students, express "opinions." A hierarchy of knowing is established in the process of teaching/learning, where one becomes better educated by becoming more "objective" and expressing less "opinion," eg., perspectivity.

A second and related feature of the treatment of perspectivity in the curriculum involves another dichotomous notion, the myth of an explicit boundary dividing ethics and science. As Bellah contends, this is a false dichotomy:

> One experiences life as flowing from ethical commitments that one has made. In this process of reception, practice, and reflection, it is quite arbitrary to decide what is cognitive and what is normative, when we are being scientific and when ethical. (1983: 373)

Perspectivity is honed at the intersection of ethical and rational reflection. As Bellah and others have argued,[6] these two are not incompatible. Yet perspectivity is invariably linked with ethical reflection, and both are assigned a subordinate role in the teaching/ learning process, if in fact they are included at all. Just as judgment is frowned upon, moral and ethical judgments are especially unsuitable in social science. But as Bellah points out, "intellectual acuteness and ethical maturity... go hand in hand. Wisdom is the traditional word that includes both (1983: 373)." Perspectivity is essential for developing ethical maturity, for one cannot assess one's stance without knowing what it is. Perspectivity, or point of view, is clarified through dialogue, yet if ethical reflection and the explicit use of perspectivity are excluded from the teaching/learning process, then the classroom is left a place of "blind observation and bland description." Unfortunately for far too many students, this has become the norm.

A third dimension of the treatment of perspectivity in the curriculum centers on who has the power to validate knowledge. As Rosaldo succinctly points out, "our questions are inevitably bound up with our politics... intellectual insight thrives in a complex relation with contemporary moral and political demands (1983: 76)."[7] In short, perspectives of those in power are given more validity, status, and credence than those of less powerful groups. In many cases, the perspectives of those in power are not seen as being perspectives at all, while those of their opponents are. For example, positivist sociology has long called itself a "science" while labeling Marxist sociology, critical sociology, and variants of interpretive sociology "perspectives." In actuality, they are all perspectives, and represent the point of view of those who developed them. Yet the contenders are not equal, and often it is not the power of the idea that holds sway, but the power of the individual or group owning the idea or perspective.[8] Worse yet, the perspectives of the powerful masquerade as universal reality. Thus, a power dynamic pervades the sociological teaching/ learning process, with perspectivity intimately involved in issues of assessing the validity of knowledge.

Fourth, excessive use of the adversary paradigm as a preferred method of classroom interaction fosters an attenuated expression of perspectivity. Moulton (1983) describes the contours of this popular framework used to stimulate "debate." The adversary paradigm assumes that the best way of evaluating an idea is to subject it to the strongest or most extreme opposition. Under this model, good discussions are essentially impassioned debates between adversaries vying to defend their own angle of vision against the verbal attacks of others. This approach virtually excludes the personal and cultural components of perspectivity because first, few individuals are hardy enough to expose these portions of self to adversarial scrutiny, and second, the particularistic can be easily discredited as mere "opinion" and not universal. Thus, what often passes for lively discussion is actually a verbal duel where neither side gains deeper understanding of the other's stance and where both merely sharpen their defensive skills for the next calculated attack.

It is difficult to root out this win-lose mentality. Unfortunately, many students only encounter perspectivity in the contexts of adversarial debates. When an instructor takes a point of view and identifies it as such, students justifiably wonder if an effort to convert them is in the works. To many, professorial perspectivity represents an unfair advantage for, to students, teachers have access to more facts, the basis on which arguments are won or lost.

Finally, students frequently equate perspectivity with bias. For those schooled in the assumption that "objective," "value-free" scholarship and teaching is less biased and "fairer" than other approaches, classrooms incorporating teacher perspectivity can appear quite threatening. Students are wary of professors who express perspectivity in teaching for, in their experiences, such professors are often biased toward those who do not share their point of view. A holistic perspectivity, by definition, is personalized and subjective, and subjectivity and fairness are popularly viewed as being an unstable combination.

It is one thing to adopt an objective research methodology, although a lively debate roars on as to whether this is even possible. It is quite another to structure the human interaction in sociology classrooms around "objective" social science's narrow vision of knowing, i.e., the denial and subordination of personal and cultural components of perspectivity and the refusal critically to examine the subjective core of "objective" social science. Yet this is exactly what happens in classrooms that deny the holistic view of perspectivity. Classrooms that deny the subjective, the particularistic, the personal, or that relegate them to subordinate roles of illustrating the important concepts, reinforce a way of knowing that trains students in the basic tenets of Eurocentric social science. In short, by covering a highly subjective process with the illusion of objectivity, the denial of perspectivity prepares students to fit into a system where a highly suspect "objectivity" is used to control, dominate, and win.

The attenuated version of perspectivity that students have come to expect in their classrooms was nurtured in this environment. Attempting to reunite and rethink perspective involves a lot more than allowing opinions into the classroom, or accumulating pedagogical tricks to make content more interesting. Rather, reclaiming perspectivity as a pedagogical tool addresses a fundamental issue of Eurocentric social science—how we view and use and feel about difference, and how this affects human action.

Perspectivity and Teaching

The goals for humanizing the process of education are well articulated and are directly applicable to humanist sociology. Giroux and Penna accurately capture the feel of this emerging humanist pedagogy.

> The values and social processes which provide the theoretical underpinnings for socialeducation include developing in students a respect for moral commitment, group solidarity, and social responsibility. In addition, a nonauthoritarian individualism should be fostered, one that maintains a balance with group cooperation and social awareness. (1983: 112)

Not only are the goals of humanist education fairly well established, implementation strategies are similarly specified.[9] Therefore, this section identifies two considerations when using perspectivity in teaching that grow from the preceding analysis.

Uncovering and Explaining Differences in Perspectivity

Karl Mannheim identifies one important contribution of perspectivity to humanist sociological pedagogy. He notes, "it becomes our task not only to indicate the fact that people in social positions think differently, but to make intelligible the causes for their different ordering of the material of experiences by different categories" (1936: 274). In other words, the existence of perspectivity must be clarified and its role in explaining differences explored.

McKelvey's (1984) discussion of the function of perspectivity (labeled "horizon" in his schema) taps the importance of the full use of perspectivity in evaluating the quality of one's own outlook and those of others. For McKelvey, perspectivity (horizon) makes understanding possible. He notes, "we select according to what is significant in light of our horizon, and we organize in a way that is meaningful in relation to our horizon" (1984: 286). In short, without the organizing framework of perspectivity, understanding would not be possible. But McKelvey also points out that perspectivity simultaneously limits understanding because individual perspectivity is primarily personal and particularistic. Hence, encounter and dialogue with others, especially trying to understand the key components of others' stances, as they see them, sharpens understanding of the individual's own angle of vision, and deepens it.

Classrooms that view investigating perspectivity itself as a valid area of sociological inquiry are more likely to avoid what Mannheim labels "talking past one another." In this situation, participants are aware that other participants come from groups different than their own, but discussions proceed as if differences are confined to the specific topic at hand. One result of this is that specific differences cannot be resolved, nor in many cases, should they. Rather, a more useful goal is for participants to try and see the topic from the stance of other groups, and understand why other outlooks are so different. This replaces heated arguments about differences with the goal of uncovering what accounts for those differences. In this sense, the classroom deals with difference without trying to control, silence, or dominate the different.

This does not mean that the task of sharing individual biographies becomes the curriculum. Students needs content, and existing sociological content, is more than adequate for this process of incorporating perspectivity in the teaching/learning process. What is different is how that content can be taught. Just as students must examine the personal and cultural components of their own and others' perspectivity, and try to assess how these experiences shape their own outlooks and those of their classmates, they must learn to view disciplinary training through the same lens. Thus, feminist course content can and should be taught to males, Blacks should be exposed to European history, and Whites should learn about African cultures. Theoretically, anything can be taught to any group—the content is not the issue as much as how that content is presented.

Teaching this way can be very demanding for all concerned. Students are asked to take risks, and to self-disclose (versus talk) much more than they are used to doing in more formal, hierarchical settings. To do this, they must be convinced that they will not be ridiculed or attacked, and that the instructor will treat their ideas fairly and seriously, even if their stance is radically different than everyone else's. Perspectivity is not evaluated by the degree that it approximates the views of those in power. Rather, perspectivity can be more clearly articulated and comprehensible to self and others, i.e., known and understood by the individual via self-reflection and dialogue. Being self-reflective by assessing the origins of one's own perspectivity, being willing to engage in dialogue with others (as compared to adversarial debates), and being able to alter one's perspective all involve hard work. In a classroom, perspectivity is not assessed by its correctness, but by its clarity, comprehensiveness, and depth.[10]

Evaluating the Adequacy of Varying Stances

It is not enough to uncover and explain differences in perspectivity among teacher, learners, and sociological course content. A second dimension of perspectivity in sociological pedagogy involves identifying a process that assesses the adequacy of varying stances on a given topic. In other words, while it is necessary to identify perspectivity's role in influencing thought, and to explain differences among what is certified as knowledge by explicating the perspectivities that nurtured such thought, if one stops analysis at this point, a kind of intellectual anarchy can result. Just how does one go about judging the merits of varying perspectives?

Positivist sociological approaches claim that the most adequate perspective on a given topic is one that approaches the ideal of a detached, unbiased point of view. Objectivity is defined to mean independence from value judgments and emotions.[11] In contrast, a different definition of "objectivity" is offered by Mannheim who suggests that this positivist ideal be replaced with the "ideal of an essentially human point of view which is within the limits of a human perspective, constantly striving to enlarge itself" (1936: 297). For Mannheim, "objectivity" is brought about by the translation of varying perspectives into the terms of one another. The stance that evolves as the most comprehensive translation at a given point in time is the most "objective" and can be judged most adequate.

This approach to judging the adequacy of varying perspectives differs from positivist analyses in several respects. First, "objectivity" is a result of human agency, of people deciding which knowledge claims are most comprehensive and adequate. This is in contrast to the notion of objectivity as being equivalent to absolute truth that exists independently of whether people know about it or not. Second, "objectivity" in Mannheim's sense is never complete. The process of determining adequacy assumes that knowledge is socially constructed, historically specific, dynamic and incomplete. Thus, an explanation for sociological phenomena is adequate only in relation to a given group at a given point in time. Third, values and emotions are included in the process of knowledge-validation. One significant implication of building dialogues around holistic perspectivities is that participants can tap various ways of knowing and this diversity can strengthen analysis.

The classroom is the ideal location for structuring such dialogues. Thus, while students certainly benefit from exposure to diverse stances, they benefit even more by translating their stances for one another with the purpose of generating a comprehensive group stance that is inclusive yet recognizes the autonomy of individual stances. The issue is less one of choosing among competing perspectives and more one of developing comprehensive analyses that account for differences without trying to eliminate them.

Concluding Remarks

One potential outcome of using perspectivity as a cornerstone of humanist sociological pedagogy involves the empowerment of learners. It has been stated that perspectivity is already in the classroom, masquerading as objectivity. The task is to identify the subjective roots of what is believed to be objective without discrediting the validity of subjectivity. In other words, the issue is not to denigrate academic sociology by revealing how "biased," "subjective," and "unfair" it really is, because, in doing this, perspectivity as a valid way of knowing is discredited as well. Rather, the task is to see the issue of how who has the power to define the norms, or impose his/her perspectivity on others, defines his/her own angle of vision as "truth." When learners realize that social "truths" are not absolute, but rather are contingent on group perspectivity and a group's power to impose its stance on others, reality ceases to be static and becomes "a reality in process." It is by recognizing that they as learners have the power, not only to accept, reject, or decide how they want to respond to other's angle of vision, but moreover, that they have the power to define their own reality, that learners are empowered.

Just as one learns to be human by interacting with others, humanist sociology is fully actualized when it fosters this type of human interaction. The sociology classroom, as one place where people come together to examine issues of human social interaction, thus has the potential of being a primary arena of activism. Reclaiming perspectivity as a valid pedagogical tool is a significant first step in counteracting the tendency to perceive the classroom as being in passive, contemplative isolation from the active "real world" that lies just outside its doors. Rather, the classroom is a primary arena of activism, a place where people deepen their understanding of the interconnections between thought and action and, in doing so, build the foundation of their own power as social actors.

Endnotes

[1]Since "humanist goals" are somewhat ambiguous in the literature, this article uses a distinction raised by the Brazilian educator, Paulo Friere. Friere (1973) points out that education has but one of two purposes—it functions either to teach people to fit into the current system or to help people change and improve their reality. Humanist sociology fits the latter category.

[2]This idea has been prominent in educational philosophy for some time. See, for example, works of the American philosopher John Dewey (1966).

[3]The definition of perspectivity used in this article derives initially from Karl Mannheim's (1936) use of "perspective" in his classic article "The Sociology of Knowledge:" C. Wright Mills' (1959) discussion of the "sociological imagination" parallels my use of the term perspectivity. For related uses, see Messer-Davidow's (1985) discussion of perspectivity and knowing, and McKelvey's (1984) use of the term "horizon."

[4]See, for example, Spelman's (1982) article on the relationship of the mind/body duality to theories of race and gender. The thought/feeling duality is discussed in Hochschild's (1975) analysis of the absence of a sociological theory of feelings and emotions. Asante (1980) evaluates the culture/nature dichotomy, and its role in colonialism. The fact/value dichotomy is explored in Bellah's (1983) analysis of the ethical aims of social inquiry, while Westkott (1979) evaluates the knowledge/judgment duality.

[5]The importance of process has resurfaced in the discussions of the "hidden curriculum" during the past decade. See the edited volume by Giroux and Purpel (1983) for a solid overview of his literature. The following statements by Giroux and Penna describe the relationship between the "hidden curriculum" and humanist education:

> We believe that a major task for social studies educators is to identify those social processes that work against the ethical and political purpose of schooling in a democratic society and construct new elements that provide the underpinnings for new social studies programs. Initially, developers will have to understand the contradictions between the official curriculum, namely the explicitly cognitive and affective goals of formal instruction, and the "hidden curriculum," namely the unstated norms, values, and beliefs that are transmitted to students through the underlying structure of meaning in both the formal content as well as the social relations of school and classroom life (1983: 101–102).

Also, see Vallance (1983) for a discussion of dimensions of the hidden curriculum.

[6]See the articles in the edited volume by Haan et al (1983).

[7]In her essay, Rosaldo confines her discussion to contemporary feminism and social science. For related discussions, see, for example, Gouldner's (1970) analysis of Western sociology, Bash's (1979) discussion of how ideology has shaped the sociology of race and ethnicity, and Handing and Hintikka's (1983) edited volume critiquing the masculinist core of social science.

[8]This situation presents a real challenge for those individuals and groups that do not share the dominant group's "perspective" on reality. Ironically, the power issues of the mainstream ideology are most likely to be seen by those groups least likely to have power to challenge the dominant ideology. Thus, Blacks see racism that escapes the attention of vast numbers of Whites, feminists perceive sexism that non-feminists experience as "normal," etc.

[9]Among some of the strategies listed by Giroux and Penna (1983), Goldsmid and Wilson (1980), and Bunch and Pollack (1983) are heterogeneous class groupings, structures that develop peer and group-leadership roles for students, reduction in extrinsic rewards (grades) whenever possible, increased group interaction experiences, and the use of self-paced assignments. For additional suggestions, see Goldsmid and Wilson (1980), Katz (1985), and any of the extensive resources of the American Sociological Associations Teaching Resources Program.

[10]Teachers are not exempt from this continual process of examining perspectivity and assessing its impact on one's attitudes and behavior. For teachers, one key part of this process is being clear about what one's own standpoint actually is. The goal is to find a balance between the propaganda of a professor whose perspectivity has become the curriculum, and the objective, controlling "scientific" sociology that currently alienates teachers and students alike. For the teacher, striking this balance involves self-reflection, and clarity about one's own judgments, values, biases, and fears as well as how these have been shaped by personal, cultural, and disciplinary experiences. This self-reflective process never ends. For me, the results of my reflection are recorded in how my syllabi, course notes, and assignments have changed over the years. Questions such as "What is it I'm actually teaching here" and "Why am I asking these questions and not others" produce different and more complex answers after each successive group of students.

[11]See Jaggar (1983), especially Chapter 11.

References

Asante, Molefi Kete. 1980. "International/intercultural Relations." Pp. 43–50 in *Contemporary Black Thought*, edited by M. Asante and A. Vandi. Beverly Hills, CA: Sage.

Bash, Harry H. 1979. *Sociology, Race and Ethnicity, A Critique of American Ideological Intrusions upon Sociological Theory*. New York: Gordon & Breach.

Bellah, Robert N. 1983. "The Ethical Aims of Social Inquiry." Pp. 360–381 in *Social Science as Moral Inquiry*, edited by N. Haan, R. Bellah, P. Rabmow and W. Sullivan. New York: Columbia University.

Brittan, Arthur and Mary Maynard. 1984. *Sexism, Racism, and Oppression*. New York: Basil Blackwell.

Bunch, Charlotte and Sandra Pollack, eds. 1983. *Learning our Way: Essays in Feminist Education*. Trumansburg, NY: The Crossing Press.

Dewey, John. 1966. *John Dewey, Selected Educational Writings*. London: Heinemann.

Eisenstein, Hester. 1983. *Contemporary Feminist Thought*. Boston: G. K. Hall.

Friere, Paulo. 1970. *The Pedagogy of the Oppressed*. New York: Herder & Herder.

Giroux, Henry and Anthony Penn. 1983. "Social Education in the Classroom: The Dynamics of the Hidden Curriculum:" Pp. 100–121 *in The Hidden Curriculum and Moral Education*, edited by H. Giroux and D. Purpel. Berkeley,CA: MeCutchan.

Giroux, Henry and David Purpel, eds. 1983. *The Hidden Curriculum and Moral Education*. Berkeley, CA: MeCutchan.

Goldsmid, Charles A. and Everett K. Wilson. 1980. *Passing on Sociology*. Belmont, CA: Wadsworth.

Gouldner, Alvin. 1970. *The Coming Crisis in Western Sociology*. New York: Avon Books.

Haan, Norma, Robert Bellah, Paul Rabinow, and William Sullivan, eds. 1983. *Social Science as Moral Inquiry*. New York: Columbia University.

Herding, Sandra and Merrill B. Hintikka, eds. 1983. *Discovering Reality*. Boston: D. Reidel Publishing.

Hochschild, Arlie Russell. 1975. "The Sociology of Feeling and Emotion: Selected Possibilities." Pp. 280–307 in *Another Voice, Feminist Perspectives on Social Life and Social Science*, edited by M. Millman and R. Kanter. Garden City, NY: Anchor.

Irele, Abiola. 1983. "Introduction." Pp. 7–32 in *African Philosophy: Myth and Reality*, edited by P. Hountondji. Bloomington: Indiana University.

Jaggar, Alison M. 1983. *Feminist Politics and Human Nature*. Totowa, NJ: Rowman & Allanheld.

Katz, Joseph, ed. 1985. *Teaching as Though Students Mattered*. San Francisco: Jossey-Bass.

Lee, Alfred McClung. 1973. *Toward Humanist Sociology*. Englewood Cliffs, NJ: Prentice-Hall.

Lorde, Audre. 1984. *Sister Outsider*. Trumansburg, NY: The Crossing Press.

Mannheim, Karl. 1936. *Ideology and Utopia*. New York: Harcourt, Brace & World.

McKelvey, Charles. 1984. "Sociological Knowing in a Humanist Society." *Humanity & Society* 8: 283–303.

Messer-Davidow, Ellen. 1985. "Knowers, Knowing, Knowledge: Feminist Theory and Education." *Journal of Thought*, forthcoming.

Mills, C. Wright. 1959. *The Sociological Imagination*. New York: Oxford.

Morgan, Gareth and Linda Smircich. 1980. "The Case for Qualitative Research." *Academy of Management Review* 5: 491–500.

Moulton, Janice. 1983. "A Paradigm of Philosophy: The Adversary Method." Pp. 149–164 in *Discovering Reality,* edited by S. Harding and M. Hintikka. Boston: D. Reidel Publishing.

Papke, Sven and Martin Oppenheimer. 1984. "Value-free Sociology—Design for Disaster, German Social Science from Reich to Federal Republic." *Humanity & Society* 5: 272–282.

Richards, Dona. 1980. "European Mythology: The Ideology of 'Progress'." Pp. 59–79 in *Contemporary Black Thought*, edited by M. Asante and A. Vandi. Beverly Hills, CA: Sage.

Rosaldo, Michelle Z. 1983. "Moral/Analytic Dilemmas Posed by the Intersection of Feminism and Social Science." Pp. 76–96 in *Social Science As Moral Inquiry*, edited by N. Haan, R. Bellah, P. Rabinow, and W. Sullivan. New York: Columbia University.

Spelman, Elizabeth V. 1982. "Theories of Race and Gender, the Erasure of Black Women." *Quest* 5: 36–62.

Vallance, Elizabeth. 1983. "Hiding the Hidden Curriculum: An Interpretation of the Language of Justification in Nineteenth Century Educational Reform." Pp. 9–27 in *The Hidden Curriculum and Moral Education*, edited by H. Giroux an Purpel. Berkeley, CA: McCutchan.

Westkott, Marcia. 1979. "Feminist Criticism of the Social Sciences." *Harvard Educational Review* 49: 422–30.

———.1983. "Women's Studies as a Strategy for Change: Between Criticism and Vision." Pp. 210–218 in *Theories of Women's Studies*, edited by G. Bowles and R. Klein. Boston: Routledge & Kegan Paul.

Rejoinder to Collins' "Perspectivity and the Activist Potential of the Sociology Classroom"[1]

Kathleen A. Tiemann
University of North Dakota

Humanism in the Work of Patricia Hill Collins

When this article appeared nearly 20 years ago, Patricia Hill Collins became one of the first in sociology to adapt the emerging critical pedagogy literature to the discipline. It is also fitting that it was published in *Humanity and Society*, the official journal of the Association for Humanist Sociology, because the organization was also an early leader in addressing critical pedagogy.

This article is a timeless reminder of something that humanist teachers know; incorporating humanistic principles in our classrooms can help empower students as learners and as social agents, but that it is not without its costs. Alfred McClung Lee (1973), one of the founders of the Association for Humanist Sociology, contended that sociology should help people realize that action and change are not only possible, but desirable. Lee's concern is apparent in Patricia Hill Collins' discussion of "perspectivity" in the teaching and learning process. By perspectivity, she means "one's angle of vision or stance" (1987: 343). Perspectivity is a holistic way of knowing that is shaped by the personal biography of each actor, "the cultural context formed by those experiences, thoughts, statuses, roles and ideas that are shared with other members of a group and that give meaning to individual biographies" and by the training provided by socializing institutions that "exposes individuals ideas, knowledge, and angles of vision that go beyond an individual's experienced personal reality" (p. 343 in original). For Hill Collins, an effective social actor understands and uses her or his individual, group, and disciplinary ways of knowing, while seeing the strengths and limitations of each. Thus, she concludes that "using one's perspectivity, engaging one's sociological imagination, can empower the individual" (p. 344 in original).

When we bring perspectivity into the classroom we disrupt its traditional hierarchical structure and students' expectations of how they should be taught. However, we also provide a climate that empowers students and creates the potential for activism. Hill Collins' argument for perspectivity is particularly important today when many authors emphasize students' passive enjoyment of technological razzle dazzle over thinking about and actively "trying on" new ideas for themselves. Indeed much of the literature published in the 1990s focused on how to convince faculty to adopt new technology in their classrooms, how to configure new technology, how to train faculty (especially those who are reluctant to embrace technology) to integrate technology into their classes and reports of how much

---

[1]This paper originally appeared in *Humanity & Society* Volume 27, Number 3, 2003.

students like multimedia presentations (Tiemann 1999). Unlike humanist reflections on teaching and learning like the one by Hill Collins, these authors pay little attention to the alienation that typically results in classrooms governed by technology and institutional constraints. In light of the recent emphasis on documenting student learning outcomes, perspectivity seems especially relevant today.

However, humanist sociologists recognize that helping students develop perspectivity is difficult because it flies in the face of their own educational experiences. As Hill Collins put it, "classrooms are designed to teach people to think and act in accordance with the wishes of those in power.... Eurocentric social science devalues perspectivity, and its classrooms merely reflect its ideological core"(p. 349 in original). This is as true of sociology classes as it is of classes taught by those in other disciplines. It is no wonder that students are leery of professors who bring perspectives to the classroom that challenge their educational experiences. This rejection of humanism comes as no surprise to those of us who participate in a rigid educational structure that rewards teaching "within the bureaucracy primarily for processing, efficiency, and compliance with institutional requirements" (Mauksch 1986: 47).

So should we abandon perspectivity and humanism in our classrooms? Should we all become what C. Wright Mills called "cheerful robots" (1951)? Let me join with Patricia Hill Colllins and shout a resounding "NO!" The article makes clear that Hill Collins has constructed a teaching role that reflects her commitment to humanist ideals as compared to the prevailing institutionally prescribed norms supportive of the status quo. This article is an impassioned plea for us to join her in this pursuit.

References

Lee, Alfred McClung. 1977. "Humanistic Sociology: Purposes and Perspectives." *Humanity & Society* 1:1–11.
Mauksch, Hans O. 1986. "Teaching within Institutional Values and Structures." *Teaching Sociology* 14: 40–49.
Mills, C. Wright. 1951. *White Collar*. New York: Oxford University Press.
Tiemann, Kathleen A. 1999. "Presidential Address: Humanistic Teaching and Technology." *Humanity & Society* 23:3–9.

3. Prison Dances:
Teaching and Learning Behind Bars[1]

Annette Kuhlmann
University of Wisconsin - Baraboo

Reflexive Statement

When I began teaching sociology and anthropology college classes in a federal prison, I had to deal for many years with a personal struggle. The people around me, the media, and politicians presented clear cut lines between law abiding citizens and criminals, who supposedly violated the law as a personal decision based on selfishness, laziness, and asocial character traits. Yet my own experiences in my prison classroom were dramatically different. Every convict had a unique story of why he was incarcerated, making generalizations impossible. Most of my students were thoughtful people, who had difficult, often abusive histories. For various reasons many of them were trapped in their life situations. This kind of stereotyping dehumanizes them and sets them up as scapegoats for other, structural problems. This article wants to convey the humanness and rawness of classroom interactions and the ultimately rewarding nature of this work for those who open up to it.

Introduction

In 2004, over 6.5 million adults were currently under some form of correctional supervision in the United States (Irwin 2004). Since February 2000, the number of those behind bars has passed the two million mark in the United States—this means that with five percent of the world's population, the U.S. has 25 percent of the world's prison population (Kappeler 2004). About 1100 of these convicts live in an upper-medium security prison for men in Wisconsin where I have been teaching classes in sociology and anthropology for over ten semesters. Classes have on average 30 students and reflect the general prison population; a majority are African Americans, mostly from the inner cities of American metropolis—in fact, their number in prison is nearly seven times that of whites nationwide (Katz 2000). Native Americans are represented in disproportionately high numbers. Because of their special legal and political status they are usually members of sovereign tribes and, therefore, largely under federal jurisdiction. There are also several students who are citizens of other countries. Some students come from middle class or affluent backgrounds, but a majority grew up in low income families. In fact, most of them are the first members of their families to take a college class. Their ages range from mid-twenties

[1]This paper originally appeared in *Humanity & Society* Volume 30, Number 2, 2006.

to late sixties, with a cluster in their late thirties. The prisoners in this institution carry an average sentence of 15 years for predominantly drug-related crimes.

The story I want to tell is about different kinds of negotiation involved in teaching and learning in a prison. All of the prisoners have their unique stories to tell about the circumstances that brought them into my classroom. Everybody involved has personal and group experiences of the barriers of race, ethnicity, gender, and class and it is unlikely that our paths would have crossed in the outside world—yet there is a desire to follow our curiosity, to be open, to connect. But this entails some risk since the wish for connection runs counter to the dynamics of prison life—especially the students have to survive within the informal rules of the prison community and the formal ones of the Bureau of Prisons. We find ways to communicate in relation to the course material. Teaching social science material necessitates dialog about world views and life experiences with prisoners unlike more commonly taught college classes. These negotiations create tensions, constantly changing efforts on the side of all the participants to reach across the great gulfs of life experiences while also protecting our personal and institutional safe spaces. The result is a dance in which every participant negotiates through taking risks, challenges, assertions, or questions—with sometimes surprising moments of humor and harmony.

The instructor, meanwhile, may be engaged in another dimension of the dance—the interplay of roles of a scholar, activist, and teacher. My academic background in sociology provided me with an overall, theoretical understanding of pertinent issues in this environment, but it was my fieldwork experiences as a foreigner and as a researcher that helped prepare me to reach my students. For many foreign sociologists and anthropologists working in this country, it is natural to change into a mode of conducting field work whenever we find ourselves in unfamiliar circumstances (DeVita et al. 2002). In my case this was reinforced through a previous year-long fieldwork project in biculturalism among a traditional Native American tribe, the Kickapoo of Oklahoma (Kuhlmann 1992). This field work was particualy applicable because my research focused on an activist methodology, Action or Collaborative Anthropology. This approach argues, among others, that the knowledge of the "natives" has, in the past, not been valued and they themselves are therefore often not aware of the importance of their knowledge and are devalued as individuals (Schlesier 1980).[1] This work led me to approach my students as members of other cultures in terms of their prison, pre-incarceration, and cultural experiences. While this stance cannot create equality, it removes some of the barriers and allows for a sense of curiosity about each other.

Language plays a particularly important role in this part of the dance. Several of the students are from other countries, some are of Native American, Hispanic, or Asian backgrounds so English is often not their first language. So when I occasionally search for an appropriate English word or do not understand a term they use, we depend on each other for support and our cultural diversities are highlighted. This carries over to other linguistic areas which otherwise could easily become problematic. The slang used in prison, which often originated in the street, is a pervasive, extended part of their communication. The students usually try carefully to translate for me and use "high English" in class or explain their terminology to me—often this is a joint effort of several students. I, in turn, do not lower my standards and use sociological terminology; for instance, I talk about "stratification" instead of "who is on top" after explaining the term. In this way I show that I trust them to be capable of using this professional language and see them as college students now and in the future.

My background in interweaving field work, scholarship, and activism not only helped me to make better connections with my convict students, my experiences in the prison, in turn, have changed my engagement with activism. In a climate of increased punitiveness, of "being tough on crime," and daily primetime television shows on crime and criminals, stereotypes of those behind bars abound in which prisoners become increasingly seen as unredeemable and "bad" people who need to be locked up (Garland 2001; Kappeler and Potter 2004; Kunz 2004; Kury 2004), it becomes a necessity to remind ourselves of the humanity of these men and women and of our own as not so different.

Getting to the Prison

The journey to this prison is surrealistic. One travels first through the scenic area of the Wisconsin Dells, then through cornfields and pine trees along rural county roads—when suddenly the low-lying prison complex emerges, complete with towers and razor wire. At the entrance to the prison complex a large sign informs us in English and in Spanish that we are now on federal property and our vehicles can be searched at any time. Visitors are greeted with a flowerbed of sage plants, an herb sacred to Native Americans, which reads "Welcome." We enter, are processed, and have our hands stamped in the lobby with invisible ink so we can be identified as visitors in case of a riot. Then we proceed through various gates to "Control" where we may feel forgotten as we wait in a cell-like enclosure for our escort. Finally accompanied out, we cross the drab prison yard where hundreds of twittering swallows nest under the eaves and small, gray clusters of prisoners huddle in khaki jackets.

When we arrive on the education floor, the scene changes. There are no guards; there is light and there are animated voices. We can see inside the bright classrooms that line the hallway since their front consists of glass windows. Students move along the hallway between the library, the classrooms and the college office with book bags slung over their shoulders; some shuffle in a tired manner, others rush to complete an errand before classes start. When I enter the hallway some students from previous semesters greet me pleasantly when they see me, there is some friendly banter. Then I enter my classroom and take a deep breath—I arrived. I am aware of my much faster paced life in contrast to the relaxed, slow moving pace of my prison students. Sometimes we talk about it.

Until 1994 several prisons offered college programs financed largely through Pell grants, a financial aid program for low-income students. But in that year President Clinton signed off the end of these grants for prison college programs, although the actual cost to taxpayers was minimal, less than one percent of the Pell grants program budget (Yarbo 1996). College education significantly reduces recidivism rates. Although the exact numbers are difficult to establish, some studies cite reductions of 40 to 50 percent (Harris 1999; Taylor 1995). According to the former program director, this college program pays for itself if it keeps three convicts out of prison for one year. As a result of these federal cuts, most of the prison college programs nationwide have disappeared. The prison college program where I teach is one of the very few that remain. However, it, too, was reduced from a baccalaureate to an associate degree program that also provides classes for vocational training and certificates. The program has lost many of its students since they now have to pay for their books and tuition while making only about 60 cents per hour "on the inside."

College Classes

The convicts call incarceration "doing time" for good reason. Time is different in a prison; it passes more slowly. Although the students are quite busy with work assignments and different prison programs, many feel that college classes allow them to do something more constructive. With a college degree they hope to have a better chance on the outside after their release. But the program also serves an additional purpose. College classes are places where the prisoners can practice being "regular" people. They are not shamed for their crime, for being felons, for having a disreputable past. We as instructors don't even know why they are incarcerated. When they are in our classroom, they can practice their social skills, gain some confidence, and learn values and habits that will help them after their release. Their voices and their usually extensive life experiences are heard and validated.[2]

In spite of these motivations, incarcerated students have a number of special problems to attend the education program. As prisoners the organization of their time is often unpredictable and beyond their control. They work not only 40 hours a week, but these hours are often irregular. In addition the students have to attend special programs and events. Because of the duration of the class session or because of the (otherwise unusual) lack of formal supervision, the students frequently leave the classroom to visit others on the floor, to talk informally in the hallways, or just to relax. When I call them on this behavior, they insist they have to visit the restroom. This response may be to show me and their fellow students that I do not have power over them or it may be a euphemism to protect me from business they are taking care of that I am safer not knowing about. In any case, this nearly constant coming and going of students is disruptive and frustrating for the instructor.

As previously noted, a majority of the students are the first in their families to attend a college class. This, combined with their often negative previous educational experiences and their status as convicted felons, leaves many of them with low self-esteem. Much of the instructor's time inside and outside the classroom is spent encouraging and coaching students. This is particularly difficult since individualized teacher-student attention is limited to the short breaks; there are no office hours, no telephone or computer contacts. Consequently, individual concerns have to be cut short or addressed in the public arena of the classroom, which takes up class time planned for other activities. This adds to the stress level for all parties.

Just how new this educational experience is, especially for minority students, can be illustrated by the following incident. One student told me in an agitated manner that my reading assignments were just too overwhelming. Apparently, judging by the non-verbal confirmation of others, he was articulating a widely shared sentiment. I explained some aspects of learning theory and assured them that their existing patterns of knowledge would expand and they would develop new cognitive categories and skills to deal with academic learning. I used their initial incarceration experiences as an example for such a process of learning a new context of thinking. The student disagreed: "No, that wasn't so different. Being in prison is like being in the street, the same guys, the only difference is there are no girls here. You have to have a business, a product to sell—but this is really different!" Again his comments were accompanied by the nodding of many heads and sounds of affirmation. It is a testament to their adaptability that the majority of students, including this prisoner, completed the next exam with exceptionally high scores.

The students' perception of continuity between their lives on the street and prison was surprising. In either case they had to deal with similar personalities—minus the presence of women—and similar challenges of finding venues for individual entrepreneurial activities. The college class room, in contrast, is the genuinely new territory. In the street and in the prison the boundaries between legal and illegal activities are fluid, the struggles to get by are the constant (Bourgeois 2000). I do not address the issue of their entrepreneurial activities in class directly. If these activities are illegal, the student will potentially get in trouble and/or possibly lie about it. If the activity is legal, the student will most likely feel it to be humiliating, service-level work and likely to lie about it.

Teaching Strategies

Teaching in this environment requires taking a different stance from the one that is needed in a regular classroom. It requires thinking constantly on one's feet, being flexible and creative, and being open to the unexpected. The students are curious about any topic in class and are intellectually astute. The diversity of applicable life experiences is extensive. But it is often quite different from those of the instructor, who has to think of examples and reference points the students can relate to. One incident, nearly stereotypical, occurred when I tried to explain correct referencing for research papers. They had a hard time understanding why such exactness was necessary and why every discipline requires a different format. When I told them that "Plagiarism is like b&e[3] in academia," the students showed signs of relief—the issue was instantly clarified.

Most of my convict students have extensive direct experiences with issues discussed in a typical sociology class. I, in contrast, knew initially little about their backgrounds. So I stated explicitly that as a German and as an academic I did not know much about their lives in prison or in the street, that I was curious, and that a greater understanding of their experiences on my part would enhance the class. My fieldwork experience in collaborative research methods among a Native American tribe helped me in this approach (Kuhlmann 1992). It had taught me that oppressed people's experiences and perspectives are usually excluded from mainstream knowledge and that members of such groups often are not aware of how much they know and the value of their knowledge. My resulting curiosity created a more open atmosphere in the prison class room. The students took their teaching seriously and used several different class assignments for this purpose. In the regular journal entries my convict students expanded on class discussions and included their own experiences in greater depth. One of the options for their research papers was to apply a theoretical concept to life in prison or even to conduct their own research project as will be described below. In meta-conversations during class sessions the students explained to me current prison dynamics. For instance, on one of the many occasions when the atmosphere in the class suddenly changed and students began to talk among themselves, I ask them what is going on. "You just dissed so-and-so." I had to ask them to repeat the sentence and then to define "dissed" to me: the term means "to disrespect." The code of respect and disrespect is important and complex in a prison, particularly when gender is factored in. A sincere apology, when appropriate, usually clears the air quickly.

In one class session the students applied the presented theoretical concepts of stratification to prison life by teaching me about the criteria of ranking used, such as physical strength and reputation or availability of resources like stamps, cigarettes, or specific brands of potato chips. Then they proceeded to take me to the classroom windows that were facing the prison yard. It happened to be "movement," the hourly ten-minute opportunity for prisoners to move from one location to another within the prison complex. My students pointed out to me the individuals, both convicts and staff, who had "juice," that is, power and high ranking in the prison social system. Some students continued this discussion in their research papers by using theoretical topics such as stratification or authoritarianism and applying it to prison life.

Invariably a student will ask, "Now what does this really mean?" In their urgency to understand the world around them and get explanations that ring true to their life experiences, these students are very direct, even blunt, when asking about the ideas addressed in class. They are not satisfied with standard explanations but insist on honest, direct, and in-depth answers. "Now, are human beings in their core good or bad?" "We are stronger than women, why shouldn't we beat them up to get them to do what we want?" They require me to be more open than I was initially used to, but they respond in kind.

The instructor has to be acutely aware of the various moods in the classroom, including hostilities between groups. Events outside class can significantly affect the students' attitudes unbeknownst to the instructor. Maybe it is early spring, the hardest time to be incarcerated, and students tend to be more tense and irritable at this time. Or, somebody may just have been caught and put in the "hole," or solitary confinement, for a violation of prison rules. The complex net of alliances, friendships, and tensions determines their lives in the prison and in the classroom, but the lines and dynamics are not necessarily obvious to the uninitiated. Members of different groups may not talk to each other or they may express hostile feelings unrelated to the class—race and gang-related issues are obvious examples—and these feelings have to be taken into account when planning class activities. For example, students from different ethnic groups tend to sit together in class; also, as instructors we do not know gang membership of our students. Assigning group work for a project can potentially be hazardous if members of different gangs and/or racial groups end up in the same group. Another sensitive issue is colors. The College program, for example, used to sell canvas book bags with the school's logo. Since the color was associated with one of the gangs, all of the bags had to be returned and exchanged for neutral white ones. The protection or possible increase of status vis-a-vis fellow convicts is a major motivator of classroom demeanor and may shape or intensify class discussions in ways otherwise not intelligible. This may include posturing behavior for the benefit of class mates which can be a source of conflict because of my role as an authority as well as a female. Therefore, I try to address any individual tensions as much as possible outside the class room setting.

The students often have creative arguments, which they present from angles unfamiliar to the instructor. Sometimes it is a challenge to balance the responsibility of maintaining a focus in the prison classroom discussions—they usually get much livelier than in a classroom on the outside—and of letting go and allowing the students to carry the conversation. For instance, we were watching the documentary "In the Spirit of Crazy Horse" which deals with the Red Power movement on the Pine Ridge reservation. In the movie a mixed-blood man sided with the FBI and the "goon squad." Several students began to talk among themselves about the film. One student asked, "How come? Why isn't he dead? Why didn't anybody kill him?" His sense of ethics, based on his experiences, was disturbed. A lively discussion on the theoretical concepts of social movements and their applications to mobilizations such as the Red Power movement and the Civil Rights movement ensued.

In the prison classroom emotions are raw and noticeably simmering under the surface. Therefore, as an instructor, I have to be able to respond on both intellectual and emotional levels and articulate new and existing conflicts in the class and about the way I feel. Boundaries have to be set especially clearly to create a context in which openness can occur. Any decision on my part is better than appearing indecisive, including an insistence on the rules when students challenge me. The greatest compliment from prisoners is to be called "tough and fair." This is illustrated in one incident at the beginning of my teaching experience in the prison, when I was still not very secure in my role. I criticized the definition of 'ideology' in the textbook we used and gave the class a different one. The students were more uncritical, sometimes even in awe, about the written word, so a few students became quite aggressive, saying, "How can you criticize the textbook?" (I'm sure this also had a gender component.) I proceeded to explain my own background in social theory, the academic tradition of peer-reviewed articles, and other matters of publication and expertise. I reasserted my definition of the term. Suddenly the whole class started to give me an ovation, which, to their enjoyment, left me quite speechless.

At times the different kinds of tensions and conflicts have other kinds of unexpected resolutions. On one occasion, a student had been especially disruptive and I told him to calm down. He attacked my response to his behavior in class, and his classmates did not react at all. In the following session, however, about half of them did not pass their copies of the regular quiz to the front row as usual, but took this opportunity to walk up to me individually to tell me how much they liked the class. It goes without saying—the tension had dissipated.

Academics and Prison Culture

Part of the challenge of teaching in a prison is constantly being prepared for the unsuspected. For example, usually about a third of the time into the semester, there are incidents where the students test me to see "what I am made of." One kind of test is kinesthetic. A prisoner, usually a tall African-American student, walks up to me to ask a question, standing very close to gauge my body reaction. (I don't know if the respective persons were conscious of their behavior or intent.) As a German, I am used to closer physical proximity than Americans and in the beginning only noticed that something had occurred because I could feel the classroom relax. Inadvertently I had done the right thing. I had not stepped back or withdrawn in other ways because he was a black male felon. Other situations become a mixture of genuine personal interest, acuteness, and testing. Out of the blue students may ask rather personal questions in a demanding manner: "Have you ever been discriminated against? Tell us about it!" "Have you ever been at an Indian ceremony?" "Have you ever been arrested?" Under other circumstances these questions would be inappropriate and too personal, in this setting I often appreciate the directness and openness. A response in kind or the maintenance of clear boundaries is usually successful. However, in some situations a question may be too unexpected or feel initially intrusive. For instant, when one student asked in the middle of class "are you all assimilated or does your being German still affect how you date people?" the questions felt intrusive to me and I reacted defensively. When I saw that his interest had been genuine and he was apparently affected by my rough response, I had to realize that my reaction came out of my own situation. His question showed a depth of real life understanding of ethnicity I was unprepared for and that I had missed, so his sensitivity had hit a nerve. The result of this realization was a particularly in depth, honest discussion on dating, gender, and ethnicity.

Sometimes the academic setting itself allows convict students to validate their own experiences in new ways and me to learn about their subculture and my own assumptions. In the beginning of every class session I give the student a short quiz about the reading. On a day when Socialization was the topic of the class, I changed the multiple choice question defining primary in contrast to secondary socialization environments to include the background of the majority of the class, i.e. inner city African Americans. "Gangs" was one possible option, though a false one. When I returned the quiz the students got agitated. They insisted that gangs were primary socialization environments. In a lively discussion, in which at least ten students participated, they explained their understanding of gangs to me. For them the gang was their family, participation in violent acts and drug dealing were secondary. Most of them had become members at the young age of six to eight years. They joined primarily because their fathers were usually permanently absent and their mothers were working and mostly not available. So other gang members took the place of a family in regard to emotional bonds but also in regard to guidance. Older gang members would teach the younger ones how to survive "in the concrete jungle" of the inner city. Furthermore, the gang provided protection, not only for the young boy or the young man, but also for his mother and sisters. Furthermore, this membership provided economic opportunity. American inner cities are characterized by job flight and lack of employment. The few legal jobs available, such as fast food restaurants, tend to be low wage and demeaning. The risks involved in drug dealing are seen as part of life, a majority of my African American and Hispanic students have been shot and have shot others. Many of them are in my classes as part of an identity crisis, they never expected to live beyond the age of 22 or 24 and had made no plans. Finally, gangs are the institutions which provide transitions in and out of prison. Most of the main gangs such as the Bloods and the Crips exist in and outside prison walls. When a person arrives in a prison, he has an instant group which will not only provide protection and membership. In times of emotional stress, such as the arrival of a "Dear John" letter, they will also provide emotional support.

There is a new sense of pride when convict students discover that their backgrounds and experiences are important and can be part of serious research as another gang related incident illustrates. This came about as a result of a discussion on research methods. After lecturing on the standard methods used in sociology I was looking for concrete examples. Since most of my convict students are incarcerated for drug and/or gang related crimes, I asked which methods would be most appropriate to study gangs: surveys, interviews, participant observation, etc. There was not much reaction to my question. But when I suggested the use of interviews, they students got suddenly agitated, several talked at once and got out of their seats. With horizontal hand signs close to their throats, they indicated that I would not survive this research method for very long. When I told them that I had no intention to conduct such research myself, but instead imagined the students in this role, there was silence—for a moment they were stunned by this new vision. I called a break, yet, instead of leaving the class room as usual, the students involved surrounded my desk and continued to talk vividly—several of them at once. They fell into a spontaneous role play, imitating various gang leaders' response to their questions and project. The outcome of the discussion was that two of the students, each one a member of the two main gangs in the prison at the time, the Bloods and the Crips, decided to prepare a collaborative research project by jointly interviewing members of each gang. By working on it together they expected to get more serious answers and to be perceived as less biased in their outcome.

The resulting twenty page paper was creative, insightful, and well articulated. It was unusual in that the students had applied their newly learned academic skills, such as writing introductions, conclusion, formal writing style, etc., without sacrificing their own voices. They first developed interview questions such as "How did you get involved in gangs?" "What attracted you to gangs?" "Where did the colors (of the gangs) come from?" "What about the killings?" "What about the people who have lost a homie (a fellow gang member) and can't let go?" "What can you tell me about some positive role models in your life?" to cite just a few. They sincerely tried to correctly apply the recently learned research methods, although they did not always do so systematically. They did not ask each gang the same interview questions. In the paper the students cited each question and each answer verbatim. In between the questions the authors offered their own interpretations and acted as cultural brokers between the gangs and the audience. For instance, the authors kept the gang terminology and provided a translation into dominant English in parenthesis or explained the concepts. For example, "straight up" means "truthfully", a "gangbanger" is "an active gang member," having "a beef" with someone is "having a problem or conflict" with this person. Other concepts were more complex. "The White situation almost has to be put into a capsule, and it can't be harped on. When you harp on something it just stagnates everything." In this quote they are expressing a street philosophy that obsessive thinking (to harp on) is detrimental to changing the situation. The term "capsule" means on one hand a form of dissociation, i.e., "package it in your mind and move on," yet it also requires context that needs to be understood and addressed. The paper showed a high degree of awareness of gang history. Both the Blood and the Crips were founded in the early 1970s, largely to organize muggings. Drugs and sophisticated weapons came later. Similarly, gang specific dress, ear piercings, colors and hand signs emerged over time. The constant was the daily discrimination and sense of social exclusion which leads to rage. In that regard they saw themselves as similar to the Irish and Italian gangs of the past. Noticeable was the distinction between the young guys and the "OGs" the original gang members or old guys. The latter were seen or saw themselves as elders, leaders who teach the young to survive, who are concerned about the community and the level of violence. Efforts to create peace between gangs was a major theme in the paper. In fact, at the end of the paper the students offered another reason for doing this project as a collaborative effort, they saw a possibility that such a joint research paper would serve gang policies. At that time there was an effort underway to broker a peace between both gangs. The authors did not list the formal names of the members interviewed, but at the end of the paper they gave a list of their street names complete with their respective membership in the various chapters of the two gangs from major cities throughout the U.S.

During the Semester: Hot Topics

There are several "hot topics" in a prison classroom: race and gender, of course, but child rearing and spirituality are at least as sensitive. Race is a central dividing force in a prison that can get a convict killed—it is intense, raw, and always present. Some of the students, whites and minorities alike, had lived in homogeneous communities and had not encountered people from other racial or ethnic groups until they came to prison. On the one hand, many of them are especially interested in other groups and their respective histories. On the other hand, students tend to sit together with others of similar racial background, and the tension between groups is always palpable. At the beginning of the semester one student often asks how I would handle incidents in which one person would say something insulting to members of another group. In regard to this concern, I ask students for a commitment not to drop this class due to conflicts without talking to me first and for an appreciation that we all were in the class to learn.

As marginalized people, critical thinking and structural explanations are more readily comprehensible to them than to the average Midwestern college student—with some exceptions. For instance, one student summed up William Wilson's (1998) work on the underclass and the connection between out-of-wedlock births and lack of jobs by saying, "Sure, you can't take love to the grocery store!" And the focus quickly moves to "how can we change it?"

Some of the most intense questions focus on child rearing. As others have pointed out, when a person is incarcerated, often his or her whole family is punished (Mauer and Chesney-Lind 2002). Families have to cope without a major income, wives live without husbands, children grow up without fathers. Some of the men feel guilt for having caused such pain, some explain their crime as a failed attempt to be a good provider in a time of declining wages. Other men have children from a previous marriage or out-of-wedlock birth and they are concerned about not being part of their upbringing. Many of the men emphasized to me that they are sending home child support payments from their meager prison income. Their interest in parenting classes and the increased number of diaper stations in the facility are further confirmations of this observation. In my classes questions related to child rearing often occur suddenly and are always intense: "How do you deal with children idealizing murderers or, more, the life style of murderers?" For many students this does not only refer to media hype, but to their own communities. Their experiences and personal struggles as well as their thoughtfulness became obvious when one of them asked, "How do you teach your children to deal with racism and protect them and not make them into racists at the same time, not teach them that all whites are bad and will hurt you?" We have not yet found good answers to these questions.

Another prison dance involves gender and sexuality. For obvious reasons it is the constant proverbial pink elephant in the classroom. Derogatory comments about women are part of prison culture, perhaps assertion of masculinity is used as a survival technique in an environment where it can be dangerous to show weakness. The students may use sexual/sexist comments to test me, such as "the chick" reference that is usually exchanged among them. This stops with a decisive comment on my part, and an ensuing discussion of the topic offers an opportunity to learn more about gender. Finding a partner after being released from prison is of great concern to the students. Living for extended periods of time without close contact to women leaves them feeling insecure about their ability to communicate with the opposite sex. Especially the white students see their chances of establishing a relationship as diminished by their felony record and limited assets as a provider. Most of the students' ideas about gender roles are quite conservative, in contrast to their views about other political issues. A majority of my convict students are unusually knowledgeable even about details of current national and international politics. They have well articulated opinions on most issues, including the war in Iraq, social welfare, education, tax cuts, etc. Mostly they are liberal opinions. At the same time there are frequent sexist remarks especially from white students and most of them have a strong sense of "women's place and men's place." They expect women to fulfill traditional gender roles, i.e., stay at home, take care of children and the elderly, clean and fix meals. There are strong negative responses to even the suggestion of doing any tasks that could be considered women's work. Yet, underlying is the awareness that their chances of acting as the sole provide through legal occupations is fairly limited and they fear a loss of power and authority in their families. The conflict between their traditional gender role expectations, often central to their male identity, and the reality of being locked into their socio-economic position with declining wages seems to be a major reason for the offenses that brought especially the white students to the prison. Discussions on these topics were sometimes a cause for side remarks by African American students, that they have fewer problems with female authority figures since they have many strong independent women in their families and communities.

It also turns out, however, that the students' views about women are more complex than I anticipated. I was surprised to find out how, for example, my students see women as powerful. On several occasions they explained to me that they viewed women's ability to express and deal with emotions, to be articulate about their feelings, and to negotiate conflict as a superior skill that leaves men at a disadvantage.

Discussions on sexuality can enter the classroom in surprising venues. In one instance I had asked the students to describe the orange each student had been required to bring to class—any other fruit or vegetable could have served the purpose of this assignment equally. I allowed them to use any format they liked, including poetry. I had effectively used this exercise numerous times in my college or Native American classrooms to illustrate differences in American Indian and Anglo-American worldviews. Here, however, the students became restless, talked to each other, and formed spontaneous groups, a response I had not encountered in this classroom before. When the exercise was completed, some students read formal, abstract descriptions. Others were more imaginative. One student read a well written but explicitly sensual poem. An open conversation about sexuality ensued, and some tried to challenge, even intimidate me, with talk of sex. Unbeknownst to me, I had hit a nerve with this assignment. Since then I have had other encounters where students responded in sexual terms when I discuss issues that were too close to home. In such cases they were intrigued that it was acceptable to rationally discuss sexuality and related issues, and in this case they were also flattered that I assumed they could write poetry. Yet the topic also left them feeling uncomfortable.

Spirituality may well be the most sensitive topic in this environment. It is a main survival tool in the prison. A special department, organized by two chaplains, houses the activities and equipments of various religions. They include not only many Christian denominations, but also several Native American religions, Buddhism, Wicca, and Rastafarians. Spiritual experiences and practice provide guidance and sustenance for some convicts, but there is also an aspect of prison politics. Active participation in any of the religious groups carries with it membership in one of the subgroups within the prison at large. These subgroups are predominantly but not only organized according to racial and ethnic lines. The emotional and political intersection is illustrated in the following incident. A colleague from a different university, who is a member of the Hopi tribe, came to give a guest lecture on the importance her tribe places on listening. She was able to make the link between listening and spirituality direct and tangible for the students. The ensuing heated discussion on the possibility of different class members attending each other's ceremonies created a moving opening of formerly rigid barriers.

The End of the Semester

The end of the semester can be an emotional time. The risks involved in the presentation of self have declined and there is a need for closure. When each student hands in his final exam, many use this opportunity for an individual goodbye. Some just want to talk for a while, others make jokes, and again others want only a sincere handshake. Most of them express gratitude for this opportunity to take a college class. During graduation ceremony it is moving to see their pride in their accomplishments and in the opportunity to publicly show their accomplishments to their families.

The nature of the classroom structure creates a need for closure and the possibility to resolve still lingering tensions. In a recent semester, on the last day of class, a student who had been particularly difficult—he frequently disrupted the class and was sometimes rude—apologized for his behavior. However, he had taken the effort to find somebody in the prison to teach him to do so in German to convince me of his sincerity and to prevent his classmates from overhearing him.

Another incident in this context illustrates student strategies. Often one student addresses a conflict for the whole group, and sometimes humor is used to defuse tension. This often occurs in a mix of manipulation and directness. On the last day of the semester I had planned to prepare the students for the final and to this end, I had brought my draft. I was sitting as usual on a table in front of the class, with several folders stacked right beside me—the bottom one contained the draft of the exam—and a few books on top. I had not moved from this place, although several students had crowded around me during the break. When I wanted to begin the review, the draft of the final was gone. Someone had to have taken it. I had checked for the draft at the beginning of the break, and one student may have seen it. I felt hurt and angry. I was forced to tell the administration and was reminded to "remember where I am." Each of the students was also searched by the prison staff.

Afterwards I talked with the students about my feelings and the bind I was now in concerning the design of the final exam so not to unfairly give advantage to the person(s) who had taken it. None of us felt good when I left that day. A few days later I resolved the problem about the final's design by turning all the previously planned multiple-choice questions into essay questions. On the day of the final, the students were worried at first, but realized that this solution mostly created more work for them. When one of the first students to complete the exam came up to the front to hand me his copy, he mumbled something. I asked him to speak up. He mumbled again. I again asked him to talk louder. Then this big, tall African-American man said, in a low but booming voice, "Look at it with love." The rest of the students smiled and snickered, and for the first time that day the atmosphere relaxed. When I arrived a week later to attend the college graduation ceremony, this same student smiled broadly at me across the big hall; he had done well on the final. After the ceremony he came over to where I was standing with other students and told me, "See, love made all the difference."

In Conclusion

Teaching in a prison is the most challenging and rewarding work I have ever done. In sociology in particular, we do not teach convict students so much content—they know about stratification, racism, deviance—but instead they can gain a context, an alternative view, a framework in which to locate their experiences, a shared language in which to think and talk about it. On many occasions students told me they found this liberating.

The students' life experiences, their ability and willingness to be present and engaged, their urgency to find answers, their emotional rawness make for an environment rich for teaching, and for learning to teach. But it also requires more involvement on the part of the instructor. Although in a different role, for one afternoon a week, I am part of their environment, I am locked up as well. The extensive diversity and varied life experiences in the classroom have to be integrated to create a learning setting. The boundaries of teaching and learning disappear. I become a learner as well as a teacher. Yet other boundaries have to be observed—I can go home after class.[4] The power differential is great but constantly shifting. Because of the nature of the situation and the people, I have to be vigilant about the undercurrents of moods and atmospheres in the classroom—often originating outside the education floor—and interpret them correctly. I need to learn from my students how to do this. The result is a dance. On one side the learning process is influenced by the negotiation of needs, including the need to connect with others with very different life experiences, not in the role of "the other" into which women, men, whites, minorities, or convicts have been cast. On the other side are the formal and informal rules of prison life. Conversational niceties and political correctness are a luxury the students can ill afford. Yet the need for specific information about the workings of the outside world, the search for a language to express and understand life experiences are urgent and require trust and the ability to listen. The moments of openness can be honest and raw, but they are moments of connection that—for an instant—bridge the barriers of class, race, nationality, and gender and transform us all.

Endnotes

[1]The success of Convict Criminology, a new direction in criminology in which former convicts who have become criminologists discuss their experiences, shows the applicability of collaborative research methodologies to other environments such as prisons (Ross and Richards 2003).

[2]For a convict's perspective on college programs, see Terry (2003).

[3]"B & e" refers to "breaking and entering" in prison lingo.

[4]For more on the issue of boundaries in prison, see Ferrell and Hamm (1998).

References

Bourgois, Philippe. 2000. "Workaday World, Crack Economy." In: J. Skolnick and E.Currie. *Crisis in American Institutions.* Boston: Allyn and Bacon.

DeVita, Philip and James Armstrong. 2002. *Distant Mirrors: America as a Foreign Culture.* Belmont, CA: Wadsworth.

Ferrell, Jeff and Mark S. Hamm (eds.). 1998. *Ethnography at the Edge: Crime, Deviance, and Field Research.* Boston: Northeastern University Press.

Garland, David. 2001. *The Culture of Control: Crime and Social Order in Contemporary Society.* Chicago, IL :University of Chicago Press.

Harris, Jean. 1999. "Jail Sentences with No End." *New York Times*, May 20:A27.

Irwin, John. 2004. *The Warehouse Prison: Disposal of the New Dangerous Class.* Los Angeles, CA: Roxbury.

Kappeler, Victor and Gary Potter. 2005. *The Mythology of Crime and Criminal Justice.* Long Grove, IL: Waveland.

Kuhlmann, Annette. 1992. "Collaborative Research in Among the Kickapoo Tribe of Oklahoma." *Human Organization.* Vol 51:3.

Kunz, Karl-Ludwig. 2004. *Kriminologie.* Bern: Haupt Verlag.

Kury, Helmut, Harald Kania, Joachim Obergfell-Fuchs. 2004. "Worüber sprechen wir, wenn wir über Punitivität sprechen? Versuch einer konzeptionellen und empirischen Begriffsbestimmung." in *Punitivität 8. Beiheft des Kriminologischen Journals.* Weinheim: Juventa.

Mauer, Marc and Meda Chesney-Lind. 2002. *Invisible Punishment: The Collateral Consequences of Mass Imprisonment.* New York: The New Press.

Pastore, Ann L. & Kathleen Maquire. 2002. *Sourcebook of Criminal Justice Statistics 2001.* Washington, DC: U.S. Dept. of Justice.

Ross, Jeffrey and Stephen Richards. 2003. *Convict Criminology.* Belmont, CA: Wadsworth.

Schlesier, Karl. 1980. "Zum Weltbild einer neuen Kulturanthropologie." *Zeitschrift für Ethnologie.* Bd. 105:1,2.

Taylor, Jon Marc. 1995. "It's Criminal to Deny Pell Grants to Prisoners." *World & I* 10:88.

Terry, Chuck. 2003. "From C-Block to Academia: You Can't Get There From Here." In J.Ross and S.Richards *Convict Criminology.* Belmont, CA: Wadsworth.

Wilson, William J. 1998. *When Work Disappears: New Implications for Race and Urban Poverty in the Global Economy.* London: London School of Economics.

Yarbo, Kathy. 1996. "Saving Money or Wasting Minds?" *Corrections* Today, Aug.:12–16.

Rejoinder to Kuhlmann's "Prison Dances: Teaching and Learning Behind Bars"

Jeffrey Cohen
Worcester State College

Annette Kuhlmann's description of travelling to and entering a prison in Wisconsin reminded me of the times I have spent travelling to and from prisons in Pennsylvania. It is not surprising that her experiences so closely match my own. The criminal justice systems we currently employ are rooted in a relatively uniform approach to imprisonment. Institutions, located in remote, almost invisible regions, serve as protective barriers between those "on the inside" and us "on the outside." The physical and geographical isolation of prisons intensify the mental and emotional isolation of convicts, creating a virtual veil of secrecy where the public remains immune to the inhumanity of prison life.

There are, however, people who break through this veil of secrecy. As Kuhlmann points out, these individuals are rewarded with rich, meaningful interactions with members of a culture and community many of us avoid. Revisiting her article provides a welcome context in which to discuss the current state of corrections in the United States. Kuhlmann's piece also represents an important call for a more humane and empowering paradigm for education in BOTH correctional and educational institutions.

Current Correctional Context

Unfortunately, many of the statistics that Kuhlmann cites in her article have continued along a trend towards increased incarceration and correctional supervision. For instance, according to the Bureau of Justice Statistics, at year-end 2007, 7.3 million people were under correctional supervision (i.e., probation, jail, prison, and parole) in the United States. If we look at incarceration figures specifically, at midyear 2008 there were 2,310,984 individuals doing time in local jails, as well as state and federal prisons, an increase of .8% from year-end 2007. Additionally, racial discrimination and disparities continue to plague correctional systems as the latest statistics show. When we consider rates of incarceration, our latest statistics show that there are 4,777 black male inmates per 100,000 black males in the population, compared to 1,760 Hispanic male inmates, and 727 white male inmates. Finally, the lack of access to Pell grants continues to place limits on the ability of inmates to pursue college education. As Kuhlmann points out in her article, without access to these grants, colleges and universities have eliminated their prison-based degree programs and many inmates who are interested in pursuing college education, which has been linked to decreased recidivism, are blocked due to the prohibitive costs. What these statistics reveal is that the prison setting continues to present unique challenges to educators and service providers who wish to engage prisoners in meaningful ways. But what Kuhlmann offers in this intimate and informative article is the groundwork for a more humane approach to the education of prisoners and, I believe, these lessons can and should be carried into classrooms "on the outside" as well.

Collaboration

Perhaps the greatest contribution of Kuhlmann's approach to prison education is her dedication to bringing forth and valuing her students' personal experiences. As she describes, this dedication to empowering her students stems from her work with collaborative research methods, aimed at giving voice to traditionally marginalized individuals. It is hard to imagine a more marginalized group than those serving time in correctional institutions. Exposing incarcerated students to education that doesn't further or enhance their alienation and marginalization poses a powerful model for disenfranchised men and women. To do so in a way that also empowers students to apply academic concepts to their own lived experiences is very difficult, but Kuhlmann's call for a truly collaborative approach provides an avenue to achieve this goal.

My own limited experience working with inmates to construct recidivism reduction courses supports this methodology. Few people are better situated to shape effective recidivism prevention programs than those who have been through the criminal justice systems in the U.S. In my view, entering this setting as an expert prepared to disseminate knowledge without recognizing the contributions of the prisoners themselves would be pedagogically perilous and in effect just another act of social injustice. Teachers inside and outside of the prison walls could benefit from a more inclusive, collaborative approach to education; one that actively engages students in the material in a way that resonates with their own experiences and allows them to be a part of a larger community.

The Ideal Classroom

Kuhlmann suggests that "teaching in this environment...requires thinking constantly on one's feet, being flexible and creative, and being open to the unexpected." In addition, she states that "most of my convict students have extensive direct experiences with issues discussed in a typical sociology class." As someone whose academic training is in criminology, I also have been impressed with the level of critical understanding that most of the inmates I have worked with bring to our discussions. The description of the classroom setting that Kuhlmann provides corresponds with what I have long held to be an ideal. I begin every semester hoping to engage with students who have direct experience with the course material and, therefore, require me to access my own creativity and openness. This also points to the unwarranted stereotyping of prisoners. Those prisoners who I have had the pleasure of working with are a testament to the enduring humanity that exists in each of us. Faced with mounting barriers, oppressive living conditions, and strict regulations on every aspect of their daily lives, these men and women continue to engage in meaningful work for the benefit of their peers and the communities that have more-or-less shunned them.

Setting Boundaries

Finally, Kuhlmann's article also touches on one of the most challenging aspects of working within the prison setting; the maintenance of clear boundaries. As she states, "in the prison classroom emotions are raw and noticeably simmering under the surface. Therefore, as an instructor, I have to be able to respond on both intellectual and emotional levels and articulate new and existing conflicts in the class and about the way I feel. Boundaries have to be set especially clearly to create a context in which openness can occur." I believe this illustrates the need for a more holistic and humane approach to education. No longer should we rely on our positioning as experts in our individual fields to disseminate information to those who seem reluctant to receive it. Instead, we must come to terms with the inherently emotional aspects of our work. Kuhlmann's description of her experiences working as a teacher in prison provides a clear illustration of how one can move between the personal and academic in ways that both maintain necessary structural power relationships (e.g., student/teacher) and promote openness and trust.

In Conclusion

In many ways, the unique challenges that Kuhlmann faced while teaching in the prison setting can inform the broader educational community. Actively engaging students continues to be a rallying cry among educators at all levels. It is clear from this article, however, that what is needed is a more open, honest, and humane approach. Simply placing the responsibility on students to be more active ignores the emotional context of the student-teacher relationship and the power structures within the classroom and broader educational and correctional systems. Without such a movement towards a more humane and open approach to prison education, policymakers and educators will lack the "right moves" to make the systemic and personal changes necessary to effectively reduce recidivism and reform our current criminal justice systems. I know that my future interactions with students inside and outside the prison setting will benefit from the lessons of this article. With any luck, I will have taken a few steps towards a more fluid and responsive dance that engages my students and my own humanity.

4. The News and the Myth of Spat-upon Vietnam Vets: What Can We Learn from the slate.com File[1]

Jerry Lembcke
Holy Cross College[2]

Reflexive Statement

Stories about spat-upon Vietnam veterans caught my attention during the Persian Gulf War when they were used by supporters of the Bush Administration to discredit the peace movement. Far from being spat on, I knew from experience that thousands of Vietnam veterans, like me, had actually been embraced by the anti-war movement which we, in turn, joined forces with. It is important to debunk the image of spat-upon veterans because, left unchallenged, it functions to displace from public memory the legacy of anti-war veterans and distorts the historical record of activists' solidarity with soldiers and veterans.

Introduction

We celebrated the 25th anniversary of the peace in Vietnam during May 2000. It was a time to remember the victory of the Vietnamese people and the courage and commitment of those in this country who opposed the war. It was also a time to reflect on how the war, and opposition to it, is remembered.

Studies of historical representation have grown during the last decade and the subject of the United States' twentieth-century wars, Vietnam in particular, figure prominently in the growth of that literature. Film, poetry, novels, and other forms of popular culture have been of special interest to scholars.[3] Here, I want to focus on the role of the print news media in popularizing an important image through which the history of the war and anti-war movement has come to be represented—the image of the spat-upon Vietnam veteran.

Journalists, of course, are not solely responsible for the widespread belief that Vietnam veterans were spat on by protesters when they returned from the war. The vilification of the anti-war movement by the Nixon Administration and the representation of the veterans' "coming home" experience by Hollywood undoubtedly contributed to that belief. And yet, these stories have an element of urban legend in the sense that they have no identifiable time and place of origin—and that makes the part played by journalists in keeping the idea of disparaged veterans alive all the more interesting.

---

[1]This paper originally appeared in *Humanity & Society* Volume 26, Number 1, 2002.

In what follows, I use a recent set of exchanges over the veracity of the spat-upon veterans' stories to document their vitality in the culture as well as to illustrate some of their more interesting dimensions. I'll close with a comment on the legacy of that image and the way it plays in the current period.

slate.com Revisits The Myth

On May 2, 2000, Jack Shafer, administrator of slate.com, an Internet news portal, wrote an editorial criticizing the print news media for their references to spat-upon veterans in stories they had carried about the 25th anniversary of the war's end. In an April 28 story, *The New York Times'* John Kifner had quoted a class of 1974 West Point cadet as saying he had been spat on and, a few days later, the *U.S. News and World Report's* Amanda Spake recalled that Vietnam vets had to change their clothes in bus stations lest they be spat on. Shafer used my book *The Spitting Image: Myth, Memory, and the Legacy of Vietnam* to upbraid Kifner, Spake, and other journalists for their perpetuation of the widely-believed but historically inaccurate idea that anti-war activists had been hostile to Vietnam veterans.

During the next four days, slate.com received nearly 300 postings on the subject, one of its largest-ever responses. The slate.com collection is the largest single data set we have for the study of the spitting stories since Chicago Tribune columnist Bob Green published a collection of letters from veterans in his 1989 book *Homecoming*.[4]

When I wrote *The Spitting Image* in the mid-1990s, I cited Greene's book not only as evidence for the existence of these stories but also for the patterns that appeared in them. As Greene pointed out, many of the stories occurred at West Coast airports and many of the incidents were accompanied by name-calling such as "baby killer." The similarity in the stories was something that raised Greene's concern that there might be an element of legend at work in their telling.

I was interested in two other patterns in his collection and, in my book, I used both as clues that the stories were even less authentic than Greene thought. I thought it particularly remarkable that eighteen of the storytellers said that the spitters were girls or women. "It's gotta be a myth," said a psychologist friend of mine who works in women's studies, "girls don't spit." And, of the twenty-two spitters identified as men, six were described as "long hairs" or "hippies," terms which, I argue in the book, are also a form of gendering.

Subsequently, I learned that stories of veterans abused by women circulated in Germany after its defeat in World War I and the alleged abuse sometimes took the form of spitting. Klaus Theweleit's study of these stories, published as *Male Fantasies: Women, Floods, Bodies, and History*, used a neo-Freudian analysis to suggest that the stories arise from the subconscious of defeated male warriors. Within this analytical framework, the vanquished soldier fears that it was his own weaknesses that betrayed him and caused his defeat and, since weakness, in Western culture, is imagined as female, the veteran imagines his betrayal in female imagery and projects that outwardly, onto others. The hostility for what the veteran fears is really within himself is aimed at "the female" in the society, making girls and women the targets of his anger. In the literature that Theweleit examined, he found veterans' stories alleging abuse by women who carried pistols beneath their skirts, images he says are the projections of male fears of women with male powers. In *The Spitting Image*, I argue that the role of women spitters in the stories is to suggest that these traitorous females also have the male power to project body fluid.

Greene's stories also struck me as loaded with exaggeration. His own disclaimers not-withstanding, some of the accounts he published were simply not believable. One of his selections was from Lou Rochat:

> In Frisco, we had… a one hour wait. I was spit on twice—once by a female hippie-type who smelled as bad as she looked and secondly by a well dressed young business type who would be called a "yuppie" today. Him I flattened with a left book in the gut and a right to his big mouth. My fellow officers and I were escorted to our plane by security. The average American in the airport only called us names… such as "Murderer," "Baby Killer," "Rapist," and "Fucking Bastard War Monger." [These] were the parting words from our fellow Americans.

Like many of the other stories, there are elements in this one suggesting that some, or all of it, is not true. It is not true, of course, that *average Americans* disparaged departing troops with obscenities. Nor is it true that he could have decked a yuppie and then been protected by "security." Altercations between uniformed military personnel and civilians were dealt with very severely by the military, making it more likely that, had Rochat really punched someone, he would have been escorted to a military lock-up, not his plane.

The gendered and even sexualized nature of many of the stories, combined with the exaggerated machismo, led me to conclude that there was something specifically masculine about them. With the insight provided by Theweleit and James William Gibson's book *Warrior Dreams*, I came to understand the spat-upon veteran stories as a genre of defeated male-warrior fantasies spawned in the post-Vietnam culture of the United States.

The Stories Get Better

Since Greene's book appeared in 1989, the stories of spat-upon Vietnam veterans have been popularized by novelists, turned into political propaganda during the Persian Gulf War, and, in turn, critiqued by me and a few other writers.[5] The widespread publicity given my book is reason enough to assume that at least some of the slate.com posters had gotten the word that the truth of their tales was being questioned. Perhaps not.

Sixty-two veterans responded to Shafer's editorial, 63% saying, yes, it happened to them. Nineteen others reported witnessing spitting incidents. The size of that response alone confirms the general tenacity of the myth. The content of the stories continues to be marked by exaggeration and clichés while gender and sexual themes remain central to their telling.[6]

Multiple spittings are a common form of exaggeration in the slate.com stories. On May 3, Spc4 Hughes (May 3) wrote:

> I and members of my company were spat-on by University of Wisconsin pro-testers while transferring from a commercial bus to waiting military vehicles in Madison in 1969. The protesters were able to get up into our faces for clear shots realizing they were safe as no soldier is going to break rank to defend himself. These brave protesters have earned their "cheesehead" nicknames.

R.H.F. wrote about his experience at Colorado State University:

> Not only for the returning, but the mere act of wearing the uniform on the campus during the early 1970s was a sure fire way to be spat upon. Often two and three times per day.

Sex and The Spitting Girl

Many veterans in the slate.com file identified their attackers as female or male hippies and their stories frequently contained sexual innuendo or overtly sexualized imagery. One of the more interesting in that regard was from C.W. Davitz (May 4) who is worth quoting at length:

> Viet Vets getting spat upon is a myth? Wrong, stud! My group of GI's had to be escorted through the San Francisco airport by cops. The "long hairs" were like a mob and were throwing bags of feces on us, eggs, & other trash at us. All the while screaming at us. One thing that still to this day stands out in my mind was this girl, filthy, sandals, the whole bit, was holding this dog in an American flag and she was giving the dog a blow job. And then she spit at us. Other people in the terminal were cheering this hippie trash as security cops surrounded us.... So don't tell me, backaroo, about "myths."

While few of us would believe this story, we nevertheless have to take seriously the subtext of female betrayal that it conveys. That gendered betrayal narrative is even clearer in a story recounted by "Viet Vet":

> Yes, I was spat upon and called baby killer and considered a second classed no brain fool for my efforts. My homecoming consisted of my girl pregnant and her hippie beau too cool to take responsibility.

The soldier betrayed by the wife or girlfriend back home is stuff of military legend, of course. Recall that Odysseus returns to find his wife, Penelope, courted by a "hoard" of young men who have moved in with her. It is possible, of course, that Viet Vet's homecoming was as he says but there is no mistaking the likeness between the scene he describes and the one in the 1987 movie *Hamburger Hill.* In the film, the protagonist has returned to his unit in Vietnam after having gone home from his first tour of duty. "I'm home from the 'Nam," he says, "I get home, the wife is sitting cross-legged on the floor, kids running around barefoot, there is a hairhead taking a leak in the john." "That," he tells his troops as they are about to go on attack, "is why I'm here."

From Spit to …

The slate.com file is also distinguishable from Greene's collection by its scatological content. While none of Greene's stories made reference to feces or urine—a potato salad was the most odious entre—several slate.com victim-veterans claimed to have been served these ultimate insults. The more interesting ones, like C.W. Davitz' (above) and the following from J.F. Burns (May 3), are gendered stories combining spit and excrement:

> Yes, Jerry, a first person story.... At that time it was a daily event at LAX for idiots to demonstrate at incoming flights... in 65 it was common to deplane down on the tarmac and walk across an open area secured by a four foot chain-link fence. It was behind those fences that the radicals gathered. That's where it happened.

> A young white blonde male and his redheaded girlfriend saw me, rushed the fence and threw a liquid concoction of a blood-like substance and human excrement in my direction. It was 50% on target. Not satisfied... the spittle was their next missile, it hit. From many people in the crowd, me and this other guy were called everything but a child of God. And, yes, Jerry, "baby killer," was one of them.

This scene—Los Angeles, the tarmac and four-foot fence, and radical greeting party—is too close for comfort to Bob's arrival home in Jane Fonda's 1978 film *Coming Home*; its fanciful quality underscored by the fact that no GIs returning from Vietnam deplaned at LAX and the unlikelihood that, even if Mr. Burns been assaulted in the manner he describes, he couldn't have known that the substance he was hit with was actually human.

The perceived need to exaggerate probably explains how it is that stories of defiled veterans got larded with excrement. It is also possible that the softening of homophobic taboos on oral and anal sex during the 1990s, and the widening acceptability of bathroom humor in television comedy and talk-show programs, has lowered the risk of adding them to other forms of popular culture. The nature of the medium, finally, might also have encouraged slate.com posters to be more vulgar than writers of letters to Greene in the mid 1980s. There is an air of anonymity and presumption of impermanence that surrounds the use of the Internet. The identity of "Viet Vet" with the pregnant girlfriend cannot be verified; his story cannot be fact-checked; he can say whatever he wants without being held accountable. For that matter, how do we know that Mr. Burns isn't really a mischievous Mr. Johnson salting our popular culture with fraudulent images he knows will get reproduced as something that really happened? [7]

The public accessibility of the slate.com file also sets it apart from Greene's collection. Whereas we can't study the letters that Greene discarded, we can look at all the 278 items evoked by Shafer's editorial and that includes over 200 items written by individuals who did not identify themselves as veterans. Moreover, Greene's findings have always been suspect because he solicited a particular response. By asking his readers if they had been spat on when they returned home, he was, in effect, leading the witnesses. If he had asked a more neutral question—what was your homecoming experience like?—he might have gotten a less dramatic but more scientifically valid result. Shafer, on the other hand, simply wrote an editorial and put it on-line. And, although his piece used my book to underwrite his assumption that the stories of abused veterans were fanciful, his criticism was directed at the news media's use of the spat-upon veteran image, not at the validity of the image itself. And he didn't ask for any response, thus making the outpouring of the sentiment he did get all the more authentic as an indicator of what a certain segment of Americans thinks about the issue of spat-upon Vietnam veterans.[8]

Spit on the Messenger

The interactive quality of the file also allows us to see beyond the stories, and their tellers, into the way that Americans talk about the stories. In that sense it is a kind of text on the popular discourse surrounding the iconic image of spat-upon Vietnam veterans. First, we can see the kind of rhetoric used to rebut the stories and how, in turn, the story tellers rejoin those objections.

Particularly interesting are the ten rejoinders that use the rhetoric of "holocaust denial" to counter my claim that the image of spat-upon Vietnam veterans is mythical. One string of exchanges went as follows:

> Pissed Off Reader (May 2) Sure, sure no one was spat upon. I suppose Jews being slaughtered in WWII is a myth too?
>
> CPT KN (May 3) This professor fits in the same mold as those who claim 6 million Jews and other groups hated by Hitler did not die in the Holocaust.
>
> J.Mingus (May 3) I think the author is suffering from a post-war syndrome... similar to the guy who doesn't believe the Jews died in the death camps of Nazi Germany.
>
> Frances Brennan (May 3) I am reminded in a small way of ignorant youth who stupidly say the holocaust never happened.
>
> G.E. McCaddon (May 4) I'll bet Shafer doesn't believe the Holocaust happened either.
>
> Marvin G. (May 4) The Holocaust was the extermination of six million people. It is a well documented proven fact. On the other hand this spitting nonsense is NOT documented, NOT proven, and certainly not relevant. If they did get spit on, so what? Spit washes off. Concentration camp tattoos don't.
>
> Richard Aubrey (May 4) I think you miss the point. I don't believe anybody really thinks Shafer doesn't believe the Holocaust. The point is a metaphor....
>
> WatsonH (May 4) Actually, I think YOU missed the point. Yes, we often try to rewrite history to reflect our personal prejudices.... But if we revise long-held beliefs that are inconsistent with new evidence, there's nothing wrong with that.... If you don't like what the author of this column has to say, offer evidence to prove him wrong or show how the research he did was flawed. But don't assume that just because he challenges a widely-held belief that he's some kind of Nazi. Making a connection between Holocaust revisionism and this column shows fuzzy thinking on any level.
>
> Richard Aubrey (May 5) I didn't connect him with the Nazis. I said the use of the Holocaust is a metaphor for screwing the pooch in the service of some idea

he prefers. That there is no "proof" is absurd. Neither he nor Lembcke could have missed the first-person stories if they'd bothered to look.

Some of the defenses of the stories took the form of personal counter-attacks on me, a kind of shoot-the-messenger approach. The common form of those was to dismiss the credibility of my work on the assumption that I'm not a Vietnam veteran (I am) and, therefore, have no basis for knowing the truth of this matter. Isaac (May 4) implied that I was a "draft-dodging hippy" while others just called me names, with Professor Nitwit (Roy Jaruk, May 3) being one of the more endearing. When Robert (May 3) politely announced that he "would like to spit on Jerry Lembcke" Reese (May 3) replied, "Well done, Robert."

Of course, the Internet allowed me to fire (not spit!) back. I made my own first-posting as the holocaust exchange was underway. I said the notion of veteran disparagement on the home front is dangerous because it keeps alive the mistaken idea that the war could have been won if we had not beaten ourselves. It is a myth that displaces the real history of the war, thus creating a blank space in our public memory that can be filled in with the old war-time U.S. propaganda line that the war was about North Vietnam having invaded the South.

My posting received over a dozen direct responses that were generally civil and thoughtful, but the file as a whole is characterized by defensiveness and verbal aggressiveness of those who believe the stories.[9] The interactive nature of the slate.com file provides a written record that, when challenged, those who hold to the truth of the spat-upon veteran stories do not back down. This provides an important clue that there is something about these stories that sets them apart from urban legend. After all, who among us would expect the teller of, say, the Hookman legend to counter-attack by inferring their critics were Nazis. And if Professor Nitwit told Robert and Reese that their story of the cat in the microwave was not true, would they threaten to put him in with the cat? I don't think so.

Journalists and The Myth

When Jack Shafer wrote his editorial, little did he know that I had been on the case of journalism's complicity with myth-mongering for a couple years. One of my favorite exchanges with *The New York Times* came in response to a business story they ran in November 2, 1998. With the headline "A Bicycle Path From Wall Street to Vietnam," and written by Laura A. Holson, the story was about Peter D. Kiernan 3d who organized a bicycle tour of Vietnam. In her report, Holson wrote that Kiernan had been moved to organize the trip when a Vietnam veteran told him he had returned from Vietnam on a stretcher with a bullet in his leg. He said, "college kids rushed up and poured rotten vegetables on him. They spat on him. He was so ashamed."

On the day Holson's story appeared, I faxed a letter saying that in my research I found no evidence that such incidents ever took place and explained that it would have been impossible for protesters with rotten vegetables to get close to a wounded soldier returning from Vietnam. Subsequently, I attempted via e-mail to engage Holson in some discussion of the issue. She did respond once with a curt "What do you want to know?" but after I told her more fully that my interest was in journalism and the myth, I never heard from her again.

Though the *Times* did not acknowledge my criticism, I nevertheless thought the presence of my position may have been felt and that maybe we had seen the last reference to spittled veterans in the pages of that paper. My optimism grew when Lars-Erik Nelson reviewed Robert Timberg's book, *John McCain: An American Odyssey* for the *New York Review of Books*, October 21, 1999. In his book, Timberg accused the anti-war movement of hostility to Vietnam veterans and said protesters had spat on men returning from the war. Reviewing the book, Nelson called Timberg's accusation a "slur that should be dealt with once and for all" and then, citing my book, went on at some length to do that.

Nelson's prominence as a writer should have insured that his Vietnam-interested colleagues at the *Times* saw his review. In my imagination, I pictured them standing around a water cooler, now chagrined that they had bought into the myth of spat-upon veterans. Alas, their imaginations proved stronger than mine for, a few months later, the *Times* staff did it again.

On February 29, 2000, *Times* columnist Clyde Haberman wrote about John McCain's run for the Republican Party's nomination for President. Since he was writing about McCain, I expect that Haberman would have read Nelson's then-recent review of Timberg's book. Nevertheless, Haberman wrote that McCain's campaign was easing the pain felt by soldiers who were ignored, even spat on, when they returned from Vietnam. I responded with a letter to the Times pointing that a 1972 Harris Poll done for the Veterans Administration found that 96% of Vietnam veterans reported receiving a "very or somewhat friendly" reception from their family and friends, while 82% said they felt just as welcomed by their age-group peers." The myth of spat-upon veterans, I said, "works to stigmatize anti-war activism and falsify our memory of the war years. It needs to be laid to rest." Since that letter was not printed either, it was no surprise to see the myth reappear in the *Times* coverage of the 25th anniversary of the war's end.[10]

Since the public conversation around spat-upon Vietnam veterans began with the work of journalist Bob Greene and has been extended through Jack Shafer's criticism of the media for reproducing the stories, it is appropriate to view them as a media phenomenon and ask what it is about them that continues to hold the fascination of reporters and editors.

The irony is that newspaper archives are themselves troves of evidence that relations between veterans and anti-war activists were mutually supportive and that thousands of GIs and veterans had joined the opposition to the war by 1970. So why are these tales believed by people who should know better?

One answer might be that the stories have been with us for a long enough time that younger writers have, in a sense, grown up with them. But there might be something more than miseducation at work. It's as if stories of spat-upon vets have become a kind of trope, a way of talking about things related to the war that we don't know how to express otherwise.

The image of spat-upon veterans is an icon through which the country constructs its memory of what the war was about and the fictive nature of that icon suggests that America has never come to grips with the war itself. Screened out by the accounts of forgotten warriors and spat-upon veterans are the politics that got us into the war and the history that thousands of GIs joined the effort to end the war; buried beneath the images of protester's animus for veterans is the history of the real war in which 3,000,000 Vietnamese died fighting for national independence.

During the closing years of the war in Vietnam, the Nixon Administration turned American war dead and POWs into excuses to continue the war. "If we quit now," I was told by my hawkish uncle when I returned from Vietnam in 1970, "those we've lost will have died in vain." Some Americans bought that reasoning and we lost another 20,000 young lives during the next three years. The same logic was used to leverage support for George I's war in the Persian Gulf. "The troops are there," we were told after August 1990, "support them." Those who didn't, were accused of spitting on "our boys," just like the protesters in the 1960s.[11]

Exploiting Victims For War: After September 11

The legacy of the spat-upon veteran myth lives in the post-9/11 American political culture. When Jay Leno returned to the air a week after the attacks, his guest was Arizona Senator John McCain. Leno introduced McCain, telling viewers that McCain's generation of veterans came home to be forgotten, and "spat on—sometimes literally." With those words, Leno reset the triggers that fellow pundits could pull to extort support for a military response to the attacks and intimidate those who dare oppose it. In short, the reinvocation of the myth reminds us that we fight wars for the victims already lost—causalities and POWs in Vietnam, the dead at the World Trade Center and Pentagon—and those who don't rally to the cause are disrespecting the sacrifices already made.[12]

Playing gatekeeper to public memory about wars is a lofty calling. Yet, that is what the those in the press establishment—and their cousins who write political commentary for late-night television hosts—assume they can do when they revisit turning points in history like the Vietnam war. That professional writers are willing to take the risks involved in doing that work is good news; the thought that they are ill prepared by background and training to sort out the influences of historical events, popular culture, and personal fantasies in the construction of memory should concern us all.

Endnotes

[1]Previous drafts of this article were presented at the New England Cultural Studies Conference, Fall 2000, the American Studies Association annual meeting, Fall 2001, and the Humanist Sociology Conference, Fall 2001

[2]Jerry Lembcke can be reached at jlembcke@holycross.edu or 508–793–3050.

[3]See, for example, H. Bruce Franklin, *Vietnam and Other American Fantasies*, University of Massachusetts Press, 2000.

[4]In the introduction to the book, Greene explained that, after hearing stories of vets being spat on, he used his column to ask veterans if they had been spat on and solicited letters from them. In response, he received hundreds of letters, some from victims of spitting, others from vets calling the stories hogwash, and still others who were neutral on the spitting issues but had other interesting coming-home stories to tell. Greene began printing the letters in his columns and then put them together for the book.

[5]Pat Conroy used the spat-upon veteran image in his novel *Beach Music*. Chapter 2 of my book *The Spitting Image* chronicles the references to spat-upon vets during the period of the Persian Gulf War. Beamish et al. (1995) also searched in vain for evidence that Vietnam veterans were spat on.

[6]The slate.com has archived only Shafer's editorial and a few of the exchanges. I have a hard copy of the entire file which is available upon request.

[7]One of my interventions in the exchange was an invitation to contact me directly with any sort of documentation such as a letter written in, say, 1969 in which the veteran reported

the attack he now remembers having occurred. I have not received a single response to that solicitation.

[8]When I asked Shafer for a demographic profile of his market he said, "Think *Atlantic Monthly* and *Harpers*."

[9]One of the more thoughtful responses came from Maturin (May 3) who wrote: "Thanks for the book, Jerry. I bought it when it first came out. It generally conforms to my own experience of the era and I have used it in an attempt to persuade my son to view the persistent contrary propaganda skeptically."

[10]My favorite instance of lapsed journalistic (and common) sense actually comes from my local paper, the Worcester, Massachusetts *Telegram and Gazette*. In a November 11, 1998 Veterans Day story, James Collins claimed his plane from Vietnam was met at Clark Airforce Base north of San Francisco by "thousands of protesters throwing Molotov cocktails." Like many of the stories, Collins' had details that were factually wrong (e.g. There is no Clark Airforce Base in the Bay Area) or too implausible to be believed. A year earlier, the same Telegram and Gazette reporter, George Griffin, had profiled another local veteran who claimed he arrived home at Boston's Logan airport and was greeted by anti-war protesters: "I got tattooed with eggs and bags of urine and s__ ," he said. As was the case with *The New York Times* stories (and others), I submitted a critical comment which was promptly rejected by the Worcester paper. My invitation to Mr. Griffin that we get together to talk about journalism's affinity for the idea of disparaged veterans went unacknowledged.

[11]Like the spat-upon veteran stories, the myth of POWs were abandoned in Southeast Asia helps sustain the betrayal narrative for why the United States lost the war. See Franklin (1992).

[12]I met the enemy in this new propaganda war three days after the attack. At a forum, I recalled the record of U.S. policies in Iraq, Palestine, and Yugoslavia that have enraged people around the globe and put us all at risk. In response, a young philosophy professor angrily accused me of blaming those lying in the rubble of the World Trade Center for their own deaths.

The responses to September 11 attacks will provide cases for the study of the militarization of culture for decades. One of the most obvious examples is the likelihood (as of January, 2002) that a commemorative statue of fire fighters raising a flag at the World Trade Center site will be built to resemble that of Marines raising the flag on Iwo Jima during World War II.

References

Beamish, Thomas D., Harvey Molotch, and Richard Flacks. 1995. "Who Supports the Troops? Vietnam, the Gulf War, and the Making of Collective Memory." *Social Problems* 42 (3):344–60.

Franklin, H. Bruce. 1992. *M.I.A., or, Mythmaking in America: How and Why Belief in Live POWs Has Possessed a Nation*. New York: Lawrence Hill Books.

Franklin, H. Bruce. 2000. *Vietnam and Other American Fantasies*. Boston: University of Massachusetts Press.

Gibson, James William. 1994. *Warrior Dreams: Violence and Manhood in Post-Vietnam America*. New York: Hill and Wang.

Greene, Bob. *Homecoming*. New York: G.P. Putnam, 1989.

Holson, Laura M. 1998. "A Bicycle Path From Wall Street to Vietnam." *The New York Times*, November 2, p. c1.

Kifner, John. "A Case Study in Disaster for Tomorrow's Generals." *The New York Times* (April 28, 2000).

Lembcke, Jerry. 1998. *The Spitting Image: Myth, Memory, and The Legacy of Vietnam*. New York: New York University Press.

Spake, Amanda. "The Healing Precess is Far From Done." *U.S. News and World Report* (May 1, 2000).

Theweleit, Klaus. *Women, Floods, Bodies, History. Vol 1 of Male Fantasies*. Minneapolis: University of Minnesota Press, 1987.

Commentary on Lembcke's "The News and the Myth of Spat-upon Vietnam Vets: What Can We Learn from the slate.com File"[1]

James W. Russell
Eastern Connecticut State University

I was active in the antiwar movement from 1964 to 1975 and never heard of a single spitting incident despite being around activists who were willing to take the most militant of actions. During one part of that time, from 1972 to the end of the war in 1975, I lived in San Francisco—the claimed site of many of the incidents. No one, but no one, in my memory ever suggested spitting as a wise reaction to returning soldiers. To the contrary, the strategic assumption was that the returning soldiers were potential recruits to the anti-war movement and thus should be treated respectfully as such.

From my direct experience I thus find compelling Jerry Lembcke's argument that it is a myth that returning soldiers were spat upon by antiwar veterans and that it is a myth that functions now to buttress public support for Washington's contemporary wars. His masterful exposure of this myth raises questions about the nature of consciousness, a key variable in any theory of the components of human societies as well as Marxist revolutionary theory.

Are the perpetrators of this myth—those who so fervently in their e-mails to Salon. com claimed to have witnessed or been the victims of such acts—knowingly engaged in spreading a lie or themselves unknowing victims of a false memory syndrome? If the latter, what Lembcke hints openly is more the case, then to what extent are all citizens vulnerable or are these only a loud vocal minority whose minds were especially open to being filled with stereotyped falsities?

In a society in which many believe in flying saucers, the existences of physical heavens and hells, sightings of the Virgin Mary and other elements of what Marx in *Economic and Philosophic Manuscripts of 1844* called "operations of the human imagination that operate independently of the individual [but] on him as alien, divine or diabolical activities," it should not be surprising that many would believe supposed eye-witness accounts of returning soldiers being spat upon. In this myth production it only takes producers—those who claimed to be witnesses or victims—and gullible believers. Lembcke does a good job in showing many of the reasons why that particular myth would be more believable in the aftermath of a losing war. It allows the public to believe that the war was lost not because we were weaker than the other side but rather because disloyal elements from within sapped our collective will to prevail and thus betrayed us. By implication the enemy within

---

[1]This paper originally appeared in *Humanity & Society* Volume 27, Number 4, 2003.

must never be allowed to again defeat us in war. The thrust of the myth and its implications are to prepare a preemptive strike on the civil liberties of war opponents.

In the case of this myth a distinction can be made between its producers and its gullible consumers. The role of the producers and perpetrators in keeping it alive is crucial. When Lembcke spoke at my university a man stood up at the end and said that he had been spat-upon. Lembcke asked to discuss the incident with him later and determined that he had never been to Vietnam! He had supposedly suffered his misfortune in Times Square. This revelation however occurred out of earshot of the audience. A number of my students in reaction papers maintained that the man had totally "blown apart" Lembcke's whole presentation since he was proof that the spitting had indeed occurred. They thus continued to consume the myth. What is disturbing is that it only took one person alleging to be a victim to reassure them that what they had assumed to be true before Lembcke's careful marshalling of counter evidence indeed was still true. Not all the students were so quick to close their ears to Lembcke's challenging of a popular myth. They were at least willing to hold on to the dissonance of the two contrary versions of what had happened a decade or so before they had been born.

The nature of consciousness is such that while there are truths that are not relative, beliefs about what is true are and it is a constant struggle to make beliefs square with what is true—in this case what is true about an important opposition movement in the ongoing history of American imperialism. That is where the importance of Lembcke's demythologizing lies. The more the reactionary bases of such myths can be exposed, the more the identifications become opportunities not only for the defensive purpose of stopping the distortion of the antiwar movement but also for raising consciousness about American imperialism and its wars.

5. Crime, Deviance and Criminal Justice: In Search of a Radical Humanistic Perspective[1,2]

David O. Friedrichs
University of Scranton

Reflexive Statement

Being among those basically quite dissatisfied with the framework, assumptions and biases of conventional mainstream criminology I was much attracted to the thought of radical criminologists which has emerged over the past ten years. At the same time certain features of this neo-Marxist analysis have been unpalatable or unacceptable to me, and unconvincing as well, and I have been unwilling to abandon some of the observations and values of liberal humanistic thought. This article reflects a personal exploration of the relationship between and synthetic potential of humanist sociology and Marxist humanism in terms of the emergence of a humanistic criminology. It makes no pretense to being more than a preliminary examination; much work remains to be done if a viable, effective radical humanistic criminology is to become a potent intellectual and moral force.

Humanism and Humanist Sociology

The search for a humanistic criminology confronts many problems and paradoxes. This article focuses especially upon the relationship of radical thought to this search. It begins, as I believe any such examination should begin, with an articulation of what is understood by the broader category "humanist sociology."[1]

"Humanism" as a philosophical outlook has had a long history. The earliest manifestations of a humanist philosophy have been traced back to the ancient Greeks (Protagoras: humanity as "the measure of all things") and Romans (Terence: I am a man and nothing that concerns a man is a matter of indifference to me") (Novak 1973: 106).[2] As Schiller has noted the term itself has been appropriated by several philosophical movements, beginning with the Renaissance challenge to traditional religious thought (1932: 542). The common point of "departure" of humanistic philosophies, according to Schiller, is that "humanity is

[1] An earlier version of this article was presented at the Annual Meeting of the Association for Humanist Sociology, University of Pittsburgh-Johnstown, PA, October 26–28, 1979. The encouraging responses of Al Lee, Stu Hills and Richard Quinney were especially appreciated.
[2] This paper originally appeared in *Humanity & Society* Volume 6, Number 3, 1982.

the central object of interest" and "the human aspect" is opposed to the supernatural and natural (542). More to the point "humanism was essentially a protest against the dehumanizing and depersonalizing procedure which seemed to characterize both the natural sciences and absolutist metaphysics" (543). In a broad sense humanism has been associated with undogmatic inquiry, rational thought, democratic values, the application of knowledge for the benefit of all mankind, human self-reliance and the power to will and shape destiny, and the proposition that happiness, reason, justice and love can only be advanced within the framework of human criteria.[3] These formulations pertain mainly to the secular and liberal version of humanism, which has indeed often been at odds with traditional religious orthodoxy and political extremists.[4] But, as A.M. Lee has pointed out, "humanism" has been identified with, and disassociated from, most traditional and contemporary "isms," from communism to Catholicism (1978: 44).[5] Humanism as a basic concern with value questions and issues of enhancing the human environment cannot be properly limited to either a liberal or a secular orientation. The position taken here is that humanism at its core involves a central concern with the human experience, the problem of human value choices, and the objective of striving for a humane civilization. Such an outlook may be adopted by people of diverse religious beliefs and political affiliations. Humanism is a call for deeper understanding, for cooperative relations and for constructive change.

Within the social sciences specifically a humanistic challenge to what Glass and Staude have called "value-free, detached, mechanistic and deterministic theories and methodologies" (1972: xi) has emerged over the past several decades. The psychological version of this challenge is well-established, inspired by the pioneering work of Carl Rogers, Abraham Maslow, J.F.T. Bugenthal, Sidney Jourard and others (described as having "a central concern with the dignity and worth of man and the development of human potentialities" [Glass and Staude 1972: xi]).

A humanistic sociological challenge to the dominant positivistic model adopted by the discipline has always existed in the writings of individual theorists, such as G.H. Mead, W.G. Sumner and C. Wright Mills (Lowry 1974: 192; Lee 1973: x). Humanistic elements, at the least, can be identified in the work of Weber and other founding fathers of contemporary sociology (Lowry 1974: 192). Humanistic sociology has been identified with elementaristic theoretical perspectives (e.g. interactionism) as well as holistic theoretical perspectives (e.g., conflict theory) (Staude 1972: 262; Lowry 1974: 196).[6] Among contemporary sociologists those identified as humanists have included conservatives (e.g., Peter Berger), liberals (e.g., Amitai Etzioni) and radicals (e.g., Alvin Gouldner) (Friedrichs 1970: 125–128). Whether these sociologists would choose to identify themselves primarily as humanist sociologists is open to question. The humanistic element which is common to their work, however, is a tendency to draw upon the literature of the humanities, and its critical style, rather than that of the natural sciences; a central concern with the human condition, including philosophical premises and problems; a recognition of the fundamental importance of the issues of values and moral commitment; a broadly defined conception of the person as subject and actor; and a basic commitment to improving and enhancing the essence of human existence.

Some sociologists—most prominently, Al and Betty Lee—have consciously adopted a humanist stance. As John Staude, among others, has noted, it could be argued that the sociological discipline as such has a decidedly humanistic dimension; but the self-consciously humanist sociologist, in his interpretation, has adopted an attitude and an emphasis pertaining to experience and personhood at the center of his study (Staude 1972: 263). Ultimately, therefore, it is neither a specific theoretical paradigm nor a particular methodology which sets the humanist sociologist apart but rather an outlook, a general set of concerns, and a moralistic involvement, or in A.M. Lee's words, an intellectual focus "upon what exists and upon what is most relevant to man" (Lee 1973: xii). The humanist sociologist tends to subscribe to an optimistic faith in the potential of individuals and society itself to transcend the status quo and to mature and develop toward higher forms of human existence, to realize more meaningful freedom, equality and dignity, and he or she is committee to studying society with these objectives in mind (Glass 1972: 9; Staude 1972: 268).

Lee summarizes a humanist view of what sociology should be as including the following elements: people-centered, egalitarian, ethical and humanly responsible, oppositional (critical), social change-oriented and "a product of carefully trained scientists who value intimate observation and creative intellectual ferment" (Lee 1978: 94). The humanist sociologist, in fact, is open to drawing upon any discipline which enhances understanding of the human experience (Stein 1974: 165) or any methodology, including traditional positivistic methods, as long as they are not used in a way which violates humanistic ethics and goals (Bowman 1973: 3). Central to Lee's conception of humanistic sociology is independence from elitist interests and a willingness to be "outsiders" to the professional establishment, with its concern for careerist interests, obtaining grants and highlighting internal debates (Lee 1979: 5–8; Lee 1976: 925–935; Lee 1973: 128). The humanist role model can be contrasted, then, with that of the technician or the organization man (Lee 1973: 122–128). Lee's point is that those actively involved in social processes may contribute more to a creative understanding of society and an advancement of humanist goals than do conservative and liberal sociologists oriented toward professional paradigms and objectives (Lee 1979: 8). Thus the humanist sociologist is concerned with how humans freely and intersubjectively formulate meaning in their existence, and how the structure of social institutions imposes limitations on human freedom. The humanist sociologist is concerned with the development of knowledge useful to people (citizens, neighbors, and consumers) rather than elitist interests and professional colleagues (Lee 1976: 935). In order to achieve this objective humanist sociologists must quite consciously avoid excessive use of abstract theory, quantitative formulations and abstruse jargon (Bowman 1573: 4). A humanist sociology must be in touch with everyday human reality.[7]

The precise boundaries (and bona fide membership) of "humanist sociology"—as a perspective—are not entirely clear, it must be conceded. The specific establishment of a humanist sociology, with a distinctive identity of its own, may be rejected by mainstream sociologists on a variety of grounds: that it is an ideological, self-righteous, posturing, ambiguous, and ineffective—even counter-productive—enterprise. In response it may be argued that the humanist goals advanced by self-identified humanist sociologists can serve as the conscience of a growing profession ever in danger of selling its soul to elitist, self-serving and oppressive social elements, and in danger as well of losing touch with the subjective reality of human existence (see Lee 1978: 24–224). The relevance of these concerns as applied to the subdisciplinary area of criminology will be obvious as we proceed here.

Humanism and Marxism: The Paradoxical Reconciliation

The question of whether a radical humanistic criminology is possible requires some preliminary attention to the broader question of the relationship between humanism and Marxism. Marxism has commonly been regarded as essentially materialistic, deterministic, and dogmatic, and very much at odds with the fundamental tenets of humanism. The emergence of a Marxist or socialistic humanism[8]—inspired in no small way by the totalitarian excesses of Stalinist Russia and other twentieth century communist states—has challenged this interpretation. This socialistic humanism looks first to the writings of the young Marx, which focused on the concept of alienation and were indisputably humanistic (see Fromm 1961). The on-going debate concerning the relationship between the thought of the "young Marx" and that of the "old Marx" is beyond the scope of this article, but the position is adopted that Marxism can be viewed openly and creatively;[9] if the emphasis and focus of Marx's later work shifted toward a more positivistic, materialist orientation we can still draw valid inspiration from the more specifically humanistic character of his earlier writing. It can also be argued that a familiarity with Marx's person and biography allows us to maintain the image of Marx as humanist. Erich Fromm, perhaps the leading Western exponent of the conception of Marx as humanist, argues that "the socialist humanism of Karl Marx was the first to declare that theory cannot be separated from practice, knowledge from action, spiritual aims from the social system" (Fromm 1965: viii). Contemporary humanistic socialism is expressed mainly in the writings of Eastern European philosophers such as George Lukacs, Gajo Petrovic, Ivan Svitak and Adam Schaff, some Western socialists such as Fromm, and Russian dissidents such as Sakharov (Gruenwald 1974: 888).[10]

The basic premise of socialist (or Marxist) humanism is succinctly stated by Svitak: "Communism without humanism is no communism and humanism without communism cannot be humanism" (1970: 158). Non-socialistic humanism is perceived as being "feeble," liberal, naive and "lacking a sociology"—insofar as it does not adequately appreciate and relate the roots of oppression to the class struggle and the structure of a capitalist system (see Goldmann, in Fromm 1965: 50; Novack 1973: 108, 131; Young 1978: 57). Every form of humanism has an ideology; the Marxist form at least acknowledges this openly (Schaff 1970: 4). An authentic and realistic humanism, then, is "amplified, deepened and enriched" through its integration with Marxist materialism, and achieves a far broader appeal by virtue of its manifest correspondence with reality and its pragmatic focus on fundamental societal transformation (Novak 1973: 105, 150).

A socialist humanism attempts to replace the inadequate *philosophical* anthropology of traditional secular humanism with a *scientific* anthropology—one rooted in the examination of actual social relationships (Kamenka 1965: 139; Svitak 1970: 160–161). In the Marxist view, human nature is not fixed but is in process; whether its egoistic or altruistic potential emerges is dependent upon the material and social environment (Nord 1974: 564; Nord 1977: 77). Marx was fundamentally humanistic because he wished to liberate men from economic necessity, to free them to realize themselves fully as human beings (Fromm, 1961: 3, 5), at home with themselves, their fellow men and with nature (Marcuse 1965: 113; Svitak 1970: 165). "Marxist" humanism (as Oskar Gruenwald puts it) turns away from abstract entities (e.g., the state, collectivities) to focus upon human beings and human *praxis*: "The idea of *praxis* implies human potentiality and capability to transform the world, that is, to change both one's self and one's environment" (Gruenwald 1978: 895; see also Svitak 1965: 165; Korac 1965: 3, 6).

A premise of Marxist theory would be that a social environment in which man can truly realize the humanistic goals of real freedom, equality and justice can only come about through a revolutionary transformation of society (Marcuse in Raines and Dean 1970: 4).[11]

In this interpretation a reciprocal relationship may be said to exist between individual and societal liberation (see Korac 1965: 10). Marxism in any form rejects the idea, advanced by some, that a humanistic capitalism is possible (see Harman 1974: 32), because for Marx a capitalist system of private ownership of property and wage workers is inherently exploitative. The many varieties of socialism and communism have differed on the extent to which the economic structure and organization must be transformed in order for a humane society to be possible (see Thomas 1965). Those who specifically identify with socialist humanism have disassociated themselves from the totalitarian and repressive corruptions of Marxism (exemplified by Stalinism) and, at heart, the utilization and justification of inhumane means toward utopian ends.[12] But the most extreme version of the humanist interpretation of Marx holds that socialism and communism are *transitory* stages toward humanism and a human society (see Gruenwald 1978: 905; Korac 1965: 8). Thus Marx has been interpreted as being a great democrat insofar as he stood for human and civil rights as the basis of political life (Svitak 1965: 171). The humanistic social sciences (especially the psychological version) have neglected socialist humanism (see Nord 1977: 76). One premise of this article is that radical criminology has also neglected to adequately integrate the framework and insights of socialist humanism into its analysis of crime and criminal justice. The foregoing exposition is directed toward helping to lay a foundation for such a fruitful integration.

Criminology: Its Non-humanistic Character and Humanistic Elements

Having identified some of the attributes of humanism, of humanistic sociology, and of socialist (or Marxist) humanism the next task is to examine a particular sub-disciplinary sociological field, criminology, in terms of its humanistic content and potential.

The general subject matter of criminology may be said to relate in an especially poignant way to the central concerns of humanism. Questions of human nature, of value choices, and of justice, for example, are very starkly represented within the realm of criminology.[13] An examination of the emergence and development of criminological theory and study—even on a cursory and superficial level—reveals a bewildering variety of premises, methods and perspectives on crime and criminal justice, some of which may be considered to include humanistic dimensions, others decidedly and often consciously non-humanistic or antihumanistic. Without in the present context attempting to examine this history one may safely assert (despite humanitarian elements of the early progressive perspective on crime) that the dominant thrust of mainstream American criminology in the twentieth century has been non-humanistic, has in fact been essentially positivistic, deterministic, uncritical, detached, and instrumentally or pragmatically oriented toward explaining and predicting crime and delinquency and developing policies for its elimination, containment or repression.[14] This mainstream paradigm has always been subject to challenge by more humanistically oriented criminological perspectives. Some contributions to the emergence (some might argue the re-emergence) of an authentically humanistic criminology can be identified.

A humanistic criminology begins with a reflexive consideration of the complex or configuration of factors which provide the foundation for the criminologist's own understanding of crime and criminal justice; the pretense of a "scientific" and wholly objective approach to these phenomena is rejected (see Friedrichs 1981a). Our understanding of violence—as an example—is experiential and ideological as well as scholarly (see Friedrichs 1981b).

Then we have renewed attention to a historical perspective. Much mainstream criminology has been essentially ahistorical. A humanistic criminology concerns itself with the development of crime patterns and criminal justice responses through time. A basic premise of such a criminology is that we cannot properly understand crime and criminal justice without incorporating into our understanding a sensitivity to the historical context (e.g., see Inciardi et. al. 1977; Conley 1977; Inciardi and Faupel 1980; Terrill 1980). A good example of such criminological research, insofar as it critically re-examines the seminal origins of the juvenile courts and generates a deeper understanding of the rationales maintaining that system, is Anthony Plattis' *The Child Savers* (1977, rev.). A sense of history is essential to a humanistic criminological perspective because it compels us to recognize that features of our present system which may be perceived as oppressive were once hailed as humanitarian reforms, and vice versa (e.g., indeterminate sentences; see Sagarin and Karmen 1978: 248).

Attention to subjective/autobiographical accounts of the experience of crime and criminal justice is important.[15] At the core of a humanistic criminology there must always exist a recognition of the actors in the crime and criminal justice drama as real people, an individuals, as human beings who choose, experience and reflect. Autobiographical accounts by "criminals" and by those on the criminal justice side—judges, lawyers, etc.—have always been available and the case history approach has a respectable history in the discipline (e.g. Sutherland 1937), but the utilization of such accounts has most commonly been subjected to secondary analysis, and accounts have been utilized to lend support to a particular theory or hypothesis. Valuing of subjective accounts simply in their own, phenomenological terms has been less common, although a number of collections of first-hand accounts have appeared in recent years (e.g. Petersen and Truzzi 1972; Denfield 1974). A humanistic criminology takes seriously the task of understanding the point of view of the actor.

Certain theoretical perspectives which have emerged in recent decades provide a foundation for a humanistic criminology. Such a criminology views the traditional meanings attached to crime as problematic, and regards the individual as an actor with some control over his response to the social environment. The emergence and development of interactionist theory, conflict theory, and phenomenological sociology, especially as applied to criminological phenomena in the 1960s and 1970s, can be mentioned in this regard. For our present purposes we need only mention the names of Lemert, Becker, Erikson, Schur, Matza, Goffman, Bittner, Douglas, Turk, Hills and the earlier work of Chambliss and Quinney as contributors or contributions to these theoretical perspectives.

"Muckraking" exposés have contributed importantly to the genesis of a humanistic criminology. This is an old and honorable tradition, of course, and one which has more often involved journalists than self-identified sociologists. From Lincoln Steffens, Upton Sinclair and Ida Tarbell, to more recent contributors to the tradition such as Jessica Mitford, Bernstein and Woodward and Jonathan Kwitny, we have been provided with frequently impassioned (no pretense of detachment need be maintained), well-written (devoid of social science jargon), investigatively sound and widely diffused critiques of crime and criminal justice—especially the injustices perpetuated by criminal justice institutions and the crimes committed by "respectable" members of society. [16] While such studies may not always correspond to the canons of acceptable social science we should be fully appreciative of their role in identifying and publicizing various manifestations of criminal injustice. It should be stressed here that, contrary to what might be a commonplace assumption, humanistic concerns need not be restricted to injustices to the accused and convicted. J.L. Barkas' *Victims* (1978) is a good recent example of a book which helps sensitize us to the injustices visited upon victims of crime and their families, and counters effectively conventional victimological research which frequently focuses on victim provocation and proneness, and does so with little attention to the very real pain suffered by victims. At the same time journalistic exposes of the juvenile offender as victim—e.g., Ken Wooden's *Weeping in the Playtime of Others* (1976)—provide us with a necessary counter-perspective. The synthesis of emotionally based anger and indignation—often rooted in personal experience—with valid sociological analysis is not easily arrived at, but may be regarded as an appropriate goal for a humanistic criminology.

Finally, interactionist and conflict theorists, as well as muckraking journalists, have directly or indirectly challenged the validity and viability of justice being realized within either the framework or the content of the existing legal order. A humanistic criminology must incorporate a theory of jurisprudence, possibly what Tigar refers to as a "jurisprudence of insurgency" (1977: 310–330). Critical evaluations of "victimless crime" laws (e.g. Schur 1965; Geis 1974; Smith and Pollack 1974), attempts to assess the attributes of a valid legal order (e.g. Fuller 1963), attention to the call for informal justice (e.g. Abel 1981), considerations of the "paradox of a life in law" (Elkins 1979), and the exploration of alternative images of the law (e.g., Bankowski and Mungham 1976) are all part of a humanistic criminological jurisprudence. This jurisprudence draws upon the contributions of legal realists in exposing the gaps between legal ideals and legal reality, and sociological jurisprudence in its concern with the social bases of law and the social consequences of legal policy. Peter D'Errico has described a humanistic approach to legal studies as critical, interdisciplinary and directed toward the development of self-knowledge (D'Errico 1979: 511). A humanistic jurisprudence is one which promotes an open inquiry and study about rather than in law, and rejects the "pathology" of legalism (513). As D'Errico puts it:

> In legal studies, our search is for a way of life and a paradigm of understanding law which does not require the acceptance of social oppression and personal repression as unalterable features of human existence. It is a search which is praxis: reflection is merged with activity so that we are neither academics separated from the "real" world, nor "activists" cut off from the process of inquiry and education. (517)

A humanistic criminology might well adopt this as a succinct statement of or maxim for its purpose.

The Call for a Humanistic Criminology

A number of contemporary criminologists have specifically called for the development of a humanistic criminology. In one of the first texts to challenge conventional positivistic and functionalist perspectives on criminality, *Crime, Power and Morality*, Stuart Hills noted the need for "fundamental alterations in the structure and character of American life"

(1971: 203) through effective mobilization of public opinion and utilization of pressure politics (203). A humanistic criminology, in Hills' conception, begins with the recognition that "many of our crime problems, are largely of our own making—a product of our value priorities, cherished social practices, legal policies, and the kind of structure that we impose on our social order" (205). A humanistic criminology focuses upon these products and ultimately attempts to contribute to the emergence of a humanistic ethic among the young, and basic "modifications" in society including redistribution of power and resources, reduction of materialistic values, and more rational application of the criminal sanction (204–205). In a more recent text (1980), Hills reissues the call for a focus on "the values of individual dignity and self-determination and the creation of a more humane and just society" (xi). He specifically applies this perspective to the understanding of various forms of deviance.

In Clayton Hartjen's conception (1978), a humanistic criminology is dedicated to protecting fundamental human rights and helping people secure these rights (226). Hartjen doesn't believe that we can or should dogmatically advance a single appropriate role for the humanistic criminologist, or a single conception of humanistic values (226). While he defines humanistic criminology as an active enterprise "involved with the world...(and) disposed to ensuring that tyranny, repression and oppression are fought on every front..." the criminologist's main task is to "achieve criminological understanding" (226). A humanistic criminology focuses on the formulation of definitions and critically examines the political state, it broadens the focus of criminological inquiry, and hopes to promote alternative conceptions of the world to its students, as well as contributing to the emergence of a society in which citizens are free from both criminal victimization and legalized oppression (222–232). Hartjen offers us, then, a generalized vision of a humanistic criminology which modifies but does not directly challenge the mainstream paradigm.[17]

A call for a humanist criminology has also been issued by Edward Sagarin and Andrew Karmen. They caution against a humanistic criminology which has become a falsely sentimental ideology—e.g., with regard to street crime (1978: 242–243). In their vision a humanist criminology must take street crime—and the experience of victimization—as well as occupational crime, seriously, and must recognize the unity and circularity which links and interrelates these quite different forms of crime (243–244). A humanist criminology must concern itself with the larger traumas endured by our society including the civil rights movement and the war in Vietnam and must ultimately address itself to the core question: How is justice to be maximized (252–254)?

A Humanist Criminology: Issues of Special Concern

A humanist criminology, then, gives priority to those problems which are restrictive to the exercise of human freedom and dignity, and to the quality of life for all members of society, rather than to those problems which are excessively abstract or are simply defined by the state itself as problems. Conventional definitions of crime are therefore regarded as problematic, although there has been some disagreement on the use of state definitions of crime. Herman and Julia Schwendinger (1970) have argued that use of legal definitions of crime has compromised and co-opted the criminological profession, and that crime can be reconceptualized in moral terms, in terms of offenses against basic human rights. In their admittedly radical view, as recently stated, "Legal definitions are ideological instrumentalities which shape and develop the language and objectives of science in such a way as to strengthen class domination" (1977: 8). They decry the lack of professional criminological concern with the crime of imperialism, for example (1977: 8). The Schwendingers claim that in a Marxist approach "the truthfulness of moral judgments about crime can only be warranted by objective criteria based on scientific knowledge about right, duty, justice and crime, originating in socially determined relationships rather than in natural laws" (1977: 10). Hartien and others have challenged the Schwendinger thesis, with Hartjen claiming that use of the legal definition does not require acceptance of the state's claim, and does not in fact preclude critical examination of how these legal definitions are formulated (1972: 62–66). Gurgin and Betsch criticize the alleged pretense of the Schwendingers in suggesting that their conception of crime can be scientifically and absolutely validated (1971: 97).

A possible resolution of the conflict outlined above doesn't necessarily require us to make a choice between legalistic and non-legalistic conceptions of crime. Rather, we can work toward the full establishment and utilization of dual conceptions of crime, the legalistic and the humanistic. That a humanist criminology should direct more attention toward imperialism, racism, sexism and the like, as morally criminal regardless of legal status, may be stressed. That objectively harmful effects of these phenomena can be identified should be apparent. That legally defined crime can be studied without necessarily abandoning humanistic values may also be conceded.

Needless to say, the concerns of the humanist criminologist and of the state may overlap in many instances; but the humanist criminologist cannot allow the state to define or delimit his objectives. This is another issue which has attracted the attention of humanistic criminologist with radical and non-radical identities, although here there is a good deal of consensus. Richard Quinney and John Galliherf, among others, have indicated the character of research and projects funded by the LEAA, a major governmental criminal justice agency (Quinney 1974: 32–43; Galliher 1979: 44–50). This government-sponsored research is most often related to specific governmental social control objectives. As Galliher observes, "The morality of social science seems purchased or influenced by the government through research grants" (48). This research cannot be regarded as humanistic or autonomous.

We have earlier indicated some elements of and contributions to the emergence of a humanistic criminology. A humanistic criminology inevitably shares many of the concerns of mainstream criminology, but may give special emphasis to some of these concerns, including: abuse and misuse of discretionary decision-making in the criminal justice system (especially discrimination re minorities); the impact of "victimless crime" laws and the general problem of humane legal reform, the rationales and dehumanizing effects (on correctional personnel and convicts) of penal sanctions, including capital punishment, and penal institutions; the experience and trauma of crime victimization; the prevalence of illegality within "respectable" (i.e., white collar, corporate and governmental) contexts; and the relationship between value patterns, liberated consciousness and criminal status (see Morain 1978). A nagging question remains, however: is a humanistic criminology but a version of liberal criminology, wedded to the same basic framework, assumptions and methodology?

The argument has been advanced (by John Galliher) that liberal criminology as such has been experiencing a decline; what has emerged in the wake of this decline, he suggests, has been a conflict between Marxist and neo-conservative "New Realists" or deterrence-oriented criminologists (1978: 245–263). While it may obviously be argued that criminology of an essentially liberal orientation is still very evident its dominance (peaking, perhaps, in the late 1950s and early 1960s) has been drastically eroded, both as a result of external political developments and the manifest failure in either deterring crime or dramatically promoting the elimination of oppressive, inequitable dimensions of criminal justice (see Bayer 1981). Furthermore, as Simon Dinitz has observed, liberal perceptions change:

> Yesterday's humaneness is today's patronization of the defenseless. The historic fight for the right to treatment has become today's struggle for the right to be left alone. (1978: 228)

For mainstream liberal-minded criminologists such as Dinitz and Donald Cressey the alleged abandonment of scholarly concern with, for example, the search for causes of crime, and the shift toward politicized theorizing, is unfortunate (Cressey 1978: 174–187; Dinitz 1978: 230). In Dinitz's view the dilemma is this: either we lower our expectations and accept social inequality, stratification, and deprivation in our social system, or we recast present society radically and dramatically" (229). Insofar as liberals are unwilling to embrace, or commit themselves to the actual implications of the latter possibility, they may have to embrace the former; the specific dilemma for the professed humanist criminologist is this: insofar as he or she is in principle unwilling to lower expectations regarding humanistic values and goals must he then embrace the radical alternatives? A consideration of radical criminology in relation to humanistic objectives is required.

The Current Status of Radical Criminology

In the original paper from which the present analysis is derived, and in two subsequently published articles (Friedrichs 1980a and 1980b), I discussed the emergence and present status of radical criminology in some detail. For reasons of space the analysis is excluded here, but interested readers are referred to those articles, other articles in the same volume (Inciardi 1980), and several books published since the compilation of the fairly extensive lists of references found in that volume (e.g., Balkan, Berger and Schmidt 1980; Tifft and Sullivan 1980; Quinney 1980; Greenberg 1981). For present purposes it can be noted that a radical, neo-Marxist criminological paradigm emerged conspicuously in the 1970s (most notably in the work of Quinney and Chambliss) which linked the nature of crime and the organization of criminal justice quite directly to the capitalist political economy. Numerous criticisms have been directed at the radical criminological enterprise; it is alleged to be in crisis (see Inciardi 1980). Radical criminology has been accused among other things—of metaphysical ambivalence, uni-dimensional analysis, insensitivity to oppressive elements of existing communist societies, and hypocrisy re the call for revolutionary change. The recent writings of self-identified radical criminologists—or their sympathizers—have been at pains to distinguish between instrumental and structural Marxism (e.g., see Beirne 1979; Hunt 1980; Greenberg 1981). The call for decentralization, community control, popular justice, and anarchy has also been quite conspicuous (e.g., see Pfohl 1981; Lee and Visano 1981; Brady 1981; Tifft and Sullivan 1980).

The two most prominent and prolific radical criminologists of the 1970s were probably Richard Quinney and William Chambliss. In his most recent specifically criminological work Quinney (1980) has developed a critique of crime and criminal justice which tran-

scends the ordinary boundaries of discussion and explores the possibilities of a reconciliation between the Marxist and the religious realms as a precondition for the realization of
authentic social justice. Chambliss (1981: 61) has recently advanced a dialectical model
of law creation which "stresses the importance of basic contradictions between ideological
commitments and social structure, as the starting point for a sociological understanding
of law creation." These two imaginative radical scholars, and others who identify with
the radical tradition, will take their work in diverse directions as we move through the
1980s. Several general observations can be proffered, however: (1) The present political
and cultural environment in America is not especially receptive to radical analysis; should
economic conditions continue to deteriorate during the Reagan administration this environment could change dramatically; (2) While radical criminologists today may subscribe to
a number of general propositions in common and share some basic premises they cannot
be characterized as belonging to a wholly unified school of thought; the intellectual styles,
logistical priorities and specific elements of analysis vary considerably, and this may be
inevitable given the socially ingrained American resistance to collectivism; and (3) the
survival and further development of radical criminology is much dependent upon its ability
to reach and persuade a significantly larger audience than it has to date. In the foreseeable
future most radical criminologists are likely, as a practical matter, to continue to be affiliated with academic institutions; this fact places certain general constraints on the extent of
direct involvement in radical action. The principal contribution of radical criminologists,
then, is likely to be in the realm of consciousness-raising activity; the ultimate effectiveness of this activity depends, of course, upon the fusion of objectively appropriate conditions with the emergence of a widely diffused, enlightened consciousness.

On the whole a radical criminology provides a basic framework for an understanding
of some fundamental sources of crime and criminal justice, or injustice, in a capitalist
society. It has not always been sufficiently sensitive to the ultimate complexities of crime
and criminal justice, the perceptions and sufferings of individual human beings, and the
inhumane potential, at least, of radical solutions.

Conclusion

It is my basic thesis here that a radical humanistic perspective in criminology is possible.
It is a perspective which emerges dialectically from a confrontation between classical radical analysis and the concerns and values of humanist sociology. A humanistic criminology
has greatest coherence and potency if it incorporates a radical understanding of the pervasive impact of a capitalist system on crime and criminal justice into its analysis; a radical
criminology achieves more validity and effectiveness insofar as it maintains fundamental
contact with humanist concerns and insights, with the complexities of the human and social
fabric. The principal danger for a humanist criminology is that it exposes and condemns
injustices in the criminal justice system without sufficient attention to the structural roots of
these injustices; for radical criminology the danger of losing sight of real people and their
feelings, of the strengths of democratic traditions, with a consequent transformation into a
uni-dimensional analysis with "Stalinist" connotations, is quite real.

Some directions for reconciling radical and humanist perspectives have already been
suggested by a number of criminologists. Joseph Scimecca (1975: 150) has argued that
more attention should be paid to C. Wright Mills' scheme which conceives of the indi-

vidual as "a rational being capable of transcending structural determinants, as capable of exercising free choice." Mills' relativistic social theory helps us to reconcile social structure with a volitional model of man; Scimecca notes Mills' attention to motive and perception of social contradictions as grounds for comprehending contemporary alienation and anti-social behavior (1976: 181–189). In the realm of practical action, as opposed to theory, Drew Humphries has observed that certain responses to the immediate situation of crime can be made without compromising radical social objectives; these include better street lighting, escort services for the elderly, and victim compensation programs (1979: 237). Such reforms are consistent with humanistic values. And Paul Lawson (1977) has explored the possibility of a humanistic socialistic perspective on prisons, drawing upon the insights of Solzhenitsyn and Cleaver.

A radical humanistic criminology must further explore a theoretical and pragmatic synthesis of radical and humanistic objectives. The perspective of Marxist humanism, outlined earlier, has something to contribute to the future development of criminology. In the United States today, with the decade of the 1980s on its way, it might be argued that both humanistic and radical analysis are not entirely in tune with the temper of the times. It may be suggested, however, that as economic conditions deteriorate and the existing system continues to fail in its attempts to both explain and control crime a radical humanistic criminology may be recognized to provide a more enduring perspective for resolving the crisis of contemporary criminal justice and for promoting the emergence of a truly just society.

Endnotes

[1]The themes explored in the next few paragraphs will be quite familiar to those who regard themselves as humanist sociologists. The discussion is included here in the hopes that this will reach a wider audience.

[2]A good discussion of the meaning of humanism and some of its more prominent varieties may be found in A. M. Lee (1978: 41–67).

[3]Based upon observations by Jacob Bronowski, Linus Pauling, Corliss Lamont, R. G. Ingersoll, Julian Huxley, Brock Chrisholm and Erich Fromm, cited by *The Humanist.*

[4]The term humanist, or "secular humanism," has become a principal target of the fundamentalist New Right and the Moral Majority; this conception of humanism as antithetical to all things Christian can, of course, be challenged (see Woodward and Salholz 1981).

[5]For a review of the bewildering variety of definitions of humanism see Smith (1981).

[6]The highly influential interactionist (societal reaction; labeling) perspective has been criticized for its neglect of the political economic structure (Pfohl 1981) and its discounting of human agency (Piven 1981).

[7]This last contention would not necessarily garner support from those who identify themselves as humanist sociologists.

[8]See Gusfield (1980) for a conception of humanistic sociology which stresses assumptions about studying humans as opposed to specific value concerns. Scimecca (1981) provides us with a recent introduction to the humanistic perspective in sociology.

[9]The term socialism is probably preferable to Marxism in this context, insofar as the emphasis should ultimately be on the nature of society rather than on the thought of a particular individual.

[10]As Gruenwald (1974: 900), among others, has noted: "Marxism is not a dogma, promulgated once and for all; on the contrary, it requires continuous creative interpretation in theory and application in practive.

[11]The attempt to reconcile Marxism with humanism is quite naturally open to challenge—as are in fact all attempts toward reconciling Marxism with another tradition of thought or belief (e.g., Christianity; see Arrupe 1981).

[12]There is, perhaps inevitably, a certain tension between those who put the highest priority on humanistic Marxist goals (e.g., Herbert Marcuse) and those who refuse to compromise on humanistic Marxist means (see Gruenwald 1974: 915). It has been recognized that a fundamental problem with an orientation toward Marxist goals is that insofar as goals are not realized we are left with the means, and therefore "the end must always be present in the means" (Danko Grlic, quoted in Gruenwald, 1974: 896; see also Korac in Fromm, 1965: 15). On the other hand the use of revolutionary violence has been defended on essentially humanist grounds insofar as it is maintained (by Marcuse, among others) that the choice is not between humanism and terror, or violence and non-violence, but "only between two modes of violence—capitalist and socialist" (Marcuse in Fromm 1965: 107).

[13]See Saragin and Kelly (1981) for a discussion of the issue of responsibility and punishment within a humanistic framework.

[14]See Gibbons (1979) for a good review of the development of criminology in America in the twentieth century.

[15]Alternatively, and relatedly, see Sagarin (1981) for a discussion of the contribution of great literature to our understanding of crime.

[16]Most journalistic coverage of crime and criminal justice is not simply ahistorical and astructural but is characterized by a class bias as well (see Humphries 1981).

[17]James Inciardi (1978: 180) has suggested, with a somewhat different emphasis, that the pursuit of knowledge regarding crime and criminal justice can and must be both pragmatic and humanistic, although the reconciliation of these objectives may be considered problematic.

References

Abel, Richard L. 1981. "Conservative Conflict and the Reproduction of Capitalism: The Role of Informal Justice," *International Journal of the Sociology of Law* 9: 245–267.

Arrupe, S.J., Pedro. 1981. "Marxist Analysis by Christians," *Catholic Mind* (September) 58–64.

Balkan, Sheila, Ronald J. Berger and Janet Schmidt. 1980. *Crime and Deviance in America: A Critical Approach.* Belmont, CA: Wadsworth Publishing Co.

Bankowski, Zenon and Geoff Mungham. 1976. *Images of Law.* London: Routledge & Kegan Paul.

Barkas, J. L. 1978. *Victims.* New York: Charles Scribners Sons.

Bayer, Ronald. 1981. "Crime, Punishment, and the Decline of Liberal Optimism," *Crime & Delinquency* 27, 2 (April): 169–190.

Beirne, Piers. 1979. "Empiricism and the Critique of Marxism on Law and Crime," *Social Problems* 26, 4 (April): 373–384.

Bowman, Claude C. 1973. *Humanistic Sociology.* New York: Appleton Century-Crofts.

Brady, James. 1981. "Toward a Popular Justice in the United States: The Dialectics of Community Action," *Contemporary Crises* 5: 155–192.

Chambliss, William. 1981. "The Criminalization of Conduct," pp. 45–64, in H. Laurence Ross (ed.) *Law and Deviance.* Beverly Hills: Sage Publications.

Conley, John. 1977. "Criminal Justice History as a Field of Research: A Review of the Literature, 1960–1975," *Journal of Criminal Justice* 5: 13–28.

Cressey, Donald. 1978. "Criminological Theory, Social Science and the Repression of Crime," *Criminology* 16, (August): 171–192.

Denfield, Duane. 1974. *Streetwise Criminology.* Cambridge, MA: Schenkman.

D'Errico, Peter. 1979. "The Law is Terror Put into Words," pp. 511–517, in J. Bonsignore et al., (eds.) *Before The Law* 2nd Edition. Boston: Houghton Mifflin.

Dinitz, Simon. 1978. "Nothing Fails Like Success," *Criminology* 16, 2 (August): 225–238.

Elkins, James R. 1979. "The Paradox of a Life in Law," *University of Pittsburgh Law Review* 40, 2 (Winter): 129–168.

Fetscher, I. 1980. "The Changing Goals of Socialism in the Twentieth Century," *Social Research 47*, 1 (Spring): 36–62.

Friedrichs, David 0. 1981. "The Problem of Reconciling Divergent Perspectives on Urban Crime: Personal Experience, Social Ideology and Scholarly Research," *Qualitative Sociology* 4, 2 (Fall): 217–228.

——. 1981. "Violence and the Politics of Crime," *Social Research* 48, 1 (Spring): 1–6.

——. 1980. "Radical Criminology in the U.S.: An Interpretive Understanding," pp. 35–60, in James A. Inciardi (ed.) *Radical Criminology: The Coming Crises.* Beverly Hills: Sage Publications.

——. 1980. "Carl Klockars vs. the 'Heavy Hitters': A Preliminary Critique," pp. 149–160, in James A. Inciardi (ed.) *Radical Criminology: The Coming Crises.* Beverly Hills: Sage Publications.

Friedrichs, Robert. 1970. *A Sociology of Sociology.* New York: Free Press.

Fromm, Erich. 1965. *Socialist Humanism: An International Symposium.* New York: Anchor.

——.1961. *Marx's Concept of Man.* New York: Frederick Ungar Publishing Co.

Fuller, Lon. 1964. *The Morality of Law.* New Haven: Yale University Press.

Galliher, John F. 1979. "Government Research Funding and Purchased Virtue: Some Examples from Criminology," *Crime & Social Justice* (Spring/ Summer): 44–50.

——. 1978. "The Life and Death of Liberal Criminology," *Contemporary Crises* 12, 3: 245–263

Geis, Gilbert. 1974. *One Eyed Justice.* New York: Drake Publishing Company.

Gibbons, Don C. 1979. *The Criminological Enterprise: Theories and Perspectives.* Englewood Cliffs: Prentice Hall.

Glass, John & J. R. Staude. 1972. *Humanistic Society: Today's Challenge to Sociology.* Pacific Palisades: Goodyear.

Goldmann, Lucien. 1965. "Socialism and Humanism," pp. 40–52, in E. Fromm (ed.) *Socialist Humanism.* New York: Anchor.

Greenberg, David F. 1981. *Crime and Capitalism.* Palo Alto, CA: Mayfield Publishing Company.

Gruenwald, 0. 1974. "Marxist Humanism," *Orbis* 18 (Fall): 888–916.

Gurgin, Vonnie and Sondra Betsch. 1971. "An Orthodox Obloquy or Seraphic Sophistry among Criminologists," *Issues in Criminology* 6, 1 (Winter): 97–101.

Gusfield, Joseph R. 1980. "The Tension between Humanism and Science: Sociology in the 1980's," *Mid-American Review of Sociology* 5, 1: 1–14.

Harman, W. W. 1974. "Humanistic Capitalism: Another Alternative," *Journal of Humanistic Psychology* 14, 1 (Winter): 5–32.

Hartjen, Clayton. 1978. *Crime & Criminalization*, 2nd ed. New York: Praeger.

——. 1972. "Legalism and Humanism: A Reply to the Schwendingers," *Issues in Criminology* 7 (Winter): 56–69.

Hills, Stuart L. 1980. *Demystifying Social Deviance.* New York: McGraw Hill.

——. 1971. *Crime, Power and Morality: The Criminal Law Process in the United States.* Scranton: Chandler Publishing Company.

Humphries, Drew. 1981. "Serious Crime, News Coverage, and Ideology: A Content Analysis of Crime Coverage in a Metropolitan Paper," *Crime & Delinquency* 27, 2 (April): 191–205.

——. 1979. "Crime and the State," Ch. 9, in A. J. Szymanski and T. G. Goertzel *Sociology: Class Consciousness and Contradictions.* New York: D. Van Nostrand.

Hunt, Alan. 1980. "The Radical Critique of Law: An Assessment," *International Journal of the Sociology of Law.* 8: 33–46.

Inciardi, James. 1980. *Radical Criminology: The Coming Crises.* Beverly Hills: Sage.

——. 1978. *Reflections on Crime.* New York: Holt, Rinehart & Winston.

—— and Charles E. Faupel. 1980. *History and Crime: Implications for Criminal Justice Policy.* Beverly Hills: Sage.

——, Alan Block & Lyle Hallowell. 1977. *Historical Approaches to Crime: Recent Strategies and Issues.* Beverly Hills: Sage.

Kamenka, Eugene. 1965. "Marxian Humanism and the Crisis in Socialist Ethics," pp. 118–130, in E. Fromm (ed.) *Socialist Humanism.* New York: Anchor.

Korac, Veljko. 1965. "In Search of Human Society," pp. 1–15, in E. Fromm (ed.) *Socialist Humanism.* New York: Anchor.

Lawson, Paul E. 1977."Toward a Humanistic Socialistic Paradigm for Prisons.*" International Journal of Criminology and Penology* 5: 285–307.

Lee, Alfred McClung. 1979. "On the Dread of Innovation in Universities," *The Humanist* (March-April): 4–8.

——. 1978. *Sociology for Whom?* New York: Oxford University Press.

——. 1976. "Sociology for Whom?" *American Sociological Review* 41: 925–936.

——. 1973. *Toward Humanist Sociology.* Englewood Cliffs, NJ: Prentice Hall.

Lee, John Alan and Livy Anthony Visano. 1981. "Official Deviance in the Legal System," pp. 215–250, in H. Laurence Ross (ed.) *Law and Deviance.* Beverly Hills: Sage.

Lowry, Ritchie. 1974. *Social Problems.* Lexington, MA: D.C. Heath.

Marcuse, Herbert. 1965. "Socialist Humanism?" pp. 107–117, in E. Fromm (ed.) *Socialist Humanism.* New York: Anchor.

Morain, Lloyd. 1978. "Criminals are People," *The Humanist* 38 (September/ October): 5–8.

Nord, W. 197. "Marxist Critique of Humanistic Psychology," *Journal of Humanistic Psychology* 17 (Winter): 75–83.

——. 1974. "The Failure of Current Applied Behavioral Science A Marxian Perspective,*" Journal of Applied Behavioral Science* 10, 4: 557–578.

Novack, George. 1973. *Humanism and Socialism.* New York: Pathfinder Press.

——. 1966. *Existentialism versus Marxism: Conflicting Views on Humanism.* New York: Delta.

Petersen, D. M. & Marcello Truzzi. 1972. *Criminal Life.* Englewood Cliffs: Prentice Hall.

Pfohl, Stephen J. 1981. "Labeling Criminals," pp. 65–98, in H. Laurence Ross (ed.) *Law and Deviance.* Beverly Hills: Sage.

Piven, Francis Fox. 1981. "Deviant Behavior and the Remaking of the World," *Social Problems* 28, 5: 489–508.

Platt, Anthony. 1977. *The Child Savers* (Revised edition). Chicago: University of Chicago Press.

Quinney, Richard. 1980. *Class, State and Crime* (Second edition). New York: Longmans.

——. 1974. *Critique of Legal Order: Crime Control in Capitalist Society.* Boston: Little Brown.

Raines, John C. & Thomas Dean. 1970. *Marxism and Radical Religion.* Philadelphia: Temple University Press.

Sagarin, Edward. 1981. *Raskolnikov and Others: Literary Images of Crime, Punishment, Redemption and Atonement.* New York: St. Martin's Press.

—— and Andrew Karmen. 1978. "Criminology and the Reaffirmation of Humanist Ideals," *Criminology* 16 (August): 239–254.

—— and Robert J. Kelly. 1981. "Responsibility and the Law: An Existential Account," pp. 21–44, in H. Laurence Ross (ed.) *Law and Deviance.* Beverly Hills: Sage.

Schaff, Adam. 1970. *Marxism and the Human Individual.* New York: McGraw Hill.

——. 1965. "Marxism and the Philosophy of Man," in E. Fromm (ed.) *Socialist Humanism.* New York: Anchor.

Schiller, F. C. S. 1932. "Humanism," pp. 537–542, in E. R. A. Seligmann & A...Johnson (eds.) *Encyclopedia of the Social Sciences*, Volume 7. New York: MacMillan.

Schur, Edwin. 1965. *Crimes Without Victims*. Englewood Cliffs, NJ: Prentice Hall.

Schwendinger, Herman & Julia Schwendinger. 1977. "Social Class and the Definition of Crime," *Crime and Social Justice* 7 (Spring/Summer): 4–13.

——. 1970. "Defenders of Order or Guardians of Human Rights?" *Issues in Criminology* 5 (Simmer): 123–157.

Scimecca, Joseph A. 1981. *Society and Freedom - An Introduction to Humanist Sociology*. New York: St. Martin's Press.

——. 1976. "Paying Homage to the Father: C. Wright Mills and Radical Sociology," *The Sociological Quarterly* 17 (Spring): 180–196.

Scimecca, Joseph A. 1975. "The Implications of the Sociology of C. Wright Mills for Modern Criminological Theory," *International Journal of Criminology & Penology* 3, 2 (May): 145–154.

Sher, Gerson S. 1978. *Marxist Humanism and Praxis*. Buffalo: Prometheus Books.

Smith, Alexander and Harriet Pollack. 1975. *Some Sins are Not Crimes*. New York: New Viewpoints.

Smith, Warren A. 1981. "Are You a Humanist: Some Authors Answer," *The Humanist* (March/April): 5–26, 54.

Staude, John R. 1972. "The Theoretical Foundations of Humanistic Sociology," pp. 262–268, in J. Glass & J. R. Staude (eds.) *Humanistic Society*. Pacific Palisades, CA: Goodyear.

Stein, Maurice. 1972. "On the Limits of Professional Thought," pp. 164–170, in J. Glass & J. R. Staude (eds.) *Humanistic Society*. Pacific Palisades, CA: Goodyear.

Sutherland, E. H. 1937. *The Professional Thief*. Chicago: University of Chicago Press.

Svitak, Ivan. 1970. *Man and His World: A Marxian View*. New York: Delta.

Terrill, Richard J. 1980. "Clio and Criminal Justice," *Criminal Justice Review* 5, 1: 81–89.

Thomas, Norman. 1965. "Humanistic Socialism and the Future," pp. 347–357, in E. Fromm (ed.) *Socialist Humanism*. New York: Anchor.

Tifft, L. and D. Sullivan. 1980. *The Struggle to Be Human: Crime, Criminology and Anarchism*. Over the Water, Sanday, Orkney: Cienfuegos Press.

Tigar, M. with M. Levy. 1977. *Law and the Rise of Capitalism*. New York: Monthly Review Press.

Wooden, Ken. 1976. *Weeping in the Playtime of Others*. New York: McGraw Hill.

Woodward K. L. & E. Salholz. 1981. "The Right's New Bogeyman," *Newsweek* (July 6): 50.

Young, T. R. 1978. *The Red Feather Dictionary of Socialist Sociology*, 2nd edition. Red Feather Institute.

Rejoinder to Friedrichs' "Crime, Deviance, and Criminal Justice: In Search of a Radical Humanistic Perspective"[1]

James David Ballard
California State University, Northridge

David O. Friedrichs wrote this reflective essay twenty-plus years ago and with the intent to create a "preliminary examination" of the potential synthesis of humanism, sociology, and Marxism as they pertain to the enterprise of criminology. His reflective statement ends with the caution that "much work remains to be done if a viable, effective radical humanistic criminology is to become a potent intellectual and moral force." In sad reflection, it seems that many ignored the promise he offers, and that the vision he had for the transformation of criminology was premature at best and wildly off target at worst.

Why have criminologists strayed from the author's potent vision of a criminology inspired to be humanistic? What can be done to resurrect this intellectual enterprise, if that is a goal for the current generation of humanists that would need to stand and be counted as the vanguard for the humanistic criminology movement? To answer these questions this rejoinder will first briefly summarize Friedrichs' vision and then offer a brief summary of contemporary social relations as related to criminological study. This rejoinder will terminate with a challenge to the body humanist to either heed his call or to fall upon their swords in the attempt to make real their convictions in everyday life.

The summary of his vision is based on the work of many fine academics and this essay stands on their shoulders. It is a monument to their life work as radicals, Marxists, and humanists, but not one without serious contemplation, reflection, and questioning of their assumptions. Friedrichs does a masterful job of interweaving various threads of theoretical discourse in such a way as to show the similarities and differences between traditional sociological discourses and his vision of a humanistic criminology.

Friedrichs' form of study was not meant to be your grandfather's criminology; it is not a paradigm based on just theology, nor is it based on some overdeveloped sense of scientific imperative. No, this form of criminology would be founded on three principles: 1) it should seek a deeper understanding of its primary focus/subject of study; 2) it would embrace, encourage, and foster cooperative relations between the humanist researcher and the field broadly defined (e.g., victims, perpetrators, processes, etc.); and 3) this discipline would seek constructive change in the social relations personified within the criminal justice system. These principles do not represent a paradigm, nor do they suggest a single theoretical or methodological vision; rather they are reflective of a moralistic vision of what should be, a call to arms for what must be, and a manifesto for what ought to be our

---

[1] This paper originally appeared in *Humanity & Society* Volume 27, Number 3, 2003.

challenge and opportunity. These assumptions clearly represent lofty goals, but given the era from which they emerge, they are also an understandable and laudable project for the academy to undertake. Have we taken the challenge posed by this vision?

So what has happened since this call to arms, since his vision was cast in the stone cold pages of *Humanity and Society*? Several trends that Friedrichs seemingly anticipated and still others that he had no way to anticipate transpired. These social events have profoundly impacted the development of criminology and criminal justice, not for the better.

First and foremost, while he foresaw the political turn to the right that was just beginning in the Reagan era (the timeframe from which he wrote), he clearly under anticipated the impact of this sea change in American society. The early years of the Reagan era were a time of transformation and characterized by high unemployment, increasing perceptions of criminality, less and less tolerance for deviance, increasing incarceration and social stratification, and other signs of social disturbances that would have been ripe for the application of the new criminology he was exposing.

Yet, in a very short period on time, the wholesale shift to the right by the nation would rapidly increase the pace and demands for more and more punishment, calls that seeming obliterated the vision and promise Friedrichs offered to the academy. The failure of the left in general (liberals, radicals, or anyone else not overtaken by the fundamental(ist) shift in society) to counteract this sea change in social relations left the potentials he identified barely breathing in academic circles.

The ascension of a right wing criminology that glorifies punishment and embraces degradation and the overwhelming social fear that accompanied such social panics as the "crack" epidemic left almost everyone who was trying to offer a unique or alternative vision of criminology holding the bag. One example is that funding for research that could have supported his ideas went to those willing to conduct atheoretical and ahistorical work in support of state institutions, the drug war, increased means and justifications for incarceration, and helping develop and implement a myriad of other social control agendas. The cooptation of criminology, and criminal justice study in particular, was so invasive and insidious, that many within this criminal enterprise fail to see how far and fast their work has been appropriated.

This cooptation was accomplished by structural means, budgets for criminal justice dramatically increased and as a means to garner a share of these funds, universities were willing and eager to become cop shops teaching Handcuffing 101, if only to build their criminal justice programs, a cash cow in many institutions. The growth in the criminal justice business was insidious since it allowed just about anyone to become a scholar in the field. The number of well trained academics willing to participate in this consumption of funds was overwhelming and rapidly grew to critical mass. They in turn produced more and more proto academics that fail to see any purpose in examining the assumptions behind their regression equations, let alone have the capacity to do as Friedrichs asks and become reflective humanists. The vicious cycle of criminology was complete and breaking this cycle will be difficult at best.

As the country sits knee deep in the right wing decadence that has beset our society, what can be done? What message does this author have for humanists today and tomorrow? First and foremost he offers a vision, sorely lacking in many contemporary academic enterprises relative to criminology. While humanists still exist, we are a fractured lot, each seeking our own academic market niche; many obsessed with eking out a career in academia. The barbarians who seemingly control our destiny are not only at the gate, but they seem to be battering on our office doors.

Few of us reside in large institutions where our research could effect changes in large-scale public policy and fewer still have the social capitol to overcome the anti-intellectual bias that has not only risen to the highest levels in the land, but invaded our everyday life. Sociologists who study criminology in general, and humanists in particular, have been marginalized almost to the point of irrelevancy. Old humanists do not just die, we fade away as more and more of the new generation is hired. They arrive amidst an era of over abundance of human capital in higher education. They are all too happy to conform since they are so happy to have jobs and quickly succumb to the humiliation rituals of tenure. Daily the academy is pull farther and farther away from Friedrichs' vision.

Bleak as this may sound, I have faith in the enterprise we have set forth as our life goal: the humanist enterprise. I have faith that we as a community of scholars can tackle the issues posed by this visionary and in the process provide for a new criminology, one that is feminist, humanist, Marxist, and anything else that will assist in the project.

But we must act and act soon. The sense of urgency that barely underlies his original writing is even more visible today. We have to find ways to share our concerns with main-stream sociology, a sociology hell bent on degrading the academy as much as the politi-cians and society does. We must rush the halls of power that have become the ASA and through our participation and advancement of scholarship, insist that the radical voices that dare to embrace a humanistic criminology not only are heard, but also heeded.

Local level praxis is not enough to overcome the trends that have marginalized almost all academics that have an alternative vision for society (or criminology). The praxis of today is even more daunting than suggested by Friedrichs. It is praxis where mountains must be moved; huge mega-cities transformed; it is utopian and pragmatic; it may be illu-sionary to most but its reality is embodied within those who read this volume.

Section 4

Confronting Politics: Local, Global and Everything In Between

Sometimes—often—public sociology comes up against political power and institutional blockades as it attempts to address social problems. At every level—the local, the global, and everything in-between—those with political clout, money and control can affect our ability to do public sociology and make the kinds of changes we want to make. The articles and rejoinders in this section examine this inevitable confrontation over ameliorating social problems in several different domains. From sports to the environment to a variety of community-based concerns, the authors in this section discuss struggles with conservative political machinations large and small, providing important guidelines for dealing with them effectively. But notable in each effort is the willingness and courage to commit to social justice regardless of the power elite, their institutions and their attendant ideologies. Each article gives us insight into the particularities of how public sociology can be deployed in struggles over everything from public financing for private sports stadiums to the success of community based organizations and sustainable development efforts. While public sociology brings research, knowledge and theory to bear on developing new tactics and strategies for addressing social problems, the core principles of humanist sociology—an ethical and unyielding commitment to human rights and social justice—persevere.

1. Popular Epidemiology and Environmental Movements: Mapping Active Narratives for Empowerment[1,2]

David N. Pellow
Northwestern University

Reflexive Statement

As an activist-scholar, I am constantly pulled between two arenas of loyalty. As an activist in the environmental movement I am urged to put my political convictions before my scholarly priorities. On the other hand, as a scholar in the academy I am expected to do the reverse. In this paper I attempt to grapple with these cross-pressures by painting a complex, seemingly contradictory picture of an environmental justice movement organization. My experience with this organization stems from my personal and professional interests in highlighting the struggles of oppressed peoples, particularly the victims of environmental racism. Using an "active narrative" approach, I explore the paths an African American environmental organization follows in its efforts to document the negative human health effects of local industrial pollution, through what is called "popular epidemiology." The active narrative flows from my work as an activist-scholar and is therefore an explicitly humanistic approach to sociology. Through this lens I conclude that popular epidemiology both empowers and disempowers social movement organizations. This observation is important because it provides a more accurate portrait of environmental movement experiences and is the result of active participation in the lives of my informants.

Popular Epidemiology and Environmental Movements: Mapping Active Narratives for Empowerment

Analyses of environmental movements have revolved around the contested terrain of scientific certainty and epidemiology in environmental health conflicts (Brown 1992; Brown and Mikkelsen 1990; Freudenberg and Steinsapir 1992; Pellow 1994). A broader, but related, discourse has emerged over the notion of environmental movement empowerment versus disempowerment (Gould, Weinberg and Schnaiberg 1993; Gould, Schnaiberg, and Weinberg 1996; Pellow 1994; Szasz 1994). While scholars of environmental movements

[1] I would like to thank the following people for reading earlier drafts of this paper: Allan Schnaiberg, Adam Weinberg, Ken Gould, Lisa Sun-Hee Park, Aldon Morris, Albert Hunter, Charles Payne, Ira Silver, and Phil Brown.
[2] This paper originally appeared in *Humanity & Society* Volume 21, Number 3, 1997.

have vigorously argued on both sides of this debate there appears to be little attention paid to the complexity with which activists are both empowered and disempowered through the use of tactics like popular epidemiology (PE).

Brown and Mikkelsen (1990) define *popular epidemiology* as "the process by which lay persons gather scientific data and other information and direct and marshal the knowledge and resources of experts to understand the epidemiology of disease" (ibid: 125–6). They argue that community groups using popular epidemiology are successfully challenging and changing the nature of scientific inquiry. The question I ask in this paper is, what are the costs and benefits to community groups using popular epidemiology? I argue that communities experience a combination of empowerment and disempowerment through this strategy. I define *empowerment* as the ability to maintain relative control over one's agenda, which often also includes the capacity to shape an adversary's agenda, thus realizing one's original goals. Conversely, disempowerment is the inability to maintain control over one's agenda, which often results in an adversary's capacity to shape that agenda, thus leaving one with few if any original goals realized. As Szasz (1994: 103) states, when a party is disempowered its power is "contain[ed] and neutralize[d]."

Theories of Citizen Science and Environmental Movement Success

A defining element of the environmental justice movement is the concern with human health (Schnaiberg and Gould 1994; Szasz 1994). While the links between a number of toxic substances and human health problems are well-established (Brown and Mikkelsen 1990), there is great uncertainty and controversy concerning the possible causation between many other toxins and illnesses (ibid). It is within this gray area of scientific uncertainty that hundreds of grassroots organizations across the United States are seeking a voice and an audience in their attempts to document environmentally-related diseases and their connections to industrial pollutants (Brown 1992; Brown and Ferguson 1995; Brown and Mikkelsen 1990; Freudenberg 1984; Szasz 1994). Phil Brown (1992) argues that activists practicing popular epidemiology draw on "cultural rationality"—a tradition-oriented, personal and protective response to toxic waste threats—to prove causation between community health problems and pollution. In so doing, he argues, activists control and change the nature of epidemiological inquiry, challenging scientific canons (Brown 1992; Brown and Ferguson 1995; Brown and Mikkelsen 1990). Although widely practiced in many forms, popular epidemiology is only one of many tactics in the environmental movement's repertoire (Freudenberg 1984). Thus, any consideration of this strategy should be grounded in a broader discussion of movement activity and efficacy.

I situate popular epidemiology within the sociological literature on environmental movements. Much of this literature is marked by what I will term the *movement empowerment perspective* (MEP). MEP proponents generally argue that, despite obstacles elites in government and industry present movement activists and organizations with, the latter often succeed in articulating and realizing their goals (Dunlap and Mertig 1982; Freudenberg 1984; Milbrath 1984). More specifically, MEP scholars report widespread environmental consciousness and commitment across demographic categories (Hamilton 1985), increasing movement activity in the form of "radical populism" (Szasz 1994) and "revolution" (Bullard 1993), instances of movement activists undergoing personal transformation (Brown and Ferguson 1995; Kroll-Smith 1994), and successful use of scientists and scientific data for social change (Brown and Mikkelsen 1990; Brown 1992; Freudenberg 1984).

While the environmental movement has achieved significant gains, I contend that the MEP is often overly celebratory. As others (Gould, Weinberg and Schnaiberg 1993: 208) have argued,

> This [positive reporting] is due, in part, to the relatively higher social rewards attached to reports of good news. It also stems from the political importance of environmental groups claiming success, as well as from political leaders who want to claim pro-environmental records...

The theoretical and empirical importance of presenting reports of *both* environmental movement successes and failures cannot be overstated. For scholars aiming to build contextualized, rich theory, the movement empowerment perspective (MEP) is often limited because, while the environment itself is considered a social problem, the environmental movement remains unproblematic.

This paper builds upon recent work by environmental sociologists who question the view that "the environmental movement is holding corporate wrongdoers accountable for their actions" (Gould 1994) and that "environmental problems are being solved" (Schnaiberg and Gould 1994: v). These studies analyze the more unpleasant realities of citizen-worker-activists organizing locally against powerful forces in a transnational political economy (Gould, Schnaiberg, and Weinberg 1996). Following this more recent framing of environmental movement strategy, I make no claims as to the success or failure of the environmental movement. Instead I maintain that, more often than not, activists experience a complex mixture of loss and triumph, empowerment and disempowerment, and that sociologists should pay more attention to these processes.

One way of exploring these processes is the use of what I term the "active narrative" approach, which draws heavily from Weinberg's (1994) concept of a "sociological narrative," as well as from research on history as story-telling (Cronon 1992), Black feminist theory (Collins 1991; Crenshaw 1993), and advocacy research (Park and Pellow 1996; Stoecker and Beckwith 1992; Stoecker 1996). Weinberg (1994: 32) writes that the sociological narrative "entails the use of pragmatic philosophical skills to tell stories that engrossingly and persuasively convey central themes that represent what has been missed by others." This narrative is a way of creating "alternative versions, which challenge readers to examine their belief structures" (ibid) to the extent that it is "possible to narrate the same evidence in radically different ways" (Cronon 1992: 1370). The role of the narrative in sociology is that it remains but one method whereby a story or multiple stories can be told, without privileging one voice over another. As Black feminist Patricia Hill Collins (1991) and critical legal theorist Kimberle Crenshaw (1993) argue, when two or more competing perspectives attempt to explain a phenomenon—such as race or gender in accounting for inequality—the traditional "either/or" dichotomy is less robust than a "both/and" orientation. Thus, for example, while an African American woman may be discriminated against on the basis of *either* her race *or* her gender, it is also the case that she experiences this treatment *both* because of her race *and* her gender.

Building on this research on narratives I also draw on the work of activist-scholars (Hall 1992; Stoecker 1996; Stoecker and Beckwith 1992; Stoecker and Bonacich 1992) who argue that one path sociologists can take to becoming "critical inquirers" (Weinberg

1994) is to become active participants in social movement infrastructures. In this way, through the articulation of an active narrative, we may add new richness to our research and to social movement repertoires. Through "participatory research" (Stoecker 1996)—the direct involvement of research informants as partners in the research act—sociologists engage in an explicitly humanistic, activist methodology.

The active narrative approach, like the sociological narrative, recognizes contradiction, paradox, and socially constructed multiple "truths." The active narrative negotiates these often dissonant pathways with the aim of providing activist-scholars and our social movement organizations many possible 'maps' toward progressive change. Building on the sociological narrative, the active narrative approach calls for direct participation in the worlds of our informants. Following this active narrative approach, environmental sociologists—many of whom are environmentalists themselves—would concern themselves with observing the successes and failures of the movement from "within" so as to offer insider perspectives with the intention of improving the possibilities of realizing effective social change. I argue that the practice of direct engagement in both social movements and in universities, is one way in which sociologists can cross many boundaries (Park and Pellow 1996) and report these multiple narratives. I should note that there are several ways social scientists can get at multiple truths within social movements without necessarily having an insider's view.

In the rest of the paper I argue that one social movement organization's experience with both empowerment and disempowerment offers lessons for the environmental movement and the discipline of sociology.

Methods

In September 1992 I joined People for Community Recovery (PCR)—a grassroots environmental organization—as a volunteer. My volunteer status was crucial in building trust and relationships with those whom I was interviewing and observing. As an activist-scholar, it was understood that, in order to gather data for my own work, I would also serve as an advocate. Thus participant observation entailed joining the organization, writing grant proposals, policy reports and surveys with fellow activists, researching environmental issues, and representing the organization at conferences. Through this intimate involvement I was able to gain access to numerous organizational meetings and documents. I complemented these data with 34 open-ended interviews, ranging from one to three hours in length, with PCR activists, Environmental Protection Agency (EPA) representatives, and environmental scientists and doctors associated with this case. The open-ended questions were organized around four main topics: each organization's mission, the reliability and limits of environmental science, pollution and waste dumping practices, and community concerns. I conducted interviews in respondents' homes, offices, and at conferences. This paper is the result of three and a half years of field work and an enduring personal commitment to environmental justice.

People for Community Recovery

In Southeast Chicago, one of the nation's most visible grassroots environmental justice organizations, People for Community Recovery (PCR), and the Environmental Protection

Agency's (EPA) branch office are involved in a decade-old conflict over the environmental health effects of locally-generated pollution. PCR is a small organization that counts about thirty active members in its coalition. Since its founding in 1982, the organization has subsisted from grant check to grant check in a public housing development isolated from the city and its various institutions. Situated in an area that activists call "the Toxic Doughnut," PCR is surrounded by a multitude of polluting industries and more than fifty landfills. The housing community there is locally referred to as "the Gardens" and is home to 10,000 residents. The Gardens also has the third highest neighborhood poverty rate in Chicago, is 98% African American (London and Puntenney 1993), and is located in the zip code with the second highest volume of toxic industrial releases in the city (Cohen 1992).

In the next section I present what I term a "chronological narrative"[1] of events that transpired between 1982 and 1995 at PCR. I follow this section with two "active narrative" perspectives that intentionally contradict and complement one another.

A Chronological Narrative

In 1982, after viewing a television news story revealing that the Southeast Side of Chicago had the highest incidence of cancer in the city, PCR's founder, Hazel Johnson, decided to conduct her own research. Mrs. Johnson had been interested in her community's health since her husband died of cancer years before. As the written history of the organization reports, Johnson

> made numerous calls around the country to learn what was going on in her own community regarding the high cancer rate. Later she connected with city and state health departments and these agencies mailed Johnson many reports on environmental problems in [her] community.... After conducting research, PCR learned that [the community] was the home of many surrounding waste disposal companies. PCR found that... low and moderate income residential communities on the Southeast Side of Chicago were being exposed to substantial amounts of toxic chemicals and their negative health impact (PCR 1993a).

Johnson immediately went about the task of canvassing door-to-door in her neighborhood, having residents complete health surveys she obtained from the EPA. The Director of Preventive Health Programs at the Department of Health at that time, described this process, wherein PCR's president,

> knew nothing about chi square, mean, mode, median or sampling error, and didn't care. She said 'I'm going to go out here and I'm going to produce a survey and I'm going to ask as many people as I can touch, what's wrong with them, how did they feel about their health, what kinds of health problems did they experience, were they seeing physicians?' And she got an overwhelming response.

Examining the eleven hundred open-ended surveys compiled, I discovered stories from each family who completed one. Without exception, every survey indicated that air pollution was perceived to be the cause of serious physical discomfort in the community. In answer to the question, "Briefly describe the problem," one respondent's survey read: "It smells like something dead, raw sewage and sulfur all mixed together, and it's unbearable to breathe. It is something followed by a haze in the sky." In answer to the question, "Known or Suspected Source?" one respondent wrote: "Calumet Industrial District Landfill, 134 Calumet Expressway, Sanitation Dept. 1300 E. 130th St." Numerous respondents wrote that the suspected pollution source was the "Sanitation District" and one specified the "Interlake Steel garbage dump at 13500 S. Perry Ave" (PCR 1984). Other respondents reported symptoms common in pollution "sacrifice zones" (Bullard 1993). The following are some typical examples:

> "I vomit, get dizzy, and also have headaches."
>
> "At night the foul smell wakes you up."
>
> "...my head has been bothering me for the past three years." (PCR 1984).

Upon completing this exercise in "shoe leather epidemiology" (Brown and Ferguson 1995), PCR released its first health study to the press in 1985. Although the survey documented many observations and conclusions of local residents, the EPA argued that it was not scientifically rigorous enough to prompt an official response. In part, this was because each "survey" was actually only an EPA complaint form and was never designed to produce any remedial governmental action—at best only further research. The EPA's Associate Regional Counselor commented that studies like PCR's are "not done in a way that meets scientific protocol and therefore [are] not given much credence." Even so, PCR was publicly credited with completing a community health study—one of the first of its kind. As *The Los Angeles Times* later reported it, PCR "came up with stunning results...the media took notice [but] the EPA... demanded more evidence" (Getlin 1993).

In January of 1992, PCR decided to accept the EPA's challenge. With the help of the University of Illinois School of Public Health, PCR designed and conducted another, more scientifically sophisticated health survey. As PCR's administrative assistant informed me:

> We got people from the University to do our health survey and it's statistically significant. But if we didn't use them it wouldn't hold any weight like those EPA complaint forms from the first survey.

In this second, university-directed study, PCR again made efforts to document the human health hazards associated with living in the community and, once again, produced "stunning results." A dozen television stations and newspapers carried the press release of the second survey. One quoted PCR president Hazel Johnson saying, "Lots of people [in this community] have asthma and respiratory problems, miscarriages" (Mahin 1993), while another reported that Johnson "has the numbers to prove what she has been saying all along" (Michaeli 1993). Yet another journalist declared "the report confirmed what residents have long reported" (Pinkney 1993).

From the second survey, the finding PCR most emphasized was that over half of the pregnancies respondents reported having during a one year period resulted in some sort of complication, mortality, or abnormality (PCR 1993b). Other figures documented that several residents suffered from asthma and "Chronic Obstructive Pulmonary Disease (COPD) which could include Emphysema or Chronic Bronchitis" (ibid: 3). All this information was outlined in pie charts and bar graphs in a six-page document.

Less than a week after PCR released this survey to the press, the EPA announced its plans to implement what it called the "South Side Initiative" a plan to reduce pollution in the area, while encouraging environmental education and economic development. The EPA wanted PCR's direct involvement in this endeavor and the group accepted. The initiative was intended to be a model for the nation. According to PCR's vice president, Cheryl,

After we published the results of the health survey, the EPA contacted PCR about the Southeast

> Chicago Initiative. They were waiting for us [to release the study]... It took people like us to do this study because the government wouldn't do it for us.

One EPA official admitted to the author that "political pressure" from groups like PCR and the NAACP provided "the catalyst for this initiative" such that the agency decided that "we need to do something about the Southeast Side." Indeed, earlier that year, in April 1993, Hazel Johnson's colleague, then NAACP executive director Benjamin Chavis, visited Chicago

> fighting what he calls environmental racism, the tendency to place landfills and toxic waste sites disproportionately in poor neighborhoods. 'Chicago's South Side has the greatest environmental degradation in the country,' he said in an interview the day after he was picked to head the NAACP (Johnson 1993).

When PCR joined the South Side Initiative, they decided to use the health data to push for more stringent pollution prevention and control standards in the area. The South Side Initiative has been underway since 1993 and is being used to seek funding for further health studies and environmental clean ups.

An Active Narrative of Movement Disempowerment

PCR's first health survey was a recording of testimonials wherein the activists and respondents demonstrated "cultural rationality" by pointing to what they, as laypersons, understood to be the community's pressing problems. Indeed, the Gardens is a community with several landfills in full view and thick plumes rising out of nearby smokestacks. Residents' drinking water is often visibly polluted and many people suffer from physical ailments (some residents require respirators). Thus, firsthand knowledge of the problems associated with living in a polluted environment is widespread. This first survey was therefore culturally empowering but structurally disempowering to PCR and the community as its design and purpose made sense to the lay public, but the response they received from the EPA did not.

Regarding the second survey, it would appear that by convincing the EPA to undertake the South Side Initiative, PCR achieved real empowerment. Numerous community organizations around the nation have replicated PCR's pattern of gathering data through external "resource mobilization" (McCarthy and Zald 1977). However, as in PCR's situation, none of the studies in these cases were conducted without the help of university or government officials. Though this survey was the result of PCR activists', local residents', and university scientists' collaborative efforts, it was the *scientists* who designed and supervised the project, and tabulated the results. The community therefore abdicated much of its control over the process as activists relinquished these tasks to professionals so as to improve the survey's "technical rationality"—a more ordered approach to toxic waste and epidemiological uncertainty.

Many social scientists maintain that lay persons respond to environmental threats with "cultural rationality"—a traditional, qualitative understanding of toxics (Brown and Mikkelsen 1990; Fitchen 1989; Krimsky and Plough 1988). Brown and Mikkelsen explicitly argue that popular epidemiology is one such response.[2] However, in PCR's case, activists tended to defer to technical rationality and scientific expertise as the pragmatic path to environmental and human health protection.

During negotiations with the EPA concerning the South Side Initiative, PCR members relied on outside technical assistance from mainly white, middle class environmental organizations and institutions. This reliance insured that PCR's participation in the conflict was largely restricted to the realm of technical rationality. For instance, a staff member of a local university's community resource center that provides PCR with technical support argued that

> the whole field, the whole environmental issues field is very complicated, very technical. In order to understand it fully you need a certain amount of training and expertise just to understand the thousands of different chemicals, the health effects. I mean you have to be a physician, a biochemist, [and] an engineer just to understand what all these things are.

Echoing this sentiment, an activist in PCR's coalition from a neighboring community commented

> that an environmental health survey is definitely an empowering mechanism as long as the questionnaire that is used is designed or approved by a professional as having scientific validity.

At a meeting called to prepare PCR activists for an upcoming negotiation with the EPA, an outside scientific advisor coached the activists:

> ...you can say... 'we want to clean up the existing contamination, we don't want to burden the people with anymore pollution in the area. We're not here to shut down industry. We're here to help industry modernize.'

Upon hearing this, and based on her own anxiety in confronting the EPA scientists, PCR's vice president jokingly asked him, "Can I dress you up as me?" During this same meeting a PCR member apologized,

> I really don't have the technical background to really start discussing this whole thing so I'll need some input.... What if at this meeting they [EPA] start shooting real technical, technical stuff and we don't have the back-up here to counteract that?

Thus, unlike some activists who become versed in the language of epidemiology (Brown and Ferguson 1995; Kroll-Smith 1994), PCR members located the sphere of expertise *outside* of their personal boundaries—an act of technical rationality. At the same time, however, these activists relied on cultural rationality to dismiss scientific claims they found unconvincing or suspicious. Thus Brown and Mikkelsen and others miss the often complex and contradictory process where activists use both cultural and technical rationality as a political strategy. This apparent contradiction allows us to consider the empowering aspects of this conflict.

An Active Narrative of Movement Empowerment

There are three principal ways in which PCR activists achieved movement empowerment. First, activists regularly questioned authority and scientific evidence. When asked how she felt about working with EPA experts, one PCR member, Ann, stated flatly:

> I resent outsiders coming in and telling me what's wrong with my community when I already know because I live and breathe it. And because they have a degree makes them smarter than me? Hell no! It just means that they just stayed in [school] longer and stood the bullshit.

At a meeting of PCR's newsletter staff, another activist suggested distributing the newsletters to doctors: "Doctors' offices would be good places. They need to know that we know there is a problem." During a meeting with the EPA, PCR's president commented upon a previous government-sponsored, city-wide health assessment that found no significant patterns of illnesses in the Gardens neighborhood:

> I didn't like what they [EPA] came up with. It was some old data saying that it wasn't that many cases of cancer within our community when we know people are dying like flies! We know that information is false!

Thus, while activists in this coalition rely on technical rationality by depending on outside experts, they also hold on firmly to cultural rationality when necessary. PCR's vice president confided to me that "if we do have the government come out here and do a study they'll get results that aren't significant." Distrust of public health officials, government scientists and corporations by activists is well-documented (Brown and Mikkelsen 1990; Brown and Ferguson 1995; Freudenberg 1984; Freudenberg and Steinsapir 1992; Pellow 1994; Szasz 1994) and is especially salient in communities of color due to the historical mistreatment these groups have experienced at the hands of government, the legal system, and industry (Bullard 1993; Freudenberg 1984).

Second, the fact that the EPA has devoted (albeit minimal) financial and human capital to launch the South Side Initiative indicates to some degree that PCR presented a public relations threat to the agency. Judging by the widespread media coverage PCR regularly attracts, this is not difficult to understand. In other words, PCR accomplished things that most likely would not have been accomplished had the organization not existed. As one health department official told me,

> If they [PCR] weren't there then there would be no attention there [on the Southeast Side]. They are the conscience of the community with respect to environmental issues. They lend a kind of agitating perspective that is necessary so that even the most minimal things get done.

Finally, as an effort to create a sense of cultural and/or racial solidarity, PCR has been able to attract the services and consultation of African American professionals—although outsiders to the community. One staff member proudly informed me of her success in recruiting a "Black militant cardiologist" to serve on the organization's Board of Directors. At times, having members of their own race on their side provided PCR with a "free space" (Evans and Boyte 1986) that they rarely felt existed with their white technical supporters. White supporters were seen as "OK" or marginally racist while the African American technical support team members were referred to as "brothers." Morris (1984) demonstrates that shared cultural symbols and histories, such as those cultivated here, can be important in sustaining movements.

Thus, within the narrow confines that define environmental problems only within scientific parameters, PCR retained some agency. Therefore, despite its disempowering experiences, PCR also found empowerment. PCR's environmental policy coordinator, Patricia, summed up these complexities in reflecting on her experiences with popular epidemiology:

> If we could have got somebody to do more research we could have gotten a hell of a lot more out of it... Not being sophisticated about how we can use the numbers to our advantage was a problem. I'm not a researcher but we needed some real professional researchers to come out and do some hard core research. We left it up to the EPA, we trusted them and they bullshitted us. *Either way, in my mind, we found, we proved there was a problem.*

This is a typical response from PCR coalition members and contains strong indicators of disempowerment and empowerment. In a technically rational fashion, Patricia locates the sphere of expertise outside herself, the organization and the community. At the same time, however, she remains confident that PCR demonstrated the existence of "a problem" where before none officially existed. This complexity and contradiction, accompanied by the author's intimate participation in the project are the crux of the active narrative approach. As a member of the academic and environmental movement communities, I am privy to these data and perspectives that other, more distanced researchers might not have access to.

Discussion

Active Narratives and Sociology

In comparing conflicting scholars' conclusions about the causes and consequences of the Dust Bowl, environmental historian William Cronon (1992:1376) writes

> [e]ach [book] implies a different possible narrative for environmental histories of the region, and different possible endings for each of those stories.... Rather than evade it [narrative]—which is in any event impossible—we must learn to use it consciously, responsibly, self-critically.

Cronon echoes the sentiments of a number of environmental sociologists (Weinberg 1994), and Black feminist scholars (Collins 1991; Crenshaw 1993) who acknowledge the power embedded in narratives and the necessity therefore to give voice to multiple, often conflicting stories. Although Phil Brown's and my own accounts of popular epidemiology's efficacy differ significantly, both stories are useful in detailing narratives from a particular scholar's perspective, in a certain context and time. Thus, if we search for the "truth" here, we will not find it, but *both* Brown's *and* my narratives are useful. In the case of PCR, the empowerment and the disempowerment narratives were both accurate, as told by the author, someone who lived and experienced them as an activist-scholar.

A growing movement of sociologists conducting advocacy or participatory research (Hall 1992; Park and Pellow 1996; Stoecker 1996; Stoecker and Bonacich 1992) have argued broadly that social scientists can and ought to make their research more relevant and more accountable to the communities we write about. In this emerging tradition, scholars are charged with the responsibility to call attention to the glamorous and not-so-glamorous elements among movement activities, with the aim of improving our own understanding of, and participation in, various social causes. Activist-scholars are increasingly involving themselves in the environmental movement's struggles through research (Brown and Mikkelsen 1990), day-to-day work (Park and Pellow 1996), joining social movement organizations, serving on advisory boards, and founding resource centers (Wright 1995). I do not anticipate that this increased involvement will necessarily lead to more critical and balanced research on environmental movements; in fact, it may have the opposite effect—that is, professionals are just as likely to present positive, successful images of the movement's efforts in order to sustain legitimacy in intellectual, philanthropic, and social movement circles. However, we might be more conscious of the possibility that if our research offers relevance to social movement organizations, philanthropic organizations, civic groups, and other citizen's forums, then public support for sociology and sociologists might be more intact. From a social science perspective, activist-scholarship by sociologists allows for previously unexplored data collection possibilities and more sophisticated reporting methods.

Conclusion

In this paper I explored the costs and benefits to a community group using popular epidemiology as a tool to make scientific and political claims about environmental illness. Based on complex assumptions activists revealed while engaged in this process and PCR's ability to exercise some agency despite considerable odds, I conclude that it is both costly and beneficial, empowering and disempowering. I grounded this discussion in a broader framework of environmental sociology and proposed that we view competing accounts of environmental strategy as narratives that may complement each other. One way to explore this complementarity is through practicing advocacy research whereby one might produce "active narratives." The two narratives I proposed saw PCR in the following ways. In the disempowered narrative, I discovered that what is experienced and determined through a social, political, historical and economic process of environmental injustice is, through popular epidemiology (i.e. the second health survey), reframed in the form of scientific documentation, mostly devoid of any sense of conflict or oppression. In the empowered narrative, however, I also discovered that PCR succeeded in placing issues on the public agenda and drew on cultural rationality and technical rationality as political resources. As an activist-scholar and member of PCR, I was in the unique position to uncover and report both stories. Sociological narrative theory provides a useful tool for moving beyond success versus failure debates and offers a way of viewing movements in their full complexity with varying degrees of gain and loss at multiple levels.

Active narratives emerge from an activist-scholar or "participatory" research tradition because they require the researcher to be closely involved with one's informants. Bunyan Bryant (1995) proposes that participatory research by activist-scholars is one way to ensure that both communities and universities survive and thrive together. Participatory research would involve partnerships between scholars and citizen-workers to democratically produce and use problem-solving knowledge relevant to particular communities. Communities might benefit greatly from this type of scholarship, which is deeply imbued with humanist values. As several universities have earmarked resources for participatory research projects, we can have hope this trend will become a mainstream practice that extends beyond the social sciences to create "communiversities" between scholars in all disciplines at every academic institution.

Endnotes

[1]In the strictest sense a chronology would be a story-less account of all possible events that take place surrounding one or more topic, time, or space (Cronon 1992: 1351). Here, however, I present a chronology as a narrative of events that seeks to view these occurrences as having happened—with an infinite number of events excluded—without analysis or judgment. Ergo the term "chronological narrative" as a chronology itself contains narratives.

[2]Personal correspondence between Phil Brown and the author, letter dated 1/21/94.

References

Brown, Phil. 1992. Popular Epidemiology and Toxic Waste Contamination: Lay and Professional Ways of Knowing. *Journal of Health and Social Behavior* 33:267–81.

Brown, Phil and Edwin Mikkelsen. 1990. *No Safe Place: Toxic Waste, Leukemia, and Community Action*. Berkeley: University of California Press.

Brown, Phil, Edwin Mikkelsen and Faith Ferguson. 1995. Making a big stink. *Gender & Society* 9:145–172.

Bryant, Bunyan, ed. 1995. *Environmental Justice*. San Francisco: Island Press.

Bullard, Robert. ed. 1993. *Confronting Environmental Racism. Boston*: South End Press.

Cohen, Linc. 1992. Waste Dumps Toxic Traps for Minorities. *The Chicago Reporter.* vol.21, no. 4, April.

Collins, Patricia Hill. 1991. *Black Feminist Thought.* New York: Unwin Hyman.

Crenshaw, Kimberle. 1993. Demarginalizing the intersection of race and sex. Pp. 383–394 in D. Kelly Weisberg, ed. *Feminist Legal Theory: Foundations*. Philadelphia: Temple University Press.

Cronon, William. 1992. A place for stories: nature, history, and narrative. *Journal of American History* March: 1347–76.

Dunlap, Riley. 1987. Polls, Pollution and politics revisited: Public opinion on the environment in the Reagan Era. *Environment* 29:32–37.

Dunlap, Riley and Angela Mertig. 1992. *American Environmentalism: The U.S. Environmental Movement, 1970–1990*. Crane Russak.

Evans, Sara and Harry Boyte. 1986. *Free Spaces*. New York: Harper and Row.

Fitchen, Janet. 1989. When Toxic Chemicals Pollute Residential Environments: The Cultural Meanings of Home and Homeownership. *Human Organization* 48:313–324.

Freudenberg, Nicholas. 1984. *Not in Our Backyards: Community Action for Health and the Environment.* New York: Monthly Review Press.

Freudenberg, Nicholas and Carol Steinsapir. 1992. *Not in our backyards.* In Riley Dunlap and Angela Mertig, eds. American Environmentalism. Philadelphia: Taylor and Francis.

Getlin, Josh. 1993. *Fighting Her Good Fight. Los Angeles Times.* February 18., section E, p.1, col.2.

Gould, Kenneth. 1994. Author Meets Critics. Roundtable at the annual meetings of the American Sociological Association, Los Angeles, August.

Gould, Kenneth, Adam Weinberg, and Allan Schnaiberg. 1993. Legitimating impotence: pyrrhic victories of the modern environmental movement. *Qualitative Sociology* 16: 207–46.

Gould, Kenneth, Allan Schnaiberg, and Adam Weinberg. 1996. *Local Environmental Struggles.* New York: Cambridge University Press.

Gould, Kenneth, Allan Schnaiberg, and Adam Weinberg. 1995. Natural Resource Use in a Transnational Treadmill. *Humboldt Journal of Social Relations* 21: 61–93.

Hall, Bud. 1992. From margins to center? the development and purpose of participatory research. *American Sociologist* Winter: 15–28.

Hamilton, Lawrence. 1985. Concern about toxic waste. *Sociological Perspectives* 28: 463–86.

Johnson, Mary. 1993. NAACP leader targets Chicago. *Chicago Sun-Times.* April 12, p. 1.

Krimsky, Sheldon and Alonzo Plough. 1988. *Environmental Hazards.* Dover, Mass: Auburn House.

Kroll-Smith, Stephen. 1994. Multiple chemical sensitivity and negotiated codes. Paper presented at the annual meetings of the American Sociological Association, Los Angeles, August.

London, Rebecca and Deborah Puntenney. 1993. *A Profile of Chicago's Poverty and Related Conditions.* Northwestern University: Center for Urban Affairs and Policy Research.

Mahin, Chris. 1993. Altgeld residents fight environmental racism. *People's Tribune*, April 26.

McCarthy, John and Mayer Zald. 1977. Resource Mobilization and Social Movements. *American Journal of Sociology* 82:1212–41.

Michaeli, Ethan. 1993. [Southeast Side] Residents face health problems. *Chicago Defender*, July 13.

Milbrath, Lester. 1984. *Environmentalists: Vanguard for a New Society.* Albany: State University of New York Press.

Morris, Aldon. 1984. *The Origins of the Civil Rights Movement.* New York: Free Press.

Park, Lisa and David N. Pellow. 1996. Washing Dirty Laundry. *Sociological Imagination* 33: 138–153.

Pellow, David N. 1994. Environmental Justice and Popular Epidemiology. Paper presented at the annual meetings of the American Sociological Association, Los Angeles, August.

People for Community Recovery. 1993. "History: PCR, Inc."

People for Community Recovery. 1984. "PCR's Health Survey."

People for Community Recovery. 1993. "PCR's Health Survey."

Pinkney, Deborah. 1993. Altgeld tenants sick of bad air. *Chicago Sun-Times.* July 10, p.3.

Schnaiberg, Allan and Kenneth Gould. 1994. *Environment and Society: The Enduring Conflict.* New York: St. Martin's Press.

Stoecker, Randy and David Beckwith. 1992. Advancing Toledo's Neighborhood Movement through Participatory Action Research. *Clinical Sociology Review.*

Stoecker, Randy, David Beckwith and Edna Bonacich. 1992. Why Participatory Research? *The American Sociologist.* Winter: 5–14.

Stoecker, Randy, David Beckwith and Edna Bonacich. 1996. Sociology and Social Action. *Sociological Imagination* 32: 3–17

Szasz, Andrew. *EcoPopulism.* Minneapolis: University of Minnesota Press.

Weinberg, Adam. 1994. Environmental Sociology and the Environmental Movement: Towards a Theory of Pragmatic Relationships of Critical Inquiry. *American Sociologist* Spring: 30–56.

Wright, Beverly. 1995. Environmental Equity Justice Centers. Pp. 57–65 in Bunyan Bryant, ed., *Environmental Justice.* San Francisco: Island Press.

Sharing Knowledge and Power: A Rejoinder to Pellow's "Popular Epidemiology and Environmental Movements"[1]

James R. Pennell
University of Indianapolis

The central theme of Pellow's article strikes at the heart of every activist sociologist's concern: how to negotiate the expert/layperson relationship in a manner that does not diminish or usurp the power of individuals or groups attempting to bring about change in some area of life that troubles them. Pellow frames his analysis strictly within the environmental movement literature, but this dilemma has been studied more broadly in terms of expert/ novice or professional/lay person relations (Abbott 1988; Habermas 1970; Habermas 1975; Stehr 1994). Pellow's account points to the need for activist sociologists and academics from other disciplines with the sociological imagination and social competence to help bridge the worlds of expert conceptions and those of everyday life. We need activist scholars with a heightened awareness of the political potential and pitfalls when different groups with different social realities come together for a common cause.

But we must be careful not to overly dichotomize or reify different social worlds in our analyses. Pellow is right that the academy continues to hold its members to a set of expectations that often works against playing an activist role or even spending time on practical, as opposed to "academic" matters. However, changes are clearly evident. Many change-oriented groups now have liaisons who negotiate between expert and lay conceptions of the world, translating language and informing parties with different experiences and conceptions about the way the other's world is understood. These are typically people who are highly attuned to different social worlds, can speak the different languages of those worlds, and do not have their perceptions and motives dominated by a single way of viewing the world. They may be researchers who work across organizations, spokespersons/media relations specialists, or lobbyists. In addition, various forms of academic knowledge have permeated everyday life and have become common knowledge. Conversely, academics live at least some part of their lives in the everyday world and are not always the cultural dopes they are often made out to be.

Changes are also evident as universities seek to attract more students and external funding from new sources by making stronger connections between academic work and practical concerns. Some of these changes may work against goals of democratic empowerment and social justice, for example, the growing corporate involvement in universities and the corporatization of the university itself (White 2000). But in an effort to make universities more relevant and attract popular media attention, opportunities have also developed

[1]This paper originally appeared in *Humanity & Society* Volume 27, Number 4, 2003.

for progressive academics to combine applied research with service to their communities. Conducting research from an openly committed perspective is not without pitfalls. Advocacy research may be rejected for taking a value-oriented stance. It may also produce findings that fail to support one's commitments. And it can just as easily be reactionary as progressive, the Hudson Institute and the American Enterprise Institute being just two of many examples.

Pellow's account gives me hope that expert and everyday worlds can be brought closer together and that academic knowledge can be used to promote social justice and protection of the environment. Although he highlights the potential loss of power that lay activists may face when needing to rely on the technical expertise of others, Pellow's narrative is really about the power of knowledge shared and the possibilities of what might be referred to as "power with" instead of power over or against. Overcoming social and environmental injustices is going to require collaboration and power sharing among activist groups and academic experts, as Pellow's account suggests. These alliances will need to be strengthened and extended across national borders as capitalist forces seek to treat knowledge as a product to be bought, sold, and used to shape and control the lives of the less powerful. Humanistically-oriented activist sociologists are well situated to be a guiding force in these important endeavors.

References

Abbott, Andrew. 1988. *The System of Professions: An Essay on the Division of Expert Labor.* Chicago: Univ. of Chicago Press.

Habermas, Jurgen. 1970. *Toward a Rational Society: Student Protest, Science, and Politics.* Jeremy J. Shapiro, Trans. Boston: Beacon Press.

—————. 1975. *Legitimation Crisis.* Thomas McCarthy, Trans. Boston: Beacon Press.

Stehr, Nico. 1994. *Knowledge Societies.* Thousand Oaks, CA: SAGE.

White, Geoffry, Ed.; with Flannery C. Hauck. 2000. *Campus, Inc.: Corporate Power in the Ivory Tower.* Amherst, NY: Prometheus Books.

2. Local Growth Coalitions, Publicly Subsidized Sports Stadiums, and Social Inequality[1]

Kevin Delaney
Temple University

Rick Eckstein
Villanova University

Reflexive Statement

Since the mid-1980s, approximately $10 billion of public money has gone toward building new professional sports stadiums in American cities (Keating 1999), while urban residents face rising inequality and inadequate social services. Most social scientific research has not adequately explained why public polices supporting new stadium construction remain popular in the face of increased community hostility and skepticism that they will improve the quality of residents' life. Using extensive, qualitative research in nine U.S. cities, we argue that "local growth coalitions" are the driving force behind these new stadium initiatives and are powerful enough to sweep aside most community opposition. By focusing on local growth coalitions, we identify how and why urban resources are diverted toward new stadiums and away from other policy initiatives. In this regard, publicly financed sports stadiums are the local equivalent of state-financed prisons and a federally-financed military, where social policies that benefit narrow class and organizational interests are rationalized as being in the entire community's best interest.

Introduction

During the last few decades, social inequality within American cities has noticeably increased, leading to a deteriorating quality of life for most poor urban residents (Jargowsky 1996, 2002; Edin and Lein 1997; Squires and O'Connor 2002; Smith and Ingham 2003). Poorer residents have been especially victimized by social problems such as inadequate public schools, dangerous housing, unreliable social services, and poor health, to name just a few (Massey and Denton 1998; Drier, Swanstrom, and Mollenkompf 2001). Social scientists have dedicated considerable effort to articulating the plethora of structural factors precipitating these problems, including (but not limited to) deindustrialization,

---

[1]This paper originally appeared in *Humanity & Society* Volume 30, Number 1, 2006.

reductions in the social safety net, regressive tax policies, and funding shifts from urban schools to urban prisons (Wilson 1996; Edin and Lein 1997; Lucas 1999; Kissane 2003; Kozol 2005). More recently, however, a new phenomenon has contributed to these intensifying urban social problems: spending public money on new professional sports stadiums.

People supporting such policies argue that new sports stadiums will actually alleviate urban social problems by stimulating local economic growth in ways that other policies (and older stadiums) cannot. This growth will supposedly stem directly from the new jobs needed to construct and operate the new stadiums, and indirectly from the ancillary economic activity generated by the stadiums and the huge numbers of people, especially tourists, who will come to watch ballgames, stay in local hotels, eat in local restaurants, and spend additional dollars throughout the city. Urban residents can allegedly reap the rewards of this increased economic activity in two ways. First, they will benefit from new employment opportunities both at the stadium and because of the stadium. Second, local government services will expand quantitatively and qualitatively as the city's revenues swell from all the new tax receipts spawned by all this stadium-based economic activity.

This belief that new stadiums will improve life for poor urban residents has greatly influenced public policy over the last two decades. In many American cities, local (and sometimes state) governments have provided large subsidies to construct new major league baseball and football stadiums, usually in the name of revitalizing that city and improving the quality of life for its residents (Austrian and Rosentraub 2003; Friedman, Andrews, and Silk 2004; Chapin 2004; Santo 2005; Tu 2005). Between 1990 and 2004, 14 new baseball stadiums and 17 new football stadiums have been built, with an additional three under construction. This is an unprecedented wave of stadium building and one analyst estimated that approximately $10 billion of public money has gone to these new stadiums since the mid-1980s (Keating 1999). While the actual costs of these stadiums are often hidden, the public has paid anywhere from 10% to 99% of new stadium costs with most contributions typically falling in the 30%-70% range (Delaney and Eckstein 2003a).

Despite these significant contributions and optimistic claims, new stadiums have not been a panacea for poor, urban residents and the social services upon which they depend. Sports economists have studied at length using social subsidies for sports facilities and have concluded, in nearly unanimous fashion, that it is not a wise use of public money (Baade and Dye 1990; Baade 1996; Noll and Zimbalist 1997; Rosentraub 1997; Zimbalist 1998; Bandow 2003; Zimbalist 2003). Most have found that stadiums create some direct economic development (mainly construction jobs) and limited indirect economic development (e.g., nearby restaurants). However, much of this growth represents shifts in spending from other areas of this city and not a net increase in revenues. On balance, these studies conclude that the revenues created by new stadiums do not lead to measurable economic growth (Baade and Dye 1990). Indeed, municipalities may actually be receiving far less net receipts after these new stadiums open due to the diversion of certain revenue streams from the old stadium (Coates and Humphreys 2000; Delaney and Eckstein 2003a).

New stadiums also have not delivered on improving social services such as education. In Cleveland, for example, the city's public schools were supposed to be a major beneficiary of public spending on a combined baseball stadium and basketball arena (Jacobs Field and Gund Arena) in the early 1990s. However, by the late 1990s, even after Jacobs Field (especially) had been continually sold out, Cleveland's public schools had not visibly improved. Cleveland's dropout rate was the highest among large cities in the state.

Dropout rates in nearby Akron, which had no new stadiums, were about one-third the rate of Cleveland in 1998, four years after the opening of Jacobs Field. Per pupil expenditures between 1994 and 1998 were increasing more than twice the rate in Akron as compared to Cleveland.[1] These troubling figures, of course, are due to many factors other than stadium funding. However, these figures are particularly ironic since during the campaign to publicly finance Cleveland's new stadiums, some advocates warned that failing to support this policy initiative would doom Cleveland into becoming "another Akron." This scapegoating of allegedly inferior cities is part of an overall strategy that plays on a community's emotional attachment to its professional sports teams (Eckstein and Delaney 2002; Ingham, Howell, and Schilperoort 1987; see also Smith and Ingham 2003).

Studying Publicly Financed Stadiums

Social scientists examining the community impact of new sports stadiums have approached the issue from two different angles. Macro-economic approaches, such as those mentioned in the previous section, generally examine aggregate economic data about employment trends, sales receipts, and tax revenue changes. These analysts use economic factors to either make a broad analysis across many cities with new stadiums (i.e., Coates and Humphreys 2000; Zimbalist 1998; Baade 1996; Baade and Dye 1990) or to examine in detail one or more cities with new stadiums (i.e. Noll and Zimbalist 1997; Rosentraub 1997). These studies are almost always quantitative and rely on a variety of statistical techniques to reach their conclusions that, in almost all cases, new stadiums have little or no impact on a local economy. Interestingly, this practically unanimous academic consensus about the negligible economic benefits of new stadiums has had little direct impact on urban policies (Delaney and Eckstein 2003b).

In addition to this macro-economic focus, there is a less common angle, which explores some of the individual and organizational behavior that precipitates new stadium construction in different U.S. cities (i.e. Cagan and Demause 1998; Euchner 1993; Keating 1997; Shropshire 1995; Spirou and Bennett 2003; Weiner 2000; Smith and Ingham 2003; Friedman, Andrews, and Silk 2004). This research is generally qualititative so, rather than examining aggregate economic data, it uses single or multiple case studies to look at political processes and grass roots activities that either support or oppose financing and constructing new stadiums. As with the macro-economic approach, this research is highly skeptical of assertions that using public dollars for new stadiums will alleviate urban problems. Also similar to the economic models, these conclusions have been ignored and/or attacked by urban policy makers (Delaney and Eckstein 2003b).

However, the two dominant intellectual approaches are becoming less helpful for understanding how and why stadiums are built with public money. One problem common to both approaches is that they cannot account for the huge variation among recent stadium initiatives. This variation is expressed in many different ways. First, although most stadium initiatives since 1993 have been successful, some have failed and for a variety of different reasons. Second, even with successful initiatives, there is significant variation in the "level" of success as measured by the percent of total costs passed on to the public. Third, the structure and strategies of the initiatives themselves have differed greatly. There are tremendous contextual differences between and among the various cities trying to build publicly financed stadiums. In short, the processes of building publicly financed stadiums, the contexts in which these stadiums are built, and the social impact of the stadiums are extremely diverse and should not be treated as a homogenous social phenomenon.

Macro-economic models do acknowledge variation among cities, but only as expressed by specific aggregate data. Such an approach overlooks how these data are embedded in a larger social context. For example, it is interesting and informative to compare labor market changes in Cincinnati and Phoenix, two cities that recently built new publicly financed stadiums. But this comparison can be interpreted differently depending on whether you look at these data by themselves or whether you consider the enormous differences between Cincinnati and Phoenix: only one is experiencing population growth; only one has a significant corporate presence; only one has a long professional sports history. These non-economic factors may have a tremendous impact on the meaning of more conventional economic factors.

The less common qualitative approach to studying publicly financed stadiums also has trouble accounting for this variation in process, outcome, and context. The primary reason is that this research usually examines single cases where comparative variation is not an issue (Friedman, Andrews, and Silk 2004; Smith and Ingham 2003; Spirou and Bennett 2003; Blair and Swindell 1997; Agostini, Quigley, and Smolensky 1997; Keating 1997; Weiner 2000; Curry, Schwirian, and Woldoff 2004). But, even research drawing on multiple cases tends to overlook the sometimes staggering, multivariate dissimilarity among cities, preferring instead to focus on a single analytical element and how this is expressed in different places (Cagan and DeMause 1998; Shropshire 1995; Euchner 1993). For instance, many of these case studies (both single and multiple) tend to explain publicly financed stadiums as examples of "corporate welfare" although the specific manifestation of this corporate welfare might differ slightly from city to city. Underlying all these manifestations, however, are the allegedly greedy team owners who hire influential lobbyists, make or withhold campaign contributions, and/or threaten to move their teams in order to squeeze out every possible public dollar for a new stadium that they claim will solve a plethora of urban social problems. In this conception, greedy owners are aided and abetted by the weak-kneed, spineless local politicians who create policies that end up harming a city's most vulnerable citizens.

This "corporate welfare" approach eschews the heterogeneous characteristics of new stadium financing and construction in different cities. For example, sometimes new publicly financed stadium are built and sometimes they are not. Sometimes the pathway to a new stadium is very smooth and sometimes it is laden with obstacles. Most importantly, sometimes team owners spearhead the drive toward new publicly financed stadiums but, increasingly, they are involved peripherally, if at all. Understanding these significant differences among cities building (or trying to build) new publicly financed stadiums requires a model that overcomes the shortcomings of relying strictly on aggregate economic data, single case studies, or univariate explanations. Such a model needs to place aggregate quantitative data within a qualitative social context, and to compare the myriad of social processes that generate both patterns and idiosyncrasies in cities building new stadiums.

Local Growth Coalitions and Publicly Financed Stadiums

We use the idea of "local growth coalitions" to explain this enormous variation between and among recent new stadium initiatives, and why local resources continue to stream toward stadium construction despite increased skepticism that this will alleviate urban inequality. This concept is an extension of the "growth machine" idea first offered in the late 1970's, and refined many times since, to explain how powerful individuals and organizations systematically benefit from urban policy making while perpetuating an ideology that these policies serve the entire local community (Molotch 1976; Whitt 1982; Molenkopf 1983; Friedland and Palmer 1984; Swanstrom 1985; Logan and Molotch 1987; Eckstein 1997; Lauria 1997; Schimmel 2002; Troutman 2004). Growth coalitions are rooted in an institutionalized relationship between locally headquartered major corporations, the local government, and the local media. They articulate and implement social policies that will supposedly stimulate local economic growth that benefits the entire community. In essence, these coalitions are arbiters of what urban economic growth should look like and how social resources should be allocated to achieve this vision.

Locally based financial corporations are often, but not always, the driving force of these coalitions, and the more powerful the local corporate community, the more powerful the local growth coalition. Local or regional government is the other key player in these alliances since it implements policies that will facilitate the coalition's vision of economic growth, especially when tax dollars are contributing to this vision. Governments may play a conspicuous or inconspicuous role in these coalitions depending on varying social circumstances. While financial institutions are often at the helm of these coalitions, non-financial local corporations are not excluded from leadership. Smaller locally based corporations, or corporations without a local headquarters, may also be part of these coalitions but rarely in leading roles. In addition, the increasingly corporate controlled media outlets in many cities are frequently involved with the local growth coalition. Even non-business organizations such as religious groups and labor unions may be part of these alliances. Interestingly, the professional sports teams are often part of these coalitions but usually do not take a leading role in promulgating the coalition's position, even on public funding for new sports stadiums. In fact, we will argue that a stadium initiative is most beneficial to the home team when that team is minimally involved in the initiative.

Even though we talk about these coalitions as if they were tangible organizations, they don't necessarily have an office or issue position papers as a single body. But, the individuals and organizations involved in these coalitions do plan, discuss, and strategize with each other in some structured fashion, and they do try to influence policy makers and the general public. For example, a foundation director in Cleveland described the power of the growth coalition in this way: "It isn't a corporate dictatorship. But yes, this is a very top down place. We set priorities. We make agendas. We line up the troops" (Adams 1998).

One highly structured forum for these discussions are the elite, CEO-only business groups present in many U.S. cities such as the Cincinnati Business Committee, Cleveland Tomorrow, Greater Philadelphia First (now extinct), Greater Denver Corporation (extinct), and the Allegheny Conference (Pittsburgh). These groups are the standard bearers of the local growth coalitions and often play a leading role in building publicly financed stadium, even if they are largely unknown to the general public. We believe that the strength and influence of these coalitions is directly proportional to the strength and influence of these "corporate roundtables." A stronger roundtable means a stronger local growth coalition, which makes it easier to divert public resources away from more pressing urban problems and toward new stadiums, even in the face of public skepticism or hostility.

We prefer talking about growth coalitions rather than growth machines for two main reasons. First, a machine sounds much more omnipotent than a coalition and we want to be clear that these alliances, while extremely powerful, do not always get their way. More importantly, the coalition idea allows for much more empirical variation in the strength and unity of the coalition. These local alliances do not all look the same even though they have many similarities. Indeed, not all cities even have growth coalitions. Some have powerful coalitions, while others have very weak ones. Some coalitions may have been powerful for many years while others may only recently have become powerful. Sometimes a coalition dies off and stays dead; sometimes it dies and rises anew. Identifying the existence of a local growth coalition, and the relative strength of any coalition, yields important insights into how cities spend their scarce resources. In short, those advocating for spending urban resources on stadiums rather than other social needs face fewer obstacles and have more success in cities with strong local growth coalitions and minimal involvement by "greedy" team owners.

Methods and Data Collection

For the last several years, we have been conducting detailed qualitative research in nine American cities. Policy makers in these cities have all engaged in protracted political battles over how best to stimulate urban economic growth and improve their cities' quality of life: by strengthening basic infrastructure such as schools and job training, by attracting new businesses through tax abatements, or by building new sports stadiums and tourist attractions. Advocates for stadium-based urban rejuvenation have clearly won seven of these nine battles where one or more new stadiums have opened between 1994 and 2004. The successful initiatives we have examined include Cleveland (2 new stadiums), Cincinnati (2), Philadelphia (2), Pittsburgh (2), Denver (2), Phoenix (1), and San Diego (1). Advocates of publicly financed stadiums have lost these battles in two cities that we have studied: Hartford and Minneapolis.

In each of these nine cities, we conducted lengthy interviews with people enmeshed in the stadium battles. In all, we talked with more than 70 political policy makers, corporate leaders, sports team executives, grass-roots activists, journalists, and academics all involved in, or greatly familiar with, these initiatives. We also toured and photographed stadium districts (both existing and proposed) to build an ethnographic picture of the alleged urban rejuvenation generated (or potentially generated) by this allocation of public resources. These primary sources of data were enhanced by a thorough review of secondary sources such as local mainstream papers, the local business press, and the many "advocacy studies" commissioned to support publicly financed stadiums. Finally, these data were augmented by more informal conversations with dozens of residents and workers in these nine cities.

Selecting these nine cities was an initially daunting task. Since we wanted to go beyond the limitations posed by aggregate economic data and single case studies, we were committed to conducting detailed, comparative, primary, qualitative research. Given the time and resource constraints associated with such a strategy, we had to make decisions among the almost 20 cities in the "population" of places where new publicly financed stadiums had been built or where people were contemplating building them. While exploring these cities through secondary sources, we discovered that each one had unique characteristics and that lumping them into a single population was oversimplifying a very complex social reality. We were initially delighted to find such variation because it reinforced our critique of existing research that overlooked the importance of these differences. However, such variation made selecting a representative sample of cities much more difficult.

In the end, we did our best to study cities that reflected variation on important issues such as: whether or not the initiatives were successful; how beneficial these outcomes were to stadium advocates; the strength of local growth coalitions; different strategies chosen by local growth coalitions or other advocates; the economic, social, and cultural characteristics of each city; and the efficacy of opposition to these initiatives in each city. While each city expresses these characteristics in idiosyncratic ways, there are still enough patterns to support our point that even in the face of public resistance, cities with strong local growth coalitions and limited sports team involvement are far more likely than others to direct social resources toward new stadiums.

Corporations and Local Growth Coalitions

The local growth coalition in Cincinnati was probably the most powerful of those we examined in this project. On the surface, it appeared that both the football Bengals and the baseball Reds demanded new stadiums and that political leaders (and the general public) eventually acquiesced. However, the CEO-only group, the Cincinnati Business Committee (CBC), worked in tandem with the local Chamber of Commerce to spearhead the campaign for new stadiums. They purposefully framed the issue as one not of economics (and therefore, not one of corporate welfare) but of city pride and appealing to a nostalgic sense of community. Their strategy avoided the pitfalls of promising stadium-generated economic development while fully manipulating the community's emotional attachment to professional sports (Eckstein and Delaney 2002; Smith and Ingham 2003). This strategy was embodied in the slogan "Keep Cincinnati a Major League City." As one leading coalition member told us:

> We have a business community, which is committed to the community; it makes a statement. Someone in a job like mine is given the privilege of shaping opinions from time to time. I can't do wonderful stuff; I'm not the genie. But every now and then you have the opportunity to tip the rock just enough and see what damage it will do. Those of us who are playing these roles, the influencers, have to sit and say 'is [a stadium] the best way to spend [all these] millions?' The answer is probably no, but who else would [make these hard decisions] over the years? All [the business community] did was put up a million bucks. The naysayers maybe had $40,000 in their campaign, certainly less than $100,000 going against our million.

Despite providing money and strategic support, the CBC stayed out of the limelight as much as possible and allowed a local county politician to spearhead the campaign for public subsidies. The teams themselves tried to maintain a low profile to avoid the "greedy owners" and "corporate welfare" accusations. According to a business leader, this was a well thought out strategy:

> [A consultant] out of Columbus came and was the brains behind things. So we had these six business leaders each with their own ideas and who could be a

spokesperson but chose not to. Didn't let ourselves get involved in a big ego hunt. We spent the next six to eight months working with the consultant, raising a million bucks so he had the resources to do what he needed to do, then being a sort of kitchen cabinet to advise. Until three days before the election, you never saw a suit.

Similarly, Pittsburgh's strong corporate community, reflected by its CEO-only group, the Allegheny Conference, played a leading role in the stadiums initiatives in that city. A sports team executive pointed to the importance of a strong corporate base for gaining sports stadium subsidies:

The corporate community here is very supportive, very supportive. That's the one thing we have going for us here. We don't have the population base but we have a very strong corporate community. [Companies like] Mellon Bank, PNC Bank, Alcoa, USX, Heinz. We've taken some hits losing Rockwell and Westinghouse [but] it's still a significant corporate community. They were very supportive of [Plan A]. We spent $6 million on the initiative. They put money up for it.

Not all cities, of course, have such powerful and unified growth coalitions. The coalition in Philadelphia is surprisingly weak, even though Philadelphia is the country's fifth largest city. Although much larger than Cincinnati, Philadelphia has few large corporations headquartered in town. The CEO-only group in Philadelphia, Greater Philadelphia First, consciously chose not to place stadium funding as a priority.[2] Instead they chose to focus on public education. This left the stadium initiative up to the mayor (first, Ed Rendell; later, John Street). As a result, a more fractious procedure ensued over where to place the stadium, leading to long delays and many public hearings. In the end, the teams got their stadiums but with some significant changes from their "wish list." For instance, the Phillies very much wanted a downtown stadium like the Pirates' PNC Park, but eventually settled for a new ballpark in the existing sports complex several miles from center city, which reduced the amount of public subsidy. A business leader drew a contrast between Pittsburgh and Philadelphia highlighting the strong, corporate led, local growth coalition.

I'm prepared to say there is a difference in [corporate] cultures in the different cities. In Pittsburgh, the [corporate community] is different. There are all sorts of ways that unfolds: culturally, politically, and in the nature of business leadership. Pittsburgh's [corporate leadership] dominates the city and the region in a way that Philadelphia's does not… Pittsburgh is not run by steel [but] by large banks. Was Core States [before its merger, the largest bank in Philadelphia] really a player in Philadelphia? Not really. You have to go back to the 1970s to find a strong banking presence in Philadelphia; all the way back to First Pennsylvania or [the Philadelphia Savings Fund Society]. To what extent does the [corporate community] still have dominant market share? In Philadelphia it does not.

In Minneapolis, a once strong growth coalition has experienced a steady decline since the 1970s. As a result, at least five stadium initiatives have languished. As in Philadelphia, few corporate titans have stepped up to take the lead on stadium subsidies. With local political elites also somewhat timid, team owners in the Twin Cities, more than any other city in our study, have taken the lead of trying to divert social resources to new stadiums. This has created a situation where cries of "corporate welfare" have much more resonance. One business leader drew a distinction between the once powerful corporate coalition that built the Metrodome (which opened in 1982) and the current vacuum of corporate leadership in the quest to build a new stadium for the baseball Twins:

> A major player in the seventies that was missing in the 1990s was the business community. In the run-up to the Dome's political passage and financial creation, a cabal of Minneapolis' major business leaders determined that they would bring the Dome downtown, by hook or by crook. They didn't jump in at the very beginning. They jumped in when the political process turned a bit haywire. But when the business leaders decided to get involved, their involvement was deep and unswerving. They seriously put their money where their mouths were.

One business leader, the publisher of the local newspaper, attempted to fill this role, but eventually backed out under criticism and has since left the Twin Cities. Even as he tried to play the leadership role, he recognized the changes in the city that diminished his power as a member of the local growth coalition:

> Most of us are hired guns. We don't own these companies and therefore many people were thinking about their business overseas and the global economy was forcing them to spend an inordinate amount of time out of this community…What was nagging at us was that the people who made things happen in this community were family-owned businesses and very wealthy entrepreneurs and families that had been here for a very long time like the Pillsburys and the Daytons and so forth and we felt we were kind of losing that kind of coalition of people who were looking out after the community.

Why Stadiums?

We think there are a number of factors that have led corporate elites to favor building new stadiums rather than, for example, putting more money into improving local education. First, corporate executives want to be able to use stadiums—especially their luxury boxes—and the aura surrounding professional sports to attract new executives. Many of the corporate executives we talked with spoke about the challenges they faced recruiting top talent to their city. This is a particularly strong sentiment in cities that are smaller and have less allure for graduates from top law schools and business schools. Business leaders in Cleveland and Cincinnati told us that when competing with firms in New York and San Francisco, these new stadiums gave them something to show off.

> What's the greatest single problem a business has today? Workforce. If you interview 50 businesses at random I'll bet 49 would say that my biggest problem is getting qualified workers. To get workers you have to get people who

want to be in your community because they love the community, it's got things to offer. As the incoming CEO of [one local] company said, I got 80 people making over $100,000 in this operation. Every one of them is young, aggressive, highly compensated people. They go to the best schools in the country, they can go anywhere they want, they are the A players in the business world. I need things that A players want. What are you going to sell [to executives you are recruiting]? You sell the city's amenities. We have a great art museum, a great orchestra, and major league sports. Nice suburbs? There are nice suburbs everywhere. So, you have to sell a package of things and that means something to these CEOs.

We can't help but wonder whether there is some gender bias here. Of course, women can be interested in professional sports, but in all our conversations with executives about recruiting "A level talent" it always seemed that they were talking about men. We aren't even sure whether the A level talent really cares all that much about the luxury boxes at the stadium, but as long as current executives believe that these future executives care, they will continue treating new stadiums as part of their recruitment effort. And why not have the local government subsidize this particular recruitment tool?

This focus on executive recruitment reflects an interesting post-industrial phenomenon. Many cities in the United States have become filled with "hollow" corporations. Hollow companies split their administration from their production with the former staying in the home city and the latter moving elsewhere in the U.S. or even offshore. Thus, when we talk about firms' headquarters being located in a city, often this simply means that the company employs several hundred, or at most a few thousand, top managerial and administrative staff who work inthe city. The production workers with their more secure wages and salaries have left town, or perhaps more accurately, their jobs have left town, leaving only low-wage work to provide support services for executives. This makes for a very polarized social class dynamic in these cities since there are well paid and poorly paid workers with fewer people in the middle.

These two polarized groups have different stakes in the city itself. For the high paid members of the local growth coalition, the city is more of a transient station for work and play before returning home to suburbia or moving on to their next outpost in another city. Their urban priorities are likely to include good roads and/or commuter rails, interesting restaurants, and cultural diversions, which might include new sports stadiums with plenty of available parking. For the minimum wage worker, the city is a more permanent place to work and live. These people's urban priorities would more likely include good schools, reliable buses, safe neighborhoods, clean streets and playgrounds, and decent grocery stores. Given this latest wave of using public dollars for private stadiums, it would seem that the interests of the growth coalition are being served more than the interests of poorer urban residents. This was clearly illustrated when a Cleveland business leader said,

Some CEOs have absolutely no exposure to the Cleveland public schools. They could be a large company but only have 100 employees here [in Cleveland] because they run companies across the country. They probably don't have a single person that ever went to the Cleveland public schools.

This is an astounding statement and would not have been made fifty years ago because these companies still had relatively well paid production workers living in Cleveland. Gone are the Fisher Body Division workers from the Euclid plant (which closed for good in 1993) as well as members of the United Steel Workers, whose Cleveland area membership dropped from 47,000 in 1980 to just over 20,000 in 1990. Urban neighborhoods, which were built around these factories, increasingly face economic and social decay when the facility leaves town. This reduces the overall tax base and puts even more strain on the public sector to maintain services (e.g., schools) and deal with the fallout (e.g., crime) from deindustrialization. Unfortunately, in cities like Cleveland, the powerful local growth coalition has been encouraging this by supporting subsidized stadiums rather than subsidized housing.

Finally, some corporate executives are simply big sports fans. They enjoy professional sports and want to be associated with building the new sports stadium. If a corporate executive wants to wear a civic hat, it is a lot harder to improve the test scores of inner city schools (although some do try) than it is to build a new stadium. They want to see a visible monument to their efforts and the stadium will serve that purpose. If you are a big-time sports fan, what better way to show your civic pride than to help get the team a new place to play and the community a new place to watch games? It would be grander still if you could manage to have the new stadium named after your company.

Politics and Local Growth Coalitions

The corporate arm of the local growth coalition has clear reasons to be interested in new publicly funded sports stadiums beyond lining the pockets of "greedy" team owners. Ultimately, however, politicians are still responsible for the actual policies that direct public dollars toward sports stadiums and away from more pressing urban challenges. In cities with weak corporate communities, the government often (but not always) becomes a more visible advocate for publicly financed stadium projects. We have discovered that this more visible role by the local government is associated with more contentious and less successful stadium initiatives (from the advocates' point of view).

For example, in cities such as Phoenix and San Diego, where the absence of large corporate headquarters contributes to a weak local growth coalition, the local government (either county or city) played a more visible role in building publicly financed stadiums. While these initiatives were ultimately successful, they faced more significant obstacles and resulted in agreements using a smaller percentage of public money. In both of these cities (and some others), those politicians who championed the new stadiums were frequently voted out of office. Why do some governors, mayors, and other political leaders want stadiums if they are politically risky, and increasingly difficult to justify as catalysts for urban economic growth?

Political actors may adopt these increasingly unpopular positions for many different reasons. Sometimes, local corporations capture policy makers through campaign contributions, relocation threats, membership on key task forces, or other overt types of influence. Some politicians are fearful of the threats (direct, implied, or imagined) that a sports team might leave town on their watch. Professional sports are different than from other kind of business in that much more attention and emotion are attached to the home team than to, say, a local supermarket. If a non-sports business that employed 150 people left town hardly anyone would even notice. But if that business were a professional sports team, it would be big news (see Smith and Ingham, 2003). This creates a context where powerful actors can manipulate and scare a community into thinking that it will become a hell-hole if their teams leave town; and that keeping them around is possible only by building them new subsidized stadiums.

In other cases, however, policy makers simply see a convergence between corporate interests and the overall community's interests without the application of any overt corporate influence. For example, Connecticut's political leaders were not pressured into thinking that luring the New England Patriots to Hartford would be a huge boost to the city's economy that could revitalize its poor public schools (Delaney and Eckstein 2003a). Neither the football Eagles nor the baseball Phillies forced Philadelphia to spend almost $500 million in public money for two new stadiums while simultaneously privatizing some of the city's public schools and threatening to close some public libraries. Thus, even without overt pressure from the corporate arm of the growth coalition, the political arm often acts in ways that serve the corporate arm's interests because they have a similar vision of appropriate growth strategies for their community.

These two dimensions of social power are by no means mutually exclusive. We saw such overlap in Cleveland with the relationship between the mayor's office and Cleveland Tomorrow, the local CEO-only group. Cleveland Tomorrow had produced an economic blueprint for the city that had the complete support of Mayor Mike White. This was not particularly surprising since the executive director of Cleveland Tomorrow at the time had previously been a senior mayoral aide. However, the mayor's new senior aide, with no direct connections to Cleveland Tomorrow, also supported this blueprint. Indeed, we would speculate that any person in this political position (in Cleveland) would support the blueprint, suggesting a systemic (rather than personal) convergence of corporate and political interests. Politicians genuinely believe that they must transform their city into a tourist destination to survive—and they are betting on stadiums to do this. Particularly in the cities that have experienced substantial economic decline, politicians are often desperate to hold on to businesses and residents. New stadiums are seen as a highly visible way to indicate that your city is still powerful and important. However, these choices end up diverting a great deal of public money to stadiums while other needs get neglected. As one critic of Cleveland's stadium policies said,

> We haven't spent money on tool-and-die, metal bending or steel, or certainly not comparable to the money we are spending reforming our image. It's at least worth a guess whether if we spent this kind of money on less spectacular, but basic, things, whether we'd put more of our industries back to work in jobs that people of this city could do.

We suggest that in cities with a strong local growth coalition, politicians can play a more subtle role in these stadium initiatives even though they may choose not to. Conversely, in cities with weak or fractured growth coalitions, the teams themselves and/or the politicians are forced to take more prominent roles. This can cause problems since, if the teams are taking the lead, they are open to attacks of holding the city hostage for a handout. If the local government takes the lead, we have discovered, it opens the entire process to the much more "messy" trappings of procedural democracy such as public hearings, and rancorous city council meetings. This can sometimes derail a stadium initiative (i.e., Minneapolis) or, at the very least, greatly slow it down (i.e., San Diego and Philadelphia). It usually also results in the teams paying for a larger share of the new stadium.

Local Growth Coalitions and the Media

Large media also play a role in creating growth ideologies connected to new stadiums. In every city we studied, the main local newspaper editorially favored using public dollars for stadiums as a mechanism for improving the overall urban landscape. In Minneapolis, for example, local newspaper publishers have historically (although not currently) played a central role in coordinating the local growth coalition around a vision of how the city should define and pursue economic growth (Weiner 2000). One business leader in San Diego told us a story where a media executive was demanding that the influential San Diego Taxpayers Association keep its concerns over public subsidies inside a task force on which its director served. In Cincinnati, during the referendum campaign to raise the local sales tax to fund these stadiums, editorials continually accentuated the positive elements of the agreements and downplayed the negative elements.

As with the political arm of the growth coalition, the media arm exercises power in both overtly and subtly. The examples mentioned above highlight the more observable pressures that powerful individuals and organizations bring to bear on social policies. However, the local media's power may also be more understated due to ideological agreement about what is best for the city's economic and social welfare. Contributing to this ideological convergence is the increasingly corporate composition of local media. As newspapers, radio outlets, and TV stations each coalesce into gargantuan media conglomerates, they begin espousing a common vision of what is needed to improve urban conditions. This vision seems increasingly about turning cities into tourist destinations and decreasingly about shoring up basic community needs such as public education.

Pittsburgh was the only city we studied where this ideological hegemony broke down. The city's largest paper, the *Post-Gazette*, was editorially supportive toward the city's new stadium plans. However, a second "mainstream" paper, the *Tribune*, was editorially hostile toward the stadium plans. Unlike in Philadelphia, where the two seemingly autonomous major papers are actually owned by the same company, Pittsburgh's two dailies are independent of each other. The *Tribune* incessantly excoriated the city's new stadium plans and anybody who championed it. The paper, along with the Allegheny Institute for Public Policy—a libertarian think tank that generally opposed most types of government spending—presented an alternative view criticizing the use of public money for new stadiums. The Allegheny Institute published dozens of position papers on the tribulations of publicly financed stadiums, which were all reported in the *Tribune* and largely ignored by the *Post-Gazette*. This created a significant obstacle to Pittsburgh's very powerful growth coalition, and the initial stadium financing plan was soundly defeated in 1997 by Pittsburgh area voters. Pittsburgh's growth coalition figured out a way to finance and build these stadiums, without a public referendum, but the process was more convoluted than if there had been no significant media opposition. If other cities had competing mainstream media voices like the one in Pittsburgh, their successful stadium campaigns might have been less successful.

Discussion

Local growth coalitions do not exist in a social vacuum. Ignoring the important social context in which these coalitions operate would make us guilty of the same univariate shortcoming we critiqued earlier. There are many other structural factors besides the existence and strength of local growth coalitions that affect how and why social resources are diverted toward new stadiums. In fact, many of these structural features actually contribute to the strength of a city's local growth coalition and possibly the very existence of a coalition. So, while the shape and form of local growth coalitions is the key to understanding new stadium initiatives, this shape and form is thoroughly intertwined with subtle structural factors.

Growth Coalitions and the Social Characteristics of Cities

One important element influencing the structure of local growth coalitions is whether or not the community is actually growing. The three rapidly growing cities we studied (Denver, Phoenix, San Diego) actually have very weak or non-existent growth coalitions. One explanation for this is that these newer cities do not need coalitions to articulate "appropriate" growth strategies and battle with competing strategies for scarce resources because, with or without new stadiums, there's plenty of growth and possibly enough fiscal pie to go around. Another explanation for the missing growth coalitions in the high growth "frontier" cities is that they have not yet developed entrenched power structures like many older northeastern and Midwestern cities. This is especially true within these cities' business communities, which are clearly not directed by a small cabal of locally headquartered companies and have no CEO-only association.

Conversely, declining cities often have very powerful local growth coalitions for the same reasons growth cities do not. First, since achieving and maintaining economic growth is problematic in these cities, the policies that may or may not stimulate growth become more critical. In these cities, there is more at stake in creating an image of a city in recovery or "on the move forward." Second, these declining cities are usually older with more established political and economic power structures—often reflected in the large number of local corporate headquarters and the presence of a CEO-only group. Given the context of economic "decline," these powerful coalitions have more ideological legitimacy (i.e., perceived expertise) about economic growth than, say, community activists or academics. The history of growth coalitions in these declining cities is also relevant to understanding new stadium dynamics. For example, Minneapolis and Hartford once had fairly powerful growth coalitions that have since become quite weak. Philadelphia, meanwhile, despite a large population, has never had a strong, corporate-driven, local growth coalition. Thus, it is not surprising that new publicly financed stadiums have not been built in Minneapolis and Hartford, and that Philadelphia's new publicly financed stadiums had a relatively hard time being built and with a relatively smaller percentage of public money.

Unique social circumstances in each city interact with growth coalitions and growth dynamics in various ways. Really, no two cities are completely alike. For instance, demographic patterns like overall population growth are quite important. Yet, even the seemingly similar population explosions in the three growth cities of Denver, Phoenix and San Diego are very different from one another. Phoenix, for example, is unique because its growing population is much older than the growing populations of Denver and San Diego. The large proportion of retirees created strong opposition to any new taxes at all, including stadium taxes.

Each city's downtown "personality" also influences the stadium building process. Some downtowns are strictly 9–5 commuter destinations while others are vibrant mixes of permanent residences and businesses open beyond banking hours. The three cities with very strong local growth coalitions (Cincinnati, Cleveland, Pittsburgh) all have sterile downtown areas that close up when the commuters return to the suburbs. Of the nine cities we studied, only Philadelphia and Denver had downtowns that were active more than 40 hours a week. This has an enormous impact on the strategies employed by local growth coalitions, and the efficacy of these strategies, at least as they pertain to publicly financed stadiums.

Resistance to Publicly Financed Stadiums

It is difficult for organized and unorganized citizens to oppose new sports stadiums, especially when up against a powerful local growth coalition. We have uncovered no discernable patterns to stadium opponents in different cities. Like the growth coalitions they battle with, the existence, shape, and form of the stadium opposition in any city is deeply tied to the social characteristics of that city. In Minneapolis, opposition coalesced around an anti-corporate welfare position that has roots in Minnesota's long-running populist tradition, and had an easy target in the team-orchestrated financing schemes. In Phoenix, a relatively elderly population generated a fairly formidable opposition rooted almost totally in an anti-tax philosophy. However, these opponents were simply ignored and their single-minded, anti-tax focus prevented them from forming more sustainable alliances with smaller bands of opponents who, for instance, didn't mind raising taxes for the city's public education system. Philadelphia's relatively middle class, residential, opposition was effective in preventing a downtown baseball stadium in their neighborhood, but was largely irrelevant to the more general issue of using public money to build the ballpark in the first place.

Opponents to Pittsburgh's stadium financing policies mounted one of the most effective opposition campaigns, although its success was only temporary. However, as mentioned earlier, the catalyst for this opposition was the unique resistance of a wealthy and powerful person who happened to own a newspaper and fund a libertarian think tank in Pittsburgh. Without this idiosyncrasy, the opposition in Pittsburgh would have been far less effective and the failed stadium financing referendum might have passed. Interestingly, Cincinnati's patchwork opposition, outspent more than 10–1 by an extremely powerful local growth coalition, might have actually won its referendum if not for the Cleveland Browns' bad timing in moving from Ohio to Baltimore (where they became the Ravens) just ten days before election day.

A city's downtown personality also greatly affects the structure and strategies of local opponents. It is different planning a new ballpark in a decrepit warehouse/parking district (Cleveland) or an industrial site (Hartford) than it is in a gentrifying, middle class, family neighborhood (Philadelphia) or a gentrifying warehouse district that is being transformed into a residential community (San Diego). It is no wonder that grass roots opposition to new stadiums has been strongest in these latter two cities because most people actually prefer going to the ballpark in someone else's neighborhood. Of course, if the local residential neighborhood is predominantly poor (Phoenix), it can mitigate the effectiveness of neighborhood opposition. Demographic characteristics also affect new stadium opposition. As mentioned, the primary opposition in Phoenix came from groups representing elderly retirees who opposed using public monies for ballparks and most anything else. Residents near (although not adjacent to) Denver's downtown baseball stadium are mostly young, single, men—a group that consistently shows strong support for new sports stadiums. This certainly contributed to the almost complete lack of organized opposition to Coors Field.

How can there be more effective opposition to spending finite social resources on stadiums rather than other urban needs? One potential reform might be to create spending limits on the referendums over stadium funding. This would at least even the playing field. Our research shows that proponents typically outspend opponents by at least a 10–1 margin and sometimes much more. At the same time, we are very aware that such reforms might not make a difference in the long run. Newspapers can still run an avalanche of editorials and reproduce home team press releases (disguised as news stories) documenting the economic pain being endured by the franchise. Corporate elites can still influence the political discussion about "correct" forms of economic growth and development. The team can continue its threat to leave the city and politicians can wring their hands over becoming a minor league city.

Creating a "Major League" City

Besides trying to win referenda, opponents of using public money for new stadiums often try to put pressure on the local sports teams who seem to benefit most from these policies. Opponents might try to publicize the finances of the team and its owners or organize a boycott of the team. But, based on what we have learned in our research, this tactic might not be very effective. For one thing, it is no surprise that the teams are trying to use tax money to build their stadiums. The teams are forever trying to maximize revenues by increasing prices on tickets and concessions, so why not try to maximize profits even more by gaining a publicly subsidized stadium. Team owners are lodged in an industry that leads them to continue to press for more than the other guy gets. So, an obvious reform, suggested by other observers, would involve pressing for changes in the overall economic structure of the sports leagues (Costas 2000; Weiner 2000). For example, national legislation limiting the amount (or percent) that a municipality can spend on a sports stadium, or laws mandating that leagues pay a substantial share of new stadium costs might alter the playing field for all teams and cities. Other possibilities include placing limits on a team's mobility (particularly after receiving a large public subsidy in the stadium) thereby undercutting the future threat to leave the hometown.

More importantly, though, our identification of the growth coalition's leading role in building publicly financed stadiums offers a very different tactic for any opposition. Opponents need to understand the role of non-sports organizations and try to raise awareness about their influence over dominant ideologies. So, instead of trying to pressure sports teams, opponents might try to pressure the other local businesses that advocate transferring urban resources from things like public education to sports stadiums. A more successful opposition will have to adapt to the shifting strategies of local growth coalitions and other stadium advocates by creating a more effective argument for why spending on basic neighborhood needs might be more important to revitalizing a city. More attention should be paid to the emotionally-charged arguments that new stadiums help create "major league" cities with both economic and cultural advantages absent from "minor league" cities. In other words, opponents must have a good response to "Keep Cincinnati a Major League City" and "Keep Cleveland from Becoming Akron." They must articulate ways that public dollars can be better spent to keep their city vibrant, and remind people that the public coffers are not bottomless. A stronger connection must be made for community development, stronger neighborhoods, lower crime, better housing, a vibrant downtown, and better schools before new ballparks. It might even be easier for opponents to highlight these community trade-offs in cities where advocates have mostly abandoned justifying new stadiums in economic terms. By admitting that new stadiums will not expand the public till, advocates can no longer make arguments that there will soon be enough money for new stadiums, and new libraries, and new public schools.

Thus, opponents must force a public realization that there are actual choices to be made about which of these amenities contributes most to enhancing urban life. At the moment, popular perceptions have been successfully manipulated to equate a major league city with major league sports played in fancy new stadiums. But this is not an inevitable connection, even though it will be hard to change. The consequences of current social policies are becoming more evident in many cities. As mentioned earlier, Cleveland's public schools have the lowest graduation rate of any city in Ohio despite having two relatively new stadiums (and a new arena). Just months after Cincinnati opened a new football stadium, and just prior to unveiling a new baseball stadium, the city erupted in a wave of ugly racial unrest sparked by the alleged brutality of a white police officer on a black citizen—in a neighborhood that was supposed to bathe in the largesse of social policies that finance new stadiums with public money (see also Smith and Ingham 2003).

Conclusion

Social scientists are practically unanimous in challenging the alleged community benefits created by new publicly financed stadiums. An increasing number of urban residents demonstrate skepticism, and often hostility, toward diverting scarce social resources away from more pressing needs. Nevertheless, despite this scientific criticism and grass roots skepticism, new stadiums continue being built with accompanying promises that they will solve a host of urban social problems. Our emphasis on the structure and strength of local growth coalitions sheds light on how and why this is happening. The most organized and powerful coalitions are able to transcend allegations of corporate welfare by taking the lead in stadium initiatives, thus allowing local team owners to play far less visible roles. These coalitions can more easily portray their interest in publicly financed stadiums as wearing their civic hats or trying to keep their city major league. In cities with weak coalitions, where the teams assume a more central role in stadium initiatives, there are often more obstacles to diverting social resources away from other urban needs.

Our emphasis on growth coalitions raises some troublesome questions about the state of democracy in American cities. These questions go beyond those explored by previous research where the focus is on greedy team owners shaking down city governments to spend public money on new stadiums rather than on, say, public education. We disagree with the assumption that local government is a neutral party that sometimes gets extorted by local sports teams or local growth coalitions. Instead, the default position of local governments (with only rare exceptions) is to believe in the wonders of publicly subsidized sports stadiums. Consequently, growth coalitions and sports teams are less likely to play the relocation card now than they were ten years ago. It is simply not necessary anymore. Local governments will act as if this threat exists, even when there is no threat. In Minnesota, for example, a governor actually advised a team owner that he should threaten to leave the city to heighten hysteria and increase support for a new stadium (Weiner 2000). This is not a team extorting a government, but a government acting in coalition with the interests of the local corporate community and, by definition, the interests of the local team owners.

From our perspective, the causes of this coalition are both political (e.g., influenced by lobbying and campaign donations) but also extra-political in the sense that many politicians have come to share in the vision of creating a tourist economy with publicly subsidized enticements to tourists to visit their city (Judd and Fainstein 1999; Friedman, Andrews, and Silk 2004). Our research suggests that these publicly subsidized sports stadiums serve the interests of the entire local corporate community and not just the parochial interests of the local sports teams, with government serving as a symbolically important rubber stamp. It's not that unusually strong organizations (including but not limited to sports teams) present an episodic challenge to local democratic institutions. Instead, corporate-dominated, local growth coalitions pose a more systemic challenge to democratic institutions, and stadium funding is perhaps the latest, most visible example of this institutionalized power.[3] We believe that using public dollars for private stadiums ends up transferring social resources from the not-so-powerful to the already powerful, much like policies that funnel huge amounts of resources toward punitive forms of internal social control (i.e., prisons) and external social control (i.e., the military). All told, such policies will continue exacerbating rather than alleviating the staggering levels of inequality in the United States, especially within its cities. If the payoff from massive investment in new stadiums doesn't produce its promised economic turnaround, urban schools will continue to deteriorate, city dwellers will continue looking to the underground economy for survival, and basic health care will continue being inaccessible to an increasing percentage of city residents. Meanwhile, billions of dollars of public money continue to be spent on stadiums that increase the wealth of team owners and other local corporate chieftains while entertaining the suburbanites and tourists who can afford tickets to the games. It may be hard work to articulate an alternative vision of a "major league city" that places the needs of residents first, but it is work that needs to be done.

Endnotes

[1]Authors' analysis of data from National Center for Education Statistics and Ohio Dept. of Education, using adjusted expenditure per pupil data and yearly dropout rate data. For the 2002–3 year, the graduation rate for the Akron district was 74.8% while for Cleveland the rate was 39.4%. Akron did have an "overall performance record" (which takes into test scores across all grade levels conducting state testing) slightly below Cleveland in 2002–3. In sum, though, it is difficult to argue that the revenues created by stadiums have enhanced the Cleveland public schools.

[2]Greater Philadelphia First no longer exists after merging with the local Chamber of Commerce in 2003.

[3]This systemic bias should not be read as inevitability. In fact, some recent events suggest that representative democracy might have another life. The mayor of Dallas (2004)

and the Washington DC City Council (2005–06) have both demonstrated unprecedented political resistance to stadium initiatives.

References

Adams, B. (1998). Cleveland: The partnership city. In Adams, B., & Parr, J. (Eds.), *Boundary crossers: Case studies of how ten of America's metropolitan regions work.* College Park, MD: Academy of Leadership.

Austrian, Z & Rosentraub, M. (2002) Cities, sports, and economic change: a retrospectiveassessment. *Journal of Urban Affairs*, 24: 549–63.

Agostini, S., Quigley, J., & Smolensky, E. (1997). Stickball in San Francisco. In Noll, R. and Zimbalist, A. (Eds.), *Sports, jobs, and taxes: The economic impact of sports teams and stadiums.* Washington, DC: Brookings Institutions Press.

Baade, R. (1996). Sports as a catalyst for metropolitan economic development. *Journal of Urban Affairs*, 18, 1–17.

Baade, R.,& Dye, R., (1990). The impact of stadiums and professional sports on metropolitan area development. *Growth and Change*, Spring: 1–14.

Bandow, D. (2003). *Surprise: stadiums don't pay after all.* Washington DC: Cato Institute.

Blair, J., & Swindell, D., (1997). Sports, politics and economics: The Cincinnati story. In Noll, R. and Zimbalist, A. (Eds.), *Sports, jobs, and taxes: The economic impact of sports teams and stadiums.* Washington, DC: Brookings Institutions Press.

Cagan, J., & DeMause, N. (1998). *Field of schemes.* Boston: Common Courage Press.

Chapin, T. (2004). Sports facilities as urban redevelopment catalysts. *Journal of the American Planning Association*, 70: 193–209.

Curry, T., Schwirian, K, and Woldoff, R. (2004). *High stakes: Big time sports and downtown redevelopment.* Columbus: Ohio State University Press.

Coates, D., & Humphreys, D. (2000). *The stadium gambit and economic development.* Regulation, 23, 15–20.

Costas, B. (2000). *Fair Ball: A Fan's Case for Baseball.* NY: Broadway Books.

Delaney, K., & Eckstein, R. (2003a). *Public Dollars, Private Stadiums.* New Brunswick: Rutgers University Press.

Delaney, K., & Eckstein, R. (2003b). The devil is in the details: Neutralizing critical studies of publicly subsidized stadiums. *Critical Sociology*, 29: 189–210.

Drier, P., Swanstrom, T., & Mollenkompf, J. (2001). *Place matters: Metropolitics for the twenty-first century.* Lawrence, KS: Univ. Press of Kansas.

Eckstein, R. (1997). *Nuclear Power and Social Power.* Philadelphia: Temple University Press.

Eckstein, R., & Delaney, K. (2002). New sports stadiums, community self esteem, and community collective conscience. *Journal of Sport and Social Issues*, 26: 235–47.

Edin, K., & Lein, L. (1997). *Making ends meet: How single mothers survive welfare and low-wage work.* NY: Russell Sage Foundation.

Euchner, C. (1993). *Playing the field: Why sports teams move and cities fight to keep them.* Baltimore: Johns Hopkins University Press.

Friedland, R., & Palmer, D. (1984). Park place and main street: Business and the urban power structure. " *Annual Review of Sociology*, 10, 395–416.

Friedman, M., Andrews, D., & Silk, M. (2004). Sport and the facade of redevelopment in the postindustrial city. *Sociology of Sport Journal*, 21, 119–134.

Ingham, A., Howell, , J., & Schilperoort, T. (1987). Professional sports and community: A review and exegesis. *Exercise and Sports Sciences Review*, 15, 427–465.

Jargowsky, P. (1996). Take the money and run: economic segregation in U.S. metropolitan areas. *American Sociological Review*, 61, 984–998.

Jargowsky, P. (2002). Sprawl, concentration of poverty, and urban inequality. In Squires, G. (ed.), *Urban sprawl: Causes, consequences, and policy responses*. Wash. DC: Urban Institute.

Judd, D., & Fainstein, S. (1999). *The Tourist City*. New Haven: Yale University Press.

Keating, R. (1999) Sports pork: The costly relationship between major league sports and government." Cato Institute: Cato Policy Analysis No. 339.

Keating, D.W. (1997). Cleveland, the "comeback city": The politics of redevelopment and sports stadiums amidst urban decline. In Lauria, M. (ed.), *Reconstructing urban regime theory: Regulating urban politics in a global economy*. Thousand Oaks, CA: Sage.

Kissane, R. (2003). What's need got to do with it? Why poor women do not use nonprofit social services." *Journal of Sociology and Social Welfare*, 30,127–148.

Kozol, J. (2005). *The shame of the nation*. New York: Random House

Lauria, M. (1997). *Reconstructing urban regime theory: Regulating urban politics in a global economy*. Thousand Oaks, CA: Sage Publications.

Logan, J., & Molotch, H. (1987). *Urban Fortunes*. Berkeley: University of California Press.

Lucas, S. (1999). *Tracking inequality: Stratification and mobility in American high schools*. New York: Teachers College Press.

Massey, D., & Denton, N. (1998). *American apartheid: Segregation and the making of the underclass*. Cambridge, MA: Harvard University Press.

Mollenkopf, J. (1983). *The contested city*. Princeton: Princeton University Press.

Molotch, H. (1976). The city as a growth machine. *American Journal of Sociology*, 82, 309–330.

Noll, R., & Zimbalist, A. (1997). Build the stadium-create the jobs! In Noll, R., & Zimbalist, A. (Eds.), *Sports, jobs, and taxes*. Washington, DC: Brookings Institute.

Rosentraub, M. (1997). *Major league losers: The real costs of sports and who's paying for it*. New York: Basic Books.

Santo, C. (2005). The economic impact of sports stadiums: recasting the analysis in context. *Journal of Urban Affairs*, 27: 177–91.

Scherer, J., & Jackson, S. (2004). From corporate welfare to national interest: Newspaper analysis of the public subsidization of NHL hockey debate in Canada. *Sociology of Sport Journal*, 21, 36–60.

Schimmel, K. (2002). The political economy of place: Urban and sports studies perspectives In J. McGuire & K. Young (Eds.), *Theory, sport, and society* (pp. 335–351). London: Elsevier Science

Shropshire, K. (1995). *The sports franchise game: Cities in pursuit of sports franchises, events, stadiums, and arenas*. Philadelphia, PA: University of Pennsylvania Press.

Smith, J., & Ingham, A. (2003) On the waterfront: Retrospectives on the relationship of sports and communities. *Sociology of Sport Journal*, 20, 252–274.

Spirou, C., & Bennett, L. (2003). *It's hardly sportin': Neighborhoods and the new Chicago*. DeKalb: Northern Illinois University Press.

Squires, G., & O'Connor, S. (2002). *Color and money: Politics and prospects for community reinvestment in urban America*. Albany: SUNY Press.

Swanstrom, T. (1985). *The crisis of growth politics: Cleveland, Kucinich, and the challenge of urban populism*. Philadelphia: Temple University Press.

Troutman, P. (2004) A growth machine's plan B: legitimating development when the value-free growth ideology is under fire. *Journal of Urban Affairs*, 26: 611–22.

Tu, C. (2005). How does a new sports stadium affect housing values? *Land Economics*, 81: 379–95.

Weiner, J. (2000). *Stadium games*. Minneapolis: University of Minnesota Press.

Whitt, J. A. (1982). *Urban elites and mass transportation: The dialectics of power*. Princeton, NJ: Princeton University Press.

Wilson, W. J. (1996). *When work disappears: The world of the new urban poor*. New York: Knopf.

Zimbalist, A. (1998) *The economics of stadiums, teams and cities*. Policy Studies Review 15:17–29.

Zimbalist, A. (2003). *May the best team win: Baseball economics and public policy*. Washington DC: Brookings.

Just like Cleveland, Only Worse: Response to Delaney and Eckstein's "Local Growth Coalitions, Publicly Subsidized Sports Stadiums, and Social Inequality"

Greta Eleen Pennell
University of Indianapolis

When the editors of this volume first asked me to write a response to Delaney and Eckstein's article I hesitated because I was unsure what insights or new sociological arguments I could add. Should I use this opportunity to enter the debate regarding the explanatory power of "local growth coalitions" relative to competing ideas such as "growth machines" or "urban regimes" (c.f. Collins 2005; Domhoff 2005)? Or perhaps I should play devil's advocate and highlight potential "trickle down" benefits afforded by using public dollars for stadium construction, thereby mapping additional avenues for further research.

Ultimately, I decided that further parsing the nuances between competing theories or setting up advocacy studies as straw men would, quite simply, miss the point. In the tradition advanced by one of AHS's founders, Alfred McClung Lee (1988), Delaney and Eckstein's work challenges us to put our sociological imaginations to work with the aim of making life more livable for all people rather than just the powerful and well-connected. With that in mind, it seemed appropriate that this rejoinder have a similar aim. Therefore, I begin by recounting what has transpired in my own city in order to illustrate how Delaney and Eckstein's findings can be used to understand and confront the challenges local growth coalitions pose to the common good.

I live in a world-class city, but it wasn't always this way. Despite being home to the "greatest spectacle in racing," the second-oldest minor league baseball franchise in professional sports, and state capital of "Hoosier Hysteria" fueled by the legacies of basketball greats Oscar Robertson, Bobby Knight, Larry Bird, and three-time American Basketball Association (ABA) champions, the Indianapolis Pacers; these celebrated sporting venues, events and the thousands of visitors they brought to the city,[1] simply weren't enough to really put Indianapolis on the map. PR efforts to raise the city's profile with catchy taglines like "Move over New York, Apple is our middle name" were (predictably) ineffective. My town might sit at the "Crossroads of America," but it was still "India-No-Place."

Then, on a cold, snowy night in 1984, our fortune changed with the arrival of several moving vans. The groundwork laid five years earlier by community leaders had paid off. The Indianapolis Colts came to town, and the city was transformed overnight from Naptown to a real "Major League City." The designation as World Class, however, would take a little longer, and cost considerably more.

Over the next twenty years, pride of place became inextricably linked with the city's distinction as the home of the Indianapolis Colts. When the team actually started posting more wins than losses and making successful runs at division titles and championships, fan fever spread throughout all economic segments of the city and much of the state. Colts blue was used to re-paint highway overpasses following repairs and the Indiana Blood Center introduced an annual "Bleed Blue" blood drive.[2] The team received the lion's share of the credit for re-establishing downtown Indy as the vibrant, cultural and commercial center of the state. In terms of the city's identity, the notoriety that had come from being home of the Indy 500 paled in comparison to being the place the Colts called home.

Reflecting on this transformation former deputy mayor, David Frick explained, "Sports was an element in our game plan to change the image of the city back in the late 1970's, early 1980's…. It was a community effort involving the major businesses in town, combing with the not-for-profit sector and the government leadership of Indianapolis, and the state itself" (as quoted in Herman 2007). Central to the plan was construction of a state-of-the art stadium that was pitched to the community as a convention center "expansion." However, from the start, right down to its interior blue and silver color scheme, this multi-purpose "auditorium" was designed to entice the Colts franchise. Hailing the Hoosier Dome as a "milestone" and a "catalyst," coalition leaders credited the stadium for changing "the world's perception of the city" (Richards 2008: 6) as well the key to their successful game plan to become a NFL city.

Once the Colts arrived, there was no going back. Bill Benner, spokesman for the Indiana Convention and Visitors Center, clearly drew the connection between Indy's image and the Colts in noting, "When the Colts came here in '84, that sent the message to the nation that we were indeed on a course to succeed in revitalizing, re-energizing, and upgrading our image" (as quoted in Herman 2007). A state senator (and chairman of the Senate Finance committee for more than thirty years) attributed Indianapolis's success to the Colts arrival, stating, "I think the Colts have elevated Indianapolis to a status among some cities in the United States. I don't know if we'll ever reach the plateau of Chicago or New York or San Francisco, but we're a co-equal with the Detroits and maybe Philadelphia and Dallas-Fort Worth" (as quoted in Herman 2007). The implication from all fronts was that clear, continued progress on this path of growth and success would be contingent on keeping the Colts here.

So, in 2002, when rumors surfaced that the Colts might be looking for greener pastures, community leaders took notice. The problem was that the old stadium was "economically obsolete," too small with too few luxury boxes to keep the bottom line sufficiently high. The team's owner lamented that much as he liked Indianapolis, team revenues lagged too far behind that of most other teams in the league.

In response, a new local growth coalition took shape. While some members were also involved in brokering the deal for the first stadium built to lure the Colts here, this coalition was not simply the power elite of days gone by. CEOs of corporate giants such as Eli Lilly and Wellpoint along with reporters and editors of the local newspaper joined forces with public and private college officials, elected officials from both sides of the aisle, directors of various non-profit groups, and radio deejays. In the end representatives from more than 450 groups came together to form the "Colts Business Alliance" in order to broker a new stadium deal to ensure the Colts would stay in Indianapolis and firmly establish Indianapolis as a "World Class" city. Mobilization of a new local growth coalition wasn't surprising.

What was surprising, however, was the speed with which the ensuing initiative for a new stadium, seemingly at any cost to local taxpayers, garnered broad support and ultimately the necessary approvals.

In the race to seal the deal on a new stadium, booster rhetoric ran rampant, bombarding the city and state with examples of how far we'd come and warnings of what we might become—another Baltimore perhaps, should we fail to build the team a new stadium. As one local business owner stated, "I remember what the Downtown was and see what it is now, and I see what it can be. This is just another way to showcase your city. I can't see anything bad about it" (as quoted by Eschbacher 2006). Another key part of the plan was to link the stadium construction to the need for expanded convention center facilities. This helped further broaden the coalition's base, drawing in people who might not care about sporting events, but viewed hosting conventions for large groups like the Southern Baptist Association or Future Farmers of America equally important for cementing our identity as "World Class." During this same time, the Colts organization remained quiet, they did not threaten to leave if the deal didn't go through, nor did they lobby for a new stadium.

In December, 2004 in front of a sold out crowd, Colts owner Jim Irsay and Indianapolis Mayor Bart Peterson proclaimed that a new deal had been reached to keep the Colts in Indianapolis. It included construction of a new $500 million stadium for the team. All but $52 million of which would come from public funds. The agreement also gave all game-day revenue, concessions, income from naming rights for the stadium, and half of all revenue from any other event at the stadium to Irsay as compensation for staying in a small market.[3] DeMause and Cagan (2008) described the arrangement as involving so much public and so little private that the term "partnership" was simply inapplicable.

Almost before the ink was dry on the new deal, cost estimates for the stadium jumped from the initial $500 million to $625 million. By January 2005 projected costs were reported as high as $675 million. Securing funding to build the stadium took center stage, while policies and initiatives for other pressing issues for the public good (i.e., upgrading the city sewer infrastructure, public transportation, environmental protection, and ensuring a sufficient tax base and revenues for schools and subsidized housing) remained in the wings. During this same time period, Indianapolis lost ground on virtually every measure of sustainability, public health or other quality of life indicators. Home to 13 active superfund sites according to the U.S. Environmental Protection Agency (EPA 2009) on one comparative ranking of US cities after another, Indianapolis was at the bottom of the list.

Construction on the stadium began in the summer of 2005 and by June 2007 cost projections were reported between $695.2–$719.6 million (Eschbacher 2007). Stadium construction was completed in 2008 at a final cost generally reported of $720 million. On the heels of the construction cost overrun came news that the operating budget was $20 million, no wait, $47 million dollars short. Apparently, the increased utilities and other variable costs associated with operating a substantially larger stadium hadn't been factored into the budget. In addition, revenues from the new food and beverage taxes levied to help pay for the stadium were coming in under projections as a result of the economic downturn. Finally, to make matters worse, the owners of the Indianapolis Pacers suggested that they too might require a new deal to stay in Indianapolis—something along the lines of excusing them from their $15 million dollar obligation to the city for their use of the field house. So, as the first season in the new stadium got underway, taxpayers learned that that bleeding blue and white just might bleed them dry.

Consistent with Delaney and Eckstein's findings, in the hands of a strong growth coalition, the stadium initiative in Indianapolis, effectively swept questions under the rug, silenced virtually any opposition, and, for all practical purposes gave away the collective store. However, it is important to remember that there were critics, protests and opposition to the stadium deals while they were being brokered. In the early 90's stadium boosters initially met with skepticism if not downright hostility when pitching the Hoosier Dome idea to civic and fraternal groups (Richards 2008). In 1997 a group of taxpayers filed a formal petition with the city council objecting to the use of tax monies to fund professional sports venues in town on the grounds that the expenditures promoted "potentially sexually discriminatory practices" (Falk 1997: D3). In 2004, when it became clear that a new local growth coalition was at work pushing the current stadium deal, activists from various community groups joined forces to ask hard questions about the plan. At the invitation of the Indiana Alliance for Democracy, Delaney and Eckstein came to Indianapolis in 2005 to present their research at a citizen's summit. While well attended by the community, only one city-county councilwoman of the nearly 50 invited elected officials, press, and other coalition members attended. Their offer to conduct an in-depth economic analysis of the deal, at no charge to the city, also fell on deaf ears. With many details of the plan veiled in secrecy, local media outlets as key players in the coalition, and the sense of urgency fueled by mayoral warnings that we couldn't afford to lose our Colts (Tully 2005: April), it was almost impossible for the other side of the story to gain any traction. According to Allen Sanderson, strong coalitions typically put such deals on the fast track "under the political cover of night before the populace catches on to what bad economic deals these type of facilities usually are" (Sanderson as quoted in McNeil 2005: B1). As the local growth coalition grew stronger, voicing opposition or even simply asking questions about the details of the plan was tantamount to sedition.

Delaney and Eckstein's analyses regarding the team's and team owners' roles in such initiatives proved especially prophetic. Throughout the early stages of the stadium deal, the Colts players, staff, and team owners maintained an extremely low profile. Later, as costs and deficits mounted and details of the deal became better reported, the Colts organization issued a letter to fans stating "The Colts never asked for a new stadium... At no time did the Colts threaten to leave Indianapolis or otherwise hold the city hostage" (Indianapolis Colts 2009). Team owner Jim Irsay has stuck with this story, maintaining that he has no intention of re-negotiating the deal or contributing additional monies to the stadium or its operation. Given his original concerns regarding lagging team revenues, recent front page news that Irsay's estimated net worth of $1.1 billion puts him in the company of the 400 richest Americans (Russell 2009) is not going over well at a time of double digit unemployment in the state.

Irsay and his organization clearly understood the importance of staying clear of any appearance of being "greedy" or indulging in "corporate welfare." However, when it comes to diverting public dollars for private interests, appearance often parts company with reality. As the details of just what the public didn't get in the deal (and what Irsay and the Colts organization did) and we could see at what cost the stadium funding came in terms of cuts in funding for parks, grants to support arts and music programs for urban children, and other agencies serving the public good, a subtle but noticeable shift in the discourse occurred. Boosters began to defect, even if only subtly, to the other side. A local sports writing asked in a column uncharacteristically critical of Colts owners, "Why are we pushing ahead to build this thing?" (Kravitz 2004). Another reporter, who previously warned readers that Indianapolis without big-time sports wasn't a pretty picture seemed to realize that without parks and police, the picture was even worse. Questioning if a "cathedral for the NFL gods" was really worth the price, the *Indianapolis Star* reporter wrote, "Nothing is fair when dealing with the NFL... We wait to see what else the Colts can squeeze out of us—on top of the stadium and so many other freebies—at a time when the city is cutting police ranks, park maintenance, street cleaning and more" (Tully 2005: Jul 29, B1). More recently some of the biggest boosters and most visible players in the coalition (i.e., Indianapolis Convention & Visitors Association) have found their own budgets slashed to make up for budgetary shortfalls for the stadium. As a result, some of these boosters have become critics, opening the door for a different kind of growth coalition, one that is at least starting to ask if there are other definitions of what it might mean to be a "world class" city.

While opponents to the stadium deal for the Indianapolis Colts lost the battle, they served to open a whole new front for dissent down the road. Ventures such as privatizing public assistance or the water company or selling off the parks are now being questioned and new coalitions forming in ways that have the potential to expand our civic capacity and encourage collective action in order to "take back the riches stolen by a few" (Pennell 2004).

The ongoing saga in Indianapolis highlights the intangible albeit powerful ways that identity and ideology drive the formation of alliances between otherwise strange bedfellows, as well as the sometimes ephemeral and/or shifting composition of these local coalitions. It is inclusion of these aspects of growth coalitions, along with the recognition that such entities are not always strong or even deeply entrenched that makes Delaney and Eckstein's work so compelling.

From my very first reading of this article, I found Delaney and Eckstein's explanation of weak and strong growth coalitions useful for explaining what had and is still happening in my hometown. Moreover, it provides a useful framework for understanding the role of other local growth coalitions in struggles that less obviously involve land use and public subsidy (i.e., charter schools), but nonetheless serve to exacerbate social, political, and economic inequality. As Delaney and Eckstein note, expanding our definition of what it means to be a "world class city" in order to better ensure that the needs of all residents are met is hard work. It is hard work that not only needs to be done, but is the heart and soul of what constitutes humanist sociology.

Endnotes

[1] Indianapolis has been home to the Indianapolis Motor Speedway and the Indianapolis Indians minor league baseball team since 1902. The Indianapolis Pacers were ABA champions in 1970, 1972, 1973; and joined the NBA in 1976.

[2] Promoting the 2009 blood drive on their website, the Indiana Blood Center proudly proclaims its fan status by acknowledging that "game days aren't for donating blood, they're for watching Colts football" and then connecting the dots between fandom and being a good citizen by reminding donors "that it is the Colts fans who are as committed to their community as they are to bleeding blue for their Indianapolis Colts... support the team and help save a life." (www.indianablood.org/donating/community/sports/Pages/Colts2009.aspx)

[3]The agreement specified that Irsay would pay $100 million toward the stadium's construction. However, the city of Indianapolis had to pay a $48 million "lease termination fee" to Irsay in order to break the contract with the team for play in the old stadium. Revenue from the naming rights total $6 million per year to Irsay. The team does pay $250,000/year in rent to play in the new stadium.

References

DeMause, N. and Cagan, J. (2008). *Field of Schemes: How the Great Stadium Swindle Turns Public Money into Private Profit: Revised and Expanded Edition.* University of Nebraska Press: Lincoln, NE.

Domhoff, W. (2005). Power at the Local Level: Growth Coalition Theory. Retrieved from http://sociology.ucsc.edu/whorulesamerica/local/growth_coalitoin_theory.html

Collins, T. (2005). The Uneven Geography of Downtown Redevelopment: Sources, Processes, and Consequences of Sports Stadium Building. Paper presented at the annual meeting of the American Sociological Association, Marriott Hotel, Loews Philadelphia Hotel, Philadelphia, PA, Aug 12, 2005. Retrieved from http://www.allacademic.com/meta/p21120_index.html

Eschbacher, K. (2006, December 21). Price Tag for Super Bowl? Up to $20M. *Indianapolis Star*.

Eschbacher, K. (2007, June 26). Stadium's Cost Will Rise, But Taxes Won't. *Indianapolis Star*. Retrieved from: docs.newsbank.com/s/Infoweb/aggdocs/Newsbank/11AOA62691-665498/OD-CB57E1DBEAF60

EPA (2009). Superfund Site Information. Retrieved from: http://cfpub.epa.gov/supercpad/cursites

Falk, S (1997, Sept. 26). Taxpayers blast use of funds for projects favoring mostly men. *Indianapolis Star*, D3.

Herman, S. (2007, January 28). "Colts Arrival Transformed Indy into Major Sports City." Associated Press: Record # D8MUGBT00

Indianapolis Colts (2009, April 24). Colts Statement on the CIB. Retrieved 10/4/09 from http://www.colts.com/sub.cfm?page=article7andnews_id=92985b3b-42db-bb6e5-392428ebd567

Kravitz, B. (2004, July 25). Where do you stand, Mr. Irsay? *Indianapolis Star*, p. C1.

McClung Lee, A. (1988). *Sociology for People: Toward a Caring Profession.* Syracuse University Press.

McNeil, M. (2005, Oct. 9). Public had little say on stadium; Residents had lots of chances to voice views, mayor says. *Indianapolis Star*, B1.

Pennell, J. (2004). Light a fuse. On *Songs of Peace and Justice [CD]*. Indianapolis, IN: Rambling Roots Records.

Richards, P. (2008, Aug. 15). The dome that put Indy on the map; Building helped transform a dying Downtown. *Indianapolis Star*, A6.

Russell, J. (2009, October 1). With $1.1B Fortune, Irsay Lands on List of Richest Americans. *Indianapolis Star*, A1.

Tully, M. (2005, June 22). Stadium deal really sweet—for Colts. *Indianapolis Star*, p. B1.

Tully, M. (2005, July 29). New stadium isn't enough to satisfy the Colts. *Indianapolis Star*, p. B1.

3. Sociology, Humanism, and the Environmental Crossroads: Bringing Nature Back In[1]

Anthony E. Ladd
Loyola University, New Orleans
1993 AHS Presidential Address

Reflexive Statement

I have been involved for the past fifteen years in exploring what I see as some of the inherently compatible theoretical linkages between the fields of sociology, philosophy, and ecology. While humanist sociologists, among others, have increasingly turned their attention to environmental issues and problems as an area worthy of academic concern, we have not seriously grappled with the historical and intellectual contradictions between the paradigmatic assumptions that underlie sociology, humanism, and Marxism, and those that facilitate ecological sustainability. While we should continue to embrace the positive thrust of humanism's quest for social emancipation and human dignity, we must also recognize—and transcend—humanism's darker themes of anthropocentrism, dominion, control, exceptionalism, and technocracy. By fostering an ecological praxis that critiques all forms of social domination, and not just those benefiting humans, I argue that we could become mentors of a deeper and profounder humanism that truly speaks to the goals of justice, wisdom, freedom, and community.

Introduction

The theme that I chose for the Association for Humanist Sociology's 1993 annual conference in New Orleans, LA was "Humanity at the Crossroads: Building a New Social Agenda for the Future." In view of our moving from a critical decade into an even more critical century, it was a title that made a lot of sense to me and seemed to very much describe what most of us in AHS are concerned with—building a more progressive and humane social order for present and future generations. As a lover of Robert Johnson's Delta Blues that evolved out of the magical and painful Mississippi River past surrounding us, I found that the title also had another appeal to me. As legend has it, Johnson's most famous song "Crossroads" is based on his journey to a rural intersection to make a pact with the devil; in exchange for his soul, the devil would grant him the power and human abilities to be the

---

[1]This paper originally appeared in *Humanity & Society* Volume 18, Number 2, 1994.

greatest blues player of all time. In real life, of course, Robert Johnson finally did achieve the immortality he sought as the king of the Delta Bluesmen. His early death—reportedly poisoned by a jealous rival—not only seemed to confirm the legend of his pact with the devil, but lived up to the mythical image of every hard-living, hard-loving blues musician from the region.

More than just great music, however, Johnson's blues—like all good parables worth considering—contain some relevant and important lessons for our times. In our quest for human control and power, in our longing for immortality and perfectibility, what will be the price that we, and the rest of the planet, will pay? As we meet tonight to celebrate sociology and the possibilities of the future, perhaps it is worth pondering what may be waiting for us ahead at the crossroads, and what kind of pact—with ourselves and with the earth—will be required to sustain the present course of human events?

To start with, even a cursory diagnosis of the current ecological health of the planet is unlikely to leave most observers feeling very sanguine. During the more than two decades since Earth Day 1970, the world lost 200 million hectares of tree cover, an area the size of the U.S. east of the Mississippi River. Deserts expanded by some 120 million hectares, more land than is currently planted in crops in China. Thousands of plant and animal species with which we shared the planet 20 years ago ceased to exist, as their habitats vanished in the face of development, agricultural expansion, and pollution. Atmospheric concentrations of carbon dioxide, the principal greenhouse gas, increased by 9 percent, while the loss of stratospheric ozone—not even imagined in the 1970's—continued. Moreover, the world's farmers lost 500 billion tons of topsoil through erosion, during the same period in which they were expected to feed an additional 1.6 billion people reproducing at a rate of 90 million a year (Brown 1993). And while I could continue to outline myriad other serious environmental crises facing us, all of them would similarly point to the central dilemma of our age: that we are pursuing an unsustainable path of satisfying our present demands at the expense of future generations. Unlike the Native Americans before us who constructed their world around the wisdom of their ancestors and the needs of generations yet unborn, most contemporary societies seem to be following a course of pillaging the past and pawning the future.

What does our current environmental (and socio-economic) crisis really mean for us? As every sociologist has been trained to understand, comprehending the world we live in today is not simply a function of gaining more facts and knowledge, but developing more relevant theories and paradigms with which to analyze the facts we already have. Socrates was right when he said that we are not so much limited in our ignorance, but rather in our *knowledge* that the world is what we think it "must" be. As sources of "mythic understanding," therefore, the dominant paradigms that we subscribe to constitute the central tenets that capture and mold our worldviews and actions (Drengson 1980: 223).

As humanist sociologists, it is our adherence to the paradigmatic assumptions underlying both sociology and humanism that differentiates us from the wider scientific community to which we belong. In our literature, we proudly declare that:

> We view people not merely as products of social faces, but also as shapers of
> social life, capable of creating social orders in which everyone's potential can
> unfold ...We share a commitment to address all facets of the human condition

in our scholarship and in our practice, and to make sociology more relevant to human needs.

In this commitment to a value-oriented, reflexive, and non-deterministic approach to the study and eradication of social injustices, we have carved out not only a unique identity for ourselves within professional sociology, but more importantly, acted to morally realign the discipline in favor of its original, reformist roots (Flynn 1987; Goodwin 1987). Clearly, we have much to feel good about: while much of sociology seems increasingly preoccupied with the manipulation of human beings to accommodate external agents of power and wealth, we still appear to have our feet planted squarely in the tradition of pursuing a more humane and emancipatory social order through critical praxis and change.

And yet, in terms of addressing the larger global dilemmas to which I referred earlier, I'm unsure whether the sociological/humanistic paradigm provides us with the worldview that we need to move us beyond the crossroads of the late 20th century, whether—if you'll pardon the ecological metaphor—we aren't missing the *forest* for the trees. Developed during an era of exuberant growth when humans seemed exempt from environmental constraints, sociology—along with many other sciences—shares a worldview which "impedes recognition of the societal significance of current ecological realities" (Catton and Dunlap 1980: 15). And though we tend to see humanism as an alternative to the over-rationalized components of sociology, it too saddles us with conceptual blinders that limit our ability to see the ramifications of an earth converted into satisfying the desires and possessions of human beings.

It is not my moot intention to remind you that our paradigms—or anyone else's—cannot be all things to all people, nor can they explain all ills. Indeed, we sociologists have yet to agree on the parameters of our own knowledge base, nor is there agreement on whether we are essentially a core or an integrative discipline in the study of human behavior (Gove 1993). Notwithstanding the inherent limitations of the discipline, as well as our own eclectic complaints and orientations about the shortcomings of sociology, I nevertheless wish to share my thoughts with you about some of the problems and prospects regarding humanist sociology's contributions to our planetary future.

The Unearthly Roots of Western Sociology

The "unearthly" traditions and perspectives of the modern social sciences like sociology stem largely from two interrelated facts: first, the extent to which our paradigms are rooted in anthropocentric Western thought where humans are viewed as separate and "above" nature; and second, the extent to which our discipline evolved during an era of anomalistic abundance and growth when ecological constraints were not salient (Dunlap 1980: 5). Building on the human-centric tenets of Judeo-Christian, Enlightenment, and Mechanistic philosophies, as well as following upon the profound cultural impacts of Europe's economic and technological expansionism into the New World, modern social thought was strongly shaped by the illusion that rapid growth and progress were not only reflective of "natural law," but a normal and perpetual state of affairs. Bolstered further by a seemingly endless supply of resources, fossil fuels, and new technologies, the scientific and industrial revolutions fed an expanding cultural mindset that growth and production could rectify all social ills (Ladd 1987).

These foregoing factors, among others, established among social scientists the assumption that the biophysical environment was virtually irrelevant as a determinant of social life, except as a utilitarian "resource" for human exploitation. Indeed, by the end of the 19th century, the social sciences were underscored by at least two interrelated worldviews, wherein humans were not only dominant over nature, but constituted an "exceptional" species that was largely exempt from the ecological laws regulating other forms of life (Dunlap 1980; Catton and Dunlap 1980).

As argued by Catton and Dunlap (1980: 17–18), the first of these paradigmatic assumptions, the Dominant Western Worldview, can be expressed by the following four beliefs:

1. People are fundamentally different from all other creatures on earth, over which they have dominion.

2. People are masters of their destiny; they can choose their goals and learn to do whatever is necessary to achieve them.

3. The world is vast, and thus provides unlimited opportunities for humans.

4. The history of humanity is one of progress; for every problem there is a solution, and thus progress need never cease.

This anthropocentric set of assumptions, built upon Western social thought from Genesis to Descartes to Locke, provided not only the cornerstones of scientific rationality, but firmly established the technological society as the ultimate conquest of Nature. While patently *regressive* from the ecological perspective, the technocratic vision was conceived of as *progressive* in its call for the continual development and expansion of the artificial environment at the expense of the natural world (Devall and Sessions 1985). As a product of 19th century Europe and early 20th century America, it should be unsurprising that sociology would also embrace this optimistic faith in social progress, views which were particularly prominent in the work of our discipline's founder, Auguste Comte (Timasheff 1967).

Perhaps even more central to the unearthly foundations of sociology, however, were its related beliefs in what has also been termed "human exceptionalism"—the view that humans, by virtue of their culture and technology, only have to adapt nature to human ends, rather than the other way around (Catton and Dunlap 1980: 19–25). Indeed, the growth of the social sciences was tied not only to their ability to distinguish social and cultural environments from biological and physical ones, but to the assumptions that such human mechanisms as institutions, language, intellect, and organization constituted the sufficient means by which Homo Sapiens adapted to the biophysical environment.

In sociology, Catton and Dunlap (1980) argue that the tradition of human exceptionalism was most directly influenced by both the Durkheimian and the social definitional legacies from which the discipline evolved. For Durkheim, of course, sociology was the study of "social facts," those social phenomena such as norms, groups, classes, institutions, etc. that were external and formative to an individual's reality. As *the* subject matter for sociology, Durkheim was emphatic in his view that social facts were *sui generis*, and thus not reducible to non-social facts like psychological, biological, or physical variables. While Durkheim's argument was historically and theoretically critical for establishing the autonomy of social phenomena and their inability to be reduced to psychological states of consciousness, its wider implication was to rule out biophysical variables as external constraints and explanations of human behavior. Packaged in the form of anti-biologism,

Durkheim's antireductionism-of-social-facts tenet also successfully generated a sociological taboo against geographical, hereditary, or environmental determinism in any form; socio-cultural and biophysical environments were thus conceptually distinct and non-reducible to each other (Catton and Dunlap 1980).

The other expression of human exceptionalism in sociology springs from the "social definitional" perspective pioneered by Weber, Mead, Cooley, Thomas, and others. In this tradition, reality is seen as a socially constructed process whereby subjective actors/actresses define the meaning of their worlds and behaviors. Objective environmental and physical properties become relevant therefore only if they are perceived as such by the participants involved. Echoing the Durkheimian perspective, the primacy of the "environment" for humans here becomes largely reduced to not only the "definition of the situation," but also to the sociocultural phenomena surrounding human thought and action (Catton and Dunlap 1980: 22).

Removed from a biophysical world made up of geography, climate, natural resources, animals, plants, and soil, the image of human societies emphasized in these sociological traditions is captured in the following beliefs of the Human Exceptionalist Paradigm (Catton and Dunlap 1980: 24–25):

1. Humans have a cultural heritage in addition to (and distinct from) their genetic inheritance, and thus are quite unlike all other animal species.

2. Social and cultural factors (including technology) are the major determinants of human affairs.

3. Social and cultural environments are the crucial context for human affairs, and the biophysical environment is largely irrelevant.

4. Culture is cumulative; thus technological and social progress can continue indefinitely, making all social problems ultimately soluble.

Thus, in the discipline's quest to establish its own autonomy in relation to the other natural and social sciences, most sociologists, as Catton and Dunlap (1980: 25) argue, "have totally ignored the biophysical environment, as if human societies somehow no longer depend on it for their physical existence and for the means of pursuing the goals they value."

Both the Dominant Western Worldview and the Human Exceptionalist Paradigm reflect, therefore, some 400 years or more of atypical historical patterns and perceptions—an "age of exuberance"—based on the illusions that humans are dominant over nature, that accelerating growth and social progress is an endless possibility, and that human culture and technology is largely exempt from ecological and biophysical constraints.

Regardless of one's particular specialty area today, both our discipline and the wider social sciences continue to be steeped in this set of domain assumptions regarding our place in Nature, as well as our power to transcend its properties.

The Dark Side of Humanism

Many of the same anthropocentric and exceptionalist assumptions underlying sociology and the social sciences also have their roots in the larger philosophy of humanism erected in the 17th century. Bridging the early Christian notions of human dominion over the world with the Enlightenment's quest for scientific rationality, humanism literally replaced the religion of creation with the religion of humanity: a supreme faith in human reason and its ability to rearrange both Nature and people so that humankind will prosper (Ehrenfeld 1978). Tuning the early Greek concept of "hubris" on its head, humanism evolved not only as a supreme belief in human power, control, and transcendence, but out of the assumption that as the center of reality, humans constituted the source of all meaning and value in the universe.

Extending both the Dominant Western/Human Exceptionalist worldviews advanced earlier by Catton and Dunlap, David Ehrenfeld (1978: 16–17) argues that humanism similarly suggests the following five corollaries:

1. All problems are soluble.
2. All problems are soluble by people.
3. Many problems are soluble by technology.
4. Those problems that are not soluble by technology alone have solutions in the social world (of politics, economics, etc.).
5. When the chips are down, we will apply ourselves and work together for a solution before it is too late.

Anthropocentric and technocratic in its outlook, humanism has historically viewed the earth primarily as a collection of natural resources to be used for the needs and desires of human beings. Through the acquisition of knowledge and scientific understanding, humanity now believes that it has the power to ensure its own salvation by recreating the earth in ways that promote human goals and values. By elevating our inventiveness to divine levels and celebrating it as infallible, humanism thus rests on an overriding faith that human civilization will dominate Nature and survive (Ehrenfeld 1978).

Conceiving this doctrine as a Janus-faced creature, philosopher Michael Zimmerman (1985: 135) has argued that humanism contains both a "positive" and a "dark" side. On the one hand, it recognizes the importance of individual freedom and affirms the dignity of humankind; on the other, it also "involves an arrogant human-centeredness that reduces the nonhuman world to the status of a commodity whose only value lies in its usefulness for human purposes." By becoming the source of all value, then, humans deprive everything else of intrinsic worth; by removing themselves from a context of limits, they in turn appear as limitless in what they can achieve. While belief in the nobility and value of humankind and a reasonable respect for our achievements and competencies is highly worthy of our consideration, humanism also serves to protect us from the "darker side of nature," and the darker side of our own self-worship (Ehrenfeld 1978: 7). As Roszak (1973: xxiv) once claimed:

> There are those who believe fervently that the good society may yet be built—
> if only our humanistic resolve is sufficiently strong. I disagree. Humanism
> is the finest flower of urban-industrial society; but the odor of alienation yet
> clings to it and to all culture and public policy that springs from it.

It is also important to view Marxism—like other materialist philosophies of the 19th and 20th centuries—as a form of humanism. Although traditional Marxism offers a viable critique of the positivist underpinnings of Rationality, as well as a passionate attack on commodification and oppression under capitalism, it too departs from the humanist worldview and the technological utopianism of mastering the earth for human ends. While Marx rejected many of the dualistic divisions between humans and Nature, he believed that the latter lacked any value in itself, except that which is objectified by human labor (Zimmerman 1983). Indeed, in his discussion of "man's inorganic body" in the Paris Manuscripts, Marx views nature solely as the "direct means of life," "the material, the object, and the instrument" of the "life activity" of "man" (Marx 1974: 67). Nature, apart from humans, is therefore only necessary as an instrument in the latter's own self-creation and reproduction; reduced to a lifeless system of objects, "Nature becomes its own gravedigger" (Clark 1993: 399).

In the *Grundrisse* (1973), moreover, Marx repeatedly argues that historical progress depends on the continual expansion of the mode of production with Nature as its raw material for labor. As Clark (1984: 105) has pointed out about the technological utopianism inherent in Marx's work:

> For all its evils, capitalism and the system of dehumanizing high technology to which it gave birth are a necessary means toward human liberation. Far from condemning the system of technology which capitalism developed, Marx contends that it must be even further expanded. The failing of capitalism does not lie in the inherent destructiveness and inhumanity of its technology, but in its incapacity to develop further this form of technology. Marx has nothing but disdain for those "utopians" and unscientific socialists who call for the immediate replacement of this technology with less dehumanizing, less manipulative and less hierarchical forms.

Despite Marx's clear denunciation of many of the ecological side-effects of capitalist agriculture and pollution (see Parsons 1977), he not only called for the removal of the fetters on the evolving mode of production, but believed that the process itself constituted the ultimate in the revolutionary liberation of human beings (Clark 1984: 106–115).

Though Engels' *Dialectics of Nature* (1940) clearly warns of the long-term costs of our boastful presumptions that we can conquer and master the earth, Trotsky (1937: 45) himself charged that "Marxism is saturated with the optimism of progress." Notwithstanding recent attempts by Neo-Marxists like O'Connor (1988) and Merchant (1989) to provide an analysis of the dialectical contradictions between capitalist production, nature, and social reproduction, Marxism still explicitly promotes the indomitable spirit of human self realization and development through the subjugation of the natural world (Clark 1993).

As Murray Bookchin (1982) has pointed out, Marxism fails to see that the rise of humanism does not eliminate all forms of domination simply through the elimination of social classes; rather, it tends to legitimize nature's domination under the veil of human emancipation. Similarly, critical of the ecological myopia underlying both capitalist and socialist models, Hazel Henderson (1981) has long argued that we need to shift the focus from the sterile debate over who *controls* the means of production, to the more crucial questions over the *consequences* of the means of production themselves.

Toward a Profounder Humanistic Sociology: Bringing Nature Back In

From the standpoint of theory and practice, then, how do concerned sociologists and humanists like ourselves begin to seriously grapple with the growing contradictions between the domain assumptions that underlie our own intellectual traditions and those that facilitate ecological sustainability? How can we use our skills to best assist in the many ecological battles that must be fought if we are to maintain the planet as a habitat that nurtures life, rather than destroys it? How do we retain the positive thrust of humanism's quest for social emancipation, while at the same time transcend its egocentric and homocentric ethos? As we stand at the environmental crossroads of the late 20th century, how do we find a way—as Joni Mitchell put it—back to the garden?

To begin to escape from our anthropocentric baggage of the past few centuries, we must first start to shift away from many of our theoretical tenets based on dominion and exceptionalism and move toward what Catton and Dunlap (1980: 33–34) term a "New Environmental Paradigm," a worldview that:

1. Stresses the interdependence of all life in our global ecosystem.

2. Acknowledges that human affairs are heavily influenced by social and cultural forces, but also stresses our relationship to the biophysical environment and the serious limitations it imposes on us.

3. Recognizes that no matter how inventive we humans tray be, our science, technology, and rationality cannot repeal ecological and thermodynamic laws; that despite our exuberant past, there are limits to the growth and sustainability of human societies.

Clearly, such a paradigm shift could lead to dramatic differences regarding the kinds of issues we deem worthy of investigation, the way we methodologically approach and practice our craft, and the kinds of educational curricula we might develop. It could serve to integrate traditional sociological concerns like class, race, gender, political economy, movements, culture, epistemology, and social constructionism into a broader, more synthetic framework. It could facilitate the recognition that nearly all our present ecological problems arise from deep-seated social conflicts, that the roots of the domination of nature he in the hierarchical domination of humans by humans, and that the future of life on this planet—like it or not—pivots on the future of society (Bookchin 1993). As we stand at a point in history in which the course of planetary evolution is being reversed, an ecologically transformed educational agenda would also help our students grasp an awareness of the connections between the nature of the earth's evolution, ecological integrity, cultural particularity, and personal uniqueness (Berry 1988; Clark 1984). By fostering an educational praxis that calls for the liberation of *all* species of life from social domination, and not just self-conscious creatures with two legs, we become mentors of not only a deeper humanism, but a more universal cosmology promoting freedom, justice, wisdom, and community.

Beyond our own classrooms and offices, such a worldview would serve to reconnect us to some of our colleagues in the natural sciences and humanities so that we could witness the revolutionary ways in which almost every traditional mode of intellectual inquiry is being transformed today by ecological constructs. Long committed to learning more and more about less and less, our current crisis calls all of us in the academy to check our egos at the door, pool our knowledge bases, and develop multidisciplinary solutions to multilateral global problems. In our Cartesian, mechanistic past, our duty as scientists was to dismantle the world into a set of fragmented objects; now we are at an historical turning point where our task must be to reassemble it again into an holistic system of organic, interconnected relationships (Capra 1982).

Returning to our own backyard for a moment, Gerhard Lenski (1986) has long urged sociology to utilize an ecological and evolutionary perspective in the study of human societies. Such a focus, he argues, would first of all compel us to pay closer attention to the dependence of human populations on the biophysical environment and its vital resource base. Secondly, an evolutionary/ecological perspective would allow us to view our current hemispheric problems in terms of the historical circumstances and colonial legacy inherited from our western European past. Third, the above contexts would restrain us from attempting to generalize too quickly or optimistically about the future direction of the planet based on the fortuity of the U.S. experience. We cannot, Lenski warns us, predict the next 200 years—or even the next two decades—based on our unique resource/population anomalies of the past two centuries. Moreover, Laska (1993) has recently observed that environmental sociology in particular offers our wider discipline a very useful vehicle for surmounting some of the criticisms concerning our intellectual core, fragmentation, integrity, and relevancy.

Reconceptualizing the construct of the "environment" for sociology will increasingly become critical if our profession is to play an activist role in solving the myriad problems inherent to societal-nature interactions.

Toward this end, let us take some cues from the work of Martin Heidegger, who not only provided a coherent critique of the ontological basis of anthropocentric humanism but offered us a *profounder* kind of humanism to emulate. For Heidegger, the environmental crisis reflects the way we understand who we are, that is, our view of ourselves as independent ego-subjects who identify with their cravings and desires and view Nature as an object to be dominated. We tend to think that we fulfill our highest possibilities by turning the world into yet another object to be devoured for our ends. But for Heidegger, our higher possibilities lie not in our domination of things, but instead in our stewardship of them where we simply "let them be" (Zimmerman 1985: 141–147). Despite the challenge that this ethic poses for object-driven and action-oriented humans, the secular disenchantment of the world cannot long continue. Heidegger's message is that our humanism will fail to *fulfill* human life, if it is blind to what *transcends* human life (Zimmerman 1983; 1993).

Almost 30 years ago, George C. Homans (1964) attacked the overly abstracted and analytical nature of social thought and called for "Bringing Men Back In" to our models of human behavior. Today, increasing numbers of environmental sociologists, ecological philosophers, process theologians, quantum physicists, and many others are similarly calling for "bringing Nature back in" to the models that attempt to understand the human community's relationship to the larger universe in which it resides. Though our recent experiment with industrial modernity has been typified by the refusal to acknowledge the reality of ecological constraints on human societies, our future will largely depend upon the catastrophic necessity of recognizing and readapting to such limits (Schnaiberg and Gould 1994: 31).

Contrary to our self-assertions since Candide, humans are "neither the measurer nor the measure" of all things, because the nature of value in the world *is* the value of Nature and its biogenic properties (Ralston 1993: 143). As humanist scholars and activists, then, let us be resolved to continue our work in building a new social agenda for the next century, one that can liberate both the dignity of individuals and the collective dreams of the masses from the social forces that thwart human potential. In so doing, however, let us first embark upon the wider task of freeing ourselves from an outdated worldview that, in the name of human emancipation, may actually exhaust the earth's resources on which such hopes depend.

References

Berry. Thomas. 1988. *The Dream of the Earth*. San Francisco: Sierra Club Books.

Bookchin. Murray. 1993. "What is Social Ecology" Pp. 354–373 in *Environmental Philosophy: From Animal Rights to Radical Ecology*. Edited by Michael E Zimmerman. J. Baird Callicott. George Sessions. Karen J. Warren. And John Clark. Englewood Cliffs. N.J.: Prentice-Hall, Inc.

_____. 1982. *The Ecology of Freedom*. Palo Alto, CA.: Cheshire Murray Books, Inc.

Brown, Lester R. 1993. "A New Era Unfolds." Pp. 3–21 in *State of the World 1993*, edited by Lester R Brown et al. New York: W. W. Norton and Co.

Capra, Fritjof. 1982. *The Turning Point: Science, Society and the Rising Culture*. New York: Simon and Schuster.

Catton, William R and Riley E. Dunlap.1980. "A New Ecological Paradigm for Post-Exuberant Sociology." *American Behavioral Scientist* 24:15–47.

Clark, John. 1993. "Marx's Inorganic Body." Pp 390–405 in *Environmental Philosophy: From Animal Rights to Radical Ecology*, edited by Michael E. Zimmerman, J. Baird Callicott, George Sessions, Karen J. Warren, and John Clark. Englewood Cliffs. N.J.: Prentice-Hall, Inc.

_____. 1984. *The Anarchist Moment: Reflections on Culture, Nature and Power*. Montreal: Black Rose Books.

Devall, Bill and George Sessions. 1985. *Deep Ecology. Living as if Nature Mattered*. Salt Lake City, Utah: Gibbs M. Smith, Inc.

Drengson, Alan R. 1980. "Shifting Paradigms: from the Technocratic to the Person-Planetary." *Environmental Ethics* 2: 221–240.

Dunlap, Riley E.1980. "Paradigmatic Change in Social Science: From Human Exceptions to an Ecological Paradigm:" *American Behavioral Scientist* 24: 5–14.

Ehrenfeld, David. 1978. *The Arrogance of Humanism*. New York: Oxford University Press.

Engels, Frederick. 1940. *Dialectics of Nature*. Edited by Clemens Dutt. New York: International Publishers.

Flynn, Charles P.1987. "Humanist Sociology and the Love Project: Some Basic Assumptions and Implications for Teaching." Pp. 15–17 in *The Humanist Sociology Resource Book*, edited by Martin D. Schwartz. Washington, D.C. ASA Teaching Resources Center.

Goodwin. Glenn A. 1987. "Toward the Articulation of a Humanist Perspective and the Teaching of Sociology." Pp. 4–8 in *The Humanist Sociology Resource Book*, edited by Martin D. Schwartz. Washington, D.C. ASA Teaching Resources Center.

Gove, Walter R. 1993. "President's Message." *The Southern Sociologist*, 25: 1–4.

Henderson, Hazel. 1981. *The Politics of the Solar Age: Alternatives to Economics*. Garden City. N.Y.: Anchor Books.

Homans, George C. 1964. "Bringing Men Back In." *American Sociological Review* 29: 809–818.

Ladd, Anthony E. 1987. "The Era of Living Dangerously: Illusions of Salvation in the Republic of Technology." *Humanity and Society* 11: 302–314.

Laska, Shirley Bradway. 1993. "Environmental Sociology and the State of the Discipline," *Social Forces* 72: 1–17.

Lenski, Gerhard. 1986. "The Garden of Eden Revisited: Resource Depletion in Ecological and Evolutionary Perspective." Pp. 14 in *Resource Dependency*, edited by Marvin Olsen. Washington. D.C.: ASA Environment and Society Section.

Marx, Karl. 1974. *Economic and Philosophical Manuscripts of 1844*. Moscow: Progress Publishers.

_____. 1973. *Grundrisse: Foundations of the Critique of Political Economy*. New York: Vintage Books.

Merchant, Carolyn. 1989. *Ecological Revolutions: Native, Gender, and Science in New England*. Chapel Hill: University of North Carolina Press.

O'Conner, James. 1998. "Capitalism, Nature, Socialism: A Theoretical Introduction." *Capitalism, Nature, Socialism* 1:11–38.

Parsons, Howard. (ed.)1977. *Marx and Engels on Ecology*. Westport, CT: Greenwood Press.

Rolston III, Holmes. 1993. "Challenges in Environmental Ethics." Pp.135–157 in *Environmental Philosophy: From Animal Rights to Radical Ecology*. edited by Michael E. Zimmerman, J. Baird Callicott, George Sessions, Karen J. Warren, and John Clark. Englewood Cliffs, NJ.: Prentice-Hall, Inc.

Roszak, Theodore. 1973. *Where the Wasteland Ends*. New York: Anchor Books.

Schnaiberg, Allan and Kenneth Alan Gould. 1994. *Environment and Society: The Enduring Conflict*. New York: St. Martin's Press.

Timasheff, Nicholas S. 1967. *Sociological Theory: Its Nature and Growth*. New York: Random House.

Trotsky, Leon. 1937. *The Revolution Betrayed*. Garden City, N.Y.: Doubleday Co.

Zimmerman, Michael E. 1993. "Rethinking the Heidegger-Deep Ecology Relationship." *Environmental Ethics* 15:195–224.

_____ . 1985. "Anthropocentric Humanism and the Arms Race." Pp. 135–149 in *Nuclear War; Philosophical Perspectives*, edited by Michael Fox and Leo Groarke. New York: Peter Lang.

_____ . 1983. "Humanism, Ontology, and the Nuclear Amts Race." *Research in Philosophy and Technology* 6: 157–172.

Toward The New Social Agenda: A Commentary on Ladd's "Sociology, Humanism, and the Environmental Crossroads"[1]

Tim Maher
University of Indianapolis

In many ways, Anthony Ladd's presidential address on the absence of an environmental consciousness in the histories of both Sociology and Humanism is still quite timely and appropriate ten years after originally presented. While some things have certainly changed in that decade, and a sociologically inspired literature has emerged (particularly in environmental racism/environmental justice), both Sociology and Humanism still struggle with how to incorporate the natural environment with the human and social environments.

Sometimes, however, an absence of clearly articulated relationships can have serious social consequences. People may fail to act because adequate guides to action are incomplete or absent altogether. In the case of sociology and the environment, the lack of such theoretical ties clearly contributed to a significant lapse in the Civil Rights Movement. Social scientists were consistently in the forefront of the movement, from W.E.B. DuBois onward. Legal protections in many areas of social life emerged from the decades long struggle. While the 1960's saw great strides in the social arena, exactly the opposite was happening in the area of the environment. Poor people, African-Americans included, always had been relegated to the least desirable land. With the rise of advanced industrialization, however, "undesirable" came to include the toxic by-products of industry and government. At the height of civil rights achievements, these victories were being silently snatched away through policies and practices driven by environmental racism. Nearly all of this occurred outside the awareness of most people, even those ultimately most devastated. While African Americans were gradually able to gain entrance to good schools and rewarding occupations, their communities continued being targeted for the disposal of the worst of society's toxic wastes (Bullard, 1993; Maher, 1998). These chemical contaminants sapped the health of individuals and whole communities, in many ways nullifying earlier gains in education and employment.

While civil rights expanded, a more insidious form of racism continued out of the view of social scientists. Social science theories failed to include such issues and, as a result, did not draw attention to corporate and governmental practices that consciously and deliberately targeted African American, Latino, Native American, and other low-income

---

[1]This paper originally appeared in *Humanity & Society* Volume 27, Number 4, 2003.

communities for poisonous dumping. Social science was not part of the solution but rather part of the problem.

Even now, it may not be sociologists and humanists that force the conceptual transformation. The anti-globalist movement, so ironically (and necessarily) global in character, is simultaneously challenging both social as well as environmental relationships (Martes 2004; Notes From Nowhere 2003). The anti-NAFTA movement brought labor and environmental movements together and in the process provided a critique of global capitalism and its antipathy toward people and the environment. In many ways the conceptual integration that both sociology and humanism desperately need is being written in such direct action, an imperfect praxis where theory may be more tentative than the action.

It is perhaps also being written in the fundamentalist Islamic rejection of Western culture and practices. Such theological critiques focus more on the West's conspicuous consumption than on its accompanying environmental destruction. Ironic again that this violent rejection of global capitalism comes from the heart of the oil fields that literally provide its fuel.

As sociologists, it is our responsibility to identify these core relationships among the natural, social, and human environments. A broadly humane and environmentally balanced society may yet emerge from the chaos and anarchy that seem to be taking hold in many parts of the world. While it has taken decades to coalesce into a "movement," the anti-global forces are now taken quite seriously. Likewise in earlier times, leaders in the West viewed Islamic fundamentalists as culturally backward but never as a real threat to our culture of conspicuous consumption. Now many of our basic rights have been taken away under the guise of countering this supposedly menacing threat.

Anthony Ladd's plea to bring the environment into sociological thinking needs to be taken seriously. Ten years ago his was an important voice, a critical warning. Today the issue is no longer academic. Without an integrated vision linking humane treatment of each other with humane treatment of the planet, the future may be written entirely by the clash of Western capitalism and fundamentalist Islam, leaving both humanism and the environment by the wayside.

It is time to recognize that society and the environment are inextricably linked. Pretending they are separate and distinct does not make them so. Pretending they are separate and distinct only diminishes our sociological possibilities and our true humanity.

References

Bullard, R. D. 1993. *Confronting Environmental Racism.* Boston: South End Press.

Ladd, Anthony. 1994. "Sociology, Humanism, and the Environmental Crossroads: Bringing Nature Back In." *Humanity & Society.* Volume 18, Number 2: 49–60.

Maher, Timothy. 1998. "Environmental Oppression: Who Is Targeted for Toxic Exposure?" *Journal of Black Studies.* Volume 28, Number 3: 357–367.

Mertes, Tom (ed.) 2004. *A Movement of Movements: Is Another World Really Possible?* New York: Verso.

Notes From Nowhere (ed.). 2003. *We Are Everywhere: the irresistible rise of global anticapitalism.* New York: Verso.

4. National Voluntary Service: A Humanist Alternative[1]

Jerold M. Starr and G. David Curry
West Virginia University

Reflexive Statement

There was a time in our lives when one of us felt that the best expression of active citizenship was to serve in the U.S. military during the Vietnam War while the other felt it was to protest the war and support relief efforts for the Vietnamese. These days we both are committed to peace and still committed to active citizenship. We personally support the promise of national voluntary service to provide job training and placement for poor youth and promote an ethic of collective responsibility for middle class youth. We are particularly concerned, however, that such a program, consistent with humanist principles, be people-centered, egalitarian and designed and administered in such a way as to maximize potential benefits for both the volunteers and service organizations.

Introduction

On October 24, 1990, the U.S. Congress passed the $287 million National and Community Service Act of 1990 and sent it to President Bush. The President had agreed to drop his opposition to stipends for young people in full-time civilian service projects in exchange for an approximately 60 percent reduction in funding. Bush then refused to sign the bill until Congress conceded him authority to nominate the 21 persons who are to administer the program. In February 1991, Congress passed the necessary technical amendments, but Bush took several months to submit any nominations for approval. The conflicts surrounding this bill are but the latest in a process that has been ongoing for six years.

In May 1985, the Ford Foundation brought together the directors of some thirty state and city youth-service programs to consider the possibility of a national youth service. Ford subsequently spent more than $1 million on various feasibility studies. Over the same period, no fewer than ten major national voluntary service bills were introduced in Congress. In fall 1989, all such bills were withdrawn in favor of Senator Edward M. Kennedy's $330 million "Service to America Act." President Bush then put forward his own $25 million Youth Engaged in Service to America or "Points of Lights Initiative" proposal. Eventually, liberal Democrat Kennedy and conservative Republican Orrin Hatch worked together to fashion a bill both Congress and the White House would pass.

---

[1]This paper originally appeared in *Humanity & Society* Volume 16, Number 3, 1992.

Continued controversy over the design and administration of the National and Community Service Act of 1990 can be expected. The issues involved are of special concern to humanists. Here we examine six questions that we feel are central to the debate over national service: (1) Who would be eligible? (2) Would such service be voluntary or mandatory? (3) What would participants be qualified and/or trained to do? (4) Which community needs would be served (especially as regards military vs. civilian service)? (5) How would participants be rewarded? And (6) How would the program be financed? We will conclude with some comments on the need for youth service programs in our own state and on the special role that sociologists can play in enhancing the success potential of such programs.

National Voluntary Service and Humanist Principles

In *Toward a Humanist Sociology,* Lee (1973) compares and contrasts three paradigms of sociology. They are distinguished primarily by their attitude toward method and the purpose of their research. The "managerial-bureaucratic" paradigm uses complex quantitative methods to serve the "functional" needs of elites who manage and manipulate the "equilibrating social order." The "problematic-technical" paradigm, exemplified by the Chicago School's approach to social problems, can be both elitist-manipulative and democratic-humanist in orientation. The practitioners of this approach accept quantification only when it appears practical for analyzing and reporting the evidence. However, when confronted with "embarrassing data involving the concerns of important vested interests," such sociologists revert to a discussion of research technique (Lee 1973: 128). They are not bureaucrats, but they are technicians.

In contrast, the humanist sociologist must "face as fully as we are able the relevant implications...of social control, conflict, and exploitation" (Lee 1973: 129). The goal of humanist sociology is "to serve the needs of [people] rather than to aid the manipulations of present elites and future tyrants..." (Lee 1973: 201).

In *Sociology for Whom?,* Lee (1978: 94) more fully explicates the paradigm of humanist sociology. What characterizes humanist sociology is that it is people-centered, egalitarian and broadly representative, ethical, critical of the status quo, dedicated to social change, and performed by sociologists who accept personal responsibility for creative intellectual work. Such work should be informed by theory. But it also should be applied to the problems of real people. To restate the issue in the terms of C. Wright Mills (1959), humanist sociologists are not primarily concerned with methodological or theoretical problems, as defined by the discipline's bureaucrats and technicians. Nor are they concerned with "social problems" as defined by society's elite consensus managers. Rather, humanist sociologists are primarily concerned with the "substantive problems" experienced by ordinary people in everyday life.

In 1976, Lee co-founded the Association for Humanist Sociology. Its mission statement establishes that humanist sociology is a sociology to serve human needs. This goal is based on a distinctive understanding of human nature and social order: humanist sociologists "view people not merely as products of social forces, but also as shapers of social life, capable of creating social orders in which everyone's potential can unfold."

This has two important implications for the subject at hand. First, we encourage sociologists to apply their skills to designing and testing models of voluntary service because such information is needed by (especially disadvantaged) youth and those who care about them. We also wish to note that this is a much more complex conceptual and methodological challenge than many academics may realize. Second, models of voluntary service for youth should include a strategy for youth-empowerment. At the least, this means youth participation in decisions about funding and budgets, setting program objectives, writing proposals and evaluating administration. Adults always should be present to train, guide and serve as resources. However, in some cases, empowerment requires that only youth have a vote on policy.

National Voluntary Service: History

The first non-military national service was mandatory for conscientious objectors under the Lincoln administration (Moskos 1988). The 1864 revision of the Union draft laws required that conscientious objectors be inducted as non-combatants. These men served as hospital workers and teachers of freed slaves. Written in 1906, William James' (1943) "Moral Equivalent of War" remains one of the best-known humanist justifications for a national youth service program.

In practice, the national service programs of the New Deal remain as models. The Civilian Conservation Corps (CCC), established in 1933, provided work and much needed financial assistance for nearly three million young men in forest and park camps. CCC members wore uniforms and lived in the field in camps containing about two hundred young men.

The CCC was soon joined by the Works Project Administration and the National Youth Administration. Nearly 14 million workers were employed by these programs. Some 30 percent of these workers were youths between the ages of 16 and 24. For them, the work camps provided an opportunity to acquire experience and develop skills denied to them by a depressed economy.

All of these programs also made significant contributions to building a prosperous nation. The CCC alone planted 2 billion trees, constructed 126,000 miles of minor roads, and improved 40 million acres of farmland (Janowitz 1983).

National Voluntary Service: Needs

Youth today also face tremendous obstacles in coming of age. In 1967, men in their early twenties earned 74 percent as much as older men. By 1988, this had dwindled to 54 percent. Over that same period, the real income of those under twenty-five years of age fell by 18 percent and home ownership fell by 33 percent. A 1988 study by the William T. Grant Foundation found that the income of families headed by 20 to 24-year-olds declined by 27 percent between 1973 and 1986. During the same period, the earnings of male high school graduates in the same age group declined by 28 percent (Olson 1990). Even college graduates are in trouble. According to the U.S. Department of Labor, about 100,000 a year cannot find suitable employment, a condition projected to last until the end of the century.

Certainly, there is an enormous need for the services of volunteers. Donald Eberly, Executive Director of the National Service Secretariat (NSS), feels that at least three million young people could be utilized productively in national service projects. Charles Moskos and the Democratic Leadership Council (DLC) estimate that useful tasks could be found for as many as four million national service participants.

In a major study, Danzig and Szanton (1986) projected a need for almost 3.3 million national service providers, broken down as follows: 1,200,000 in health care, 820,000 in child care, 250,000 in criminal justice, 165,000 in environmental conservation and 100,000 in libraries and museums. That same year, NSS estimated that if we just took an enrollment equal to the one million 18–24 year olds in active duty military service, we could employ them as follows: troops and teacher aids (200,000), conservation workers (200,000), senior citizen aides (150,000), day-care aides (100,000), literacy aides (80,000), health and hospital aides (80,000), police and library aides (50,000), pollution monitors (40,000), volunteers in new areas (100,000).

Voluntarism in America

Americans have favored the idea of national voluntary service for youth for over half a century. A 1936 Gallup Poll found that 82 percent of the public favored continuation of the Civilian Conservation Corps. A 1966 Gallup poll found that 72 percent of the public favored requiring all young men to give two years of either military or nonmilitary service.

Throughout the United States, people of all ages are involved in some kind of volunteer service activity. The Labor Department's Bureau of Labor Statistics reported that 38 million Americans (nearly one in five) did some volunteer work in the year ending May 1990. The largest proportion of these volunteers (37%) worked through churches and religious organizations. The second largest group (15%) worked with schools or other education programs. In 1989, according to the American Council on Education survey of the nation's incoming college freshmen, 62 percent had performed volunteer work in high school.

Unfortunately, there have been few programmatic efforts to recruit, train and utilize youthful volunteers. Many more volunteer programs are based in schools. Susan Dodge (1990: A1) observed that "a growing number of colleges are making a formal commitment to community service by encouraging their students to sign up for local volunteer projects." And Wendy Kopp, a Princeton University student, raised $1 million to fund a teacher corps called Teach for America, in which recent college graduates teach at rural and inner-city public school systems in different parts of the country. While in service, corps participants are able to defer repayment of federal college loans.

In 1984, Wayne Meisel and a group of recent college graduates launched the Campus Outreach Opportunity League (COOL) as a national vehicle to promote student community involvement (Loeb 1984). By 1989, COOL had a 600-school network. The breadth of the group's appeal is reflected in Meisel's receipt of praise from activist Jonathan Kozol, a Presidential Volunteer Action Award with a congratulatory telegram from Barbara Bush and a 1988 grant from the conservative Coors Corporation.

From 1989 to 1991, the Student Environmental Action Coalition (SEAL) grew to more than 1,000 campus chapters nationwide. In October 1990, SEAC sponsored a conference that attracted more than 7,600 students from 1,100 schools in all 50 states and 11 countries. The conference launched a corporate accountability campaign to expose the environmental degradation caused by multi-national corporations. Another group, Campus Compact, has about 150 member schools where the presidents have agreed to institutionalize service-teaming on campus.

There are calls for more of the same. A People for the American Way survey of 405 social studies teachers and 1,106 youths aged 15 to 25 found that 74 percent of the teachers and 51 percent of the students support the idea of schools making some sort of community service a requirement for graduation. James Kielsmeier, President of the National Youth Leadership Council, feels that school-based youth service programs can have a significant impact on school reform. He says, "It really helps us to rethink the place of young people in society. Instead of being part of the problem in schools, young people can become part of the solution in their communities." Marian Wright Edelman, President of the Children's Defense Fund, has proposed, "Adults should train children to believe that service is the rent we pay for living" (Buchanan 1989: 21).

1990 National and Community Service Act

The 1990 National and Community Service Act has three parts, each of which receives 30 percent of the total budget, disbursed over a three year period. First, the Act will provide up to 75 percent of the operating costs of full-time service programs such as the CCC and CVC. Second, the Act will support up to eight demonstration projects in order to test the suitability of various designs for large-scale national service programs. For example, in some projects persons serve part-time for at least three years, in some they serve full-time for between one and two years, and in some senior citizens serve for periods yet to be designated. Third, the Act will support school and college students engaged in service learning activities for academic credit. The remaining 10 percent of the funds are to be used for a variety of national level projects to be administered by a commission on National and Community Service, an independent government agency led by a 21–member Board of Directors, appointed by the President with the advice and consent of the Senate.

As mentioned, the Act represents the latest compromise after several years of competing bills differing by objectives, scope, scale, costs and benefits. Such controversies will continue and it is imperative that humanist sociologists get involved in the debate. Here we examine the six questions we feel are central to the debate over the future of national service.

National Voluntary Service: Humanist Concerns

(1) Who would be eligible?

Age. The Act allocates most of its funds for youth programs. Moskos (1988) justifies this emphasis on youth because, practically speaking, young people have fewer commitments to and are less essential to employers and family members. Youth also are more in need of work experience and skill development. Conversely, some physical work (e.g., conservation and the military) is more ably performed by youth as compared to older people. Also, some youth need more time to grow up after leaving school and before starting marriage and career. National service could provide that needed moratorium. Finally, "Focusing national service on youth makes it a rite of passage toward adult citizenship, dramatizing its importance" (Moskos 1988: 3).

All of the above are compelling reasons for making national voluntary service available to all interested youth. However, we also would make a claim on behalf of older Americans. Most of them have few or no work or family commitments. Many of them have skills and experiences that would make important contributions to community needs. And they need to experience active citizenship every bit as much as young people. Finally, involving both youth and the elderly in common projects would create cross-generational interaction and learning that would enhance the perspectives of both age groups and better prepare them for their distinct life course developmental challenges.

One also could make a case for making eligible middle-aged adults who, due to unexpected unemployment or the desire to seek new experiences and directions in life, wish to participate in national voluntary service. If we are serious about lifelong learning and active citizenship, then service throughout life is the only viable humanist alternative.

Gender. Some programs have been characterized by explicit or implicit gender discrimination. For example, the New Deal's Civilian Conservation Corps (CCC) was for males only. While the California Conservation Corps is only 25 percent female, young women make up 50 percent or more of the composition of contemporary urban-based programs (Moskos 1988: 69). We recognize that there will be some natural selection into projects on the basis of interests and aptitudes that are gender related. However, we see no justification for eligibility criteria based on gender for any service, including the military.

Social Class. Another important consideration is the social class background of program participants. Some see national voluntary service primarily as a way to promote civic virtue among middle class youth who are perceived as apathetic and self-involved. Early twentieth century national service programs, like the Plattsburg movement, were dominated by participants from upper-class backgrounds. The Peace Corps, the most significant national voluntary service program of recent years, has been criticized for its preponderance of "middle class college types" and relative absence of minorities and lower class whites.

Certainly, apathy is also widespread. Buchanan (1989) points out that in the 1986 midterm election, fewer than 17 percent of 18 to 24-year-olds voted. In the 1988 presidential election, only 36 percent turned out; down 5 percent from 1984. A *Times Mirror* Center for People and the Press study of 18 to 19-year-olds (Oreskes 1990: Al) concluded that this generation "knows less, cares less, votes less and is less critical of its leaders and institutions than young people in the past." Quite startling are decreases between 1965 and 1990 for the proportions of those under 35 obtaining news information from all three sources, newspapers (68% to 30%), radio (58% to 57%), and TV (52% to 41%). Thus, we concur with those who wish to address the withdrawal of alienated youth by challenging them with needed community service. Such service can help youth develop self-esteem and facilitate the transition to adulthood (Staff 1992).

Others are interested in national voluntary service primarily in terms of labor force integration for disadvantaged youth. New Deal programs drew participants from the Great Depression's growing pool of poor and unemployed. For years, minority youth labor force participation has decreased and unemployment increased. There are more young black men in prison than in college. In fact, the U.S. criminal justice system imprisons, jails, probates or paroles 25 percent of all black males between the ages of 20 and 29. As the recession grows, this situation will become worse. For too long now, the only option for minority youth aspiring to transcend poverty has been the military. Of all American troops serving in the Persian Gulf War, 104,000 or 25 percent were black, twice their share of the relevant age group.

Lynn Olson (1990: 1) writes, "Almost half of American high school students hope to go from school directly into the workforce. But finding and keeping a job—particularly one with the possibility of career advancement—has proven an elusive goal for the approximately 20 million non-college-bound youths between the ages of 16 and 24."

The "school-to-work transition" in the United States is the "worst in the industrialized world," according to Marc S. Tucker, president of the National Center on Education and the Economy. According to former Secretary of Labor Elizabeth H. Dole, the United States is one of the few western nations without a formal school-to-work transition (Olson 1990). Moskos (1988: 200) proposes that national service could rescue our "unemployed, unassimilated, and embittered underclass."

To be sure, programs to improve the lot of the disadvantaged cost money. However, during the Great Depression, the Roosevelt Administration was willing to spend seven percent of the federal budget on youth programs. Today, the Bush Administration spends only 0.5 percent and many needy youth are neglected. The cost of our neglect is crime, drug addiction, and other problems. Criminologist William Oliver states: "Our churches and community organizations must create programs that match black boys with black men who define manhood in terms of studying and working hard, self-discipline and providing for the emotional and material needs of their families" (Muwakkil 1988).

The Children's Defense Fund has called for strengthening and expanding youth-service programs to benefit at-risk youths. By participation in service programs, the report argues, disadvantaged youths will build their self-esteem, thus increasing the "hope factor" that could help them improve their lives. Thus, while we applaud the effort to promote active citizenship among affluent youth, as humanists, we call for a special emphasis in national youth service on job training, creation and placement for America's disadvantaged, especially minority, youth.

(2) Would such service be voluntary or mandatory?

On no other question is the humanist alternative more unambiguous. National service must not be coercive. Moreover, any kind of economically based coercion is as morally intolerable as mandatory service.

The legislation proposed by the Democratic Leadership Council in 1988 cancelled current school aid programs and made assistance contingent on national voluntary service. Many rejected this bill on the grounds that it discriminated against the poor. Danzig and Szanton (1986) favor a program that places a surtax on the income of all citizens. Those who serve in a "universal" program of national service are excused from this surtax. Again, the less affluent, for whom any tax causes greater deprivation, are treated unfairly. Any program that requires service, even if in exchange for educational grants or loans, promotes social class discrimination. Money spent for education should be seen as an investment in our nation's future, not as a means to recruit low-wage labor. Rewards for service provided should be separate from other government benefits and the same for persons from all social backgrounds.

(3) What would participants be qualified and/or trained to do?

As mentioned, we support voluntary service proposals that promote labor force integration for disadvantaged youth. On the other hand, we also must heed the warning of Martien

Taylor (1989) that we not ignore the seriousness of the problems for those who are to be served. She states, "A community of people cannot be used as a training ground for citizenship. Enlisting students to clean up parks and repair houses is one theory, but loosing thousands of reluctant, untrained volunteers to learn 'on' people is not only irresponsible, but dangerous. We need to be sensitive to how service affects those who are served. A bad volunteer is far worse than no volunteer at all" (Taylor 1989: 16).

Still another concern is that a large influx of low-paid young volunteers in some fields, such as day care, literacy and health care, could displace workers and undercut the wages of professionals. As humanists, we respect the role of labor unions and social-service professionals in meeting community needs. Any program that undermines their position would not be acceptable.

As for the training component, any program that proposes to rescue youth from poverty would have to tackle the problem of how to make many "labor intensive" tasks into opportunities to develop marketable skills. This would require attention to all aspects of project design. Here there is a special role to play for building in youth empowerment. For example, engaging volunteers in project planning and decision-making would teach useful administrative skills. Also, bringing experienced service providers into the process as consultants would provide youth with role models and career counseling during the work and, possibly, job placement upon graduation.

(4) Which community needs would be served?

The 1990 Act does not include military service and authorities have expressed confidence in the ability of America's all volunteer force to meet the country's military needs. Nevertheless, some progressives fear that the National Service Act could be a possible Trojan Horse for a program to restore involuntary military conscription.

Jo Becker (1989) notes that in 1989 the Army failed to meet its recruitment quota for the first time since 1980. The number of 18-year-old men will drop 30 percent between 1989 and 1992. A 21 percent decline in the 15–24 year-old population is projected to occur between 1980 and 1992, from 42.7 million to 34 million. According to Bill Galvin of the Central Committee of Conscientious Objectors (CCCO), 55 percent of eligible and available males will need to enlist to meet military quotas set for the 1990s. The military also projects a severe shortage of medical personnel. In fact, a health professionals draft has been developed which would function similarly to the regular draft. Under this plan, a wide variety of health professionals aged 20 to 44 would be required to register.

The military interest in national voluntary service was underlined in 1990 when a Department of Defense appropriations bill proposed a commission on National Service. One of the responsibilities of the commission was to evaluate future military personnel needs and to what extent these needs might be met through a national service program that offers special education and other incentives to participants in return for military service. Commenting on the 1990 Kennedy Bill, the Army Secretariat stated that the continued "success" of the all-volunteer force requires that any federal programs strongly tilt benefits toward military rather than civilian service. Indeed, one factor promoting military recruitment in the 1980s was the Reagan administration's shift of school grants and loans from the Pell program to RO.T.C.

As mentioned, Moskos and the DLC proposed making educational assistance totally dependent on national voluntary service. They did so on the premise that this would improve the quality of the military. In Moskos' view, the current market model military is per capita more expensive than any military in history. Moreover, the educational levels and aptitude scores are lower in today's military than for any later twentieth century U.S. force. A 1977 Gallup poll found that if national service were compulsory, 40 percent of youth would choose military over civilian service. However, a 1979 Gallup poll reported that youth from the upper half of the income distribution would be inclined to choose civilian service over military service by a ten-to-one ratio. Thus, it seems that rigging the system to upgrade the troops might be futile.

It appears that many youth from less advantaged backgrounds enlist in the military because they think they have no other strategy for escaping poverty and are persuaded by slick advertising appeals that they will develop marketable skills while in the military. We urge that the U.S. standing military be reduced to post Cold War requirements and that deception as a strategy for recruitment be abandoned. The hard fact is that few of the skills learned in the military are transferable to civilian occupations. Obviously, trained pilots can anticipate lucrative careers in commercial aviation. The much greater number of infantrymen, however, gain no advantages in searching for a career. While military service may have helped World War II veterans get ahead, Villamez and Kasarda (1976) show that Korean veterans fare only about the same as their non-veteran contemporaries in terms of income and jobs. While cautioning that their findings are premature, Villamez and Kasarda found evidence that Vietnam veterans suffered in terms of career and income in comparison to their non-veteran peers.

Those hardest hit by the negative career impact of military service are minorities. Josefina Card's (1983) data on 1963 male high school seniors found a specific dollar loss in income per year that can be attributed to military service for the cohort. Using Social Security Administration records, Angrist (1990) found that "the annual earnings loss to white veterans is on the order of $3,500 current dollars, or roughly 15 percent of yearly wage and salary earnings in the early 1980s." A recent Human Resources Research Organization report (McAllister 1990) concludes, "Regardless of speculation as to 'why not,' the military doesn't appear to be the panacea for struggling youth." A national service program that respects humanist principles would not have a detrimental impact on the career opportunities of youth who participate.

(5) How would participants be rewarded?

The 1990 Act legislates "a living allowance not less than 100 percent of the poverty line for a single individual and not more than 100 percent of the amount such participant would have earned if such participant had been paid at a rate equal to the minimum wage for a 40-hour work week." In addition, participants would also receive health insurance. Postservice benefits include education and training benefits for each participant "in an amount not less than $50 per week nor more than $100 per week."

Whether or not this constitutes sufficient compensation should be evaluated. Theologian John Swomley raises a serious concern: "When government demands for civilian service at a low rate of pay are an alternative to the provision of needed jobs at living wages, and when such demands are masked by talk of citizenship, obligation and patriotism, government is simply exploiting youth for the benefit of affluent adults." From a humanist perspective, we oppose the disproportionate burden that a low level of compensation imposes on participants from lower class backgrounds.

This concern has a practical as well as ethical basis. If service compensation is set too low, programs would be disrupted by lower class participants leaving to respond to needs at home. Poor GIs explained their higher rate of desertion during the Vietnam War in terms of "problems at home" (Curry 1985). The CCC has averaged 71 percent attrition over twelve months and the CVC 59 percent over nine months. Given the initial investment in training, high attrition rates seriously reduce the cost-effectiveness of any program.

(6) What would a national youth service cost and how would it be financed?

A broad-based voluntary national service program could draw some 1.6 million youth between the ages of 16 and 20 and cost about $11 billion a year. This would represent just one percent of the $1.1 trillion 1991 federal budget. Thus, $287 million over three years is only a small step. Nevertheless, given the relatively small scale of existing programs, Eberly wrote to us that "passage of the national service law is the most significant step toward national service since creation of the Peace Corps nearly 30 years ago." Indeed, as Eberly also pointed out to us, if state and local programs of full-time youth service had continued at just their rate of expansion through the 1980s, another 240 years would have had to pass until they reached the level attained by the CCC in its first three months!

We feel that an adequate accounting of all the costs of national voluntary service must include more than just the costs of program establishment and operation. There also are the compensating costs of public service tasks undone or done by others at presumably greater expense and the direct and indirect costs of neglecting the needs of youth.

Brenner (1975) has estimated the costs of youth unemployment and concludes that a one percent rise for those 15–24 years of age, relative to those twenty-five and older, leads to a six to eight percent rise in prostitution, forcible rape, auto theft and criminal homicide and a two to four percent rise in robbery and assault. The bill for one year of juvenile incarceration averages $18,000. In a "state training school" the bill averages $40,000 to $45,000 a year.

Service performed by the ACTION national service project has been assessed at 190 percent of the program's cost; President Carter's conservation corps at 100 percent of cost. The unemployment rate among ACTION participants was 70 percent at entry, but fell to 18 percent just six months after completion of service. That means lower crime and welfare costs and more tax revenue for government.

There also are long-term benefits from subsidized volunteerism. A 1986 ACTION poll of participants in Young Volunteers Program, a national program enrolling about 40,000 young people, ages 14 to 22 from low-income families, revealed that 73 percent expected to continue to do volunteer work as adults. Ninety-one percent said that they would encourage others to be volunteers.

The 1991 Act also promotes partnerships with local governments and private donors to cover costs. In order to qualify for federal support, state and local full-time volunteer programs must meet at least 25 percent of their own costs. The multiplier formula typically encourages contributions.

Municipalities interested in starting a youth service program can apply to organizations like Public/Private Ventures (Philadelphia) or the National Association of Service and Conservation Corps (Washington). The latter's Urban Corps Expansion Project provides $10,000 grants to cities to design programs to serve 18–25 year-olds not in school and unemployed. Some 75 cities currently are enrolled.

What Can Sociologists Do to Help?

We work in West Virginia in the Central Appalachian region. Wilson (1987) has acknowledged that the white Appalachian unemployed may also fit the criteria for what he calls the new "underclass," typically composed of inner-city minority youth. West Virginia is an especially depressed state. Its labor force participation rate is the nation's lowest and it still has unemployment above the national average. West Virginia workers are out of work longer than any workers in the country and the state has the second highest poverty rate in the nation. One consequence is that the health status of West Virginians is ranked second worst in the nation. A major pattern of response has been for young people to leave the state in search of gainful employment, in the process abandoning the elderly who must then care for their own transportation, health care and physical labor needs.

We hope to promote voluntary service for youth in West Virginia, drawing on our state's share of the funds from the 1990 National and Community Service Act. Our contribution would be to develop a system for generating volunteers, identifying their skills and needs, developing a pool of jobs, identifying their characteristics, and creating a data retrieval system that would facilitate matching volunteers with jobs. This involves an active outreach and effective computer programming.

Unfortunately, this has been done too seldom in the past and the consequences have been failure for both youth and the organizations where they have volunteered. Writing about the programs of the Comprehensive Employment Training Act (CETA), Cooper (1987) notes that even under "the best of intentions, the quick-hire mandate of CETA meant in many cases that the jobs were found and the individuals forced to fit, rather than tailoring jobs to meet the job potential and training needs of the unemployed." In 1977, Eberly (1977) reported that, if national youth service were suddenly to become a reality, "the number of openings that could be filled in the next three months is not more than 250,000. It will take some time to translate national or local needs into actual positions within organizations."

Sociologists could help in this area by developing guidelines for organizational applications. Such guidelines would require organizations to develop positions that are needed, would develop skills and have adequate supervision and resources attached. If done properly, this would constitute a very useful exercise for organizations to reevaluate their missions, objectives, resources, needs and programs.

Having volunteers go through a similar process would better ensure self-assessment that could clarify individual aspirations, expectations and needs. This would make for better choices and lessen the possibility of disappointment leading to alienation, lack of work discipline, frustrated organizational needs, poor evaluations and lowered self-esteem.

One highly successful model was developed for The Program for Local Service (PLS) in the Seattle, Washington area. Eberly (1973) has described the process in detail. In sum, (1) about 80 percent of 18–25 year olds in the area were invited, with emphasis on youth in low-income areas; (2) applications were screened for eligibility on the basis of age, geographic area and health; (3) sponsors were identified and invited to apply for volunteers; (4) these applications also were screened for eligibility; (5) the pool of available positions were listed in a directory for purposes of self-matching; (6) organizations agreed to contribute a $150 program fee; (7) a one-day orientation session was held for volunteers to hear about the program, get practice in interviewing and complete one-page resumes; (8) volunteers made appointments for interviews, with "brokers" and "matchmakers" on hand to facilitate appointments and even the interview itself, if requested; (9) applicants took a voucher and memorandum of agreement to the interview to be negotiated according to the sponsor's needs and the applicant's talents and interests. The agreement spelled out the duties of the participant and the supervisory and training responsibilities of the sponsor; (10) agreements were checked at the PIS office for compliance with the law and program regulations. Once an applicant's agreement was certified, s(he) was invited to a three-day pre-service training session and the year of service began within a few days. Within five months, 372 persons became PLS volunteers at 137 sponsoring agencies.

A truly national or, at the least, statewide matching program also would be possible through a telephone and computer network designed for that purpose. While a physical interview to finalize agreement ultimately would be required, a good deal of screening and negotiation could be conducted in advance to increase the chances of a good match.

Once programs are operating, there would be a need to evaluate the quality of their administration and their impacts upon participants and the community. Surveys of participants could be designed and administered before, during and after their service to determine what benefits, if any, they realize. Assessments by peers, immediate supervisors, parents, academic advisors and/or subsequent employers could be used to supplement the self-assessments and interpret changing test scores. Community impacts could be assessed by standard cost-benefit calculations. The latter could be used to justify applications for funding and appeals for organizational participation and public support. The latter also could be used to improve on the design of positions and processes for integrating volunteers so as to maximize benefits for both individuals and organizations. Where possible, experiments in youth empowerment could be conducted to expand the potential for human development through voluntary service. Research in this area would draw from and contribute to what we know about innovative models of workplace democracy and their relative productivity.

The research described above will not be published in the American Sociological Review or any of the discipline's elite journals. However, as Lee (1978: 218) has urged us, "Hopefully, members of the Association for Humanist Sociology will long be more concerned with developing a socially useful sociology than with trying to take seats at the tired old entrepreneurial games played by the cliques who rule so many of our organizations."

In contrast, "humanist sociologists can...develop pertinent information that might become very useful in popular struggles to achieve a more egalitarian and participatory society" (Lee 1978: 100). Among the many ways that sociologists can serve people, Lee (1973: 200) cites "providing information, theory, and counsel to educators, psychotherapists, social workers, social planners, and major policymakers in government, business, and voluntary organizations."

We have communities desperately in need of services, many Americans willing to serve, and millions of youth desperately in need of skills and work experience. While our formal national, state and local budgets already are severely strained, we have a wealth of human resources yet to be tapped. The possibilities for good work are almost limitless. That makes it an especially inviting problem for humanist sociologists.

References

Angrist, Joshua D. 1990. "Lifetime Earnings and Vietnam Era Draft Lottery." *The American Economic Review* 80(3): 313–336.

Becker, Jo. 1989. "Volunteer or Else! National Service Legislation." *The Nonviolent Activist* (Sept.): 7.

Buchanan, John H. 1989. "The Value of Community Service Programs." *Education Week* (April 5): 21.

Card, Josefina. 1983. *Lives after Vietnam: The Personal Impact of Military Service*. Lexington, Mass.: Lexington Books.

Chira, Susan. 1990. "Princeton Students' Brainstorm: A Peace Corps to Train Teachers." *New York Times* (June 21): Al, B9.

Chute, Eleanor. 1990. "Pool of College Grads Drying Up Jobs." *The Pittsburgh Press* (July 1): A8.

Coalition for National Service. 1988. *National Service: An Action Agenda for the 1990's*. Washington, D.C.: National Service Secretariat.

Cooper, Scott. 1987. "The Next Public Works Program." *Social Policy*. (Winter): 14–19.

Curry, G. David 1985. *Sunshine Patriots Punishment and the Vietnam Offender*. South Bend: Notre Dame University Press.

Danzig, Richard, and Peter Szanton. 1986. *National Service: What Would It Mean?* Lexington, Mass.: Lexington Books.

Dodge, Susan. 1990. "Colleges Urge Students Do Community Service Work; Some Even Require It." *The Chronicle of Higher Education* (June 6): Al.

Eberly, Donald J. 1990. Memo on national service. Unpublished.

_____. 1977. "A Universal Youth Service." *Social Policy*. (January/February): 1–5.

Education Week. 1990. "Schools Fail to Provide Skills for Work, Report Says." (April 18): 11.

Gailey, Phil. 1988. "Reviving a Love of Duty." *St. Petersburgh Times*. (March 20).

Hanham, Robert, and Spiker, Scott. 1990. "A Fresh Look at Unemployment in West Virginia." *The West Virginia Public Affairs Reporter* 7 (2).

Hedin, Diane. 1987. "Students as Teachers: A Tool for Improving Schools." *Social Policy* (Winter): 42–47.

Howe, Neal and William Strauss. 1991. "America's 13 Generation." *Pittsburgh Post Gazette* (March 13).

James, William. 1943. "The Moral Equivalent of War." *Essays on Faith and Morals*. New York: Longman, Greens.

Janowitz, Morris. 1983. *The Reconstruction of Patriotism: Education for Civic Consciousness*. Chicago: University of Chicago Press.

Jennings, Lisa. 1991. "Youth Volunteer Service Taking Center Stage in Capital." *Education Week* (Feb. 22): 1–20.

_____. 1989. "Kennedy Unveils $330–Million Plan for Volunteers." *Education Week* (August 2): 1–25.

_____. 1989. "Kennedy Youth-Service Plan Would Involve Schools." *Education Week* (June 14): 15.

_____. 1989. "Action on Youth Service is Bottled Up Pending Clearer Signal from President." *Education Week* (May 17): 20–22.

Lee, Alfred McClung. 1978. *Sociology for Whom?* New York: Oxford University Press.

_____. 1973. *Toward Humanist Sociology*. Englewood Cliffs, New Jersey: Prentice Hall.

Loeb, Paul Rogat. 1990. "Serve the People." *Mother Jones* (July/August): 1822.

Mills, C. Wright. 1959. *The Sociological Imagination*. New York: Oxford University Press.

Monaghan, Peter. 1988. "Democratic Lawmakers Campaign for Plan to Link Student Aid to National Service." *Chronicle of Higher Education* (October 26): A25.

Moskos, Charles C. 1988. *A Call to Civic Service: National Service for Country and Community*. New York: The Free Press.

Muwakkil, Salim. 1988. "Getting Black Males Off the Endangered Species List." *In These Times* (22 June).

National and Community Service Act of 1989. Committee on Labor and Human Resources. U.S. Senate. 101st Congress, Report 101–176.

Olson, Lynn. 1990. "Federal Agencies Sound the Alarm over the `School-to Work Transition'." *Education Week* (May 23): 1, 19.

Oreskes, Michael. 1990. "Profiles of Today's Youths: Many Just Don't Seem to Care." *The New York Times* (June 28): A1, A11.

Reeves, Frank. 1990. "W. Va. Needs More U.S. Aid for Services, Caperton Says." *Charleston Post-Gazette.* (26 April).

Schapiro, Renie. 1990. "Assignment Making A Difference" *Teacher Magazine* (February): 60–65.

Schine, Joan. 1990. "A Rationale for Youth Community Service." *Social Policy.* 30(4): 5–11.

Smith, P.K. 1983. *Tutoring: A National Perspective.*

Starr, Jerold M. 1992. "Peace Corps Service as a Turning Point." Submitted for publication.

Taylor, Martien. 1989. Untitled comment. Fellowship. (October/ November): 16–17.

Villemez, William, and Kasarda, John. 1976. "Veteran Status and Socioeconomic Attainment." *Armed Forces and Society.* (3).

West, Peter. 1989. "Senators Unveil 2 Bills to Bolster Teaching Ranks." *Education Week* (Oct. 14): 1–22.

Wiggenbach, Charles E. 1961. *Guide to the Peace Corps: Who, How, and Where.* New York: McGraw-Hill Book Co.

Zlatos, Bill. 1990. "More Students Get Credit for Helping Others." *The Pittsburgh Press,* (January 28): B1.

The Dialectical Dance between Amelioration and Transformation: Contemplating "National Voluntary Service: A Humanist Alternative" a Decade Later[1]

James R. Pennell
University of Indianapolis

It seems fitting and somewhat ironic that *Humanity and Society* revisits Starr and Curry's work on national voluntary service in the wake of the George W. Bush administration's budget slashing of AmeriCorps—a program benefiting young adults, cash-strapped non-profit organizations, and their communities. The United States continues to struggle with economic and political circumstances that make job prospects for youth, the poor, and even the middle class seem rather gloomy. Many seniors well into their retirement years are working at Wal-Mart just to make ends meet (not for the good times Wal-Mart's advertisements depict). Government programs, services, and financial support get cut while spending for the U.S. war machine expands.

Starr and Curry wrote during a period of guarded optimism, marked by federal efforts to expand health care availability and extend a variety of educational opportunities to the masses. We are clearly in much more myopic times today. The "faith-based" initiatives of the current administration hearken back to the assumptions about and approaches to addressing poverty from a century ago, with Salvation Army-style charities being provided federal funds to purchase the religious commitments of the poor by using food, clothing, and shelter to barter for souls.

Despite these circumstances, Starr and Curry's analysis and recommendations are still highly relevant. Their work reflects the strength of humanist sociology as they advocate and model sociologists acting as designers, researchers, leaders, and partners in the development of a more just and humane world. Their thinking is inclusive, cutting across lines of class, age, gender, ethnicity, and institution. They are critical of military spending crowding out funding for social services, a message the current Bush administration seems willing to ignore at its—and our—peril. It is sad that Starr and Curry's insights and wisdom have not found their way into the thinking of mainstream politicians. This is sociology at its best and why many of us entered the field.

Yet one thing continues to trouble me. It applies not only to Starr and Curry's article, but to the written and service work of many humanist sociologists, including myself. We at times play down, and in many cases ignore, the general decline of good-paying, full-time jobs when we talk about the benefits of service as job training and entry-level employ-

---

[1]This paper originally appeared in *Humanity & Society* Volume 27, Number 1, 2003.

ment. As Aronowitz and DiFazio (1994) argue, we may be attempting to address a future world of work that will not exist. Humanity, including professional sociologists and others involved in social engineering, may need to consider a world that is not organized primarily around individuals' contribution to production. We must start asking hard questions about the work opportunities available in a late-capitalist economy and how service programs contribute to, or impede, the ability and willingness of people to create a world with reduced economic, social, and political inequities.

To be sure, Starr and Curry recognize that volunteer service should not just be job training. They consider the possible impact of a volunteer force on the paid work force and potential democratizing and empowering elements of volunteer service. But they, and we perhaps, too easily revert to status-quo conceptions and concerns of things "as they are" out of what is probably practical necessity. It may be that widespread, highly inclusive voluntary service will help build the insight and will-to-act that will result in social transformation toward a more equitable, humane, and just society in which work and material concerns do not dominate our thinking. But the path from service that is predominately ameliorative of problems to service that contributes to transformation on a broad scale is difficult to conceptualize, even if many of us are attempting to do that (Dolgon 2002; Kahne and Westheimer 1999; Maher, Pennell, and Osterman 2003). It is the same problem faced by those who advocate education as the path to transformation while the educational system continues to serve the existing political and economic system.

Perhaps this is what makes humanist sociology different than other sociologies described by Al Lee and summarized by Starr and Curry (370–371 in original). There is a willingness to deal with real, immediate, messy problems and issues as best as one can (as opposed to using theory, research, objectivity/neutrality, scientific uncertainty, and professional status to distance oneself), while keeping the possibility of a better world in mind and looking for ways to connect immediate responses with that vision of the future. Clearly, Starr and Curry are attempting this. Perhaps that is the best any of us can do if we want our work to be relevant to others who do not share our values and vision of the future, especially those who control the instruments of power.

Humanist sociologists have yet to find a way to shift thinking on a broad scale from treating social problems as personal failures to attacking problems as social in origin and requiring public solutions. Voluntary national service may help develop that understanding, even if the "official" justification for funding it is workforce development or some other status-quo conception. Still, humanist sociologists are willing to do the dialectical dance between actions justified on pragmatic grounds and actions that embody a higher vision (see Dolgon [2002] for a more developed discussion of this "praxis"). This intellectual and political "flexibility" can be confusing and somewhat frustrating for our audiences and ourselves. But humanist sociology refuses to reduce social reality to simplistic conceptions and prescriptions. We continue to engage in the messy, often frustrating struggles for a better, more just, more equitable, and ultimately more free and democratic world.

References

Aronowitz, Stanley, and William DiFazio. 1994. *The Jobless Future: Sci-Tech and the Dogma of Work.* Minneapolis: University of Minnesota Press.

Dolgon, Corey. 2002. "In Search of 'Cognitive Consonance:' Humanist Sociology and Service Learning." *Humanity and Society* 26 (2):129–50.

Kahne, Joseph and Joel Westheimer. 1999. "In the Service of What? The Politics of Service Learning." In *Service Learning for Youth Empowerment and Social Change*, edited by Jeff Claus and Curtis Ogden. New York: Peter Lang.

Maher, Timothy, James R. Pennell, and Lisa Osterman. 2003. "Sociology in the Neighborhood." Paper presented at the Southern Sociological Society Annual Meeting, New Orleans, LA, March 27–29.

5. Collaborations for Change: Who Is Playing and Who Is Winning in Community-Based Organization Led Development in Rural Appalachia[1]

Chris Baker
Walters State Community College

Reflexive Statement

As a graduate student at the University of Tennessee, I was drawn to the idea of the application of academic research for solving social problems and creating social change. The experiences in a graduate program dedicated to participatory research and grassroots community development left me with a greater understanding of the abilities of communities to define and solve their own needs. Through the increased involvement with Appalachian studies, my research goals have centered on the changing development options of disenfranchised communities in the region. Like many who work on community development issues, my experiences have made me keenly aware of the conflicts and contradictions between community-based organizations, activists, and scholars. As academia and non-profits move toward a greater role in addressing community needs these conflicts are becoming more evident. My involvement with this research began in 1996 as an assistant professor of sociology at West Virginia University Institute of Technology (WVUIT). There I worked with the Southern Appalachian Labor School (SALS) attending board meetings, evaluating programs, and operating a service learning program. What emerged from this work is a community development model showing the strengths and difficulties of integrating multiple resources and groups to help facilitate grassroots development. The paper discusses SALS's role in addressing basic needs, fostering indigenous leadership, facilitating service learning programs, and increasing local participation in development policy including generating networks needed to transform those involved and assist rural communities in the modern economy.

Introduction

Grassroots Community Based Organizations (CBOs) are the most prolific and least understood model of community development (Stoecker 1994, 2004). The multiplicity of goals and types of these organizations often complicates measuring their effectiveness. Furthermore, the involvement of researchers and the incorporation of participatory and com-

---

[1]This paper originally appeared in *Humanity & Society* Volume 29, Number 3–4, 2005.

munity based research methods varies within each organization. There is little research dedicated to how well community organizations and nonprofits are able to utilize resources and take advantage of the increased opportunities provided by federal and state programs and college-based service learning programs. Yet significant research shows CBOs have the capacity to facilitate grassroots based change and alter the way disenfranchised communities see development (Fisher 1993; Horton and Friere 1990; Hinsdale et al. 1995; Seitz 1995; Smith 2002).

In addition to solving basic needs, the involvement of multiple groups in community development has been shown to create both personal and social changes for participants. A number of educators point to the crucial role service learning can play in critical thinking. Moreover, the incorporation of grassroots groups into service learning initiatives can facilitate critical reflection and pedagogy (Horton and Freire 1990), generate a greater understanding of and commitment to civil society (Bellah et al. 1996) and lead to a broader concept of community and cultural diversity (Rhoads 1997). In Appalachia, Reid and Taylor (2002) argue that critical thinking and exposure to the region's oppositional politics to global capitalism is a crucial experience for its college students.

In this paper I look at SALS programs and the collaborations that result from the increased participation of multiple levels of society in grassroots led development. I point out some of the most visible gains in the areas of basic needs and social capital and the impact of participation on volunteers and participants. I use a case study to analyze the initiatives at the center. With programs involved in housing, basic provisions, healthcare, child and family services, and job training, SALS generates broad networks connecting resources and development initiatives through a community center approach. Three aspects of SALS are looked at. First, I overview the gains made by program participants, volunteers, and communities in the areas of social capital, basic provisions, and housing. Second, I focus on the collaborations and partnerships that have emerged involving nonprofit and private organizations, service learning and volunteer programs, and state and federal agencies. Finally, I address how the CBO approach effects participation on service learning and volunteer groups.

Data collection was conducted beginning in 1996 using content analysis, participant and direct observation, surveys, and interviews. I conducted formal and informal interviews at West Virginia University Institute of Technology (WVUIT), the SALS Community Center, and at Fayette County housing sites with participants from SALS, YouthBuild, AmeriCorp, visiting college volunteers, service learning programs, and in the Global Volunteers program. Surveys and interviews were directed toward goals, program satisfaction, and reflection on volunteer activities. Along with content analysis, I conducted fieldwork and participant observation while participating as an AmeriCorp and YouthBuild evaluator, service learning coordinator, and lecturer on Appalachian culture between 1995 and 2000. Participant observation provided in-dept understanding of the coordination of programs through observation at board meetings, staff meetings, on-site activities, dedications, training sessions, and community festivals.

Grassroots Appalachia

Since the 1960s, academics, nonprofits, and community activist organizations in rural Appalachia have worked creatively together incorporating grassroots and participatory research perspectives to address underdevelopment and systematic inequality. The work has centered on critiques of the region's experiences with modernity and capitalism drawing on feminism, narrative analysis, and critical perspectives. Focusing on social and economic justice, the region's activism has often conflicted with power brokers (ALOTF 1982; Fisher 1993; Gaventa 2002; Hay and Reichel 1997; Horton and Freire 1990; Lewis et al. 1978; 2003; Seitz 1995). Many of these grassroots groups have faced what Helen Lewis calls the "NGO Ceiling" in which good community based projects have been prevented from scaling-up to official structures and impacting long term planning and policy making (Taylor 2001: 28). Key to the grassroots efforts has been the development of indigenous leadership and community based solutions. While the region's organizations represent a wide range of groups and issues, women have been at the center of much of the community-level activism addressing poverty and solutions to development through the region's tight-knit community networks and institutions (Appleby 1999; Hinsdale et al. 1995; Lewis et al. 1978; 2003; Smith 1998).

Other approaches by the region's community-based organizations include the expansion of collaborations and the generation of new programs through mainstream development initiatives, including empowerment zones and enterprise communities or EZ/ECs. The emerging collaborations are generating partnerships with for-profit companies, state and federal programs, service learning, and volunteer groups in an effort to combat social problems, provide services, and develop social capital (Taylor and Cook 2001). Couto's (1999) *Making Democracy Work Better: Mediating Structures, Social Capital, and Democratic Prospect* represents the most recent comprehensive work analyzing Appalachia's grassroots organizations. Using Nisbet's concept of mediating structures, Couto chronicles how grassroots organizations are empowering local people and linking communities with resources throughout the region. For isolated rural communities negatively affected by economic change, nonprofits and community groups have become important providers of basic needs such as housing, social services, childcare, and social capital. In a similar vein, Anglin (2002: 574) looks at how small scale communities are able to address basic needs using grassroots approaches in rural Kentucky. She points to the success of the Blair Development Association (BDA) and the Eastern Kentucky Project in dealing with multiple political and economic issues in Blair County, Kentucky. Both groups have developed local and community-centered programs addressing childcare, transportation, housing, and industrial recruitment.

Along with community based organizations, increasingly, activist scholars throughout the country are linking service learning programs to collaborative partnerships transforming civic engagement into long term social changes (Maher et al. 2003). New programs in Appalachian schools engaged in service learning are developing college courses and curriculum with initiatives addressing the regions' problems. For example in southwest Virginia, Emory and Henry College's new Appalachian Center for Community Service works directly with low-income coalfield communities. These experiences are behind a new education for social change within what Stanley and Fisher call a place based education (2001: 20).

By drawing on multiple resources and levels of society, CBOs are in a position to assist underprivileged communities to address their needs and make development policy accountable to local communities. Who decides how funds are used and who participates in decision-making in recent initiatives such as EZ/ECs are open questions. One of the goals of the EZ/EC is to catalyze systemic change in how localities address social problems and how community groups, nonprofits, private firms, and public agencies interact (Baum 1999; Gaventa et al. 1995; Herring et al. 1998; HUD 1994). Involvement in mainstream development can lead grassroots groups to a larger voice in development decision making. Along with the Clinton era EZ/EC legislation, the growing popularity of participatory research is leading to continued pressure to incorporate all levels of society in development decisions. Key aspects of participatory research center on how ordinary people define services and their distribution, and how they affect social policy formation (Cornwall and Gaventa 2001). Early results of studies on the effectiveness of the EZ/EC show mixed results with variations between sites and use of resources. Of the goals of the programs, i.e. economic opportunity, sustainable community development, community based partnerships, and strategic vision for change, much of the emphasis has been on job growth and business development (American City and County 2002). In looking at the early results of EZ/EC programs, Gaventa et al. (1995: 118), document that while some cases exhibited top down tendencies,

> In other cases, however, private nonprofit organizations took the lead and successfully galvanized and sustained broad based community involvement. For some organizations, such widespread community participation provided focus and established momentum that they previously failed to achieve.

Defining the Problem: Rural Poverty and its Consequences

The problems faced by Central Appalachia's rural communities are complex. Even though the region's overall poverty rate has been reduced in the last twenty years, its distressed rural counties continue to stand apart (ARC 2000). Largely unrecognized, rural poverty is at the base of many social problems (Moore 2001). Rural communities suffer more chronic poverty with larger working poor populations than urban areas. Moreover, distressed communities house a disproportionate number of unskilled single women, children, and the elderly resulting in a higher proportion of those residents who possess a limited amount of education, experience in accessing government programs, and fiscal resources (Findeis and Jensen 1998; Trent et al. 2004). Wealth inequality remains central to the region's poverty. Rural communities continue to combat the effects of declining coal and heavy industries, coal camp housing, absentee land ownership, and divided local politics, and they also continue to be plagued by large tracts of undertaxed, unimproved land (ALOFT 1982; Baun 1997; Billings and Blee 2000; Couto 1995; Lewis et al. 1978; Rasmussen 1995).

Eastern Kentucky and West Virginia's rural populations have been hard hit by economic decline. Many rural communities increasingly depend on growing low-wage service sector employment (ARC 2000; Mencken 1997). West Virginia's top employers are Wal-Mart followed by the state. Formerly employed in heavy industry, rural workers now find themselves in service, tourists, and prison occupations. Telemarketing jobs in Charleston alone outnumber mining jobs throughout the state of West Virginia. The remaining coal mining jobs pay an average of $50,300 opposed to the $24,700 made by the average West Virginian (West Virginia Mining and Reclamation Association 1999). The emerging information/service economy has negatively affected lower-educated rural workers who historically were well paid in heavy industry jobs. Because of the concentration of opportunities for male workers in heavy industry, West Virginia has historically had a low female labor force participation rate (Baker 2002; Ewen 1995, 1996; Ewen and Lewis 1999; Maggard 1994; Mencklen 1997)

The above trends have left contemporary rural communities in the region facing less economic opportunity, substandard housing, and declining schools and infrastructure. Due to these trends, the region's population has experienced a dramatic shift that underlies a crisis in available human capital. Heavy industries have also left West Virginia communities facing the nation's highest disability rates. The lack of employment has facilitated the out-migration of young, educated workers. The state has one of the nation's highest populations over 65 and is last in median income and percent of the labor force employed (United Mine Workers Journal May-June, 2000: 8). While over one in four of its working aged men are disabled, West Virginia's child population declined 28 percent between 1980 and 2000. Overall, one out of three children in central Appalachia is below the poverty line (Wilson 2002). With welfare reform and as companies have become less involved in resource provision and community involvement how will rural communities already in crisis adapt to postindustrial economic transformation? One answer to this question comes in the outcomes of the increased involvement of nonprofit organizations in mainstream development initiatives.

Waltzing with Hegemony

SALS was created in the mid-1970s in order to address contract and labor disputes and other adult education initiatives for mine workers. In 1981, SALS received its 501 C (3) nonprofit classification. John David, a Professor of Economics at WVUIT, developed and currently directs SALS. Since 1995, SALS has been headquartered at a former school building at the Loup Creek Community Center. The center is located in the Beards Fork community in rural Fayette County. The county is divided by the New River Gorge with Beards Fork and surrounding coal camps rural enclaves between the Kanawha Valley and Charleston and Oak Hill/Fayetteville in the eastern part of the county. With the decline of the coal industry, the county has started promoting tourism along the New River Gorge (Colias 2002). Along an isolated mountainous stretch off Route 61 between Oak Hill and Montgomery, the community center serves twelve different former coal camp communities with a playground, dining room, meeting rooms, childcare rooms, group sleep area, and kitchen. Recently SALS remodeled the former Beards Fork Church of God into an annex to house visiting volunteers (SALS Journal Fall/Winter 2004). The SALS board is a coalition representing activist groups, education, human services, labor, and other organizations. Through their affiliations, board members incorporate college presidents, governors, union leaders, and congressmen into direct support for the programs. SALS uses grants to fund most of the programs. Under the direction of John David, the staff writes grants, coordinates outside and local volunteers, and operates the programs and numerous partnerships with local agencies and companies. Helen Powell, the SALS board chair, helped draft the Coal Mine Health and Safety Act and the 1972 Black Lung Amendments and is the former social services coordinator of Fayette County Child Development Inc or HeadStart. Other board members represent the Catholic Church, WVU extension, the United Mine Workers, and a number of local community organizations. SALS operates a worker education program around the idea of forming a union of communities including families, children, and seniors (SALS 25th Anniversary Publication, May 11, 2002). Labor education is incorporated into training, ceremonies, and community programs.

The community center is the base of multiple programs, and often has overlapping funding sources, agencies, and participants. The programs operate in two EZ/EC zones. They include the Upper Kanawha Valley Enterprise Community (UKVEC) and the Central Appalachian Empowerment Zone or CAEZ. The CAEZ is a designated rural Enterprise Community covering five counties in rural southwest West Virginia. In its planning stage, the CAEZ held 83 public meetings involving 1,400 citizens in 28 committees (West Virginia Enterprise Communities 2000). The UKVEC originated in 1999 and its lead entity is the Kanawha County Commission centered in Charleston. SALS programs fall into the following categories: housing, educational training, worker education, community center, and community service. The community center combines food distribution, 21st Century Community Center, Starting Points and MIHOW, senior health, and after school and summer services in the same building. The largest program at the center, YouthBuild trains high school dropouts to build houses and take GED classes at Fayette County's vocational technical school. YouthBuild, a Housing and Urban Development (HUD) program, provides up to $400,000 each cycle for training high school dropouts. YouthBuild participants have daily contact with SALS staff, community members, college students, and other volunteers groups (*Fayette Tribune* Dec 25, 1998; Casto 2000; *SALS Journal* Fall/Winter 2004).

Community service programs based at the center are Global Volunteers, Group Work Camp, College Workcamp Program, and AmeriCorps—USA, Learn and Serve, and VISTA. Several college volunteer groups use the programs for alternative spring break and service learning programs. The center offers six on-going housing programs designed to build new homes for low income residents (New Page Housing), provide rehabilitations in the CAEZ (New River Safe Housing) and in the UKVEZ (Coalfield Housing). SALS also works with the West Virginia Housing Development Fund and is a Community Housing Development Organization or (CHDO) designation.

Building Social and Human Capital

> We are dealing with people who have had problems all through their lives.
>
> —Kathryn South, SALS Staff

The political economy of rural Central Appalachia has left a population with less access to social capital and fewer institutions that link communities to available resources. In addition to these realities, the postindustrial economy provides fewer available resources for communities and workers (Couto 1999). Historically, West Virginia's heavy industries provided unionized jobs requiring little formal education. Today, one out of four people in the state over the age of 25 do not have a high school degree. 27 percent of Fayette County adults lack basic reading, writing, and computational skills (*Charleston Gazette* March 28, 1998). Research on social capital suggests that rural areas faced with rigid stratification and a small middle class are less able to generate the changes needed to create community level social capital or generate an environment able to create positive experiences for young people (Duncan 2001). Studies also suggest that community based organizations can be an important component for building social capital in poor neighborhoods (Gittell and Thompson 2001; Stoecker 2004). In this section, I look at how the SALS Community Center and its programs affect social capital formation.

Participant observation reveals that when combined with programs and services, the presence of large networks at the community center increases participants trust with others through contact with cultural diversity, new ideas, social institutions, government agencies, and professionals. SALS programs reaffirms that operating the programs at a community center level offers experiences that are needed to generate social capital for troubled youth. The community center concentrates a large number of volunteers and people from outside the community who provide mentors for local youth and Youthbuild participants. Often teen parents, YouthBuild participants face dropping out of high school, criminality, and other social pathologies. Local retirees at the community center and program leaders provide informal supervision and occupational guidance. Staff and the Beards Fork Community Organization members Floyd McKnight and Kenneth Fox often police the center. SALS is on its sixth YouthBuild grant with funding of approximately $450,000 per cycle. On average twenty participants are enrolled in YouthBuild with over half receiving a GED (YouthBuild Evaluation, 2000; HUD Report July 2003). YouthBuild participants have to pass drug tests to stay in the program. SALS construction coordinator, Vickie Smith, spends time with as many as six crews at different sites during an average day (Casto 2000). Besides GED training, participants receive mentoring in career counseling, homebuilding and life skills. Examples of life skills and topics covered at the center include conflict resolution, AIDS, CPR, and cultural diversity. Most participants take multiple attempts at their GED and younger participants are more likely to finish. Some members are suspended, quit, or take jobs without finishing their GED.

The empowerment of women in community development plays an important role in community organizing and grassroots based change especially in the Appalachian region (Appleby 1999; Briscoe et al. 2000, Lewis et al. 2003; Stoecker and Stall 1998). Participant observation in this study also reveals women playing an important role in social capital formation. The involvement of women from the community, in Americorp and Youthbuild programs, and as volunteers from the outside has been central to SALS community centered organizing strategy. Women make up most of the staff positions and engage the family and church networks needed to identify problems in the communities. Black lung widows and single parents have a strong presence in rural West Virginia and are often the most at risk for poverty in the community. SALS also employees a female construction coordinator. Staff jobs are retained locally by community members some with college degrees or other training. Jennifer Hamm is a certified housing counselor at the center who has worked with the other education programs. She became involved with housing after the experience of working with youth. "I'd go see these kids and there would be rain pouring in through the roofs. The houses were falling apart. The children with low reading skills are the same ones living in these houses, so I wanted to fix that" (*Charleston Daily Mail* June 15, 2001). There are four fulltime VISTA coordinators. Skills obtained in the VISTA jobs include procuring home loans, coordinating work crews, and serving as after school program directors. Staff and community participants work with state and federal agencies and private companies including lending institutions like Fannie Mae, WV Housing Development Fund, and the USDA Rural Development, Federal Home Loan Bank, and local banks.

SALS programs offer local program participants the opportunity to go outside the region, often for the first time. Staff and the participants travel to organizational and professional meetings, leadership conferences, and state and national rallies and ceremonies. Cultural integration is also one of the organizations' goals. Historically, the Beards Fork community was segregated by race along the forks. Today, at the community center black and white families work together. The integration of different age groups also supports community integration with senior programs operating beside youth based programs at the center. Yearly celebrations at the center celebrate Black History Month along with the now 14th annual Solidarity Cultural Festival celebrating workers held every spring. The center celebrates the annual Martin Luther King, Jr. Service Day by special projects and continuing ongoing work.

The presence of community center staff, visiting volunteers, and program participants generates an active social environment. AmeriCorps surveys found the most cited gains were learning about other cultures, human needs, making friends, and serving the community (AmeriCorps Evaluation 1998). Volunteers also become aware of the class system. Open-ended responses by the AmeriCorps participants revealed that personal gains were made in the area of human relationships. This is the same for skills. When asked what skills were obtained from the programs, participants provided the following responses:

> "Learning to work with difficult people. With Teams. Problem Solving."
>
> "Community—getting along with different people."
>
> "How to build a home, How to be sociable with people, How to use my art."

Members also responded to how the experience has created new goals.

> "Because I now realize that I want my own shop so I can go out on my own and help people"
>
> "Because I can work through my problems now and I enjoying working with people."
>
> "Learning to work with young people, mentoring young people."
>
> "My future goals are still far from me but learning to do things inside the home was very interesting and helpful to myself." (AmeriCorp Evaluation 1998).

Heritage preservation is a goal at the center. All groups experience lectures, presentations, and art exhibits on labor, coal camps, Appalachian culture, economics, community lore, and oral narratives. The inclusion of WVUIT professors and local retirees into the programs provide perspectives from the social sciences, engineering, and health and human services. Community ceremonies include new house dedications, Christmas present drives, and graduations. The center often hosts international visitors from Ireland and Africa. The speakers and guests at ceremonies have included the president of United Mine Workers, Cecil Roberts, folk singers, social activists, college presidents, state officials, and Vermont's Bread and Puppet Theatre. Next, I look at the programs used at SALS to address basic needs.

Basic Services and the Provision of Needs

Addressing basic needs and service delivery is a challenge in poor rural areas. Census data for the surrounding Loup Creek Catchment area reveals per-capita income of between $7,000 and $8,000 dollars a year with a third of the population below the poverty line.

Local schools have up to 80 percent of students in free breakfast/lunch programs (*Charleston Gazette* Sept 1, 2000). The concentration of the elderly, retirees, the disabled, and single mothers in an isolated rural area means many families lack transportation and do not receive health and dental care, before and after school services, and social services. This has become even more difficult with welfare reform and as health care providers and social services have restructured through consolidation and centralization. Increasingly, basic services are located outside of rural communities (Murty 2001). In addition, the closing of blacklung clinics and tightening of eligibility for benefits has narrowed the options of blacklung victims.

This research points to multiple roles carried out by the community center replacing the declining community services once available in a successful economy. Current and past programs serving families include School Day Plus, a latch key program reaching 20 children, and Energy Express a summer camp program for 40 children. With SALS as Fayette counties only Energy Express program it provides breakfast and lunch, transportation, and nutrition counseling. Currently, the center operates the after school program, Accent Education. The program serves snacks and dinner and focuses on assisting school age children with homework, computer technology, fine arts, and public speaking (*Fayette Tribune* November 13, 2003).

The community center has an ABC room for young children. Parents are encouraged to participate in the programs with their children. Over 3000 meals are served for six weeks each summer at the center. The programs also provide computer, cultural diversity, and communication skills (*Fayette Tribune* July 1, 2002; *SALS Journal* Spring 2000). The above programs utilize volunteers and donated books and computers (*Fayette Tribune* July 1, 2002; SALS Board Meeting 2000).

SALS provides information on available services and programs to the community. The center identifies and links specific families who are in crisis to available resources. The center has seven bulletin boards in the area that describe its programs. The center links local families to human service programs such as the Mothers, Infants, Health Outreach Worker Program (MIHOW). Health services at the center are through its partnership with 21st Century Community Center, the New River Health Association, and Fayette County Schools. Other health services provided at the center include promoting free dental cleaning and x-rays provided for participants at WVUIT. The inclusion of the National Blacklung Association (NBA) on the SALS board helps local victims of the disease to gain support and information on clinics and eligibility. A former president of the NBA and board member Mike South, assisted local black victims with benefits and lobbied for support of clinics at the center until his recent death from the disease. Today, John Cline from the Fayette County Black Lung Association serves on the SALS board (*Charleston Gazette* April 17, 2002; *SALS Journal* 2000; *SALS Journal* 2004).

SALS uses donated vehicles to transport the elderly, shut-ins, participants, and volunteers. It also houses a Senior Health Program providing health workshops and health bingo along with transportation for basic needs. Many families in the area are in hollows off main roads several miles from the larger towns of Montgomery, Oak Hill, Fayetteville, and Beckley. The community center approach is effective given the geography. The center serves as a site for the Self-Help and Resource Exchange (SHARE) program offering reduced cost groceries for between 50 and 100 people a month. SHARE distributes groceries to people for reduced costs, food stamps, or free with community service. The community center offers a centralized location for SHARE distribution and delivery (*SALS Journal* 2000). The board routinely acts on cases of indigent care and temporary homelessness by providing or directing individuals toward services. The social networks created by the programs helps identify needy and ill residents throughout the community. Substandard housing represents one of the most pressing basic needs in the area. In the next section, I look at the housing programs operated at the center.

Providing Communities with Housing

As a middle class housing boom helps drive the economy throughout the country, the crisis in affordable and safe housing in rural America remains virtually invisible. A recent HUD study reveals 30 million Americans in poor, inefficient housing (Auvil 2001). West Virginia's housing crisis dates back to the coal camp regime policies of renting to mining families. As labor practices changed in the 1960s, housing was privatized. Today, 77 percent of the residents in the state own their own homes with many in the coalfields remaining substandard. Early coal camp housing often lacked foundations, solid floors, inside walls, modern plumbing, and insulation. Consequently, contemporary families in southwest West Virginia, often live in dangerous, substandard housing (Auvil 2001; Spence 1979). Addressing the region's housing crisis is a key to developing its communities. Housing programs involve numerous community members and economic sectors. Programs in the region such as The Federal of Appalachian Housing Enterprises (FAHE) have been shown to successfully generate development within poor communities. FAHE has been described as able to make "social capital float uphill" (Couto 1999: 163).

The negative effects of substandard housing fall disproportionately on the disabled, elderly widows and young families with children in developmental stages (Auvil 2001; HUD 2001). Local families often cannot afford repairs and also have trouble finding contractors who will work on small projects. A SALS construction supervisor describes the contractor market, "Most of the local contractors don't want smaller repair jobs. They're dirty, they are time consuming, and they don't know what they are going to get into until they are there" (*Beckley Register Herald* Aug 7, 1996). The housing programs rehabilitate and weatherize eligible houses, build new houses, and relocate rehabilitated manufactured homes. Crews engage in all aspects of construction and removal. Every rehab is different with most requiring insulation, windows, new doors, and wiring. Rehabs are based on five year forgivable loans and new homes are set up on payments of less than $100 a month for 20 years. The SALS staff determines eligibility within the service area and then works with the mortgage company and the homeowner. The programs seek to provide affordable mortgages through HUD and Fannie Mae low cost loan programs. The goal is to provide mortgages based on the ability to pay. Homeowners receive low cost loans as long as they live in their homes. The New River Safe Housing Program uses West Virginia Housing Development grants to find and purchase homes for rehabilitation. The CAEZ and Fayette County help provide Small Cities Block Grants to SALS for its housing program (Benedum 2000). HUD also works with local governments to purchase foreclosed homes for rehabilitation (*Charleston Gazette* mail Sept 3, 2000). Another housing initiative is the locating of donated manufactured homes from the WV Manufactured Home Association and Excel Modular Home Units to qualified members of local communities (*SALS Journal* 2004).

Starting in 2000, the ongoing housing projects have been aided by Group Work-camps. In July of 2000, 800 volunteers from the U.S. and Canada repaired over 50 homes and in 2001 over 100 in Fayette and Kanawha counties through SALS programs. SALS and UKVEC organize the groups which includes the providing of temporary living space donated by local high schools and WVUIT (*The Beckley Register-Herald* July 26, 2000; *Charleston Gazette* June 14, 2001). The housing programs were diverted to flood relief in July 2001 as a once-in-a-century flood destroyed communities in the area. Due in part to logging operations, the flood washed away a number of homes, bridges, and roads in the Loop Creek area. Workcamp volunteers were used for the initial rescues and in the subsequent summers to rebuild water damaged housing (*Charleston Gazette* mail July 15, 2001). In total between July 2001 to 2002 over 800 work camp and 200 college volunteers weatherized 104 homes, helped construct four homes, installed five modu-craft units, and rehabilitated several others. Between January and November of 2003, 1500 volunteers worked on homes. For 2004, over 1700 volunteers worked with SALS housing programs (*Charleston Gazette* July 15, 2001; *Benedum Foundation* October 12, 2002; *Fayette Tribune* March 13, 2003; *Montgomery Herald* August 13, 2003; *SALS Journal* 2004).

Nonprofit housing programs are addressing the housing crisis in rural West Virginia. The key is their ability to generate broad scale participation both from residents in need and volunteer labor. The next section focuses on the partnerships and collaborations involved in the center's programs.

Community Partnerships and Advocacy

The SALS board and the networks established through its programs have expanded community partnerships with universities, extensions, and colleges. Also one of the goals of the EZ/EC is to create partnerships linking resources and providers. The WVU-W.K. Kellogg foundation initiated community service projects with SALS beginning in 1999. The goal of service learning is to enhanced civic responsibility not just through volunteering but with course material (Bringle and Hatcher 1996). University service learning initiatives provide an available labor force. A number of partnerships have been made possible by the programs. Most volunteer programs at the center are alternative spring break programs geared toward providing general labor. SALS utilizes service learning in program marketing, site planning, handicap ramp design, health care, basic nutrition, child care and education, dental care, and preventive health clinics. Students engaged in service learning from WVUIT and West Virginia University is from programs in health services, nursing, engineering, sociology, and economics. Health services majors developed and coordinated projects for emergence medical services, wellness, CPR, and workers compensation (*Kellogg Report* 1999).

Along with service learning, SALS is connected with multiple religious organizations and networks. Denominations and churches sending volunteers to the center include Presbyterian, Lutheran, Catholic, Episcopal, Methodist, and Church of Christ. Christian Endeavor and Group Workcamp volunteers are hosted at the center. Group Workcamp is hosted through the Commission of Religion on Appalachia or CORA and Church World Service. Group Workcamps is a Colorado based nonprofit group sending volunteers to 48 states each summer (*SALS Journal* 2004). The community center is also involved in local church projects. Other ties that have emerged through the programs include the support of the West Virginia Council of Churches for the 2001 flood relief operations (Interview with John David, October 25, 2001). Private companies participate in SALS programs through the use of tax credits and direct donations of goods and services. Designed to encourage donations, tax credits allow businesses to donate surplus material and services. Nonprofits are given an allotment of credits and it is the responsibility of the programs to access companies. Tax credits are managed through the state's Neighborhood Investment Program, where 50 percent of the donated value can be used to reduce income tax. In 2003, the state has 102 applicants for $2 million in credits (*Fayette Tribune* December 9, 2002). Staff at the center network and solicit to find businesses that will provide donations. Participation by for-profit companies is prominent in the case of SALS's programs. The organization effectively uses state of West Virginia tax credits in part because of the diversity of programs. SALS draws donations from banks, mobile home dealers, hospitals, gas companies, and other corporations. Recent tax credits have been used to obtain need vehicles (*SALS Journal* 2004).

Donations are in the form of cash, cars, vans, computers, carpet, clothes, food, insulation, paint, building material, mobile homes, books, and office equipment. Nonprofit organizations like Gifts in Kind also contribute materials. The U.S. Department of Agriculture donated $26,000 in 2000 for a new van for the Energy Express program (*SALS Journal* 2000). When large amounts of material are donated, storage is often a problem with institutions such as the Beards Fork volunteer fire department holding material on site.

Partnerships with Nonprofits and Community Based Organizations

Nonprofit coalitions are another level of partnerships supporting the program initiatives. SALS has on staff an issues coordinator, Gary Zuckett, who along with other board members, link the center with the Commission on Religion in Appalachia (CORA), West Virginia Health Care Reform Coalition, the West Virginia Environmental Council, People's Election Reform Coalition, and the West Virginia Rainbow Coalition (see Table 1). The partnerships address universal health care, tort reform, and support for environmental issues. Examples of activism include advocating the extension of welfare benefits, marching in opposition to the KKK, opposing strip mining, and supporting efforts to impose weight limits on trucks. SALS has also co-sponsored three of the nonprofit theater Appalshop documentaries including Coal Bucket Outlaw, Ethel Coffee Austin, and Stranger with a Camera.

The community center approach has proven effective in identifying at-risk community members in need of services. Advocacy at the center includes assistance for flood victims for FEMA signup, CHIP (Children Healthcare Initiative Program), and eligibility for child assistance with DHHR. In April of 2002, the Welfare Law Center filed briefs on behalf of SALS against the state's cutting off of hardship welfare cases. The brief argued that the state has imposed stricter requirements than federal law mandates and violated children's equal protection rights and due process (*Charleston Gazette* April 14, 2002). The center distributes information on earned income tax credits for low-income families. Nonprofit groups also connect the community with the actions of the legislature and its impact of rural communities outside of Charleston. Next, I overview how the integration of multiple social networks shapes the experiences of those involved in the programs at the center.

TABLE 1   Partnerships

Nonprofits/Volunteer Coalitions	For Profit Partnerships	State/Federal
West Virginia Rainbow Coalition	United National Bank	West Virginia University W.K. Kellogg Community Partnership
Good Shepherd Mission	One Valley Bank	Head Start
Concerned Citizens to Save Fayette County	City National Bank	West Virginia State Employees Association
Commission on Religion in Appalachia	Columbia Natural Resources	Central Appalachian Empowerment Zone
Association for Community based Education	Montgomery General Hospital	Upper Kanawha Valley Enterprise Zone
West Virginia People's Election Reform	Lowe's	Department of Housing and Urban Development
Global Volunteers	Wal-Mart	West Virginia Housing Development
Gifts in Kind Organization	West Virginia Manufactured Housing Association	Governor's Cabinet On Children and Families
Coalition for a Tobacco Free West Virginia	AT&T	Appalachian Regional Commission
WorkCamp Volunteers	MADD Mobile Homes	Corporation of National Service—Americorps
Claude W. Benedum Foundation	William Jones Mobile Homes	USDA Rural Development
United Mine Workers	Economy Heating	WVU Extension
United Way	Owens Corning	YouthBuild USA
WV Healthy Kids Coalition	Adventures Mountain River Outfitters	Kanawha/Fayette County Schools
Group Workcamps	Excel Homes	Valley/East Bank High Schools
WV Health Care Reform Coalition		WIA Workforce Investment Act

Experiences of the Heart: Community Service, Volunteering, and Social Development

> I picked up many pointers on tearing down, then building up the walls of a house, dry-walling, wiring, and avoiding incarceration.

> —Bryan Gibson, (Team Coming Soon, AmeriCorps Portfolios: 23)

SALS facilitates service learning and volunteering by coordinating volunteer groups and resources within programs. The integration of programs, individuals from the community, service learning, and other volunteer groups at a community center sets the stage for transformational collaborations involving life changing experiences, exploring long term commitments, and fundamental changes in institutions (see Mahler et al. 2003). What have volunteers gained from participating in the community development programs at SALS? Measuring the outcomes of community service is proving difficult (Thomson and Perry 1998). The AmeriCorps program has been critiqued as a service program with an educational component. While many students cannot use the program to fully fund a college degree they are assisting community programs like SALS to survive along with getting education credit. John David comments on the role of AmeriCorps, "If we had to rely on regular volunteers showing up every morning, the whole thing wouldn't stay glued together…People just can't take months away from their lives to renovate houses" (Selingo 1998: A40). Surveys given to the global volunteers, visiting Americorps NCC, and local AmeriCorps Learn and Serve provide evidence of what volunteers receive from their experience in community level programs.

Evidence from the surveys suggests that while rural communities lack economic capital, they offer volunteers alternative experiences through civic involvement with tight-knit community bonds embedded in rural social structure and the natural environment. Participants in service learning gain a broader sense of Appalachia's history and culture along with the issues reflective of global capitalism and confrontational politics. They see firsthand the failure of the economy, the effects from the neglect of basic needs and social capital for communities, and the process of renewal. During their stay, AmeriCorps and other volunteers travel to surrounding rural communities, towns, and recreational areas. They support local diners and attend church services. Volunteers experience rural community solidarity and West Virginia's natural ecology through hiking and rafting. The trip includes exposure to American's most dramatic waterfalls, state parks, and natural areas. By using volunteers from more than one age group, region of country, religious affiliation, and culture, contact with different people is accelerated. For instance, during the flood of June 2001, program volunteers, and staff ended up cut off from the main road without power for an extended period. The community center was used for "serving gigantic community meals" (*Charleston Gazette* mail June 15, 2001).

The themes emerging from the service learning surveys relate to personal transformation, community and the social bond, and consciousness of social conditions, ecology, and diversity. Most of the AmeriCorps participants and visiting college students represent young people in college looking for diversity and life experiences. AmeriCorps participants, from outside the area, spending weeks in coal communities engage in self-transformation in a place foreign to them. Survey responses include:

> The most important thing that I did while I was here was to take a look at my life. I asked myself a lot of different questions concerning a lot of different aspects of my life. I might not have come up with all the answers, but I did some re-prioritizing of the important things in my life.

> There was lessons everyday I was there. From when to keep my mouth shut… to appreciating the moon and the stars, mountains, and land, or how I need to simply my life. (Emily, AmeriCorps Portfolios, Team #4, 2000)

> I became very emotionally attached to my sheetrock, and every piece had to be exactly in place. (Rachel, AmeriCorps Portfolios, Team #4, 2000)

Volunteering also allows students to get a greater sense of the historical factors behind uneven development and the human side of underdevelopment. The labor education is exemplified at the housing sites. Comments reveal the participants learn about social disorganization, poverty, and human suffering. These are experiences Rhoads (1997) sees as crucial for mythbreaking. Comments include:

> The owners of the houses in Mossy and Page have thanked us for their now beautiful homes. They are now living in homes with roofs that will not cave in, walls that will not crumble, and wires that will not catch fire. (Team Coming Soon, AmeriCorps Portfolios, 1998)

> I enjoy that we get direct results from our work. We have created a house that will be nice to live in out of a shanty. (En Fuego, AmeriCorps Portfolios, 1998).

> We have spent six weeks renovating houses, helping run shelters in a state of emergency, reaching out to the community, and helping those in need. This project has left a permanent impact on our lives. (Team Coming Soon, AmeriCorps Portfolios, 1998).

For older adults in the Minnesota based Global Volunteers, the stay in West Virginia and the programs were different than their daily lives. Global volunteers pay $450 to volunteer at a number of venues around the world. Beards Fork has become the destination for executives from Disney and IBM, military commanders, teachers, pet groomers, managers, state agricultural commissioners, photographers, and bankers. Surveys of Global Volunteers show differing responses in their awareness of problems faced by YouthBuild participants. Some respondents wanted to change how the programs were run and the participant's attitudes. They were concerned about the slow pace of work, and YouthBuild participants' behavior. The surveys revealed that the visiting Global Volunteers also experienced West Virginia's community solidarity. Comments from global volunteers on West Virginia include,

> Very warm, genuine friendliness and concern.... I thought it was very beneficial in 'team building' to be housed in a community building instead of a hotel/motel.

> Everyone was so nice here; they all really embraced the group and made us feel welcome. Even people, who didn't really know what we were doing here, were very friendly.... They treated us like family.

After her third whitewater trip, eight-one-year old volunteer Betty Mein offered, "everyone thinks I should be petrified, so they are watching after me" (*Montgomery Herald* August 16, 2003).

Conclusion

This research suggests the following findings. First, nonprofit organizations working with EZ/EC zones and other collaborations can successfully initiate rural community development and expand participation. Second, the interactive community center proves to be an effective tool for identifying problems, fostering indigenous leadership, and generating available resources required to address social problems and basic needs, empower local communities, and eventually make changes in large-scale institutions. Third, qualitative research suggests that the multiple groups and community integration involved in the programs further enriches the experience of service learning, volunteers, and participants. The multiplicity of groups becomes a tool for both transforming the experiences of service learning and local communities. The programs both build community and use community as a learning tool. In addition, the use of labor history, multiculturalism, and cultural heritage preservation provides a vehicle for understanding large-scale structures and cultural hegemony. Exposure to everyday life in West Virginia's tight-knit communities breaks down myths of rural America and its low income communities.

The paper has laid out a case for future support and an expanded role for nonprofit organizations in development policy. It also points to important distinctions and issues related to the nonprofit CBO approach to community development. The reliance on grants and volunteer grant writing is evident in the type of resources and the combinations of programs available at SALS. SALS is effective because of the determination of its leadership and community participants, the multiplicity of the groups involved in its programs, and the integration of charities, local resources, and available state and federal programs. The model presented here demonstrates the level of involvement and some of the resources that need to be in place for a CBO to meet its goals. Community participation in the development programs at the center is a key factor in the execution of programs. Particularly the strong presence of women and families and the emphasis on cultural integrity in the problem posing and solving process break down gender barriers and better address family needs. The inclusion of local voices in development transforms visitors, solidifies communities, and challenges stereotypes of rural Appalachia and America.

The next step is to connect the blocks into regional and sustainable networks capable of articulating political and economic change or scaling-up. Gaventa (1998: 153) lays out the road participatory based organizations face:

> The challenge that is before us now is how to build upon the successes of participatory development that have occurred at the micro and macro levels to take them to a larger scale-to incorporate participation into the development and implementation of national policies and large-scale institutions.

Scaling up will require larger coalitions. Citing Bill Horton, Steve Fisher points to Appalachia's need for "coalitions of opposition, coalitions of advocacy, and coalitions of alternatives" (Fisher 1999:1). SALS not only engages in broad local capacity building it also incorporates the business sector, volunteers, and nonprofits into a debate on rural Appalachia's development plight. These groups represent sectors of the population essential to institutional change.

References

Anglin, Mary K. 2002. "Lessons from Appalachia in the 20th Century: Poverty, Power, and the 'Grassroots.'" *American Anthropologist* 104: (2) 565–582.

Appalachian Landownership Task Force. 1983. *Who Owns Appalachia?* Lexington: UK Press.

Appalachian Regional Commission. 2000. Recent Trends in Poverty in the Appalachian Region: The Implications of the U.S. Census Bureau Small Area Income and Poverty Estimates on the Appalachian Regional Commission Distressed Counties Designation. (The Applied Population Laboratory)

Appleby, Monica Kelly. 1999. "Women and Revolutionary Relations." Pp. 171–184. in *Neither Separate Nor Equal: Women, Race, and Class in the South ed. Barbara Ellen Smith* (Philadelphia Temple University Press).

American City and County (2002) "Study Find EZ/EC Program Results Mixed." April 1.

Auvil, Ken. 2001. "Nation, State Should focus on Affordable Housing." *Charleston Gazette* April 16.

Baker, Chris. 2002. "Community Development and the Prison Industry in Rural Appalachia." *Mountain Promises* The Newsletter of the Brushy Fork Institute 13:2–6.

Baum, Howell. 1999. "Education and the Empowerment Zone: Ad Hoc Development of an Interorganizational Domain." *Journal of Urban Affairs* 1:290–309.

Bellah, Robert N. Richard Madsen, William M. Sullivan, Ann Swindler, and Steven Tipton. 2006. *Habits of the Heart: Individualism and Commitment in American Life.* Berkley: University of California Press.

Benedum Foundation. 2000. Annual Report Working Together for West Virginia's Children Families.

Billings, Dwight and Kathleen M. Blee. 2000. *The Road to Poverty: The Making of Hardship in Appalachia.* New York: Cambridge University Press.

Billings, Dwight. Gurney Norman and Katherine Ledford. 1999. *Confronting Appalachian Stereotypes: Backtalk from an American Region.* Lexington: University of Kentucky.

Braun, Denny. 1997. *The Rich Get Richer: The Rise of Income Inequality in the US and the World.* Chicago: Nelson Hall.

Bringle, R.C. and J.A.Hatcher. 1996. "Implementing Service-Learning in Higher Learning in Higher Education." *Journal of Higher Education* 67:221–239.

Briscoe, Lori, Erica S. Collins, Amanda Deal, Ron Hancocke, Kristyn McGraw. 2000. "Unruly Woman: An Interview with Helen Lewis." *Appalachian Journal* 2:164–189.

Casto, James E. 2000. "Learning Skills, Building Futures." *Appalachia: The Journal of the Appalachian Regional Commission. 33*: Sept-Dec

Colias, Christopher. 2002. "Almost Heaven Still? Post-industrial Development and Local Response in Fayette County, West Virginia." *Journal of Appalachian Studies* 8:91–119.

Cornwall, Andrea and John Gaventa. 2001. From Users and Choosers to Makers and Shapers: Repositioning Participation in Social Policy. (Working Paper Institute of Development Studies: Brighton, England).

Couto, Richard. 1995. Spatial Distribution of Wealth and Poverty in Appalachia. *Journal of Appalachian Studies* Fall Pp. 99–120.

Couto, Richard. 1999. *Making Democracy Work Better: Medicating Structures, Social Capital, and the Democratic Prospect.* Chapel Hill: The University of North Carolina Press.

Duncan, Cynthia. 2001. "Social Capital in America's Poor Rural Communities" Pp.60–88. *In Social Capital and Poor Communities.* eds. Susan Saegert, J. Phillip Thompson, Mark R. Warren. New York: Russell Sage Foundation.

Ewen, Linda Ann. 1996. "Sustaining the Myth of the Black Underclass Ignoring West Virginia." *West Virginia Sociological Review.* 2: 14–29.

Ewen, Linda Ann. 1995. Underdevelopment and Tanzania and West Virginia. *West Virginia Sociological Review* 1: 34–47.

Ewen. Linda Ann and Julia A. Lewis 1999. "Buffalo Creek Revisited. *" Appalachian Journal* Fall.

Findeis, Jill L. and Leif Jensen. 1998. "Employment Opportunities in Rural Areas: Implications for Poverty in a Changing policy Environment." *American Journal of Agricultural Economics* 80:1000–8.

Fisher, Steve. 1993. ed. *Fighting Back in Appalachia: Traditions of Resistance and Change.* Philadelphia: Temple University Press.

Fisher, Steve. 1999. "President's Message" Appalink 22: 1.

Gaventa, John. 1998. "The Scaling-up and Institutionalization of PRA: Lessons and Challenges." Pp. 153–166 in *Who Changes? Institutionalizing Participation in Development.* London: Intermediate Technology Publications.

Gaventa, John. Janice Morrissey, Wanda Edwards. 1995. "Empowering People: Goals and Realities." *Forum for Applied Research and Public Policy.* Winter

Gaventa, John. 2002. "Appalachian Studies in Global Context: Reflections on the Beginnings Challenges for the Future." *Journal of Appalachian Studies* 8:79–90.

Gittell, Ross and J Phillip Thompson. 2001. "Making Social Capital Work: Social Capital and Community Economic Development" Pp. 115–135 in *Social Capital and Poor Communities* eds. Susan Saegert, J.Phillip Thompson, Mark R. Warren. New York: Russell Sage Foundation.

Hay, Fred and Mary Reichel. 1997. "From Activist to Academic: An Evolutionary Model for the Bibliography of Appalachian Studies." *Journal of Appalachian Studies* 3: 211–230.

Herring, Cedric. Michael Bennett. Doug Gills. Noah. Temaner Jenkins. 1998. *Empowerment in Chicago Grassroots Participation in Economic Development and Poverty Alleviation.* Chicago: University of Illinois Press.

Horton, Miles and Paulo Freire.1990. *We Make the Road by Walking.* Conversations. Philadelphia: Temple University Press.

Kellogg Year End Report. 1999. W.K. Kellogg/West Virginia University Community Partnership Program.

Lee, K.W. 1969. "Fair Elections in West Virginia" *Appalachian Outlook.* April.

Lewis, Helen M. Linda Johnson and Donald Askins.1978. *Colonialism in Modern America: The Appalachian Case.* Boone.

Lewis, Helen. Monica Applyby. Rosemary Radford Ruether. 2003. *Mountain Sisters: From Convent to Community in Appalachia.* Lexington: The University of Kentucky Press.

Maggard, W. Sally. 1994. "From Farm to Coal Camp to Back Office and McDonald's: Living in the Midst of Appalachia's Latest Transformation." *Journal of the Appalachian Studies Association* 6:14–38.

Mahler, Tomothy. James Pennell and Lisa Osterman. 2003. "Sociology in the Neighborhood: A University-Community Collaboration Model for Transformative Change. *Humanity and Society* 27: 50–66.

Mencken, Carson 1997. "Regional Differences in Socioeconomic Well-Being in Appalachia" *Sociological Focus* 30:79–97.

Moore, Robert. ed. 2001. "Introduction" Pp. 1–20. in *The Hidden America: Social Problems in Rural America for the Twenty-First Century.* Selinsgrove: Susquehanna University Press.

Murty, Susan. 2001. "Regionalization and Rural Service Delivery" Pp. 199–218. In *The Hidden America: Social Problems in Rural America for the Twenty-First Century,* ed. Robert Moore. Selinsgrove: Susquehanna University Press.

Putnam, Robert B. 1992. *Making Democracy Work: Civic Traditions in Modern Italy.* Princeton: The University of Princeton Press.

Reid, Herbert and Betsy Taylor. 2002. "Appalachia as a Global Region: Toward Critical Regionalism and Civic Professionalism." *Journal of Appalachian Studies* 8:9–32.

Rhoads, Robert. 1997. *Community Service and Higher Learning.* Albany: State University of New York Press.

Seitz, Virginia. 1995. *Women, Development, and Communities for Empowerment in Appalachia.* SUNY Press.

Selingo, Jeffery. 1998. "AmeriCorps at 5 Years: A Success, but Not the Way Clinton Hoped" *The Chronicle of Higher Education* September 25.

Simon, Richard. 1981. "Uneven Development and the Case of West Virginia: Going Beyond the Colonial Model" *Appalachian Journal* Spring Pp. 165–185.

Smith, Barbara Ellen. 1998. "Walk-ons in the third Act: The Role of Women in Appalachian Historiography" *Journal of Appalachian Studies* 4:5–28.

Smith, Barbara Ellen. 2002. "The Place of Appalachia." *Journal of Appalachian Studies* Spring 8: 42–49.

Spence, Beth. 1979. "More Than a Shortage—A National Disgrace." *Mountain Life and* Work Jan Pp.4–8

Stanley, Talmage A. and Stephen L. Fisher. 2001. "Partners, Neighbors, and Friends: The Practice of a Place-Based Education." *Practicing* Anthropology 23:19–23.

Stoecker, Randy. 1994. *Defending Community: The Struggle for Alternative Redevelopment in Cedar-Riverside*. Philadelphia: Temple University Press.

Stoecker, Randy and Susan Stall. 1998. "Community Organizing or Organizing Community? Gender and the Crafts of Empowerment." *Gender and Society* 6:729–56.

Stoecker, Randy. 2004. "The Mystery of the Missing Social Capital and the Ghost of Social Structure: Why Community Development Can't Win." in *Community-Based Organizations The Intersection of Social Capital and Local Context in Contemporary Urban Society.* Pp. 53–66 ed. Robert Mark Silverman. Detroit: Wayne State University Press.

Taylor, Betsy. 2001. "A Place-Based University?: The Land Grant Mission in the 21th Century." *Practicing Anthropology* 23:24–8.

Thomson, Ann Marie and James L. Perry. 1998. "Can AmeriCorps Build Communities?" *Nonprofit and Voluntary Sector Quarterly* Vol. 27 No. 4 399–420.

Trent, Charles. Richard Caputo, and Chris Baker. 2004. "Poverty as a Social Problem: A Call for Social Action." In *Society for the Study of Social Problems: Agenda for Social Justice* Pp. 17–21. eds, Robert Perricci, Kathleen Ferraro, JoAnn Miller. Paula C. Rodriguez Rust (The Society for the Study of Social Problems).

Wilson, Rick. 2002. "Economic Development Review Long Overdue in West Virginia" *Charleston Gazette* Jan 2.

Rejoinder to Baker's "Collaborations for Change: Who Is Playing and Who Is Winning in Community-Based Organization Led Development in Rural Appalachia"

Emma Bailey
Western New Mexico University

Chris Baker suggests all who play win when it comes to collaborations between community-based organizations (CBOs), other non-profit organizations, for profit organizations and service learning based programs. Indeed, Baker addresses the very thing that I, as the coordinator for my university's community initiative with The Volunteer Center of Grant County (TVC) for food security and service learning programs, state as good, solid reasons for faculty to use Community Based Learning (CBL) in their courses. And he states the very reasons I give to the administration to encourage them to support these types of programs for students and faculty. The community receives needed work, faculty can use innovative and critical pedagogical techniques, the university builds collaborative and lasting community alliances, and students can expand their horizons beyond the classroom and begin to envision a place for themselves in the community. So, it does seem as though all who play win.

Clearly the CBOs benefit, as in the case of the Southern Appalachian Labor School (SALS) which Baker illustrates. The identified work just could not be done in such large blocks if it were not for the numerous volunteers and the hours they work. As Baker states, "In July of 2000, 800 volunteers from the U.S. and Canada repaired over 50 homes and in 2001 over 100 in Fayette and Kanasha counties through SALS programs" (2005: 339). In much the same way, our partner organization, TVC, depends on community members, students, and university employees to pack over 300 weekend food backpacks each week for children in Grant County. CBOs' programs exist to meet a need in their communities, but the success of the programs often depend on volunteers, service learning students, immersion programs, etc. And similar to SALS, many CBOs, like TVC, use AmeriCorps in place of regular staff. These full-time volunteers, as Baker indicates, give some stability and "glue" to organizations that depend on episodic volunteers for most of their programming.

The community, in which the CBOs work, clearly benefits as these organizations work towards providing services that otherwise may not be available. CBOs engage in community development that brings change for community members in terms of housing, access to food, and economic and social capital. In addition, other organizations (non- and for-profit) can reap benefits through the collaboration with CBOs by learning about issues in their community they wouldn't otherwise know about. In turn, this collaboration also enhances the students' experiences as they learn how various organizations work together. For example, through my institution's partnership with TVC students learn that the success of the programs requires community involvement at all levels—in-kind donations from organizations, corporate sponsorships, local funding, state and federal grants, volunteer hours and SL/CBL projects that engage students in providing services.

As an educator, among other things, one of the winners that keeps pulling me back into using SL/CBL projects is the benefit for students themselves. When I use SL/CBL projects in a course, I give up my need to be the students' only conduit to knowledge. When I unleash students from the classroom and usher them into the community, I no longer control outcomes. Yet, as Baker attests, students can learn how to be engaged citizens and come to have a broader understanding of community, cultural diversity, and oppositional politics, and participate in social change. The benefit to students is so great that even though I cannot control outcomes, I continue to encourage students as they give and receive from the community. My goal is to have them think critically about the course material and the "world" they have just encountered. As Baker indicates, students can learn valuable skills that they otherwise would not have developed and begin to see the role they want to have in the community after graduation. Like the students Baker cites, students in SL/CBL projects at my institution exclaim, "Wow! I had no idea these problems really existed here" and "I really did write and administer a survey to help an organization know how to help the community."

So, it does seem that all who play win…and yet, the humanistic endeavor begs the question, Is the game itself creating such organizational co-dependency on the structural status quo that players are prevented from addressing systemic change? For example, CBOs relationship with AmeriCorps volunteers provides some stable staff and an opportunity for young people, but if CBOs get trapped into a string of part-time employees humanists can ask three questions. Is the relationship one where the need of the CBO feeds the bureaucratic reality and vice-versa? And to what extent can we speak to the value of the work of the CBO when there is no permanent employee to work towards change? What social conditions prevent the CBO from having permanent staff, which may be supplemented by AmeriCorps volunteers? Similarly, the cycle of grants never fully frees an organization to do the work they see necessary in part because of the energy diverted to the grant writing process itself. There is also the more philosophical reality that the funding often sets parameters regarding the work of CBOs. It is highly likely that a CBO receives money (directly or indirectly) from an organization that creates the very problem the CBOs are working to correct.

As an educator, I believe in the power of SL/CBL projects for students. As a humanist, I wonder how to keep from being a part of a dependent relationship where collaborations lead to winners. Collaborations may build bigger and better CBOs, but should this be the goal of the project? If it is, then ultimately will we be like the enthusiastic food pantry volunteer who finds the experience so stimulating she hopes her children will have the same volunteer opportunity when they grow up? As an educator and a humanist is it not necessary for me to ask how we might eliminate the need for a food pantry? I want my students to look at root causes or social conditions that lead to the need of a CBO not just participate in SL/CBL projects in order for them to have a winning experience of collaborating with CBOs. In the end, we need to redefine a winning collaboration as one that plans for its own end. If we question the system and look for the root causes that give rise to the need for the CBO, then we can work towards systemic change that will eliminate our collaboration. Now that's what I call winning.

Section 5

Big Ideas:
Humanist Sociology and
the Future of the Public

Many people, even those whose political ideologies and professional bent make them sympathetic to public sociology, proclaim that by allowing social "causes" or community-based or non-governmental organizations to collaborate in the design and analysis of sociological research is to destine one's efforts to provinciality at best, obscurity at worst, and in any case, it's not real sociology. "Real sociology," they claim, is that which relates to grand theory and changes the ways in which sociologists think about their work for generations.

Such proclamations remind Corey Dolgon, one of the editors of this volume, of his graduate school days, when a prominent social scientist told some of his fellow students in a cultural studies reading group that they shouldn't get bogged down in community engagement as a source for intellectual practice. Dolgon and his cohort claimed that the field of cultural studies itself had been formed first by people like Raymond Williams and E.P. Thompson (no intellectual slouches) as they developed and operated worker education programs after WWII. The field then expanded as radical scholars like Stuart Hall and others in the Center for Contemporary Cultural Studies created new theories and inquiries based on their experiences participating in anti-racist and progressive social movements in some of London's poorest neighborhoods. These local political engagements were the fuel of intellectual theory, Dolgon argued, and such theory then informed the practical work of engagement. The mentor's response was to suggest that as intellectuals our job was simply the theory part and we should leave the engagement part to activists. Mary Chayko, this anthology's co-editor, along with probably most members of the AHS, has heard such entreaties many times over the years as well, in settings that range from classrooms and faculty offices to the wider world in which our research is conducted and our lives are lived.

Of course, intellectuals can be—are—activists. In this section of the book we present authors who understand intellectual and practical political engagement as part of the same enterprise. There is no sociological theory that can take place outside of the human social and political condition—what Marx called the "sensuousness of human activity." Far from

359

humanist, public sociology limiting or somehow making suspect the breadth and depth of our sociological work, political and social engagement strengthens it. The embrace of the sensuous, everyday world and its attendant social problems feeds our theoretical inclinations, shapes our understanding of the present and fuels our visions of the kind of world we want to create. Amidst the masses of people struggling to change their conditions and build a better society, the authors in this last section of the book find the bone and sinew of big ideas about possible futures. These are philosophers who not only work to understand the world, but try to change it.

1. A Different Kind of Sociological Society[1,2]

Alfred McClung Lee
Brooklyn College and the CUNY Graduate Center

Even though it is recorded that Aesop said it more than 2500 years ago, he was probably not the first to perceive that sheep's clothing may hide a wolf. In folk sayings, this wisdom often takes the form given it in Gilbert and Sullivan's "H. M. S. Pinafore" (1878: 122): "Things are seldom what they seem."

The phenomena behind this folk sagacity intrigue many humanist sociologists. On the whole, however, novelists and psychologists give more persistent attention than do a great many sociologists to what personal masks and institutional facades may hide or disguise. Too many sociologists assume that offhand expressions of opinion by a stranger can be used as data on which to predict probable behavior. Too many presuppose that a person or group will behave in terms of the same apparent set of values or use the same types of procedure in different social contexts. Too many work on the basis of the inaccurate notion that the public image a person or institution projects is dependably something more than a mask or a facade. Too many think that they can learn somehow about the nature of social behavior without empathy, without participant observation of a patient and continuing sort, and without testing generalizations in actual social practice.

Contrasts exist between the superficial and transient on the one hand and the wholeness of personal behavior and of social processes on the other. Unfortunately for our students, our academic disciplines, and our society, too few teachers understand and accept what they might accomplish by helping their students perceive and experience such contrasts. They can do this by stimulating enlightening new experiences. They can arouse enthusiasm for a good poem or other work of art. They can provide opportunities for fresh exploration of diverse social situations. They can encourage creative efforts at interpretation and explanation. It is too easy merely to try to cram student minds with textbook details, classifications, characterizations, and methods.

Too many teachers believe that they serve their students and society best by helping those in their classes to become dependably formed technicians who have unquestioningly assimilated details and methods without learning to suspect their validity. Such teachers are often fearful of the consequences to themselves and their students of the young being encouraged to reach out for new perceptions and new insights. Such teachers would deny that they dread novelty or creativity, but they are highly protective of the existing "system" (Lee 1970: 209–215). They do not wish to suggest that they would shake "the apple cart." They do not comprehend that they are thus serving not their students and society but the needs of currently entrenched power manipulators for an oversupply of indoctrinated tools.

---

[1] Speech at founding conference, Association of Humanist Sociology, Miami University, Oxford, Ohio, Saturday, October 30, 1976.
[2] This paper originally appeared in *Humanity & Society* Volume 1, Number 1, 1977.

The teachers themselves have long since wittingly or unwillingly come to serve as minions for power manipulators. Too many sociologists are thus little more than intellectual equivalents of routine postage stamp collectors, and they are comfortable with students who hope to emulate them.

A sociological teacher can help open new worlds of experience for students by encouraging them to perceive empathetically and thus to understand the thoughts and activities of people in diverse groups. Then the behavior of their own and of many other groups can become vivid to them in the group members' own terms. How much more useful are such experiences than exercises with methodologies that trivialize social problems and with jargonized restatements of traditional justifications for the current social class structure.

What does all this mean in terms of the sociological discipline and profession as a human enterprise faced with the bureaucratic, technocratic, plutocratic, and imperialistic problems of the last quarter of this century? How do our professional and scientific societies help sociologists to face these problems—if they do? Or have such organizations merely become parts of the symptoms of those problems? What kind of professional body should we humanist sociologists now create which can mean something more to us and to society at large than the existing organizations in our general field? What can such a new body mean to the sociological discipline in general and to its own members as sociologists and as people?

These are complex questions. They depend upon so many human variables. I shall outline how I would like to see them answered. I trust that you all will have given and will continue to give them your own serious consideration and will come up with your own answers as well as with still other questions.

Our oldest and largest professional body, the American Sociological Association, has passed its seventieth birthday. In all those years, it has never represented the needs and interests of American society generally and many of the concerns of those working in our discipline. Constructive pressures from groups of social problems researchers and activists, from radicals, from Blacks and other nonwhites, and from women have gradually forced some democratization of the ASA, but it and its journals and other projects are still largely in the hands of entrepreneurs of so-called "research" institutes in search of grants and contracts. That control group is a tightly knit, self-designated, self-perpetuating, and self-verifying ideological elite.

Myths of legitimacy having the powerful influence over the ill-informed that they do, far too many sociologists permit and accept the ASA and our major regional organizations to serve as the definers of the terms of status scrambles within our profession. The ASA elite provides the peer review committees who pass on article and book manuscripts for ASA publications and for non-experimentally-minded editors of periodicals and book publishing outfits otherwise owned. This elite also attempts to control review committees for other goodies, such as grants and contracts. In fact, it tries to give the impression that it controls all the gates to paths upward in the sociological profession. This is nonsense. American society is too complex for them. They are what the Chinese like to call "paper tigers." There are a great many other journals and book publishers as well as experimentally-minded foundation executives. From my own experiences as department chairperson and a professional society critic and participant, I would like to assure you all that the control claims for the ASA ideological elite have some substance but that a great many people have gotten ahead and even gained great distinction in our field by ignoring those gates and their vaunted gatekeepers! I have been informed that more than one-third of the full professors of sociology in this country do not bother to belong to the ASA! Many of them never have belonged. People of lesser academic rank often join for just a year now and then in order to give a paper. Student membership is not high.

The American Sociological Association and the major regional societies are enmeshed deeply in the bureaucratic, technocratic, plutocratic, and imperialistic structure of our society as it is today. Their ruling cliques are dedicated consciously or unconsciously to the reinforcement of our decadent social structure, self-destructive though it be. The existing social scientific societies are parts of the problems sociologists should be probing in their efforts to make human society livable and hopefully more self-fulfilling for a great many more people.

What we need is a professional body that will bring together those who are not impressed by the deceptive appearances of an exclusive control of sociological legitimacy by our existing organizations. I hope that the Association of Humanist Sociology will affiliate people whose curiosity is constantly jogged by the realization that "Things are seldom what they seem." Above all else, I trust that this Association will attract to it those whose dedication is to a sociology committed to the service of humanity, to the agelong high road of humanist social investigation and social theory. This means, as I see it, a sociology in which a humanist ethic is accepted as a self-imposed mandate. That ethic implies not only service to broad human interests but also accuracy in observation, distrust of trick formulas and pretentious methodologies, search for the most tenable and practical theories, and freedom from an acceptance of outside controls over one's "scientific" work.

The rationalizing and even the justifying of outside controls over "scientific research" projects has become a sophisticated organizational activity. Thus, all too often, the "ethics" committees in sociological and other societies devote themselves to the construction of public relations casuistries from which to fabricate profitable public images for the service of special interests. They try to justify or obscure the propagandistic distortion of data, as currently in the busing and the intelligence testing controversies, rather than to define and maintain scientific ideals (Form 1976; Pettigrew and Green 1976; Lee 1976: 9). Let us try to provide an honest alternative to such hypocrisies. Let us freely criticize unethical practices now taking place in our discipline. This will reveal sharply conflicting views on ethics, and that is so much the better for the future of sociology.

The building of an Association of Humanist Sociology is not going to be easy. It is going to be controversial. Like the Society for the Study of Social Problems in its early days, it may be looked upon as a threat to the discipline's alleged "integrity," that is to say, to sociology's repute with administrators fearful of any novelty that might conceivably rock the societal or even a college's boat. I wish that the Society for the Study of Social Problems had not become so "respectable" (Colvard 1976; Lee and Lee 1976), and I trust that the Association of Humanist Sociology's members will long be more concerned with developing a socially useful sociology than with trying to take seats at the tired old entrepreneurial games played by the disciplinary cliques who rule so many of our organizations.

In building the Association of Humanist Sociology, we can learn much from both the successes and the failures of the Association for Humanistic Psychology. I am happy to be a member of the AHP, but I do not offer it as a model for the AHS. Our two disciplines are too dissimilar, and, as I said, we need to benefit from both the successes and the failures of the AHP. In writing a communication for the AHP Newsletter of January 1972, Rollo May (1972: 89) warned AHP members not to concern themselves with the formation of a Division of Humanistic Psychology within the American Psychological Association. As May put it, the AHP members "represent the New Underground in psychology and I think that is a crucial function, as necessary for APA as for ourselves."

I surely agree with Rollo May and other humanistic psychologists that they and we should build and maintain autonomous organizations. But I would not at all agree that humanist sociology is a "New Underground" movement in sociology comparable to humanistic psychology in the psychological field. Quite the contrary! We represent the great traditions of social philosophy and sociology as far back as they stretch. Our intellectual ancestors include such stalwarts as the sophist Protagoras of ancient Greece who is looked upon as having furnished a philosophic basis for democracy. Little wonder that the elitists, Aristophanes and Plato, did what they could to try to destroy the influence of the sophists. More than any other statement, Protagoras's "Man is the measure of all things" echoes "the most characteristic and most seminal of all Greek contributions to civilization," as the classics scholar Moses Hadas (1967: 8) puts it in his *The Living Tradition*. Hadas (1967: 9) adds, "It is easy to see why the doctrine must have been abhorrent to men who favored other-worldly religion or conservative politic s for it was potentially subversive of all institutions and usages and all authority."

Down through the various periods of humanist flowering in South Italy and Sicily, in Asia Minor and Alexandria, among the Jews and Arabs of northern Africa and Europe, in the Great Renaissance beginning in fourteenth century Florence and spreading throughout Europe by the seventeenth century, and in the subsequent rise of modern social science and sociology, humanist social thought has been the high road of social intellectual exploration and of aid to humanity (Lee 1975).

The partial eclipse of humanist social science in this century and especially since the depression of the 1930's has not at all driven us underground. It takes more than the faddish scientism of Lester F. Ward, George A. Lundberg, Paul F. Lazarsfeld, and Samuel A. Stouffer to displace the great contributions to social thought and human welfare of the humanist theorists and activists. Now that the various forms of neo-positivism have more and more thoroughly demonstrated their dehumanizing character, their class orientations and other special interest proclivities, and their progagandistic uses, humanist sociology is staging a great comeback for which this Association can provide a useful medium and focal point. The sociologies of Karl Marx and Frederick Engels, of Sigmund Freud, of the older W. G. Sumner, the anti-plutocrat and anti-imperialist, of Florian Znaniecki and W. I. Thomas, of Pitirim A. Sorokin, of C. Wright Mills, of W. E. B. DuBois, and of Willard Waller—not to mention the many outstanding humanist sociologists now alive—represent no "underground" movement in sociology. Neglected though they may be by ASA establishment figures, trivialized though they many times may be by their so-called interpreters in our textbooks, and whether or not you agree with them at all or in detail, they are great lights of our discipline.

The communication of Rollo May about the Association for Humanistic Psychology from which I read a few remarks contains another warning that is probably not necessary for humanist sociologists. At least I hope not. But I think that we might well bear it in mind. May (1972: 89) was especially concerned with an anti-intellectual tone he detected in AHP circles, a tendency "to leave out the thinking, reflecting, historical man and put in only the feeling, touching man."

The great differences between our disciplines make this possibility less of a threat to the AHS. At the same time, in our contrasts with the ASA, I would put the anti-intellectualism on the ASA side, not on ours. Where so many currently prestigious sociologists are heedless of historical, cultural, and sometimes even situational contexts, humanist sociologists have often been notably sophisticated about social processes through time, about cultural differences among societies and among groups and classes within a society, about control structures and class conflict, and about the significance of environmental and technological changes. We are also aware that we must somehow perceive people and groups as totally as possible in their changing social environments. We must try to see whole people who feel, experience, decide, think, and reflect.

The permissive experimentalism of the Association for Humanistic Psychology made it grow very rapidly. It originated with a small group of deeply concerned psychologists who were vividly aware of the artificialities and dehumanizing tendencies of "regular" psychology as exemplified by the APA and its current divisions. As A. H. Maslow (1963: 167) listed his own suggestions "for maintaining openness and flexibility in our organization," he expressed the hope that ASP would: "(1) retain a shifting and fluctuating organizational situation; (2) define the organization in terms of the problems; (3) develop an intellectual movement *without* a leader." In other words, AHP was begun by psychologists who wanted to provide a more personalized organization as a means of transforming psychology into a science more relevant to people.

Then a variety of appliers, therapists, and even enjoyers, watchers, and sympathizers joined themselves to the original corps of researchers and analyzers. They now even include various types of mystics and other cultists. As Maslow (1968: 168) also suggested, there should be no effort to exclude anyone who might wish to join the organization, but he pointed out that AHP "could have 'scientific' members and meetings and other meetings for trying out new techniques." That would avoid a confusion of goals.

I hope that the Association of Humanist Sociology will be equally open and permissive in its membership and programming. Whether or not this will mean that we will have to find ways to live with a variety of cults remains to be seen, even foreseen. Humanist sociology does not have the wide range of clinical organizations such as the National Training Laboratories and Esalen which might seize upon AHS as a medium for publicity and recruitment. There are cultish religious-humanist sociologists, but maybe they will continue to find themselves more at home in such bodies as the Association for the Sociology of Religion and some denominational groups. What may happen in consequence of its inclusiveness does not alarm me so long as the AHS maintains a firm commitment to broad humanitarian concerns and does not become a medium for promulgating rigid intellectual tools and precise strategies for special-interest manipulators.

From the psychologists, we certainly can borrow and use such key conceptions as Maslow's (1964) "self-actualization," a human goal to be sought and achieved through "peak experiences." This is a human struggle for identity, dignity, and self-expression to which humanist sociologists can contribute significantly but differently from humanistic psychologists, belletrists, social philosophers, poets, painters, and novelists.

This is a great challenge that faces us as humanist sociologists. Let me spell out some challenges related to this one. Let me try to be more specific as to lines along which we might well work:

1. Let us create first of all a professional society of cooperative friends rather than one of competitive prima donnas.

2. Let us be critical of the abuses of privilege in our discipline and especially of the exploitation of junior colleagues and graduate students.

3. Let us not look upon the published work of any writer as "holy writ." Let us be wide-ranging in our search for facts and ideas. Just because a sociologist of the past could not transcend his racist, sexist, or class-centered conditioning does not mean that she or he might not have left behind some challenging ideas and possibly collections of data. In other words, it is easy and—I believe—justifiable to make a case against Herbert Spencer or Vilfredo Pareto, but it is also profitable to study their writings at first hand. I am sure that Marx, Sumner, Cooley, and Weber would regard a lot of their printed ideas as old hat" today if they were still at work among us. It is ridiculous to get into long exegetical debates as to what Marx or Sumner or Cooley or Weber "really" meant about something. The important thing is what do given phenomena, actions, processes mean to you and me and to people generally today and tomorrow. Fortunately, we have such a tool as *Sociological Abstracts* to help us find what we might need in the international maze of sociological contributions. That service will also bring abstracts of our own writings to the attention of those who use principal research libraries throughout the whole world.

4. Let us examine critically the stylish fads and suspect theories that sweep across our field. I refer especially at this time to the current resurgence of a sophisticated racism led by certain academicians and echoed by those who are making political or economic capital out of so-called "reverse discrimination," agitations against the use of busing for desegregation, and class-biased and ethnocentric I Q. tests (Pettigrew & Green 1976; Lee 1976: 9). Criminologists who have dug deeply enough into the statistics of their field know that crime statistics are largely arbitrary fictions set by the current notions of expediency of those who compile them. Their basic weakness lies in the class and race biases in the detection and recording of crimes. All sorts of allegations are then based upon them. Marriage and divorce figures may be more accurate in a formal sense, but analyses of their significance often have little reference to actual human behavior.

5. Let us try to see social problems as something more than developments that irritate the inhabitants of our white suburban ghettos and our carefully guarded urban apartment skyscrapers. Visit our prisons. You will get the impression that criminals are disproportionately nonwhite. And yet it is no great secret that anti-social conspiracies, law violations, interpersonal violence, theft, and all the rest take place in all social circles, classes, and neighborhoods. Those responsible get differential treatment. Our prisons are the end product of a society shot through with white racism and middle-class centeredness subservient to upper-class controls. Why do our newspapers and our other mass media see busing to end racial segregation only from the standpoint of the alleged evils of white flight and not from the standpoint, among others, of Black deprivation in jobs, housing, health care, as well as education? Is a white middleclass ghetto a fit place in which to raise children who will presumably be able to take their places one day as impartial judges, broadminded educators,

and intelligent and fair administrators in what is so often called our "democratic" society? Are we as educators concerned enough with the anti-intellectual roles, even the socially subversive roles that college social sororities and fraternities prepare our students to play in American society?

6. Let us look at the worldwide problem of colonialist and neocolonialist exploitation, at the millions who lack not only civil rights and dignity but food a.;d shelter. The problem centers especially in the United States, and this is all the more reason for us to recognize it and to preoccupy ourselves with it. A visitor from Bombay, a sociologist of note, said to me recently, "Why do we Indians have to accept American sociology as if it were something other than apologetics for American plutocracy and for plutocratic imperialism?" When I myself lectured abroad in such countries as Bangladesh, India, and Syria and even in parts of Europe, I had great difficulty in establishing my credibility—to the extent that I did so at all. The United States is the principal base of the multinational corporations, as foreigners see us, and those corporations owe loyalty to nothing other than their own boards of directors who treat the United States and other country governments as tools for domination and exploitation. I was thus suspect of being a propagandistic tool of a governmental agency in the service of those multinational corporations. The members of those supranational boards live in such an abstract world that they do not have to confront the suffering their decisions precipitate or observe personally how much blood their decisions may make flow. Certainly the Jews, Christians, and Muslims in the Middle East are not fighting each other in consequence of religious mandates. They are fighting for human dignity, for civil rights, for reasonable security for themselves and their families, but their loyalties and their struggles are exploited by remote military-industrial interests to carry on their vast games of power manipulation. Let us help Americans see their share in these manipulations. Let us suggest the disastrous future toward which we appear to be drifting.

I could go on and on with the challenges that confront us, but I will mention only one more:

7. Let us explore more carefully and then publicize the manipulative strategies and propagandas to which so much of our mass media, politics, religious apologetics, and formal education are devoted. Who is selling what to whom and at what costs and for what purposes? Sociology textbooks appear to be giving less and less space to the nature of public discussion and opinion and to the ways in which specialists manipulate them. In preparing our sociology students to live effectively and constructively in a world that constantly experiences Watergates but only occasionally is told about them, we need to discover all we can about how human beings are made into tools and societies are subjected to costly and even catastrophic scenarios.

Let us hope that we are launching an Association of Humanist Sociology which will have some such idealism, which will bring a lot of us together in non-competitive comradeship, and which will help keep more sociological research and teaching on the great humanist high road.

References

Colvard, Richard, ed. 1976. "SSSP as a Social Movement." *Social Problems*, 24: 1–142.

Form, W. H., Secretary. 1976. "Minutes of the Third Meeting of the 1976 ASA Council." *ASA Footnotes*, 4: 5 (may): 8–9.

Gilbert, W. S., and Arthur Sullivan. 1878. "H.M.S. Pinafore," pp. 101–137 in *The Complete Plays of Gilbert and Sullivan*. New York: Modern Library, n.d.

Guion, Carol, and Tina Kelly, eds. 1976. *Satan is Left-Handed*. San Francisco: Association for Humanistic Psychology.

Hadas, Moses. 1967. *The Living Tradition*. New York: New American Library. Lee, A. McC. 1970. Multivalent Man. 2nd ed. New York: George Braziller.

——. 1975. "Humanism as Demystification." *Sociological Analysis & Theory*, 5: 267–288.

——. 1976. "Valedictory: A Report on the Year 1975–76." *ASA Footnotes* 4: 6 (August): 1, 9–10.

Lee, Elizabeth B. and A. McC. Lee. 1976. "The Society for the Study of Social Problems: Parental Recollections and Hopes." *Social Problems* 24: 4–14.

Maslow, A. H. 1963. Paraphrased quotation, p. 167 in "Culled From the Archives." Guion & Kelly, 1976: 167–169.

——. 1964. *Religions, Values and Peak-Experiences*. Columbus: Ohio State University Press.

——. 1968. Paraphrased quotation, pp. 167–168 in ''Culled From the Archives." Guion & Kelly, 1976: 167–169.

May, Rollo. 1972. "Rollo May Writes." Guion & Kelly, 1976: 89–90.

Pettigrew, T. F. , and R. L. Green. 1976. "School Desegregation in Large Cities." *Harvard Educational Review*, 46: 1–53.

Humanist Sociology in the Wake of Al Lee[1]

Timothy Black
University of Hartford

At the founding conference in 1976, Al Lee provided a strong rationale for a new sociological organization that would challenge the formulaic, unreflective practices of a sociology obsessed with its own professional existence and recognition as a social science. In the 27 years that have elapsed since Lee's inspiring speech, the need for humanist sociology could not be more urgent. Most sociologists rarely step outside the professional parameters established by the discipline and by the academy to actively seek social change or to locate their own work in a collectively established vision of a better world. Few interact directly with marginalized or oppressed groups furthering an empathetic understanding of the social world and broadening the prospects for informed social action. Instead, most sociologists remain safely rooted behind a facade of science, indulging professional status as it has been defined within the discipline and the university, and accepting the dispassionate and benign routines of privileged academics. Peering across the sociological landscape today, Al Lee would no doubt shake his head in disgust and find little to cheer about. But taking refuge in convenient cynicism or indolent whining was not his style; finding an alternative was.

Lee understood, perhaps foremost, that effective challenges to power require organization. The Association for Humanist Sociology is an attempt to provide an organization for teacher-scholars and scholar-activists to forge new ways of practicing sociology that is distinct from a sociology "enmeshed deeply in the bureaucratic, technocratic, plutocratic, and imperialistic structure of our society…." Working within universities and colleges that increasingly resemble corporate organizations, with a top-down management structure, a contingency workforce, and a reward structure that reflects market interests, humanist teacher-scholars search for public spaces within universities to engage students about the social processes that shape their lives and reproduce social inequalities. They nurture critical thinking among students and often link students to progressive organizations in the community where they can put their ideas into practice. They join students in democratically organized groups on campus to bring in speakers, plan actions, and to create alternative identities and ways of interacting on campus.

Humanist scholar-activists confront similar challenges, both on campus and within the sociology profession. As universities have become leaner and meaner "cutting costs, raising tuition and increasing dependence on corporate donations" programs that do not meet a market-inspired vision are often marginalized and even at risk of elimination. Women's studies, Labor studies, Latino and African American studies programs struggle to maintain a funding base and decent space on campus. Sociology, itself, was threatened in the '80s as enrollments declined and a few universities experimented with eliminating the major

---

[1] This paper originally appeared in *Humanity & Society* Volume 27, Number 3, 2003.

altogether. The sociology profession responded in predictable ways, it shored up its professional image and attempted to legitimate itself as a science. Applied sociology programs grew and revenue streams along with it, as the discipline became more grant and contract oriented, more state and foundation dependent. Top sociological journals emphasized scientific methods, which usually meant the quantitative analysis of large, national data bases created through survey methods. And tenure and promotion decisions increasingly required large numbers of publications in these journals. In the panic of legitimating our profession, even smaller colleges and universities adopted similar models for assessing "excellence" in the field. In short, the profession has become Al Lee's nightmare.

Humanist scholar-activists work against these trends. They refuse assembly line sociology, and instead, adopting Lee's creed that "Things are seldom what they seem," they explore social issues and social problems in a broader context of social injustice and establish theories that help us to see how social science is implicated within the processes that reproduce social privilege, power and status. The humanist scholar-activist eschews the armchair model of research, but also the objective field researcher model, and instead works together with progressive groups struggling to create alternative economic and social forms of existence and writes from a perspective that confronts power and nurtures social change. The humanist scholar-activist doesn't simply "study" disadvantaged groups, but interacts with them in an effort to understand the processes that foster social inequality and the psychological consequences that result from these processes, all in an effort to better inform human struggle. Finally, the humanist scholar-activist very often adopts the role of the public intellectual, in which he or she seeks a variety of forums to engage the public, whether through local speaking engagements, local newspapers and radio, alternative journals, or books published through trade presses.

Al Lee's founding speech provided both an ideological and political framework for the AHS. He attempted to radicalize the discipline, to formulate a vision of sociology grounded in the struggle for social justice. But Lee also understood well the need for an institutional base through which a set of practices could be established that provided an alternative way of doing and thinking about sociology that explicitly challenged the assumptions and values of mainstream sociology. Central to these practices is the association's journal Humanity and Society, which provides the institutional space for scholar-activists to present their work and, in doing so, to forge a new path for a sociology integrated into the struggle for meaningful social change. Lee's vision was that the AHS would become a place for teacher-scholars and scholar-activists to come together to find meaningful camaraderie, inspiration, legitimacy, vision, identity and hope. After all, practicing humanist sociology can be a lonely endeavor in a hostile landscape, often mitigated only by a passion for social justice and an organization that helps to keep that passion alive.

2. An Alternative to Corporate Capitalism and State Socialism[1]

Frank Lindenfeld
Bloomsburg University[1]
1996 AHS Presidential Address

Reflexive Statement

This paper reflects my longstanding interest in worker co-ops, workplace democracy, and societal alternatives to corporate capitalism and state socialism. Cooperatively organized economies, in my opinion, provide a social framework which promotes humanistic values including empowerment, equality, social justice, and genuine political democracy.

Much of my work on cooperatives has taken place within the context of a scattered network of friends and colleagues. At the 1979 meetings of AHS I made a brief presentation about the sugar worker cooperatives in Jamaica; there I met anthropologist Monica Frölander-Ulf, with whom I then did a study of those co-ops (Frölander-Ulf and Lindenfeld 1985). A few years earlier, I had begun working with the short-lived national Federation for Economic Democracy, whose Chair was William F. Whyte, and whose Director was C. George Benello (also an AHS member). I helped found a local affiliate of the federation, which subsequently became the technical assistance group PACE of Philadelphia. With George, Len Krimerman and others I edited the bimonthly *Changing Work* and later worked with Len on the successor *Grassroots Economic Organizing Newsletter*, as well as on an anthology on workplace democracy (Krimerman and Lindenfeld 1992). After George's untimely death, I also helped edit a collection of his essays on grassroots and workplace democracy (Krimerman, Lindenfeld, Korty, and Benello 1991).

Introduction

Corporate capitalism sucks. Major corporations poison our environment with toxic wastes, they market products known to be defective or even lethal, and they devastate our communities through plant closings that idle thousands. At the same time, the corporations and the wealthy pay reduced taxes, shifting the burden onto the rest of us. How can they get away with this? In part, they succeed because they fund politicians of both major parties who are in positions to protect their interests. Fifteen percent of the population—some 40 million Americans, including at least 16 million children—live in poverty, while wealth is increasingly concentrated in the hands of a small elite. The CEO of Coca Cola

---

[1]This paper originally appeared in *Humanity & Society* Volume 27, Number 4, 2003.

has accumulated nearly $1 billion in deferred compensation all by himself! (*The New York Times*: 10/13/96)

To mitigate some of the worst excesses of capitalism, reform movements have pushed for various health and welfare programs, though the U.S. has lagged far behind west European industrial countries in the scope and quality of its welfare policies. By the mid 1990s, the already flimsy and badly frayed social safety net of ours was further torn apart by bipartisan welfare cuts concurrent with our government's continued lavish AFDC program, aka Aid For Dependent Corporations.

In Europe, capitalism was challenged by revolutionaries as well, as anarchist, socialist and communist movements struggled to replace capitalism with a better system. Beginning with the revolution of 1917, the Russian Communist Party set up a state socialist economy, later expanded to other countries in the Soviet orbit. Its top-down socialism was not much of an improvement over capitalism, and the Stalinist excesses were far worse. The people of central and Eastern Europe deposed the Communists when they had an opportunity to do so. Their motto was, state socialism sucks! The basic flaw of the Communist systems (including Yugoslavia) was the combination of socialism with an authoritarian political system.

A major problem with corporate capitalism and state socialism is that they are both based on the concentration of economic power in the hands of a small elite unaccountable to the rest of us. Economic systems are not limited to these two choices, however. There is a third way, referred to variously as the social economy (Bruyn and Meehan 1987) or the cooperative commonwealth. The building blocks for this alternative already exist in the cooperative movement, which broadly speaking includes consumer and worker co-ops, employee owned companies, credit unions, community development loan funds, service credit systems and local barter and service exchange networks.

A major landmark of the cooperative movement was the co-op store initiated in 1844 by a group of unemployed flannel weavers in Rochdale, England. Since then, there has been an extensive development of consumer and worker cooperatives, including the 19th century U.S. worker co-ops supported by the militant Knights of Labor trade union, the collective settlements or kibbutzim in Israel that go back to 1911, and the post-World War II development of the influential Mondragon network in Spain and the legion of several thousand worker co-ops in the Emilia Romagna region of northern Italy.

I will begin here with a discussion of the Rochdale Pioneers, whose cooperative ideas can be traced back to the writings of Robert Owen in 1820. Then I will discuss the characteristics of worker co-ops, look at three contemporary cooperative networks, and examine the recent development of service exchange and barter networks. Finally, I will come back to the problem of putting the pieces together to build a cooperative commonwealth.

The Rochdale Pioneers

The first cooperatives represented a peaceful attempt to build an alternative economic system by organizing peoples' institutions that would co-exist alongside capitalist ones, and which would gradually expand to involve the majority of the population as cooperative producers and consumers. The Rochdale Cooperative of 1844 began in the aftermath of a bitter strike.

At the end of an unsuccessful weavers' strike in 1843, twenty seven men and ne woman (Ann Tweedale) found themselves blacklisted; they could not get any kind of work. They formed a collective discussion group, "The Equitable Society of Rochdale Pioneers," which spent months discussing how their political beliefs could best be translated into action (Giese: 1982).

The goals of the Rochdale Pioneers were far reaching and visionary; they set out to build not only consumer co-ops, but also housing co-ops and manufacturing co-ops leading ultimately to a worker-controlled economy. This was their program, stated in their own words:

- The establishment of a store for the sale of provisions, clothing, etc.
- The purchasing or erecting of a number of houses, in which…members desiring to assist each other in improving their domestic and social conditions may reside.
- The manufacture of such articles as the society may determine…for the employment of…members as may be without employment, or who may be suffering in consequence of repeated reduction in their wages.
- The society shall purchase or rent…land which shall be cultivated by the members who may be out of employment, or whose labor may be badly remunerated.
- As soon as practicable, this society shall…arrange the powers of production, distribution, education and government, or in other words…establish a self-supporting colony of united interest, and assist other societies in establishing such colonies.

In 1854, the Rochdale Pioneers also founded a cooperative cotton mill, with 100 workers putting up most of the capital. The mill was so successful that the Pioneers decided to expand it. They built a new, larger factory in 1859. To obtain the necessary capital, they sold 1000 shares. Many were bought by outsiders, who soon held a majority. The interests of the outside shareholders and the mill worker-owners were in conflict, however, and within three years the outsiders, intent on profiting from their investment, transformed the business into a capitalist company.

Cooperative Principles

Here I will discuss briefly some major cooperative principles with illustrations from the Rochdale Pioneers as well as from contemporary worker co-ops. The Rochdale mill was vulnerable to takeover by capitalists when it violated the bedrock cooperative principle of democratic control: to avoid this, Ellerman (1990) suggests worker co-ops separate *personal rights* such as the right to elect Directors and set policy, from *property rights* such as the right to receive a return on share capital invested and to receive a share of the profits. Each worker has one vote as part of their membership. This vote is a personal right that cannot be given or sold to outsiders. Under certain conditions, members can sell their shares, usually only back to the co-op. But they can never sell their voting rights, just as U.S. citizens cannot sell their right to participate in elections to foreigners. (This differs sharply from capitalist corporations where stockholders' influence is generally proportional to the money they invested—the more money, the greater their voting power). In addition to the one member, one vote rule, worker cooperatives differ in several other crucial respects from capitalist corporations. I list these here, with the reminder that this is an ideal-typical description not necessarily reflected in all details by all worker cooperatives.

1. *Co-ops Embody Diverse Social Goals Beyond Mere Profit.* Worker co-ops balance profit with an emphasis on worker and community welfare and economic sustainability. They seek to:

   a. Generate community employment, maintain existing jobs and create good new jobs;
   b. Provide high quality services and safe, durable and healthy products without harm to workers or the environment;
   c. Empower worker-members by encouraging their education, personal growth, and their learning new skills; and
   d. Maximize member participation in the organizational decision making process.

2. *Co-ops Avoid Hiring Non-Member Labor.* Co-ops avoid employing non-members, though they may hire temporaries to meet unexpected or seasonal demand. Without such a rule, co-ops degenerate into workers' capitalist organizations where a privileged group of worker-owners profits from the labor of hired help.

3. *Co-ops Provide Equitable Compensation and Job Security.* Worker co-ops strive to offer members adequate pay and benefits, as well as steady, interesting and challenging work. When business is slow, hours of work are reduced for all instead of laying off some. Co-ops usually maintain only modest pay differentials between managers and others. The Israeli kibbutzim do not pay their worker-members any wages; all jobs are equally valued, and all members entitled to the same benefits. In the Mondragon network, the highest paid get no more than six times the earnings of the lowest paid worker.

4. *Co-op Profits Belong To Their Worker-Members.* In worker co-ops, profits are shared by worker-members equally or in proportion to hours worked. The Mondragon co-ops, for example, allocate 10% of their profits to education, 20% is reinvested in the business, and the rest kept in the form of internal capital accounts held for each worker-member. These accounts, which can grow to $50,000 or more, are refunded to members as an extra bonus on retirement.

5. *Co-ops Are Democratically Managed.* Worker co-ops do need coordinators or managers; missing are the middle managers and foremen whose job it is to make sure employees are not goofing off or stealing from the company. In worker co-ops, managers are responsible to a democratically elected Board, and ultimately to the membership. The relationship between workers and managers is based upon mutual respect and trust. Worker-members or their elected delegates have a say at all levels of the organization, from the work group level all the way up to the Board of Directors. To handle the inevitable disagreements between managers and workers, many co-ops have special grievance committees.

6. *Co-ops Generally Limit Their Size.* Though some have as many as 1000 members, many worker co-ops remain small by choice. Most of the northern Italian co-ops

have fewer than 50 members, for example. An optimum size limit is probably closer to 200, because organizations under that size are better able to provide for maximum member participation in decision-making.

Next, I will turn to three contemporary networks of consumer and worker cooperatives that embody the principles discussed above: the Mondragon co-ops in Spain, the Seikatsu clubs of Japan, and Co-op Atlantic in Canada.

Three Contemporary Co-op Networks

The Mondragon Co-ops

The Mondragon cooperative network is an impressive social achievement. It accounts for a considerable slice of production and distribution in the Spanish Basque provinces. Its sales exceed $5 billion a year and its associated co-ops provide jobs for about 30,000 members. The Mondragon co-ops are collectively owned, and based on cooperative principles. The size and scale of this cooperative system are such that we can begin to talk about its becoming a credible challenge to capitalist institutions. From a modest beginning of one stove factory begun in the 1950s by several graduates of a technical school founded by local priest Jose Arizmendi, the network has expanded to dozens of industrial co-ops and a growing chain of consumer markets. It also embraces numerous second order co-ops, including educational institutions, its own social security and health system, and its own bank. The bank and its entrepreneurial department have played a crucial role in coordination and in pro-active planning for the development of new cooperatives (see Whyte and Whyte 1988; and Morrison 1991).

In the early 1990s, the network reorganized itself as the Mondragon Cooperative Corporation (MCC), with three broad divisions: an industrial group, a financial group, and a distribution group. The industrial group includes the flagship FAGOR enterprises which produce everything from auto parts and refrigerators to machine tools and robots. The financial group is led by the cooperative bank, the Caja Laboral Popular. The mainstay of the distribution group is Eroski, a growing chain of consumer co-ops.

The recent growth of Eroski is impressive. Retailing is the fastest growing part of the MCC. With the help of investment funds from the Caja, the distribution group has been expanding each year, setting up more and more supermarkets including the giant size ones or hypermarkets. Hundreds of co-op markets now provide employment for some 10,000 persons (Ormaechea et al. 1995).

The MCC seems to have successfully met the challenge of the integration of Spain into the European Common Market, but there are signs it is wavering from its cooperative principles. The investments of the Caja no longer exclusively promote cooperative development. Moreover, as the retail network continues its breakneck expansion, its democratic features are in danger of being watered down. One issue is the hiring of non-member workers, whose numbers appear to be growing. Another relates to annual membership meetings. Because of the large numbers involved, MCC members do not meet together in a general assembly of the whole. Rather, they meet in different geographical regions to choose delegates who in turn elect the Board of Directors.

The Seikatsu Anti-Consumerist Buying Clubs

A contrasting model is provided by the Seikatsu buying clubs in Japan. These democratically organized clubs strive to provide high quality food at reasonable prices through advance orders. They avoid unnecessary product proliferation. Instead of carrying dozens of types of rice, soy sauce, etc., they offer only one or two of each. Products detrimental to the environment are not sold. Membership in the clubs represents more than a commitment to obtain healthy food at reasonable prices; it signifies adherence to a lifestyle and philosophy that opposes consumerism and supports the movement to build a sustainable economy based on ecological values. Beginning with one local group organized in Tokyo in 1965 to provide quality milk for their children, Seikatsu has grown to a quarter of a million member families that together purchase about $1 billion annually. The clubs began to forge links with producers early in their development:

They realized that the big dairy companies were not to be trusted and they began their own line of natural milk. Making direct links to small dairies, they contracted to purchase projected amounts of quality products at stabilized prices: an alternative marketing system emerged. That same system has been extended to all foods necessary for a healthy life— rice, eggs, vegetables, fish—and to non-agricultural products, e.g. appliances, clothes, books, and even concert tickets. Seikatsu has its own product line of about 60 items, owns two dairies and a beef ranch, and contracts for some 30% of its produce from organic farmers. In 1985, one Seikatsu branch began its own soap factory, rejecting chemical detergents in favor of environmentally friendly ingredients such as recycled cooking oil (Matsuoksa, Stone and Krimerman 1994).

Seikatsu has initiated the development of new worker co-ops to provide various goods and services including food products, home health care for the aged and infirm, lunch services and retail stores. By 1994 there were 161 affiliated worker cooperatives which provided employment for over 4000 members.

The basis for the Seikatsu clubs are local "hans," groups of 8–10 families whose housewife-representatives meet monthly to order food as well as to discuss issues of common concern. The clubs also produce for their own guaranteed market those products they cannot obtain from commercial sources.

Each of the more than 26,000 hans elects a representative to their local branch. The branches in turn elect regional representatives to the General Assembly which chooses the overall Board of Directors. The Seikatsu clubs have sponsored various campaigns to promote ecologically sound public policies, such as the one which persuaded the Tokyo city government to reject the use of rain forest lumber for municipal public works. By 1993, some 75 Seikatsu sponsored candidates had been elected to local government seats.

Co-op Atlantic

A final example of a large-scale cooperative network is Co-op Atlantic in Canada, which combines some features of both Mondragon and Seikatsu (Morrison 1994–5). Co-op Atlantic is an umbrella organization governed by representatives of member co-ops. It is a second order co-op, serving 161 member organizations with management training, planning assistance and coordination. Its members include 88 retail cooperatives—which account for a fifth of all food sales in the Atlantic provinces—as well as housing, agricultural, fishing and production co-ops. The network has over 5,000 workers and sales approaching

$500 million. The co-op membership includes about 170,000 families. Co-op Atlantic is continuing to plan and implement integrated, community based cooperative development on an economy-wide scale for this poor and underdeveloped region (Stone 1995).

These examples demonstrate the benefits of size and scale that facilitate networking to form local and regional development associations of worker and consumer cooperatives. Networking helps create jobs, promotes organizational stability, combines buying power, and maximizes the group's influence on the rest of the society. Another feature of these models is their vertical integration—the use of collective buying power to encourage the development of cooperatively run businesses that supply them with items the members want, at the same time helping to create local jobs.

The experience of Mondragon shows that the establishment of second order cooperatives—organizations that provide services to member co-ops, especially educational, management and financial services—is crucial for the growth of the cooperative sector. Much of the dynamism of the Mondragon system resulted from the role of the Caja Laboral Popular in attracting savings deposits, lending money to its member cooperatives, and providing them with entrepreneurial services. It will be important for the U.S. cooperative movement to create and nurture numerous community development financial institutions that can perform a similar function.

Local Exchange Systems and Barter Networks

Another aspect of cooperativism is the moneyless exchange system, based on mutual aid and barter (Cahn and Rowe 1992; Greco 1994; Offe and Heinze 1992). Like the consumer cooperatives, such exchanges were also promoted by the visionary writings of Robert Owen. Exchange systems flourished in the U.S. as part of the self help movement during the depression of the 1930s (Offe and Heinze ch.5). Barter networks are based on the fact that many unemployed, retired and poor persons lack money to buy even essentials but have time, skills, goods and services they are able and willing to trade with others.

Community barter networks promote local trade without the exchange of official currency or checks. The exchanges are based on agreement by local community residents and businesses to accept payment for goods or services in the form of promises such as IOUs, scrip, or credits entered on a computer. These systems go well beyond two person barter and may involve networks of hundreds or thousands of community members.

The barter works like this: Amy washes laundry for Bob, in exchange for some cash and some scrip. Bob fixes Carl's car; he receives money for the parts and scrip for his labor. Carl pays for meals at Daphne's restaurant with scrip. The restaurant pays waitress Ellen partly in cash, partly in scrip, etc. Most networks periodically publish directories that list services or goods offered. The most successful networks include local businesses that agree to accept at least part of their customers' payments through some form of barter exchange.

Such exchange networks have many benefits. They promote community cohesion and local development. They provide some needed goods and services—such as day care and elder care—to those who do not have enough money to buy them. Local businesses can increase the number of their customers and the amount purchased by each; governments can stretch the use of scarce tax dollars as volunteers perform services that might otherwise have to be paid out of public funds. (A major objection to service credit systems is that they may encourage governments to further skimp on welfare services.) Unemployed and retired participants can gain a sense of empowerment by participating in barter networks. Moreover, locally traded credits keep resources circulating within the community, encouraging people to patronize local sources rather than buying from outside the community.

Three general forms of barter networks have emerged: service credit systems, local currency or scrip systems, and local exchange trading systems. In service credit systems participants perform services for other network members, such as home care, chauffeuring, or tutoring, expecting that other network participants will provide services for them when they themselves need help. Service credit networks, including the time dollar systems inspired by Edgar Cahn, have been organized in dozens of U.S. localities, primarily as a way to provide services to the elderly. Volunteers provide care in return for credits they can redeem in future or donate to a nonprofit group or to a relative for their use. Each hour volunteered earns the same credit, regardless of the expertise or skill used in that hour, and credits are generally redeemable only within a defined local community.

In local currency systems, participants exchange goods and services with each other, paying with scrip. One of the most advanced is Ithaca Hours which began in 1991. The non-profit group distributes and maintains a local currency called Ithaca Hours. Each Hour note is considered the equivalent of about $10 in official U.S. currency. The free bimonthly newspaper, Ithaca Money, is distributed locally. Those who list their services in it and agree to accept partial or full payment in the alternative currency receive two Hour notes for the first ad; if the ad is repeated four times they receive two additional Hours. The group donates 10% of its Hours to local nonprofit organizations chosen at its meetings. As of 1996, Ithaca Hours has been able to attract about 80 retailers and over 160 other local businesses and professional services as members. The local credit union accepts the payment of loan fees in Ithaca Hours and some restaurants accept 100% payment in the local currency. Some employees have also agreed to accept part of their wages in the form of Ithaca Hours. As of 1996, the cumulative volume of trade in Ithaca Hours exceeded $500,000. The idea has been copied in dozens of other U.S. communities.

Local exchange trading systems (LETS) are similar to alternative currency systems but don't use cash or scrip. Instead, they maintain a computerized accounting of the flow of the alternative debits and credits—the amounts of services and goods purchased by members from others in the network and the amounts paid to the others in the form of goods and services provided to them. In contrast to service credit systems where all volunteer hours count equally, alternative currency and LETS networks accept exchanges where more highly skilled persons receive a greater number of credits per hour than less skilled ones. In principle, both scrip systems and LETS could use locally accepted credit cards to further stimulate trade among members. LETS have spread in Canada, Australia, New Zealand, and England. The largest LETS in Auckland, New Zealand, reached 2,000 members by 1996.

Service credit systems and alternative currencies by themselves will not, of course, replace the corporate capitalist system. Nevertheless, they can help build the economic strength of local communities, empower local residents, and mitigate some of the consequences of poverty and unemployment. Such barter exchange networks are one of the ingredients than can be used to build the cooperative commonwealth.

Political Neutrality: A Questionable Principle

One vexing issue for the cooperative movement is that of political neutrality. Despite their origin as a working class organizatica directly opposed to capitalism, the Rochdale Pioneers adopted a rule of political neutrality. The cooperatives that followed in their footsteps embraced that principle, but I believe that has been a mistake. Neutrality makes sense if your goal is to go after the greatest possible number of customers to increase sales, but detracts from building a self-conscious cooperative movement. Cooperatives would do better to pursue what Charles Hampden-Turner termed political marketing, attracting and keeping customers loyal to the cooperative ideal even if they have to pay a penny or two more for some products. Cooperatives are based on a participatory ethos and a democratic value system that runs counter to the capitalist principles of hierarchy and control by the wealthy. Worker and consumer cooperatives represent an alternative to corporate capitalism. As potential agents of social transformation, cooperatives are political in their very existence. They embody the kind of participatory democratic structures that would predominate in a cooperatively organized world, countering the worker alienation characteristic of both corporate capitalist and state socialist systems. At the same time, the struggle to establish cooperatives and broaden them into mutually supporting networks is in itself part of the process of building that cooperative world. As networks of cooperatives and democratically managed organizations proliferate, they may reach enough of a critical mass to transform the entire society into the cooperative commonwealth foreseen by the Rochdale Pioneers. This brings us to the matter of building a cooperative system within existing capitalist societies.

Building A Cooperative Commonwealth

The cooperative movement needs to move forward on two feet. One foot consists of alternative economic institutions—worker and consumer co-ops, community development financial institutions and barter networks. The movement needs to forge linkages between these organizations to form second order co-ops and federations. The other foot consists of a broad scale coalition of anti-corporate people's political organizations. Such a political thrust is needed to challenge the entrenched power of the transnational corporations and open them up to democratic control by their employees, as well as to modify the legal and tax framework to make it more friendly to cooperatives. This might be done by taking over one of the existing political parties, but it is much more likely that we will need to develop a new movement outside the existing major party framework, building a progressive third party or coalition. The seeds of such a political development are now beginning to sprout— as in the Green Party, the Alliance, the New Party and the Labor Party. To become more effective, these groups will need to work together. The opposition to corporate capitalist dominance cannot afford the internecine squabbles that split the socialist and other left movements over most of their history. That political opposition must also be based on interracial coalitions. The 19th century Populist movement began to unite black and white farmers and workers and posed a strong challenge to the then existing establishment (Goodwyn 1976); that challenge was defused and splintered by a number of factors, one of which was racism encouraged and funded by the capitalists and wealthy landowners.

There is not necessarily any one best version of a cooperative economy, nor any one best path to get there, so what follows should be seen as a general vision rather than a blueprint.

Such a social economy would be a mixed system where worker-owned and controlled cooperatives predominate but where there are also small private enterprises as well as public services provided by local or regional governments in such fields as education, transportation, communication, energy production, education, day care, and health care. The cooperative economy would consist mainly of small and medium size worker co-ops, typically with less than 50 workers, though there might also be some much larger ones. These co-ops would join together to create an array of second order cooperatives and federations to provide various types of business services including banking, managerial training, health care, etc.

Some financial alternatives already exist: the Cooperative Bank, community development credit unions, microenterprise funds, and community development loan funds in the U.S., and the Canadian labor investment funds. A major cornerstone would be educational institutions that promote cooperativism and provide training for co-op managers. It will take a major educational effort to crack the hegemony of capitalist ideas, spreading an alternative cooperative ideology.

One role that humanist sociology can play is taking part in this educational effort. Working with the cooperative movement, we can initiate participatory and applied sociological research projects around building cooperative alternatives. We can organize technical assistance programs and take pro-active roles in promoting worker ownership and control, as the Ohio Employee Ownership Center has been doing. We can work with progressive political coalitions and parties to help develop policy initiatives, strategies for sharing the wealth, and strategies for gaining more access for cooperative ideologies and anti corporate programs to TV and other mass media.

A cooperative economy would be based on a foundation of local production for local and regional consumption, especially for such basic needs as food and shelter, though there would also be some trade with other regions and countries. The tax structure would give preferential treatment to cooperative businesses as well as to pension plans and venture funds that invest in a diversified portfolio of cooperative businesses, and would reward ecologically friendly and sustainable business practices. The legal structure would allow the charter or continuation of corporations only if they provided for substantial employee ownership and control.

The cooperative commonwealth will be enhanced by the organization of local barter and volunteer networks to enable those with more time than money to obtain necessary services and products through exchange with other community residents. It will be greatly enhanced by the provision of government social welfare benefits such as regional or national health insurance and a guaranteed minimum income combined with a progressive tax system that transfers income from wealthy families and corporations to those less fortunate. Such a tax system could favor corporations that embrace genuine worker ownership and control and democratic management systems, and impose heavy taxes on those that do not implement such measures. This could further be supplemented by a tax on wealth and on the movement of capital to other countries.

Conclusion

The cooperative commonwealth is a desirable and feasible alternative to corporate capitalism and state socialism. The cooperative networks mentioned above, Mondragon, Seikatsu, and Co-op Atlantic, point the way. We need to emulate such examples in the U.S., though I do not have any blueprint for how that will happen. To accomplish the goal of building a cooperative economy will require economic initiatives as well as a political movement. On the economic side, the challenge will be to build numerous regionally based clusters of worker co-ops and second order cooperative institutions. This means supporting the development of schools and colleges that spread cooperative ideas and practices, and offer cooperative education and training for prospective co-op managers. It will include the gradual conversion of existing companies to employee ownership, as well as the startup of new cooperative enterprises. And it will involve the strengthening of existing community development financial institutions and the formation of new ones to provide venture and loan capital to worker cooperatives.

On the political side, we need a people's movement to democratize the economy, like that of the Populists of the 1890s (Goodwyn 1976). Such a movement would push for reforms to limit the power and privileges of the transnational corporations, and link up with similar movements throughout the globe. It might seek a constitutional amendment to keep corporations from claiming rights guaranteed to material persons, and an absolute ban on corporate contributions to political parties, political action committees, and candidates. Such a movement would also strive for new and additional tax incentives to promote employee ownership and control, heavier progressive corporate taxes and taxes on wealthy individuals and foundations, and use of public funds to strengthen community-based intermediary and technical assistance organizations.

Through a combination of local economic initiatives to build co-ops and the support of a broad based anti-corporate political movement, we could indeed transform the U.S. into a cooperative commonwealth where the extremes of wealth and poverty have been abolished and where local economic resources are used to benefit all.

References

Bruyn, Severyn T. and James Meehan. 1987. *Beyond the Market and the State*. Philadelphia: Temple University Press.

Cahn, Edgar and Jonathan Rowe. 1992. *Time Dollars: The New Currency that Enables Americans to Turn their Hidden Resource—Time—into Personal Security & Community Renewal*. Emmaus, PA: Rodale Press.

Ellerman, David. 1990. *The Democratic Worker Owned Firm: A New Model for the East and West*. Winchester, MA: Unwin Hyman.

Frölander-Ulf, Monica and Frank Lindenfeld. 1985. *A New Earth: The Jamaican Sugar Worker Cooperatives, 1975–1981*. Lanham, MD: University Press of America.

Giese, Paula. 1982. "How the Old Coops Went Wrong," in Frank Lindenfeld and Joyce Rothschild-Whitt (eds) *Workplace Democracy and Social Change*. Boston: Porter Sargent.

Goodwyn, Lawrence. 1976. *Democratic Promise: The Populist Movement in America*. New York: Oxford U. press.

Greco, Thomas H. Jr. 1994. New *Money for Healthy Communities*. Tucson, AZ: T.H. Greco.

Krimerman, Len and Frank Lindenfeld (eds). 1992. *When Workers Decide: Workplace Democracy takes Root in North America*. Philadelphia: New Society Press.

Krimerman, Len, Frank Lindenfeld, Carol Korty and Julian Benello (eds). 1991. *From the Ground Up: Essays on Grassroots and Workplace Democracy*, Boston: South End Press.

Matsuoka, Kazumi, Bob Stone and Len Krimerman. 1994. "Seikatsu as a Cooperative Model: 'From the Kitchen to the World,' Three Decades of Cooperative Development" *Grassroots Economic Organizing Newsletter* (GEO), #12, March/April.

Morrison, Roy. 1991. *We Build the Road as We Travel*. Mondragon: A Cooperative Solution. Philadelphia: New Society Press.

Morrison, Roy. 1994–5. "Co-op Atlantic: Cooperation in Atlantic Canada," *Grassroots Economic Organizing Newsletter* (GEO) # 15, December/January.

Offe, Claus and Rolf G. Heinze. 1992. *Beyond Employment: Time, Work and the Informal Economy*. Philadelphia: Temple University Press.

Ormaechea, Jose M. et al. 1995. "1994: Las Cuentas de MCC" *Trabajo y Union Lankide*, #387, January.

Stone, Bob. 1994–5. "Co-op Atlantic's Ambitious Plan for Atlantic Canada," *Grassroots Economic Organizing Newsletter* (GEO) #15, December/January.

Whyte, William F. and Kathleen K. Whyte. 1988. *Making Mondragon: The Growth and Dynamics of the Worker Cooperative Complex*. Ithaca, NY: ILR Press.

Reflections on Lindenfeld's
"The Cooperative Commonwealth"[1]

Corey Dolgon
Stonehill College

Frank Lindenfeld is my hero. Anyone who can begin an address with such clarity as "corporate capitalism sucks," is someone I want as a mentor. It is important to note that the qualifier "corporate" is not some kind of equivocation on Frank's part stemming from his admiration for capitalism writ small (yeoman farmers, small business people, and the other kinds of hard working, decent folks that Right-Wing thugs tout out when they want to slash inheritance taxes). No, Lindenfeld's mission is clearly anti-capitalist to the extent that he recognizes both capitalism's important temporal and progressive place in the trajectory of world history as well as the reality of its powerful material and ideological position in the world today. His alternative, however, is neither a kinder, gentler capitalism nor the traditional Marxist offering of State Socialism.

Instead, Frank presents a vision of a cooperative commonwealth which seems part Wobbly-dreamt, commonwealth of toil and part populist-driven market democracy. Yet his vision is not steeped in the past; it is inspired by vigorous research into a host of examples (both large and small) of groups that are succeeding in creating democratic systems of economic production and distribution today. In fact, while Frank's most well-known work has been primarily on the idea of workplace democracy (Lindenfeld 1992, 2003), here he proposes that the cooperative commonwealth will be "enhanced by the organization of local barter and volunteer networks, [as well as] by the provision of government social welfare benefits" such as national health insurance and a guaranteed minimum income. In other words, this alternative system of production and distribution really does move beyond anarcho-syndicalism and cooperative marketing to include an entirely new economic, political and cultural organization of society.

Such a revolution requires a serious reorganization of social institutions and cultural values, but Lindenfeld brings us along slowly and surely by demonstrating that there are both historical roots for and current examples of successful cooperative efforts. He begins by outlining the classic Rochdale Cooperative of mid 19th Century England and laying out seven operational principles inspired by Rochdale that distinguish worker cooperatives from capitalist corporations. The major one, that of one worker one vote, tears at the heart of capitalist power where authority comes not from the democratic rights of an individual's work and production, but from the bourgeois right of private ownership and monetary investment. Lindenfeld outlines other cooperative principles, all of which challenge both the structural and ideological premises of capitalism by demoting profit as the

---

[1]This paper originally appeared in *Humanity & Society* Volume 27, Number 4, 2003.

primary goal, committing themselves to democratic management, equitable compensation, and the closed shop. Finally, Frank demonstrates how these principles have been achieved in various degrees by contemporary projects in Mondragon, Spain, Japan and Canada, as well as through bartering networks and local exchange systems in Ithaca, New York and Auckland, New Zealand.

What seems to me most innovative about Frank's work in this piece is his willingness to address the problem of politics, both as a philosophical and practical matter for cooperatives to address. He recognizes that Rochdale and its followers adopted a rule of political neutrality. Lindenfeld contends that was a mistake, reminding us that "as potential agents of social transformation, cooperatives are political in their very existence." While they "embody the kind of participatory democratic structures that would predominate in a cooperatively organized world…the struggle to establish cooperatives and broaden them into mutually supporting networks is in itself part of the process of building that cooperative world." Here, Frank incorporates our own humanist principles to the cooperative movement, reminding us that we cannot rationalize inactivity with narratives of neutrality or objectivity when the world is on fire.

Lindenfeld completes this integration of humanist values into the cooperative commonwealth vision by concluding that the movement needs "two feet," one representing alternative economic institutions, but the other seeking "a broad scale coalition of anti-corporate people's political organizations" to develop the "political thrust needed to challenge the entrenched power of the transnational corporation…" Frank's cooperative commonwealth is no wimpy group of swap meet hounds nor is it an eclectic collection of bohemian artists and professional intellectuals making their own scrip; his is a vision of an activist and engaged mass of democratically infused workers out to reshape both themselves and the world. An inspiring vision indeed.

As a final note, I want to add that this article was originally Frank's presidential address to the Association for Humanist Sociology, and as such, was also a reflection of what he as an individual has meant to both the organization in particular, and the project of humanist sociology in general. While his research on cooperatives and alternative economic institutions remains vital, he also continues to be a committed activist/scholar of the first order. And, as a humanist scholar—if his exemplary efforts towards researching and building a revolutionary cooperative commonwealth weren't enough—he's just an outright generous, kind, yet principled man—the very model of a humanist.

Thus, I know he won't mind my one critical observation or at least concern, about the cooperative movement in both theory and practice. A few years ago I was involved with a group of custodians at Long Island University's Southampton College who had been outsourced to an outside management company by the administration. The move resulted in their loss of benefits and threats of union busting (Dolgon 2000, 2001). A group of faculty, students and community members had organized to challenge the decision, and along with the custodians fought an 18-month (eventually successful) battle to get them re-hired by the College. A colleague of mine from LIU's flagship campus, C.W. Post—and a fellow co-op traveler of Frank's—wrote us a letter of support and tried to persuade the custodians that the best way to fight their battle might be to form a workers' cooperative. After discussing the letter with the custodians, I wrote back thanking him for his support, but explained that as employees of the larger management company, they had little bargaining power to change any of their work conditions, let alone try to institute a small cooperative arrangement. I suggested that once they were rehired by the College, such avenues would be interesting ones to explore.

I also suggested that a campaign by supportive students and faculty from the other LIU campuses could be crucial to the campaign and that we could discuss strategies for bringing the fight to the wider community. But we never heard from him again. Of course, I don't know what actions he may or may not have taken on his own, but we were never able to get visible pressure from faculty and students at other LIU campuses. All this to say that there is nothing inherently transformative, either on a systemic or on a cultural and political consciousness level, about cooperatives. What distinguishes Lindenfeld's work is his willingness to infuse the movement with a political awareness and a humanistic commitment to complete radical social change.

Stuart Hall once finished a long analysis of cultural studies by saying that, in the end, if it didn't have to do with socialism, he "didn't give a damn." I usually err on that side of the political and intellectual equation myself. But if I were to give up such a vision of socialism and be convinced that an alternative such as a cooperative commonwealth might have the political commitment and social engagement powerful enough to bring about real radical democratic and systemic change, Frank Lindenfeld could do it.

References

Dolgon, Corey. 2000. "Justice for Janitors: Organizing Against Outsourcing at Southampton College," in *Campus, Inc.*, edited by Geoff White. Amhers, NY: Prometheus Books.

Dolgon, Corey. 2001. "Building Community amid the Ruins: Strategies for Struggle from the Coalition for Justice at Southampton College," in *Forging Radical Alliances*, edited by Jill Bystydzeinski and Steve Schacht. Rowman & Littlefield.

Lindenfeld, Frank. 1982. *Workplace Democracy and Social Change*. Porter Sargent Pub.

Lindenfed, Frank, and Krimerman, Len. 1990. *When Workers Decide: Workplace Democracy Takes Root in America*. Philadelphia: New Society Publishers.

3. Scholar Activism: Popular Education and Social Transformation[1]

Walda Katz-Fishman
Project South and Howard University

Ralph C. Gomes
Howard University

Jerome Scott
Project South

Tomas Encarnacion
Project South

> Philosophers have only interpreted the world in various ways; the point, however, is to change it.

> —Karl Marx, *Theses on Feuerbach*

Reflexive Statement

We share pieces of our lives, study and struggles that explain how activism and, especially, how working for fundamental social change became vital to who we are as scholars, teachers and fighters for justice and equality. We do this in the context of our political biographies, our understanding of Marxism—the unity of theory and practice—and our political practice as part of the social struggle to transform capitalist globalization, neoliberalism and the political repression and destruction they bring to our lives, our society and our planet. We believe and act on our understanding that abundance exists—only the market prevents its distribution—and work to help educate and organize today's movement.

For us, this "movement" is one movement that is growing and deepening. It is a movement of organizations—not individuals—that work on many fronts, e.g. jobs at a living wage, affordable housing, quality and free education, anti-war and anti-prison-industrial complex, gender-race-class justice, indigenous treaty rights, youth organizing, immigrant rights, universal single-payer health care, environmental justice, and so forth. Increasingly those of us in struggle see the need to connect our various struggles, to develop a shared analysis of the systemic causes of our problems, to vision the world we are fighting for, and to prepare for an action and education strategy for the long haul.[1]

---

[1]This paper originally appeared in *Humanity & Society* Volume 30, Number 2, 2006.

This developing movement challenges property relations of global capitalism and white supremacy—the primary tactic of global capital in its divide and conquer strategy, as well as patriarchy, homophobia, and all oppressions that are embedded in and reproduced by this increasingly brutal and violent system. We are part of bottom-up movement building that is locally grounded, nationally networked and globally connected, e.g., anti-poverty and workers struggles, and struggles against all forms of oppression in our communities.

We begin with our political biographies—our formative years—that helped shape us as sociologists, activists, movement builders and revolutionaries. We show how the experiences we had early on led to deepening our theoretical study and political activism in many spaces. We also examine how such work inspired the evolution of Project South: Institute for the Elimination of Poverty and Genocide. Over the last nineteen years, Project South has been central to our intellectual and political work in communities and classrooms, and in linking theory and practice through popular education to develop new collective leadership for our emerging movement. Finally, we share lessons learned as scholar activists and movement builders in this movement moment. We hope our experiences and lessons are helpful to others in traversing this exciting but often challenging terrain. Our participation in building today's bottom-up movement for justice, equality and popular democracy has been and remains essential to our intellectual and political lives and struggles.

How We Became Activists and Movement Builders: Social History and Our Political Biographies

Our political biographies answer the question in each of our lives of how we became political—first as activists, then as movement builders and finally as popular educators. Though each of us comes from very different social locations—race/nationality, class, gender—all of our stories share themes of going from circumstances that fostered questioning the society around us, to activism and theoretical study, and to acting on the unity of theory and practice in today's struggle for justice and equality.

Ralph Gomes' Political Biography

My life as a political activist began during my youth with the formation of the People's Progressive Party (PPP) of Guyana. I grew up in Guyana—a former English colony located on the northeast coast of South America. Blacks and East Indians constituted the coastal labor for the sugar plantations as well as the urban labor force that met the needs of the colonialists. During the early 1950s East Indians and Blacks, under the leadership of two western educated Marxists, Forbes Burnham (1970) and Cheddi Jagan (1954, 1975), were involved in many social struggles for citizens' rights—e.g., civil rights, political rights, social rights, and human rights—and for workers' rights. They were fighting for self-determination through independence from an oppressive colonial system and for workers' rights to organize and assemble, to have universal education and other social welfare benefits, and to exercise universal suffrage. In their struggles the Guyanese people used a range of tactics including civil disobedience, selective attacks against colonial institutions and organized strikes and demonstrations.

During these struggles, a comprehensive national front emerged. It initially took the form of the Political Action Committee (PAC), which later facilitated the emergence of the mass-based Peoples' Progressive Party (PPP) with the aim of mobilizing and educating the masses for political-oriented actions toward independence. The socialist ideology of the PPP called for an end to the colonial system which exploited the human and natural resources of Guyana, and sought to install in its place a socialist government. The mass-based PPP was made up of formerly powerless urban workers (mainly Afro-Guyanese) and rural peasants (mainly Indo-Guyanese). Because we were geographically dispersed and lacked access to communication technology, the party was organized into many small political groups throughout the country. We discussed and analyzed a range of issues, e.g., workers rights to organize trade unions, universal education and other welfare benefits, and universal suffrage and grassroots activism. These issues were crystallized by the PPP into a clear political line for independence and an anti-imperialist stand. Guyana obtained self-government in 1953 and independence in 1966.

Many of the political study group meetings were held in our home, and my father encouraged me to participate. This was my baptism into activism. The important lesson here is that the struggle was carried out by an organization—the PPP—with a clear political line—independence and anti-imperialism. This was coupled with study—Marxist theory guiding the political analysis of the society and world capitalism—and praxis, i.e., grassroots activism. My college years in Puerto Rico, Wisconsin and Pennsylvania were filled with various study groups and only occasional activism. In the 1970s I moved to Howard University, Washington, DC and became a support group member of the Workers People Alliance (WPASG)—an anti-imperialist movement organization—formed by Walter Rodney and other progressives in Guyana. We had to be a member of at least one movement organization in the community we lived in. In addition to study and activism in the WPASG, I was involved with several US-based political movement organizations, including Project South and the Center for Urban Progress at Howard University. Participation in study groups clarified my knowledge and deepened my commitment to struggle on behalf of the poor and the working class. Study—theory—and practical work in the community greatly influenced my research, teaching and writing. I was able to influence students and community members to become activists in pursuit of social justice, equality and genuine democracy.

In essence, my scholarship itself is a kind of activism. I have always had two main goals in my research and scholarship: to make my publications useful for people studying race, ethnicity and class in domestic and global perspectives and to make my publications relevant to people's everyday practice. For example, my work has emphasized how the American electoral system has been stacked against groups such as Blacks and Latinos, that this is the inevitable result of a class system and politics geared against those at the bottom, and that electoral-representative processes in the United States cannot guarantee or even promote substantive social and economic equality for the working class and people of color in America. (For other examples, see Gomes and Williams 1995; Gomes and Katz-Fishman 1989a; Gomes and Katz-Fishman 1989b.)

The most important point of these writings is not their clarification of the theory of race and class, but the practical directions they provide activists, administrators, and students who seek a society that is truly equal. Anyone who reads my scholarship understands that I am advocating struggle not just or even primarily against particular elected officials of the American state (the superstructure), but against American capitalism (the structure) itself and its global consequences.

Walda Katz-Fishman's Political Biography

When I think about how I became who and what I am, I see three stages—coming to social consciousness, to class consciousness, and finally to revolutionary consciousness and the praxis that goes with each stage.

Social consciousness and activism was the stage of my growing up in New Orleans as part of a privileged Jewish family in the 1940s-60s. It was the era of Jim Crow—apartheid southern style—and the struggles and reform victories of the civil rights movement. I experienced and came to understand that something was terribly wrong in American society. Daily, I saw rigid racial division and white supremacy, as well as anti-Jewish prejudice and discrimination, extreme economic injustice and the most decadent class privilege. I also saw the power to dominate that came with being a man.

I learned from the activism of my parents to actively oppose injustice and work for change—whatever the consequences. Through civic, electoral and Jewish organizations they challenged Jim Crow segregation and worked for civil and voting rights, and faced the attacks of the very active and aggressive White Citizens Council in Louisiana. My mother also taught me that it was okay to differ with our parents on political questions. She was an ardent Stevenson supporter while her mother, my grandmother, supported Eisenhower. So, while my parents were social justice reformers, I began down a more radical road to Marxism.

Emersion in the working class reality and culture of Detroit, where I was a graduate student at Wayne State and first read Marx and Engels, brought me to class consciousness and anti-imperialist activism. I was immediately drawn to their dialectical and materialist conception of history, their analysis of alienation, exploitation and oppression, and their optimism in the struggle for human liberation. It became my worldview because it explained so clearly my life experiences and the social world in which I had grown up, gave me a direction for the future, and gave me the intellectual tools to participate in the anti-war (Vietnam) and anti-imperialist movement and to take on my professors when they asked me "why?"

In 1970, I moved to Washington, D.C. and began teaching at Howard University. I knew I had to be involved in organized political struggle to be part of the historical process. I also knew that I had to dig into the space I was in everyday—the university and the profession—if I was to survive as a Marxist in a still very anti-communist world without alienating myself from who and what I really was. By the late 1970s I finished my Ph.D. and began to ground myself in political study circles, revolutionary organizations, and progressive sociological and scholar organizations. I was into the stage of revolutionary consciousness and movement building. Unity of theory and practice—testing theory in the cauldron of social struggle—was essential to my life as a scholar, teacher and activist.

In the 1980s, I did homeless and anti-poverty organizing and was a founding member of Project South. Then as now, I taught social theory and social inequality classes, always rooting analysis is in theory and struggle—as worldview and as guide to fundamental social transformation. Classes are spaces where we all learn and can correct the errors of our mis-education and expose the lies of the ruling class. My political practice is grounded in theory and, like theory itself, is an essential part of the seamless fabric of my scholarship, my teaching, and my life.

Jerome Scott's Political Biography

My life as a revolutionary and social analyst has taken several dramatic turns mainly because of my struggle to understand and resolve the problems confronting me and people like me. I grew up in the poorest area of the poor inner city of Detroit in the 1940s-60s. It was Detroit's "black bottom." My life embodied all of the consequences of race and class in the 1960s. Like too many working class black youth, then and now, I enlisted in the military thinking this was the "way out." In early 1966 I was shipped out to Vietnam where I was a power production specialist—running the power generators for the camp in Dangha, five miles from the DMZ border dividing North and South Vietnam. My "aha" moment came when I realized I knew nothing about Vietnam and why the U.S. was waging a vicious war against the communist North Vietnamese. It got more intense when I found flyers on the road from the camp to the town that asked: "Black soldier why is it that in Vietnam you march at the front of the line and at home you march at the end of the line?" At that moment I determined that never again would I find myself in a situation that I knew nothing about. And so I began my journey of politicization and study.

When I returned to the U.S. in early 1967, I was stationed in Mississippi. *I had gone from one war zone—Vietnam—to another—the U.S. South—but they had taken away my gun.* I was on a weekend pass in the town of Laurel and saw the National Guard protecting scabs (workers crossing the union picket line) at the pulp wood factory where the workers were on strike. Coming from Detroit where workers, unions and picket lines were respected, this was unbelievable. That was the moment I decided I eventually wanted to do organizing work in the U.S. South—it was a whole other world.

I ended up in the auto plants of Detroit in late 1967 where I joined and became an organizer for the League of Revolutionary Black Workers. Our struggle was for equality for black workers in plants and in the union (United Auto Workers). Politics was in the air and in 1971 the League split over strategy and tactics—national versus local organizing and the allocation of resources. I was part of those who went on an 18–month study of theory—nationalism, Maoism, Trotskyism, Marxist-Leninism, etc.—in search of an explanation to our situation as black workers in America. In this process many of us became Marxist-Leninists and revolutionaries.

I worked at the Chrysler Detroit Forge Plant and led the last wildcat strike there in 1973. The strike successfully shut down the entire Chrysler production system in the United States because Detroit Forge was the only plant in the U.S. that made certain engine parts such as rods and caps, crank shafts, and cam shafts. I was arrested, fired and then tried for inciting illegal strikes in my plant and other plants. I was found guilty and was banned for life from ever coming within 1,000 feet of any Chrysler facility in the world.

Perhaps the best organizing job I ever had was my next job as a bartender at the Van Lynch Bar, which was outside the 1,000–foot ban, but was within a few blocks of four Chrysler plants—my former plant Detroit Forge, Eldon Gear and Axel, Plymouth Assembly Plant, and Lynch Road Forge. I was now "famous" because of the successful wildcat strike. So my bartender job was an incredible opportunity to organize workers from the four plants close by who came to the bar for lunch and after work. I was organizing them into their plant-based Revolutionary Union Movements (RUMs) fighting for better union representation, working conditions, and wages and benefits. (For more about the wildcat strike, the League of Revolutionary Black Workers and RUMs see Georgakas and Surkin [1998] and Thompson [2001].)

In 1976, I moved to Chicago where I did community organizing and political education in the revolutionary movement. Acting on my desire to return to the South and given the opportunity, I headed to Atlanta in 1979. There I worked for the Equal Rights Congress organizing around uniting various people of color communities—Black, Latino and Native American. I was an organizer for the "I'll vote on" campaign in 1986 to support voting rights in West Alabama—the struggle that gave rise to Project South. In 1989, after the Up & Out of Poverty Now! network was formed in Philadelphia, I became the lead organizer for the southern region. In 1991 we did an evaluation of our work and found that continuous political and economic education and occasional research was missing. Project South was asked to fill that gap—and the rest is history.

How Project South Reflects the Unity of Theory and Practice in Today's Moment of Bottom-Up Movement Building for Justice and Equality

We all became politically aware as part of key struggles of the times—anti-Jim Crow, anti-colonial, anti-war and anti-imperialist and the struggles for racial, class and national liberation. We studied theory—Marxism—and we were part of various political formations, from reform to revolutionary, in which we strived in different ways to politically educate ourselves and, through collective action, to realize our dreams. And yet for each of us today our work with Project South is central to our intellectual and political work and our struggle for human liberation.

By the mid-1980s, we had all connected and were working in small collectives. Marxism (Berberoglu 1998; Hennessy and Ingraham 1997; Keat and Urry 1975) offered us a powerful tool for analysis. But we needed to create an organizational forum and space where we could bring our two communities—scholar and student activists and low-income and people of color activists—together to work in building a bottom-up movement for justice, equality and popular democracy.

To analyze where the movement building process was and to guide our political work, we developed the timeline and CVS model—social history and consciousness, vision and strategy stages—of movement building. While Marxism/historical materialism as theory and science guided our political practice and the work of Project South, we knew we had to develop popular education tools to make this analysis more accessible to grassroots and low-income organizations with which we were working. The first popular education tool we developed was the social history timeline; and it remains at the center of our popular education and movement building work today. Social history helps us see the process of social change—i.e. where we have come from, how our past shapes our present, and what lessons we need to take from our past and present to move into the future. Our social history timeline also lifts up three key structures and processes that profoundly impact our lives—economics, politics and power, and popular struggles and movements.

We begin with people telling their stories and sharing their lived experience. These realities are located on the social history timeline that includes three interacting dimensions: economic history—money, markets, technology and economic elite interests and realities; popular movement history—the bottom-up struggles and demands of exploited and oppressed people; and government policy history—the power relations and policies resulting from these conflicting interests and forces. People in struggle today are able to see their daily realities within this big picture context of structures and systems and to derive lessons learned for today's struggles from the victories and losses of earlier movements as well as from the long term thinking and planning of the ruling class.[2]

Combined with the social history timeline we developed, the CVS (consciousness, vision and strategy) model of movement building and popular education provide tools to understand and talk about movement building in our daily work. The CVS model presents movement building as an ongoing process that has definite, but overlapping, stages of development. These we can identify through people's actions and their thinking about the problems they are confronting, the proposed solutions to their problems, and their plan to get there.

In the consciousness stage people experience more and more problems and crises in their lives because of the objective conditions of global capitalism and they join organizations to fight back, to hold on to what they have, or to make short-term gains. Eventually in this stage people and organizations must look to connections among problems and systemic root causes. In the vision stage, people and their organizational leadership understand systemic root causes and begin to vision the world we are fighting for—i.e., what our communities will look like when we have resolved our problems and have fundamentally transformed societies worldwide. The final stage is the strategy stage, which is a movement-wide coordinated plan to organize and educate for the long-haul struggle to make the vision a reality.[3]

Based on our participation in the social struggle, we found movement building to be in the consciousness stage in the 1990s and first years of the 21st century. So the primary work we had to do was consciousness-raising—deepening peoples' understanding of the root causes of the problems affecting our communities locally, nationally and globally, their systemic and historical nature, and to begin to think about solutions, short-term, but especially long-term. In 2004 we held our first popular education gathering to look at "vision"—the Midnite School—and we have been using more vision tools in our workshops (Project South 2004).

Our current mission and vision, as most recently formulated in our 2005 strategic planning process, are the following:

> **Mission:** Project South is a southern-based, leadership development organization creating spaces for movement building. We work with communities pushed forward by the struggle to strengthen leadership and provide popular political and economic education for personal and social transformation. We build relationships with organizations and networks across the U.S. and global south to inform our local work and to engage in bottom-up movement building for justice and equality.

> **Vision:** The world we are fighting for will evolve from the continuous struggle of liberated people. Cooperative, globally-interconnected communities protect, produce, distribute, and sustain the resources of the earth on the basis of need. Our society values the power of diversity and difference, and all humanity is free to develop to its fullest potential.

We offer the following by way of a brief synopsis of the history, work and commitments of Project South:

We must know history and be grounded in the movement building moment.

Project South was born out of the social struggles of the 1980s-90s, in response to global capitalism in the electronic age, and the beginning of the neo-liberal attack on the gains of the New Deal and civil rights eras. In 1986, in the west Alabama Blackbelt, the FBI launched the largest investigation of alleged vote fraud by historic civil rights activists who had authored the Voting Rights Act. Project South joined activists from across the South and the country in the "I'll vote on campaign" to defend voting rights that had been won only twenty years earlier. Central to our original purpose was to educate a new generation of movement leaders about the strategic role of the South in U.S. history—as a site of heroic resistance and victory in the face of enormous exploitation and repression.

Project South's niche and division of labor became political and economic education for leadership development and building the capacity of the social and economic justice movement that was beginning to form—with many fronts of struggle and new and older groups alike networking, dialoguing and joining forces. The movement was local and national, with a strong southern base, and took on a global character with the Zapatista rebellion in Chiapas in response to NAFTA. We formulated the timeline and CVS model to analyze and contextualize the movement building process (see previous discussion; Katz-Fishman and Scott 2005b). Our thinking was "outside the box." We understood that the technological revolution—electronics, computers, robots, etc.—was labor-replacing and created many problems for working people. At the same time, it created an abundance of goods and services and made possible an end to scarcity—and thus to poverty, inequality and all the related social and political ills—once capitalism and private productive property were also transformed to a cooperative and shared economy. Our challenge was to bring this analysis to the consciousness and vision stages in the movement building process (Katz-Fishman 2004c, 2005a, 2005b; Mertes 2004).

At first we were "talking heads," using a lecture format to tell people what we knew. Then we moved to interactive workshops "the same old way." We had dialogue with people, but we still did most of the telling and the workshop participants still did most of the listening. It was better than "talking heads," but did not yet draw on the experience, knowledge and wisdom in the room. In 1990 and 1991, Project South organized two Southern Up & Out of Poverty Now! summit gatherings, bringing together low-income and grassroots activists and organizations from across the South in two days of workshops to network, share experiences and figure out next steps. We organized an international conference in 1992 at Howard University—500 Years of Resistance: The Columbus Legacy and the African, Searching for the Truth and Fighting for the Future—that brought together grassroots movement leaders, student and scholar activists for three days of workshops and sharing.

Our next major gathering, in 1995 at the University of Tennessee, Knoxville, focused on *Clinton's Midterm Report Card*; and highlighted the extremely adverse impact of many Clinton policies (NAFTA, welfare elimination, etc.). Project South also organized regular educational events for grassroots, student and scholar activists—book clubs in Atlanta and "teaching & organizing for justice" (TOJ) book and video forums in Washington, D.C. from the mid-1990s on. In D.C. the TOJ are co-sponsored by the sociology graduate student organization (OGS) at Howard University and the Sociology Department and Office of Multicultural Affairs at American University. We now use popular education tools ("aha" moments and small group work) for the TOJ and graduate and undergraduate students do the facilitation (see discussion in *Today's Globalization* on "aha" and small group processes—Katz-Fishman and Scott 2005b).

In 1996, the boards of Project South and our longest and closest partner, Georgia Citizens Coalition on Hunger, did a joint educational workshop to examine different models of popular education to guide us in moving forward. We looked at three popular education traditions. Freire's *Pedagogy of Hope: Reliving Pedagogy of the Oppressed* (1994) located popular education at the center of oppressed peoples' struggles in Brazil, throughout Latin America and among radical educators and movement builders worldwide. Myles Horton's *The Long Haul: An Autobiography* (1990) shared the story of the folk school tradition and the Highlander Center outside Knoxville, TN that played an important strategic and popular education role in the southern labor and civil rights movements. And bell hooks' *Teaching to Transgress: Education as the Practice of Freedom* (1994) brought radical pedagogy to the classroom experience. Based on our study, we formulated a Project South definition and method of popular education (see below) rooted in history and the struggle for social transformation and liberation.[4]

We began using popular education methods in all our workshops and developing popular education curriculum for communities and classrooms. *Project South* organized popular education institutes in 1997, 1999 and 2001, a membership gathering in 2000, BAMs—building a movement popular education skills weekend retreats—beginning in 2003 and a Midnite School for visioning in 2004 (Project South 2004).

The Youth Council was formed in 2001 to do leadership development and popular education skills building among Atlanta youth and to network with youth elsewhere. We published our first popular education workbook in 1998, a second in 2001, published single theme toolkits beginning in 2002, and the *Roots of Terror* workbook in 2004. From 1996 to 2004 we did participatory action research and publications in Atlanta and D.C.[5]

We formed relationships and partnerships with activists in low-income and people of color organizations, and in labor and scholar/student organizations concentrated in the southeastern U.S. Our most consistent working relationships have being with Georgia Citizens Coalition on Hunger (Hunger Coalition) and Southern Up & Out of Poverty Now, with 1199 SEIU—Service Employees International Union—Florida, with scholar and student activists at Howard University and American University, and with tenants in Columbia Heights, Washington, DC facing gentrification beginning in 1999. We have worked with many organizations across the country; and beginning in 2002 we participated internationally with COMPA (Convergence of Movements of Peoples of the Americas), GGJ (Grassroots Global Justice Alliance) and the World Social Forum process.

We are formed by and bring together diverse activist communities of low-income and working folks and of scholars and students based on relationships of trust and equality in a community-based reality.

Our strategy in Project South is to form a bridge from different activist spaces—community, labor, student/scholar, etc.—to a movement building space that is anchored in the community and the larger social struggle. This is a space that offers a team model and a practice of how scholars and students work with low-income grassroots members and activists—long term, trust building, mutual respect for each other's experience and knowledge, sharing of resources, etc.

We strive to model the world we are trying to create—a world with many voices, faces and struggles melded into a powerful bottom-up movement to end all forms of exploitation and oppression. Our organization and the movement we are part of building challenges all forms of privilege and power. An essential part of the movement building process is to "walk the talk"—to struggle within our movement for equality among us despite our historic differences. If we do not do this work as we build our movement we will not be able to realize our vision of justice and equality.

One of the greatest difficulties we face is having people confront the various forms of privilege—class, race, gender, nationality, sexuality, etc.—that are so deeply embedded in society and culture and try to move beyond these divisions to a place of learning and working together to create a totally new world. This means low-income activists moving beyond the frenzy of daily survival in a capitalist world to see the big picture. It means much the same for student and scholar activists who need to go beyond the day-to-day rat race of formal education and moving up the career ladder to see what is common in their lives with low-income communities and how we all might together build a movement for transformation.

Our core work is education—and especially popular political and economic education for developing new leadership and long-haul movement building.

Building a broad and deep mass movement for social transformation requires an educational method and curriculum to do this work—and popular education is the answer. Popular education connects lived experience with social history—economic, political, cultural and popular struggles. It embodies the unity of theory and practice through an intentional process that combines social struggle with economic and political analysis and strategic thinking. Following our study of popular education in 1996 Project South formulated the following definition and model of popular education that is uniquely ours. It first appeared in *Popular Education for Movement Building: A Project South Resource Guide,* Vol. II (Horowitz de Garcia et. al 2001: 9) and is reprinted in all Project South popular education curriculum (Katz-Fishman and Scott 2004a, 2004b and 2005b).

What is Popular Education?

1. Popular education, n. *[Education for liberation]*—Popular education is essential in developing new leadership to build a bottom-up movement for fundamental social change, justice and equality; see also liberation, revolution, social and economic equality.

2. *[Accessible and relevant]*—We begin by telling our stories, sharing and describing our lives, experiences, problems and how we feel about them.

3. *[Interactive]*—We learn by doing: participating in dialogue and activities that are fun, including cultural arts such as drama, drawing, music, poetry and video.

4. *[Education with an attitude]*—We are not neutral: through dialogue and reflection we are moved to act collectively—creating change that will solve the problems of those at the bottom in our communities, those of us who are most oppressed, exploited, and marginalized.

5. *[Egalitarian]*—We are equal. All of us have knowledge to share and teach. All of us

are listeners and learners, creating new knowledge and relationships of trust as we build for our future.

6. *[Historic]*—We see our experience within history, indicating where we have come from and where we are going.

7. *[Inclusive]*—We see ourselves in relation to all people, including those of different ethnic groups and nationalities, social classes, ages, genders, sexualities and abilities.

8. *[Consciousness raising]*—We critically analyze our experiences, explaining the immediate causes of our problems and discovering the deeper root causes in the structures of the economy, political institutions and culture.

9. *[Visionary]*—We are hopeful, creating an optimistic vision of the community and global society we want for ourselves and our families.

10. *[Strategic]*—We are moved to collective action, developing a plan for short-term actions to address the immediate causes of our problems, and for long-term movement building to address the root causes of our problems.

11. *[Involves the whole person]*—We use our head for analysis, reflection and consciousness; our heart for feeling and vision; and our feet for collective action for the short term and the long haul.

We use Project South popular education methods and curriculum in our classrooms as well as community spaces. We offer interactive methods and historical timelines to share experiences and knowledge on many topics—e.g., globalization, democracy, roots of terror, movement building. We model for students and colleagues as well as community members a participatory (vs. lecture-oriented) approach to learn about the critical issues confronting our communities and a way to build our movement for social change. Because we use similar popular education methods and curriculum in classroom and community, we are preparing all of us for a way of knowing, sharing, learning and acting in a more egalitarian way.

In the final analysis, we do popular education work to develop new leadership from our diverse communities—low-income, labor, student and scholar, etc.—for building today's movement. The popular education process is key to the progression of movement building from the consciousness stage to the vision and strategy stages.

As much as we are passionate about popular education as a key tool for leadership development and movement building—our biggest challenge in this work is convincing others. Folks believe they cannot take time from the frenetic pace of organizing, mobilizing, protesting, meeting, lobbying, and the "banking method of teaching" to reflect, to see the big picture, to dream another world and create the vision and strategy to get there. Our task is to convince folks that not to do this is the greatest danger we face.

Why Activism and Movement Building are Vital to our Being as Sociologists & Fighters for Justice & Equality: Lessons Learned

We share lessons learned—how our lived experience, social history, study and social struggle intertwined to move each of us—to bring us together and to inform our work in Project South. Each of these lessons is the result of a long-term and ongoing process.

> *Lesson:* Change that is personal and consciousness raising and that calls for systemic transformation comes from the "outside in." We are part of a much bigger picture and our intellectual and political development is informed by that big picture and our willingness to be part of political organizations, study and struggle.

We found ourselves in the midst of struggles of the day—anti-colonial/anti-imperialist, anti-Jim Crow/anti-white supremacy, anti-war, and struggles for equality and workers rights, especially black workers. Without grounding in this bigger picture, we would not have become what we are. But what really set us down the path of ongoing analysis, activism and movement building was theoretical study of Marxism/historical materialism. This provided a worldview and ideological clarity to sustain us intellectually and politically from the struggles of the 1950s-70s to the struggles of the 21st century. We grasped the necessity of the unity of theory and practice, of activism and scholarship in the context of social history. And we came to theory out of struggle—to better understand the systemic nature of the problems and to answer practical questions of strategy and tactics in the political organizations of which we were, and remain, a part.

So, the process for us was and is "outside in." Social struggles and movement building that are part of the big picture outside the university and other worksites set the conditions for activism and consciousness-raising for us, and for others, inside these spaces. This was the reality in the 1960s-70, and we argue it is the reality today as the movement for local-global justice, equality and popular democracy grows. To do this work long-term and holistically—so we are not alienated in our teaching, scholarship and practice—means that as scholar, student and community activists we must be connected and grounded in political organizations, study and struggles in the larger community.

> *Lesson:* We must be part of teams or collectives. We cannot do this work alone, in isolation, because that is unsafe and will not work.

Being political also means having a plan and a strategy for survival in our immediate work environment so that we can continue to educate and organize for social change. Not being isolated or allowing ourselves to be isolated in our department or work place, classrooms, professional spaces and in the larger community and struggle is crucial.

The McCarthy period may be over and the Soviet Union as a world power may be gone, but anti-communism is alive and well in America. Our understanding of anti-communism is rooted in the classical definition of communism offered by Marx and Engels (1967: 26): "Communism is for us not a stable state which is to be established, an *ideal* to which reality will have to adjust itself. We call communism the *real* movement which abolishes the present state of things." Thus, any struggle or movement that is dealing not simply with this or that effect of capitalism, e.g., poverty, unemployment, global warming, homelessness, sexism or racism, etc., but is linking these effects to the system itself and is anti-capitalist at its core is viewed as dangerous by the ruling class. War, the prison-industrial complex, surveillance, censorship, and other forms of state control express the volatile nature of politics today and the new form of anti-communism in U.S. society. Many of us know that the U.S. Patriot Act is not about "external terrorism," but is about the ruling class trying to silence dissent and opposition within. And the movement builders are their "enemy" (Katz-Fishman and Scott 2004a).

Essential to our survival as scholar and community activists and movement builders working in both spaces—the campus and the larger community—has been and is our work in teams. We organized our teams as collectives that provided a needed base of support among progressive sectors of the scholarly/professional community and grounding in the rising local-global justice and equality movement of the 1990s and 21st century. We had and still have clear tasks and division of labor so we can collectively do more than any one of us could do alone.

Concretely, Ralph and Walda, shortly after joining the sociology faculty at Howard University in the early 1970s, found we shared a Marxist perspective and participation in political organizations. We formed a collective to organize and share intellectual and political work, including Project South work. Jerome and Walda connected in 1986 in west Alabama during the vote fraud struggles. Jerome was a community organizer on the ground and Walda helped organize a contingent of student and community activists from the DC area. We formed a collective that was part of the founding of Project South and that modeled our team concept of grassroots and scholar activists working as equals and working consistently in both spaces.

The key point is that you cannot do this work alone. If you are the only one in your department or work place the very first thing is to look for a "partner"—someone who generally shares progressive views and an activist approach to teaching and social change. It is really important to find this "other" before venturing too far into activism and linking the classroom to the larger social struggle. Teams and collectives also provide the space for conversations about planning and evaluating what we are doing so we can be more strategic in our social change work—whether on campus, in the profession or in community.

> *Lesson:* Students are very often open and critical. Sharing, teaching, mentoring, modeling scholar activism and movement building offers another way of building the movement.

Leadership development—"reproducing ourselves" intellectually and politically, passing on what we know and nurturing a new generation of thinkers, activists and movement builders—is another essential lesson. Part of our intentional collective process was figuring out how to do the teaching, mentoring, modeling and political practice in our classrooms and linking that to the struggles in low-income and oppressed communities. This means, of course, being in and having ongoing relationships with these communities and activists who are also thinkers and movement builders.

"Teaching as practice" means consciously challenging the ideology, lies and the general miseducation we are all exposed to on a daily basis. It is sharing our ideological outlook and commitment to justice, equality and struggle and, in this way, shaping the outlook of new leadership among progressive and activist students and scholars. This work is also base-building—i.e., building a strong student base as well as a base in the larger community. In developing a student base we taught and still do teach all theoretical perspectives, but honestly share our own perspective of Marxism as what we believe best explains society, social history and social change. We reinforce each other's teaching. As students go from one class to another, their thinking about the social world becomes clearer through this process. This was and is especially the case for graduate students because we work and dialogue with them over a multi-year process as they shape their theoretical and ideological outlook on the world and begin to develop a political practice.

It is not the courses we teach (social theory, poverty and social inequality), but how and what we teach in our courses. We teach from the perspective of the unity of theory and practice, and social struggle as the real test of social theory. We began many years ago teaching Marxism as one of several theoretical perspectives in social analysis, then moved to using popular education methods as well as popular education curriculum developed by scholar and grassroots activists in Project South (see www.projectsouth.org for details). As the world has changed and the movement has grown (see, e.g., Katz-Fishman and Scott 2004c, 2005a, 2005b; Mertes 2004), we also bring this reality into our classrooms, we model by example and invite our students to leave the comfort zone of the classroom to be part of the movement building process.

Over the years, four of Walda's and Ralph's former students have become movement builders and popular educators and now serve on the board of Project South. In the early 1990s, Stan Mosley and M. Bahati Kuumba were both doctoral students in Sociology at Howard. Stan was part of student and grassroots activist delegations to the Up & Out of Poverty Now! southern summits, became the first part-time staffer for Project South in Washington, D.C., and worked on our popular education curriculum. When he graduated and moved on to the University of Maryland Eastern Shore criminal justice and sociology faculty, he also joined the board of Project South. Bahati was on the organizing committee for the 500 Years of Resistance Conference. She graduated and moved on to the sociology department at Buffalo State where she was part of the Resurge action research collective, and was a scholar activist in classroom and community. Bahati also became a Project South board member. She now brings popular education and movement building work to her current position at Spellman College in Atlanta as Associate Director of the Women's Resource and Research Center, to her teaching, and to her global networking, especially in South Africa. Bahati has also contributed to Project South's popular education curriculum.

In the mid-1990s Eshanda Fennell and Tomas Enrique Encarnacion were undergraduate students in sociology at Howard and participated in the Project South ToJ—teaching and organizing for justice—workshops and book forums. Both Eshanda and Tomas continued their graduate studies at Howard. Eshanda became a Project South board member while she was a graduate student; and did her M.A. thesis on the struggles for quality education in post-apartheid South Africa based on her research there. She is an educator in the Pennsylvania school system and a dynamic popular educator and movement builder. Tomas, a native of the Dominican Republic, became a Project South staffer while completing his M.A. and Ph.D. degrees. He joined the Project South board when he left his staff position, is a skilled popular educator in the classroom and in community, and is committed to building a local-global movement for justice and equality. We share Tomas' story.

Tomas Encarnacion's Political Autobiography

I was born and grew up in the southern part of the Dominican Republic, bordering the Republic of Haiti. During my childhood and adolescent years I witnessed political repression, economic exploitation and social disenfranchisement of the Dominican working class and Haitian immigrants. My parents were part of the Partido de la Revolution Dominicana (Party of the Dominican Revolution), which, at that time, was a leftist party associated with the International Socialist Movement. I often participated in the political discussions held at my home and neighbors' homes.

My parents encouraged me to be part of the youth movement and gave me permission to be part of civic youth organizations and religious groups guided by liberation theology. Through my participation in these political discussions, organizations and religious groups, I became politically aware of the need for the Dominican working class to take leadership into their own hands. I often asked myself and my parents, elders and religious leaders: Why were there so many poor people and so very few rich and wealthy? Why were Haitians being transported in cage-trucks to the Dominican sugarcane plantations? Why did my mom have to work long hours making cotton mattresses and not make enough for us to eat? Why did I have to go to school with "broken" shoes? Why did we have no electricity? Why did we have to walk miles to get two gallons of drinkable water? Why…?

I believed the answer to my questions rested in the "Christianization" of the poor, i.e., offering them a helping hand through "God's charity work." I wanted to become a priest. I was 18 years old when, in 1987, I had the opportunity to travel to Haiti with the intention of becoming a missionary priest. During my short time in Port Au Prince, I witnessed the most extreme exploitation of the Haitian people by the Haitian elites, led by the outgoing Duvalier family. I soon noticed that my helping hand was considered a threat to Haitian elite's security, and was not welcomed. I asked: "Why were so many Haitians so poor while so few Haitians were so rich?" I was told not to ask, but to pray.

I returned home to the Dominican Republic to decide whether or not the priesthood was for me. I sought the advice of one my parish priests and shared with him my call to do God's work. After a few hours, he told me that God did not want me to be a bridge between the poor and the rich and that the priesthood was not for me. I was called to do God's work by working with the poor so they would liberate themselves. He told me to keep searching and never to stop asking the question "why," that I would one day find the answer.

Soon after that, in 1988, I migrated with six other siblings to the United States to meet my father. He had migrated years before, leaving behind my mother and one sister. Upon arrival my siblings and I were given jobs at a factory making plastic containers where my father worked. We woke up at 5 a.m. to be at the factory by 6:45 a.m. We worked long hours in the factory assembly line and were told not to take breaks so we could meet the quota for plastic containers. Once again, I questioned my father: "Why were we doing this?" It was my understanding that my family and I were coming to the United States in search of a better life.

After many arguments with my father, I decided to go to Washington, D.C. to visit one of my brothers who lived there with his wife. My brother and his wife encouraged me to stay. I was 21 years old. I immediately searched for a job and enrolled in school to get my high school diploma and learn English as a second language. I often left my house at 7 a.m. and returned by 10 p.m., Monday through Friday, but never stopped asking the question "why?" In 1990, I enrolled in the University of the District of Columbia to pursue a B.A. degree in leisure studies. For the next five years I attended classes three days a week, taking one or two classes each semester. In 1996, I transferred to Howard University to purse a degree in sociology. It was at Howard that I was exposed to the idea of movement building for social and economic justice in my social theory class taught by Professor Walda Katz-Fishman.

To my surprise, in the city of Washington, D.C., there were people who, like me, questioned the status quo. But, unlike me, some had already found the answer to the question "why?" that intrigued me for so many years. Professor Katz-Fishman invited us—students—to participate in a forum that an organization called Project South was giving in the community close to campus. I was interested by the explanation to my questions. I soon began to participate in other Project South activities. I went on to finish my M.A. and Ph.D. in sociology at Howard, became a member and the second local paid staff of Project South, and currently serve on the board. Today, my lived experience, educational background and community activism has molded me into a scholar activist and popular educator for social and economic justice!

The Effects on Students, Colleagues, and Other Activists

Quite a few other Howard students, through their participation in Project South popular education programs such as the ToJ, through using the popular education curriculum in class, and from seeing scholar activism modeled have become more deeply committed to working for social change. They have learned the importance of popular education as a tool for leadership development and movement building for justice and equality; and they have developed a more critical consciousness and a more radical vision. This is also the case for American University students, several of whom have interned with Project South and worked with us on campus and in the community.

Our colleagues also "validated" our work when Walda and Jerome won the American Sociological Association Award for the Public Understanding of Sociology in August 2004 for their work in Project South. Progressive and activist colleagues and students alike value Project South as a bridge from classroom to community spaces where low-income and grassroots activists come together with student and scholar activists to understand the systemic roots of the problems we face, to create a bold vision of the future we are fighting for, and to build a broad movement to make it happen.

> *Lesson:* We have to connect to, support and help create progressive and activist spaces among other scholars and scholar and student activists in the profession.

Professional spaces—though not themselves "movement" spaces—are spaces for intellectual struggle, spaces to educate and learn, spaces to build support for those of us more deeply involved in political struggle and even to support the movement itself. To be a part of and to nurture these spaces—professional associations and journals and the more progressive locations within them and other scholar activist spaces—is also critical for survival on campus, for professional participation, for publishing and office holding and, ultimately, for getting jobs and for tenure. And as long as this is the economic and political reality of our work lives, we have to cultivate and support these "professional" spaces and at the same time try to make them ever more open to movement building from the bottom-up.

Professionally, we connected to and continue to be part of many radical and progressive spaces—e.g., the Union of Radical Sociologists early on; Southern Sociological Society

Radical Caucus (in "the day"); American Sociological Association sections on Marxist Sociology, Race and Ethnic Minorities, Race, Class, Gender and recently Labor; Society for the Study of Social Problems; Association for Humanist Sociology and its journal *Humanity and Society*; Sociologists for Women in Society, Association for Black Sociology; and Sociologists without Borders, among others. We held office, served on committees to develop and give awards recognizing community and student activism for social justice, organized sessions, staffed tables, brought our students and community activists into these spaces, and shared our analysis and the necessity for activist students and scholars to connect to the broader bottom-up movement arising in society and continue to do many of these things.

> *Lesson:* Grounding in political collectives and organizations in the larger society is critical for staying clear, optimistic and active. This can also be a base of support and protection.

Though we have touched on this, we want to emphasize how important it is to understand and act on the unity of theory and practice—to be grounded in the big picture and in community-based and movement-centered collectives and organizations.

Some progressive scholars and students may first study Marxism or other radical theory in an academic setting and then go into the community in search of struggles or ways to do activism, advocacy and service. Activist and radical sociologists may also teach "activism" and radical analysis in their classes. But too often they do not commit to being part of political organizations that are firmly grounded in the larger community and society and that are about movement building for social transformation.

For us, "armchair" Marxism and revolutionary Marxism are fundamentally different. Armchair Marxism can change consciousness, but that consciousness must be connected to a vision of the world we are fighting for, social struggle in building social movements and a clear strategy. In revolutionary Marxism, the real test of social theory is the struggle as it is unfolding and ultimately the historical process.

Clearly, we cannot expect universities—designed to reproduce ideological hegemony of the ruling class and the systemic *status quo* to be the site of movement building for fundamental social change. Educational institutions are part of the arsenal of the ruling class and the curriculum is a curriculum for "social control" not for "social transformation," despite the space for a few of us under the guise of "academic freedom" to teach the truth about capitalism, white supremacy and patriarchy, etc. Those of us wanting to work for social transformation can sometimes find each other in that setting and nurture a new generation of activists. But we cannot put movement building at the center of our intellectual and political work within the structure of the university. To achieve that goal, we need to be based in those spaces where movement building is at the center and where the struggle for systemic change—anti-capitalist, anti-white supremacist, anti-patriarchal and for equality and justice—is embraced and nurtured. So we formed Project South as a vision and a strategy for movement building.

We urge all of you to be part of the movement building process. We stand at a critical moment in our history-the vision we are creating for ourselves and our world must compel us and our communities to act, to take us to the next stage of social development and human liberation.[6]

Endnotes

[1] See, for example, Project South's Today's Globalization, Katz-Fishman and Scott 2005b; "A Movement Rising," Katz-Fishman and Scott, 2004c; and *A Movement of Movements*, Mertes 2004.

[2] For our most recent social history timeline and for a longer discussion on how to use the timeline as an educational and political strategy tool, see *Today's Globalization*, 2nd ed. (Katz-Fishman and Scott 2005b).

[3] For the theoretical foundations of the CVS model see Marx and Engels (1998) and Lenin (1978); and for a longer discussion about how we use the CVS model and tools in Project South see *Today's Globalization*, 2nd edition (Katz-Fishman and Scott 2005b).

[4] As a southern organization we were aware of the Highlander Center—a historic popular education and strategy center for southern labor and civil rights movement building. And we studied the history of Highlander when we read Myles Horton's *The Long Haul: An Autobiography* in the mid-1990s. Our origins, however, were independent of the Highlander Center. Though in the mid to late 1990s and early 2000s we have worked collaboratively with Highlander Center on several projects and have been in each other's spaces often. We suggest reading Myles Horton's *The Long Haul* (1990), which we did in Project South, for a deeper understanding of the history and work of the Highlander Center.

[5] To learn more about our current popular education BAMs and curriculum, please visit www.projectsouth.org.

[6] We invite you to join Project South: Institute for the Elimination of Poverty and Genocide and make it happen! The national office is located at 9 Gammon Ave., Atlanta, GA. The address of the Washington office is: 1525 Newton St. NW, Washington, DC. To join us or for more information, go to www.projectsouth.org or call us at 404–622–0602.

References

Berberoglu, Berch. 1998. *An Introduction to Classical and Contemporary Social Theory: A Critical Perspective, 2nd edition*. Dix Hills, NY: General Hall.

Burnham, Forbes. 1970. *A Destiny to Mould: Selected Discourses by the Prime Minister of Guyana*. Compiled by C. A. Nascimento and R. A. Burrowes. Caribbean: Longman.

Freire, Paulo. 1995 [1970]. *Pedagogy of the Oppressed*. New York: Continuum.

Freire, Paulo. 1994. *Pedagogy of Hope: Reliving Pedagogy of the Oppressed*. New York: Continuum.

Georgakas, Dan and Marvin Surkin. 1998. *Detroit: I Do Mind Dying, A Study in Urban Revolution, updates edition*. Cambridge, MA: South End Press.

Gomes, Ralph, Walda Katz-Fishman, J. Scott, and R. Newby. 1989a. "The Politics of Race and Class in City Hall: Race, Politics, and the Class Question" in *Research in Urban Sociology, Vol 1*. Jerry Lembcke and Ray Hutchinson, eds. Greenwich, CT: JAI Press, Inc., pp. 135–177.

Gomes, Ralph and Walda Katz-Fishman. 1989b. "A Critique of the Truly Disadvantaged: A Historical Materialist Perspective." *Journal of Sociology and Social Work*. Vol XIV(4): 77–98.

Gomes, Ralph and Linda Faye Williams (eds.). 1995. *From Exclusion to Inclusion: The Long Struggle for African American Political Power*. Westport, CT: Praeger.

Hennessy, Rosemary and Chrys Ingraham, eds. 1997. *Materialist Feminism: A Reader in Class, Difference, and Women's Lives*. New York, NY: Routledge.

Hooks, Bell. 1994. *Teaching to Transgress: Education as the Practice of Freedom*. New York: Routledge.

Horowitz de Garcia, Dan, W. Katz-Fishman, A. Illenberger, K. Rajanna & J. Scott (editors & authors). 2001. *Popular Education for Movement Building: A Project South Resource Guide, Vol. II.* Atlanta: Project South.

Horton, Myles (with Judith Kohl & Herbert Kohl). 1990. *The Long Haul: An Autobiography.* New York: Doubleday.

Jagan, Cheddi. 1954. *Forbidden Freedom: The Story of British Guiana.* London: Lawrence and Wishart;

Jagan, Cheddi. 1975. *The West on Trial: The Fight for Guyana's Freedom.* Berlin: Seven Seas.

Katz-Fishman, Walda and Jerome Scott, et. al. 2004a. *The Roots of Terror: Yesterdays Struggles, Todays Lessons, Tomorrows Victories, 2nd edition.* Atlanta: Project South.

Katz-Fishman, Walda and Jerome Scott, et. al. 2004b. *It Ain't Just About a Vote: Defining Democracy for Movement Building.* Atlanta: Project South.

Katz-Fishman, Walda and Jerome Scott. 2004c. "A Movement Rising" in *An Invitation to Public Sociology.* American Sociological Association. Washington, DC, pp. 53–55.

Katz-Fishman, Walda and Jerome Scott. 2005a. "Global Capitalism, Class Struggle, and Social Transformation" in *Globalization and Change: The Transformation of Global Capitalism.* Berch Berberoglu, ed. Lanham, MD: Lexington Books, pp. 123–140.

Katz-Fishman, Walda and Jerome Scott, et. al. 2005b. *Today's Globalization, 2nd edition.* Atlanta: Project South.

Keat, Russell and John Urry. 1975. *Social Theory as Science.* Boston: Routledge & Kegan Paul.

Kelley, Robin. 2002. *Freedom Dreams: The Black Radical Imagination.* Boston: Beacon Press.

Lenin, V.I. 1978 [1961]. *What Is To Be Done? Burning Questions of Our Movement.* New York: International Publishers.

Marx, Karl and Frederick Engels. 1967. *The German Ideology.* New York: International Publishers.

Marx, Karl and Frederick Engels. 1986. *Selected Works.* New York: International Publishers.

Marx, Karl and Frederick Engels. 1998 [1848]. *The Communist Manifesto.* New York: Verso.

Mertes, Tom (editor). 2004. *A Movement of Movements: Is Another World Really Possible?* New York: Verso.

Peery, Nelson. 2002. *The Future is Up to Us: A Revolutionary Talking Politics with the American People.* Chicago: Speakers for a New America.

Project South. 2004. The *Midnite School: Creating a Vision for Our Movement—Report back from Project South Gathering 2004.* Atlanta, GA: Project South.

Project South. www.projectsouth.org (popular education curriculum, programs, membership).

Ransby, Barbara. 2003. *Ella Baker and the Black Freedom Movement: A Radical Democratic Vision.* Chapel Hill, NC: U of North Carolina Press.

Thompson, Heather Ann. 2001. Whose *Detroit? Politics, Labor, and Race in a Modern American City.* Ithaca, NY: Cornell University Press.

Rejoinder to "Scholar-Activism: Popular Education and Social Transformation"

Chris Dale and Dennis Kalob
New England College

In our view, the point of humanist sociology is to participate in the process of building a more just, humane society—not simply to study society (as the mainstream definition of the field suggests). Humanist sociology makes no pretense at being value-neutral. To the contrary, it is predicated on the observation/premise that a wide gap exists between a humanistic vision of society (universal access to decent jobs, housing, education and health care; the non-violent mediation of conflict, etc.) and contemporary social conditions. Humanist sociologists have a responsibility to help close this gap. Social justice activism (broadly interpreted) is, then, at the very heart of humanist sociology.

This vision of sociology is not new. In fact, some of the discipline's early U.S. pioneers viewed sociology as a value-committed enterprise and demanded that it embrace social activism. Jane Addams, in particular, made this case and lived her life accordingly (Deegan 1988; Scimecca and Goodwin 2003). Of course, her groundbreaking work, like that of others who wed scholarship to activism, soon fell from grace as the university-based men who came to dominate the field insisted on an academic, narrowly scientific and politically sanitized characterization of sociology.

In more recent years, voices from within mainstream sociology have indicated that there may after all be room for, even merit in, a humanist vision of sociology. Former ASA Presidents Joe Feagin, who enunciated a "liberation sociology," and Michael Burawoy, who called for a more public sociology (notably including what he has termed an "organic public sociology") have been particularly important in this regard. Still, contemporary humanist sociology stands apart. While Feagan and Burawoy see sociology as fundamentally rooted in academia, contemporary humanist sociologists see the field as equally grounded in academic settings (universities, research institutes, etc.) *and* in a rich array of groups and organizations that are engaged in social justice work (Dale and Kalob 2006). Moreover, while mainstream sociology allows for various kinds of "sociological practice" that may challenge or serve the *status quo*, humanist sociology is unequivocally committed to changing the current system of privilege and power and building a more just society.

Wherever the field as a whole might be heading, we do know for sure that humanist sociology, as we have described it, is very much alive and thriving. Examples of a thoughtful and engaged humanist sociology abound. Certainly some are described in an article we chose to include in the special (May 2006) edition of *Humanity and Society* that we edited: "Scholar Activism: Popular Education and Social Transformation" by Walda Katz-Fishman, Ralph Gomes, Jerome Scott and Tomas Encarnacion. Two of these authors are primarily anchored in a university (Katz-Fishman and Gomes teach at Howard University), while the other two have been primarily anchored in the community (Scott and Encarnacion have been at Project South). All four have backgrounds in sociology and all four are activists, primarily working with Project South. Katz-Fishman was actually a founder of Project South and has worked in that activist organization since its beginning in 1986, while also being a member of the faculty in the Department of Sociology at Howard.

Starting with their reflexive statement, Katz-Fishman et al. make it very clear that they fully embrace humanist sociology as their orientation. They identify themselves as scholar activists who regard as "vital" their work to build a broad movement for "fundamental social change." Sparing us stale academic reservations or caveats, the authors indicate up front, that they are deeply and passionately immersed in the struggle against oppression and injustice. And, as they see it, this inevitably means challenging the vested interests associated with capitalist property relations, the war system, patriarchy, white supremacy, and other structures of domination.

In an informative and refreshingly humanistic break from standard academic protocol, the authors share their respective political biographies. In doing so, they provide the reader with insights into the evolution of their radical / progressive political consciousness. While each author describes a unique and fascinating journey to political consciousness and social activism, their stories reveal a common commitment to a dialectic of study (including formal and grassroots education), reflection and praxis. This is precisely what humanist sociology calls for—a blending of social inquiry and social action in the pursuit of social justice.

Gomes tells of his early political baptism sitting in on study group meetings of the (socialist) People's Progressive Party at his parents' home in Guyana, while Katz-Fishman recalls her parents' civil rights activism in rigidly segregated New Orleans where she grew up. Scott, we learn, grew up in Detroit's poorest Black neighborhood, enlisted in the military to escape poverty, and was shipped off to Vietnam. Questions about the war, class and racial justice surfaced in Vietnam, and only intensified when (in early 1967) he returned to a U.S. base in Laurel, Mississippi. Scott went on to devote many years to union and community organizing in Detroit, Chicago and Atlanta, where he eventually connected with Project South. Encarnacion's story, which appears somewhat later in the article, begins in the Dominican Republic, where he was exposed to leftist political discussions held in his parents' home and neighborhood, and where he witnessed the exploitation and repression of the Dominican working class and Haitian immigrants. At 19, he and his siblings joined their father in the U.S., where they all worked long hours in a local assembly plant. Disillusioned with his new life in the U.S., Encarnacion embarked on a path that led him to Howard, a sociology class with Katz-Fishman, a doctorate in sociology, and a commitment to Project South—first as a staff member, then as a member of the board.

As the authors point out, Project South grew out of a popular struggle to protect voting rights in Alabama's Blackbelt during the mid-1980s. It is a Washington- and Atlanta-based organization that uses popular education techniques to empower communities and build movements for justice. Not unlike the renowned Highlander Center, it helps to train and connect activists by organizing workshops, retreats, video forums and other events/activities. Project South pursues popular education and movement-building in alliance with a host of anti-poverty, tenant-rights, labor, student and other progressive organizations. Katz-Fishman, Gomes, Scott and Encarnacion have played various roles in the Project South over the years—from staff organizers and facilitators to board members and grant writers.

The authors identify education as their "core work." In their vision of education, scholars do not operate in ivory tower isolation, competing with "colleagues" for status and the recognition of research that is typically of interest to (and relevance for) a tiny "community" of fellow intellectuals. Rather, scholars work collectively with each other, with students, and with community members in the pursuit of social justice. And they do this, in part, by creating spaces—oases of solidarity, if you will—where scholar activism is actively nurtured and encouraged. (One such space, we might note, is the Association for Humanist Sociology.) Crucial, too, are on-going efforts to reach out and establish deep, sustainable working relationships with grassroots political organizations and initiatives.

What Katz-Fishman, Gomes, Scott and Encarnacion describe in this article exemplifies, in our view, the very essence of humanist sociology. They offer a rich and inspiring model for working creatively and collaboratively—with scholars, students and community members—to forge a better, much more humane, world.

References

Dale, Chris and Dennis Kalob. 2006. "Embracing Social Activism: Sociology in the Service of Social Justice and Peace," *Humanity and Society* 30, 2, May: 121–152.

Deegan, Mary Jo. 1988. *Jane Addams and the Men of the Chicago School, 1892–1918*. Transaction Books: New Brunswick, NJ.

Scimecca, Joseph and Glenn Goodwin. 2003. "Jane Addams: The First Humanist Sociologist," *Humanity and Society* 27, 2, May: 143–157.

4. Confronting Structures of Power: Toward a Humanist Sociology for the 21st Century[1]

Ashley W. Doane, Jr.
University of Hartford
1999 AHS Presidential Address

Reflexive Statement

My election as AHS President presented an intellectual challenge. I was excited by the opportunity to serve, but at the same time perplexed by the problem of what to say in a presidential address. I made an immediate decision not to talk about my own research. As fascinated as I am with the issues that I study, it felt incredibly self-indulgent to use the occasion to impose them upon everyone in a plenary session. My election as AHS President (Fall 1997) and my term of office (1999) coincided with a number of significant events in my professional life: I was newly tenured (1997), facing my first sabbatical (Spring 1999), and beginning (Fall 1999) a term as department chair. My election also represented a transition for AHS as an organization in that I am the first president who did not join the organization until the 1990s, and the first who never met Al Lee. These thoughts triggered a period of reflection on my professional career amid the realization that—the fates willing—my career is less than half over. Rather than a benediction, I began to view this address as a "halftime talk," an opportunity to focus on future directions for myself, for AHS, and for sociology in general. What I present here is a reflection on the current state of humanist sociology and, more importantly, the direction that I think humanist sociology needs to follow in the twenty-first century.

Introduction

What is the mission of sociology—or, more to the point, of humanist sociology? Certainly this is a question that is both global and complex. I also recognize that this is a question with which we have all wrestled. At the 1995 AHS Annual Meeting, then president Tom Arcaro (1996) asked, "What is Humanistic Sociology, Anyway?" Last month, a student who is here attending her first AHS meeting told me that when she registered at the hotel, the reservation clerk asked her, "what is humanist sociology?" I have no doubt that we will continue to consider this issue in the years to come.

It is not my purpose for AHS to become mired in searching for the perfect answer. Indeed, I suspect that the 150 persons in this room could produce at least twice as many

[1]This paper originally appeared in *Humanity &Society* Volume 24, Number 2, 2000.

answers. In our literature, we describe ourselves as sociologists concerned with issues of peace, social justice, and inequality. I tell my students that humanist sociologists believe that sociology should be used to address human needs and to solve social problems, or as AHS cofounder Al Lee (1978: 93) put it, "to serve people, not their manipulators." At other times, I have described humanist sociology as a "sociology that matters," a sociology that "makes a difference," a sociology that passes the "who cares" test, and as a sociology that "confronts structures of power."

In selecting "Confronting Structures of Power" as the theme for this meeting, I wanted to recognize that as we prepare to enter a new century, forces of capitalist accumulation, globalization, and technological change are triggering transformations and crises in human social arrangements. I wanted to emphasize that if we intend to pursue social justice in this rapidly changing world, then there is much to be done. We need to challenge systems of oppression (especially, but not exclusively, those of capitalism, racism, and sexism) and to refine our critique of practices that limit human potential. We need to explore and to expose the myths and practices (e.g., in education, the media, and the workplace) that legitimize and perpetuate social inequalities. We need concepts, ideas, and discourses to inspire a new critical pedagogy and to create new alternatives to the existing order. We need to analyze grassroots organizations and social movements to develop new and effective strategies for social change in a changing environment. Certainly, now is the time for humanist sociologists to revisit and renew their shared commitment to confronting structures of power.

I believe that AHS and its members reflect much of what is positive about sociology. As scholars and researchers, we criticize a sociology that dehumanizes "subjects" and accepts the status quo—and we combine sociology with activism and involvement in grassroots movements. As teachers, we inspire students to develop their "sociological imaginations" and a humanistic ethos—and to become involved in addressing social problems. The work presented at this conference—the individual witnessing, the structural analyses, and the strategies for social change—leaves me truly honored to be AHS president.

As an organization, AHS stands in sharp contrast to other sociological associations. For example, in a recent resolution regarding the public role of the organization, the American Sociological Association (ASA) asserted (1999: 3) that ASA Council or member-initiated resolutions should restrict ASA policy pronouncements to "issues consonant with its mission of advancing and protecting the well-being of the discipline" (e.g., funding, data collection, human subjects protection) and to clarifying policy "about how the Association should conduct its own business" (e.g., meeting location, investments). From my perspective, this sounds more like a craft guild than a sociological association—and I am proud to say, "that is not AHS!" Such actions on the part of our largest sociological organization underscore the increasing importance of AHS in the tumultuous times to come.

The Crisis of Marginalization

Despite these kind words, it is important to recognize that we face a crisis: we are becoming increasingly marginal. The scope of this marginalization is profound. Those of us who are left/progressive/humanistic find ourselves on the fringes of politics. Sociology as a discipline has a limited impact on public discourse regarding social issues. And certainly AHS exists on the fringe of the discipline of sociology: the status of AHS was reflected in the title of John and James Galliher's (1995) book on the careers of Al and Betty Lee, *Marginality and Dissent in Twentieth-Century American Sociology.*

How has this come to pass? The answer, in my opinion, requires an analysis of the political economy of knowledge and information. Over the past century—and especially over the past two decades—we have witnessed the increasing centralization of economic resources in the hands of transnational corporations, and the resulting concentration of economic and political power. Included in this process is the increasing centralization of the means of production and distribution of knowledge, as print and electronic media are controlled by a shrinking number of giant corporations (cf. McChesney 1999). Beyond the control of information, this economic power has become virtually a determining factor in politics through lobbying and campaign contributions, as Jim Hightower (1997) so eloquently described for us at last year's annual meeting in Austin. The growing economic power of capital is manifest in a variety of other ways, including the hiring of anti-union consultants, multimillion dollar advertising campaigns presented in the guise of grassroots discourse (e.g., "Citizens For Better Medicare" as a front for the pharmaceutical industry), and the funding of social conservatives on the religious right.

The core symptom is that we have become marginal, even irrelevant, with respect to public debate. *We have lost control of the public discourse,* something that we ought to be able to influence. The effects of this loss of control are profound, creating—to borrow from Marcuse (1964)—a "one-dimensional" discourse. Look at the media "experts," the "talking heads" and columnists. Who passes for a progressive voice? Consider the framing of public issues, the use of terms such as "special interests," "identity politics," "family values," "reverse discrimination," and "military intervention." Why are vouchers able to be cast as "educational reform" and the flat tax as "economic justice?" What was the outcome of the lengthy attack on welfare and the demonization of the poor—the attempt to divide the working class by pitting its poorest members against other fractions? One prominent result was welfare "reform" legislation, which itself was hidden in Orwellian "Newspeak" as "The Personal Responsibility and Work Opportunity Act of 1996." And most important of all, what about the questions that are never raised? Who attacks the rich? Who exposes the mechanisms through which those with wealth and power manipulate social institutions to obtain more wealth and power?

We have even—to a frightening degree—lost control of the discourse within and about the academy. Perhaps the most striking examples of this are the effectiveness of charges of "political correctness," of external attacks on "tenured radicals" and individual courses and instructors. Structurally, we have experienced the increasing use and exploitation of part-time faculty—and we have been unable to mount an effective counterattack. More challenges loom on the horizon: the growing attack on tenure, the emergence of externally imposed "performance standards, and the increase in corporate support for distance learning.

How has this happened? First, we have been "outgunned." In addition to the corporate control of the production and distribution of knowledge, one important dynamic has been the power (grounded in corporate and elite wealth) of conservative foundations and think tanks to frame public debate and set the social agenda. Who anoints (and funds) spokespersons such as the Thernstroms and Dinesh D'Souza? Why was a racist book such as *The Bell*

Curve (Herrnstein and Murray 1994) given so much publicity? While a few have examined this phenomenon, most notably Jean Stefancic and Richard Delgado (1996) in *No Mercy* and Stephen Steinberg (1995) in *Turning Back* (see also Alterman 1999), we must do more to contest the influence of these institutions.

This imbalance of power has also influenced the intellectual discourse within sociology. In a recent article in the *Chronicle of Higher Education*, current American Sociological Association President—and someone whom I personally respect—Joe Feagin (1999) commented on the recent conflict over the editorship of the American Sociological Review. Feagin noted that "traditional elites in large institutions control important discourse and decisions." He described how federal agencies, foundations, and corporations have shaped the evolution and research agendas of major Ph.D. granting departments. These departments, in turn, control the major sociological organizations and publications and act as gatekeepers for the profession.

Feagin's statement, while remarkable for an ASA president, is not new. Al Lee (1978: 27, 180–219), criticized the editorial practices of the American Sociological Association and presented a critique of the "ideological elite" over 20 years ago. It is the ongoing reality of academic sociology. This reality is particularly evident to AHS members. We are not members of the sociological elite; instead, we stand on the margins of the discipline. Most of us have limited institutional resources, labor-intensive academic posts, and time-consuming community involvements. This makes it difficult to "confront structures of power."

To be fair, we have also been outmaneuvered. Take, for example, the ability of conservatives to grasp public attention with glib rhetoric, "sound bites," and the attractive framing of issues. There are reasons why persons such as Pat Buchanan and Rush Limbaugh have such substantial appeal to the disaffected. I know that sociological and structural explanations are inherently more abstract—certainly this is not news to anyone who has taught introductory sociology—but we who consider ourselves progressives have not done a particularly good job of presenting our case.

At the same time, I do not mean to be a voice of doom. As Beth Hess (1999) noted in her extremely thoughtful 1998 SSSP (Society for the Study of Social Problems) presidential address, "Breaking and Entering the Establishment: Committing Social Change and Confronting the Backlash," the efforts of many of us over the past decades have in some ways altered the discourse and changed the collective vision of what is possible. We have also seen important changes within sociology—the expansion of critical perspectives, the focus on race, class, and gender—although these have yet to appear in a significant way in the mainstream journals. I do disagree with Hess on one important point: if I were going to select a 1998 annual meeting theme to guide social change, I think that Kathy Tiemann's theme for the AHS meeting in Austin—"Taking Humanism to the Streets"—is a more promising strategy than "breaking and entering the establishment." I do not believe that we can change structures of power from the inside.

I am also heartened by the increase in student activism. The expansion of graduate student organizations, the anti-sweatshop campaigns, and organizations to support workers on campus are all promising developments. The plans for protest at next month's World Trade Organization conference in Seattle demonstrate that the word is getting out, and that the influence of the globalization of capitalism is becoming more visible. Even the labor movement is showing signs of resurgence. There will be voices making noise in the twenty-first century.

Where Do We Go From Here? Toward the 21st Century

So where do we go from here? First, we need to recognize our role—realistically. Perhaps this is the time-tempered view of a "forty-something," as opposed to the "anything is possible" view of the sociology undergraduate, but it contains an important truth. Most of us *chose* to be academics or academics/activists, not organizers or revolutionaries. I know that early in my career I had a choice between a position as a researcher and one as a community organizer—and I chose to do research. Our academic roles have limits, obligations, and distractions, for example, the struggle for tenure. Yet we must also recognize the inherent possibilities, the freedom and resources that we do have: time, a platform, access to students, and access to information.

Whatever we do, *we need to engage in the public debate on social issues.* In my own research, writing, and community involvement, I have come to appreciate the political importance of discourse —ideas, words, and images. For example, I have examined whiteness (Doane 1997a, 1997b), and how its hidden nature perpetuates racial inequality. I have studied school desegregation (Doane 1996), and how catchphrases are used to rally (and legitimize) opposition. I am currently investigating (Doane 1999) the meanings attached to "racism," and how "color-blind" ideology serves as a tool for maintaining racial domination.

What I have learned underscores the importance of naming—and of framing. We need to change the discourse, to paint "color-blindness" as racism, to make "corporate welfare" a catchphrase, and to make "lobbyist" an anathema. We need to illuminate structures of power. As Marx highlighted the structures of oppression inherent in capitalism, we can provide similarly important insights. What remains of the progressive media produces some good investigative reporting, but it takes sociologists to place events in their larger social context. We also need to dispel myths—to use Kathie Gaianguest's 1992 AHS annual meeting theme. In *Toward Humanist Sociology*, Al Lee (1973) recognized the importance of myths in legitimizing social structures. Consequently, we need to challenge the lies and distortions that perpetuate inequality-the "free market," the "opportunity society," and "color blindness." We need to show how economic power is making a mockery of political democracy, as is becoming increasingly evident in the preparation for the 2000 presidential election. We need to challenge the incredible Supreme Court decisions that give money the protections of speech (*Buckley v. Valeo*) and give corporations the rights of individuals.

These are things that we can do. As academics, words and ideas are our tools. We certainly ought to be able to learn how to create progressive and resonant catchphrases and to package key sociological insights in readily digestible form. We also ought to be able to use our understanding of popular culture and social movements to guide strategies for social change. If Rush Limbaugh and the religious right can mobilize public opinion and grassroots movements, we certainly ought to be able to do the same. In the larger public arena, we need to become players.

In an important article, "Going Public: How Sociology Might Matter Again," my friend and colleague Tim Black (1999) asserts that sociologists need to become "public intellectuals" and return to our tradition of addressing public issues. This point is absolutely crucial for our future. Each of us should make our voice heard in electronic and print media and in public forums. Here at this meeting, we have been distributing some information developed by Jerry Starr that contains a means for making our voices heard through the Institute for Public Accuracy. I hope that each and every one of you will take advantage of this important opportunity. Once again, this insight is rooted in the humanist intellectual heritage. In

Sociology for Whom, Al Lee (1978: 97) noted that "humanist sociologists themselves, as servants of humanity rather than of ruling elites, are responsible for interpreting and promulgating their findings as widely as they can. They recognize that significant changes in public policy can come from popular education, organization, and education."

But talk is not enough! We need to build structures of liberation in order to confront structures of oppression. As teachers, we must create structures for students to develop a critical perspective—a sociological imagination (Mills 1959)—and to engage the community. For example, service learning is something that many of us practice effectively with our students, but we need to develop ways to expand this process beyond the individual "volunteer" model. I would like to see the development of organizational models for service learning that encourage students to become involved with social movement organizations, progressive labor unions, and even the creation of social change structures on campus.

As researchers, we need to continue to practice a sociology that matters: one that exposes and challenges power, and one that serves human interests. We need to expand the use of methods such as participatory action research and community based research. And of equal or greater importance: we need to disseminate our results to the broadest possible audience. We cannot continue to talk only to each other—to preach to the saved. Sociological research can be a powerful tool for exposing the social structures that maintain inequality and oppression, but only if people have access to the information.

It is also important for us to work for structural change within the academy. Tim Black's article contained another important insight: we need to build structures that recognize the kind of sociology that most of us practice. We need to fight within the academy for recognition of work with the community, the time-consuming demands of service-learning, the value of nontraditional scholarship, and the worth of public intellectuals. All of these certainly "matter" more than an article in a peer-reviewed journal. But as Richard Janikowski (1999) noted in a session on Thursday, community-based research does not translate well into an academic reward structure. Those of us who have tenure—or positions of leadership—have a special obligation to press this issue. We must create space for the practice of humanist sociology. We're *sociologists*—we of all people ought to appreciate how social structures shape behavior.

Our Own Structure: AHS and the 21st Century

As we move into a new century, we need to confront our own structure. AHS is a wonderful community whose members support each other as teachers, scholars, activists, and as persons. We hold an annual meeting that re-energizes us for another year of struggle. In 1978, Al Lee (1978: 221) described AHS as "a society of cooperative friends in search of social knowledge." That description certainly fits us well today. As I said earlier, I am proud of us for practicing a sociology that matters—often in less-than-friendly environments.

At the same time, I do not believe that we have realized our full potential. I know that there are some obvious limits such as size, resources, and time. After a year as President, no one is more painfully aware of this than I am. Nevertheless, we can do more! We must do more! Not enough happens between meetings. We need to become a year-round organization if we are to have any impact. We also need to continue to improve the health of our organization—to restore lines of communication that have too often foundered, and to address a turnover of membership that is much too high. These tasks are crucial if we are to survive. While resources may be limited, there are also new opportunities. Electronic communication and the Internet are giving us some new ways to spread our ideas and to communicate with each other. We need to take advantage of this resource to build a structure that will promote humanist sociology in the 21st century.

If we are to fulfill our mission, it is essential that we make our voice heard as an organization. Within the discipline, we need to establish lines of communication with other progressive groups—Association of Black Sociologists, Sociologists for Women in Society, the ASA Section on Marxist Sociology. Perhaps together we can speak out on the issues affecting our discipline and counteract the influence of the "traditional elites in large institutions."

As an organization, we also need to put forth a humanist/progressive perspective on social issues. ASA has abdicated the area of policy statements, but we should move forward. The AHS constitution includes a director of media relations. I think that it is time to reinvigorate this position—which has been unfilled since I joined the organization. I have already spoken this evening about the critical need for sociologists to become involved in public discourse. Why not have AHS policy statements on Kosovo, the WTO, campaign finance reform, and other important social issues?

Finally, we need to build coalitions and alliances with other progressive groups—activists, labor unions, community groups. It is not enough to come to town, talk, and then leave. Our understanding of social change should make it clear that as academics we cannot change society by ourselves. SAWSJ—Scholars, Artists, and Writers for Social Justice—and its work to build alliances between intellectuals, organizers, unions, and activists is a good role model. We must explore how we can use the resources that we have to provide support (ideas, data, credibility, cover, and physical assistance) to our allies in the quest for a more just society. I believe that AHS can play an important role, but we need to begin showing up on radar screens.

I don't claim to have all of the answers, or even to have asked all of the questions. This is a task for AHS as a community, a task that I hope we can begin tonight. As I look toward the future, I have drawn strength from our location here in Memphis. Our visit to the National Civil Rights Museum presented us with a striking example of the effectiveness of grassroots struggles against structures of power and oppression, in this case the institutional racism that has shaped and continues to infect U.S. society. There are so many other examples: the local involvement in the Underground Railroad, the courageous voice of Ida B. Wells speaking out against lynching, and the sanitation workers who fought the city power structure in the name of economic justice. And of course there is Dr. King, who (in an often historically overlooked aspect of his work) recognized the essential link between economic justice and racial justice. Perhaps knowing the price that he would pay, he came to Memphis to support the sanitation workers in their struggle and he left us with an inspirational legacy with which to face future challenges.

As humanist sociologists, we need to work together to face the challenges of the new century. As we search for the strength to do so, we should reach back to the words of Karl Marx (1970 [1846], p. 158), whom I think captured the essence of humanist sociology in his famous *11th Thesis on Fuerbach*:

> The philosophers have only *interpreted* the world differently; the point is, to *change* it.

References

Alterman, Eric. 1999. "The 'Right' Books and Big Ideas: Conservative Foundations Lavishly Subsidize Author; While the Left Loses Out." *The Nation*, November 22, 1999: 16–21.

Arcaro, Tom. 1996. "What is Humanistic Sociology, Anyway?" *Humanity & Society* 20(2): 5–13.

American Sociological Association. 1999. "Council Renews Call for Input on ASA Policy on Policymaking." *Footnotes* 27(7): 3.

Black, Timothy. 1999. "Going Public: How Sociology Might Matter Again." *Sociological Inquiry* 69: 257–275.

Doane, Ashley W. 1996. "Contested Terrain: Negotiating Racial Understandings in Public Discourse." *Humanity & Society* 20(4): 32–51.

Doane, Ashley W. 1997a. "White Identity and Race Relations in the 1990s." Pp. 151–159 in *Current Social Problems*, edited by Gregg Lee Carter. Boston, MA: Allyn & Bacon.

Doane, Ashley W. 1997b. "Dominant Group Ethnic Identity in the United States: The Role of Hidden Ethnicity in Intergroup Relations." *Sociological Quarterly* 38: 375–397.

Doane, Ashley W. 1999. "What is Racism? Racial Discourse and the Politics of Race." Paper presented at the annual meeting of the Society for the Study of Social Problems, Chicago, IL, August 5–7, 1999.

Feagin, Joe R. 1999. "Soul-Searching in Sociology: Is the Discipline in Crisis?" *Chronicle of Higher Education*, October 15, 1999: B4–B6.

Galliher, John F. and James M. Galliher. 1995. *Marginality and Dissent in 20th Century American Sociology: The Case of Elizabeth Briant Lee and Alfred McClung Lee*. Albany, NY: State University of New York Press.

Herrnstein Richard J. and Charles Murray. 1994. *The Bell Curve: Intelligence and Class Structure in American Life*. New York: The Free Press.

Hess, Beth B. 1999. "Breaking and Entering the Establishment: Committing Social Change and Confronting the Backlash." *Social Problems* 46: 1–12.

Hightower, Jim. 1997. There's *Nothing in the Middle of the Road But Yellow Stripes and Dead Armadillos*. New York: Harper Perennial.

Janikowski, Richard. 1999. "Community Justice: Federal Support for Local Research and Problem Solving." Panel discussion at the Annual Meeting of the Association for Humanist Sociology, Memphis, TN, November 4–7, 1999.

Lee, Alfred McClung. 1973. *Toward Humanist Sociology*. Englewood Cliffs, NJ: Prentice-Hall.

Lee, Alfred McClung. 1978. *Sociology for Whom? New York*: Oxford University Press.

Marcuse, Herbert. 1964. *One Dimensional Man: Studies in the Ideology of Advanced Industrial Society*. London: Sphere.

Marx, Karl. 1970 [1846]. *The Essential Marx*. Ernst Fischer (ed.) Anna Bostock (trans.) New York: Seabury Press.

McChesney, Robert W. 1999. *Rich Media, Poor Democracy: Communication Politics in Dubious Times*. Champaign, IL: University of Illinois Press.

Mills, C. Wright. 1959. *The Sociological Imagination*. New York: Oxford University Press.

Stefancic, Jean and Richard Delgado. 1996. *No Mercy: How Conservative Think Tanks and Foundations Changed America's Social Agenda*. Philadelphia, PA: Temple University Press.

Steinberg, Stephen. 1995. Turning *Back: The Retreat from Racial Justice in American Thought and Policy*. Boston, MA: Beacon.

Even More So: A Commentary on the 1999 AHS Presidential Address[2]

Dan Santoro
University of Pittsburgh at Johnstown

When my good friend Woody Doane delivered his 1999 Presidential Address, "Confronting Structures of Power: Toward a Humanist Sociology for the 21st Century," he said, "I wanted to recognize that as we prepare to enter a new century, forces of capitalist accumulation, globalization, and technological change are triggering transformations and crises in human social arrangements." This is in many ways what sociology is all about. The writers of our discipline's classical tradition, Marx, Weber, and Durkheim were concerned in their various ways with these same issues: the consequences of capitalist production and commercialization, industrialization, technological change, the power of corporate and state organizations, and imperialism, which we now call globalization. These issues and the crises that they brought with them are still of concern to us yet the stakes seem even higher today. In re-reading Doane's statement I am inclined to agree and add only "and now even more so."

In the wake of the collapse of the Soviet Union and the re-arrangement of the world's furniture symbolized by the removal of the Berlin Wall, Frances Fukuyama (1992) proclaimed a new millennium, the victory of market capitalism and liberal "democracy". The East-West conflict was over. With no ideological conflicts left to resolve, we would enter a new age in which the dreams of the modernization theorists would soon be realized. Fukuyama's book became a best-seller within the U.S. State Department and politicians and policy-makers spoke confidently of a "peace dividend." Fukuyama's The End of History proclaimed the "victory of the VCR" and a "new age of boredom" which he equated with prosperity and peace.

History however, is not marked by the turning of the pages of a calendar but by transforming events. As it turns out, we are anything but bored. The euphoria of the end of the Cold War would be short-lived. The first Iraq War put an end to it and began to show us that the century to come would be shaped by the imperial ambitions of the world's remaining superpower. This coupled with the continued dismantling of the welfare state would usher in the "New American Century." The 21st century, for which Doane's address was preparing us, began, to my mind with the events of September 11, 2001. Not because they represented something new, but because they signify the human costs of sixty years of failed Cold War policy upon which Chalmers Johnson's (2000), Blowback, continues to serve as a stern warning.

I mention all of this because there is nothing in the coming of the 21st century that has made any part of Woody Doane's message any less relevant. His call to confront structures

[2]This paper originally appeared in *Humanity & Society* Volume 27, Number 4, 2003.

of power and his definition of humanist sociology as a sociology which in fact "speaks truth to power," is still meaningful. If anything is different, it is that in doing so, we face a greater sense of urgency. Woody called upon humanist sociologists to "revisit and renew their shared commitment to confronting structures of power." But, what does confronting structures of power mean in the post-9/11 world?

In many ways it means the same thing it meant in 1999. We should continue to engage in public debate on pressing issues and to "challenge systems of oppression". We should continue, in the words of Kathy Tiemann to "take humanism to the streets" outside of our purely academic role. And, "as academics, words and ideas are our tools." Our academic roles provide us with "time, a platform, access to students, and access to information." For most of our students, we are, the alternative media and this bears a certain responsibility. To teach is to be an activist. Woody identified the creation of opportunities for students to develop critical perspectives as an important "structure of liberation."

This, of course, is easier said than done. Woody (1999) pointed out that as humanist educators and activists we face a "crisis of marginalization" where, "The scope of marginalization is profound. Those of us who are left/progressive/humanistic find ourselves on the fringes of politics.... The core symptom is that we have become marginal, even irrelevant, with respect to public debate." The political and organizational culture in which we live continues to be marked by increasing concentration of corporate media, the corporatization of the university, and an intensely more one-dimensional discourse.

Sociology itself has always, it seems, been marginal. Claude S. Fischer (1990) pointed out that mainstream media supports traditional medical and psychological definitions and assessments of social problems, framing them as problems of "broken" individuals in need of "cure" or therapy. For humanist academics and activists the difficulty is much worse. Doane said, "If Rush Limbaugh and the religious right can mobilize public opinion and grassroots movements, we certainly ought to be able to do the same. In the larger public arena, we need to become players." We need, in other words, to become "public intellectuals." There are indeed reasonable voices coming through the din of cable news and print media. But at the moment, there just are not enough Jim Hightowers and Michael Moores. Certainly, not everyone can be Michael Moore or Jim Hightower, and the obstacles seem imposing indeed when one considers that not even Phil Donahue could hold a place on second-tier cable television because his message is too "controversial."

So, an unfriendly political culture is nothing new. But what has changed profoundly since 1999 is that our current political culture is defined by such things as the USA Patriot Act which holds its own particular dangers to those of us inside and outside the academy. We now live in a world that more closely resembles McCarthyism than any time since the days when the mere mention of dissent was criminalized. What is most frightening is the undeniable fact that the state now has at its disposal the technical means of surveillance that J. Edgar Hoover might only have dreamed of. There is potential (and I emphasize the word "potential") for great evil. The ante has most certainly been upped. In this new world, the attack on free speech in general, and tenure and academic freedom in particular, will continue apace as will the growing trend toward "distance learning" as universities seek not only new revenue streams but a means to exert control over the voice of the professoriate (Noble 2001). So, the crisis of marginalization that Woody explained so eloquently will intensify.

But the news is not all bad. Woody drew inspiration from the increase in student activism, the anti-globalization movement, anti-sweatshop campaigns, and the resurgence of the labor movement. Let's remember also, that since Woody delivered his address we all witnessed and even became part of the largest single anti-war movement ever seen—a movement that was and is global in scope. As far as the organization of our own profession, Woody wrote that the "ASA has abdicated the area of policy statements, but we should move forward" (1999: 235 in original). Since then, we have witnessed this mainstream organization which has acted more as a "craft guild than a sociological association" (p. 239) elect Michael Burowoy as its president but more importantly, actually issue a statement critical of U.S. policy towards Iraq creating much controversy within its ranks. I myself rejoined ASA just to have the opportunity to sign that petition.

In the end, humanist sociology stands for what C. Wright Mills called a "value-relevant" sociology. I think we have a pretty good idea what that means. But perhaps, the best statement of what that means comes from the historian Howard Zinn who, one might say, was calling for a value relevant history. In his opening chapter to *A People's History of the United States*, Zinn (1999: 10) wrote,

> The history of any country, presented as the history of a family, conceals fierce conflicts of interest (sometimes exploding, most often repressed) between conquerors and conquered, masters and slaves, capitalists and workers, dominators and dominated in race and sex. And in such a world of conflict, a world of victims and executioners, it is the job of thinking people, as Albert Camus suggested, not to be on the side of the executioners.

As humanist sociologists, we struggle to live up to the words of Albert Camus and to practice, as my friend Woody Doane says, "A sociology that matters—often in less-than-friendly environments" (1999: 234). The environments will continue to become even more unfriendly. But, a humanist sociology, by definition, is not on the side of the executioners. This simple fact just does not change.

References

Doane, Ashley W. 1999. "Confronting Structures of Power: Toward a Humanist Sociology for the 21st Century." *Humanity & Society* 24 (3): 228–236.

Fischer, Claude S. 1990. "Entering Sociology into Public Discourse." In Albert Hunter (ed.) *The Rhetoric of Social Research Understood and Believed.* New Brunswick: Rutgers University Press.

Fukuyama, Frances. 1992. *The End of History and the Last Man.* New York: The Free Press.

Johnson, Chalmers. 2000. Blowback: The Cost and Consequences of American Empire. New York: Henry Holt and Company.

Noble, David F. 2001. *Digital Diploma Mills: The Automation of Higher Education.* New York: Monthly Review Press.

Zinn, Howard. 1999. *A People's History of the United States: 1492–Present.* New York: HarperCollins.

5. Don't Celebrate, Organize! A Public Sociology to Fan the Flames of Discontent

Corey Dolgon
Stonehill College
2008 AHS Presidential Address

The radical intellectual, struggling for her own place in an academy already under siege by market forces and political interference, may lack the stomach for engaging in external conflicts that are deemed "controversial" by the media projectors of the status quo; for even radical intellectuals must eat; and to eat means to affiliate with aggregates of intellectual organization and power (universities), if one wants to teach… Nothing written in this essay will relieve the tension between one's fear and one's conscience, for nothing is more controversial in the American context than the state's role in determining whether its purported citizens should live or die.

Mumia Abu-Jamal, "Intellectuals and the Gallows."

For a mass of people to be led to think coherently, and in the same coherent fashion, about the real present world is a "philosophical event" far more important and "original" than the discovery by some philosophical "genius" of a truth which remains the property of a small group of intellectuals.

Antonio Gramsci, *The Prison Notebooks*

But you and I we've been through that and this is not our fate.
So let us not talk falsely now, the hour is getting late.

Bob Dylan, *All Along the Watchtower*

A New America?

Four years ago, sitting in an internet café in Sydney, Australia, I wrote the following:

December 2004 seemed like a good time to leave America. The naked emperor had just beaten the swift boat vets for truth's whipping boy, retaining the former's place as sham figurehead for the Haliburton-Jesus Saves-AmeriKKKa first cartel. A lot of people were disillusioned and talked about getting out and giving up. I was torn. On the one hand, it was literally stomach wrenching and figuratively heart-breaking to see the American public (whomever this public was) accept and re-elect a regime that promised more fascism at home and neo-imperialism abroad. Besides, how could people vote for such a dim-witted twit whose frat boy smirk and Beavis and Butthead snicker are like some pathological twitch betraying a dangerous mix of inferiority and entitlement, arrogance and incompetence?

On the other hand, the whole 2004 campaign became such a cynical enterprise; it reminded me that regardless of who won, the United States remained a country far from fulfilling any serious commitment to equality, democracy, and human rights. The real struggles for social justice would not be resolved by an electoral campaign, although some progressive policies may have found more sympathetic ears in a Kerry administration—some court appointments might have been less draconian. An emboldened Bush seemed even more dangerous, but the war in Iraq would continue either way; the war on the poor would continue either way; the war on women and people of color at home and abroad would continue either way; regardless of who won the 2004 election. Whether one left the country or not, giving up was never an option.

Tonight we stand here on the precipice of a new day in America. Despite the fact that it took botched wars in Afghanistan and Iraq, an economic meltdown of epic proportions whose devastation is still not done, and a campaign that cost over 2 billion dollars (one where even Dan Rather suggested the most important questions may be, "who's giving this money to whom, expecting what in return?") still, we are on the precipice. Regardless of our sometimes hyper-critical vistas as *academics*, anyone who voted on Election Day sensed the change around them—new voters willing to wait in line for as long as it took. New faces seemingly enfranchised not just at the polls but in a sense of ownership—however slight and symbolic—over the larger systems and structures in their lives.

Or maybe it was that somehow this election brought out some counterintuitive constructions of community and solidarity from a variety of contradictory places. Here are some examples: First a piece from a self-proclaimed white, middle-age swing voter from North Carolina that appeared in the *Christian Science Monitor*. As a Conservative, suburban professional whose taxes will undoubtedly go up under an Obama Presidency, Jonathan Curley (2008) writes:

So you can imagine my surprise when my wife suggested we spend a Saturday morning canvassing for Obama. I have never canvassed for any candidate. But I did, of course, what most middle-aged married men do: what I was told. At the Obama headquarters, we stood in a group to receive our instructions. I watched a campaign organizer match up a young black man who looked to be college age with a white guy about my age to canvass together. It should not have been a big thing, but the beauty of the image did not escape me.

Instead of walking the tree-lined streets near our home, my wife and I were instructed to canvass a housing project. A middle-aged white couple with clipboards could not look more out of place in this predominantly black neighborhood. We knocked on doors and voices from behind carefully locked doors shouted, "Who is it?" "We're from the Obama campaign." And just like that doors opened and folks with wide smiles came out on the porch to talk.

Grandmothers kept one hand on their grandchildren and made sure they had all the information they needed for their son or daughter to vote for the first time. Young people came to the door rubbing sleep from their eyes to find out where they could vote early, to make sure their vote got counted. I learned in just those three hours that this election is not about what we think of as the "big things."

I've learned that this election is about the heart of America. It's about the young people who are losing hope and the old people who have been forgotten. It's about those who have worked all their lives and never fully realized the promise of America, but see that promise for their grandchildren in Barack Obama. I saw hope in the eyes and faces in those doorways. My wife and I went out last weekend to knock on more doors. But this time, not because it was her idea. I don't know what it's going to do for the Obama campaign, but it's doing a lot for me.

Second, a piece from a 40–something, white, Lesbian, NGO administrator and environmental educator whose politics are Left but whose roots are in semi-rural, blue-collar Western Michigan.

The house was down a dirt road in the middle of New Hampshire, far from the noise of the highway 89 but not out of earshot of the election. Paul's door was 42nd of 51 we knocked on. It was a brilliant fall day, shirtsleeve weather. I looked at my list. Paul was 83 and "undeclared," not meaning, necessarily, he was undecided, but rather registered as an independent voter. We slowly walked up to the house, a ramshackle affair with cars and toys and old equipment strewn everywhere. A dog was barking furiously, pulling on his chain, and blocking the front door. I hollered hello over the dog's racket. Paul came from around back. His Carhartt jacket was covered in grease, what I took to be its regular condition.

I shook his hand and asked if he had made up his mind about whom he was voting for. "Well," he said, inflecting the word with in an unmistakably New Hampshire way, "I'm thinking McCain." Then he made sure he had my attention and said, "It's nothing about race. We have to protect our country. I'm a WWII vet." We talked about the wars in Iraq and Afghanistan, his service, and then I asked if he had other concerns. "Well, I worked for 30 years at the mill and when it went bankrupt, I lost my pension. I've sold hotdogs at the fair and started a sheet metal company. None of it worked out for me. Sold my equipment. Now I live on social security." And so we talked about the presidential candidate's different approaches to social security. We talked more about his lost pension, the economy, how his daughter, who lives with him, is voting (Obama). We talked so long the dog stopped barking and the evening cool air had me reaching for a sweater.

When I got back to the car, I circled "leaning Obama" on my tally sheet. We had 9 houses to go and it was getting dark. But we kept at it. We were feeling pretty good about the swing of this swing state.

And finally, here is a piece by radical Black sociologist, Rodney Coates, about voting on Election Day in his Southwestern Ohio neighborhood.

My wife and I, fearing extremely long lines, got to the polling station 15 minutes early. And there, at 6:15 a.m. was a long line that trailed throughout the corridors of Independence Elementary School. Not surprisingly, many of our neighbors were there ahead of us. So, we took our place, and waited and we talked.

A father had brought his 1 year old daughter. She was a cutie. But there was no accounting for taste as she, upon seeing me, leaned over wanting to be held [by me]. So, I did. We talked, my neighbors and I, about how this was the first time that many of us had seen such long lines. We were witnessing something different, something wonderful, something as yet undetermined—we were watching history be made.

As I looked over at my neighbors, I remembered that many had McCain/Palin signs right along with others, such as mine, which were for Obama/Biden. The strange thing was not the differences but the continued neighborly interactions that transpired. We continued our conversations as we worked in our yards, watched the kids play, as we also discussed our very different political views, and our reasons for our support…and I realized something—no matter who won, no matter the outcome—we were and would remain neighbors.

You know neighbors—when the snow falls 8 inches, they would be there helping each other dig out. Neighbors—when someone get's locked out, this is where you go. Neighbors—when someone is sick, someone brings over soup. Neighbors –when trouble comes, when disaster strikes they are ready to lend a hand. Yea—I got more than my supply of boy scout pop-corn, girl scout cookies, booster candy bars, and football support magazines—and yea, no matter what happens, I still have my neighbors. As different and extreme as politics, religion, occupation, race, and America can make it—but these are my neighbors nevertheless and my friends.

In each case the reader learns something about the ways in which this campaign and its practices have either created or highlighted a sense of community, of neighborhood, of the public. Only the hardest of hearts and dourest of Marxists could keep from being swept up by *some* semblance of hope. Many members of the Association for Humanist Sociology would agree with Eduardo Bonilla Silva's (2008) critique of those who "drank the Hope Liquor": that those who in their desire for a truly progressive leader overlooked the fact that Obama's policies were not all that progressive. Still, most of us voted for Obama and did so with at least a smidgeon of optimism. Even Alan Spector—always a beacon for the staunch political realities of material conditions and structural oppression and power—seemed moved by what he saw at an Obama rally in Indiana. We truly have a sense of hope, at least auspicious if not audacious.

But as Dennis Kalob, Eduardo Bonilla-Silva and many others have suggested at this conference, we must be more than just vigilant, we must maintain our activism and even intensify our struggles. One of the great difficulties with electoral politics is that even victories can be deceptive. While certainly many will find a sense of affirmation and triumph in what Obama represents (his representation a contested symbol to be sure), the future is only ripe with *possibility*—what we might achieve through struggle. Bonilla-Silva effectively explained how Obama had become a kind of progressive blank slate upon which many left-leaning activists and academics painted what they wanted to see him be, not necessarily who he was or, more importantly, what he stood for. For Bonilla-Silva, an Obama presidency is plagued by the political pitfalls of a continued color-blind racism now under the guise of a new post-racial America. For some whites, Obama's victory "confirmed THEIR BELIEF that America is beyond race," while for others "Obama became the 'Magic Negro'—a term from film studies that refers to black characters in movies whose main purpose is to help whites deal with their issues. In this case, voting for Obama allowed many whites to feel like they were cleansing their racial soul, repenting for their racial sins, and getting admission into racial heaven! Obama became whites' EXCEPTIONAL black man—the model to follow if blacks want to achieve in Amerika!" (Bonilla-Silva 2008)

Thus, despite the great hope and sense of promise, if we don't recognize this new day as only a place to start to build the movements for social justice we know we need, this new day in the U.S could turn out to be, in the words of Boston novelist Nick Flynn, "just another bullshit night in suck city." My message in this address tonight, as I channel Joe Hill via Joe the Plumber, is "Don't Celebrate, Organize!"

A New Sociology?

And as I consider what we have tried to accomplish at this 2008 AHS conference whose theme explores the development of "Public Sociology"—I am moved to utter a resonant phrase, "Don't institutionalize, organize!" Let me begin this section on Public Sociology itself by stating unequivocally that Humanist Sociology is Public Sociology. In point of fact, Public Sociology is Humanist Sociology. We were here first. I say this only half-kidding as clearly the roots of both public *and* humanist sociology go back a long way and share many of the same progenitors and political struggles. There really is no need for competition and the recent turn towards public sociology ought to be mostly welcomed and celebrated by those of us in the Association for Humanist Sociology. The trend towards public sociology has resulted in greater resources and support for connecting our scholarly work as researchers, writers, and teachers to civic engagement and activism. Under the guise of public sociology, the American Sociological Association has offered a larger professional and credentialed landscape for sociologists to link our work with progressive groups, non-profits and non-governmental organizations, more popular and alternative media, and a variety of different practical and political venues, all in the name of making our work more public (Clawson et al. 2007).

For the AHS, born with a mission to be a group of public sociologists whose personal values and professional endeavors would be inextricably fused, this turn has been a vindication of sorts. The important, politically engaged work that we have been promoting for over thirty years has now made its way into the professional mainstream, and we should be actively affirming the changes and embracing the organizations and institutions that now tout public sociology. I write this, in part, because these movements are really an affirmation that what we've been doing for years made a difference, kept a flame burning, and has been part of pushing the boundaries that resulted in a focus on "the public." One could say that we also stand at the precipice of a new day for sociology as well (Ballard 2002).

But when I say half-kidding, I do so because I believe that this turn towards public sociology demands a serious vigilance and activism on our part. Our embrace must be a critical embrace, as the mainstream's version of public sociology does not make AHS redundant or insignificant; in fact, I would argue we have an even more important role now than ever in addressing the mainstream of our discipline. Just as our forbearers asked "Sociology for whom?" and "Sociology for What?" we must ask "which public" are we interested in engaging and for "what purpose?" Certainly, some work practiced under the "public sociology" banner demonstrates the kind of humanistic and progressive work AHS has always supported. This conference has included some excellent examples such as what Charlotte Ryan and others have done at the Media Research Action Project, working with progressive community groups to develop effective media strategies (Ryan and Gamson 2009). Another example is Tim Woods (2008) and his students' efforts to work with both low-income housing residents and local governments to develop increased housing opportunities for poor people. Or Ben Shepard's (2005) work in New York where organizing efforts around community gardens link local residents' struggle with larger urban politics around gentrification and uneven development. If these kinds of projects represent the face of public sociology, then I expect most of us in AHS will find many reasons to embrace it.

But as public sociology struggles for legitimacy and people initiate efforts to institutionalize it in various forms, it is clear that a healthy dose of constructive criticism and debate is still warranted. In the handful of major public sociology books and dozen or so relevant articles published over the past two years, there is scant reference to the actual political and social engagements of scholars. Meanwhile, the most notable products coming out of the ASA's Public Sociology Task Force appear to be a discussion and recommendations on "the *recognition and validation* of on-going public sociology...developing guidelines for *evaluating* public sociology as a scholarly enterprise...[and] proposing *incentives and rewards* for doing public sociology." Not that any of these three areas couldn't present useful information and help promote the work that many of us have done for years. From a humanist perspective, however, I don't think our primary concerns have ever been recognition and validation, incentives and rewards, or the primacy of professional evaluation. Even the face of public sociology can get swallowed up in disciplinary and institutional navel gazing of academics. But institutionalizing a progressive or radical project is tricky business.

One of the first professional articles I ever published was for *Humanity and Society* on the evolution, pitfalls and promise of cultural studies as a radical field of research and political struggle. I was part of a group of graduate students at the University of Michigan who had been inspired by the work coming out of the British Centre for Contemporary Cultural Studies. Cultural Studies seemed to promote a kind of active engagement *with* cultural politics, not just an analytical study *of* it. But as soon as students started to take our research into the streets, we were reprimanded by some of the faculty leading our study group. They contended that our role was to generate theory, not activism. As some of us dug further into the developing field, we realized that, just as its major figures were hosting conferences and starting institutes, publishing journals and attaining a kind of *star* status, the activism that had inspired their initial work—participatory action methods and theories steeped in political strategy and struggle—had waned. What had begun as popular education projects after WWII and had been re-energized by anti-racist struggles in the 1960s, had by the 1980s become institutionalized and "declawed" (Dolgon 1997).

In trying to understand what had happened, I turned to one of cultural studies' founders, Raymond Williams. In general, Williams bemoaned the fact that the histories of such intellectually engaged innovations eventually get told by the few scholars involved who published books. Their accounts, their texts, became the documents that others then read and respond to, and the professional fetish for texts distorted not only the actual history, but the ways in which the practice of popular education informed the theory about cultural politics itself. Williams (1997) distinguished between the *project* of cultural studies—born out of political struggles to educate a working class (and conversely be educated by the working class)—and the *formation* of cultural studies as a field with texts, institutes, etc. He argued that, as texts took over as the centerpiece of the formation, the field changed. Williams wrote:

> I often feel sad about the many people who were active in that field at that time who didn't publish, but who did as much as any of us did to establish this work. Only when it reached the national publishing level or was adopted in the university was this work perceived as existing at all. [People chose] alternative sites to do their work in distinctly as a vocation rather than a profession.

In other words, the institutionalizing of the project developed at the same time that the project itself was being distorted by professionalization and efforts to institutionalize. Williams concludes that, while institutionalizing such efforts has the advantage of being more professional, better resourced, and more organized, "there remains the problem of forgetting the real project."

Years later, I would use this evolutionary tale to analyze what I thought was happening to a new field promoting civic engagement, that of service learning. Many have written of the birth and growth of service learning as a pedagogy that incorporates students' community service with course curriculum. Many of the field's founders claim their own historical experience with engaged learning came from participating in the social movements of the 1960s. Yet, as service learning gained a kind of ascendency within the academy, like cultural studies, it was "declawed." In part, institutionalization within the academy has the kind of conservatizing force that Al Lee predicted, restricting radical pedagogy with the trappings and demands of funders, administrators and major journals and the practices of professionalism. Private-sector funding promotes service projects shaped by a charity paradigm instead of fundamental social change. Administrative and professional concerns influence a fetish for assessing student outcomes instead of measuring the real political impact on communities. The radical project of educating students while participating in socially transformative work has evolved into an institutional formation where student learning and teaching excellence are often exalted (and funded and promoted) for their noblesse-oblige, not for their social impact or contribution to social justice (Dolgon 2002).

My point in offering these two examples is to suggest that now is the moment to engage with public sociology as a project while we can influence the current phase of its development. Public sociology, like the Obama Phenomenon, is nothing more than open space—ripe with possibilities—but with no inherent guarantees of ideological or humanist commitments towards social justice. I would suggest that Joe Feagin's (2001) presidential address was, in fact, a much more radical proposition for sociology as a discipline than was Burawoy's on public sociology. It was Feagin who essentially articulated the primary decision that we must all make as social scientists: "In practice, social scientists can accept the prevailing nation-state or bureaucratic-capitalistic morality or they can resist this morality by making a commitment to social justice and human rights." I would suggest that public sociology's greatest promise lies in its ability to adopt and adapt such a moral framework and find ways in which to infuse its research and engagement with such commitments.

But why should we as humanist sociologists be interested in such an enterprise anyway? After all, that is what this organization has been about since its inception. This has been our project. Our formation has evolved primarily in opposition to the mainstream of the discipline whose "fat cat" professionalism aligned itself with nationalism and market capitalism at the same time it secured its perimeters by promoting value-free positivism. Certainly Bonilla-Silva's biggest applause line at his AHS 2008 plenary related to his own repudiation of ASA and the types of research it produces and authorizes. While I agree with much of this assessment and welcome his new AHS membership, I want to suggest that there are three reasons why now is a crucial time for us to rethink our relationship with ASA in general and public sociology in particular.

1. ASA has a tremendous amount of resources, power and legitimacy. If we intend to pursue our AHS mission and values of making the world a better place, we strengthen the possibilities of having such an impact when we bolster our movement with more resources. While I am not suggesting that we might reach our goals more efficiently and effectively if we were to embed ourselves into the publication of the mainstream elite journals such as the *American Sociological Review* or *American Journal of Sociology*, I am suggesting that the wildly popular growth of a journal such as *Contexts* is one of those signs of major shifts within the discipline—like an Obama victory. Public sociology's success is evidence of some of those same progressive shifts that offer progressive promise. But they don't guarantee progressive policies or progressive change. To ignore the *potential* of expanding our vision of an engaged and value infused social science seems remiss. I would also add that *now* is the time! As public sociology enters its next formational stage, it is the humanist social justice commitment that must shape it or forever remain on the outside as gadfly instead of on the inside shaping it future.

2. Some of the most important resources are people—primarily graduate students and younger faculty who are most likely entering into sociology careers because of desires to use their social science for good. But graduate school and early professional pressures quickly suck the socialistic life blood out of them. By re-relating with ASA we make inroads into recruiting people we barely see in the nooks and crannies of academia. Public sociology, as it formalizes and institutionalizes, promises to widen those nooks and crannies, where young scholar activists with the fortitude to maintain social justice commitments may find homes. It is here that AHS in particular, and humanist sociology in general, can provide the kind of moral

and political compass necessary to nurture such fortitude. And here I think even Burawoy (2004) would agree as he suggests that for public sociology to succeed it must transcend the handcuffs of value neutrality and embrace devoutly humanistic goals.

3. Meanwhile, one of AHS's strengths has always been its own recognition of itself as a public. Never have I been associated with a group that tried so hard and so earnestly to use both its analytical tools and its shared values to practice what it preaches. We don't always succeed—in fact, sometimes we fail miserably. But we never stop trying, reflecting and recommitting ourselves to our mission. And in doing so, we educate each other and further inform and shape what may very well be an articulation of what we would like to see the larger community look like. After all, we may be committed to social justice, but we don't know exactly what that socially-just society is until we work together to create it.

As an organization, AHS pursues such a goal, but as Walda Katz-Fishman and Jerome Scott et al. (2006) have written, "the analytical and methodological tools of social analysis are not the private property of academics—rather theory and practice are two aspects of a powerful dialectical unity coming out of and continuously tested in the struggle to end oppression." The "other world that is possible" will be shaped by those working in concert to challenge the one we have now. To carry on that challenge, AHS can no longer remain a small, insular club thumbing our noses at the professional elite. It is time to restore our numbers, solidify our links to practitioners and activists, and challenge the mainstream confidently and directly—not in the smallest of margins, but on the main stage. A strong relationship with public sociology may give us an entrée onto that stage.

A New Dream?

Towards the end of Lenin's "What is to Be Done?" he calls on intellectuals to worry less about "raising the activities of the masses of workers...and think more about raising [intellectuals] own activity." In part, intellectuals needed to produce the kind of political knowledge and historical and current information necessary for the revolution. But intellectuals also needed to engage the movement themselves. I believe this is still true, but I am weary of sociologist's ability to lead these revolutions and movements. We must engage them, but I don't think we understand them well enough yet to lead. While our ability to analyze and deconstruct maybe vital parts of creating a necessary critical consciousness, our "dialectical negation" too often comes off as just negative and our penchant for caveats doesn't always inspire.

Thus, for all of Bonilla-Silva's excellent insights, I don't think he fully recognizes the role that *hope,* inspired by Obama's campaign, could play in seriously organizing a social movement. To some degree sociologists may be imprisoned by our inability to embrace hope because it is too easily doused by the drop of a bomb or the slash of a pen. As sociologists, we tend to be so critical and so good at pointing out the intricacies of power and politics, that we have trouble building from social critique to social action. When Bonilla-Silva calls for the power of social movements, we nod, we smile, we clap, and we cheer—but what do we do?

Our fallen comrade, Frank Lindenfeld, was ahead of his time in recognizing that the intellectual failures of objectivity and the scientific method, as well as the institutional failures of professionalism and bureaucracy, were endemic to the larger social, political and economic systems that circumscribe our life and work. Thus, Frank knew that regardless of how smart we might be, academics could not think or write ourselves out of war, oppression, inequality, or human suffering and the systems that support them. Frank knew that our theories and arguments needed to be informed by and engaged with political movements for social justice. Frank's intellectual life and work was always an outgrowth of his commitment to the struggle for a better world. After decades of identity politics and postmodernism and post-feminism and post-Marxism, it seems that cutting edge progressive and radical scholars are rediscovering the importance of mass movements and realizing the revolution will not be theorized. Without movement organizing and real connections to political struggle our public intellectualism may be moot. Frank wrote about these dynamics twenty years ago.

Recently, radical historian Robin D.G. Kelley wrote that too often our standards for evaluating social movements pivot around whether or not they succeed in realizing their visions rather than on the merits of the power of the visions themselves. By such a measure virtually every radical movement failed. Yet, it is precisely these alternative visions and creams that inspire new generations to continue to struggle for change!" In many ways I think Frank would have echoed these sentiments. In *Radical Perspectives on Social Problems* (1987) Frank wrote, "This anthology is intended to be a utopian antidote, an interpretation of the social world dedicated to the possibility and the desirability of radical change. My aim is to help cultivate the utopian sensibility: the ability to look at social patterns and to see not only as they are and as they have been, but as they might be if..." We cannot organize, we cannot struggle, we cannot change the world without these visions, without what Kelley calls "Freedom Dreams"—without hope.

But Obama was never our real hope; his campaign was never the source of freedom dreams to inspire a new mass movement for social justice. As was true in the brief stories I opened with, and the countless others that I have heard from friends and colleagues around the nation, the hope came from the walking and talking and acting with others who also wanted change. A sense of hope arose out of the conversations and commitment, the camaraderie and community that developed as people canvassed together, stood together, watched together, spoke together, and in concert created a new sense of what America might look like—what America might mean. We now have an opportunity to continue building on these connections and inspiring new utopian visions of what a socially just world might look like.

As humanist sociologists, we kept such a flame alive within our discipline for many years. The rise of public sociology will not necessarily be the professional savior for progressive scholar activists hoping to influence the mainstream of our discipline. But like the Obama phenomenon, there seems to be a renewed sense of hope and optimism that sociology is once again a more receptive place for scholars engaged with local and global activism. And as with the Obama victory, I want to argue that public sociology is a sign of an opportunity to nurture the real spirit, the real hope, the real fuel for freedom dreams that comes from sociologists working in concert with neighborhoods and activists around the world. This is the fuel that fans the flames of discontent; it accelerates sparks into roaring fires that rise from the hearths of yearning and blazes new freedom trails across the planet.

References

Ballard, Chet. "An epistle on the origin and early history of the Association for Humanist Sociology," *The American Sociologist*, Volume 33, Number 4. (2002)

Bonilla-Silva, Eduardo. "The 2008 Elections and the Future of Anti-Racism in 21st Century Amerika or How We Got Drunk with Obama's *Hope Liquor* and Failed to See Reality." Plenary presented to the Association for Humanist Sociology 2008 Annual Meeting, Boston, MA.

Burawoy, Michael. "Public Sociologies: Contradictions, Dilemmas, and Possibilities." *Social Forces*, Volume 82, Number 4, June 2004.

Clawson, Dan et al. (eds). *Public Sociology: Fifteen Eminent Sociologists Debate Politics and the Profession in the Twenty-First Century.* (University of California Press, 2007)

Curley, Jonathan. "My wife made me canvass for Obama; here's what I learned," *Christian Science Monitor* (11/3/2008).

Dolgon, Corey. "The United Colors of Cultural Studies: The Politics of Politics in the Academy," *Humanity and Society*, Volume 21, Number 4, November, 1997.

Dolgon, Corey. "In Search of 'Cognitive Consonance': Humanist Sociology and Service Learning" *Humanity and Society*, Volume 26, Number 2, 2002.

Feagin, Joe. "Social Justice and Sociology: Agendas for the Twenty-First Century," *American Sociological Review* 66 (February 2001):

Katz-Fishman, Walda, Jerome Scott, Ralph Gomes, and Tomas Encarnacion. "Scholar Activism: Popular Education and Social Transformation," *Humanity and Society*, Volume 30, Number 2 (2006).

Kelley, Robin D.G. Freedom *Dreams: Te Black Radical Imagination.* (Boston, Beacon Press, 2003)

Lindenfeld, Frank. *Radical Perspectives on Social Problem.* New York: General Hall, 2006.

Ryan, Charlotte and William Gamson, "Are Frames Enough?" in *Social Movements Reader: Cases and Concepts, Second Edition.* Edited by Jeff Goodwin and James Jasper, Oxford: Wiley-Blackwell, 2009.

Shepard, Benjamin. "Four Narratives of Anti-Poverty Community Mobilization: Housing Works, FIERCE, Human Rights Watch, and the More Gardens Coalition," Comm-Org Papers website, http://comm-org.wisc/papers2006/shepard.htm (2006).

Williams, Raymond. *The Politics of Modernism* (London: Verso Press, 1989).

Woods, Tim. "Student Engagement and Community Change," Paper presented to the Association for Humanist Sociology 2008 Annual Meeting, Boston, MA.

Celebrate, Then Keep Organizing!
A Rejoinder to Dolgon's
"Don't Celebrate, Organize!
A Public Sociology to Fan the Flames
of Discontent"

James R. Pennell
University of Indianapolis

Before responding to this article, following the Association for Humanist Sociology tradition of offering a reflexive statement to situate one's values in relation to a topic, I will start with the disclaimer that Corey Dolgon is my friend and a colleague in the efforts to use sociological knowledge to make a fairer, more peaceful, and just world. We share similar dreams for families, communities, and the larger world. So the thinking he offers in his article is no surprise to me. This does not mean we are always in complete agreement, especially on the difficult issues and gray areas that challenge all scholars and defy an absolute answer to Lenin's question of "what is to be done?"

Given the restrictions of length, I won't restate Corey's arguments or provide a comprehensive analysis of them, but simply offer a few comments. I agree that the Obama election and public sociology are promising developments, with all the qualifications he musters and then some. Sociological theory provides some insight into these developments. Political process or opportunity theory (Tarrow 1983) suggests the pendulum of opportunity (public opinion and institutional openings) shifts back and forth, and some historical moments provide better opportunities for social change in a progressive direction than others. Patterns of ups, downs, and transformations are replete through history. One set of shifts and the circumstances created commonly spurs the next round of challenges and dreams for the future. For those of us who mourned when the bombs fell on Baghdad in March, 2003, and found it difficult to speak loudly without being shouted down by a large percentage of the confused and angry masses (and unfortunately the very large majority of elected representatives who should have known better), it was small comfort to know that Bush's time for scrutiny and criticism would surely come. But it did.

I think Corey was too easy on Eduardo Bonilla-Silva's dismissal of the possibilities that exist with the election of Obama. Eduardo argued that "Obama's election does NOT mean the end of racism, is unlikely to bring meaningful social and economic change, may continue and even expand American imperialist foreign policy, and, more significantly for me, BLUR the space to talk about race in the public square" (2008, emphasis in original). He suggested intellectuals may have bought into the "Obama-hope-liquor," and have ignored how Obama's election offers little in the way of real change. His election may even provide ammunition for those who think race no longer matters, ignoring the subtle ways racism contributes to continuing inequities.

Granted, racism has not ended. And yes, we should keep a critical skepticism of politicians and the promises they proffer, especially given the piles of money and influence that taint their judgment. But we must see their lofty promises and vague positions within the context of a world that has moved forward in its awareness of human rights, even as the large majority continues to suffer and be deceived for the benefit of the few. Politicians such as Obama have to make choices about what they say and do and how far they can go in the here and now. What they do at a given moment may advance a cause or undermine it. Taking a strong, absolute position that draws a line in the sand may end with a sandstorm that suffocates their best intentions. Even we sociologists, whether busily climbing the professional ladder at prestigious schools or working for change in smaller, typically more conservative schools and communities, must pick and choose our battles. Perhaps, as Eduardo suggests, Obama has no causes other than to placate the corporate elite and political mainstream—the price that must be paid to gain and hold high office. I'm not ready to accept that yet, although I agree that we should not relax our expectations or voices, and these voices are stronger when they are organized.

I agree with Corey that institutional pressures in universities tend to work against those things that will help intellectuals make a difference in our communities. And the step by the American Sociological Association toward opening our work up to the possibility of making a difference is a positive one. I am not personally interested in the ASA and its battles, but I am glad Corey and others are since progressive change happens in multiple contexts and in multiple ways. I don't see the ASA as a potential long-term "partner" for other organizations seeking progressive social change. It may serve as a potential resource at times, but its mission is to advance sociology and sociologists first, not struggle in pursuit of a better world. The move to include what it refers to as public sociology is certainly a positive addition to its portfolio of pursuits in its search for greater institutional power relative to other disciplines. And there may be collateral benefits to those of us spending more of our time on the streets and in classrooms. Other social science disciplines, psychology and economics most prominently, attract resources in part due to their claims of practical relevance. Of course, much of that work is as irrelevant to creating a better world as the majority of articles in the *American Sociological Review*.

The strength of the Association for Humanist Sociology is not a result of institutional power within the academic-industrial complex. It comes from the ideas, encouragement, and yes, modest but important organizational and professional resources we provide to each other. Some of us will keep the AHS home fires burning in our sites of struggle while others take our vision to the lion's den of mainstream sociology. There are many publics and powerful actors to engage, and the way forward must be formulated from the circumstances we are given. Eduardo is right that we are most likely only slightly better off with Obama as President. But that is a small step in a better direction than we were headed. So, to take slight exception to Corey's title, I say celebrate when we can, let those fleeting moments sustain us, and incorporate the possibilities they hold into our difficult work.

References

Bonilla-Silva, Eduardo. 2008. "The 2008 elections and the future of anti-racism in 21st century amerika, or how we got drunk with obama's *hope liquor* and failed to see reality." Presentation at the annual meeting of the Association for Humanist Sociology, Boston, MA, November 6–9.

Tarrow, Sidney. 1983. "Struggling to reform: Social movements and policy change during cycles of protest." Ithaca, NY: Cornell University Press.